UNIX® SYSTEM V RELEASE 4

Programmer's Reference Manual: Operating System API

for Intel Processors

Copyright © 1992, 1991 UNIX System Laboratories, Inc.
Copyright © 1990, 1989, 1988, 1987, 1986, 1985, 1984 AT&T
All Rights Reserved
Printed in USA

Published by Prentice Hall, Inc.
A Simon & Schuster Company
Englewood Cliffs, New Jersey 07632

No part of this publication may be reproduced or transmitted in any form or by any means—graphic, electronic, electrical, mechanical, or chemical, including photocopying, recording in any medium, taping, by any computer or information storage and retrieval systems, etc., without prior permissions in writing from UNIX System Laboratories, Inc. (USL).

IMPORTANT NOTE TO USERS

While every effort has been made to ensure the accuracy and completeness of all information in this document, USL assumes no liability to any party for any loss or damage caused by errors or omissions or by statements of any kind in this document, its updates, supplements, or special editions, whether such errors, omissions, or statements result from negligence, accident, or any other cause. USL further assumes no liability arising out of the application or use of any product or system described herein; nor any liability for incidental or consequential damages arising from the use of this document. **USL disclaims all warranties regarding the information contained herein, whether expressed, implied or statutory, including implied warranties of merchantability or fitness for a particular purpose**. USL makes no representation that the interconnection of products in the manner described herein will not infringe on existing or future patent rights, nor do the descriptions contained herein imply the granting of any license to make, use or sell equipment constructed in accordance with this description.

USL reserves the right to make changes to any products herein without further notice.

TRADEMARKS

UNIX is a registered trademark of UNIX System Laboratories, Inc. in the USA and other countries.
WE is a registered trademark of AT&T.
XENIX is a registered trademark of Microsoft Corporation.

10 9 8 7 6 5 4 3 2 1

ISBN 0-13-951294-2

PRENTICE HALL

ORDERING INFORMATION

UNIX® SYSTEM V, RELEASE 4 DOCUMENTATION

To order single copies of UNIX® SYSTEM V, Release 4 documentation, please call (201) 767-5937.

ATTENTION DOCUMENTATION MANAGERS AND TRAINING DIRECTORS:
For bulk purchases in excess of 30 copies please write to:
Corporate Sales
Prentice Hall
Englewood Cliffs, N.J. 07632
Or call: (201) 461–8441

ATTENTION GOVERNMENT CUSTOMERS: For GSA and other pricing information please call (201) 767-5994.

Prentice-Hall International (UK) Limited, *London*
Prentice-Hall of Australia Pty. Limited, *Sydney*
Prentice-Hall Canada Inc., *Toronto*
Prentice-Hall Hispanoamericana, S.A., *Mexico*
Prentice-Hall of India Private Limited, *New Delhi*
Prentice-Hall of Japan, Inc., *Tokyo*
Simon & Schuster Asia Pte. Ltd., *Singapore*
Editora Prentice-Hall do Brasil, Ltda., *Rio de Janeiro*

Preface

UNIX System V Reference Manuals describe the interfaces and execution behavior of each System V component. The components of UNIX System V include the graphical user interface (GUI), Shell command line interface, application program interface (API) and Device Driver Interface/Driver Kernel Interface (DDI/DKI), as well as device special files, header files and other system files. The following table summarizes the general categories of manual pages:

Table 1: Manual Page Categories

Description	Section Reference
□ *Shell & Command Line Interface*	
— General Purpose Utilities	1
— Maintenance Utilities	1M
□ *Application Program Interface (API)*	
— UNIX System Calls	2
— C Language Libraries	3
□ *System Files & Devices*	
— System File Formats	4
— Miscellaneous Facilities	5
— Special Files (Devices)	7
□ *Device Driver Interface/Driver Kernel Interface (DDI/DKI)*	
— DDI/DKI Driver Data Definitions	D1
— DDI/DKI Driver Entry Point Routines	D2
— DDI/DKI Kernel Utility Routines	D3
— DDI/DKI Kernel Data Structures	D4
— DDI/DKI Kernel Defines	D5

Reference Manuals supply technical reference information that describes the source-code interfaces and run-time behavior of each component of System V on a component by component basis. As concise reference material, manual pages assume some familiarity with the information.

Preface

Organization of the Reference Manuals

Each section in a Reference Manual consists of a number of independent entries called "manual pages." A "Table of Contents" precedes each manual page section. Within each section, manual pages are arranged in alphabetical order based on the name of the component described by that manual page. Some manual pages may describe several commands, functions, or other type of system facility. In such cases, the manual page appears only once in a table of contents, alphabetized under its "primary" name, the name that appears at the upper corners of each manual page. For each Reference Manual, a "Permuted Index" of all manual pages for that manual is provided at the back of the book.

This latest edition of the UNIX System V Release 4 Reference Manuals has reorganized the reference manuals to make it easier to identify which manual contains a given manual page, and to locate the manual page within that manual. The new organization of the UNIX System V Reference Manuals

- includes all reference manual pages found in various Programmer's Guides in the Reference Manuals
- makes each manual page unique, rather than repeating it in different Reference Manuals
- sorts each section together, rather than breaking it out by subsection, for example, all of Section 1, including subsections 1C, 1F, 1M, and 1N
- precedes each section with its own table of contents

The set of UNIX System V Reference Manuals organizes the manual pages into volumes aligned with the different types of interfaces that make up UNIX System V Release 4. Manual pages for the same type of components are found in the same volume, and components of different types are found in separate volumes. For example, you will no longer find programming commands (cc, make, and so on) in the *Programmer's Reference Manual*. Those commands have been moved to join Section 1 commands in the *User's Reference Manual/System Administrator's Reference Manual*. At the same time, all Section 4, 5 and 7 manual pages, which describe various system files and special files (devices) and were previously located in the *Programmer's Reference Manual* or the *System Administrator's Reference Manual*, have been consolidated in a new, separate volume entitled *System Files and Devices Reference Manual*. The table on the following page lists the contents of the new complete set of Reference Manuals:

Table 2: The UNIX System V Release 4 Reference Manual Set

Reference Manual	Description	Sections
User's Reference Manual/ System Administrator's Reference Manual (Commands a – l and m – z)	General-Purpose User Commands Basic Networking Commands Form and Menu Language Interpreter System Maintenance Commands Enhanced Networking Commands	1 1C 1F 1M 1N
Programmer's Reference Manual: Operating System API	System Calls BSD System Compatibility Library Standard C Library Executable and Linking Format Library General-Purpose Library Math Library Networking Library Standard I/O Library Specialized Library	2 3 3C 3E 3G 3M 3N 3S 3X
Programmer's Reference Manual: Windowing System API	X Window System Library X Window System Toolkit OPEN LOOK Intrinsics Toolkit	3X11 3Xt 3W
System Files and Devices Reference Manual	System File Formats Miscellaneous Facilities Special Files (Devices)	4 5 7
Device Driver Interface/ Driver Kernel Interface Reference Manual	DDI/DKI Driver Data Definitions DDI/DKI Driver Entry Point Routines DDI/DKI Kernel Utility Routines DDI/DKI Kernel Data Structures DDI/DKI Kernel Defines	D1 D2 D3 D4 D5

Preface

Reference Manual Index

A "Permuted Index" for this reference manual is provided at the back. The Permuted Index is a list of keywords, alphabetized in the second of three columns, together with the context in which each keyword is found. The manual page that produced an entry is listed in the right column.

Entries are identified with their section numbers shown in parentheses. This is important because there is considerable duplication of names among the sections, arising principally from commands and functions that exist only to exercise a particular system call.

The index is produced by rotating the NAME section of each manual page to alphabetize each keyword in it. Words that cannot fit in the middle column are rotated into the left column. If the entry is still too long, some words are omitted, and their omission is indicated with a slash ("/").

Here is an example of some of the entries produced for the manual pages rand(3C), sleep(1), sleep(3), and sleep(3C):

Figure 1: Sample of a Permuted Index

generator	rand, srand simple random number	rand(3C)
srand simple	random number generator rand, ...	rand(3C)
rand, srand	simple random number generator	rand(3C)
interval	sleep suspend execution for an	sleep(1)
interval	sleep suspend execution for an	sleep(3)
interval	sleep suspend execution for an	sleep(3C)
generator rand,	srand simple random number	rand(3C)

Table of Contents

Introduction to the Operating System API

Section 1 – Programming Commands

intro(1)	introduction to programming commands
admin(1)	create and administer SCCS files
ar(1)	maintain portable archive or library
as(1)	assembler
cb(1)	C program beautifier
cc(1)	C compiler
cdc(1)	change the delta comment of an SCCS delta
cflow(1)	generate C flowgraph
cof2elf(1)	COFF to ELF object file translation
comb(1)	combine SCCS deltas
convert(1)	convert archive files to common formats
cscope(1)	interactively examine a C program
ctrace(1)	C program debugger
cxref(1)	generate C program cross-reference
delta(1)	make a delta (change) to an SCCS file
dis(1)	object code disassembler
dump(1)	dump selected parts of an object file
get(1)	get a version of an SCCS file
help(1)	ask for help with message numbers or SCCS commands
install(1M)	install commands
ld(1)	link editor for object files
ldd(1)	list dynamic dependencies
lex(1)	generate programs for simple lexical tasks
lint(1)	a C program checker
lorder(1)	find ordering relation for an object library
lprof(1)	display line-by-line execution count profile data
m4(1)	macro processor
make(1)	maintain, update, and regenerate groups of programs
mcs(1)	manipulate the comment section of an object file
nm(1)	print name list of an object file
prof(1)	display profile data
prs(1)	print an SCCS file
regcmp(1)	regular expression compile
rmdel(1)	remove a delta from an SCCS file
sact(1)	print current SCCS file editing activity

Table of Contents

sccsdiff(1) .... compare two versions of an SCCS file
sdb(1) .... symbolic debugger
size(1) .... print section sizes in bytes of object files
strip(1) .... strip symbol table, debugging and line number information from an object file
tsort(1) .... topological sort
unget(1) .... undo a previous get of an SCCS file
val(1) .... validate an SCCS file
vc(1) .... version control
what(1) .... print identification strings
x286emul(1) .... emulate XENIX 80286
yacc(1) .... yet another compiler-compiler

Section 2 – System Calls

intro(2) .... introduction to system calls and error numbers
access(2) .... determine accessibility of a file
acct(2) .... enable or disable process accounting
adjtime(2) .... correct the time to allow synchronization of the system clock
alarm(2) .... set a process alarm clock
brk, sbrk(2) .... change data segment space allocation
chdir, fchdir(2) .... change working directory
chmod, fchmod(2) .... change mode of file
chown, lchown, fchown(2) .... change owner and group of a file
chroot(2) .... change root directory
chsize(2) .... change the size of a file
close(2) .... close a file descriptor
creat(2) .... create a new file or rewrite an existing one
creatsem(2) .... create an instance of a binary semaphore
dup(2) .... duplicate an open file descriptor
errno(2) .... complete list of the error numbers and their names
exec: execl, execv, execle, execve, execlp, execvp(2) .... execute a file
exit, _exit(2) .... terminate process
fcntl(2) .... file control
fork(2) .... create a new process
fpathconf, pathconf(2) .... get configurable pathname variables
fsync(2) .... synchronize a file's in-memory state with that on the physical medium
ftime(2) .... get time and date
getcontext, setcontext(2) .... get and set current user context

2   Programmer's Reference Manual: Operating System API

getdents(2)	read directory entries and put in a file system independent format
getgroups, setgroups(2)	get or set supplementary group access list IDs
getmsg(2)	get next message off a stream
getpid, getpgrp, getppid, getpgid(2)	get process, process group, and parent process IDs
getrlimit, setrlimit(2)	control maximum system resource consumption
getsid(2)	get session ID
getuid, geteuid, getgid, getegid(2)	get real user, effective user, real group, and effective group IDs
ioctl(2)	control device
kill(2)	send a signal to a process or a group of processes
link(2)	link to a file
lock(2)	lock a process in primary memory
locking(2)	lock or unlock a file region for reading or writing
lseek(2)	move read/write file pointer
memcntl(2)	memory management control
mincore(2)	determine residency of memory pages
mkdir(2)	make a directory
mknod(2)	make a directory, or a special or ordinary file
mknod(2)	make a directory, or a special or ordinary file
mmap(2)	map pages of memory
mount(2)	mount a file system
mprotect(2)	set protection of memory mapping
msgctl(2)	message control operations
msgget(2)	get message queue
msgop: msgsnd, msgrcv(2)	message operations
munmap(2)	unmap pages of memory
nap(2)	suspend execution for a short interval
nice(2)	change priority of a time-sharing process
open(2)	open for reading or writing
opensem(2)	open a semaphore
p_online(2)	turn a processor online or offline
pause(2)	suspend process until signal
pipe(2)	create an interprocess channel
plock(2)	lock into memory or unlock process, text, or data
poll(2)	input/output multiplexing
priocntl(2)	process scheduler control
priocntlset(2)	generalized process scheduler control
processor_bind(2)	bind a process to a processor
processor_info(2)	get information about one processor
profil(2)	execution time profile

Table of Contents

ptrace(2)	process trace
putmsg(2)	send a message on a stream
rdchk(2)	check to see if there is data to be read
read(2)	read from file
readlink(2)	read the value of a symbolic link
rename(2)	change the name of a file
rmdir(2)	remove a directory
sdenter, sdleave(2)	synchronize access to a shared data segment
sdget, sdfree(2)	attach and detach a shared data segment
sdgetv(2)	synchronize shared data access
semctl(2)	semaphore control operations
semget(2)	get set of semaphores
semop(2)	semaphore operations
setpgid(2)	set process group ID
setpgrp(2)	set process group ID
setsid(2)	set session ID
setuid, setgid(2)	set user and group IDs
shmctl(2)	shared memory control operations
shmget(2)	get shared memory segment identifier
shmop: shmat, shmdt(2)	shared memory operations
sigaction(2)	detailed signal management
sigaltstack(2)	set or get signal alternate stack context
signal, sigset, sighold, sigrelse, sigignore, sigpause(2)	simplified signal management
sigpending(2)	examine signals that are blocked and pending
sigprocmask(2)	change or examine signal mask
sigsem(2)	signal a process waiting on a semaphore
sigsend, sigsendset(2)	send a signal to a process or a group of processes
sigsuspend(2)	install a signal mask and suspend process until signal
stat, lstat, fstat(2)	get file status
stat, lstat, fstat(2)	get file status
statvfs, fstatvfs(2)	get file system information
stime(2)	set time
swapctl(2)	manage swap space
symlink(2)	make a symbolic link to a file
sync(2)	update super block
sysfs(2)	get file system type information
sysi86(2)	machine specific functions
sysinfo(2)	get and set system information strings

termios: tcgetattr, tcsetattr, tcsendbreak, tcdrain, tcflush, tcflow, cfgetospeed,
    cfgetispeed, cfsetispeed, cfsetospeed, tcgetpgrp, tcsetpgrp, tcgetsid(2)
    .... general terminal interface
time(2) .... get time
times(2) .... get process and child process times
uadmin(2) .... administrative control
ulimit(2) .... get and set user limits
umask(2) .... set and get file creation mask
umount(2) .... unmount a file system
uname(2) .... get name of current UNIX system
unlink(2) .... remove directory entry
ustat(2) .... get file system statistics
utime(2) .... set file access and modification times
vfork(2) .... spawn new process in a virtual memory efficient way
wait(2) .... wait for child process to stop or terminate
waitid(2) .... wait for child process to change state
waitpid(2) .... wait for child process to change state
waitsem, nbwaitsem(2) .... await and check access to a resource governed by a semaphore
write, writev(2) .... write on a file

Section 3 – Library Functions

intro(3) .... introduction to functions and libraries
a64l, l64a(3C) .... convert between long integer and base-64 ASCII string
abort(3C) .... generate an abnormal termination signal
abs, labs(3C) .... return integer absolute value
accept(3N) .... accept a connection on a socket
addseverity(3C) .... build a list of severity levels for an application for use with fmtmsg
alloca(3) .... memory allocator
assert(3X) .... verify program assertion
atexit(3C) .... add program termination routine
basename(3G) .... return the last element of a path name
bessel: j0, j1, jn, y0, y1, yn(3M) .... Bessel functions
bgets(3G) .... read stream up to next delimiter
bind(3N) .... bind a name to a socket
bsearch(3C) .... binary search a sorted table
bstring: bcopy, bcmp, bzero, ffs(3) .... bit and byte string operations
bufsplit(3G) .... split buffer into fields

Table of Contents

byteorder, htonl, htons, ntohl, ntohs(3N)
.... convert values between host and network byte order
catgets(3C) .... read a program message
catopen, catclose(3C) .... open/close a message catalog
clock(3C) .... report CPU time used
connect(3N) .... initiate a connection on a socket
conv: toupper, tolower, _toupper, _tolower, toascii(3C) .... translate characters
copylist(3G) .... copy a file into memory
crypt, setkey, encrypt(3C) .... generate encryption
crypt(3X) .... password and file encryption functions
ctermid(3S) .... generate file name for terminal
ctime, localtime, gmtime, asctime, tzset(3C) .... convert date and time to string
ctype: isdigit, isxdigit, islower, isupper, isalpha, isalnum, isspace, iscntrl, ispunct,
   isprint, isgraph, isascii(3C) .... character handling
curs_addch: addch, waddch, mvaddch, mvwaddch, echochar, wechochar(3X)
   .... add a character (with attributes) to a curses window and advance cursor
curs_addchstr: addchstr, addchnstr, waddchstr, waddchnstr, mvaddchstr,
   mvaddchnstr, mvwaddchstr, mvwaddchnstr(3X)
   .... add string of characters (and attributes) to a curses window
curs_addstr: addstr, addnstr, waddstr, waddnstr, mvaddstr, mvaddnstr,
   mvwaddstr, mvwaddnstr(3X)
   .... add a string of characters to a curses window and advance cursor
curs_attr: attroff, wattroff, attron, wattron, attrset, wattrset, standend, wstandend,
   standout, wstandout(3X) .... curses character and window attribute control routines
curs_beep: beep, flash(3X) .... curses bell and screen flash routines
curs_bkgd: bkgdset, wbkgdset, bkgd, wbkgd(3X)
   .... curses window background manipulation routines
curs_border: border, wborder, box, hline, whline, vline, wvline(3X)
   .... create curses borders, horizontal and vertical lines
curs_clear: erase, werase, clear, wclear, clrtobot, wclrtobot, clrtoeol, wclrtoeol(3X)
   .... clear all or part of a curses window
curs_color: start_color, init_pair, init_color, has_colors, can_change_color,
   color_content, pair_content(3X) .... curses color manipulation routines
curs_delch: delch, wdelch, mvdelch, mvwdelch(3X)
   .... delete character under cursor in a curses window
curs_deleteln: deleteln, wdeleteln, insdelln, winsdelln, insertln, winsertln(3X)
   .... delete and insert lines in a curses window
curs_getch: getch, wgetch, mvgetch, mvwgetch, ungetch(3X)
   .... get (or push back) characters from curses terminal keyboard

Table of Contents

curs_getstr: getstr, wgetstr, mvgetstr, mvwgetstr, wgetnstr(3X)
.... get character strings from curses terminal keyboard
curs_getyx: getyx, getparyx, getbegyx, getmaxyx(3X)
.... get curses cursor and window coordinates
curs_inch: inch, winch, mvinch, mvwinch(3X)
.... get a character and its attributes from a curses window
curs_inchstr: inchstr, inchnstr, winchstr, winchnstr, mvinchstr, mvinchnstr, mvwinchstr, mvwinchnstr(3X)
.... get a string of characters (and attributes) from a curses window
curs_initscr: initscr, newterm, endwin, isendwin, set_term, delscreen(3X)
.... curses screen initialization and manipulation routines
curs_inopts: cbreak, nocbreak, echo, noecho, halfdelay, intrflush, keypad, meta, nodelay, notimeout, raw, noraw, noqiflush, qiflush, timeout, wtimeout, typeahead(3X) .... curses terminal input option control routines
curs_insch: insch, winsch, mvinsch, mvwinsch(3X)
.... insert a character before the character under the cursor in a curses window
curs_instr: insstr, insnstr, winsstr, winsnstr, mvinsstr, mvinsnstr, mvwinsstr, mvwinsnstr(3X) .... insert string before character under the cursor in a curses window
curs_instr: instr, innstr, winstr, winnstr, mvinstr, mvinnstr, mvwinstr, mvwinnstr(3X) .... get a string of characters from a curses window
curs_kernel: def_prog_mode, def_shell_mode, reset_prog_mode, reset_shell_mode, resetty, savetty, getsyx, setsyx, ripoffline, curs_set, napms(3X)
.... low-level curses routines
curs_move: move, wmove(3X) .... move curses window cursor
curs_outopts: clearok, idlok, idcok immedok, leaveok, setscrreg, wsetscrreg, scrollok, nl, nonl(3X) .... curses terminal output option control routines
curs_overlay: overlay, overwrite, copywin(3X)
.... overlap and manipulate overlapped curses windows
curs_pad: newpad, subpad, prefresh, pnoutrefresh, pechochar(3X)
.... create and display curses pads
curs_printw: printw, wprintw, mvprintw, mvwprintw, vwprintw(3X)
.... print formatted output in curses windows
curs_refresh: refresh, wrefresh, wnoutrefresh, doupdate, redrawwin, wredrawln(3X) .... refresh curses windows and lines
curs_scanw: scanw, wscanw, mvscanw, mvwscanw, vwscanw(3X)
.... convert formatted input from a curses widow
curs_scr_dump: scr_dump, scr_restore, scr_init, scr_set(3X)
.... read (write) a curses screen from (to) a file
curs_scroll: scroll, srcl, wscrl(3X) .... scroll a curses window

Table of Contents

curs_slk: slk_init, slk_set, slk_refresh, slk_noutrefresh, slk_label, slk_clear, slk_restore, slk_touch, slk_attron, slk_attrset, slk_attroff(3X) .... curses soft label routines

curs_termattrs: baudrate, erasechar, has_ic, has_il, killchar, longname, termattrs, termname(3X) .... curses environment query routines

curs_termcap: tgetent, tgetflag, tgetnum, tgetstr, tgoto, tputs(3X) .... curses interfaces (emulated) to the termcap library

curs_terminfo: setupterm, setterm, set_curterm, del_curterm, restartterm, tparm, tputs, putp, vidputs, vidattr, mvcur, tigetflag, tigetnum, tigetstr(3X) .... curses interfaces to terminfo database

curs_touch: touchwin, touchline, untouchwin, wtouchln, is_linetouched, is_wintouched(3X) .... curses refresh control routines

curs_util: unctrl, keyname, filter, use_env, putwin, getwin, delay_output, flushinp(3X) .... miscellaneous curses utility routines

curs_window: newwin, delwin, mvwin, subwin, derwin, mvderwin, dupwin, wsyncup, syncok, wcursyncup, wsyncdown(3X) .... create curses windows

curses(3X) .... CRT screen handling and optimization package

cuserid(3S) .... get character login name of the user

dbm: dbminit, dbmclose, fetch, store, delete, firstkey, nextkey(3) .... data base subroutines

decimal_to_floating: decimal_to_single, decimal_to_double, decimal_to_extended(3) .... convert decimal record to floating-point value

dial(3C) .... establish an outgoing terminal line connection

difftime(3C) .... computes the difference between two calendar times

directory: opendir, readdir, telldir, seekdir, rewinddir, closedir(3C) .... directory operations

directory: opendir, readdir, telldir, seekdir, rewinddir, closedir(3C) .... directory operations

dirname(3G) .... report the parent directory name of a file path name

div, ldiv(3C) .... compute the quotient and remainder

dlclose(3X) .... close a shared object

dlerror(3X) .... get diagnostic information

dlopen(3X) .... open a shared object

dlsym(3X) .... get the address of a symbol in shared object

doconfig(3N) .... execute a configuration script

drand48, erand48, lrand48, nrand48, mrand48, jrand48, srand48, seed48, lcong48(3C) .... generate uniformly distributed pseudo-random numbers

dup2(3C) .... duplicate an open file descriptor

econvert, fconvert, gconvert, seconvert, sfconvert, sgconvert(3) .... output conversion

ecvt, ecvtl, fcvt, fcvtl, gcvt, gcvtl(3C) .... convert floating-point number to string

elf(3E) .... object file access library

elf_begin(3E) .... make a file descriptor

elf_cntl(3E) .... control a file descriptor

elf_end(3E) .... finish using an object file
elf_errmsg, elf_errno(3E) .... error handling
elf_fill(3E) .... set fill byte
elf_flagdata, elf_flagehdr, elf_flagelf, elf_flagphdr, elf_flagscn, elf_flagshdr(3E)
.... manipulate flags
elf_fsize: elf32_fsize(3E) .... return the size of an object file type
elf_getarhdr(3E) .... retrieve archive member header
elf_getarsym(3E) .... retrieve archive symbol table
elf_getbase(3E) .... get the base offset for an object file
elf_getdata, elf_newdata, elf_rawdata(3E) .... get section data
elf_getehdr: elf32_getehdr, elf32_newehdr(3E) .... retrieve class-dependent object file header
elf_getident(3E) .... retrieve file identification data
elf_getphdr: elf32_getphdr, elf32_newphdr(3E)
.... retrieve class-dependent program header table
elf_getscn, elf_ndxscn, elf_newscn, elf_nextscn(3E) .... get section information
elf_getshdr: elf32_getshdr(3E) .... retrieve class-dependent section header
elf_hash(3E) .... compute hash value
elf_kind(3E) .... determine file type
elf_next(3E) .... sequential archive member access
elf_rand(3E) .... random archive member access
elf_rawfile(3E) .... retrieve uninterpreted file contents
elf_strptr(3E) .... make a string pointer
elf_update(3E) .... update an ELF descriptor
elf_version(3E) .... coordinate ELF library and application versions
elf_xlate: elf32_xlatetof, elf32_xlatetom(3E) .... class-dependent data translation
end, etext, edata(3C) .... last locations in program
erf, erfc(3M) .... error function and complementary error function
ethers(3N) .... Ethernet address mapping operations
exp, expf, cbrt, log, logf, log10, log10f, pow, powf, sqrt, sqrtf(3M)
.... exponential, logarithm, power, square root functions
fattach(3C)
.... attach a STREAMS-based file descriptor to an object in the file system name space
fclose, fflush(3S) .... close or flush a stream
fdetach(3C) .... detach a name from a STREAMS-based file descriptor
ferror, feof, clearerr, fileno(3S) .... stream status inquiries
ffs(3C) .... find first set bit
floatingpoint(3) .... IEEE floating point definitions
floor, floorf, ceil, ceilf, copysign, fmod, fmodf, fabs, fabsf, rint, remainder(3M)
.... floor, ceiling, remainder, absolute value functions

Table of Contents

floating_to_decimal: single_to_decimal, double_to_decimal, extended_to_decimal(3)
.... convert floating-point value to decimal record
fmtmsg(3C) .... display a message on stderr or system console
fopen, freopen, fdopen(3S) .... open a stream
fopen, freopen, fdopen(3S) .... open a stream
form_cursor: pos_form_cursor(3X) .... position forms window cursor
form_data: data_ahead, data_behind(3X)
.... tell if forms field has off-screen data ahead or behind
form_driver(3X) .... command processor for the forms subsystem
form_field: set_form_fields, form_fields, field_count, move_field(3X) .. connect fields to forms
form_field_attributes: set_field_fore, field_fore, set_field_back, field_back,
    set_field_pad, field_pad(3X) .... format the general display attributes of forms
form_field_buffer: set_field_buffer, field_buffer, set_field_status, field_status,
    set_max_field(3X) .... set and get forms field attributes
form_field_info: field_info, dynamic_field_info(3X) .... get forms field characteristics
form_field_just: set_field_just, field_just(3X) .... format the general appearance of forms
form_field_new: new_field, dup_field, link_field, free_field,(3X)
.... create and destroy forms fields
form_field_opts: set_field_opts, field_opts_on, field_opts_off, field_opts(3X)
.... forms field option routines
form_field_userptr: set_field_userptr, field_userptr(3X)
.... associate application data with forms
form_field_validation: set_field_type, field_type, field_arg(3X)
.... forms field data type validation
form_fieldtype: new_fieldtype, free_fieldtype, set_fieldtype_arg,
    set_fieldtype_choice, link_fieldtype(3X) .... forms fieldtype routines
form_hook: set_form_init, form_init, set_form_term, form_term, set_field_init,
    field_init, set_field_term, field_term(3X)
.... assign application-specific routines for invocation by forms
form_new: new_form, free_form(3X) .... create and destroy forms
form_new_page: set_new_page, new_page(3X) .... forms pagination
form_opts: set_form_opts, form_opts_on, form_opts_off, form_opts(3X)
.... forms option routines
form_page: set_form_page, form_page, set_current_field, current_field,
    field_index(3X) .... set forms current page and field
form_post: post_form, unpost_form(3X) .... write or erase forms from associated subwindows
form_userptr: set_form_userptr, form_userptr(3X) .... associate application data with forms
form_win: set_form_win, form_win, set_form_sub, form_sub, scale_form(3X)
.... forms window and subwindow association routines
forms(3X) .... character based forms package

10   Programmer´s Reference Manual: Operating System API

fpgetround, fpsetround, fpgetmask, fpsetmask, fpgetsticky, fpsetsticky(3C)
.... IEEE floating-point environment control
fread, fwrite(3S) .... binary input/output
frexp, frexpl, ldexp, ldexpl, logb, modf, modff, modfl, nextafter, scalb, scalbl(3C)
.... manipulate parts of floating-point numbers
fseek, rewind, ftell(3S) .... reposition a file pointer in a stream
fsetpos, fgetpos(3C) .... reposition a file pointer in a stream
ftime(3C) .... get date and time
ftw, nftw(3C) .... walk a file tree
gamma, lgamma(3M) .... log gamma function
getc, getchar, fgetc, getw(3S) .... get character or word from a stream
getcwd(3C) .... get pathname of current working directory
getdate(3C) .... convert user format date and time
getdtablesize(3) .... get descriptor table size
getenv(3C) .... return value for environment name
getgrent, getgrgid, getgrnam, setgrent, endgrent, fgetgrent(3C) .... get group file entry
gethostent, gethostbyaddr, gethostbyname, sethostent, endhostent(3N)
.... get network host entry
gethostid(3) .... get unique identifier of current host
gethostname, sethostname(3) .... get/set name of current host
getitimer, setitimer(3C) .... get/set value of interval timer
getlogin(3C) .... get login name
getmntent, getmntany(3C) .... get mnttab file entry
getnetconfig(3N) .... get network configuration database entry
getnetent, getnetbyaddr, getnetbyname, setnetent, endnetent(3N) .... get network entry
getnetpath(3N) .... get netconfig entry corresponding to NETPATH component
getopt(3C) .... get option letter from argument vector
getpagesize(3) .... get system page size
getpass(3C) .... read a password
getpeername(3N) .... get name of connected peer
getpriority, setpriority(3) .... get/set program scheduling priority
getprotoent, getprotobynumber, getprotobyname, setprotoent, endprotoent(3N)
.... get protocol entry
getpw(3C) .... get name from UID
getpwent, getpwuid, getpwnam, setpwent, endpwent, fgetpwent(3C)
.... manipulate password file entry
getrusage(3) .... get information about resource utilization
gets, fgets(3S) .... get a string from a stream
getservent, getservbyport, getservbyname, setservent, endservent(3N) .... get service entry
getsockname(3N) .... get socket name

Table of Contents

getsockopt, setsockopt(3N) .... get and set options on sockets
getspent, getspnam, setspent, endspent, fgetspent, lckpwdf, ulckpwdf(3C)
.... manipulate shadow password file entry
getsubopt(3C) .... parse suboptions from a string
gettimeofday, settimeofday(3C) .... get or set the date and time
gettimeofday, settimeofday(3) .... get or set the date and time
gettxt(3C) .... retrieve a text string
getusershell, setusershell, endusershell(3) .... get legal user shells
getut: getutent, getutid, getutline, pututline, setutent, endutent, utmpname(3C)
.... access utmp file entry
getutx: getutxent, getutxid, getutxline, pututxline, setutxent, endutxent,
    utmpxname, getutmp, getutmpx, updwtmp, updwtmpx(3C) .... access utmpx file entry
getvfsent, getvfsfile, getvfsspec, getvfsany(3C) .... get vfstab file entry
getwd(3) .... get current working directory pathname
gmatch(3G) .... shell global pattern matching
grantpt(3C) .... grant access to the slave pseudo-terminal device
hsearch, hcreate, hdestroy(3C) .... manage hash search tables
hypot(3M) .... Euclidean distance function
ieee_functions, fp_class, isnan, copysign, scalbn(3M)
.... miscellaneous functions for IEEE arithmetic
ieee_handler(3M) .... IEEE exception trap handler function
index, rindex(3) .... string operations
inet: inet_addr, inet_network, inet_makeaddr, inet_lnaof, inet_netof, inet_ntoa(3N)
.... Internet address manipulation
initgroups(3C) .... initialize the supplementary group access list
insque, remque(3C) .... insert/remove element from a queue
isastream(3C) .... test a file descriptor
isencrypt(3G) .... determine whether a character buffer is encrypted
isnan, isnand, isnanf, isnanl, finite, finitel, fpclass, fpclassl, unordered,
    unorderedl(3C) .... determine type of floating-point number
killpg(3) .... send signal to a process group
l3tol, ltol3(3C) .... convert between 3-byte integers and long integers
libwindows(3X) .... windowing terminal function library
listen(3N) .... listen for connections on a socket
localeconv(3C) .... get numeric formatting information
lockf(3C) .... record locking on files
lsearch, lfind(3C) .... linear search and update
maillock(3X) .... manage lockfile for user's mailbox
makecontext, swapcontext(3C) .... manipulate user contexts
makedev, major, minor(3C) .... manage a device number

12 Programmer's Reference Manual: Operating System API

malloc, free, realloc, calloc, memalign, valloc,(3C) .... memory allocator
malloc, free, realloc, calloc, mallopt, mallinfo(3X) .... memory allocator
matherr(3M) .... error-handling function
mbchar: mbtowc, mblen, wctomb(3C) .... multibyte character handling
mbstring: mbstowcs, wcstombs(3C) .... multibyte string functions
mctl(3) .... memory management control
memory: memccpy, memchr, memcmp, memcpy, memmove, memset(3C)
 .... memory operations
menu_attributes: set_menu_fore, menu_fore, set_menu_back, menu_back,
 set_menu_grey, menu_grey, set_menu_pad, menu_pad(3X)
 .... control menus display attributes
menu_cursor: pos_menu_cursor(3X) .... correctly position a menus cursor
menu_driver(3X) .... command processor for the menus subsystem
menu_format: set_menu_format, menu_format(3X)
 .... set and get maximum numbers of rows and columns in menus
menu_hook: set_item_init, item_init, set_item_term, item_term, set_menu_init,
 menu_init, set_menu_term, menu_term(3X)
 .... assign application-specific routines for automatic invocation by menus
menu_item_current: set_current_item, current_item, set_top_row, top_row,
 item_index(3X) .... set and get current menus items
menu_item_name: item_name, item_description(3X) .... get menus item name and description
menu_item_new: new_item, free_item(3X) .... create and destroy menus items
menu_item_opts: set_item_opts, item_opts_on, item_opts_off, item_opts(3X)
 .... menus item option routines
menu_item_userptr: set_item_userptr, item_userptr(3X)
 .... associate application data with menus items
menu_item_value: set_item_value, item_value(3X) .... set and get menus item values
menu_item_visible: item_visible(3X) .... tell if menus item is visible
menu_items: set_menu_items, menu_items, item_count(3X)
 .... connect and disconnect items to and from menus
menu_mark: set_menu_mark, menu_mark(3X) .... menus mark string routines
menu_new: new_menu, free_menu(3X) .... create and destroy menus
menu_opts: set_menu_opts, menu_opts_on, menu_opts_off, menu_opts(3X)
 .... menus option routines
menu_pattern: set_menu_pattern, menu_pattern(3X)
 .... set and get menus pattern match buffer
menu_post: post_menu, unpost_menu(3X)
 .... write or erase menus from associated subwindows
menu_userptr: set_menu_userptr, menu_userptr(3X) ... associate application data with menus

Table of Contents

menu_win: set_menu_win, menu_win, set_menu_sub, menu_sub, scale_menu(3X)
.... menus window and subwindow association routines
menus(3X) .... character based menus package
mkdirp, rmdirp(3G) .... create, remove directories in a path
mkfifo(3C) .... create a new FIFO
mkstemp(3) .... make a unique file name
mktemp(3C) .... make a unique file name
mktime(3C) .... converts a tm structure to a calendar time
mlock, munlock(3C) .... lock (or unlock) pages in memory
mlockall, munlockall(3C) .... lock or unlock address space
monitor(3C) .... prepare execution profile
mp: madd, msub, mult, mdiv, mcmp, min, mout, pow, gcd, rpow, msqrt, sdiv,
    itom, xtom, mtox, mfree(3X) .... multiple precision integer arithmetic
msync(3C) .... synchronize memory with physical storage
ndbm: dbm_clearerr, dbm_close, dbm_delete, dbm_error, dbm_fetch, dbm_firstkey,
    dbm_nextkey, dbm_open, dbm_store(3) .... data base subroutines
netdir_getbyname, netdir_getbyaddr, netdir_free, netdir_mergeaddr, taddr2uaddr,
    uaddr2taddr, netdir_perror, netdir_sperror(3N)
.... generic transport name-to-address translation
nice(3C) .... change priority of a process
nl_langinfo(3C) .... language information
nlist(3E) .... get entries from name list
nlist(3) .... get entries from symbol table
nlsgetcall(3N) .... get client's data passed via the listener
nlsprovider(3N) .... get name of transport provider
nlsrequest(3N) .... format and send listener service request message
offsetof(3C) .... offset of structure member
p2open, p2close(3G) .... open, close pipes to and from a command
panel_above: panel_above, panel_below(3X) .... panels deck traversal primitives
panel_move: move_panel(3X) .... move a panels window on the virtual screen
panel_new: new_panel, del_panel(3X) .... create and destroy panels
panel_show: show_panel, hide_panel, panel_hidden(3X) .. panels deck manipulation routines
panel_top: top_panel, bottom_panel(3X) .... panels deck manipulation routines
panel_update: update_panels(3X) .... panels virtual screen refresh routine
panel_userptr: set_panel_userptr, panel_userptr(3X)
.... associate application data with a panels panel
panel_window: panel_window, replace_panel(3X)
.... get or set the current window of a panels panel
panels(3X) .... character based panels package
pathfind(3G) .... search for named file in named directories

perror(3C) .... print system error messages
popen, pclose(3S) .... initiate pipe to/from a process
printf, fprintf, sprintf(3S) .... print formatted output
printf, fprintf, sprintf, vprintf, vfprintf, vsprintf(3S) .... formatted output conversion
psignal, psiginfo(3C) .... system signal messages
psignal, sys_siglist(3) .... system signal messages
ptsname(3C) .... get name of the slave pseudo-terminal device
publickey: getpublickey, getsecretkey(3N) .... retrieve public or secret key
putc, putchar, fputc, putw(3S) .... put character or word on a stream
putenv(3C) .... change or add value to environment
putpwent(3C) .... write password file entry
puts, fputs(3S) .... put a string on a stream
putspent(3C) .... write shadow password file entry
qsort(3C) .... quicker sort
raise(3C) .... send signal to program
rand, srand(3C) .... simple random-number generator
rand, srand(3C) .... simple random number generator
random, srandom, initstate, setstate(3)
 .... better random number generator; routines for changing generators
realpath(3C) .... returns the real file name
reboot(3) .... reboot system or halt processor
recv, recvfrom, recvmsg(3N) .... receive a message from a socket
regcmp, regex(3G) .... compile and execute regular expression
regex, re_comp, re_exec(3) .... regular expression handler
regexpr: compile, step, advance(3G) .... regular expression compile and match routines
remove(3C) .... remove file
resolver, res_mkquery, res_send, res_init, dn_comp, dn_expand(3N) .... resolver routines
rexec(3N) .... return stream to a remote command
rpc(3N) .... library routines for remote procedure calls
rpc_clnt_auth: auth_destroy, authnone_create, authsys_create,
 authsys_create_default(3N)
 .... library routines for client side remote procedure call authentication
rpc_clnt_calls: clnt_call, clnt_freeres, clnt_geterr, clnt_perrno, clnt_perror,
 clnt_sperrno, clnt_sperror, rpc_broadcast, rpc_call(3N)
 .... library routines for client side calls
rpc_clnt_create: clnt_control, clnt_create, clnt_destroy, clnt_dg_create,
 clnt_pcreateerror, clnt_raw_create, clnt_spcreateerror, clnt_tli_create,
 clnt_tp_create, clnt_vc_create(3N)
 .... library routines for dealing with creation and manipulation of CLIENT handles

Table of Contents

rpc_svc_calls: rpc_reg, svc_reg, svc_unreg, xprt_register, xprt_unregister(3N) .... library routines for registering servers
rpc_svc_create: svc_create, svc_destroy, svc_dg_create, svc_fd_create, svc_raw_create, svc_tli_create, svc_tp_create, svc_vc_create(3N) .... library routines for dealing with the creation of server handles
rpc_svc_err: svcerr_auth, svcerr_decode, svcerr_noproc, svcerr_noprog, svcerr_progvers, svcerr_systemerr, svcerr_weakauth(3N) .... library routines for server side remote procedure call errors
rpc_svc_reg: svc_freeargs, svc_getargs, svc_getreqset, svc_getrpccaller, svc_run, svc_sendreply(3N) .... library routines for RPC servers
rpc_xdr: xdr_accepted_reply, xdr_authsys_parms, xdr_callhdr, xdr_callmsg, xdr_opaque_auth, xdr_rejected_reply, xdr_replymsg(3N) .... XDR library routines for remote procedure calls
rpcbind: rpcb_getmaps, rpcb_getaddr, rpcb_gettime, rpcb_rmtcall, rpcb_set, rpcb_unset(3N) .... library routines for RPC bind service
rusers(3N) .... return information about users on remote machines
rwall(3N) .... write to specified remote machines
scandir, alphasort(3) .... scan a directory
scanf, fscanf, sscanf(3S) .... convert formatted input
secure_rpc: authdes_seccreate, authdes_getucred, getnetname, host2netname, key_decryptsession, key_encryptsession, key_gendes, key_setsecret, netname2host, netname2user, user2netname(3N) .... library routines for secure remote procedure calls
select(3C) .... synchronous I/O multiplexing
send, sendto, sendmsg(3N) .... send a message from a socket
setbuf, setvbuf(3S) .... assign buffering to a stream
setbuf, setbuffer, setlinebuf, setvbuf(3S) .... assign buffering to a stream
setbuffer, setlinebuf(3S) .... assign buffering to a stream
setjmp, longjmp(3C) .... non-local goto
setjmp, longjmp, _setjmp, _longjmp, sigsetjmp, siglongjmp(3) .... non-local goto
setlocale(3C) .... modify and query a program's locale
setregid(3) .... set real and effective group IDs
setreuid(3) .... set real and effective user IDs
shutdown(3N) .... shut down part of a full-duplex connection
sigblock, sigmask(3) .... block signals
sigfpe(3) .... signal handling for specific SIGFPE codes
siginterrupt(3) .... allow signals to interrupt system calls
signal(3) .... simplified software signal facilities
sigpause(3) .... automically release blocked signals and wait for interrupt
sigsetjmp, siglongjmp(3C) .... a non-local goto with signal state

sigsetmask(3) .... set current signal mask
sigemptyset, sigfillset, sigaddset, sigdelset, sigismember(3C) .... manipulate sets of signals
sigstack(3) .... set and/or get signal stack context
sigvec(3) .... software signal facilities
sinh, sinhf, cosh, coshf, tanh, tanhf, asinh, acosh, atanh(3M) .... hyperbolic functions
sleep(3C) .... suspend execution for interval
sleep(3) .... suspend execution for interval
socket(3N) .... create an endpoint for communication
socketpair(3N) .... create a pair of connected sockets
spray(3N) .... scatter data in order to check the network
sputl, sgetl(3X) .... access long integer data in a machine-independent fashion
ssignal, gsignal(3C) .... software signals
stdio(3S) .... standard buffered input/output package
stdipc: ftok(3C) .... standard interprocess communication package
str: strfind, strrspn, strtrns(3G) .... string manipulations
strccpy: streadd, strcadd, strecpy(3G) .. copy strings, compressing or expanding escape codes
strcoll(3C) .... string collation
strerror(3C) .... get error message string
strftime, cftime, ascftime(3C) .... convert date and time to string
string: strcat, strdup, strncat, strcmp, strncmp, strcpy, strncpy, strlen, strchr,
    strrchr, strpbrk, strspn, strcspn, strtok, strstr(3C) .... string operations
string: strcasecmp, strncasecmp(3) .... string operations
strtod, strtold, atof(3C) .... convert string to double-precision number
strtol, strtoul, atol, atoi(3C) .... convert string to integer
strxfrm(3C) .... string transformation
swab(3C) .... swap bytes
syscall(3) .... indirect system call
sysconf(3C) .... retrieves configurable system variables
sysconf(3C) .... retrieves configurable system variables
syslog, openlog, closelog, setlogmask(3) .... control system log
system(3S) .... issue a shell command
t_accept(3N) .... accept a connect request
t_alloc(3N) .... allocate a library structure
t_bind(3N) .... bind an address to a transport endpoint
t_close(3N) .... close a transport endpoint
t_connect(3N) .... establish a connection with another transport user
t_error(3N) .... produce error message
t_free(3N) .... free a library structure
t_getinfo(3N) .... get protocol-specific service information
t_getstate(3N) .... get the current state

Table of Contents

t_listen(3N) .... listen for a connect request
t_look(3N) .... look at the current event on a transport endpoint
t_open(3N) .... establish a transport endpoint
t_optmgmt(3N) .... manage options for a transport endpoint
t_rcv(3N) .... receive data or expedited data sent over a connection
t_rcvconnect(3N) .... receive the confirmation from a connect request
t_rcvdis(3N) .... retrieve information from disconnect
t_rcvrel(3N) .... acknowledge receipt of an orderly release indication
t_rcvudata(3N) .... receive a data unit
t_rcvuderr(3N) .... receive a unit data error indication
t_snd(3N) .... send data or expedited data over a connection
t_snddis(3N) .... send user-initiated disconnect request
t_sndrel(3N) .... initiate an orderly release
t_sndudata(3N) .... send a data unit
t_sync(3N) .... synchronize transport library
t_unbind(3N) .... disable a transport endpoint
tam(3X) .... TAM transition libraries
tcsetpgrp(3C) .... set terminal foreground process group id
times(3C) .... get process times
timezone(3C) .... get time zone name given offset from GMT
tmpfile(3S) .... create a temporary file
tmpnam, tempnam(3S) .... create a name for a temporary file
trig: sin, sinf, cos, cosf, tan, tanf, asin, asinf, acos, acosf, atan, atanf, atan2,
    atan2f(3M) .... trigonometric functions
truncate, ftruncate(3C) .... set a file to a specified length
tsearch, tfind, tdelete, twalk(3C) .... manage binary search trees
ttyname, isatty(3C) .... find name of a terminal
ttyslot(3C) .... find the slot in the utmp file of the current user
ualarm(3) .... schedule signal after interval in microseconds
ungetc(3S) .... push character back onto input stream
unlockpt(3C) .... unlock a pseudo-terminal master/slave pair
usleep(3) .... suspend execution for interval in microseconds
utimes(3) .... set file times
vprintf, vfprintf, vsprintf(3S) .... print formatted output of a variable argument list
wait, wait3, WIFSTOPPED, WIFSIGNALED, WIFEXITED(3)
    .... wait for process to terminate or stop
xdr(3N) .... library routines for external data representation
xdr_admin: xdr_getpos, xdr_inline, xdrrec_eof, xdr_setpos(3N)
    .... library routines for external data representation

xdr_complex: xdr_array, xdr_bytes, xdr_opaque, xdr_pointer, xdr_reference,
    xdr_string, xdr_union, xdr_vector, xdr_wrapstring(3N)
    .... library routines for external data representation
xdr_create: xdr_destroy, xdrmem_create, xdrrec_create, xdrstdio_create(3N)
    .... library routines for external data representation stream creation
xdr_simple: xdr_bool, xdr_char, xdr_double, xdr_enum, xdr_float, xdr_free,
    xdr_int, xdr_long, xdr_short, xdr_u_char, xdr_u_long, xdr_u_short,
    xdr_void(3N) .... library routines for external data representation
ypclnt, yp_get_default_domain, yp_bind, yp_unbind, yp_match, yp_first, yp_next,
    yp_all, yp_order, yp_master, yperr_string, ypprot_err(3N) .... NIS client interface
yp_update(3N) .... change NIS information

Section 4 − File Formats

intro(4) .... introduction to file formats
a.out(4) .... ELF (Executable and Linking Format) files
acct(4) .... per-process accounting file format
admin(4) .... installation defaults file
aliases, addresses, forward(4) .... addresses and aliases for sendmail
ar(4) .... archive file format
archives(4) .... device header file
binarsys(4) .... remote system information for the ckbinarsys command
boot(4) .... boot
compver(4) .... compatible versions file
copyright(4) .... copyright information file
core(4) .... core image file
cron(4) .... cron
depend(4) .... software dependencies files
dfstab(4) .... file containing commands for sharing resources
dir (s5)(4) .... format of s5 directories
dir (ufs)(4) .... format of ufs directories
dirent(4) .... file system independent directory entry
dump(4) .... dump
ethers(4) .... Ethernet address to hostname database or domain
/dev/fd(4) .... file descriptor files
filehdr(4) .... file header for common object files
fs (bfs)(4) .... format of the bfs file system volume
fs (s5)(4) .... format of s5 file system volume

Table of Contents

fs (ufs)(4) .... format of ufs file system volume
fspec(4) .... format specification in text files
fstypes(4) .... file that registers distributed file system packages
group(4) .... group file
hosts(4) .... host name data base
hosts.equiv, .rhosts(4) .... trusted hosts by system and by user
inetd.conf(4) .... Internet servers database
inittab(4) .... script for init
inode (bfs)(4) .... format of a bfs i-node
inode (s5)(4) .... format of an s5 i-node
inode (ufs)(4) .... format of a ufs inode
issue(4) .... issue identification file
limits(4) .... header file for implementation-specific constants
login(4) .... login default file
loginlog(4) .... log of failed login attempts
mailcnfg(4) .... initialization information for mail and rmail
mailsurr(4) .... surrogate commands for routing and transport of mail
mapchan(4) .... Format of tty device mapping files
mdevice (4) .... file format
mdevice (4) .... file format
mfsys (4) .... file format
mnttab(4) .... mounted file system table
mtune(4) .... file format
netconfig(4) .... network configuration database
netmasks(4) .... network mask data base
netrc(4) .... file for ftp remote login data
networks(4) .... network name data base
passwd(4) .... password file
pathalias(4) .... alias file for FACE
pkginfo(4) .... package characteristics file
pkgmap(4) .... package contents description file
pnch(4) .... file format for card images
/proc(4) .... process file system
profile(4) .... setting up an environment at login time
protocols(4) .... protocol name data base
prototype(4) .... package information file
publickey(4) .... public key database
resolv.conf(4) .... configuration file for name server routines
rfmaster(4) .... Remote File Sharing name server master file
routing(4) .... system supporting for packet network routing

rpc(4) .... rpc program number data base
rt_dptbl(4) .... real-time dispatcher parameter table
sccsfile(4) .... format of SCCS file
sdevice (4) .... file format
services(4) .... Internet services and aliases
sfsys (4) .... file format
shadow(4) .... shadow password file
sharetab(4) .... shared file system table
space(4) .... disk space requirement file
stat(4) .... data returned by stat system call
strcf(4) .... STREAMS Configuration File for STREAMS TCP/IP
strftime(4) .... language specific strings
stune (4) .... file format
su(4) .... su
syslog.conf(4) .... configuration file for syslogd system log daemon
term(4) .... format of compiled term file
terminfo(4) .... terminal capability data base
timezone(4) .... set default system time zone
ts_dptbl(4) .... time-sharing dispatcher parameter table
ttydefs(4) .... file contains terminal line settings information for ttymon
ttysrch(4) .... directory search list for ttyname
unistd(4) .... header file for symbolic constants
updaters(4) .... configuration file for Network Information Service (NIS) updating
utmp, wtmp(4) .... utmp and wtmp entry formats
utmpx, wtmpx(4) .... utmpx and wtmpx entry formats
vfstab(4) .... table of file system defaults
ypfiles(4) .... the Network Information Service (NIS) database and directory structure

Section 5 – Miscellaneous Facilities

intro(5) .... introduction to miscellany
ascii(5) .... map of ASCII character set
environ(5) .... user environment
eqnchar(5) .... special character definitions for eqn
fcntl(5) .... file control options
iconv(5) .... code set conversion tables
jagent(5) .... host control of windowing terminal
langinfo(5) .... language information constants

Table of Contents

layers(5) .... protocol used between host and windowing terminal under layers(1)
man(5) .... macros to format Reference Manual pages
math(5) .... math functions and constants
me(5) .... macros for formatting papers
ms(5) .... text formatting macros
nl_types(5) .... native language data types
prof(5) .... profile within a function
regexp: compile, step, advance(5) .... regular expression compile and match routines
siginfo(5) .... signal generation information
signal(5) .... base signals
stat(5) .... data returned by stat system call
stdarg(5) .... handle variable argument list
term(5) .... conventional names for terminals
types(5) .... primitive system data types
ucontext(5) .... user context
values(5) .... machine-dependent values
varargs(5) .... handle variable argument list
wstat(5) .... wait status
xtproto(5) .... multiplexed channels protocol used by xt driver

Permuted Index

Introduction

This reference manual describes the C language interface used by application programs to access the operating system services of UNIX System V Release 4. The UNIX operating system application program interface (API) described in this reference manual includes UNIX system calls and C library functions. (For a general overview of the UNIX system, see the *Product Overview*.)

Not all facilities, features, and functions described in this manual are available in every UNIX system implementation. Some of the features require additional facilities that may not exist on your system.

Organization of this Reference Manual

This manual contains the following sections (all section 3 manual pages are sorted alphabetically in one section):

Table 1: Operating System API Components

Section	Component Type
2	System Calls
3	BSD System Compatibility Library
3C	Standard C Library
3E	Executable and Linking Format Library
3G	General Purpose Library
3M	Math Library
3N	Networking Library
3S	Standard I/O Library
3X	Specialized Library

Section 2 – System Calls describes the access to the services provided by the UNIX system kernel, including the C language interface.

Section 3 – Library Functions describes the available general library routines. In many cases, several related routines are described on the same manual page. Their binary versions reside in various system libraries. See intro(3) for descriptions of these libraries and the files in which they are stored.

Manual Page Format

Manual pages follow a common format; although, some manual pages may omit some sections:

- The NAME section names the component(s) and briefly states its purpose.
- The SYNOPSIS section specifies the C language programming interface(s).
- The DESCRIPTION section details the behavior of the component(s).
- The EXAMPLES section gives examples, caveats and guidance on usage.
- The FILES section gives the file names that are built into the program.
- The SEE ALSO section lists related component interface descriptions.
- The DIAGNOSTICS section outlines return values and error conditions.

The NAME section lists the names of components described in that manual page with a brief, one-line statement of the nature and purpose of those components.

The SYNOPSIS section summarizes the component interface by compactly representing the order of any arguments for the component, the type of each argument (if any) and the type of value the component returns.

The DESCRIPTION section specifies the functionality of components without stipulating the implementation; it excludes the details of how UNIX System V implements these components and concentrates on defining the external features of a standard computing environment instead of the internals of the operating system, such as the scheduler or memory manager. Portable software should avoid using any features or side-effects not explicitly defined.

The SEE ALSO section refers the reader to other related manual pages in the UNIX System V Reference Manual Set as well as other documents. The SEE ALSO section identifies manual pages by the title that appears in the upper corners of each page of a manual page.

Some manual pages cover several commands, functions or other UNIX System V components; in which case, those components defined along with other related components share the same manual page title. For example, many references to the function `fwrite` cite `fread(3S)` because the function `fwrite` is described with the function `fread` in the manual page entitled `fread(3S)`.

How to Use a Manual Page

The manual page for each function describes how you should use the function in your program. As an example, we'll look at the strcmp function, which compares character strings. The function is described on the string(3C) manual page in Section 3 of the *Programmer's Reference Manual: Operating System API*. Related functions are described there as well, but only the sections relevant to strcmp are shown in the following figure.

Figure 1: Excerpt from string(3C) Manual Page

```
NAME
        string: strcat, strdup, strncat, strcmp, strncmp, strcpy, strncpy, strlen,
        strchr, strrchr, strpbrk, strspn, strcspn, strok - string operations.

SYNOPSIS
        #include <string.h>

        ...

        int strcmp(const char *sptr1, const char *sptr2);

        ...
DESCRIPTION

        ...

        strcmp compares its arguments and returns an integer less than, equal to, or
        greater than 0, according as the first argument is lexicographically less than,
        equal to, or greater than the second.

        ...
```

As shown, the DESCRIPTION section tells you what the function or macro does. It's the SYNOPSIS section, though, that contains the critical information about how you use the function or macro in your program. Note that the first line in the SYNOPSIS is

        #include <string.h>

That means that you should include the header file string.h in your program because it contains useful definitions or declarations relating to strcmp.

Introduction

In fact, `string.h` contains the `strcmp` "function prototype" as follows:

```
extern int strcmp(const char *, const char *);
```

A function prototype describes the kinds of arguments expected and returned by a C language function. Function prototypes afford a greater degree of argument type checking than old-style function declarations, and reduce the chance of using the function incorrectly. Including `string.h`, assures that the C compiler checks calls to `strcmp` against the official interface. You can, of course, examine `string.h` in the standard place for header files on your system, usually the `/usr/include` directory.

The SYNOPSIS for a C library function closely resembles the C language declaration of the function and its arguments. The SYNOPSIS tells the reader:

- the type of value returned by the function;
- the arguments the function expects to receive when called, if any;
- the argument types.

For example, the SYNOPSIS for the macro `feof` is:

```
#include <stdio.h>
int feof(FILE *sfp);
```

The SYNOPSIS section for `feof` shows that:

- The macro `feof` requires the header file `stdio.h`
- The macro `feof` returns a value of type `int`
- The argument *sfp* is a pointer to an object of type `FILE`

To use `feof` in a program, you need only write the macro call, preceded at some point by the `#include` control line, as in the following:

```
#include <stdio.h>    /* include definitions */
main() {
   FILE *infile;      /* define a file pointer */
   while (!feof(infile)) {   /* until end-of-file */
      /* operations on the file */
   }
}
```

The format of a SYNOPSIS section only resembles, but does not duplicate, the format of C language declarations. To show that some components take varying numbers of arguments, the SYNOPSIS section uses additional conventions not found in actual C function declarations:

- Text in `constant width` represents source-code typed just as it appears.
- Text in *italic* usually represents substitutable argument prototypes.
- Square brackets [ ] around arguments indicate optional arguments.
- Ellipses ... indicate that the previous arguments may repeat.
- If the type of an argument may vary, the SYNOPSIS omits the type.

For example, the SYNOPSIS for the function `printf` is:

```
#include <stdio.h>
int printf(const char *fmt [ , arg ... ]);
```

The SYNOPSIS section for `printf` shows that the argument *arg* is optional, may be repeated and is not always of the same data type. The DESCRIPTION section of the manual page provides any remaining information about the function `printf` and the arguments to it.

The DIAGNOSTICS section specifies return values and possible error conditions. Text in the DIAGNOSTICS section takes a conventional form which describes the return value in case of successful completion followed by the consequences of an unsuccessful completion, as in the following example:

On success, `lseek` returns the value of the resulting file-offset, as measured in bytes from the beginning of the file.

On failure, `lseek` returns -1, it does not change the file-offset, and `errno` equals:

`EBADF` if `fildes` is not a valid open file-descriptor.

`EINVAL` if whence is not `SEEK_SET`, `SEEK_CUR` or `SEEK_END`.

`ESPIPE` if `fildes` denotes a pipe or FIFO.

The `errno.h` header file defines symbolic names for error conditions described in `intro`(2) of the *Programmer's Reference Manual: Operating System API*.

Introduction _____

The SEE ALSO section may refer to manual pages in another reference manual. References to manual pages with section numbers other than those found in this volume mean that the component is described in another volume of the reference manual set. You can find the appropriate volume by checking the section numbers printed on the spine of each volume. Specifically, you'll find all section 1 manual pages (including sections 1, 1C, 1F, 1M and 1N) in the *User's Reference Manual/System Administrator's Reference Manual*. You'll find section 4, 5 and 7 references in the *System Files and Devices Reference Manual*.

Section 1 – Programming Commands

intro(1)	introduction to programming commands
admin(1)	create and administer SCCS files
ar(1)	maintain portable archive or library
as(1)	assembler
cb(1)	C program beautifier
cc(1)	C compiler
cdc(1)	change the delta comment of an SCCS delta
cflow(1)	generate C flowgraph
cof2elf(1)	COFF to ELF object file translation
comb(1)	combine SCCS deltas
convert(1)	convert archive files to common formats
cscope(1)	interactively examine a C program
ctrace(1)	C program debugger
cxref(1)	generate C program cross-reference
delta(1)	make a delta (change) to an SCCS file
dis(1)	object code disassembler
dump(1)	dump selected parts of an object file
get(1)	get a version of an SCCS file
help(1)	ask for help with message numbers or SCCS commands
install(1M)	install commands
ld(1)	link editor for object files
ldd(1)	list dynamic dependencies
lex(1)	generate programs for simple lexical tasks
lint(1)	a C program checker
lorder(1)	find ordering relation for an object library
lprof(1)	display line-by-line execution count profile data
m4(1)	macro processor
make(1)	maintain, update, and regenerate groups of programs
mcs(1)	manipulate the comment section of an object file
nm(1)	print name list of an object file
prof(1)	display profile data
prs(1)	print an SCCS file
regcmp(1)	regular expression compile
rmdel(1)	remove a delta from an SCCS file
sact(1)	print current SCCS file editing activity
sccsdiff(1)	compare two versions of an SCCS file
sdb(1)	symbolic debugger
size(1)	print section sizes in bytes of object files
strip(1)	strip symbol table, debugging and line number information from an object file

Section 1 — Programming Commands

tsort(1) .... topological sort
unget(1) .... undo a previous get of an SCCS file
val(1) .... validate an SCCS file
vc(1) .... version control
what(1) .... print identification strings
x286emul(1) .... emulate XENIX 80286
yacc(1) .... yet another compiler-compiler

Where To Find Section 1 Manual Pages

 Section 1 manual pages describing programming commands have been moved to the *User's Reference Manual/System Administrator's Reference Manual*. See the "Preface" for a description of the design changes to this Reference Manual set.

Section 2 – System Calls

intro(2)	introduction to system calls and error numbers
access(2)	determine accessibility of a file
acct(2)	enable or disable process accounting
adjtime(2)	correct the time to allow synchronization of the system clock
alarm(2)	set a process alarm clock
brk, sbrk(2)	change data segment space allocation
chdir, fchdir(2)	change working directory
chmod, fchmod(2)	change mode of file
chown, lchown, fchown(2)	change owner and group of a file
chroot(2)	change root directory
chsize(2)	change the size of a file
close(2)	close a file descriptor
creat(2)	create a new file or rewrite an existing one
creatsem(2)	create an instance of a binary semaphore
dup(2)	duplicate an open file descriptor
errno(2)	complete list of the error numbers and their names
exec: execl, execv, execle, execve, execlp, execvp(2)	execute a file
exit, _exit(2)	terminate process
fcntl(2)	file control
fork(2)	create a new process
fpathconf, pathconf(2)	get configurable pathname variables
fsync(2)	synchronize a file's in-memory state with that on the physical medium
ftime(2)	get time and date
getcontext, setcontext(2)	get and set current user context
getdents(2)	read directory entries and put in a file system independent format
getgroups, setgroups(2)	get or set supplementary group access list IDs
getmsg(2)	get next message off a stream
getpid, getpgrp, getppid, getpgid(2)	get process, process group, and parent process IDs
getrlimit, setrlimit(2)	control maximum system resource consumption
getsid(2)	get session ID
getuid, geteuid, getgid, getegid(2)	get real user, effective user, real group, and effective group IDs
ioctl(2)	control device
kill(2)	send a signal to a process or a group of processes
link(2)	link to a file
lock(2)	lock a process in primary memory
locking(2)	lock or unlock a file region for reading or writing
lseek(2)	move read/write file pointer
memcntl(2)	memory management control

Section 2 – System Calls

mincore(2)	determine residency of memory pages
mkdir(2)	make a directory
mknod(2)	make a directory, or a special or ordinary file
mknod(2)	make a directory, or a special or ordinary file
mmap(2)	map pages of memory
mount(2)	mount a file system
mprotect(2)	set protection of memory mapping
msgctl(2)	message control operations
msgget(2)	get message queue
msgop: msgsnd, msgrcv(2)	message operations
munmap(2)	unmap pages of memory
nap(2)	suspend execution for a short interval
nice(2)	change priority of a time-sharing process
open(2)	open for reading or writing
opensem(2)	open a semaphore
p_online(2)	turn a processor online or offline
pause(2)	suspend process until signal
pipe(2)	create an interprocess channel
plock(2)	lock into memory or unlock process, text, or data
poll(2)	input/output multiplexing
priocntl(2)	process scheduler control
priocntlset(2)	generalized process scheduler control
processor_bind(2)	bind a process to a processor
processor_info(2)	get information about one processor
profil(2)	execution time profile
ptrace(2)	process trace
putmsg(2)	send a message on a stream
rdchk(2)	check to see if there is data to be read
read(2)	read from file
readlink(2)	read the value of a symbolic link
rename(2)	change the name of a file
rmdir(2)	remove a directory
sdenter, sdleave(2)	synchronize access to a shared data segment
sdget, sdfree(2)	attach and detach a shared data segment
sdgetv(2)	synchronize shared data access
semctl(2)	semaphore control operations
semget(2)	get set of semaphores
semop(2)	semaphore operations
setpgid(2)	set process group ID
setpgrp(2)	set process group ID

Section 2 - System Calls

setsid(2)	set session ID
setuid, setgid(2)	set user and group IDs
shmctl(2)	shared memory control operations
shmget(2)	get shared memory segment identifier
shmop: shmat, shmdt(2)	shared memory operations
sigaction(2)	detailed signal management
sigaltstack(2)	set or get signal alternate stack context
signal, sigset, sighold, sigrelse, sigignore, sigpause(2)	simplified signal management
sigpending(2)	examine signals that are blocked and pending
sigprocmask(2)	change or examine signal mask
sigsem(2)	signal a process waiting on a semaphore
sigsend, sigsendset(2)	send a signal to a process or a group of processes
sigsuspend(2)	install a signal mask and suspend process until signal
stat, lstat, fstat(2)	get file status
stat, lstat, fstat(2)	get file status
statvfs, fstatvfs(2)	get file system information
stime(2)	set time
swapctl(2)	manage swap space
symlink(2)	make a symbolic link to a file
sync(2)	update super block
sysfs(2)	get file system type information
sysi86(2)	machine specific functions
sysinfo(2)	get and set system information strings
termios: tcgetattr, tcsetattr, tcsendbreak, tcdrain, tcflush, tcflow, cfgetospeed, cfgetispeed, cfsetispeed, cfsetospeed, tcgetpgrp, tcsetpgrp, tcgetsid(2)	general terminal interface
time(2)	get time
times(2)	get process and child process times
uadmin(2)	administrative control
ulimit(2)	get and set user limits
umask(2)	set and get file creation mask
umount(2)	unmount a file system
uname(2)	get name of current UNIX system
unlink(2)	remove directory entry
ustat(2)	get file system statistics
utime(2)	set file access and modification times
vfork(2)	spawn new process in a virtual memory efficient way
wait(2)	wait for child process to stop or terminate
waitid(2)	wait for child process to change state
waitpid(2)	wait for child process to change state

Section 2 – System Calls

waitsem, nbwaitsem (2) .... await and check access to a resource governed by a semaphore
write, writev (2) .... write on a file

intro(2)

NAME
intro – introduction to system calls and error numbers

SYNOPSIS
#include <errno.h>

DESCRIPTION
This section describes all of the system calls. Most of these calls have one or more error returns. An error condition is indicated by an otherwise impossible returned value. This is almost always −1 or the NULL pointer; the individual descriptions specify the details. An error number is also made available in the external variable errno. errno is not cleared on successful calls, so it should be tested only after an error has been indicated.

Each system call description attempts to list all possible error numbers. The following is a complete list of the error numbers and their names as defined in <errno.h>.

1 EPERM Not super-user
    Typically this error indicates an attempt to modify a file in some way forbidden except to its owner or the super-user. It is also returned for attempts by ordinary users to do things allowed only to the super-user.

2 ENOENT No such file or directory
    A file-name is specified and the file should exist but doesn't, or one of the directories in a path-name does not exist.

3 ESRCH No such process
    No process can be found corresponding to that specified by PID in the kill or ptrace routine.

4 EINTR Interrupted system call
    An asynchronous signal (such as interrupt or quit), which the user has elected to catch, occurred during a system service routine. If execution is resumed after processing the signal, it will appear as if the interrupted routine call returned this error condition.

5 EIO I/O error
    Some physical I/O error has occurred. This error may in some cases occur on a call following the one to which it actually applies.

6 ENXIO No such device or address
    I/O on a special file refers to a subdevice which does not exist, or exists beyond the limit of the device. It may also occur when, for example, a tape drive is not on-line or no disk pack is loaded on a drive.

7 E2BIG Arg list too long
    An argument list longer than ARG_MAX bytes is presented to a member of the exec family of routines. The argument list limit is the sum of the size of the argument list plus the size of the environment's exported shell variables.

8 ENOEXEC Exec format error
: A request is made to execute a file which, although it has the appropriate permissions, does not start with a valid format.

9 EBADF Bad file number
: Either a file descriptor refers to no open file, or a read [respectively, write] request is made to a file that is open only for writing (respectively, reading).

10 ECHILD No child processes
: A wait routine was executed by a process that had no existing or unwaited-for child processes.

11 EAGAIN No more processes
: For example, the fork routine failed because the system's process table is full or the user is not allowed to create any more processes, or a system call failed because of insufficient memory or swap space.

12 ENOMEM Not enough space
: During execution of an exec, brk, or sbrk routine, a program asks for more space than the system is able to supply. This is not a temporary condition; the maximum size is a system parameter. The error may also occur if the arrangement of text, data, and stack segments requires too many segmentation registers, or if there is not enough swap space during the fork routine. If this error occurs on a resource associated with Remote File Sharing (RFS), it indicates a memory depletion which may be temporary, dependent on system activity at the time the call was invoked.

13 EACCES Permission denied
: An attempt was made to access a file in a way forbidden by the protection system.

14 EFAULT Bad address
: The system encountered a hardware fault in attempting to use an argument of a routine. For example, errno potentially may be set to EFAULT any time a routine that takes a pointer argument is passed an invalid address, if the system can detect the condition. Because systems will differ in their ability to reliably detect a bad address, on some implementations passing a bad address to a routine will result in undefined behavior.

15 ENOTBLK Block device required
: A non-block file was mentioned where a block device was required (for example, in a call to the mount routine).

16 EBUSY Device busy
: An attempt was made to mount a device that was already mounted or an attempt was made to unmount a device on which there is an active file (open file, current directory, mounted-on file, active text segment). It will also occur if an attempt is made to enable accounting when it is already enabled. The device or resource is currently unavailable.

17 EEXIST   File exists
   An existing file was mentioned in an inappropriate context (for example, call to the `link` routine).

18 EXDEV   Cross-device link
   A link to a file on another device was attempted.

19 ENODEV   No such device
   An attempt was made to apply an inappropriate operation to a device (for example, read a write-only device).

20 ENOTDIR Not a directory
   A non-directory was specified where a directory is required (for example, in a path prefix or as an argument to the `chdir` routine).

21 EISDIR   Is a directory
   An attempt was made to write on a directory.

22 EINVAL   Invalid argument
   An invalid argument was specified (for example, unmounting a non-mounted device), mentioning an undefined signal in a call to the `signal` or `kill` routine.

23 ENFILE   File table overflow
   The system file table is full (that is, SYS_OPEN files are open, and temporarily no more files can be opened).

24 EMFILE   Too many open files
   No process may have more than OPEN_MAX file descriptors open at a time.

25 ENOTTY   Not a typewriter
   A call was made to the `ioctl` routine specifying a file that is not a special character device.

26 ETXTBSY Text file busy
   An attempt was made to execute a pure-procedure program that is currently open for writing. Also an attempt to open for writing or to remove a pure-procedure program that is being executed.

27 EFBIG   File too large
   The size of a file exceeded the maximum file size, FCHR_MAX [see `getrlimit`].

28 ENOSPC   No space left on device
   While writing an ordinary file or creating a directory entry, there is no free space left on the device. In the `fcntl` routine, the setting or removing of record locks on a file cannot be accomplished because there are no more record entries left on the system.

29 ESPIPE   Illegal seek
   A call to the `lseek` routine was issued to a pipe.

30 EROFS   Read-only file system
   An attempt to modify a file or directory was made on a device mounted read-only.

31 EMLINK Too many links
   An attempt to make more than the maximum number of links, LINK_MAX, to a file.

32 EPIPE Broken pipe
   A write on a pipe for which there is no process to read the data. This condition normally generates a signal; the error is returned if the signal is ignored.

33 EDOM Math argument out of domain of func
   The argument of a function in the math package (3M) is out of the domain of the function.

34 ERANGE Math result not representable
   The value of a function in the math package (3M) is not representable within machine precision.

35 ENOMSG No message of desired type
   An attempt was made to receive a message of a type that does not exist on the specified message queue [see msgop(2)].

36 EIDRM Identifier removed
   This error is returned to processes that resume execution due to the removal of a message or semaphore identifier from the system [see msgop(2), semop(2), msgctl(2), and semctl(2)].

37 ECHRNG Channel number out of range

38 EL2NSYNC Level 2 not synchronized

39 EL3HLT Level 3 halted

40 EL3RST Level 3 reset

41 ELNRNG Link number out of range

42 EUNATCH Protocol driver not attached

43 ENOCSI No CSI structure available

44 EL2HLT Level 2 halted

45 EDEADLK Deadlock condition
   A deadlock situation was detected and avoided. This error pertains to file and record locking.

46 ENOLCK No record locks available
   There are no more locks available. The system lock table is full [see fcntl(2)].

47–49 Reserved

58–59 Reserved

60 ENOSTR Device not a stream
   A putmsg or getmsg system call was attempted on a file descriptor that is not a STREAMS device.

61 ENODATA No data available

62 ETIME Timer expired
   The timer set for a STREAMS ioctl call has expired. The cause of this error is device specific and could indicate either a hardware or software failure, or perhaps a timeout value that is too short for the specific operation. The status of the ioctl operation is indeterminate.

63 ENOSR Out of stream resources
   During a STREAMS open, either no STREAMS queues or no STREAMS head data structures were available. This is a temporary condition; one may recover from it if other processes release resources.

64 ENONET Machine is not on the network
   This error is Remote File Sharing (RFS) specific. It occurs when users try to advertise, unadvertise, mount, or unmount remote resources while the machine has not done the proper startup to connect to the network.

65 ENOPKG Package not installed
   This error occurs when users attempt to use a system call from a package which has not been installed.

66 EREMOTE Object is remote
   This error is RFS specific. It occurs when users try to advertise a resource which is not on the local machine, or try to mount/unmount a device (or path-name) that is on a remote machine.

67 ENOLINK Link has been severed
   This error is RFS specific. It occurs when the link (virtual circuit) connecting to a remote machine is gone.

68 EADV Advertise error
   This error is RFS specific. It occurs when users try to advertise a resource which has been advertised already, or try to stop RFS while there are resources still advertised, or try to force unmount a resource when it is still advertised.

69 ESRMNT Srmount error
   This error is RFS specific. It occurs when an attempt is made to stop RFS while resources are still mounted by remote machines, or when a resource is readvertised with a client list that does not include a remote machine that currently has the resource mounted.

70 ECOMM Communication error on send
   This error is RFS specific. It occurs when the current process is waiting for a message from a remote machine, and the virtual circuit fails.

71 EPROTO Protocol error
   Some protocol error occurred. This error is device specific, but is generally not related to a hardware failure.

74 EMULTIHOP Multihop attempted
   This error is RFS specific. It occurs when users try to access remote resources which are not directly accessible.

76 EDOTDOT Error 76
   This error is RFS specific. A way for the server to tell the client that a process has transferred back from mount point.

77 EBADMSG Not a data message
   During a read, getmsg, or ioctl I_RECVFD system call to a STREAMS device, something has come to the head of the queue that can't be processed. That something depends on the system call:
   read: control information or a passed file descriptor.
   getmsg: passed file descriptor.
   ioctl: control or data information.

78 ENAMETOOLONG File name too long
   The length of the path argument exceeds PATH_MAX, or the length of a path component exceeds NAME_MAX while _POSIX_NO_TRUNC is in effect; see limits(4).

79 EOVERFLOW
   Value too large for defined data type.

80 ENOTUNIQ Name not unique on network
   Given log name not unique.

81 EBADFD File descriptor in bad state
   Either a file descriptor refers to no open file or a read request was made to a file that is open only for writing.

82 EREMCHG Remote address changed

83 ELIBACC Cannot access a needed shared library
   Trying to exec an a.out that requires a static shared library and the static shared library doesn't exist or the user doesn't have permission to use it.

84 ELIBBAD Accessing a corrupted shared library
   Trying to exec an a.out that requires a static shared library (to be linked in) and exec could not load the static shared library. The static shared library is probably corrupted.

85 ELIBSCN .lib section in a.out corrupted
   Trying to exec an a.out that requires a static shared library (to be linked in) and there was erroneous data in the .lib section of the a.out. The .lib section tells exec what static shared libraries are needed. The a.out is probably corrupted.

86 ELIBMAX Attempting to link in more shared libraries than system limit
   Trying to exec an a.out that requires more static shared libraries than is allowed on the current configuration of the system. See the *System Administrator's Guide*.

87 ELIBEXEC Cannot exec a shared library directly
   Attempting to exec a shared library directly.

88 EILSEQ Error 88
: Illegal byte sequence. Handle multiple characters as a single character.

89 ENOSYS Operation not applicable

90 ELOOP Number of symbolic links encountered during path-name traversal exceeds MAXSYMLINKS

91 ESTART Error 91
: Interrupted system call should be restarted.

92 ESTRPIPE Error 92
: Streams pipe error (not externally visible).

93 ENOTEMPTY Directory not empty

94 EUSERS Too many users
: Too many users.

95 ENOTSOCK Socket operation on non-socket
: Self-explanatory.

96 EDESTADDRREQ Destination address required
: A required address was omitted from an operation on a transport endpoint. Destination address required.

97 EMSGSIZE Message too long
: A message sent on a transport provider was larger than the internal message buffer or some other network limit.

98 EPROTOTYPE Protocol wrong type for socket
: A protocol was specified that does not support the semantics of the socket type requested.

99 ENOPROTOOPT Protocol not available
: A bad option or level was specified when getting or setting options for a protocol.

120 EPROTONOSUPPORT Protocol not supported
: The protocol has not been configured into the system or no implementation for it exists.

121 ESOCKTNOSUPPORT Socket type not supported
: The support for the socket type has not been configured into the system or no implementation for it exists.

122 EOPNOTSUPP Operation not supported on transport endpoint
: For example, trying to accept a connection on a datagram transport endpoint.

123 EPFNOSUPPORT Protocol family not supported
: The protocol family has not been configured into the system or no implementation for it exists. Used for the Internet protocols.

124 EAFNOSUPPORT Address family not supported by protocol family
: An address incompatible with the requested protocol was used.

125 EADDRINUSE   Address already in use
    User attempted to use an address already in use, and the protocol does not allow this.
126 EADDRNOTAVAIL   Cannot assign requested address
    Results from an attempt to create a transport endpoint with an address not on the current machine.
127 ENETDOWN   Network is down
    Operation encountered a dead network.
128 ENETUNREACH   Network is unreachable
    Operation was attempted to an unreachable network.
129 ENETRESET   Network dropped connection because of reset
    The host you were connected to crashed and rebooted.
130 ECONNABORTED   Software caused connection abort
    A connection abort was caused internal to your host machine.
131 ECONNRESET   Connection reset by peer
    A connection was forcibly closed by a peer. This normally results from a loss of the connection on the remote host due to a timeout or a reboot.
132 ENOBUFS   No buffer space available
    An operation on a transport endpoint or pipe was not performed because the system lacked sufficient buffer space or because a queue was full.
133 EISCONN   Transport endpoint is already connected
    A connect request was made on an already connected transport endpoint; or, a sendto or sendmsg request on a connected transport endpoint specified a destination when already connected.
134 ENOTCONN   Transport endpoint is not connected
    A request to send or receive data was disallowed because the transport endpoint is not connected and (when sending a datagram) no address was supplied.
143 ESHUTDOWN   Cannot send after transport endpoint shutdown
    A request to send data was disallowed because the transport endpoint has already been shut down.
144 ETOOMANYREFS   Too many references: cannot splice
145 ETIMEDOUT   Connection timed out
    A connect or send request failed because the connected party did not properly respond after a period of time. (The timeout period is dependent on the communication protocol.)
146 ECONNREFUSED   Connection refused
    No connection could be made because the target machine actively refused it. This usually results from trying to connect to a service that is inactive on the remote host.

147 EHOSTDOWN   Host is down
: A transport provider operation failed because the destination host was down.

148 EHOSTUNREACH   No route to host
: A transport provider operation was attempted to an unreachable host.

149 EALREADY   Operation already in progress
: An operation was attempted on a non-blocking object that already had an operation in progress.

150 EINPROGRESS   Operation now in progress
: An operation that takes a long time to complete (such as a `connect`) was attempted on a non-blocking object.

151 ESTALE   Stale NFS file handle

DEFINITIONS

Background Process Group
Any process group that is not the foreground process group of a session that has established a connection with a controlling terminal.

Controlling Process
A session leader that established a connection to a controlling terminal.

Controlling Terminal
A terminal that is associated with a session. Each session may have, at most, one controlling terminal associated with it and a controlling terminal may be associated with only one session. Certain input sequences from the controlling terminal cause signals to be sent to process groups in the session associated with the controlling terminal; see `termio`(7).

Directory
Directories organize files into a hierarchical system where directories are the nodes in the hierarchy. A directory is a file that catalogues the list of files, including directories (sub-directories), that are directly beneath it in the hierarchy. Entries in a directory file are called links. A link associates a file identifier with a file-name. By convention, a directory contains at least two links, . (dot) and .. (dot-dot). The link called dot refers to the directory itself while dot-dot refers to its parent directory. The root directory, which is the top-most node of the hierarchy, has itself as its parent directory. The path-name of the root directory is / and the parent directory of the root directory is /.

Downstream
In a stream, the direction from stream head to driver.

Driver
In a stream, the driver provides the interface between peripheral hardware and the stream. A driver can also be a pseudo-driver, such as a multiplexor or log driver [see `log`(7)], which is not associated with a hardware device.

Effective User ID and Effective Group ID
An active process has an effective user ID and an effective group ID that are used to determine file access permissions (see below). The effective user ID and effective group ID are equal to the process's real user ID and real group ID

respectively, unless the process or one of its ancestors evolved from a file that had the set-user-ID bit or set-group ID bit set [see exec(2)].

File Access Permissions

Read, write, and execute/search permissions on a file are granted to a process if one or more of the following are true:

> The effective user ID of the process is super-user.

> The effective user ID of the process matches the user ID of the owner of the file and the appropriate access bit of the "owner" portion (0700) of the file mode is set.

> The effective user ID of the process does not match the user ID of the owner of the file, but either the effective group ID or one of the supplementary group IDs of the process match the group ID of the file and the appropriate access bit of the "group" portion (0070) of the file mode is set.

> The effective user ID of the process does not match the user ID of the owner of the file, and neither the effective group ID nor any of the supplementary group IDs of the process match the group ID of the file, but the appropriate access bit of the "other" portion (0007) of the file mode is set.

Otherwise, the corresponding permissions are denied.

File Descriptor

A file descriptor is a small integer used to do I/O on a file. The value of a file descriptor is from 0 to (NOFILES−1). A process may have no more than NOFILES file descriptors open simultaneously. A file descriptor is returned by system calls such as open, or pipe. The file descriptor is used as an argument by calls such as read, write, ioctl, and close.

File-Name

Names consisting of 1 to NAME_MAX characters may be used to name an ordinary file, special file or directory.

These characters may be selected from the set of all character values excluding \0 (null) and the ASCII code for / (slash).

Note that it is generally unwise to use *, ?, [, or] as part of file-names because of the special meaning attached to these characters by the shell [see sh(1)]. Although permitted, the use of unprintable characters in file-names should be avoided.

A file-name is sometimes referred to as a path-name component. The interpretation of a path-name component is dependent on the values of NAME_MAX and _POSIX_NO_TRUNC associated with the path prefix of that component. If any path-name component is longer than NAME_MAX and _POSIX_NO_TRUNC is in effect for the path prefix of that component [see fpathconf(2) and limits(4)], it shall be considered an error condition in that implementation. Otherwise, the implementation shall use the first NAME_MAX bytes of the path-name component.

Foreground Process Group

Each session that has established a connection with a controlling terminal will distinguish one process group of the session as the foreground process group of the controlling terminal. This group has certain privileges when accessing its controlling terminal that are denied to background process groups.

Message
In a stream, one or more blocks of data or information, with associated STREAMS control structures. Messages can be of several defined types, which identify the message contents. Messages are the only means of transferring data and communicating within a stream.

Message Queue
In a stream, a linked list of messages awaiting processing by a module or driver.

Message Queue Identifier
A message queue identifier (msqid) is a unique positive integer created by a msgget system call. Each msqid has a message queue and a data structure associated with it. The data structure is referred to as msqid_ds and contains the following members:

```
struct   ipc_perm msg_perm;
struct   msg *msg_first;
struct   msg *msg_last;
ushort   msg_cbytes;
ushort   msg_qnum;
ushort   msg_qbytes;
pid_t    msg_lspid;
pid_t    msg_lrpid;
time_t   msg_stime;
time_t   msg_rtime;
time_t   msg_ctime;
```

Here are descriptions of the fields of the msqid_ds structure:

msg_perm is an ipc_perm structure that specifies the message operation permission (see below). This structure includes the following members:

```
uid_t    cuid;   /* creator user id */
gid_t    cgid;   /* creator group id */
uid_t    uid;    /* user id */
gid_t    gid;    /* group id */
mode_t   mode;   /* r/w permission */
ushort   seq;    /* slot usage sequence # */
key_t    key;    /* key */
```

*msg_first is a pointer to the first message on the queue.

*msg_last is a pointer to the last message on the queue.

msg_cbytes is the current number of bytes on the queue.

msg_qnum is the number of messages currently on the queue.

msg_qbytes is the maximum number of bytes allowed on the queue.

msg_lspid is the process ID of the last process that performed a `msgsnd` operation.

msg_lrpid is the process id of the last process that performed a `msgrcv` operation.

msg_stime the time of the last `msgsnd` operation.

msg_rtime the time of the last `msgrcv` operation.

msg_ctime the time of the last `msgctl` operation that changed a member of the above structure.

Message Operation Permissions

In the `msgop` and `msgctl` system call descriptions, the permission required for an operation is given as {*token*}, where *token* is the type of permission needed, interpreted as follows:

```
00400   READ by user
00200   WRITE by user
00040   READ by group
00020   WRITE by group
00004   READ by others
00002   WRITE by others
```

Read and write permissions on a `msqid` are granted to a process if one or more of the following are true:

The effective user ID of the process is super-user.

The effective user ID of the process matches `msg_perm.cuid` or `msg_perm.uid` in the data structure associated with `msqid` and the appropriate bit of the "user" portion (0600) of `msg_perm.mode` is set.

The effective group ID of the process matches `msg_perm.cgid` or `msg_perm.gid` and the appropriate bit of the "group" portion (060) of `msg_perm.mode` is set.

The appropriate bit of the "other" portion (006) of `msg_perm.mode` is set.

Otherwise, the corresponding permissions are denied.

Module

A module is an entity containing processing routines for input and output data. It always exists in the middle of a stream, between the stream's head and a driver. A module is the STREAMS counterpart to the commands in a shell pipeline except that a module contains a pair of functions which allow independent bidirectional (downstream and upstream) data flow and processing.

Multiplexor

A multiplexor is a driver that allows streams associated with several user processes to be connected to a single driver, or several drivers to be connected to a single user process. STREAMS does not provide a general multiplexing driver, but does provide the facilities for constructing them and for connecting multiplexed configurations of streams.

Orphaned Process Group
A process group in which the parent of every member in the group is either itself a member of the group, or is not a member of the process group's session.

Path-Name
A path-name is a null-terminated character string starting with an optional slash (/), followed by zero or more directory names separated by slashes, optionally followed by a file-name.

If a path-name begins with a slash, the path search begins at the root directory. Otherwise, the search begins from the current working directory.

A slash by itself names the root directory.

Unless specifically stated otherwise, the null path-name is treated as if it named a non-existent file.

Process ID
Each process in the system is uniquely identified during its lifetime by a positive integer called a process ID. A process ID may not be reused by the system until the process lifetime, process group lifetime and session lifetime ends for any process ID, process group ID and session ID equal to that process ID.

Parent Process ID
A new process is created by a currently active process [see fork(2)]. The parent process ID of a process is the process ID of its creator.

Privilege
Having appropriate privilege means having the capability to override system restrictions.

Process Group
Each process in the system is a member of a process group that is identified by a process group ID. Any process that is not a process group leader may create a new process group and become its leader. Any process that is not a process group leader may join an existing process group that shares the same session as the process. A newly created process joins the process group of its parent.

Process Group Leader
A process group leader is a process whose process ID is the same as its process group ID.

Process Group ID
Each active process is a member of a process group and is identified by a positive integer called the process group ID. This ID is the process ID of the group leader. This grouping permits the signaling of related processes [see kill(2)].

Process Lifetime
A process lifetime begins when the process is forked and ends after it exits, when its termination has been acknowledged by its parent process. See wait(2).

Process Group Lifetime
A process group lifetime begins when the process group is created by its process group leader, and ends when the lifetime of the last process in the group ends or when the last process in the group leaves the group.

Read Queue
In a stream, the message queue in a module or driver containing messages moving upstream.

Real User ID and Real Group ID
Each user allowed on the system is identified by a positive integer (0 to MAXUID) called a real user ID.

Each user is also a member of a group. The group is identified by a positive integer called the real group ID.

An active process has a real user ID and real group ID that are set to the real user ID and real group ID, respectively, of the user responsible for the creation of the process.

Root Directory and Current Working Directory
Each process has associated with it a concept of a root directory and a current working directory for the purpose of resolving path-name searches. The root directory of a process need not be the root directory of the root file system.

Saved User ID and Saved Group ID
The saved user ID and saved group ID are the values of the effective user ID and effective group ID prior to an exec of a file whose set user or set group file mode bit has been set [see exec(2)].

Semaphore Identifier
A semaphore identifier (semid) is a unique positive integer created by a semget system call. Each semid has a set of semaphores and a data structure associated with it. The data structure is referred to as semid_ds and contains the following members:

```
struct   ipc_perm sem_perm;   /* operation permission struct */
struct   sem *sem_base;       /* ptr to first semaphore in set */
ushort   sem_nsems;           /* number of sems in set */
time_t   sem_otime;           /* last operation time */
time_t   sem_ctime;           /* last change time */
                              /* Times measured in secs since */
                              /* 00:00:00 GMT, Jan. 1, 1970 */
```

Here are descriptions of the fields of the semid_ds structure:

sem_perm is an ipc_perm structure that specifies the semaphore operation permission (see below). This structure includes the following members:

```
uid_t    uid;      /* user id */
gid_t    gid;      /* group id */
uid_t    cuid;     /* creator user id */
gid_t    cgid;     /* creator group id */
mode_t   mode;     /* r/a permission */
ushort   seq;      /* slot usage sequence number */
key_t    key;      /* key */
```

intro (2)

sem_nsems is equal to the number of semaphores in the set. Each semaphore in the set is referenced by a nonnegative integer referred to as a sem_num. sem_num values run sequentially from 0 to the value of sem_nsems minus 1.

sem_otime the time of the last semop operation.

sem_ctime the time of the last semctl operation that changed a member of the above structure.

A semaphore is a data structure called sem that contains the following members:

```
ushort   semval;    /* semaphore value */
pid_t    sempid;    /* pid of last operation */
ushort   semncnt;   /* # awaiting semval > cval */
ushort   semzcnt;   /* # awaiting semval = 0 */
```

semval is a non-negative integer that is the actual value of the semaphore.

sempid is equal to the process ID of the last process that performed a semaphore operation on this semaphore.

semncnt is a count of the number of processes that are currently suspended awaiting this semaphore's semval to become greater than its current value.

semzcnt is a count of the number of processes that are currently suspended awaiting this semaphore's semval to become 0.

Semaphore Operation Permissions

In the semop and semctl system call descriptions, the permission required for an operation is given as {*token*}, where *token* is the type of permission needed interpreted as follows:

```
00400   READ by user
00200   ALTER by user
00040   READ by group
00020   ALTER by group
00004   READ by others
00002   ALTER by others
```

Read and alter permissions on a semid are granted to a process if one or more of the following are true:

The effective user ID of the process is super-user.

The effective user ID of the process matches sem_perm.cuid or sem_perm.uid in the data structure associated with semid and the appropriate bit of the "user" portion (0600) of sem_perm.mode is set.

The effective group ID of the process matches sem_perm.cgid or sem_perm.gid and the appropriate bit of the "group" portion (060) of sem_perm.mode is set.

The appropriate bit of the "other" portion (06) of sem_perm.mode is set. Otherwise, the corresponding permissions are denied.

Session

A session is a group of processes identified by a common ID called a session ID, capable of establishing a connection with a controlling terminal. Any process that is not a process group leader may create a new session and process group, becoming the session leader of the session and process group leader of the process group. A newly created process joins the session of its creator.

Session ID

Each session in the system is uniquely identified during its lifetime by a positive integer called a session ID, the process ID of its session leader.

Session Leader

A session leader is a process whose session ID is the same as its process and process group ID.

Session Lifetime

A session lifetime begins when the session is created by its session leader, and ends when the lifetime of the last process that is a member of the session ends, or when the last process that is a member in the session leaves the session.

Shared Memory Identifier

A shared memory identifier (shmid) is a unique positive integer created by a shmget system call. Each shmid has a segment of memory (referred to as a shared memory segment) and a data structure associated with it. (Note that these shared memory segments must be explicitly removed by the user after the last reference to them is removed.) The data structure is referred to as shmid_ds and contains the following members:

```
struct ipc_perm  shm_perm;      /* operation permission struct */
int              shm_segsz;     /* size of segment */
struct region    *shm_reg;      /* ptr to region structure */
char             pad[4];        /* for swap compatibility */
pid_t            shm_lpid;      /* pid of last operation */
pid_t            shm_cpid;      /* creator pid */
ushort           shm_nattch;    /* number of current attaches */
ushort           shm_cnattch;   /* used only for shminfo */
time_t           shm_atime;     /* last attach time */
time_t           shm_dtime;     /* last detach time */
time_t           shm_ctime;     /* last change time */
                                /* Times measured in secs since */
                                /* 00:00:00 GMT, Jan. 1, 1970 */
```

Here are descriptions of the fields of the shmid_ds structure:

shm_perm is an ipc_perm structure that specifies the shared memory operation permission (see below). This structure includes the following members:

```
uid_t    cuid;    /* creator user id */
gid_t    cgid;    /* creator group id */
uid_t    uid;     /* user id */
gid_t    gid;     /* group id */
mode_t   mode;    /* r/w permission */
ushort   seq;     /* slot usage sequence # */
key_t    key;     /* key */
```

shm_segsz specifies the size of the shared memory segment in bytes.

shm_cpid is the process ID of the process that created the shared memory identifier.

shm_lpid is the process ID of the last process that performed a shmop operation.

shm_nattch is the number of processes that currently have this segment attached.

shm_atime the time of the last shmat operation [see shmop(2)].

shm_dtime the time of the last shmdt operation [see shmop(2)].

shm_ctime the time of the last shmctl operation that changed one of the members of the above structure.

Shared Memory Operation Permissions

In the shmop and shmctl system call descriptions, the permission required for an operation is given as {token}, where token is the type of permission needed interpreted as follows:

```
00400    READ by user
00200    WRITE by user
00040    READ by group
00020    WRITE by group
00004    READ by others
00002    WRITE by others
```

Read and write permissions on a shmid are granted to a process if one or more of the following are true:

The effective user ID of the process is super-user.

The effective user ID of the process matches shm_perm.cuid or shm_perm.uid in the data structure associated with shmid and the appropriate bit of the "user" portion (0600) of shm_perm.mode is set.

The effective group ID of the process matches shm_perm.cgid or shm_perm.gid and the appropriate bit of the "group" portion (060) of shm_perm.mode is set.

The appropriate bit of the "other" portion (06) of shm_perm.mode is set.

Otherwise, the corresponding permissions are denied.

Special Processes
  The process with ID 0 and the process with ID 1 are special processes referred to as proc0 and proc1; see kill(2). proc0 is the process scheduler. proc1 is the initialization process (init); proc1 is the ancestor of every other process in the system and is used to control the process structure.

STREAMS
  A set of kernel mechanisms that support the development of network services and data communication drivers. It defines interface standards for character input/output within the kernel and between the kernel and user level processes. The STREAMS mechanism is composed of utility routines, kernel facilities and a set of data structures.

Stream
  A stream is a full-duplex data path within the kernel between a user process and driver routines. The primary components are a stream head, a driver and zero or more modules between the stream head and driver. A stream is analogous to a shell pipeline except that data flow and processing are bidirectional.

Stream Head
  In a stream, the stream head is the end of the stream that provides the interface between the stream and a user process. The principal functions of the stream head are processing STREAMS-related system calls, and passing data and information between a user process and the stream.

Super-user
  A process is recognized as a super-user process and is granted special privileges, such as immunity from file permissions, if its effective user ID is 0.

Upstream
  In a stream, the direction from driver to stream head.

Write Queue
  In a stream, the message queue in a module or driver containing messages moving downstream.

access(2)

NAME
access – determine accessibility of a file

SYNOPSIS
#include <unistd.h>

int access(const char *path, int amode);

DESCRIPTION
path points to a path name naming a file. access checks the named file for accessibility according to the bit pattern contained in *amode*, using the real user ID in place of the effective user ID and the real group ID in place of the effective group ID. The bit pattern contained in *amode* is constructed by an OR of the following constants (defined in <unistd.h>):

R_OK	read
W_OK	write
X_OK	execute (search)
E_OK	use effective ID
F_OK	check existence of file

Access to the file is denied if one or more of the following are true:

EACCES	Search permission is denied on a component of the path prefix.
EACCES	Permission bits of the file mode do not permit the requested access.
EFAULT	*path* points outside the allocated address space for the process.
EINTR	A signal was caught during the access system call.
ELOOP	Too many symbolic links were encountered in translating *path*.
EMULTIHOP	Components of *path* require hopping to multiple remote machines.
ENAMETOOLONG	The length of the *path* argument exceeds {PATH_MAX}, or the length of a *path* component exceeds {NAME_MAX} while _POSIX_NO_TRUNC is in effect.
ENOTDIR	A component of the path prefix is not a directory.
ENOENT	Read, write, or execute (search) permission is requested for a null path name.
ENOENT	The named file does not exist.
ENOLINK	*path* points to a remote machine and the link to that machine is no longer active.
EROFS	Write access is requested for a file on a read-only file system.

SEE ALSO
chmod(2), stat(2)

"File Access Permission" in intro(2)

DIAGNOSTICS
If the requested access is permitted, a value of 0 is returned. Otherwise, a value of −1 is returned and errno is set to indicate the error.

NAME

acct – enable or disable process accounting

SYNOPSIS

    #include <unistd.h>

    int acct(const char *path);

DESCRIPTION

acct enables or disables the system process accounting routine. If the routine is enabled, an accounting record will be written in an accounting file for each process that terminates. The termination of a process can be caused by one of two things: an exit call or a signal [see exit(2) and signal(2)]. The effective user ID of the process calling acct must be superuser.

path points to a pathname naming the accounting file. The accounting file format is given in acct(4).

The accounting routine is enabled if *path* is non-zero and no errors occur during the system call. It is disabled if *path* is (char *)NULL and no errors occur during the system call.

acct will fail if one or more of the following are true:

EACCES	The file named by *path* is not an ordinary file.
EBUSY	An attempt is being made to enable accounting using the same file that is currently being used.
EFAULT	*path* points to an illegal address.
ELOOP	Too many symbolic links were encountered in translating *path*.
ENAMETOOLONG	The length of the *path* argument exceeds {PATH_MAX}, or the length of a *path* component exceeds {NAME_MAX} while _POSIX_NO_TRUNC is in effect.
ENOTDIR	A component of the path prefix is not a directory.
ENOENT	One or more components of the accounting file pathname do not exist.
EPERM	The effective user of the calling process is not superuser.
EROFS	The named file resides on a read-only file system.

SEE ALSO

exit(2), signal(2)

acct(4) in the *System Administrator's Reference Manual*

DIAGNOSTICS

Upon successful completion, a value of 0 is returned. Otherwise, a value of −1 is returned and errno is set to indicate the error.

NAME

adjtime – correct the time to allow synchronization of the system clock

SYNOPSIS

```
#include <sys/time.h>
```

```
int adjtime(struct timeval *delta, struct timeval *olddelta);
```

DESCRIPTION

adjtime adjusts the system's notion of the current time, as returned by gettimeofday(3C), advancing or retarding it by the amount of time specified in the struct timeval pointed to by *delta*.

The adjustment is effected by speeding up (if that amount of time is positive) or slowing down (if that amount of time is negative) the system's clock by some small percentage, generally a fraction of one percent. Thus, the time is always a monotonically increasing function. A time correction from an earlier call to adjtime may not be finished when adjtime is called again. If *delta* is 0, then *olddelta* returns the status of the effects of the previous adjtime call and there is no effect on the time correction as a result of this call. If *olddelta* is not a NULL pointer, then the structure it points to will contain, upon return, the number of seconds and/or microseconds still to be corrected from the earlier call. If *olddelta* is a NULL pointer, the corresponding information will not be returned.

This call may be used in time servers that synchronize the clocks of computers in a local area network. Such time servers would slow down the clocks of some machines and speed up the clocks of others to bring them to the average network time.

Only the super-user may adjust the time of day.

The adjustment value will be silently rounded to the resolution of the system clock.

RETURN

A 0 return value indicates that the call succeeded. A −1 return value indicates an error occurred, and in this case an error code is stored into the global variable errno.

ERRORS

The following error codes may be set in errno:

EFAULT   *delta* or *olddelta* points outside the process's allocated address space, or *olddelta* points to a region of the process' allocated address space that is not writable.

EPERM   The process's effective user ID is not that of the super-user.

SEE ALSO

gettimeofday(3C)
date(1) in the *User's Reference Manual*

alarm(2)

NAME
alarm – set a process alarm clock

SYNOPSIS
    #include <unistd.h>

    unsigned alarm(unsigned sec);

DESCRIPTION
alarm instructs the alarm clock of the calling process to send the signal SIGALRM to the calling process after the number of real time seconds specified by *sec* have elapsed [see `signal(2)`].

Alarm requests are not stacked; successive calls reset the alarm clock of the calling process.

If *sec* is 0, any previously made alarm request is canceled.

fork sets the alarm clock of a new process to 0 [see `fork(2)`]. A process created by the exec family of routines inherits the time left on the old process's alarm clock.

SEE ALSO
fork(2), exec(2), pause(2), signal(2), sigset(2)

DIAGNOSTICS
alarm returns the amount of time previously remaining in the alarm clock of the calling process.

brk(2)

NAME
brk, sbrk – change data segment space allocation

SYNOPSIS
    #include <unistd.h>

    int brk(void *endds);

    void *sbrk(int incr);

DESCRIPTION
brk and sbrk are used to change dynamically the amount of space allocated for the calling process's data segment [see exec(2)]. The change is made by resetting the process's break value and allocating the appropriate amount of space. The break value is the address of the first location beyond the end of the data segment. The amount of allocated space increases as the break value increases. Newly allocated space is set to zero. If, however, the same memory space is reallocated to the same process its contents are undefined.

brk sets the break value to *endds* and changes the allocated space accordingly.

sbrk adds *incr* bytes to the break value and changes the allocated space accordingly. *incr* can be negative, in which case the amount of allocated space is decreased.

brk and sbrk will fail without making any change in the allocated space if one or more of the following are true:

ENOMEM   Such a change would result in more space being allocated than is allowed by the system-imposed maximum process size [see ulimit(2)].

EAGAIN   Total amount of system memory available for a read during physical IO is temporarily insufficient [see shmop(2)]. This may occur even though the space requested was less than the system-imposed maximum process size [see ulimit(2)].

SEE ALSO
exec(2), shmop(2), ulimit(2), end(3C)

DIAGNOSTICS
Upon successful completion, brk returns a value of 0 and sbrk returns the old break value. Otherwise, a value of −1 is returned and errno is set to indicate the error.

chdir(2)

NAME
chdir, fchdir – change working directory

SYNOPSIS
    #include <unistd.h>

    int chdir(const char *path);

    int fchdir(int fildes);

DESCRIPTION
chdir and fchdir cause a directory pointed to by *path* or *fildes* to become the current working directory, the starting point for path searches for path names not beginning with /. *path* points to the path name of a directory. The *fildes* argument to fchdir is an open file descriptor of a directory.

In order for a directory to become the current directory, a process must have execute (search) access to the directory.

chdir will fail and the current working directory will be unchanged if one or more of the following are true:

EACCES	Search permission is denied for any component of the path name.
EFAULT	*path* points outside the allocated address space of the process.
EINTR	A signal was caught during the execution of the chdir system call.
EIO	An I/O error occurred while reading from or writing to the file system.
ELOOP	Too many symbolic links were encountered in translating *path*.
ENAMETOOLONG	The length of the *path* argument exceeds {PATH_MAX}, or the length of a *path* component exceeds {NAME_MAX} while _POSIX_NO_TRUNC is in effect.
ENOTDIR	A component of the path name is not a directory.
ENOENT	Either a component of the path prefix or the directory named by *path* does not exist or is a null pathname.
ENOLINK	*path* points to a remote machine and the link to that machine is no longer active.
EMULTIHOP	Components of *path* require hopping to multiple remote machines and file system type does not allow it.

fchdir will fail and the current working directory will be unchanged if one or more of the following are true:

EACCES	Search permission is denied for *fildes*.
EBADF	*fildes* is not an open file descriptor.

EINTR		A signal was caught during the execution of the `fchdir` system call.
EIO		An I/O error occurred while reading from or writing to the file system.
ENOLINK		*fildes* points to a remote machine and the link to that machine is no longer active.
ENOTDIR		The open file descriptor *fildes* does not refer to a directory.

SEE ALSO
    chroot(2)

DIAGNOSTICS
    Upon successful completion, a value of zero is returned. Otherwise, a value of −1 is returned and `errno` is set to indicate the error.

chmod(2)

NAME
chmod, fchmod – change mode of file

SYNOPSIS
```
#include <sys/types.h>
#include <sys/stat.h>

int chmod(const char *path, mode_t mode);

int fchmod(int fildes, mode_t mode);
```

DESCRIPTION
chmod and fchmod set the access permission portion of the mode of the file whose name is given by *path* or referenced by the descriptor *fildes* to the bit pattern contained in *mode*. If *path* or *fildes* are symbolic links, the access permissions of the target of the symbolic links are set. Access permission bits are interpreted as follows:

S_ISUID	04000	Set user ID on execution.
S_ISGID	020#0	Set group ID on execution if # is 7, 5, 3, or 1
		Enable mandatory file/record locking if # is 6, 4, 2, or 0
S_ISVTX	01000	Save text image after execution.
S_IRWXU	00700	Read, write, execute by owner.
S_IRUSR	00400	Read by owner.
S_IWUSR	00200	Write by owner.
S_IXUSR	00100	Execute (search if a directory) by owner.
S_IRWXG	00070	Read, write, execute by group.
S_IRGRP	00040	Read by group.
S_IWGRP	00020	Write by group.
S_IXGRP	00010	Execute by group.
S_IRWXO	00007	Read, write, execute (search) by others.
S_IROTH	00004	Read by others.
S_IWOTH	00002	Write by others
S_IXOTH	00001	Execute by others.

Modes are constructed by OR'ing the access permission bits.

The effective user ID of the process must match the owner of the file or the process must have the appropriate privilege to change the mode of a file.

If the process is not a privileged process and the file is not a directory, mode bit 01000 (save text image on execution) is cleared.

If neither the process nor a member of the supplementary group list is privileged, and the effective group ID of the process does not match the group ID of the file, mode bit 02000 (set group ID on execution) is cleared.

If a 0410 executable file has the sticky bit (mode bit 01000) set, the operating system will not delete the program text from the swap area when the last user process terminates. If a 0413 or ELF executable file has the sticky bit set, the operating system will not delete the program text from memory when the last user process terminates. In either case, if the sticky bit is set the text will already be available (either in a swap area or in memory) when the next user of the file executes it, thus making execution faster.

chmod(2)

If a directory is writable and has the sticky bit set, files within that directory can be removed or renamed only if one or more of the following is true [see unlink(2) and rename(2)]:

- the user owns the file
- the user owns the directory
- the file is writable by the user
- the user is a privileged user

If the mode bit 02000 (set group ID on execution) is set and the mode bit 00010 (execute or search by group) is not set, mandatory file/record locking will exist on a regular file. This may affect future calls to open(2), creat(2), read(2), and write(2) on this file.

Upon successful completion, chmod and fchmod mark for update the st_ctime field of the file.

chmod will fail and the file mode will be unchanged if one or more of the following are true:

EACCES	Search permission is denied on a component of the path prefix of *path*.
EFAULT	*path* points outside the allocated address space of the process.
EINTR	A signal was caught during execution of the system call.
EIO	An I/O error occurred while reading from or writing to the file system.
ELOOP	Too many symbolic links were encountered in translating *path*.
EMULTIHOP	Components of *path* require hopping to multiple remote machines and file system type does not allow it.
ENAMETOOLONG	The length of the *path* argument exceeds {PATH_MAX}, or the length of a *path* component exceeds {NAME_MAX} while _POSIX_NO_TRUNC is in effect.
ENOTDIR	A component of the prefix of *path* is not a directory.
ENOENT	Either a component of the path prefix, or the file referred to by *path* does not exist or is a null pathname.
ENOLINK	*fildes* points to a remote machine and the link to that machine is no longer active.
EPERM	The effective user ID does not match the owner of the file and the process does not have appropriate privilege.
EROFS	The file referred to by *path* resides on a read-only file system.

fchmod will fail and the file mode will be unchanged if:

EBADF	*fildes* is not an open file descriptor
EIO	An I/O error occurred while reading from or writing to the file system.

chmod(2)

EINTR A signal was caught during execution of the fchmod system call.

ENOLINK *path* points to a remote machine and the link to that machine is no longer active.

EPERM The effective user ID does not match the owner of the file and the process does not have appropriate privilege.

EROFS The file referred to by *fildes* resides on a read-only file system.

SEE ALSO

chown(2), creat(2), fcntl(2), mknod(2), open(2), read(2), stat(2), write(2), mkfifo(3C), stat(5)

chmod(1) in the *User's Reference Manual*

The "File and Record Locking" chapter in the *Programmer's Guide: System Services and Application Packaging Tools*

DIAGNOSTICS

Upon successful completion, a value of 0 is returned. Otherwise, a value of −1 is returned and errno is set to indicate the error.

chown(2)

NAME
chown, lchown, fchown – change owner and group of a file

SYNOPSIS
```
#include <unistd.h>
#include <sys/stat.h>

int chown(const char *path, uid_t owner, gid_t group);

int lchown(const char *path, uid_t owner, gid_t group);

int fchown(int fildes, uid_t owner, gid_t group);
```

DESCRIPTION
The owner ID and group ID of the file specified by *path* or referenced by the descriptor *fildes*, are set to *owner* and *group* respectively. If *owner* or *group* is specified as −1, the corresponding ID of the file is not changed.

The function lchown sets the owner ID and group ID of the named file just as chown does, except in the case where the named file is a symbolic link. In this case lchown changes the ownership of the symbolic link file itself, while chown changes the ownership of the file or directory to which the symbolic link refers.

If chown, lchown, or fchown is invoked by a process other than super-user, the set-user-ID and set-group-ID bits of the file mode, S_ISUID and S_ISGID respectively, are cleared [see chmod(2)].

The operating system has a configuration option, {_POSIX_CHOWN_RESTRICTED}, to restrict ownership changes for the chown, lchown, and fchown system calls. When {_POSIX_CHOWN_RESTRICTED} is not in effect, the effective user ID of the process must match the owner of the file or the process must be the super-user to change the ownership of a file. When {_POSIX_CHOWN_RESTRICTED} is in effect, the chown, lchown, and fchown system calls, for users other than super-user, prevent the owner of the file from changing the owner ID of the file and restrict the change of the group of the file to the list of supplementary group IDs.

Upon successful completion, chown, fchown and lchown mark for update the st_ctime field of the file.

chown and lchown fail and the owner and group of the named file remain unchanged if one or more of the following are true:

EACCES	Search permission is denied on a component of the path prefix of *path*.
EFAULT	*path* points outside the allocated address space of the process.
EINTR	A signal was caught during the chown or lchown system calls.
EINVAL	*group* or *owner* is out of range.
EIO	An I/O error occurred while reading from or writing to the file system.

chown(2)

ELOOP	Too many symbolic links were encountered in translating *path*.
EMULTIHOP	Components of *path* require hopping to multiple remote machines and file system type does not allow it. Too many symbolic links were encountered in translating *path*.
ENAMETOOLONG	The length of the *path* argument exceeds {PATH_MAX}, or the length of a *path* component exceeds {NAME_MAX} while _POSIX_NO_TRUNC is in effect.
ENOLINK	*path* points to a remote machine and the link to that machine is no longer active.
ENOTDIR	A component of the path prefix of *path* is not a directory.
ENOENT	Either a component of the path prefix or the file referred to by *path* does not exist or is a null pathname.
EPERM	The effective user ID does not match the owner of the file or the process is not the super-user and {_POSIX_CHOWN_RESTRICTED} indicates that such privilege is required.
EROFS	The named file resides on a read-only file system.

fchown fails and the owner and group of the named file remain unchanged if one or more of the following are true:

EBADF	*fildes* is not an open file descriptor.
EINVAL	*group* or *owner* is out of range.
EPERM	The effective user ID does not match the owner of the file or the process is not the super-user and {_POSIX_CHOWN_RESTRICTED} indicates that such privilege is required.
EROFS	The named file referred to by *fildes* resides on a read-only file system.
EINTR	A signal was caught during execution of the system call.
EIO	An I/O error occurred while reading from or writing to the file system.
ENOLINK	*fildes* points to a remote machine and the link to that machine is no longer active.

SEE ALSO
chmod(2)
chown(1), chgrp(1) in the *User's Reference Manual*

DIAGNOSTICS
Upon successful completion, a value of 0 is returned. Otherwise, a value of −1 is returned and errno is set to indicate the error.

chroot(2)

NAME
chroot – change root directory

SYNOPSIS
`#include <unistd.h>`

`int chroot(const char *path);`

DESCRIPTION
path points to a path name naming a directory. chroot causes the named directory to become the root directory, the starting point for path searches for path names beginning with /. The user's working directory is unaffected by the chroot system call.

The effective user ID of the process must be super-user to change the root directory.

The .. entry in the root directory is interpreted to mean the root directory itself. Thus, .. cannot be used to access files outside the subtree rooted at the root directory.

chroot will fail and the root directory will remain unchanged if one or more of the following are true:

ELOOP	Too many symbolic links were encountered in translating *path*.
ENAMETOOLONG	The length of the *path* argument exceeds {PATH_MAX}, or the length of a *path* component exceeds {NAME_MAX} while _POSIX_NO_TRUNC is in effect.
EFAULT	*path* points outside the allocated address space of the process.
EINTR	A signal was caught during the chroot system call.
EMULTIHOP	Components of *path* require hopping to multiple remote machines and file system type does not allow it.
ENOLINK	*path* points to a remote machine and the link to that machine is no longer active.
ENOTDIR	Any component of the path name is not a directory.
ENOENT	The named directory does not exist or is a null pathname.
EPERM	The effective user ID is not super-user.

SEE ALSO
chdir(2)

DIAGNOSTICS
Upon successful completion, a value of 0 is returned. Otherwise, a value of −1 is returned and errno is set to indicate the error.

chsize(2) (Application Compatibility Package)

NAME
chsize – change the size of a file

SYNOPSIS
cc [*flag* . . .] *file* . . . −lx
```
int chsize (int fildes, long size);
```

DESCRIPTION
fildes is a file descriptor obtained from a create, open, dup, fcntl, or pipe system call. chsize changes the size of the file associated with the file descriptor *fildes* to be exactly *size* bytes in length. The routine either truncates the file, or pads it with an appropriate number of bytes. If *size* is less than the initial size of the file, then all allocated disk blocks between *size* and the initial file size are freed.

The maximum file size as set by ulimit(2) is enforced when chsize is called, rather than on subsequent writes. Thus chsize fails, and the file size remains unchanged if the new changed file size would exceed the ulimit.

DIAGNOSTICS
Upon successful completion, a value of 0 is returned. Otherwise, the value −1 is returned and errno is set to indicate the error.

SEE ALSO
creat(2), dup(2), lseek(2), open(2), pipe(2), ulimit(2)

NOTES
In general if chsize is used to expand the size of a file, when data is written to the end of the file, intervening blocks are filled with zeros. In a some cases, reducing the file size may not remove the data beyond the new end-of-file.

NAME

close – close a file descriptor

SYNOPSIS

```
#include <unistd.h>
int close(int fildes);
```

DESCRIPTION

fildes is a file descriptor obtained from a creat, open, dup, fcntl, pipe, or ioctl system call. close closes the file descriptor indicated by *fildes*. All outstanding record locks owned by the process (on the file indicated by *fildes*) are removed.

When all file descriptors associated with the open file description have been closed, the open file description is freed.

If the link count of the file is zero, when all file descriptors associated with the file have been closed, the space occupied by the file is freed and the file is no longer accessible.

If a STREAMS-based [see intro(2)] *fildes* is closed, and the calling process had previously registered to receive a SIGPOLL signal [see signal(2)] for events associated with that stream [see I_SETSIG in streamio(7)], the calling process will be unregistered for events associated with the stream. The last close for a stream causes the stream associated with *fildes* to be dismantled. If O_NDELAY and O_NONBLOCK are clear and there have been no signals posted for the stream, and if there are data on the module's write queue, close waits up to 15 seconds (for each module and driver) for any output to drain before dismantling the stream. The time delay can be changed via an I_SETCLTIME ioctl request [see streamio(7)]. If O_NDELAY or O_NONBLOCK is set, or if there are any pending signals, close does not wait for output to drain, and dismantles the stream immediately.

If *fildes* is associated with one end of a pipe, the last close causes a hangup to occur on the other end of the pipe. In addition, if the other end of the pipe has been named [see fattach(3C)], the last close forces the named end to be detached [see fdetach(3C)]. If the named end has no open processes associated with it and becomes detached, the stream associated with that end is also dismantled.

The named file is closed unless one or more of the following are true:

EBADF   *fildes* is not a valid open file descriptor.

EINTR   A signal was caught during the close system call.

ENOLINK   *fildes* is on a remote machine and the link to that machine is no longer active.

SEE ALSO

creat(2), dup(2), exec(2), fcntl(2), intro(2), open(2), pipe(2), signal(2), signal(5), streamio(7)

fattach(3C), fdetach(3C) in the *Programmer's Guide: Networking Interfaces*

DIAGNOSTICS
Upon successful completion, a value of 0 is returned. Otherwise, a value of −1 is returned and errno is set to indicate the error.

creat(2)

NAME
creat – create a new file or rewrite an existing one

SYNOPSIS
```
#include <sys/types.h>
#include <sys/stat.h>
#include <fcntl.h>

int creat(const char *path, mode_t mode);
```

DESCRIPTION
creat creates a new ordinary file or prepares to rewrite an existing file named by the path name pointed to by *path*.

If the file exists, the length is truncated to 0 and the mode and owner are unchanged.

If the file does not exist the file's owner ID is set to the effective user ID of the process. The group ID of the file is set to the effective group ID of the process, or if the S_ISGID bit is set in the parent directory then the group ID of the file is inherited from the parent directory. The access permission bits of the file mode are set to the value of *mode* modified as follows:

> If the group ID of the new file does not match the effective group ID or one of the supplementary group IDs, the S_ISGID bit is cleared.

> All bits set in the process's file mode creation mask are cleared [see umask(2)].

> The "save text image after execution bit" of the mode is cleared [see chmod(2) for the values of mode].

Upon successful completion, a write-only file descriptor is returned and the file is open for writing, even if the mode does not permit writing. The file pointer is set to the beginning of the file. The file descriptor is set to remain open across exec system calls [see fcntl(2)]. A new file may be created with a mode that forbids writing.

The call creat (*path, mode*) is equivalent to:

> open (*path*, O_WRONLY | O_CREAT | O_TRUNC, *mode*)

creat fails if one or more of the following are true:

EACCES	Search permission is denied on a component of the path prefix.
EACCES	The file does not exist and the directory in which the file is to be created does not permit writing.
EACCES	The file exists and write permission is denied.
EAGAIN	The file exists, mandatory file/record locking is set, and there are outstanding record locks on the file [see chmod(2)].
EFAULT	*path* points outside the allocated address space of the process.

creat(2)   **creat(2)**

EISDIR	The named file is an existing directory.
EINTR	A signal was caught during the `creat` system call.
ELOOP	Too many symbolic links were encountered in translating *path*.
EMFILE	The process has too many open files [see `getrlimit(2)`].
ENAMETOOLONG	The length of the *path* argument exceeds {PATH_MAX}, or the length of a *path* component exceeds {NAME_MAX} while _POSIX_NO_TRUNC is in effect.
ENOTDIR	A component of the path prefix is not a directory.
ENOENT	A component of the path prefix does not exist.
ENOENT	The path name is null.
EROFS	The named file resides or would reside on a read-only file system.
ETXTBSY	The file is a pure procedure (shared text) file that is being executed.
ENFILE	The system file table is full.
ENOLINK	*path* points to a remote machine and the link to that machine is no longer active.
EMULTIHOP	Components of *path* require hopping to multiple remote machines.
ENOSPC	The file system is out of inodes.

SEE ALSO
    chmod(2), close(2), dup(2), fcntl(2), getrlimit(2), lseek(2), open(2), read(2), umask(2), write(2), stat(5)

DIAGNOSTICS
    Upon successful completion a non-negative integer, namely the lowest numbered unused file descriptor, is returned. Otherwise, a value of −1 is returned, no files are created or modified, and errno is set to indicate the error.

NAME
creatsem – create an instance of a binary semaphore

SYNOPSIS
cc [*flag* ...] *file* ... -lx
int creatsem(char *sem_name, int mode);

DESCRIPTION
creatsem defines a binary semaphore named by *sem_name* to be used by waitsem and sigsem to manage mutually exclusive access to a resource, shared variable, or critical section of a program. creatsem returns a unique semaphore number, *sem_num*, which may then be used as the parameter in waitsem and sigsem calls. Semaphores are special files of 0 length. The filename space is used to provide unique identifiers for semaphores. *mode* sets the accessibility of the semaphore using the same format as file access bits. Access to a semaphore is granted only on the basis of the read access bit; the write and execute bits are ignored.

A semaphore can be operated on only by a synchronizing primitive, such as waitsem or sigsem, by creatsem which initializes it to some value, or by opensem which opens the semaphore for use by a process. Synchronizing primitives are guaranteed to be executed without interruption once started. These primitives are used by associating a semaphore with each resource (including critical code sections) to be protected.

The process controlling the semaphore should issue:

   sem_num = creatsem("semaphore", mode);

to create, initialize, and open the semaphore for that process. All other processes using the semaphore should issue:

   sem_num = opensem("semaphore");

to access the semaphore's identification value. Note that a process cannot open and use a semaphore that has not been initialized by a call to creatsem, nor should a process open a semaphore more than once in one period of execution. Both the creating and opening processes use waitsem and sigsem to use the semaphore *sem_num*.

DIAGNOSTICS
creatsem returns the value −1 if an error occurs. If the semaphore named by *sem_name* is already open for use by other processes, errno is set to EEXIST. If the file specified exists but is not a semaphore type, errno is set to ENOTNAM. If the semaphore has not been initialized by a call to creatsem, errno is set to EINVAL.

SEE ALSO
opensem(2), sigsem(2), waitsem(2)

NOTES
After a creatsem, you must do a waitsem to gain control of a given resource.

dup(2)

NAME
dup – duplicate an open file descriptor

SYNOPSIS
`#include <unistd.h>`

`int dup(int fildes);`

DESCRIPTION
fildes is a file descriptor obtained from a `creat`, `open`, `dup`, `fcntl`, `pipe`, or `ioctl` system call. `dup` returns a new file descriptor having the following in common with the original:

> Same open file (or pipe).
>
> Same file pointer (that is, both file descriptors share one file pointer).
>
> Same access mode (read, write or read/write).

The new file descriptor is set to remain open across exec system calls [see `fcntl(2)`].

The file descriptor returned is the lowest one available.

`dup` will fail if one or more of the following are true:

EBADF	*fildes* is not a valid open file descriptor.
EINTR	A signal was caught during the `dup` system call.
EMFILE	The process has too many open files [see `getrlimit(2)`].
ENOLINK	*fildes* is on a remote machine and the link to that machine is no longer active.

SEE ALSO
`close(2)`, `creat(2)`, `exec(2)`, `fcntl(2)`, `getrlimit(2)`, `open(2)`, `pipe(2)`, `dup2(3C)`, `lockf(3C)`

DIAGNOSTICS
Upon successful completion a non-negative integer, namely the file descriptor, is returned. Otherwise, a value of −1 is returned and `errno` is set to indicate the error.

errno(2)

NAME
errno – complete list of the error numbers and their names

SYNOPSIS
#include <errno.h>

DESCRIPTION
Each system call description attempts to list all possible error returns. The following is a complete list of the error numbers and their names as defined in <errno.h>.

1 EPERM   Not super-user
> Typically this error indicates an attempt to modify a file in some way forbidden except to its owner or the super-user. It is also returned for attempts by ordinary users to do things allowed only to the super-user.

2 ENOENT   No such file or directory
> A file-name is specified and the file should exist but doesn't, or one of the directories in a path-name does not exist.

3 ESRCH   No such process
> No process can be found corresponding to that specified by PID in the kill or ptrace routine.

4 EINTR   Interrupted system call
> An asynchronous signal (such as interrupt or quit), which the user has elected to catch, occurred during a system service routine. If execution is resumed after processing the signal, it will appear as if the interrupted routine call returned this error condition.

5 EIO   I/O error
> Some physical I/O error has occurred. This error may in some cases occur on a call following the one to which it actually applies.

6 ENXIO   No such device or address
> I/O on a special file refers to a subdevice which does not exist, or exists beyond the limit of the device. It may also occur when, for example, a tape drive is not on-line or no disk pack is loaded on a drive.

7 E2BIG   Arg list too long
> An argument list longer than ARG_MAX bytes is presented to a member of the exec family of routines. The argument list limit is the sum of the size of the argument list plus the size of the environment's exported shell variables.

8 ENOEXEC   Exec format error
> A request is made to execute a file which, although it has the appropriate permissions, does not start with a valid format.

9 EBADF   Bad file number
> Either a file descriptor refers to no open file, or a read [respectively, write] request is made to a file that is open only for writing (respectively, reading).

10 ECHILD No child processes
   A wait routine was executed by a process that had no existing or unwaited-for child processes.

11 EAGAIN No more processes
   For example, the fork routine failed because the system's process table is full or the user is not allowed to create any more processes, or a system call failed because of insufficient memory or swap space.

12 ENOMEM Not enough space
   During execution of an exec, brk, or sbrk routine, a program asks for more space than the system is able to supply. This is not a temporary condition; the maximum size is a system parameter. The error may also occur if the arrangement of text, data, and stack segments requires too many segmentation registers, or if there is not enough swap space during the fork routine. If this error occurs on a resource associated with Remote File Sharing (RFS), it indicates a memory depletion which may be temporary, dependent on system activity at the time the call was invoked.

13 EACCES Permission denied
   An attempt was made to access a file in a way forbidden by the protection system.

14 EFAULT Bad address
   The system encountered a hardware fault in attempting to use an argument of a routine. For example, errno potentially may be set to EFAULT any time a routine that takes a pointer argument is passed an invalid address, if the system can detect the condition. Because systems will differ in their ability to reliably detect a bad address, on some implementations passing a bad address to a routine will result in undefined behavior.

15 ENOTBLK Block device required
   A non-block file was mentioned where a block device was required (for example, in a call to the mount routine).

16 EBUSY Device busy
   An attempt was made to mount a device that was already mounted or an attempt was made to unmount a device on which there is an active file (open file, current directory, mounted-on file, active text segment). It will also occur if an attempt is made to enable accounting when it is already enabled. The device or resource is currently unavailable.

17 EEXIST File exists
   An existing file was mentioned in an inappropriate context (for example, call to the link routine).

18 EXDEV Cross-device link
   A link to a file on another device was attempted.

19 ENODEV No such device
   An attempt was made to apply an inappropriate operation to a device (for example, read a write-only device).

20 ENOTDIR Not a directory
: A non-directory was specified where a directory is required (for example, in a path prefix or as an argument to the `chdir` routine).

21 EISDIR Is a directory
: An attempt was made to write on a directory.

22 EINVAL Invalid argument
: An invalid argument was specified (for example, unmounting a non-mounted device), mentioning an undefined signal in a call to the `signal` or `kill` routine.

23 ENFILE File table overflow
: The system file table is full (that is, SYS_OPEN files are open, and temporarily no more files can be opened).

24 EMFILE Too many open files
: No process may have more than OPEN_MAX file descriptors open at a time.

25 ENOTTY Not a typewriter
: A call was made to the `ioctl` routine specifying a file that is not a special character device.

26 ETXTBSY Text file busy
: An attempt was made to execute a pure-procedure program that is currently open for writing. Also an attempt to open for writing or to remove a pure-procedure program that is being executed.

27 EFBIG File too large
: The size of a file exceeded the maximum file size, FCHR_MAX [see `getrlimit`].

28 ENOSPC No space left on device
: While writing an ordinary file or creating a directory entry, there is no free space left on the device. In the `fcntl` routine, the setting or removing of record locks on a file cannot be accomplished because there are no more record entries left on the system.

29 ESPIPE Illegal seek
: A call to the `lseek` routine was issued to a pipe.

30 EROFS Read-only file system
: An attempt to modify a file or directory was made on a device mounted read-only.

31 EMLINK Too many links
: An attempt to make more than the maximum number of links, LINK_MAX, to a file.

32 EPIPE Broken pipe
: A write on a pipe for which there is no process to read the data. This condition normally generates a signal; the error is returned if the signal is ignored.

errno(2)

33 EDOM   Math argument out of domain of func
    The argument of a function in the math package (3M) is out of the domain of the function.

34 ERANGE Math result not representable
    The value of a function in the math package (3M) is not representable within machine precision.

35 ENOMSG No message of desired type
    An attempt was made to receive a message of a type that does not exist on the specified message queue [see msgop(2)].

36 EIDRM   Identifier removed
    This error is returned to processes that resume execution due to the removal of a message or semaphore identifier from the system [see msgop(2), semop(2), msgctl(2), and semctl(2)].

37 ECHRNG Channel number out of range

38 EL2NSYNC Level 2 not synchronized

39 EL3HLT Level 3 halted

40 EL3RST Level 3 reset

41 ELNRNG Link number out of range

42 EUNATCH Protocol driver not attached

43 ENOCSI No CSI structure available

44 EL2HLT Level 2 halted

45 EDEADLK Deadlock condition
    A deadlock situation was detected and avoided. This error pertains to file and record locking.

46 ENOLCK No record locks available
    There are no more locks available. The system lock table is full [see fcntl(2)].

47–49 Reserved

58–59 Reserved

60 ENOSTR Device not a stream
    A putmsg or getmsg system call was attempted on a file descriptor that is not a STREAMS device.

61 ENODATA No data available

62 ETIME   Timer expired
    The timer set for a STREAMS ioctl call has expired. The cause of this error is device specific and could indicate either a hardware or software failure, or perhaps a timeout value that is too short for the specific operation. The status of the ioctl operation is indeterminate.

63 ENOSR Out of stream resources
   During a STREAMS open, either no STREAMS queues or no STREAMS head data structures were available. This is a temporary condition; one may recover from it if other processes release resources.

64 ENONET Machine is not on the network
   This error is Remote File Sharing (RFS) specific. It occurs when users try to advertise, unadvertise, mount, or unmount remote resources while the machine has not done the proper startup to connect to the network.

65 ENOPKG Package not installed
   This error occurs when users attempt to use a system call from a package which has not been installed.

66 EREMOTE Object is remote
   This error is RFS specific. It occurs when users try to advertise a resource which is not on the local machine, or try to mount/unmount a device (or path-name) that is on a remote machine.

67 ENOLINK Link has been severed
   This error is RFS specific. It occurs when the link (virtual circuit) connecting to a remote machine is gone.

68 EADV Advertise error
   This error is RFS specific. It occurs when users try to advertise a resource which has been advertised already, or try to stop RFS while there are resources still advertised, or try to force unmount a resource when it is still advertised.

69 ESRMNT Srmount error
   This error is RFS specific. It occurs when an attempt is made to stop RFS while resources are still mounted by remote machines, or when a resource is readvertised with a client list that does not include a remote machine that currently has the resource mounted.

70 ECOMM Communication error on send
   This error is RFS specific. It occurs when the current process is waiting for a message from a remote machine, and the virtual circuit fails.

71 EPROTO Protocol error
   Some protocol error occurred. This error is device specific, but is generally not related to a hardware failure.

74 EMULTIHOP Multihop attempted
   This error is RFS specific. It occurs when users try to access remote resources which are not directly accessible.

76 EDOTDOT Error 76
   This error is RFS specific. A way for the server to tell the client that a process has transferred back from mount point.

77 EBADMSG Not a data message
   During a read, getmsg, or ioctl I_RECVFD system call to a STREAMS device, something has come to the head of the queue that can't be processed. That something depends on the system call:
   read: control information or a passed file descriptor.

getmsg: passed file descriptor.
ioctl: control or data information.

78 ENAMETOOLONG File name too long
   The length of the path argument exceeds PATH_MAX, or the length of a path component exceeds NAME_MAX while _POSIX_NO_TRUNC is in effect; see limits(4).

79 EOVERFLOW
   Value too large for defined data type.

80 ENOTUNIQ Name not unique on network
   Given log name not unique.

81 EBADFD File descriptor in bad state
   Either a file descriptor refers to no open file or a read request was made to a file that is open only for writing.

82 EREMCHG Remote address changed

83 ELIBACC Cannot access a needed shared library
   Trying to exec an a.out that requires a static shared library and the static shared library doesn't exist or the user doesn't have permission to use it.

84 ELIBBAD Accessing a corrupted shared library
   Trying to exec an a.out that requires a static shared library (to be linked in) and exec could not load the static shared library. The static shared library is probably corrupted.

85 ELIBSCN .lib section in a.out corrupted
   Trying to exec an a.out that requires a static shared library (to be linked in) and there was erroneous data in the .lib section of the a.out. The .lib section tells exec what static shared libraries are needed. The a.out is probably corrupted.

86 ELIBMAX Attempting to link in more shared libraries than system limit
   Trying to exec an a.out that requires more static shared libraries than is allowed on the current configuration of the system. See the *System Administrator's Guide*.

87 ELIBEXEC Cannot exec a shared library directly
   Attempting to exec a shared library directly.

88 EILSEQ Error 88
   Illegal byte sequence. Handle multiple characters as a single character.

89 ENOSYS Operation not applicable

90 ELOOP Number of symbolic links encountered during path-name traversal exceeds MAXSYMLINKS

91 ESTART Error 91
   Interrupted system call should be restarted.

errno(2)

92 ESTRPIPE Error 92
   Streams pipe error (not externally visible).

93 ENOTEMPTY Directory not empty

94 EUSERS Too many users
   Too many users.

95 ENOTSOCK Socket operation on non-socket
   Self-explanatory.

96 EDESTADDRREQ Destination address required
   A required address was omitted from an operation on a transport endpoint. Destination address required.

97 EMSGSIZE Message too long
   A message sent on a transport provider was larger than the internal message buffer or some other network limit.

98 EPROTOTYPE Protocol wrong type for socket
   A protocol was specified that does not support the semantics of the socket type requested.

99 ENOPROTOOPT Protocol not available
   A bad option or level was specified when getting or setting options for a protocol.

120 EPROTONOSUPPORT Protocol not supported
   The protocol has not been configured into the system or no implementation for it exists.

121 ESOCKTNOSUPPORT Socket type not supported
   The support for the socket type has not been configured into the system or no implementation for it exists.

122 EOPNOTSUPP Operation not supported on transport endpoint
   For example, trying to accept a connection on a datagram transport endpoint.

123 EPFNOSUPPORT Protocol family not supported
   The protocol family has not been configured into the system or no implementation for it exists. Used for the Internet protocols.

124 EAFNOSUPPORT Address family not supported by protocol family
   An address incompatible with the requested protocol was used.

125 EADDRINUSE Address already in use
   User attempted to use an address already in use, and the protocol does not allow this.

126 EADDRNOTAVAIL Cannot assign requested address
   Results from an attempt to create a transport endpoint with an address not on the current machine.

127 ENETDOWN Network is down
   Operation encountered a dead network.

128 ENETUNREACH Network is unreachable
   Operation was attempted to an unreachable network.

129 ENETRESET Network dropped connection because of reset
   The host you were connected to crashed and rebooted.

130 ECONNABORTED Software caused connection abort
   A connection abort was caused internal to your host machine.

131 ECONNRESET Connection reset by peer
   A connection was forcibly closed by a peer. This normally results from a loss of the connection on the remote host due to a timeout or a reboot.

132 ENOBUFS No buffer space available
   An operation on a transport endpoint or pipe was not performed because the system lacked sufficient buffer space or because a queue was full.

133 EISCONN Transport endpoint is already connected
   A connect request was made on an already connected transport endpoint; or, a sendto or sendmsg request on a connected transport endpoint specified a destination when already connected.

134 ENOTCONN Transport endpoint is not connected
   A request to send or receive data was disallowed because the transport endpoint is not connected and (when sending a datagram) no address was supplied.

143 ESHUTDOWN Cannot send after transport endpoint shutdown
   A request to send data was disallowed because the transport endpoint has already been shut down.

144 ETOOMANYREFS Too many references: cannot splice

145 ETIMEDOUT Connection timed out
   A connect or send request failed because the connected party did not properly respond after a period of time. (The timeout period is dependent on the communication protocol.)

146 ECONNREFUSED Connection refused
   No connection could be made because the target machine actively refused it. This usually results from trying to connect to a service that is inactive on the remote host.

147 EHOSTDOWN Host is down
   A transport provider operation failed because the destination host was down.

148 EHOSTUNREACH No route to host
   A transport provider operation was attempted to an unreachable host.

149 EALREADY Operation already in progress
   An operation was attempted on a non-blocking object that already had an operation in progress.

150 EINPROGRESS   Operation now in progress
    An operation that takes a long time to complete (such as a `connect`) was attempted on a non-blocking object.

151 ESTALE   Stale NFS file handle

exec(2)

NAME
exec: execl, execv, execle, execve, execlp, execvp – execute a file

SYNOPSIS
    #include <unistd.h>

    int execl (const char *path, const char *arg0, ..., const char
        *argn, (char *)0);

    int execv (const char *path, char *const *argv);

    int execle (const char *path, const char *arg0, ..., const char
        *argn, (char *0), const char *envp[]);

    int execve (const char *path, char *const *argv, char *const
        *envp);

    int execlp (const char *file, const char *arg0, ..., const char
        *argn, (char *)0);

    int execvp (const char *file, char *const *argv);

DESCRIPTION
exec in all its forms overlays a new process image on an old process. The new process image is constructed from an ordinary, executable file. This file is either an executable object file, or a file of data for an interpreter. There can be no return from a successful exec because the calling process image is overlaid by the new process image.

An interpreter file begins with a line of the form

   #! *pathname* [*arg*]

where *pathname* is the path of the interpreter, and *arg* is an optional argument. When an interpreter file is exec'd, the system execs the specified interpreter. The pathname specified in the interpreter file is passed as *arg0* to the interpreter. If *arg* was specified in the interpreter file, it is passed as *arg1* to the interpreter. The remaining arguments to the interpreter are *arg0* through *argn* of the originally exec'd file.

When a C program is executed, it is called as follows:

    int main (int argc, char *argv[], char *envp[]);

where *argc* is the argument count, *argv* is an array of character pointers to the arguments themselves, and *envp* is an array of character pointers to the environment strings. As indicated, *argc* is at least one, and the first member of the array points to a string containing the name of the file.

path points to a path name that identifies the new process file.

file points to the new process file. If *file* does not contain a slash character, the path prefix for this file is obtained by a search of the directories passed in the PATH environment variable [see environ(5)]. The environment is supplied typically by the shell [see sh(1)].

If the new process file is not an executable object file, execlp and execvp use the contents of that file as standard input to sh(1).

The arguments *arg0*, . . ., *argn* point to null-terminated character strings. These strings constitute the argument list available to the new process image. Minimally, *arg0* must be present. It will become the name of the process, as displayed by the ps command. Conventionally, *arg0* points to a string that is the same as *path* (or the last component of *path*). The list of argument strings is terminated by a (char *) 0 argument.

argv is an array of character pointers to null-terminated strings. These strings constitute the argument list available to the new process image. By convention, *argv* must have at least one member, and it should point to a string that is the same as *path* (or its last component). *argv* is terminated by a null pointer.

envp is an array of character pointers to null-terminated strings. These strings constitute the environment for the new process image. *envp* is terminated by a null pointer. For execl, execv, execvp, and execlp, the C run-time start-off routine places a pointer to the environment of the calling process in the global object extern char **environ, and it is used to pass the environment of the calling process to the new process.

File descriptors open in the calling process remain open in the new process, except for those whose close-on-exec flag is set; [see fcntl(2)]. For those file descriptors that remain open, the file pointer is unchanged.

Signals that are being caught by the calling process are set to the default disposition in the new process image [see signal(2)]. Otherwise, the new process image inherits the signal dispositions of the calling process.

If the set-user-ID mode bit of the new process file is set [see chmod(2)], exec sets the effective user ID of the new process to the owner ID of the new process file. Similarly, if the set-group-ID mode bit of the new process file is set, the effective group ID of the new process is set to the group ID of the new process file. The real user ID and real group ID of the new process remain the same as those of the calling process.

If the effective user-ID is root or super-user, the set-user-ID and set-group-ID bits will be honored when the process is being controlled by ptrace.

The shared memory segments attached to the calling process will not be attached to the new process [see shmop(2)].

Profiling is disabled for the new process; see profil(2).

The new process also inherits the following attributes from the calling process:

    nice value [see nice(2)]
    scheduler class and priority [see priocntl(2)]
    process ID
    parent process ID
    process group ID
    supplementary group IDs

exec(2)

       semadj values [see semop(2)]
       session ID [see exit(2) and signal(2)]
       trace flag [see ptrace(2) request 0]
       time left until an alarm clock signal [see alarm(2)]
       current working directory
       root directory
       file mode creation mask [see umask(2)]
       resource limits [see getrlimit(2)]
       utime, stime, cutime, and cstime [see times(2)]
       file-locks [see fcntl(2) and lockf(3C)]
       controlling terminal
       process signal mask [see sigprocmask(2)]
       pending signals [see sigpending(2)]

Upon successful completion, exec marks for update the st_atime field of the file. Should the exec succeed, the process image file is considered to have been open()-ed. The corresponding close() is considered to occur at a time after this open, but before process termination or successful completion of a subsequent call to exec.

exec will fail and return to the calling process if one or more of the following are true:

EACCES	Search permission is denied for a directory listed in the new process file's path prefix.
E2BIG	The number of bytes in the new process's argument list is greater than the system-imposed limit of 5120 bytes. The argument list limit is sum of the size of the argument list plus the size of the environment's exported shell variables.
EACCES	The new process file is not an ordinary file.
EACCES	The new process file mode denies execution permission.
EAGAIN	Total amount of system memory available when reading via raw I/O is temporarily insufficient.
EFAULT	Required hardware is not present.
EFAULT	An *a.out* that was compiled with the MAU or 32B flag is running on a machine without a MAU or 32B.
EFAULT	An argument points to an illegal address.
EINTR	A signal was caught during the exec system call.
ELIBACC	Required shared library does not have execute permission.
ELIBEXEC	Trying to exec(2) a shared library directly.
ELOOP	Too many symbolic links were encountered in translating *path* or *file*.
EMULTIHOP	Components of *path* require hopping to multiple remote machines and the file system type does not allow it.

exec(2)

ENAMETOOLONG The length of the *file* or *path* argument exceeds {PATH_MAX}, or the length of a *file* or *path* component exceeds {NAME_MAX} while _POSIX_NO_TRUNC is in effect.

ENOENT One or more components of the new process path name of the file do not exist or is a null pathname.

ENOTDIR A component of the new process path of the file prefix is not a directory.

ENOEXEC The exec is not an execlp or execvp, and the new process file has the appropriate access permission but an invalid magic number in its header.

ETXTBSY The new process file is a pure procedure (shared text) file that is currently open for writing by some process.

ENOMEM The new process requires more memory than is allowed by the system-imposed maximum MAXMEM.

ENOLINK *path* points to a remote machine and the link to that machine is no longer active.

SEE ALSO

alarm(2), exit(2), fcntl(2), fork(2), getrlimit(2), nice(2), priocntl(2), ptrace(2), semop(2), signal(2), sigpending(2), sigprocmask(2), times(2), umask(2), lockf(3C), system(3S), a.out(4), environ(5)
sh(1), ps(1) in the *User's Reference Manual*

DIAGNOSTICS

If exec returns to the calling process, an error has occurred; the return value is −1 and errno is set to indicate the error.

exit(2)

NAME
exit, _exit – terminate process

SYNOPSIS
    #include <stdlib.h>

    void exit(int status);

    #include <unistd.h>

    void _exit(int status);

DESCRIPTION
_exit terminates the calling process with the following consequences:

All of the file descriptors, directory streams and message catalogue descriptors open in the calling process are closed.

A SIGCHLD signal is sent to the calling process's parent process.

If the parent process of the calling process has not specified the SA_NOCLDWAIT flag [see sigaction(2)], the calling process is transformed into a "zombie process." A zombie process is a process that only occupies a slot in the process table. It has no other space allocated either in user or kernel space. The process table slot that it occupies is partially overlaid with time accounting information [see <sys/proc.h>] to be used by the times system call.

The parent process ID of all of the calling process's existing child processes and zombie processes is set to 1. This means the initialization process [see intro(2)] inherits each of these processes.

Each attached shared memory segment is detached and the value of shm_nattach in the data structure associated with its shared memory identifier is decremented by 1.

For each semaphore for which the calling process has set a semadj value [see semop(2)], that semadj value is added to the semval of the specified semaphore.

If the process has a process, text, or data lock, an *unlock* is performed [see plock(2)].

An accounting record is written on the accounting file if the system's accounting routine is enabled [see acct(2)].

If the process is a controlling process, SIGHUP is sent to the foreground process group of its controlling terminal and its controlling terminal is deallocated.

If the calling process has any stopped children whose process group will be orphaned when the calling process exits, or if the calling process is a member of a process group that will be orphaned when the calling process exits, that process group will be sent SIGHUP and SIGCONT signals.

The C function exit(3C) calls any functions registered through the atexit function in the reverse order of their registration. The function _exit circumvents all such functions and cleanup.

The symbols EXIT_SUCCESS and EXIT_FAILURE are defined in stdlib.h and may be used as the value of *status* to indicate successful or unsuccessful termination, respectively.

SEE ALSO
acct(2), intro(2), plock(2), semop(2), sigaction(2), signal(2), times(2), wait(2), atexit(3C)

NOTES
See signal(2) NOTES.

fcntl(2)

NAME
fcntl – file control

SYNOPSIS
```
#include <sys/types.h>
#include <fcntl.h>
#include <unistd.h>

int fcntl (int fildes, int cmd, . . . /* arg */);
```

DESCRIPTION
fcntl provides for control over open files. *fildes* is an open file descriptor [see intro(2)].

fcntl may take a third argument, *arg*, whose data type, value and use depend upon the value of *cmd*. *cmd* specifies the operation to be performed by fcntl and may be one of the following:

F_DUPFD   Return a new file descriptor with the following characteristics:

         Lowest numbered available file descriptor greater than or equal to the integer value given as the third argument.

         Same open file (or pipe) as the original file.

         Same file pointer as the original file (that is, both file descriptors share one file pointer).

         Same access mode (read, write, or read/write) as the original file.

         Shares any locks associated with the original file descriptor.

         Same file status flags (that is, both file descriptors share the same file status flags) as the original file.

         The close-on-exec flag [see F_GETFD] associated with the new file descriptor is set to remain open across exec(2) system calls.

F_GETFD   Get the close-on-exec flag associated with *fildes*. If the low-order bit is 0, the file will remain open across exec. Otherwise, the file will be closed upon execution of exec.

F_SETFD   Set the close-on-exec flag associated with *fildes* to the low-order bit of the integer value given as the third argument (0 or 1 as above).

F_GETFL   Get *fildes* status flags.

F_SETFL   Set *fildes* status flags to the integer value given as the third argument. Only certain flags can be set [see fcntl(5)].

F_FREESP   Free storage space associated with a section of the ordinary file *fildes*. The section is specified by a variable of data type struct flock pointed to by the third argument *arg*. The data type struct flock is defined in the <fcntl.h> header file [see fcntl(5)] and contains the following members: l_whence is 0, 1, or 2 to indicate that the relative offset l_start will be measured from the start of the file, the current position, or the end of the file, respectively. l_start is the offset from the position specified in l_whence. l_len is the size of the section. An l_len of 0 frees up to the end of the file; in this case, the end of file (i.e., file size) is set to the beginning of the section freed. Any data previously written into this section is no longer accessible.

The following commands are used for record-locking. Locks may be placed on an entire file or on segments of a file.

F_SETLK   Set or clear a file segment lock according to the flock structure that *arg* points to [see fcntl(5)]. The *cmd* F_SETLK is used to establish read (F_RDLCK) and write (F_WRLCK) locks, as well as remove either type of lock (F_UNLCK). If a read or write lock cannot be set, fcntl will return immediately with an error value of −1.

F_SETLKW   This *cmd* is the same as F_SETLK except that if a read or write lock is blocked by other locks, fcntl will block until the segment is free to be locked.

F_GETLK   If the lock request described by the flock structure that *arg* points to could be created, then the structure is passed back unchanged except that the lock type is set to F_UNLCK and the l_whence field will be set to SEEK_SET.

If a lock is found that would prevent this lock from being created, then the structure is overwritten with a description of the first lock that is preventing such a lock from being created. The structure also contains the process ID and the system ID of the process holding the lock.

This command never creates a lock; it tests whether a particular lock could be created.

F_RSETLK   Used by the network lock daemon, lockd(3N), to communicate with the NFS server kernel to handle locks on NFS files.

F_RSETLKW   Used by the network lock daemon, lockd(3N), to communicate with the NFS server kernel to handle locks on NFS files.

F_RGETLK   Used by the network lock daemon, lockd(3N), to communicate with the NFS server kernel to handle locks on NFS files.

A read lock prevents any process from write locking the protected area. More than one read lock may exist for a given segment of a file at a given time. The file descriptor on which a read lock is being placed must have been opened with read access.

A write lock prevents any process from read locking or write locking the protected area. Only one write lock and no read locks may exist for a given segment of a file at a given time. The file descriptor on which a write lock is being placed must have been opened with write access.

fcntl (2)   fcntl (2)

The `flock` structure describes the type (l_type), starting offset (l_whence), relative offset (l_start), size (l_len), process ID (l_pid), and system ID (l_sysid) of the segment of the file to be affected. The process ID and system ID fields are used only with the F_GETLK *cmd* to return the values for a blocking lock. Locks may start and extend beyond the current end of a file, but may not be negative relative to the beginning of the file. A lock may be set to always extend to the end of file by setting l_len to 0. If such a lock also has l_whence and l_start set to 0, the whole file will be locked. Changing or unlocking a segment from the middle of a larger locked segment leaves two smaller segments at either end. Locking a segment that is already locked by the calling process causes the old lock type to be removed and the new lock type to take effect. All locks associated with a file for a given process are removed when a file descriptor for that file is closed by that process or the process holding that file descriptor terminates. Locks are not inherited by a child process in a fork(2) system call.

When mandatory file and record locking is active on a file [see chmod(2)], creat(2), open(2), read(2) and write(2) system calls issued on the file will be affected by the record locks in effect.

fcntl will fail if one or more of the following are true:

EACCES   *cmd* is F_SETLK, the type of lock (l_type) is a read lock (F_RDLCK) and the segment of a file to be locked is already write locked by another process, or the type is a write lock (F_WRLCK) and the segment of a file to be locked is already read or write locked by another process.

EAGAIN   *cmd* is F_FREESP, the file exists, mandatory file/record locking is set, and there are outstanding record locks on the file.

EAGAIN   *cmd* is F_SETLK or F_SETLKW and the file is currently being mapped to virtual memory via mmap [see mmap(2)].

EBADF   *fildes* is not a valid open file descriptor.

EBADF   *cmd* is F_SETLK or F_SETLKW, the type of lock (l_type) is a read lock (F_RDLCK), and *fildes* is not a valid file descriptor open for reading.

EBADF   *cmd* is F_SETLK or F_SETLKW, the type of lock (l_type) is a write lock (F_WRLCK), and *fildes* is not a valid file descriptor open for writing.

EBADF   *cmd* is F_FREESP, and *fildes* is not a valid file descriptor open for writing.

EDEADLK   *cmd* is F_SETLKW, the lock is blocked by some lock from another process, and if fcntl blocked the calling process waiting for that lock to become free, a deadlock would occur.

EDEADLK   *cmd* is F_FREESP, mandatory record locking is enabled, O_NDELAY and O_NONBLOCK are clear and a deadlock condition was detected.

EFAULT		*cmd* is F_FREESP and the value pointed to by the third argument *arg* resulted in an address outside the process's allocated address space.
EFAULT		*cmd* is F_GETLK, F_SETLK or F_SETLKW and the value pointed to by the third argument resulted in an address outside the program address space.
EINTR		A signal was caught during execution of the fcntl system call.
EIO		An I/O error occurred while reading from or writing to the file system.
EMFILE		*cmd* is F_DUPFD and the number of file descriptors currently open in the calling process is the configured value for the maximum number of open file descriptors allowed each user.
EINVAL		*cmd* is F_DUPFD and the third argument is either negative, or greater than or equal to the configured value for the maximum number of open file descriptors allowed each user.
EINVAL		*cmd* is not a valid value.
EINVAL		*cmd* is F_GETLK, F_SETLK, or F_SETLKW and the third argument or the data it points to is not valid, or *fildes* refers to a file that does not support locking.
ENOLCK		*cmd* is F_SETLK or F_SETLKW, the type of lock is a read or write lock, and there are no more record locks available (too many file segments locked) because the system maximum has been exceeded.
ENOLINK		*fildes* is on a remote machine and the link to that machine is no longer active.
ENOLINK		*cmd* is F_FREESP, the file is on a remote machine, and the link to that machine is no longer active.
EOVERFLOW		*cmd* is F_GETLK and the process ID of the process holding the requested lock is too large to be stored in the *l_pid* field.

SEE ALSO
close(2), creat(2), dup(2), exec(2), fork(2), open(2), pipe(2), fcntl(5)
The "File and Record Locking" chapter.

DIAGNOSTICS
On success, fcntl returns a value that depends on *cmd*:

F_DUPFD	A new file descriptor.
F_GETFD	Value of flag (only the low-order bit is defined). The return value will not be negative.
F_SETFD	Value other than −1.
F_FREESP	Value of 0.

F_GETFL	Value of file status flags. The return value will not be negative.
F_SETFL	Value other than −1.
F_GETLK	Value other than −1.
F_SETLK	Value other than −1.
F_SETLKW	Value other than −1.

On failure, fcntl returns −1 and sets errno to indicate the error.

NOTES

In the future, the variable errno will be set to EAGAIN rather than EACCES when a section of a file is already locked by another process. Therefore, portable application programs should expect and test for either value.

fork(2)

NAME
fork – create a new process

SYNOPSIS
    #include <sys/types.h>
    #include <unistd.h>

    pid_t fork(void);

DESCRIPTION
fork causes creation of a new process. The new process (child process) is an exact copy of the calling process (parent process). This means the child process inherits the following attributes from the parent process:

- real user ID, real group ID, effective user ID, effective group ID
- environment
- close-on-exec flag [see exec(2)]
- signal handling settings (i.e., SIG_DFL, SIG_IGN, SIG_HOLD, function address)
- supplementary group IDs
- set-user-ID mode bit
- set-group-ID mode bit
- profiling on/off status
- nice value [see nice(2)]
- scheduler class [see priocntl(2)]
- all attached shared memory segments [see shmop(2)]
- process group ID
- session ID [see exit(2)]
- current working directory
- root directory
- file mode creation mask [see umask(2)]
- resource limits [see getrlimit(2)]
- controlling terminal

Scheduling priority and any per-process scheduling parameters that are specific to a given scheduling class may or may not be inherited according to the policy of that particular class [see priocntl(2)].

The child process differs from the parent process in the following ways:

The child process has a unique process ID which does not match any active process group ID.

The child process has a different parent process ID (i.e., the process ID of the parent process).

The child process has its own copy of the parent's file descriptors and directory streams. Each of the child's file descriptors shares a common file pointer with the corresponding file descriptor of the parent.

All semadj values are cleared [see semop(2)].

Process locks, text locks and data locks are not inherited by the child [see plock(2)].

fork(2)

The child process's tms structure is cleared: tms_utime, stime, cutime, and cstime are set to 0 [see times(2)].

The time left until an alarm clock signal is reset to 0.

The set of signals pending for the child process is initialized to the empty set.

Record locks set by the parent process are not inherited by the child process [see fcntl(2)].

fork will fail and no child process will be created if one or more of the following are true:

EAGAIN	The system-imposed limit on the total number of processes under execution by a single user would be exceeded.
EAGAIN	Total amount of system memory available when reading via raw I/O is temporarily insufficient.
ENOMEM	There is not enough swap space.

SEE ALSO

alarm(2), exec(2), fcntl(2), getrlimit(2), nice(2), plock(2), priocntl(2), ptrace(2), semop(2), shmop(2), signal(2), times(2), umask(2), wait(2), system(3S).

DIAGNOSTICS

Upon successful completion, fork returns a value of 0 to the child process and returns the process ID of the child process to the parent process. Otherwise, a value of (pid_t)−1 is returned to the parent process, no child process is created, and errno is set to indicate the error.

fpathconf(2)

NAME
fpathconf, pathconf – get configurable pathname variables

SYNOPSIS
```
#include <unistd.h>

long fpathconf (int fildes, int name);
long pathconf (char *path, int name);
```

DESCRIPTION

The functions fpathconf and pathconf return the current value of a configurable limit or option associated with a file or directory. The *path* argument points to the pathname of a file or directory; *fildes* is an open file descriptor; and *name* is the symbolic constant (defined in unistd.h) representing the configurable system limit or option to be returned.

The values returned by pathconf and fpathconf depend on the type of file specified by *path* or *fildes*. The following table contains the symbolic constants supported by pathconf and fpathconf along with the POSIX defined return value. The return value is based on the type of file specified by *path* or *fildes*.

Value of *name*	See Note
_PC_LINK_MAX	1
_PC_MAX_CANNON	2
_PC_MAX_INPUT	2
_PC_NAME_MAX	3,4
_PC_PATH_MAX	4,5
_PC_PIPE_BUF	6
_PC_CHOWN_RESTRICTED	7
_PC_NO_TRUNC	3,4
_PC_VDISABLE	2

Notes:

1 If *path* or *fildes* refers to a directory, the value returned applies to the directory itself.

2 The behavior is undefined if *path* or *fildes* does not refer to a terminal file.

3 If *path* or *fildes* refers to a directory, the value returned applies to the filenames within the directory.

4 The behavior is undefined if *path* or *fildes* does not refer to a directory.

5 If *path* or *fildes* refers to a directory, the value returned is the maximum length of a relative pathname when the specified directory is the working directory.

6   If *path* or *fildes* refers to a pipe or FIFO, the value returned applies to the FIFO itself. If *path* or *fildes* refers to a directory, the value returned applies to any FIFOs that exist or can be created within the directory. If *path* or *fildes* refer to any other type of file, the behavior is undefined.

7   If *path* or *fildes* refers to a directory, the value returned applies to any files, other than directories, that exist or can be created within the directory.

The value of the configurable system limit or option specified by *name* does not change during the lifetime of the calling process.

fpathconf fails if the following is true:

EBADF   *fildes* is not a valid file descriptor.

pathconf fails if one or more of the following are true:

EACCES   search permission is denied for a component of the path prefix.

ELOOP   too many symbolic links are encountered while translating *path*.

EMULTIHOP   components of *path* require hopping to multiple remote machines and file system type does not allow it.

ENAMETOOLONG
        the length of a pathname exceeds {PATH_MAX}, or pathname component is longer than {NAME_MAX} while (_POSIX_NO_TRUNC) is in effect.

ENOENT   *path* is needed for the command specified and the named file does not exist or if the *path* argument points to an empty string.

ENOLINK   *path* points to a remote machine and the link to that machine is no longer active.

ENOTDIR   a component of the path prefix is not a directory.

Both fpathconf and pathconf fail if the following is true:

EINVAL   if *name* is an invalid value.

SEE ALSO
sysconf(3C), limits(4)

DIAGNOSTICS
If fpathconf or pathconf are invoked with an invalid symbolic constant or the symbolic constant corresponds to a configurable system limit or option not supported on the system, a value of *-1* is returned to the invoking process. If the function fails because the configurable system limit or option corresponding to *name* is not supported on the system the value of errno is not changed.

fsync(2)

NAME
fsync – synchronize a file's in-memory state with that on the physical medium

SYNOPSIS
```
#include <unistd.h>

int fsync(int fildes);
```

DESCRIPTION
fsync moves all modified data and attributes of *fildes* to a storage device. When fsync returns, all in-memory modified copies of buffers associated with *fildes* have been written to the physical medium. fsync is different from sync, which schedules disk I/O for all files but returns before the I/O completes.

fsync should be used by programs that require that a file be in a known state. For example, a program that contains a simple transaction facility might use fsync to ensure that all changes to a file or files caused by a given transaction were recorded on a storage medium.

fsync fails if one or more of the following are true:

EBADF	*fildes* is not a valid file descriptor open for writing.
ENOLINK	*fildes* is on a remote machine and the link on that machine is no longer active.
EINTR	A signal was caught during execution of the fsync system call.
EIO	An I/O error occurred while reading from or writing to the file system.

DIAGNOSTICS
Upon successful completion, a value of 0 is returned. Otherwise, a value of −1 is returned and errno is set to indicate the error.

NOTES
The way the data reach the physical medium depends on both implementation and hardware. fsync returns when the device driver tells it that the write has taken place.

SEE ALSO
sync(2)

NAME

ftime – get time and date

SYNOPSIS

cc [flag . . .] file . . . -lx [library . . .]

#include <sys/times.h>

ftime(struct timeb *tp);

DESCRIPTION

ftime returns the time in a structure (see DIAGNOSTICS below). ftime will fail if *tp* points to an illegal address [EFAULT].

DIAGNOSTICS

The ftime entry fills in a structure pointed to by its argument, as defined by sys/timeb.h:

```
/* Structure returned by ftime system call */
struct timeb {
    long time;
    unsigned short millitm;
    short   timezone;
    short   dstflag;
};
```

Note that the timezone value is a system default timezone and not the value of the TZ environment variable.

The structure contains the time since the 00:00:00 GMT, January 1, 1970 up to 1000 milliseconds of more-precise interval, the local time zone (measured in minutes of time westward from Greenwich), and a flag that, if nonzero, indicates that Daylight Saving time applies locally during the appropriate part of the year.

SEE ALSO

cc(1), stime(2), ctime(3C)

NOTES

Since ftime does not return the correct timezone value, its use is not recommended. See ctime(3C) for accurate use of the TZ variable.

NAME

getcontext, setcontext – get and set current user context

SYNOPSIS

    #include <ucontext.h>

    int getcontext(ucontext_t *ucp);

    int setcontext(ucontext_t *ucp);

DESCRIPTION

These functions, along with those defined in makecontext(3C), are useful for implementing user level context switching between multiple threads of control within a process.

getcontext initializes the structure pointed to by *ucp* to the current user context of the calling process. The user context is defined by ucontext(5) and includes the contents of the calling process's machine registers, signal mask and execution stack.

setcontext restores the user context pointed to by *ucp*. The call to setcontext does not return; program execution resumes at the point specified by the context structure passed to setcontext. The context structure should have been one created either by a prior call to getcontext or makecontext or passed as the third argument to a signal handler [see sigaction(2)]. If the context structure was one created with getcontext, program execution continues as if the corresponding call of getcontext had just returned. If the context structure was one created with makecontext, program execution continues with the function specified to makecontext.

NOTES

When a signal handler is executed, the current user context is saved and a new context is created by the kernel. If the process leaves the signal handler via longjmp(3C) the original context will not be restored, and future calls to getcontext will not be reliable. Signal handlers should use siglongjmp(3C) or setcontext instead.

DIAGNOSTICS

On successful completion, setcontext does not return and getcontext returns 0. Otherwise, a value of -1 is returned and errno is set to indicate the error.

SEE ALSO

sigaction(2), sigaltstack(2), sigprocmask(2), makecontext(3C), ucontext(5)

getdents(2)

NAME
getdents – read directory entries and put in a file system independent format

SYNOPSIS
```
#include <sys/dirent.h>

int getdents (int fildes, struct dirent *buf, size_t nbyte);
```

DESCRIPTION
fildes is a file descriptor obtained from a creat, open, dup, fcntl, pipe, or ioctl system call.

getdents attempts to read *nbyte* bytes from the directory associated with *fildes* and to format them as file system independent directory entries in the buffer pointed to by *buf*. Since the file system independent directory entries are of variable length, in most cases the actual number of bytes returned will be strictly less than *nbyte*. See dirent(4) to calculate the number of bytes.

The file system independent directory entry is specified by the dirent structure. For a description of this see dirent(4).

On devices capable of seeking, getdents starts at a position in the file given by the file pointer associated with *fildes*. Upon return from *getdents*, the file pointer is incremented to point to the next directory entry.

This system call was developed in order to implement the readdir routine [for a description, see directory(3C)], and should not be used for other purposes.

getdents will fail if one or more of the following are true:

EBADF	*fildes* is not a valid file descriptor open for reading.
EFAULT	*buf* points outside the allocated address space.
EINVAL	*nbyte* is not large enough for one directory entry.
ENOENT	The current file pointer for the directory is not located at a valid entry.
ENOLINK	*fildes* points to a remote machine and the link to that machine is no longer active.
ENOTDIR	*fildes* is not a directory.
EIO	An I/O error occurred while accessing the file system.

SEE ALSO
directory(3C)

dirent(4) in the *System Administrator's Reference Manual*

DIAGNOSTICS
Upon successful completion a non-negative integer is returned indicating the number of bytes actually read. A value of 0 indicates the end of the directory has been reached. If the system call failed, a −1 is returned and errno is set to indicate the error.

getgroups(2)

NAME
getgroups, setgroups – get or set supplementary group access list IDs

SYNOPSIS
    #include <unistd.h>

    int getgroups(int gidsetsize, gid_t *grouplist)

    int setgroups(int ngroups, const gid_t *grouplist)

DESCRIPTION
getgroups gets the current supplemental group access list of the calling process and stores the result in the array of group IDs specified by *grouplist*. This array has *gidsetsize* entries and must be large enough to contain the entire list. This list cannot be greater than {NGOUPS_MAX}. If *gidsetsize* equals 0, getgroups will return the number of groups to which the calling process belongs without modifying the array pointed to by *grouplist*.

setgroups sets the supplementary group access list of the calling process from the array of group IDs specified by *grouplist*. The number of entries is specified by *ngroups* and can not be greater than {NGROUPS_MAX}. This function may be invoked only by the super-user.

getgroups will fail if:

EINVAL   The value of *gidsetsize* is non-zero and less than the number of supplementary group IDs set for the calling process.

setgroups will fail if:

EINVAL   The value of *ngroups* is greater than {NGROUPS_MAX}.

EPERM   The effective user ID is not super-user.

Either call will fail if:

EFAULT   A referenced part of the array pointed to by *grouplist* is outside of the allocated address space of the process.

SEE ALSO
chown(2), getuid(2), setuid(2), initgroups(3C)
groups(1) in the *User's Reference Manual*

DIAGNOSTICS
Upon successful completion, getgroups returns the number of supplementary group IDs set for the calling process and setgroups returns the value 0. Otherwise, a value of −1 is returned and errno is set to indicate the error.

NAME

getmsg – get next message off a stream

SYNOPSIS

```
#include <stropts.h>

int getmsg(int fd, struct strbuf *ctlptr,
           struct strbuf *dataptr, int *flagsp);

int getpmsg(int fd, struct strbuf *ctlptr,
            struct strbuf *dataptr, int *bandp, int *flagsp);
```

DESCRIPTION

getmsg retrieves the contents of a message [see intro(2)] located at the stream head read queue from a STREAMS file, and places the contents into user specified buffer(s). The message must contain either a data part, a control part, or both. The data and control parts of the message are placed into separate buffers, as described below. The semantics of each part is defined by the STREAMS module that generated the message.

The function getpmsg does the same thing as getmsg, but provides finer control over the priority of the messages received. Except where noted, all information pertaining to getmsg also pertains to getpmsg.

fd specifies a file descriptor referencing an open stream. *ctlptr* and *dataptr* each point to a strbuf structure, which contains the following members:

```
int maxlen;    /* maximum buffer length */
int len;       /* length of data */
char *buf;     /* ptr to buffer */
```

buf points to a buffer in which the data or control information is to be placed, and maxlen indicates the maximum number of bytes this buffer can hold. On return, len contains the number of bytes of data or control information actually received, or 0 if there is a zero-length control or data part, or -1 if no data or control information is present in the message. *flagsp* should point to an integer that indicates the type of message the user is able to receive. This is described later.

ctlptr is used to hold the control part from the message and *dataptr* is used to hold the data part from the message. If *ctlptr* (or *dataptr*) is NULL or the maxlen field is −1, the control (or data) part of the message is not processed and is left on the stream head read queue. If *ctlptr* (or *dataptr*) is not NULL and there is no corresponding control (or data) part of the messages on the stream head read queue, len is set to −1. If the maxlen field is set to 0 and there is a zero-length control (or data) part, that zero-length part is removed from the read queue and len is set to 0. If the maxlen field is set to 0 and there are more than zero bytes of control (or data) information, that information is left on the read queue and len is set to 0. If the maxlen field in *ctlptr* or *dataptr* is less than, respectively, the control or data part of the message, maxlen bytes are retrieved. In this case, the remainder of the message is left on the stream head read queue and a non-zero return value is provided, as described below under DIAGNOSTICS.

By default, `getmsg` processes the first available message on the stream head read queue. However, a user may choose to retrieve only high priority messages by setting the integer pointed by *flagsp* to `RS_HIPRI`. In this case, `getmsg` processes the next message only if it is a high priority message. If the integer pointed by *flagsp* is 0, `getmsg` retrieves any message available on the stream head read queue. In this case, on return, the integer pointed to by *flagsp* will be set to `RS_HIPRI` if a high priority message was retrieved, or 0 otherwise.

For `getpmsg`, the flags are different. *flagsp* points to a bitmask with the following mutually-exclusive flags defined: `MSG_HIPRI`, `MSG_BAND`, and `MSG_ANY`. Like `getmsg`, `getpmsg` processes the first available message on the stream head read queue. A user may choose to retrieve only high-priority messages by setting the integer pointed to by *flagsp* to `MSG_HIPRI` and the integer pointed to by *bandp* to 0. In this case, `getpmsg` will only process the next message if it is a high-priority message. In a similar manner, a user may choose to retrieve a message from a particular priority band by setting the integer pointed to by *flagsp* to `MSG_BAND` and the integer pointed to by *bandp* to the priority band of interest. In this case, `getpmsg` will only process the next message if it is in a priority band equal to, or greater than, the integer pointed to by *bandp*, or if it is a high-priority message. If a user just wants to get the first message off the queue, the integer pointed to by *flagsp* should be set to `MSG_ANY` and the integer pointed to by *bandp* should be set to 0. On return, if the message retrieved was a high-priority message, the integer pointed to by *flagsp* will be set to `MSG_HIPRI` and the integer pointed to by *bandp* will be set to 0. Otherwise, the integer pointed to by *flagsp* will be set to `MSG_BAND` and the integer pointed to by *bandp* will be set to the priority band of the message.

If `O_NDELAY` and `O_NONBLOCK` are clear, `getmsg` blocks until a message of the type specified by *flagsp* is available on the stream head read queue. If `O_NDELAY` or `O_NONBLOCK` has been set and a message of the specified type is not present on the read queue, `getmsg` fails and sets `errno` to `EAGAIN`.

If a hangup occurs on the stream from which messages are to be retrieved, `getmsg` continues to operate normally, as described above, until the stream head read queue is empty. Thereafter, it returns 0 in the `len` fields of *ctlptr* and *dataptr*.

`getmsg` or `getpmsg` will fail if one or more of the following are true:

EAGAIN	The `O_NDELAY` or `O_NONBLOCK` flag is set, and no messages are available.
EBADF	*fd* is not a valid file descriptor open for reading.
EBADMSG	Queued message to be read is not valid for `getmsg`.
EFAULT	*ctlptr*, *dataptr*, *bandp*, or *flagsp* points to a location outside the allocated address space.
EINTR	A signal was caught during the `getmsg` system call.

getmsg(2)   **getmsg(2)**

        EINVAL   An illegal value was specified in *flagsp*, or the stream referenced by *fd* is linked under a multiplexor.

        ENOSTR   A stream is not associated with *fd*.

getmsg can also fail if a STREAMS error message had been received at the stream head before the call to getmsg. The error returned is the value contained in the STREAMS error message.

SEE ALSO

    intro(2), poll(2), putmsg(2), read(2), write(2)
    Programmer's Guide: STREAMS

DIAGNOSTICS

Upon successful completion, a non-negative value is returned. A value of 0 indicates that a full message was read successfully. A return value of MORECTL indicates that more control information is waiting for retrieval. A return value of MOREDATA indicates that more data are waiting for retrieval. A return value of MORECTL | MOREDATA indicates that both types of information remain. Subsequent getmsg calls retrieve the remainder of the message. However, if a message of higher priority has come in on the stream head read queue, the next call to getmsg will retrieve that higher priority message before retrieving the remainder of the previously received partial message.

getpid(2)

NAME
getpid, getpgrp, getppid, getpgid – get process, process group, and parent process IDs

SYNOPSIS
```
#include <sys/types.h>
#include <unistd.h>
```

pid_t getpid(void);

pid_t getpgrp(void);

pid_t getppid(void);

pid_t getpgid(pid_t pid);

DESCRIPTION
getpid returns the process ID of the calling process.

getpgrp returns the process group ID of the calling process.

getppid returns the parent process ID of the calling process.

getpgid returns the process group ID of the process whose process ID is equal to *pid*, or the process group ID of the calling process, if *pid* is equal to zero.

getpgid will fail if one or more of the following is true:

EPERM   The process whose process ID is equal to *pid* is not in the same session as the calling process, and the implementation does not allow access to the process group ID of that process from the calling process.

ESRCH   There is no process with a process ID equal to *pid*.

SEE ALSO
exec(2), fork(2), getpid(2), getsid(2), intro(2), setpgid(2), setsid(2) setpgrp(2), signal(2)

DIAGNOSTICS
Upon successful completion, getpgid returns a process group ID. Otherwise, a value of (pid_t) −1 is returned and errno is set to indicate the error.

getrlimit(2) getrlimit(2)

NAME
getrlimit, setrlimit – control maximum system resource consumption

SYNOPSIS
```
#include <sys/time.h>
#include <sys/resource.h>

int getrlimit(int resource, struct rlimit *rlp);

int setrlimit(int resource, const struct rlimit *rlp);
```

DESCRIPTION
Limits on the consumption of a variety of system resources by a process and each process it creates may be obtained with getrlimit and set with setrlimit.

Each call to either getrlimit or setrlimit identifies a specific resource to be operated upon as well as a resource limit. A resource limit is a pair of values: one specifying the current (soft) limit, the other a maximum (hard) limit. Soft limits may be changed by a process to any value that is less than or equal to the hard limit. A process may (irreversibly) lower its hard limit to any value that is greater than or equal to the soft limit. Only a process with an effective user ID or superuser can raise a hard limit. Both hard and soft limits can be changed in a single call to setrlimit subject to the constraints described above. Limits may have an infinite value of RLIM_INFINITY. *rlp* is a pointer to struct rlimit that includes the following members:

```
rlim_t    rlim_cur;    /* current (soft) limit */
rlim_t    rlim_max;    /* hard limit */
```

rlim_t is an arithmetic data type to which objects of type int, size_t, and off_t can be cast without loss of information.

The possible resources, their descriptions, and the actions taken when current limit is exceeded, are summarized in the table below:

Resources	Description	Action
RLIMIT_CORE	The maximum size of a core file in bytes that may be created by a process. A limit of 0 will prevent the creation of a core file.	The writing of a core file will terminate at this size.
RLIMIT_CPU	The maximum amount of CPU time in seconds used by a process.	SIGXCPU is sent to the process. If the process is holding or ignoring SIGXCPU, the behavior is scheduling class defined.
RLIMIT_DATA	The maximum size of a process's heap in bytes.	brk(2) will fail with errno set to ENOMEM.

Resources	Description	Action
RLIMIT_FSIZE	The maximum size of a file in bytes that may be created by a process. A limit of 0 will prevent the creation of a file.	SIGXFSZ is sent to the process. If the process is holding or ignoring SIGXFSZ, continued attempts to increase the size of a file beyond the limit will fail with errno set to EFBIG.
RLIMIT_NOFILE	The maximum number of open file descriptors that the process can have.	Functions that create new file descriptors will fail with errno set to EMFILE.
RLIMIT_STACK	The maximum size of a process's stack in bytes. The system will not automatically grow the stack beyond this limit.	SIGSEGV is sent to the process. If the process is holding or ignoring SIGSEGV, or is catching SIGSEGV and has not made arrangements to use an alternate stack [see sigaltstack(2)], the disposition of SIGSEGV will be set to SIG_DFL before it is sent.
RLIMIT_VMEM	The maximum size of a process's mapped address space in bytes.	brk(2) and mmap(2) functions will fail with errno set to ENOMEM. In addition, the automatic stack growth will fail with the effects outlined above.

Because limit information is stored in the per-process information, the shell built-in ulimit must directly execute this system call if it is to affect all future processes created by the shell.

The value of the current limit of the following resources affect these implementation defined constants:

Limit	Implementation Defined Constant
RLIMIT_FSIZE	FCHR_MAX
RLIMIT_NOFILE	OPEN_MAX

RETURN VALUE

Upon successful completion, the functions getrlimit and setrlimit return a value of 0; otherwise, they return a value of −1 and set errno to indicate an error.

ERRORS

Under the following conditions, the functions getrlimit and setrlimit fail and set errno to:

EINVAL   if an invalid *resource* was specified; or in a setrlimit call, the new rlim_cur exceeds the new rlim_max.

EPERM   if the limit specified to setrlimit would have raised the maximum limit value, and the caller is the superuser

SEE ALSO

malloc(3C), open(2), sigaltstack(2), signal(5)

getsid(2)

NAME
getsid – get session ID

SYNOPSIS
    #include <sys/types.h>

    pid_t getsid(pid_t *pid*);

DESCRIPTION
The function `getsid` returns the session ID of the process whose process ID is equal to *pid*. If *pid* is equal to (pid_t)0, `getsid` returns the session ID of the calling process.

RETURN VALUE
Upon successful completion, the function `getsid` returns the session ID of the specified process; otherwise, it returns a value of (pid_t)-1 and sets `errno` to indicate an error.

ERRORS
Under the following conditions, the function `getsid` fails and sets `errno` to:

EPERM if the process whose process ID is equal to *pid* is not in the same session as the calling process, and the implementation does not allow access to the session ID of that process from the calling process.

ESRCH if there is no process with a process ID equal to *pid*.

SEE ALSO
exec(2), fork(2), getpid(2), setpgid(2), setsid(2)

NAME

getuid, geteuid, getgid, getegid – get real user, effective user, real group, and effective group IDs

SYNOPSIS

```
#include <sys/types.h>
#include <unistd.h>
```

uid_t getuid (void);

uid_t geteuid (void);

gid_t getgid (void);

gid_t getegid (void);

DESCRIPTION

getuid returns the real user ID of the calling process.

geteuid returns the effective user ID of the calling process.

getgid returns the real group ID of the calling process.

getegid returns the effective group ID of the calling process.

SEE ALSO

intro(2), setuid(2)

ioctl(2)

NAME
ioctl – control device

SYNOPSIS
#include <unistd.h>

int ioctl (int fildes, int request, ... /* arg */);

DESCRIPTION

ioctl performs a variety of control functions on devices and STREAMS. For non-STREAMS files, the functions performed by this call are device-specific control functions. *request* and an optional third argument with varying type are passed to the file designated by *fildes* and are interpreted by the device driver. This control is not frequently used on non-STREAMS devices, where the basic input/output functions are usually performed through the read(2) and write(2) system calls.

For STREAMS files, specific functions are performed by the ioctl call as described in streamio(7).

fildes is an open file descriptor that refers to a device. *request* selects the control function to be performed and depends on the device being addressed. *arg* represents a third argument that has additional information that is needed by this specific device to perform the requested function. The data type of *arg* depends upon the particular control request, but it is either an int or a pointer to a device-specific data structure.

In addition to device-specific and STREAMS functions, generic functions are provided by more than one device driver, for example, the general terminal interface [see termio(7)].

ioctl fails for any type of file if one or more of the following are true:

EBADF   *fildes* is not a valid open file descriptor.

ENOTTY   *fildes* is not associated with a device driver that accepts control functions.

EINTR   A signal was caught during the ioctl system call.

ioctl also fails if the device driver detects an error. In this case, the error is passed through ioctl without change to the caller. A particular driver might not have all of the following error cases. Under the following conditions, requests to device drivers may fail and set errno to:

EFAULT   *request* requires a data transfer to or from a buffer pointed to by *arg*, but some part of the buffer is outside the process's allocated space.

EINVAL   *request* or *arg* is not valid for this device.

EIO   Some physical I/O error has occurred.

ENXIO   The *request* and *arg* are valid for this device driver, but the service requested can not be performed on this particular subdevice.

ENOLINK   *fildes* is on a remote machine and the link to that machine is no longer active.

STREAMS errors are described in streamio(7).

SEE ALSO
streamio(7) in the *Programmer's Guide: STREAMS*
termio(7) in the *System Administrator's Reference Manual*

DIAGNOSTICS
Upon successful completion, the value returned depends upon the device control function, but must be a non-negative integer. Otherwise, a value of −1 is returned and errno is set to indicate the error.

kill(2)

NAME
kill – send a signal to a process or a group of processes

SYNOPSIS
    #include <sys/types.h>
    #include <signal.h>

    int kill (pid_t pid, int sig);

DESCRIPTION
kill sends a signal to a process or a group of processes. The process or group of processes to which the signal is to be sent is specified by *pid*. The signal that is to be sent is specified by *sig* and is either one from the list given in signal [see signal(5)], or 0. If *sig* is 0 (the null signal), error checking is performed but no signal is actually sent. This can be used to check the validity of *pid*.

The real or effective user ID of the sending process must match the real or saved [from exec(2)] user ID of the receiving process unless the effective user ID of the sending process is superuser, [see intro(2)], or *sig* is SIGCONT and the sending process has the same session ID as the receiving process.

The process with ID 0 and the process with ID 1 are special processes [see intro(2)] and will be referred to below as proc0 and proc1, respectively.

If *pid* is greater than 0, *sig* will be sent to the process whose process ID is equal to *pid*. *pid* may equal 1.

If *pid* is negative but not (pid_t)-1, *sig* will be sent to all processes whose process group ID is equal to the absolute value of *pid* and for which the process has permission to send a signal.

If *pid* is 0, *sig* will be sent to all processes excluding proc0 and proc1 whose process group ID is equal to the process group ID of the sender. Permission is needed to send a signal to process groups.

If *pid* is (pid_t)-1 and the effective user ID of the sender is not superuser, *sig* will be sent to all processes excluding proc0 and proc1 whose real user ID is equal to the effective user ID of the sender.

If *pid* is (pid_t)-1 and the effective user ID of the sender is superuser, *sig* will be sent to all processes excluding proc0 and proc1.

kill will fail and no signal will be sent if one or more of the following are true:

EINVAL	*sig* is not a valid signal number.
EINVAL	*sig* is SIGKILL and *pid* is (pid_t)1 (that is, *pid* specifies proc1).
ESRCH	No process or process group can be found corresponding to that specified by *pid*.
EPERM	The user ID of the sending process is not privileged, and its real or effective user ID does not match the real or saved user ID of the receiving process, and the calling process is not sending SIGCONT to a process that shares the same session ID.

kill(2)

SEE ALSO
getpid(2), intro(2), setpgrp(2), signal(2), getsid(2), sigsend(2), sigaction(2)
kill(1) in the *User's Reference Manual*

NOTES
sigsend is a more versatile way to send signals to processes. The user is encouraged to use sigsend instead of kill.

DIAGNOSTICS
Upon successful completion, a value of 0 is returned. Otherwise, a value of −1 is returned and errno is set to indicate the error.

link(2)

NAME
link – link to a file

SYNOPSIS
    #include <unistd.h>

    int link(const char *path1, const char *path2);

DESCRIPTION

path1 points to a path name naming an existing file. *path2* points to a path name naming the new directory entry to be created. link creates a new link (directory entry) for the existing file and increments its link count by one.

Upon successful completion, link marks for update the st_ctime field of the file. Also, the st_ctime and st_mtime fields of the directory that contains the new entry are marked for update.

link will fail and no link will be created if one or more of the following are true:

EACCES	A component of either path prefix denies search permission.
EACCES	The requested link requires writing in a directory with a mode that denies write permission.
EEXIST	The link named by *path2* exists.
EFAULT	*path* points outside the allocated address space of the process.
EINTR	A signal was caught during the link system call.
ELOOP	Too many symbolic links were encountered in translating *path*.
EMLINK	The maximum number of links to a file would be exceeded.
EMULTIHOP	Components of *path* require hopping to multiple remote machines and file system type does not allow it.
ENAMETOOLONG	The length of the *path1* or *path2* argument exceeds {PATH_MAX}, or the length of a *path1* or *path2* component exceeds {NAME_MAX} while _POSIX_NO_TRUNC is in effect.
ENOTDIR	A component of either path prefix is not a directory.
ENOENT	*path1* or *path2* is a null path name.
ENOENT	A component of either path prefix does not exist.
ENOENT	The file named by *path1* does not exist.
ENOLINK	*path* points to a remote machine and the link to that machine is no longer active.
ENOSPC	the directory that would contain the link cannot be extended.
EPERM	The file named by *path1* is a directory and the effective user ID is not super-user.

link(2)

EROFS	The requested link requires writing in a directory on a read-only file system.
EXDEV	The link named by *path2* and the file named by *path1* are on different logical devices (file systems).

SEE ALSO
    unlink(2)

DIAGNOSTICS
    Upon successful completion, a value of 0 is returned. Otherwise, a value of −1 is returned and errno is set to indicate the error.

lock(2) (Application Compatibility Package) lock(2)

NAME
    lock – lock a process in primary memory

SYNOPSIS
    cc [*flag* . . .] *file* . . . -lx
    int lock(flag);

DESCRIPTION
    If the *flag* argument is nonzero, the process executing this call will not be swapped unless it is required to grow. If the argument is zero, the process is unlocked. This call may only be executed by the super-user. If someone other than the super-user tries to execute this call, a value of −1 is returned and the errno is set to EPERM.

locking(2)   (Application Compatibility Package)   locking(2)

NAME
locking – lock or unlock a file region for reading or writing

SYNOPSIS
cc [*flag* . . .] *file* . . . -lx
locking (int fildes, int mode, long size);

DESCRIPTION
locking allows a specified number of bytes in a file to be controlled by the locking process. Other processes which attempt to read or write a portion of the file containing the locked region may sleep until the area become unlocked depending upon the mode in which the file region was locked.

A process that attempts to write to or read a file region that has been locked against reading and writing by another process (using the LK_LOCK or LK_NBLCK mode) with sleep until the region of the file has been released by the locking process.

A process that attempts to write to a file region that has been locked against writing by another process (using the LK_RLCK or LK_NBRLCK mode) will sleep until the region of the file has been released by the locking process, but a read request for that file region will proceed normally.

A process that attempts to lock a region of a file that contains areas that have been locked by other processes will sleep if it has specified the LK_LOCK or LK_RLCK mode in its lock request, but will return with the error EACCES if it specified LK_NBLCK or LK_NBRLCK.

fildes is the value returned from a successful create, open, dup, or pipe system call.

mode specifies the type of lock operation to be performed on the file region. The available values for mode are:

LK_UNLCK	0	Unlocks the specified region. The calling process releases a region of the file it has previously locked.
LK_LOCK	1	Locks the specified region. The calling process will sleep until the entire region is available if any part of it has been locked by a different process. The region is then locked for the calling process and no other process may read or write in any part of the locked region (lock against read and write).
LK_NBLCK	2	Locks the specified region. If any part of the region is already locked by a different process, return the error EACCES instead of waiting for the region to become available for locking (nonblocking lockrequest).
LK_RLCK	3	Same as LK_LOCK except that the locked region may be read by other processes (read permitted lock).
LK_NBRLCK	4	Same as LK_NBLCK except that the locked region may be read by other processes (nonblocking, read permitted lock).

The `locking` utility uses the current file pointer position as the starting point for the `locking` of the file segment. So a typical sequence of commands to lock a specific range within a file might be as follows:

```
fd=open("datafile",O_RDWR);
lseek(fd, 200L, 0);
locking(fd, LK_LOCK, 200L);
```

Accordingly, to lock or unlock an entire file a seek to the beginning of the file (position 0) must be done and then a `locking` call must be executed with a size of 0.

size is the number of contiguous bytes to be locked for unlocked. The region to be locked starts at the current offset in the file. If *size* is 0, the entire file is locked or unlocked. *size* may extend beyond the end of the file, in which case only the process issuing the lock call may access or add information to the file within the boundary defined by *size*.

The potential for a deadlock occurs when a process controlling a locked area is put to sleep by accessing another process's locked area. Thus calls to `locking`, `read`, or `write` scan for a deadlock prior to sleeping on a locked region. An EDEADLK error return is made if sleeping on the locked region would cause a deadlock.

Lock requests may, in whole or part, contain or be contained by a previously locked region for the same process. When this occurs, or when adjacent regions are locked, the regions are combined into a single area if the mode of the lock is the same (that is, either read permitted or regular lock). If the mode of the overlapping locks differ, the locked areas will be assigned assuming that the most recent request must be satisfied. Thus if a read only lock is applied to a region, or part of a region, that had been previously locked by the same process against both reading and writing, the area of the file specified by the new lock will be locked for read only, while the remaining region, if any, will remain locked against reading and writing. There is no arbitrary limit to the number of regions which may be locked in a file.

Unlock requests may, in whole or part, release one or more locked regions controlled by the process. When regions are not fully released, the remaining areas are still locked by the process. Release of the center section of a locked area requires an additional locked element to hold the separated section. If the lock table is full, an error is returned, and the requested region is not released. Only the process which locked the file region may unlock it. An unlock request for a region that the process does not have locked, or that is already unlocked, has no effect. When a process terminates, all locked regions controlled by that process are unlocked.

If a process has done more than one open on a file, all locks put on the file by that process will be released on the first close of the file.

Although no error is returned if locks are applied to special files or pipes, read/write operations on these types of files will ignore the locks. Locks may not be applied to a directory.

SEE ALSO
   close(2) creat(2), dup(2), lseek(2), open(2), read(2), write(2)

DIAGNOSTICS
   locking returns the value (int)-1 if an error occurs. If any portion of the region has been locked by another process for the LK_LOCK and LK_RLCK actions and the lock request is to test only, errno is set to EAGAIN. If locking the region would cause a deadlock, errno is set to EDEADLK If an internal lock cannot be allocated, errno is set to ENOLCK.

lseek(2)

NAME
lseek - move read/write file pointer

SYNOPSIS
    #include <sys/types.h>
    #include <unistd.h>

    off_t lseek (int fildes, off_t offset, int whence);

DESCRIPTION
fildes is a file descriptor returned from a creat, open, dup, fcntl, pipe, or ioctl system call. lseek sets the file pointer associated with *fildes* as follows:

> If *whence* is SEEK_SET, the pointer is set to *offset* bytes.
>
> If *whence* is SEEK_CUR, the pointer is set to its current location plus *offset*.
>
> If *whence* is SEEK_END, the pointer is set to the size of the file plus *offset*.

On success, lseek returns the resulting pointer location, as measured in bytes from the beginning of the file. Note that if *fildes* is a remote file descriptor and *offset* is negative, lseek returns the file pointer even if it is negative.

lseek allows the file pointer to be set beyond the existing data in the file. If data are later written at this point, subsequent reads in the gap between the previous end of data and the newly written data will return bytes of value 0 until data are written into the gap.

lseek fails and the file pointer remains unchanged if one or more of the following are true:

EBADF	*fildes* is not an open file descriptor.
ESPIPE	*fildes* is associated with a pipe or fifo.
EINVAL	*whence* is not SEEK_SET, SEEK_CUR, or SEEK_END. The process also gets a SIGSYS signal.
EINVAL	*fildes* is not a remote file descriptor, and the resulting file pointer would be negative.

Some devices are incapable of seeking. The value of the file pointer associated with such a device is undefined.

SEE ALSO
creat(2), dup(2), fcntl(2), open(2)

DIAGNOSTICS
Upon successful completion, a non-negative integer indicating the file pointer value is returned. Otherwise, a value of -1 is returned and errno is set to indicate the error.

memcntl(2)

NAME
memcntl – memory management control

SYNOPSIS
```
#include <sys/types.h>
#include <sys/mman.h>

int memcntl(caddr_t addr, size_t len, int cmd, caddr_t arg,
        int attr, int mask);
```

DESCRIPTION
The function memcntl allows the calling process to apply a variety of control operations over the address space identified by the mappings established for the address range [*addr, addr + len*).

addr must be a multiple of the pagesize as returned by sysconf(3C). The scope of the control operations can be further defined with additional selection criteria (in the form of attributes) according to the bit pattern contained in *attr*.

The following attributes specify page mapping selection criteria:

    SHARED   Page is mapped shared.
    PRIVATE   Page is mapped private.

The following attributes specify page protection selection criteria:

    PROT_READ   Page can be read.
    PROT_WRITE   Page can be written.
    PROT_EXEC   Page can be executed.

The selection criteria are constructed by an OR of the attribute bits and must match exactly.

In addition, the following criteria may be specified:

    PROC_TEXT   process text
    PROC_DATA   process data

where PROC_TEXT specifies all privately mapped segments with read and execute permission, and PROC_DATA specifies all privately mapped segments with write permission.

Selection criteria can be used to describe various abstract memory objects within the address space on which to operate. If an operation shall not be constrained by the selection criteria, *attr* must have the value 0.

The operation to be performed is identified by the argument *cmd*. The symbolic names for the operations are defined in sys/mman.h as follows:

    MC_LOCK   Lock in memory all pages in the range with attributes *attr*. A given page may be locked multiple times through different mappings; however, within a given mapping, page locks do not nest. Multiple lock operations on the same address in the same process will all be removed with a single unlock operation. A page locked in one process and mapped in another (or visible through a different mapping in the locking process) is locked in memory as long as the locking process does neither an implicit nor explicit unlock operation. If a locked mapping is removed, or a page is deleted through file removal or truncation, an unlock operation is implicitly performed. If a writable MAP_PRIVATE page in the address range is changed, the lock will be transferred to the private page.

At present *arg* is unused, but must be 0 to ensure compatibility with potential future enhancements.

MC_LOCKAS
Lock in memory all pages mapped by the address space with attributes *attr*. At present *addr* and *len* are unused, but must be NULL and 0 respectively, to ensure compatibility with potential future enhancements. *arg* is a bit pattern built from the flags:

MCL_CURRENT	Lock current mappings
MCL_FUTURE	Lock future mappings

The value of *arg* determines whether the pages to be locked are those currently mapped by the address space, those that will be mapped in the future, or both. If MCL_FUTURE is specified, then all mappings subsequently added to the address space will be locked, provided sufficient memory is available.

MC_SYNC
Write to their backing storage locations all modified pages in the range with attributes *attr*. Optionally, invalidate cache copies. The backing storage for a modified MAP_SHARED mapping is the file the page is mapped to; the backing storage for a modified MAP_PRIVATE mapping is its swap area. *arg* is a bit pattern built from the flags used to control the behavior of the operation:

MS_ASYNC	perform asynchronous writes
MS_SYNC	perform synchronous writes
MS_INVALIDATE	invalidate mappings

MS_ASYNC returns immediately once all write operations are scheduled; with MS_SYNC the system call will not return until all write operations are completed.

MS_INVALIDATE invalidates all cached copies of data in memory, so that further references to the pages will be obtained by the system from their backing storage locations. This operation should be used by applications that require a memory object to be in a known state.

MC_UNLOCK
Unlock all pages in the range with attributes *attr*. At present *arg* is unused, but must be 0 to ensure compatibility with potential future enhancements.

MC_UNLOCKAS
Remove address space memory locks, and locks on all pages in the address space with attributes *attr*. At present *addr*, *len*, and *arg* are unused, but must be NULL, 0 and 0 respectively, to ensure compatibility with potential future enhancements.

memcntl(2)

The *mask* argument must be zero; it is reserved for future use.

Locks established with the lock operations are not inherited by a child process after fork. memcntl fails if it attempts to lock more memory than a system-specific limit.

Due to the potential impact on system resources, all operations, with the exception of MC_SYNC, are restricted to processes with superuser effective user ID. The memcntl function subsumes the operations of plock and mctl.

RETURN VALUE

Upon successful completion, the function memcntl returns a value of 0; otherwise, it returns a value of -1 and sets errno to indicate an error.

ERRORS

Under the following conditions, the function memcntl fails and sets errno to:

EAGAIN	if some or all of the memory identified by the operation could not be locked when MC_LOCK or MC_LOCKAS is specified.
EBUSY	if some or all the addresses in the range [*addr, addr + len*) are locked and MC_SYNC with MS_INVALIDATE option is specified.
EINVAL	if *addr* is not a multiple of the page size as returned by sysconf.
EINVAL	if *addr* and/or *len* do not have the value 0 when MC_LOCKAS or MC_UNLOCKAS is specified.
EINVAL	if *arg* is not valid for the function specified.
EINVAL	if invalid selection criteria are specified in *attr*.
ENOMEM	if some or all the addresses in the range [*addr, addr + len*) are invalid for the address space of the process or pages not mapped are specified.
EPERM	if the process's effective user ID is not superuser and one of MC_LOCK, MC_LOCKAS, MC_UNLOCK, MC_UNLOCKAS was specified.

SEE ALSO

mmap(2), mprotect(2), plock(2), sysconf(2), mlock(3C), mlockall(3C), msync(3C)

mincore(2)

NAME
mincore – determine residency of memory pages

SYNOPSIS
    #include <unistd.h>
    int mincore(caddr_t addr, size_t len, char *vec);

DESCRIPTION
mincore returns the primary memory residency status of pages in the address space covered by mappings in the range [addr, addr + len). The status is returned as a character-per-page in the character array referenced by *vec (which the system assumes to be large enough to encompass all the pages in the address range). The least significant bit of each character is set to 1 to indicate that the referenced page is in primary memory, 0 if it is not. The settings of other bits in each character are undefined and may contain other information in future implementations.

mincore returns residency information that is accurate at an instant in time. Because the system may frequently adjust the set of pages in memory, this information may quickly be outdated. Only locked pages are guaranteed to remain in memory; see memcntl(2).

RETURN VALUE
mincore returns 0 on success, −1 on failure.

ERRORS
mincore fails if:

EFAULT	*vec includes an out-of-range or otherwise inaccessible address.
EINVAL	addr is not a multiple of the page size as returned by sysconf(3C).
EINVAL	The argument len has a value less than or equal to 0.
ENOMEM	Addresses in the range [addr, addr + len) are invalid for the address space of a process, or specify one or more pages which are not mapped.

SEE ALSO
mlock(3C), mmap(2), sysconf(3C)

mkdir(2)

NAME
mkdir – make a directory

SYNOPSIS
```
#include <sys/types.h>
#include <sys/stat.h>

int mkdir(const char *path, mode_t mode);
```

DESCRIPTION
mkdir creates a new directory named by the path name pointed to by *path*. The mode of the new directory is initialized from *mode* [see chmod(2) for values of mode]. The protection part of the *mode* argument is modified by the process's file creation mask [see umask(2)].

The directory's owner ID is set to the process's effective user ID. The directory's group ID is set to the process's effective group ID, or if the S_ISGID bit is set in the parent directory, then the group ID of the directory is inherited from the parent. The S_ISGID bit of the new directory is inherited from the parent directory.

If *path* is a symbolic link, it is not followed.

The newly created directory is empty with the exception of entries for itself (.) and its parent directory (. .).

Upon successful completion, mkdir marks for update the st_atime, st_ctime and st_mtime fields of the directory. Also, the st_ctime and st_mtime fields of the directory that contains the new entry are marked for update.

mkdir fails and creates no directory if one or more of the following are true:

EACCES	Either a component of the path prefix denies search permission or write permission is denied on the parent directory of the directory to be created.
EEXIST	The named file already exists.
EFAULT	*path* points outside the allocated address space of the process.
EIO	An I/O error has occurred while accessing the file system.
ELOOP	Too many symbolic links were encountered in translating *path*.
EMLINK	The maximum number of links to the parent directory would be exceeded.
EMULTIHOP	Components of *path* require hopping to multiple remote machines and the file system type does not allow it.
ENAMETOOLONG	The length of the *path* argument exceeds {PATH_MAX}, or the length of a *path* component exceeds {NAME_MAX} while _POSIX_NO_TRUNC is in effect.

ENOENT	A component of the path prefix does not exist or is a null pathname.
ENOLINK	*path* points to a remote machine and the link to that machine is no longer active.
ENOSPC	No free space is available on the device containing the directory.
ENOTDIR	A component of the path prefix is not a directory.
EROFS	The path prefix resides on a read-only file system.

DIAGNOSTICS

Upon successful completion, a value of 0 is returned. Otherwise, a value of −1 is returned, and errno is set to indicate the error.

SEE ALSO

chmod(2), mknod(2), umask(2), stat(5)

mknod(2)

NAME
mknod – make a directory, or a special or ordinary file

SYNOPSIS
```
#include <sys/types.h>
#include <sys/stat.h>

int mknod(const char *path, mode_t mode, dev_t dev);
```

DESCRIPTION
mknod creates a new file named by the path name pointed to by *path*. The file type and permissions of the new file are initialized from *mode*.

The file type is specified in *mode* by the S_IFMT bits, which must be set to one of the following values:

S_IFIFO	fifo special
S_IFCHR	character special
S_IFDIR	directory
S_IFBLK	block special
S_IFREG	ordinary file

The file access permissions are specified in *mode* by the 0007777 bits, and may be constructed by an OR of the following values:

S_ISUID	04000	Set user ID on execution.
S_ISGID	020#0	Set group ID on execution if # is 7, 5, 3, or 1
		Enable mandatory file/record locking if # is 6, 4, 2, or 0
S_ISVTX	01000	Save text image after execution.
S_IRWXU	00700	Read, write, execute by owner.
S_IRUSR	00400	Read by owner.
S_IWUSR	00200	Write by owner.
S_IXUSR	00100	Execute (search if a directory) by owner.
S_IRWXG	00070	Read, write, execute by group.
S_IRGRP	00040	Read by group.
S_IWGRP	00020	Write by group.
S_IXGRP	00010	Execute by group.
S_IRWXO	00007	Read, write, execute (search) by others.
S_IROTH	00004	Read by others.
S_IWOTH	00002	Write by others
S_IXOTH	00001	Execute by others.

The owner ID of the file is set to the effective user ID of the process. The group ID of the file is set to the effective group ID of the process. However, if the S_ISGID bit is set in the parent directory, then the group ID of the file is inherited from the parent. If the group ID of the new file does not match the effective group ID or one of the supplementary group IDs, the S_ISGID bit is cleared.

The access permission bits of *mode* are modified by the process's file mode creation mask: all bits set in the process's file mode creation mask are cleared [see umask(2)]. If *mode* indicates a block or character special file, *dev* is a configuration-dependent specification of a character or block I/O device. If *mode* does not indicate a block special or character special device, *dev* is ignored. See makedev(3C).

mknod checks to see if the driver has been installed and whether or not it is an old-style driver. If the driver is installed and it is an old-style driver, the minor number is limited to 255. If it's not an old-style driver, then it must be a new-style driver or uninstalled, and the minor number is limited to the current value of the MAXMINOR tunable. Of course, this tunable is set to 255 by default. If the range check fails, mknod fails with EINVAL.

mknod may be invoked only by a privileged user for file types other than FIFO special.

If *path* is a symbolic link, it is not followed.

mknod fails and creates no new file if one or more of the following are true:

EEXIST	The named file exists.
EINVAL	*dev* is invalid.
EFAULT	*path* points outside the allocated address space of the process.
ELOOP	Too many symbolic links were encountered in translating *path*.
EMULTIHOP	Components of *path* require hopping to multiple remote machines and the file system type does not allow it.
ENAMETOOLONG	The length of the *path* argument exceeds {PATH_MAX}, or the length of a *path* component exceeds {NAME_MAX} while _POSIX_NO_TRUNC is in effect.
ENOTDIR	A component of the path prefix is not a directory.
ENOENT	A component of the path prefix does not exist or is a null pathname.
EPERM	The effective user ID of the process is not super-user.
EROFS	The directory in which the file is to be created is located on a read-only file system.
ENOSPC	No space is available.
EINTR	A signal was caught during the mknod system call.
ENOLINK	*path* points to a remote machine and the link to that machine is no longer active.

SEE ALSO
chmod(2), exec(2), umask(2), makedev(3C), mkfifo(3C), fs(4), stat(5)
mkdir(1) in the *User's Reference Manual*

DIAGNOSTICS
Upon successful completion a value of 0 is returned. Otherwise, a value of −1 is returned and errno is set to indicate the error.

NOTES
If mknod creates a device in a remote directory using Remote File Sharing, the major and minor device numbers are interpreted by the server.

mknod(2) (Application Compatibility Package)

NAME
mknod – make a directory, or a special or ordinary file

SYNOPSIS
```
#include <sys/types.h>
#include <osfcn.h>
#include <sys/stat.h>

int mknod (const char *path, mode_t mode, dev_t dev);
```

DESCRIPTION
mknod creates a new file named by the path name pointed to by *path*. The file type and permissions of the new file are initialized from *mode*.

The file type is specified in *mode* by the S_IFMT bits, which must be set to one of the following values:

S_IFIFO	fifo special
S_IFCHR	character special
S_IFDIR	directory
S_IFBLK	block special
S_IFREG	ordinary file
S_IFNAM	name special file

The file access permissions are specified in *mode* by the 0007777 bits, and may be constructed by an OR of the following values:

S_ISUID	04000	Set user ID on execution.
S_ISGID	020#0	Set group ID on execution if # is 7, 5, 3, or 1
		Enable mandatory file/record locking if # is 6, 4, 2, or 0
S_ISVTX	01000	Save text image after execution.
S_IRUSR	00400	Read by owner.
S_IWUSR	00200	Write by owner.
S_IXUSR	00100	Execute (search if a directory) by owner.
S_IRWXG	00070	Read, write, execute by group.
S_IRGRP	00040	Read by group.
S_IWGRP	00020	Write by group.
S_IXGRP	00010	Execute by group.
S_IRWXO	00007	Read, write, execute (search) by others.
S_IROTH	00004	Read by others.
S_IWOTH	00002	Write by others
S_IXOTH	00001	Execute by others.

The owner ID of the file is set to the effective user ID of the process. The group ID of the file is set to the effective group ID of the process. However, if the S_ISGID bit is set in the parent directory, then the group ID of the file is inherited from the parent. If the group ID of the new file does not match the effective group ID or one of the supplementary group IDs, the S_ISGID bit is cleared.

Values of *mode* other than those above are undefined and should not be used. The access permission bits of *mode* are modified by the process's file mode creation mask: all bits set in the process's file mode creation mask are cleared [see umask(2)]. For block and character special files, *dev* is the special file's device number. For name special files, *dev* is the file type of the name file, either a

XENIX shared data file or a XENIX semaphore. Otherwise, *dev* is ignored. See mkdev(3C).

mknod may be invoked only by the privileged user for file types other than FIFO special.

mknod fails and creates no new file if one or more of the following are true:

EEXIST	The named file exists.
EINVAL	Invalid *arg* value.
EFAULT	*path* points outside the allocated address space of the process.
ELOOP	Too many symbolic links were encountered in translating *path*.
EMULTIHOP	Components of *path* require hopping to multiple remote machines.
ENAMETOOLONG	The length of the *path* argument exceeds {PATH_MAX}, or the length of a *path* component exceeds {NAME_MAX} while (_POSIX_NO_TRUNC) is in effect.
ENOTDIR	A component of the path prefix is not a directory.
ENOENT	A component of the path prefix does not exist or is a null pathname.
EPERM	The effective user ID of the process is not super-user.
EROFS	The directory in which the file is to be created is located on a read-only file system.
ENOSPC	No space is available.
EINTR	A signal was caught during the mknod system call.
ENOLINK	*path* points to a remote machine and the link to that machine is no longer active.

SEE ALSO
creatsem(2), sdget(2)
chmod(2), exec(2), umask(2), mkfifo(3C), stat(5) in the *Programmer's Reference Manual*
fs(4) in the *System Administrator's Reference Manual*
mkdir(1) in the *User's Reference Manual*

DIAGNOSTICS
Upon successful completion a value of 0 is returned. Otherwise, a value of −1 is returned and errno is set to indicate the error.

NOTES
If mknod creates a device in a remote directory using Remote File Sharing, the major and minor device numbers are interpreted by the server.

Semaphore files should be created with the creatsem system call. Shared data files should be created with the sdget system call.

mmap(2)

NAME
mmap – map pages of memory

SYNOPSIS
```
#include <sys/types.h>
#include <sys/mman.h>
```
```
caddr_t mmap(caddr_t addr, size_t len, int prot, int flags, int fd,
    off_t off);
```

DESCRIPTION
The function mmap establishes a mapping between a process's address space and a virtual memory object. The format of the call is as follows:

pa = mmap(*addr*, *len*, *prot*, *flags*, *fd*, *off*);

mmap establishes a mapping between the process's address space at an address *pa* for *len* bytes to the memory object represented by the file descriptor *fd* at offset *off* for *len* bytes. The value of *pa* is an implementation-dependent function of the parameter *addr* and values of *flags*, further described below. A successful mmap call returns *pa* as its result. The address ranges covered by [*pa*, *pa* + *len*) and [*off*, *off* + *len*) must be legitimate for the possible (not necessarily current) address space of a process and the object in question, respectively. mmap cannot grow a file.

The mapping established by mmap replaces any previous mappings for the process's pages in the range [*pa*, *pa* + *len*).

The parameter *prot* determines whether read, write, execute, or some combination of accesses are permitted to the pages being mapped. The protection options are defined in <sys/mman.h> as:

PROT_READ	Page can be read.
PROT_WRITE	Page can be written.
PROT_EXEC	Page can be executed.
PROT_NONE	Page can not be accessed.

Not all implementations literally provide all possible combinations. PROT_WRITE is often implemented as PROT_READ|PROT_WRITE and PROT_EXEC as PROT_READ|PROT_EXEC. However, no implementation will permit a write to succeed where PROT_WRITE has not been set. The behavior of PROT_WRITE can be influenced by setting MAP_PRIVATE in the *flags* parameter, described below.

The parameter *flags* provides other information about the handling of the mapped pages. The options are defined in <sys/mman.h> as:

MAP_SHARED	Share changes.
MAP_PRIVATE	Changes are private.
MAP_FIXED	Interpret addr exactly.

MAP_SHARED and MAP_PRIVATE describe the disposition of write references to the memory object. If MAP_SHARED is specified, write references will change the memory object. If MAP_PRIVATE is specified, the initial write reference will create a private copy of the memory object page and redirect the mapping to the copy. Either MAP_SHARED or MAP_PRIVATE must be specified, but not both. The mapping type is retained across a fork(2).

Note that the private copy is not created until the first write; until then, other users who have the object mapped MAP_SHARED can change the object.

MAP_FIXED informs the system that the value of *pa* must be *addr*, exactly. The use of MAP_FIXED is discouraged, as it may prevent an implementation from making the most effective use of system resources.

When MAP_FIXED is not set, the system uses *addr* in an implementation-defined manner to arrive at *pa*. The *pa* so chosen will be an area of the address space which the system deems suitable for a mapping of *len* bytes to the specified object. All implementations interpret an *addr* value of zero as granting the system complete freedom in selecting *pa*, subject to constraints described below. A non-zero value of *addr* is taken to be a suggestion of a process address near which the mapping should be placed. When the system selects a value for *pa*, it will never place a mapping at address 0, nor will it replace any extant mapping, nor map into areas considered part of the potential data or stack segments.

The parameter *off* is constrained to be aligned and sized according to the value returned by sysconf. When MAP_FIXED is specified, the parameter *addr* must also meet these constraints. The system performs mapping operations over whole pages. Thus, while the parameter *len* need not meet a size or alignment constraint, the system will include, in any mapping operation, any partial page specified by the range [*pa*, *pa* + *len*).

The system will always zero-fill any partial page at the end of an object. Further, the system will never write out any modified portions of the last page of an object which are beyond its end. References to whole pages following the end of an object will result in the delivery of a SIGBUS signal. SIGBUS signals may also be delivered on various file system conditions, including quota exceeded errors.

RETURN VALUE

On success, mmap returns the address at which the mapping was placed (*pa*). On failure it returns (caddr_t)-1 and sets errno to indicate an error.

ERRORS

Under the following conditions, mmap fails and sets errno to:

EAGAIN	The mapping could not be locked in memory or MAP_FIXED was not specified and there is insufficient room in the address space to effect the mapping.
EBADF	*fd* is not open.
EACCES	*fd* is not open for read, regardless of the protection specified, or *fd* is not open for write and PROT_WRITE was specified for a MAP_SHARED type mapping.
ENXIO	Addresses in the range [*off*, *off* + *len*) are invalid for *fd*.
EINVAL	The arguments *addr* (if MAP_FIXED was specified) or *off* are not multiples of the page size as returned by sysconf.
EINVAL	The field in *flags* is invalid (neither MAP_PRIVATE or MAP_SHARED).

EINVAL	The argument *len* has a value less than or equal to 0.
ENODEV	*fd* refers to an object for which mmap is meaningless, such as a terminal.
ENOMEM	MAP_FIXED was specified and the range [*addr*, *addr* + *len*) exceeds that allowed for the address space of a process, or MAP_FIXED was not specified and there is insufficient room in the address space to effect the mapping.

NOTES

mmap allows access to resources via address space manipulations instead of the read/write interface. Once a file is mapped, all a process has to do to access it is use the data at the address to which the object was mapped. Consider the following pseudo-code:

```
fd = open(...)
lseek(fd, offset)
read(fd, buf, len)
/* use data in buf */
```

Here is a rewrite using mmap:

```
fd = open(...)
address = mmap((caddr_t) 0, len, (PROT_READ | PROT_WRITE),
          MAP_PRIVATE, fd, offset)
/* use data at address */
```

SEE ALSO

fcntl(2), fork(2), lockf(3C), mlockall(3C), mprotect(2), munmap(2), plock(2), sysconf(2)

mount(2)

NAME
mount – mount a file system

SYNOPSIS
```
#include <sys/types.h>
#include <sys/mount.h>
```
int mount (const char *spec, const char *dir, int mflag,
　　.../* char *fstyp, const char *dataptr, int datalen*/);

DESCRIPTION

mount requests that a removable file system contained on the block special file identified by *spec* be mounted on the directory identified by *dir*. *spec* and *dir* are pointers to path names. *fstyp* is the file system type number. The sysfs(2) system call can be used to determine the file system type number. If both the MS_DATA and MS_FSS flag bits of *mflag* are off, the file system type defaults to the root file system type. Only if either flag is on is *fstyp* used to indicate the file system type.

If the MS_DATA flag is set in *mflag* the system expects the *dataptr* and *datalen* arguments to be present. Together they describe a block of file-system specific data at address *dataptr* of length *datalen*. This is interpreted by file-system specific code within the operating system and its format depends on the file system type. If a particular file system type does not require this data, *dataptr* and *datalen* should both be zero. Note that MS_FSS is obsolete and is ignored if MS_DATA is also set, but if MS_FSS is set and MS_DATA is not, *dataptr* and *datalen* are both assumed to be zero.

After a successful call to mount, all references to the file *dir* refer to the root directory on the mounted file system.

The low-order bit of *mflag* is used to control write permission on the mounted file system: if 1, writing is forbidden; otherwise writing is permitted according to individual file accessibility.

mount may be invoked only by the super-user. It is intended for use only by the mount utility.

mount fails if one or more of the following are true:

EBUSY	*dir* is currently mounted on, is someone's current working directory, or is otherwise busy.
EBUSY	The device associated with *spec* is currently mounted.
EBUSY	There are no more mount table entries.
EFAULT	*spec*, *dir*, or *datalen* points outside the allocated address space of the process.
EINVAL	The super block has an invalid magic number or the *fstyp* is invalid.
ELOOP	Too many symbolic links were encountered in translating *spec* or *dir*.

ENAMETOOLONG	The length of the *path* argument exceeds {PATH_MAX}, or the length of a *path* component exceeds {NAME_MAX} while _POSIX_NO_TRUNC is in effect.
ENOENT	None of the named files exists or is a null pathname.
ENOTDIR	A component of a path prefix is not a directory.
EPERM	The effective user ID is not super-user.
EREMOTE	*spec* is remote and cannot be mounted.
ENOLINK	*path* points to a remote machine and the link to that machine is no longer active.
EMULTIHOP	Components of *path* require hopping to multiple remote machines and the file system type does not allow it.
ENOTBLK	*spec* is not a block special device.
ENXIO	The device associated with *spec* does not exist.
ENOTDIR	*dir* is not a directory.
EROFS	*spec* is write protected and *mflag* requests write permission.
ENOSPC	The file system state in the super-block is not FsOKAY and *mflag* requests write permission.

SEE ALSO

sysfs(2), umount(2)

mount(1M), fs(4) in the *System Administrator's Reference Manual*

DIAGNOSTICS

Upon successful completion a value of 0 is returned. Otherwise, a value of −1 is returned and errno is set to indicate the error.

NAME
mprotect – set protection of memory mapping

SYNOPSIS
    #include <sys/types.h>
    #include <sys/mman.h>

    int mprotect(caddr_t addr, size_t len, int prot);

DESCRIPTION
The function mprotect changes the access protections on the mappings specified by the range [addr, addr + len) to be that specified by prot. Legitimate values for prot are the same as those permitted for mmap and are defined in sys/mman.h as:

    PROT_READ   /* page can be read */
    PROT_WRITE   /* page can be written */
    PROT_EXEC   /* page can be executed */
    PROT_NONE   /* page can not be accessed */

RETURN VALUE
Upon successful completion, the function mprotect returns a value of 0; otherwise, it returns a value of –1 and sets errno to indicate an error.

ERRORS
Under the following conditions, the function mprotect fails and sets errno to:

EACCES if prot specifies a protection that violates the access permission the process has to the underlying memory object.

EAGAIN if prot specifies PROT_WRITE over a MAP_PRIVATE mapping and there are insufficient memory resources to reserve for locking the private page.

EINVAL if addr is not a multiple of the page size as returned by sysconf.

EINVAL The argument len has a value less than or equal to 0.

ENOMEM if addresses in the range [addr, addr + len) are invalid for the address space of a process, or specify one or more pages which are not mapped.

When mprotect fails for reasons other than EINVAL, the protections on some of the pages in the range [addr, addr + len) may have been changed. If the error occurs on some page at addr2, then the protections of all whole pages in the range [addr, addr2] will have been modified.

SEE ALSO
memcntl(2), mmap(2), plock(2), mlock(3C), mlockall(3C), sysconf(3C)

msgctl(2)

NAME
msgctl – message control operations

SYNOPSIS
```
#include <sys/types.h>
#include <sys/ipc.h>
#include <sys/msg.h>

int msgctl(int msqid, int cmd, .../* struct msqid_ds *buf */);
```

DESCRIPTION
msgctl provides a variety of message control operations as specified by *cmd*. The following *cmd*s are available:

IPC_STAT   Place the current value of each member of the data structure associated with *msqid* into the structure pointed to by *buf*. The contents of this structure are defined in intro(2).

IPC_SET   Set the value of the following members of the data structure associated with *msqid* to the corresponding value found in the structure pointed to by *buf*:
```
msg_perm.uid
msg_perm.gid
msg_perm.mode /* only access permission bits */
msg_qbytes
```
This *cmd* can only be executed by a process that has an effective user ID equal to either that of super user, or to the value of msg_perm.cuid or msg_perm.uid in the data structure associated with *msqid*. Only super user can raise the value of msg_qbytes.

IPC_RMID   Remove the message queue identifier specified by *msqid* from the system and destroy the message queue and data structure associated with it. This *cmd* can only be executed by a process that has an effective user ID equal to either that of super user, or to the value of msg_perm.cuid or msg_perm.uid in the data structure associated with *msqid*.

msgctl fails if one or more of the following are true:

EACCES   *cmd* is IPC_STAT and operation permission is denied to the calling process [see intro(2)].

EFAULT   *buf* points to an illegal address.

EINVAL   *msqid* is not a valid message queue identifier.

EINVAL   *cmd* is not a valid command.

EINVAL   *cmd* is IPC_SET and msg_perm.uid or msg_perm.gid is not valid.

EOVERFLOW   *cmd* is IPC_STAT and *uid* or *gid* is too large to be stored in the structure pointed to by *buf*.

msgctl(2)

  EPERM   *cmd* is IPC_RMID or IPC_SET. The effective user ID of the calling process is not that of super user, or the value of msg_perm.cuid or msg_perm.uid in the data structure associated with *msqid*.

  EPERM   *cmd* is IPC_SET, an attempt is being made to increase to the value of msg_qbytes, and the effective user ID of the calling process is not that of super user.

SEE ALSO
  intro(2), msgget(2), msgop(2)

DIAGNOSTICS
  Upon successful completion, a value of 0 is returned. Otherwise, a value of −1 is returned and errno is set to indicate the error.

msgget(2)

NAME
msgget – get message queue

SYNOPSIS
```
#include <sys/types.h>
#include <sys/ipc.h>
#include <sys/msg.h>

int msgget(key_t key, int msgflg);
```

DESCRIPTION
msgget returns the message queue identifier associated with *key*.

A message queue identifier and associated message queue and data structure [see intro(2)] are created for *key* if one of the following are true:

    key is IPC_PRIVATE.

    key does not already have a message queue identifier associated with it, and (*msgflg*&IPC_CREAT) is true.

On creation, the data structure associated with the new message queue identifier is initialized as follows:

    msg_perm.cuid, msg_perm.uid, msg_perm.cgid, and msg_perm.gid are set to the effective user ID and effective group ID, respectively, of the calling process.

    The low-order 9 bits of msg_perm.mode are set to the low-order 9 bits of *msgflg*.

    msg_qnum, msg_lspid, msg_lrpid, msg_stime, and msg_rtime are set to 0.

    msg_ctime is set to the current time.

    msg_qbytes is set to the system limit.

msgget fails if one or more of the following are true:

EACCES	A message queue identifier exists for *key*, but operation permission [see intro(2)] as specified by the low-order 9 bits of *msgflg* would not be granted.
ENOENT	A message queue identifier does not exist for *key* and (*msgflg*&IPC_CREAT) is false.
ENOSPC	A message queue identifier is to be created but the system-imposed limit on the maximum number of allowed message queue identifiers system wide would be exceeded.
EEXIST	A message queue identifier exists for *key* but (*msgflg*&IPC_CREAT) and (*msgflg*&IPC_EXCL) are both true.

SEE ALSO
intro(2), msgctl(2), msgop(2), stdipc(3C)

DIAGNOSTICS
Upon successful completion, a non-negative integer, namely a message queue identifier, is returned. Otherwise, a value of −1 is returned and errno is set to indicate the error.

msgop(2)

NAME
msgop: msgsnd, msgrcv − message operations

SYNOPSIS
    #include <sys/types.h>
    #include <sys/ipc.h>
    #include <sys/msg.h>

    int msgsnd(int msqid, const void *msgp,
        size_t msgsz, int msgflg);

    int msgrcv(int msqid, void *msgp,
        size_t msgsz, long msgtyp, int msgflg);

DESCRIPTION
msgsnd sends a message to the queue associated with the message queue identifier specified by *msqid*. *msgp* points to a user defined buffer that must contain first a field of type long integer that will specify the type of the message, and then a data portion that will hold the text of the message. The following is an example of members that might be in a user defined buffer.

    long mtype;   /* message type */
    char mtext[];   /* message text */

mtype is a positive integer that can be used by the receiving process for message selection. mtext is any text of length *msgsz* bytes. *msgsz* can range from 0 to a system imposed maximum.

msgflg specifies the action to be taken if one or more of the following are true:

> The number of bytes already on the queue is equal to msg_qbytes [see intro(2)].

> The total number of messages on all queues system-wide is equal to the system-imposed limit.

These actions are as follows:

> If (*msgflg*&IPC_NOWAIT) is true, the message is not sent and the calling process returns immediately.

> If (*msgflg*&IPC_NOWAIT) is false, the calling process suspends execution until one of the following occurs:

>> The condition responsible for the suspension no longer exists, in which case the message is sent.

>> *msqid* is removed from the system [see msgctl(2)]. When this occurs, errno is set to EIDRM, and a value of −1 is returned.

>> The calling process receives a signal that is to be caught. In this case the message is not sent and the calling process resumes execution in the manner prescribed in signal(2).

msgsnd fails and sends no message if one or more of the following are true:

EINVAL	*msqid* is not a valid message queue identifier.
EACCES	Operation permission is denied to the calling process [see intro(2)].
EINVAL	*mtype* is less than 1.
EAGAIN	The message cannot be sent for one of the reasons cited above and (*msgflg*&IPC_NOWAIT) is true.
EINVAL	*msgsz* is less than zero or greater than the system-imposed limit.
EFAULT	*msgp* points to an illegal address.

Upon successful completion, the following actions are taken with respect to the data structure associated with *msqid* [see intro(2)].

msg_qnum is incremented by 1.

msg_lspid is set to the process ID of the calling process.

msg_stime is set to the current time.

msgrcv reads a message from the queue associated with the message queue identifier specified by *msqid* and places it in the user defined structure pointed to by *msgp*. The structure must contain a message type field followed by the area for the message text (see the structure mymsg above). mtype is the received message's type as specified by the sending process. mtext is the text of the message. *msgsz* specifies the size in bytes of mtext. The received message is truncated to *msgsz* bytes if it is larger than *msgsz* and (*msgflg*&MSG_NOERROR) is true. The truncated part of the message is lost and no indication of the truncation is given to the calling process.

msgtyp specifies the type of message requested as follows:

If *msgtyp* is 0, the first message on the queue is received.

If *msgtyp* is greater than 0, the first message of type *msgtyp* is received.

If *msgtyp* is less than 0, the first message of the lowest type that is less than or equal to the absolute value of *msgtyp* is received.

msgflg specifies the action to be taken if a message of the desired type is not on the queue. These are as follows:

If (*msgflg*&IPC_NOWAIT) is true, the calling process returns immediately with a return value of −1 and sets errno to ENOMSG.

If (*msgflg*&IPC_NOWAIT) is false, the calling process suspends execution until one of the following occurs:

A message of the desired type is placed on the queue.

msqid is removed from the system. When this occurs, errno is set to EIDRM, and a value of −1 is returned.

The calling process receives a signal that is to be caught. In this case a message is not received and the calling process resumes execution in the manner prescribed in signal(2).

msgrcv fails and receives no message if one or more of the following are true:

EINVAL	*msqid* is not a valid message queue identifier.
EACCES	Operation permission is denied to the calling process.
EINVAL	*msgsz* is less than 0.
E2BIG	The length of *mtext* is greater than *msgsz* and (*msgflg*&MSG_NOERROR) is false.
ENOMSG	The queue does not contain a message of the desired type and (*msgtyp*&IPC_NOWAIT) is true.
EFAULT	*msgp* points to an illegal address.

Upon successful completion, the following actions are taken with respect to the data structure associated with *msqid* [see intro (2)].

msg_qnum is decremented by 1.

msg_lrpid is set to the process ID of the calling process.

msg_rtime is set to the current time.

SEE ALSO
intro(2), msgctl(2), msgget(2), signal(2)

DIAGNOSTICS
If msgsnd or msgrcv return due to the receipt of a signal, a value of −1 is returned to the calling process and errno is set to EINTR. If they return due to removal of *msqid* from the system, a value of −1 is returned and errno is set to EIDRM.

Upon successful completion, the return value is as follows:

msgsnd returns a value of 0.

msgrcv returns the number of bytes actually placed into *mtext*.

Otherwise, a value of −1 is returned and errno is set to indicate the error.

munmap(2)

NAME
munmap – unmap pages of memory

SYNOPSIS
    #include <sys/types.h>
    #include <sys/mman.h>

    int munmap(caddr_t addr, size_t len);

DESCRIPTION
The function munmap removes the mappings for pages in the range [*addr, addr + len*). Further references to these pages will result in the delivery of a SIGSEGV signal to the process.

The function mmap often performs an implicit munmap.

RETURN VALUE
Upon successful completion, the function munmap returns a value of 0; otherwise, it returns a value of –1 and sets errno to indicate an error.

ERRORS
Under the following conditions, the function munmap fails and sets errno to:

EINVAL if *addr* is not a multiple of the page size as returned by sysconf.

EINVAL if addresses in the range [*addr, addr + len*) are outside the valid range for the address space of a process.

EINVAL The argument *len* has a value less than or equal to 0.

SEE ALSO
mmap(2), sysconf(3C)

NAME
nap – suspend execution for a short interval

SYNOPSIS
cc [*flag* . . .] *file* . . . -lx
```
long nap (long period);
```

DESCRIPTION
The current process is suspended from execution for at least the number of milliseconds specified by *period*, or until a signal is received.

DIAGNOSTICS
On successful completion, a long integer indicating the number of milliseconds actually slept is returned. If the process received a signal while napping, the return value will be −1, and errno will be set to EINTR.

SEE ALSO
sleep(2)

NOTES
This function is driven by the system clock, which in most cases has a granularity of tens of milliseconds.

nice(2)

NAME
nice − change priority of a time-sharing process

SYNOPSIS
    #include <unistd.h>

    int nice(int incr);

DESCRIPTION
nice allows a process in the time-sharing scheduling class to change its priority. The `priocntl` system call is a more general interface to scheduler functions.

nice adds the value of *incr* to the nice value of the calling process. A process's nice value is a non-negative number for which a more positive value results in lower CPU priority.

A maximum nice value of 39 and a minimum nice value of 0 are imposed by the system. (The default nice value is 20.) Requests for values above or below these limits result in the nice value being set to the corresponding limit.

EPERM	nice fails and does not change the nice value if *incr* is negative or greater than 39 and the effective user ID of the calling process is not super-user.
EINVAL	nice fails if called by a process in a scheduling class other than time-sharing.

SEE ALSO
exec(2), priocntl(2)

nice(1) in the *User's Reference Manual*

DIAGNOSTICS
Upon successful completion, `nice` returns the new nice value minus 20. Otherwise, a value of −1 is returned and `errno` is set to indicate the error.

open(2)

NAME
open – open for reading or writing

SYNOPSIS
    #include <sys/types.h>
    #include <sys/stat.h>
    #include <fcntl.h>

    int open (const char *path, int oflag, ... /* mode_t mode */);

DESCRIPTION
path points to a path name naming a file. open opens a file descriptor for the named file and sets the file status flags according to the value of *oflag*. *oflag* values are constructed by OR-ing Flags from the following list (only one of the first three flags below may be used):

O_RDONLY   Open for reading only.

O_WRONLY   Open for writing only.

O_RDWR   Open for reading and writing.

O_NDELAY or O_NONBLOCK

     These flags may affect subsequent reads and writes [see read(2) and write(2)]. If both O_NDELAY and O_NONBLOCK are set, O_NONBLOCK will take precedence.

     When opening a FIFO with O_RDONLY or O_WRONLY set:

         If O_NDELAY or O_NONBLOCK is set: An open for reading-only will return without delay; an open for writing-only will return an error if no process currently has the file open for reading.

         If O_NDELAY and O_NONBLOCK are clear: An open for reading-only will block until a process opens the file for writing; an open for writing-only will block until a process opens the file for reading.

     When opening a block-special or character-special file:

         If O_NDELAY or O_NONBLOCK is set: The open will return without waiting for the device to be ready or available; subsequent behavior of the device is device specific.

         If O_NDELAY and O_NONBLOCK are clear: The open will block until the device is ready or available.

O_APPEND   If set, the file pointer will be set to the end of the file prior to each write.

O_SYNC   When opening a regular file, this flag affects subsequent writes. If set, each write(2) will wait for both the file data and file status to be physically updated.

O_NOCTTY   If set and the file is a terminal, the terminal will not be allocated as the calling process's controlling terminal.

O_CREAT   If the file exists, this flag has no effect, except as noted under O_EXCL below. Otherwise, the file is created and the owner ID of the file is set to the effective user ID of the process, the group ID of the file is set to the effective group ID of the process, or if the S_ISGID bit is set in the directory in which the file is being created, the file's group ID is set to the group ID of its parent directory. If the group ID of the new file does not match the effective group ID or one of the supplementary groups IDs, the S_ISGID bit is cleared. The access permission bits of the file mode are set to the value of *mode*, modified as follows [see creat(2)]:

> All bits set in the file mode creation mask of the process are cleared [see umask(2)].
>
> The "save text image after execution bit" of the mode is cleared [see chmod(2)].

O_TRUNC   If the file exists, its length is truncated to 0 and the mode and owner are unchanged. O_TRUNC has no effect on FIFO special files or directories.

O_EXCL   If O_EXCL and O_CREAT are set, open will fail if the file exists. The check for the existence of the file and the creation of the file if it does not exist is atomic with respect to other processes executing open naming the same filename in the same directory with O_EXCL and O_CREAT set.

When opening a STREAMS file, *oflag* may be constructed from O_NDELAY or O_NONBLOCK OR-ed with either O_RDONLY, O_WRONLY , or O_RDWR. Other flag values are not applicable to STREAMS devices and have no effect on them. The values of O_NDELAY and O_NONBLOCK affect the operation of STREAMS drivers and certain system calls [see read(2), getmsg(2), putmsg(2), and write(2)]. For drivers, the implementation of O_NDELAY and O_NONBLOCK is device specific. Each STREAMS device driver may treat these options differently.

When open is invoked to open a named stream, and the connld module [see connld(7)] has been pushed on the pipe, open blocks until the server process has issued an I_RECVFD ioctl [see streamio(7)] to receive the file descriptor.

If *path* is a symbolic link and O_CREAT and O_EXCL are set, the link is not followed.

The file pointer used to mark the current position within the file is set to the beginning of the file.

The new file descriptor is the lowest numbered file descriptor available and is set to remain open across exec system calls [see fcntl(2)].

Certain flag values can be set following open as described in fcntl(2).

If O_CREAT is set and the file did not previously exist, upon successful completion open marks for update the st_atime, st_ctime and st_mtime fields of the file and the st_ctime and st_mtime fields of the parent directory.

open(2)

If O_TRUNC is set and the file did previously exist, upon successful completion open marks for update the st_ctime and st_mtime fields of the file.

The named file is opened unless one or more of the following are true:

EACCES	The file does not exist and write permission is denied by the parent directory of the file to be created.
EACCES	O_TRUNC is specified and write permission is denied
EACCES	A component of the path prefix denies search permission.
EACCES	*oflag* permission is denied for an existing file.
EAGAIN	The file exists, mandatory file/record locking is set, and there are outstanding record locks on the file [see chmod(2)].
EAGAIN	O_NDELAY or O_NONBLOCK is set, the named file is a STREAMS device and there is another process trying to open it at the same time.
EEXIST	O_CREAT and O_EXCL are set, and the named file exists.
EFAULT	*path* points outside the allocated address space of the process.
EINTR	A signal was caught during the open system call.
EIO	A hangup or error occurred during the open of the STREAMS-based device.
EISDIR	The named file is a directory and *oflag* is write or read/write.
ELOOP	Too many symbolic links were encountered in translating *path*.
EMFILE	The process has too many open files [see getrlimit(2)].
EMULTIHOP	Components of *path* require hopping to multiple remote machines and the file system does not allow it.
ENAMETOOLONG	The length of the *path* argument exceeds {PATH_MAX}, or the length of a *path* component exceeds {NAME_MAX} while {_POSIX_NO_TRUNC} is in effect.
ENFILE	The system file table is full.
ENOENT	O_CREAT is not set and the named file does not exist.
ENOENT	O_CREAT is set and a component of the path prefix does not exist or is the null pathname.
ENOLINK	*path* points to a remote machine, and the link to that machine is no longer active.
ENOMEM	The system is unable to allocate a send descriptor.
ENOSPC	O_CREAT and O_EXCL are set, and the file system is out of inodes.

ENOSPC	O_CREAT is set and the directory that would contain the file cannot be extended.
ENOSR	Unable to allocate a stream.
ENOTDIR	A component of the path prefix is not a directory.
ENXIO	The named file is a character special or block special file, and the device associated with this special file does not exist.
ENXIO	O_NDELAY or O_NONBLOCK is set, the named file is a FIFO, O_WRONLY is set, and no process has the file open for reading.
ENXIO	A STREAMS module or driver open routine failed.
EROFS	The named file resides on a read-only file system and either O_WRONLY, O_RDWR, O_CREAT, or O_TRUNC is set in *oflag* (if the file does not exist).
ETXTBSY	The file is a pure procedure (shared text) file that is being executed and *oflag* is write or read/write.

SEE ALSO
intro(2), chmod(2), close(2), creat(2), dup(2), exec(2), fcntl(2), getrlimit(2), lseek(2), read(2), getmsg(2), putmsg(2), stat(2), umask(2), write(2), stat(5).

DIAGNOSTICS
Upon successful completion, the file descriptor is returned. Otherwise, a value of −1 is returned and errno is set to indicate the error.

NAME

opensem – open a semaphore

SYNOPSIS

cc [*flag* . . .] *file* . . . −lx

int opensem(char *sem_name);

DESCRIPTION

opensem opens a semaphore named by *sem_name* and returns the unique semaphore identification number *sem_num* used by waitsem and sigsem. creatsem should always be called to initialize the semaphore before the first attempt to open it.

DIAGNOSTICS

opensem returns a value of −1 if an error occurs. If the semaphore named does not exist, errno is set to ENOENT. If the file specified is not a semaphore file (that is, a file previously created by a process using a call to creatsem), errno is set to ENOTNAM. If the semaphore has become invalid due to inappropriate use, errno is set to ENAVAIL.

SEE ALSO

creatsem(2), sigsem(2), waitsem(2)

NOTES

It is not advisable to open the same semaphore more than once. Although it is possible to do this, it may result in a deadlock.

NAME
p_online − turn a processor online or offline

SYNOPSIS
    #include <sys/types.h>
    #include <sys/processor.h>

    p_online (processorid_t processorid, int flag);

DESCRIPTION
p_online brings a processor online or takes it offline. When a processor is online, it is performing normal operations, scheduling and executing processes, and servicing any I/O devices to which it has access.

If flag is P_ONLINE, the named processor is brought online. If the processor was already online, nothing is done. The previous state of the processor (P_ONLINE or P_OFFLINE) is returned.

If flag is P_OFFLINE, the named processor is shut down and taken offline. If the processor was already offline, nothing is done. The previous state of the processor is returned. An attempt to take a processor offline may fail for several reasons:

> One or more processes are bound to the processor.
>
> The processor is the only online processor.
>
> The processor performs some essential system function which cannot be taken over by another processor.

The calling process must have superuser privileges to bring a processor online or take it offline.

DIAGNOSTICS
p_online returns P_ONLINE or P_OFFLINE on success, or −1 on failure. Failure may result from:

- EPERM — The calling process does not have appropriate privileges.
- EINVAL — The processorid does not refer to an existing processor, or the processor for P_OFFLINE cannot be taken offline, or the flag has an invalid value.
- EBUSY — The processorid for P_OFFLINE refers to a processor with processes bound to it.
- EIO — The processor to which processorid refers is non-operational.

SEE ALSO
offline(1M), online(1M)

NAME

pause – suspend process until signal

SYNOPSIS

```
#include <unistd.h>

int pause(void);
```

DESCRIPTION

pause suspends the calling process until it receives a signal. The signal must be one that is not currently set to be ignored by the calling process.

If the signal causes termination of the calling process, pause does not return.

If the signal is caught by the calling process and control is returned from the signal-catching function [see signal(2)], the calling process resumes execution from the point of suspension; with a return value of −1 from pause and errno set to EINTR.

SEE ALSO

alarm(2), kill(2), signal(2), sigpause(2), wait(2)

NAME
pipe – create an interprocess channel

SYNOPSIS
`#include <unistd.h>`

`int pipe(int fildes[2]);`

DESCRIPTION
pipe creates an I/O mechanism called a pipe and returns two file descriptors, *fildes*[0] and *fildes*[1]. The files associated with *fildes*[0] and *fildes*[1] are streams and are both opened for reading and writing. The O_NDELAY and O_NONBLOCK flags are cleared.

A read from *fildes*[0] accesses the data written to *fildes*[1] on a first-in-first-out (FIFO) basis and a read from *fildes*[1] accesses the data written to *fildes*[0] also on a FIFO basis.

The FD_CLOEXEC flag will be clear on both file descriptors.

Upon successful completion pipe marks for update the st_atime, st_ctime, and st_mtime fields of the pipe.

pipe fails if:

EMFILE   If {OPEN_MAX}−1 or more file descriptors are currently open for this process.

ENFILE   A file table entry could not be allocated.

SEE ALSO
fcntl(2), getmsg(2), poll(2), putmsg(2), read(2), write(2), streamio(7).

sh(1) in the *User's Reference Manual*.

DIAGNOSTICS
Upon successful completion, a value of 0 is returned. Otherwise, a value of −1 is returned and errno is set to indicate the error.

NOTES
Since a pipe is bi-directional, there are two separate flows of data. Therefore, the size (st_size) returned by a call to fstat(2) with argument *fildes*[0] or *fildes*[1] is the number of bytes available for reading from *fildes*[0] or *fildes*[1] respectively. Previously, the size (st_size) returned by a call to fstat() with argument *fildes*[1] (the write-end) was the number of bytes available for reading from *fildes*[0] (the read-end).

plock(2)

NAME
plock – lock into memory or unlock process, text, or data

SYNOPSIS
```
#include <sys/lock.h>
```
```
int plock(int op);
```

DESCRIPTION
plock allows the calling process to lock into memory or unlock its text segment (text lock), its data segment (data lock), or both its text and data segments (process lock). Locked segments are immune to all routine swapping. The effective user ID of the calling process must be super-user to use this call. plock performs the function specified by *op*:

PROCLOCK	Lock text and data segments into memory (process lock).
TXTLOCK	Lock text segment into memory (text lock).
DATLOCK	Lock data segment into memory (data lock).
UNLOCK	Remove locks.

plock fails and does not perform the requested operation if one or more of the following are true:

EPERM	The effective user ID of the calling process is not super-user.
EINVAL	*op* is equal to PROCLOCK and a process lock, a text lock, or a data lock already exists on the calling process.
EINVAL	*op* is equal to TXTLOCK and a text lock, or a process lock already exists on the calling process.
EINVAL	*op* is equal to DATLOCK and a data lock, or a process lock already exists on the calling process.
EINVAL	*op* is equal to UNLOCK and no lock exists on the calling process.
EAGAIN	Not enough memory.

SEE ALSO
exec(2), exit(2), fork(2), memcntl(2)

DIAGNOSTICS
Upon successful completion, a value of 0 is returned to the calling process. Otherwise, a value of −1 is returned and errno is set to indicate the error.

NOTES
memcntl is the preferred interface to process locking.

poll(2)

NAME
poll – input/output multiplexing

SYNOPSIS
    #include <stropts.h>
    #include <poll.h>

    int poll(struct poll *fds, size_t nfds, int timeout);

DESCRIPTION
poll provides users with a mechanism for multiplexing input/output over a set of file descriptors that reference open files. poll identifies those files on which a user can send or receive messages, or on which certain events have occurred.

fds specifies the file descriptors to be examined and the events of interest for each file descriptor. It is a pointer to an array with one element for each open file descriptor of interest. The array's elements are pollfd structures, which contain the following members:

    int fd;   /* file descriptor */
    short events;   /* requested events */
    short revents;   /* returned events */

fd specifies an open file descriptor and events and revents are bitmasks constructed by an OR of any combination of the following event flags:

- POLLIN   Data other than high priority data may be read without blocking. For STREAMS, this flag is set even if the message is of zero length.

- POLLRDNORM   Normal data (priority band = 0) may be read without blocking. For STREAMS, this flag is set even if the message is of zero length.

- POLLRDBAND   Data from a non-zero priority band may be read without blocking For STREAMS, this flag is set even if the message is of zero length.

- POLLPRI   High priority data may be received without blocking. For STREAMS, this flag is set even if the message is of zero length.

- POLLOUT   Normal data may be written without blocking.

- POLLWRNORM   The same as POLLOUT.

- POLLWRBAND   Priority data (priority band > 0) may be written. This event only examines bands that have been written to at least once.

- POLLERR   An error has occurred on the device or stream. This flag is only valid in the revents bitmask; it is not used in the events field.

- POLLHUP   A hangup has occurred on the stream. This event and POLLOUT are mutually exclusive; a stream can never be writable if a hangup has occurred. However, this event and POLLIN, POLLRDNORM, POLLRDBAND, or POLLPRI are not mutually exclusive. This flag is only valid in the revents bitmask; it is not used in the events field.

POLLNVAL   The specified fd value does not belong to an open file. This flag is only valid in the revents field; it is not used in the events field.

For each element of the array pointed to by *fds*, poll examines the given file descriptor for the event(s) specified in events. The number of file descriptors to be examined is specified by *nfds*.

If the value fd is less than zero, events is ignored and revents is set to 0 in that entry on return from poll.

The results of the poll query are stored in the revents field in the pollfd structure. Bits are set in the revents bitmask to indicate which of the requested events are true. If none are true, none of the specified bits are set in revents when the poll call returns. The event flags POLLHUP, POLLERR, and POLLNVAL are always set in revents if the conditions they indicate are true; this occurs even though these flags were not present in events.

If none of the defined events have occurred on any selected file descriptor, poll waits at least *timeout* milliseconds for an event to occur on any of the selected file descriptors. On a computer where millisecond timing accuracy is not available, *timeout* is rounded up to the nearest legal value available on that system. If the value *timeout* is 0, poll returns immediately. If the value of *timeout* is INFTIM (or −1), poll blocks until a requested event occurs or until the call is interrupted. poll is not affected by the O_NDELAY and O_NONBLOCK flags.

poll fails if one or more of the following are true:

EAGAIN   Allocation of internal data structures failed, but the request may be attempted again.
EFAULT   Some argument points outside the allocated address space.
EINTR   A signal was caught during the poll system call.
EINVAL   The argument *nfds* is greater than {OPEN_MAX}.

SEE ALSO
intro(2), getmsg(2), getrlimit(2), putmsg(2), read(2), write(2)

Programmer's Guide: STREAMS

DIAGNOSTICS
Upon successful completion, a non-negative value is returned. A positive value indicates the total number of file descriptors that has been selected (that is, file descriptors for which the revents field is non-zero). A value of 0 indicates that the call timed out and no file descriptors have been selected. Upon failure, a value of −1 is returned and errno is set to indicate the error.

priocntl(2)

NAME
priocntl – process scheduler control

SYNOPSIS
```
#include <sys/types.h>
#include <sys/priocntl.h>
#include <sys/rtpriocntl.h>
#include <sys/tspriocntl.h>

long priocntl(idtype_t idtype, id_t id, int cmd, ... /* arg */);
```

DESCRIPTION
priocntl provides for control over the scheduling of active processes.

Processes fall into distinct classes with a separate scheduling policy applied to each class. The two classes currently supported are the real-time class and the time-sharing class. The characteristics of these classes are described under the corresponding headings below. The class attribute of a process is inherited across the fork and exec(2) system calls. priocntl can be used to dynamically change the class and other scheduling parameters associated with a running process or set of processes given the appropriate permissions as explained below.

In the default configuration, a runnable real-time process runs before any other process. Therefore, inappropriate use of real-time processes can have a dramatic negative impact on system performance.

priocntl provides an interface for specifying a process or set of processes to which the system call is to apply. The priocntlset system call provides the same functions as priocntl, but allows a more general interface for specifying the set of processes to which the system call is to apply.

For priocntl, the *idtype* and *id* arguments are used together to specify the set of processes. The interpretation of *id* depends on the value of *idtype*. The possible values for *idtype* and corresponding interpretations of *id* are as follows:

P_PID   *id* is a process ID specifying a single process to which the priocntl system call is to apply.

P_PPID *id* is a parent process ID. The priocntl system call applies to all processes with the specified parent process ID.

P_PGID *id* is a process group ID. The priocntl system call applies to all processes in the specified process group.

P_SID   *id* is a session ID. The priocntl system call applies to all processes in the specified session.

P_CID   *id* is a class ID (returned by priocntl PC_GETCID as explained below). The priocntl system call applies to all processes in the specified class.

P_UID   *id* is a user ID. The priocntl system call applies to all processes with this effective user ID.

P_GID   *id* is a group ID. The priocntl system call applies to all processes with this effective group ID.

P_ALL   The priocntl system call applies to all existing processes. The value of *id* is ignored. The permission restrictions described below still apply.

An *id* value of P_MYID can be used in conjunction with the *idtype* value to specify the calling process's process ID, parent process ID, process group ID, session ID, class ID, user ID, or group ID.

In order to change the scheduling parameters of a process (using the PC_SETPARMS command as explained below) the real or effective user ID of the process calling priocntl must match the real or effective user ID of the receiving process or the effective user ID of the calling process must be super-user. These are the minimum permission requirements enforced for all classes. An individual class may impose additional permissions requirements when setting processes to that class and/or when setting class-specific scheduling parameters.

A special sys scheduling class exists for the purpose of scheduling the execution of certain special system processes (such as the swapper process). It is not possible to change the class of any process to sys. In addition, any processes in the sys class that are included in a specified set of processes are disregarded by priocntl. For example, an *idtype* of P_UID and an *id* value of zero would specify all processes with a user ID of zero except processes in the sys class and (if changing the parameters using PC_SETPARMS) the init process.

The init process is a special case. In order for a priocntl call to change the class or other scheduling parameters of the init process (process ID 1), it must be the only process specified by *idtype* and *id*. The init process may be assigned to any class configured on the system, but the time-sharing class is almost always the appropriate choice. (Other choices may be highly undesirable; see the *System Administrator's Guide* for more information.)

The data type and value of *arg* are specific to the type of command specified by *cmd*.

The following structure is used by the PC_GETCID and PC_GETCLINFO commands.

```
typedef struct {
    id_t    pc_cid;                      /* Class id */
    char    pc_clname[PC_CLNMSZ];        /* Class name */
    long    pc_clinfo[PC_CLINFOSZ];      /* Class information */
} pcinfo_t;
```

pc_cid is a class ID returned by priocntl PC_GETCID. pc_clname is a buffer of size PC_CLNMSZ (defined in sys/priocntl.h) used to hold the class name (RT for real-time or TS for time-sharing).

pc_clinfo is a buffer of size PC_CLINFOSZ (defined in sys/priocntl.h) used to return data describing the attributes of a specific class. The format of this data is class-specific and is described under the appropriate heading (REAL-TIME CLASS or TIME-SHARING CLASS) below.

The following structure is used by the PC_SETPARMS and PC_GETPARMS commands.

```
typedef struct {
    id_t    pc_cid;                     /* Process class */
    long    pc_clparms[PC_CLPARMSZ];    /* Class-specific params */
} pcparms_t;
```

pc_cid is a class ID (returned by priocntl PC_GETCID). The special class ID PC_CLNULL can also be assigned to pc_cid when using the PC_GETPARMS command as explained below.

The pc_clparms buffer holds class-specific scheduling parameters. The format of this parameter data for a particular class is described under the appropriate heading below. PC_CLPARMSZ is the length of the pc_clparms buffer and is defined in sys/priocntl.h.

Commands

Available priocntl commands are:

PC_GETCID

Get class ID and class attributes for a specific class given class name. The *idtype* and *id* arguments are ignored. If *arg* is non-null, it points to a structure of type pcinfo_t. The pc_clname buffer contains the name of the class whose attributes you are getting.

On success, the class ID is returned in pc_cid, the class attributes are returned in the pc_clinfo buffer, and the priocntl call returns the total number of classes configured in the system (including the sys class). If the class specified by pc_clname is invalid or is not currently configured the priocntl call returns −1 with errno set to EINVAL. The format of the attribute data returned for a given class is defined in the sys/rtpriocntl.h or sys/tspriocntl.h header file and described under the appropriate heading below.

If *arg* is a NULL pointer, no attribute data is returned but the priocntl call still returns the number of configured classes.

PC_GETCLINFO

Get class name and class attributes for a specific class given class ID. The *idtype* and *id* arguments are ignored. If *arg* is non-null, it points to a structure of type pcinfo_t. pc_cid is the class ID of the class whose attributes you are getting.

On success, the class name is returned in the pc_clname buffer, the class attributes are returned in the pc_clinfo buffer, and the priocntl call returns the total number of classes configured in the system (including the sys class). The format of the attribute data returned for a given class is defined in the sys/rtpriocntl.h or sys/tspriocntl.h header file and described under the appropriate heading below.

If *arg* is a NULL pointer, no attribute data is returned but the `priocntl` call still returns the number of configured classes.

PC_SETPARMS
Set the class and class-specific scheduling parameters of the specified process(es). *arg* points to a structure of type `pcparms_t`. `pc_cid` specifies the class you are setting and the `pc_clparms` buffer contains the class-specific parameters you are setting. The format of the class-specific parameter data is defined in the `sys/rtpriocntl.h` or `sys/tspriocntl.h` header file and described under the appropriate class heading below.

When setting parameters for a set of processes, `priocntl` acts on the processes in the set in an implementation-specific order. If `priocntl` encounters an error for one or more of the target processes, it may or may not continue through the set of processes, depending on the nature of the error. If the error is related to permissions (EPERM), `priocntl` continues through the process set, resetting the parameters for all target processes for which the calling process has appropriate permissions. `priocntl` then returns −1 with `errno` set to EPERM to indicate that the operation failed for one or more of the target processes. If `priocntl` encounters an error other than permissions, it does not continue through the set of target processes but returns the error immediately.

PC_GETPARMS
Get the class and/or class-specific scheduling parameters of a process. *arg* points to a structure of type `pcparms_t`.

If `pc_cid` specifies a configured class and a single process belonging to that class is specified by the *idtype* and *id* values or the `procset` structure, then the scheduling parameters of that process are returned in the `pc_clparms` buffer. If the process specified does not exist or does not belong to the specified class, the `priocntl` call returns −1 with `errno` set to ESRCH.

If `pc_cid` specifies a configured class and a set of processes is specified, the scheduling parameters of one of the specified processes belonging to the specified class are returned in the `pc_clparms` buffer and the `priocntl` call returns the process ID of the selected process. The criteria for selecting a process to return in this case is class dependent. If none of the specified processes exist or none of them belong to the specified class the `priocntl` call returns −1 with `errno` set to ESRCH.

If `pc_cid` is PC_CLNULL and a single process is specified the class of the specified process is returned in `pc_cid` and its scheduling parameters are returned in the `pc_clparms` buffer.

PC_ADMIN
This command provides functionality needed for the implementation of the dispadmin(1M) command. It is not intended for general use by other applications.

REAL-TIME CLASS

The real-time class provides a fixed priority preemptive scheduling policy for those processes requiring fast and deterministic response and absolute user/application control of scheduling priorities. If the real-time class is configured in the system it should have exclusive control of the highest range of scheduling priorities on the system. This ensures that a runnable real-time process is given CPU service before any process belonging to any other class.

The real-time class has a range of real-time priority (rt_pri) values that may be assigned to processes within the class. Real-time priorities range from 0 to x, where the value of x is configurable and can be determined for a specific installation by using the priocntl PC_GETCID or PC_GETCLINFO command.

The real-time scheduling policy is a fixed priority policy. The scheduling priority of a real-time process is never changed except as the result of an explicit request by the user/application to change the rt_pri value of the process.

For processes in the real-time class, the rt_pri value is, for all practical purposes, equivalent to the scheduling priority of the process. The rt_pri value completely determines the scheduling priority of a real-time process relative to other processes within its class. Numerically higher rt_pri values represent higher priorities. Since the real-time class controls the highest range of scheduling priorities in the system it is guaranteed that the runnable real-time process with the highest rt_pri value is always selected to run before any other process in the system.

In addition to providing control over priority, priocntl provides for control over the length of the time quantum allotted to processes in the real-time class. The time quantum value specifies the maximum amount of time a process may run assuming that it does not complete or enter a resource or event wait state (sleep). Note that if another process becomes runnable at a higher priority the currently running process may be preempted before receiving its full time quantum.

The system's process scheduler keeps the runnable real-time processes on a set of scheduling queues. There is a separate queue for each configured real-time priority and all real-time processes with a given rt_pri value are kept together on the appropriate queue. The processes on a given queue are ordered in FIFO order (that is, the process at the front of the queue has been waiting longest for service and receives the CPU first). Real-time processes that wake up after sleeping, processes which change to the real-time class from some other class, processes which have used their full time quantum, and runnable processes whose priority is reset by priocntl are all placed at the back of the appropriate queue for their priority. A process that is preempted by a higher priority process remains at the front of the queue (with whatever time is remaining in its time quantum) and runs before any other process at this priority. Following a fork(2) system call by a real-time process, the parent process continues to run while the child process (which inherits its parent's rt_pri value) is placed at the back of the queue.

The following structure (defined in sys/rtpriocntl.h) defines the format used for the attribute data for the real-time class.

```
typedef struct {
    short    rt_maxpri;    /* Maximum real-time priority */
} rtinfo_t;
```

The priocntl PC_GETCID and PC_GETCLINFO commands return real-time class attributes in the pc_clinfo buffer in this format.

rt_maxpri specifies the configured maximum rt_pri value for the real-time class (if rt_maxpri is x, the valid real-time priorities range from 0 to x).

The following structure (defined in sys/rtpriocntl.h) defines the format used to specify the real-time class-specific scheduling parameters of a process.

```
typedef struct {
    short    rt_pri;       /* Real-Time priority */
    ulong    rt_tqsecs;    /* Seconds in time quantum */
    long     rt_tqnsecs;   /* Additional nanoseconds in quantum */
} rtparms_t;
```

When using the priocntl PC_SETPARMS or PC_GETPARMS commands, if pc_cid specifies the real-time class, the data in the pc_clparms buffer is in this format.

The above commands can be used to set the real-time priority to the specified value or get the current rt_pri value. Setting the rt_pri value of a process that is currently running or runnable (not sleeping) causes the process to be placed at the back of the scheduling queue for the specified priority. The process is placed at the back of the appropriate queue regardless of whether the priority being set is different from the previous rt_pri value of the process. Note that a running process can voluntarily release the CPU and go to the back of the scheduling queue at the same priority by resetting its rt_pri value to its current real-time priority value. In order to change the time quantum of a process without setting the priority or affecting the process's position on the queue, the rt_pri field should be set to the special value RT_NOCHANGE (defined in sys/rtpriocntl.h). Specifying RT_NOCHANGE when changing the class of a process to real-time from some other class results in the real-time priority being set to zero.

For the priocntl PC_GETPARMS command, if pc_cid specifies the real-time class and more than one real-time process is specified, the scheduling parameters of the real-time process with the highest rt_pri value among the specified processes are returned and the process ID of this process is returned by the priocntl call. If there is more than one process sharing the highest priority, the one returned is implementation-dependent.

The rt_tqsecs and rt_tqnsecs fields are used for getting or setting the time quantum associated with a process or group of processes. rt_tqsecs is the number of seconds in the time quantum and rt_tqnsecs is the number of additional nanoseconds in the quantum. For example setting rt_tqsecs to 2 and rt_tqnsecs to 500,000,000 (decimal) would result in a time quantum of two and one-half seconds. Specifying a value of 1,000,000,000 or greater in the rt_tqnsecs field results in an error return with errno set to EINVAL. Although the resolution of the tq_nsecs field is very fine, the specified time quantum length is rounded up by the system to the next integral multiple of the system clock's resolution. For example, the finest resolution currently available on a system is 10 milliseconds (1 "tick"). Setting rt_tqsecs to 0 and rt_tqnsecs to 34,000,000 would specify a time quantum of 34 milliseconds, which would be rounded up to 4 ticks (40 milliseconds) on that system. The maximum time quantum that can be specified is implementation-specific and equal to LONG_MAX ticks (defined in limits.h). Requesting a quantum greater than this maximum results in an error return with errno set to ERANGE (although infinite quantums may be requested using a special value as explained below). Requesting a time quantum of zero (setting both rt_tqsecs and rt_tqnsecs to 0) results in an error return with errno set to EINVAL.

The rt_tqnsecs field can also be set to one of the following special values (defined in sys/rtpriocntl.h), in which case the value of rt_tqsecs is ignored.

RT_TQINF	Set an infinite time quantum.
RT_TQDEF	Set the time quantum to the default for this priority [see rt_dptbl(4)].
RT_NOCHANGE	Don't set the time quantum. This value is useful when you wish to change the real-time priority of a process without affecting the time quantum. Specifying this value when changing the class of a process to real-time from some other class is equivalent to specifying RT_TQDEF.

In order to change the class of a process to real-time (from any other class) the process invoking priocntl must have super-user privileges. In order to change the priority or time quantum setting of a real-time process the process invoking priocntl must have super-user privileges or must itself be a real-time process whose real or effective user ID matches the real of effective user ID of the target process.

The real-time priority and time quantum are inherited across the fork(2) and exec(2) system calls.

TIME-SHARING CLASS

The time-sharing scheduling policy provides for a fair and effective allocation of the CPU resource among processes with varying CPU consumption characteristics. The objectives of the time-sharing policy are to provide good response time to interactive processes and good throughput to CPU-bound jobs while providing a degree of user/application control over scheduling.

The time-sharing class has a range of time-sharing user priority (see ts_upri below) values that may be assigned to processes within the class. A ts_upri value of zero is defined as the default base priority for the time-sharing class. User priorities range from $-x$ to $+x$ where the value of x is configurable and can be determined for a specific installation by using the priocntl PC_GETCID or PC_GETCLINFO command.

The purpose of the user priority is to provide some degree of user/application control over the scheduling of processes in the time-sharing class. Raising or lowering the ts_upri value of a process in the time-sharing class raises or lowers the scheduling priority of the process. It is not guaranteed, however, that a process with a higher ts_upri value will run before one with a lower ts_upri value. This is because the ts_upri value is just one factor used to determine the scheduling priority of a time-sharing process. The system may dynamically adjust the internal scheduling priority of a time-sharing process based on other factors such as recent CPU usage.

In addition to the system-wide limits on user priority (returned by the PC_GETCID and PC_GETCLINFO commands) there is a per process user priority limit (see ts_uprilim below), which specifies the maximum ts_upri value that may be set for a given process; by default, ts_uprilim is zero.

The following structure (defined in sys/tspriocntl.h) defines the format used for the attribute data for the time-sharing class.

typedef struct {
    short   ts_maxupri;   /* Limits of user priority range */
} tsinfo_t;

The priocntl PC_GETCID and PC_GETCLINFO commands return time-sharing class attributes in the pc_clinfo buffer in this format.

ts_maxupri specifies the configured maximum user priority value for the time-sharing class. If ts_maxupri is x, the valid range for both user priorities and user priority limits is from $-x$ to $+x$.

The following structure (defined in sys/tspriocntl.h) defines the format used to specify the time-sharing class-specific scheduling parameters of a process.

typedef struct {
    short   ts_uprilim;   /* Time-Sharing user priority limit */
    short   ts_upri;   /* Time-Sharing user priority */
} tsparms_t;

When using the priocntl PC_SETPARMS or PC_GETPARMS commands, if pc_cid specifies the time-sharing class, the data in the pc_clparms buffer is in this format.

For the priocntl PC_GETPARMS command, if pc_cid specifies the time-sharing class and more than one time-sharing process is specified, the scheduling parameters of the time-sharing process with the highest ts_upri value among the specified processes is returned and the process ID of this process is returned by the priocntl call. If there is more than one process sharing the highest user priority, the one returned is implementation-dependent.

Any time-sharing process may lower its own ts_uprilim (or that of another process with the same user ID). Only a time-sharing process with super-user privileges may raise a ts_uprilim. When changing the class of a process to time-sharing from some other class, super-user privileges are required in order to set the initial ts_uprilim to a value greater than zero. Attempts by a non-super-user process to raise a ts_uprilim or set an initial ts_uprilim greater than zero fail with a return value of -1 and errno set to EPERM.

priocntl(2)

Any time-sharing process may set its own ts_upri (or that of another process with the same user ID) to any value less than or equal to the process's ts_uprilim. Attempts to set the ts_upri above the ts_uprilim (and/or set the ts_uprilim below the ts_upri) result in the ts_upri being set equal to the ts_uprilim.

Either of the ts_uprilim or ts_upri fields may be set to the special value TS_NOCHANGE (defined in sys/tspriocntl.h) in order to set one of the values without affecting the other. Specifying TS_NOCHANGE for the ts_upri when the ts_uprilim is being set to a value below the current ts_upri causes the ts_upri to be set equal to the ts_uprilim being set. Specifying TS_NOCHANGE for a parameter when changing the class of a process to time-sharing (from some other class) causes the parameter to be set to a default value. The default value for the ts_uprilim is 0 and the default for the ts_upri is to set it equal to the ts_uprilim which is being set.

The time-sharing user priority and user priority limit are inherited across the fork and exec system calls.

RETURN VALUE

Unless otherwise noted above, priocntl returns a value of 0 on success. priocntl returns −1 on failure and sets errno to indicate the error.

ERRORS

priocntl fails if one or more of the following are true :

EPERM	The calling process does not have the required permissions as explained above.
EINVAL	The argument *cmd* was invalid, an invalid or unconfigured class was specified, or one of the parameters specified was invalid.
ERANGE	The requested time quantum is out of range.
ESRCH	None of the specified processes exist.
EFAULT	All or part of the area pointed to by one of the data pointers is outside the process's address space.
ENOMEM	An attempt to change the class of a process failed because of insufficient memory.
EAGAIN	An attempt to change the class of a process failed because of insufficient resources other than memory (for example, class-specific kernel data structures).

SEE ALSO

dispadmin(1M), exec(2), fork(2), nice(2), priocntl(1), priocntlset(2), rt_dptbl(4), ts_dptbl(4)

priocntlset(2)

NAME
priocntlset – generalized process scheduler control

SYNOPSIS
```
#include <sys/types.h>
#include <sys/procset.h>
#include <sys/priocntl.h>
#include <sys/rtpriocntl.h>
#include <sys/tspriocntl.h>

long priocntlset(procset_t *psp, int cmd, ... /* arg */);
```

DESCRIPTION
priocntlset changes the scheduling properties of running processes. priocntlset has the same functions as the priocntl system call, but a more general way of specifying the set of processes whose scheduling properties are to be changed.

cmd specifies the function to be performed. *arg* is a pointer to a structure whose type depends on *cmd*. See priocntl(2) for the valid values of *cmd* and the corresponding *arg* structures.

psp is a pointer to a procset structure, which priocntlset uses to specify the set of processes whose scheduling properties are to be changed.

```
typedef struct procset {
    idop_t     p_op;        /* operator connecting left/right sets */
    idtype_t   p_lidtype;   /* left set ID type */
    id_t       p_lid;       /* left set ID */
    idtype_t   p_ridtype;   /* right set ID type */
    id_t       p_rid;       /* right set ID */
} procset_t;
```

p_lidtype and p_lid specify the ID type and ID of one ("left") set of processes; p_ridtype and p_rid specify the ID type and ID of a second ("right") set of processes. ID types and IDs are specified just as for the priocntl system call. p_op specifies the operation to be performed on the two sets of processes to get the set of processes the system call is to apply to. The valid values for p_op and the processes they specify are:

POP_DIFF   set difference: processes in left set and not in right set

POP_AND   set intersection: processes in both left and right sets

POP_OR   set union: processes in either left or right sets or both

POP_XOR   set exclusive-or: processes in left or right set but not in both

The following macro, which is defined in procset.h, offers a convenient way to initialize a procset structure:

```
#define    setprocset(psp, op, ltype, lid, rtype, rid) \
    (psp)->p_op       = (op), \
    (psp)->p_lidtype  = (ltype), \
    (psp)->p_lid      = (lid), \
    (psp)->p_ridtype  = (rtype), \
    (psp)->p_rid      = (rid),
```

DIAGNOSTICS
`priocntlset` has the same return values and errors as `priocntl`.

SEE ALSO
priocntl(2)

priocntl(1) in the *User's Reference Manual*

NAME
processor_bind – bind a process to a processor

SYNOPSIS
    #include <sys/types.h>
    #include <sys/procset.h>
    #include <sys/processor.h>

    int processor_bind(idtype_t idtype, id_t pid,
    processorid_t processorid, processorid_t *obind);

DESCRIPTION
processor_bind binds a process to a specific processor. idtype must be set to P_PID and pid is a process ID specifying the process to be bound. When the process identified by pid has been bound, it will execute only on the processor specified by processorid (even if other processors are available), except briefly, if the process requires a resource which only another processor can provide. The processor may continue to run other processes in addition to the one specified by pid. The processor_bind call will fail if the process specified by pid is bound exclusively to another processor or if there are already processes exclusively bound to the processor specified by processorid.

The processor_bind call is not guaranteed to be synchronous with the binding operation. If the binding operation cannot be completed immediately the call may return before the operation completes. Any delay between the return of the function and the completion of the operation will, typically, be of very short duration.

If processorid is PBIND_NONE, the specified process is unbound; that is, it is made free to run on any processor.

If the process specified by pid is already bound to a different processor, the binding for that process will be changed to the processor specified by processorid. If obind is not NULL and the process is currently bound to a processor, that processorid is returned by obind.

The bind state of a process is inherited by any children created by a fork(2) call, and does not change across a call to exec(2).

In order to bind or unbind a process, the real or effective user ID of the caller must match the real or saved [from exec(2)] user ID of the process being bound or unbound, or the caller must have superuser privileges.

DIAGNOSTICS
Returns a value of zero on success, or a negative value on failure. Failure may result from:

EPERM   The calling process does not have appropriate privileges.

EINVAL An invalid idtype or processorid was specified, or the specified processor is currently offline.

ESRCH   No process can be found with a process ID corresponding to pid.

EBUSY	The process specified by pid is bound exclusively to another processor or there are already processes exclusively bound to the processor specified by processorid.
EFAULT	obind is non-NULL and points to an invalid address.
EIO	The specified processor is not operational.

SEE ALSO

pbind(1M), pexbind(1M)

processor_info(2) (Multiprocessing) processor_info(2)

NAME
processor_info – get information about one processor

SYNOPSIS
#include <sys/types.h>
#include <sys/processor.h>

int processor_info (processorid_t processorid, processor_info_t *infop)

DESCRIPTION
processor_info obtains information about a single processor in the system. The information is returned in the processor_info_t structure pointed to by infop. This structure contains the following fields:

int pi_state
: Either P_ONLINE or P_OFFLINE. If the processor is offline, the other fields are meaningless.

char pi_processor_type[16]
: A null terminated ASCII string specifying the type of processor; one of i386, i486, i860.

char pi_fputypes[32]
: A null terminated ASCII string specifying the type of floating point hardware available. The string consists of zero or more floating point identifier strings, separated by commas. Each of the floating point identifier strings may be one of i387, w1167.

int pi_clock
: The frequency of the processor clock, in megahertz, rounded to the nearest integer.

DIAGNOSTICS
processor_info returns 0 on success, or -1 on failure. Failure may result from:

EFAULT
: The infop pointer points to an invalid memory address.

EINVAL
: The processorid does not refer to an existing processor.

EIO
: The processor to which processorid refers is not operational.

SEE ALSO
pinfo(1M)

profil(2)

NAME
profil – execution time profile

SYNOPSIS
```
#include <unistd.h>
```
void profil(unsigned short *buff, size_t bufsiz, int offset, unsigned scale);

DESCRIPTION
profil provides CPU-use statistics by profiling the amount of CPU time expended by a program. profil generates the statistics by creating an execution histogram for a current process. The histogram is defined for a specific region of program code to be profiled, and the identified region is logically broken up into a set of equal size subdivisions, each of which corresponds to a count in the histogram. With each clock tick, the current subdivision is identified and its corresponding histogram count is incremented. These counts establish a relative measure of how much time is being spent in each code subdivision. The resulting histogram counts for a profiled region can be used to identify those functions that consume a disproportionately high percentage of CPU time.

buff is a buffer of *bufsiz* bytes in which the histogram counts are stored in an array of unsigned short int.

offset, *scale*, and *bufsiz* specify the region to be profiled.

offset is effectively the start address of the region to be profiled.

scale, broadly speaking, is a contraction factor that indicates how much smaller the histogram buffer is than the region to be profiled. More precisely, *scale* is interpreted as an unsigned 16-bit fixed-point fraction with the decimal point implied on the left. Its value is the reciprocal of the number of bytes in a subdivision, per byte of histogram buffer. Since there are two bytes per histogram counter, the effective ratio of subdivision bytes per counter is one half the scale.

Several observations can be made:

> the maximal value of *scale*, 0xffff (approximately 1), maps subdivisions 2 bytes long to each counter.

> the minimum value of *scale* (for which profiling is performed), 0x0002 (1/32,768), maps subdivision 65,536 bytes long to each counter.

> the default value of *scale* (currently used by cc –qp), 0x4000, maps subdivisions 8 bytes long to each counter.

The values are used within the kernel as follows: when the process is interrupted for a clock tick, the value of *offset* is subtracted from the current value of the program counter (pc), and the remainder is multiplied by *scale* to derive a result. That result is used as an index into the histogram array to locate the cell to be incremented. Therefore, the cell count represents the number of times that the process was executing code in the subdivision associated with that cell when the process was interrupted.

scale can be computed as (*RATIO* * 0200000L), where *RATIO* is the desired ratio of *bufsiz* to profiled region size, and has a value between 0 and 1. Qualitatively speaking, the closer *RATIO* is to 1, the higher the resolution of the profile information.

bufsiz can be computed as (*size_of_region_to_be_profiled* * *RATIO*).

SEE ALSO
  prof(1), times(2), monitor(3C)

NOTES
  Profiling is turned off by giving a *scale* of 0 or 1, and is rendered ineffective by giving a *bufsiz* of 0. Profiling is turned off when an exec(2) is executed, but remains on in both child and parent processes after a fork(2). Profiling is turned off if a *buff* update would cause a memory fault.

ptrace(2)

NAME
ptrace – process trace

SYNOPSIS
```
#include <unistd.h>
#include <sys/types.h>
```

int ptrace(int request, pid_t pid, int addr, int data);

DESCRIPTION
ptrace allows a parent process to control the execution of a child process. Its primary use is for the implementation of breakpoint debugging [see sdb(1)]. The child process behaves normally until it encounters a signal [see signal(5)], at which time it enters a stopped state and its parent is notified via the wait(2) system call. When the child is in the stopped state, its parent can examine and modify its "core image" using ptrace. Also, the parent can cause the child either to terminate or continue, with the possibility of ignoring the signal that caused it to stop.

The *request* argument determines the action to be taken by ptrace and is one of the following:

- 0   This request must be issued by the child process if it is to be traced by its parent. It turns on the child's trace flag that stipulates that the child should be left in a stopped state on receipt of a signal rather than the state specified by *func* [see signal(2)]. The *pid*, *addr*, and *data* arguments are ignored, and a return value is not defined for this request. Peculiar results ensue if the parent does not expect to trace the child.

The remainder of the requests can only be used by the parent process. For each, *pid* is the process ID of the child. The child must be in a stopped state before these requests are made.

- 1, 2   With these requests, the word at location *addr* in the address space of the child is returned to the parent process. If instruction and data space are separated, request 1 returns a word from instruction space, and request 2 returns a word from data space. If instruction and data space are not separated, either request 1 or request 2 may be used with equal results. The *data* argument is ignored. These two requests fail if *addr* is not the start address of a word, in which case a value of −1 is returned to the parent process and the parent's errno is set to EIO.

- 3   With this request, the word at location *addr* in the child's user area in the system's address space [see <sys/user.h>] is returned to the parent process. The *data* argument is ignored. This request fails if *addr* is not the start address of a word or is outside the user area, in which case a value of −1 is returned to the parent process and the parent's errno is set to EIO.

- 4, 5   With these requests, the value given by the *data* argument is written into the address space of the child at location *addr*. If instruction and data space are separated, request 4 writes a word into instruction space, and request 5 writes a word into data space. If instruction and data space are not separated, either request 4 or request 5 may be used with equal results. On success, the value written into the address space of

		the child is returned to the parent. These two requests fail if *addr* is not the start address of a word. On failure a value of −1 is returned to the parent process and the parent's errno is set to EIO.
	6	With this request, a few entries in the child's user area can be written. *data* gives the value that is to be written and *addr* is the location of the entry. The few entries that can be written are the general registers and the condition codes of the Processor Status Word.
	7	This request causes the child to resume execution. If the *data* argument is 0, all pending signals including the one that caused the child to stop are canceled before it resumes execution. If the *data* argument is a valid signal number, the child resumes execution as if it had incurred that signal, and any other pending signals are canceled. The *addr* argument must be equal to 1 for this request. On success, the value of *data* is returned to the parent. This request fails if *data* is not 0 or a valid signal number, in which case a value of −1 is returned to the parent process and the parent's errno is set to EIO.
	8	This request causes the child to terminate with the same consequences as exit(2).
	9	This request sets the trace bit in the Processor Status Word of the child and then executes the same steps as listed above for request 7. The trace bit causes an interrupt on completion of one machine instruction. This effectively allows single stepping of the child.

To forestall possible fraud, ptrace inhibits the set-user-ID facility on subsequent exec(2) calls. If a traced process calls exec(2), it stops before executing the first instruction of the new image showing signal SIGTRAP. ptrace in general fails if one or more of the following are true:

EIO	*request* is an illegal number.
ESRCH	*pid* identifies a child that does not exist or has not executed a ptrace with request 0.
EPERM	the invoking subject does not have the appropriate MAC privileges.

SEE ALSO
sdb(1), exec(2), signal(2), wait(2)

putmsg(2)

NAME
putmsg – send a message on a stream

SYNOPSIS
```
#include <stropts.h>

int putmsg(int fd, const struct strbuf *ctlptr,
           const struct strbuf *dataptr, int flags);

int putpmsg(int fd, const struct strbuf *ctlptr,
            const struct strbuf *dataptr, int band, int flags);
```

DESCRIPTION
putmsg creates a message from user-specified buffer(s) and sends the message to a STREAMS file. The message may contain either a data part, a control part, or both. The data and control parts to be sent are distinguished by placement in separate buffers, as described below. The semantics of each part is defined by the STREAMS module that receives the message.

The function putpmsg does the same thing as putmsg, but provides the user the ability to send messages in different priority bands. Except where noted, all information pertaining to putmsg also pertains to putpmsg.

fd specifies a file descriptor referencing an open stream. *ctlptr* and *dataptr* each point to a strbuf structure, which contains the following members:

```
int maxlen;     /* not used */
int len;        /* length of data */
void *buf;      /* ptr to buffer */
```

ctlptr points to the structure describing the control part, if any, to be included in the message. The buf field in the strbuf structure points to the buffer where the control information resides, and the len field indicates the number of bytes to be sent. The maxlen field is not used in putmsg [see getmsg(2)]. In a similar manner, *dataptr* specifies the data, if any, to be included in the message. *flags* indicates what type of message should be sent and is described later.

To send the data part of a message, *dataptr* must not be NULL and the len field of *dataptr* must have a value of 0 or greater. To send the control part of a message, the corresponding values must be set for *ctlptr*. No data (control) part is sent if either *dataptr* (*ctlptr*) is NULL or the len field of *dataptr* (*ctlptr*) is set to −1.

For putmsg(), if a control part is specified, and *flags* is set to RS_HIPRI, a high priority message is sent. If no control part is specified, and *flags* is set to RS_HIPRI, putmsg fails and sets errno to EINVAL. If *flags* is set to 0, a normal (non-priority) message is sent. If no control part and no data part are specified, and *flags* is set to 0, no message is sent, and 0 is returned.

The stream head guarantees that the control part of a message generated by putmsg is at least 64 bytes in length.

For putpmsg, the flags are different. *flags* is a bitmask with the following mutually-exclusive flags defined: MSG_HIPRI and MSG_BAND. If *flags* is set to 0, putpmsg fails and sets errno to EINVAL. If a control part is specified and *flags* is set to MSG_HIPRI and *band* is set to 0, a high-priority message is sent. If *flags* is set to MSG_HIPRI and either no control part is specified or *band* is set to a non-zero value, putpmsg() fails and sets errno to EINVAL. If flags is set to MSG_BAND, then a message is sent in the priority band specified by *band*. If a control part and data part are not specified and *flags* is set to MSG_BAND, no message is sent and 0 is returned.

Normally, putmsg() will block if the stream write queue is full due to internal flow control conditions. For high-priority messages, putmsg() does not block on this condition. For other messages, putmsg() does not block when the write queue is full and O_NDELAY or O_NONBLOCK is set. Instead, it fails and sets errno to EAGAIN.

putmsg or putpmsg also blocks, unless prevented by lack of internal resources, waiting for the availability of message blocks in the stream, regardless of priority or whether O_NDELAY or O_NONBLOCK has been specified. No partial message is sent.

putmsg fails if one or more of the following are true:

EAGAIN   A non-priority message was specified, the O_NDELAY or O_NONBLOCK flag is set and the stream write queue is full due to internal flow control conditions.

EBADF   *fd* is not a valid file descriptor open for writing.

EFAULT   *ctlptr* or *dataptr* points outside the allocated address space.

EINTR   A signal was caught during the putmsg system call.

EINVAL   An undefined value was specified in *flags*, or *flags* is set to RS_HIPRI and no control part was supplied.

EINVAL   The stream referenced by *fd* is linked below a multiplexor.

EINVAL   For putpmsg, if *flags* is set to MSG_HIPRI and *band* is nonzero.

ENOSR   Buffers could not be allocated for the message that was to be created due to insufficient STREAMS memory resources.

ENOSTR   A stream is not associated with *fd*.

ENXIO   A hangup condition was generated downstream for the specified stream, or the other end of the pipe is closed.

ERANGE   The size of the data part of the message does not fall within the range specified by the maximum and minimum packet sizes of the topmost stream module. This value is also returned if the control part of the message is larger than the maximum configured size of the control part of a message, or if the data part of a message is larger than the maximum configured size of the data part of a message.

putmsg also fails if a STREAMS error message had been processed by the stream head before the call to putmsg. The error returned is the value contained in the STREAMS error message.

SEE ALSO
getmsg(2), intro(2), poll(2), putmsg(2), read(2), write(2)
Programmer's Guide: STREAMS

DIAGNOSTICS
Upon successful completion, a value of 0 is returned. Otherwise, a value of −1 is returned and errno is set to indicate the error.

rdchk(2) (Application Compatibility Package) rdchk(2)

NAME
    rdchk − check to see if there is data to be read

SYNOPSIS
    cc [*flag* . . .] *file* . . . −lx
    rdchk(int fdes);

DESCRIPTION
    rdchk checks to see if a process will block if it attempts to read the file designated by *fdes*. rdchk returns 1 if there is data to be read or if it is the end of the file (EOF). In this context, the proper sequence of calls using rdchk is:

        if(rdchk(fildes) > 0)
            read(fildes, buffer, nbytes);

DIAGNOSTICS
    rdchk returns −1 if an error occurs (for example, EBADF), 0 if the process will block if it issues a read and 1 if it is okay to read. EBADF is returned if a rdchk is done on a semaphore file or if the file specified doesn't exist.

SEE ALSO
    read(2)

NAME
read – read from file

SYNOPSIS
```
#include <sys/types.h>
#include <sys/uio.h>
#include <unistd.h>

int read(int fildes, void *buf, unsigned nbyte);

int readv(int fildes, struct iovec *iov, int iovcnt);
```

DESCRIPTION
read attempts to read *nbyte* bytes from the file associated with *fildes* into the buffer pointed to by *buf*. If *nbyte* is zero, read returns zero and has no other results. *fildes* is a file descriptor obtained from a creat, open, dup, fcntl, pipe, or ioctl system call.

On devices capable of seeking, the read starts at a position in the file given by the file pointer associated with *fildes*. On return from read, the file pointer is incremented by the number of bytes actually read.

Devices that are incapable of seeking always read from the current position. The value of a file pointer associated with such a file is undefined.

readv performs the same action as read, but places the input data into the *iovcnt* buffers specified by the members of the *iov* array: *iov*[0], *iov*[1], ..., *iov*[*iovcnt*−1].

For readv, the iovec structure contains the following members:

```
addr_t    iov_base;
size_t    iov_len;
```

Each iovec entry specifies the base address and length of an area in memory where data should be placed. readv always fills one buffer completely before proceeding to the next.

On success, read and readv return the number of bytes actually read and placed in the buffer; this number may be less than *nbyte* if the file is associated with a communication line [see ioctl(2) and termio(7)], or if the number of bytes left in the file is less than *nbyte*, or if the file is a pipe or a special file. A value of 0 is returned when an end-of-file has been reached.

read reads data previously written to a file. If any portion of an ordinary file prior to the end of file has not been written, read returns the number of bytes read as 0. For example, the lseek routine allows the file pointer to be set beyond the end of existing data in the file. If additional data is written at this point, subsequent reads in the gap between the previous end of data and newly written data return bytes with a value of 0 until data is written into the gap.

A read or readv from a STREAMS [see intro(2)] file can operate in three different modes: byte-stream mode, message-nondiscard mode, and message-discard mode. The default is byte-stream mode. This can be changed using the I_SRDOPT ioctl(2) request [see streamio(7)], and can be tested with the I_GRDOPT ioctl(2) request. In byte-stream mode, read and readv usually retrieve data from the stream until they have retrieved *nbyte* bytes, or until there is no more data to be retrieved. Byte-stream mode usually ignores message boundaries.

In STREAMS message-nondiscard mode, read and readv retrieve data until they have read *nbyte* bytes, or until they reach a message boundary. If read or readv does not retrieve all the data in a message, the remaining data is replaced on the stream and can be retrieved by the next read or readv call. Message-discard mode also retrieves data until it has retrieved *nbyte* bytes, or it reaches a message boundary. However, unread data remaining in a message after the read or readv returns is discarded, and is not available for a subsequent read, readv, or getmsg [see getmsg(2)].

When attempting to read from a regular file with mandatory file/record locking set [see chmod(2)], and there is a write lock owned by another process on the segment of the file to be read:

> If O_NDELAY or O_NONBLOCK is set, read returns −1 and sets errno to EAGAIN.
>
> If O_NDELAY and O_NONBLOCK are clear, read sleeps until the blocking record lock is removed.

When attempting to read from an empty pipe (or FIFO):

> If no process has the pipe open for writing, read returns 0 to indicate end-of-file.
>
> If some process has the pipe open for writing and O_NDELAY is set, read returns 0.
>
> If some process has the pipe open for writing and O_NONBLOCK is set, read returns −1 and sets errno to EAGAIN.
>
> If O_NDELAY and O_NONBLOCK are clear, read blocks until data is written to the pipe or the pipe is closed by all processes that had opened the pipe for writing.

When attempting to read a file associated with a terminal that has no data currently available:

> If O_NDELAY is set, read returns 0.
>
> If O_NONBLOCK is set, read returns −1 and sets errno to EAGAIN.
>
> If O_NDELAY and O_NONBLOCK are clear, read blocks until data becomes available.

When attempting to read a file associated with a stream that is not a pipe or FIFO, or terminal, and that has no data currently available:

> If O_NDELAY or O_NONBLOCK is set, read returns −1 and sets errno to EAGAIN.
>
> If O_NDELAY and O_NONBLOCK are clear, read blocks until data becomes available.

When reading from a STREAMS file, handling of zero-byte messages is determined by the current read mode setting. In byte-stream mode, read accepts data until it has read *nbyte* bytes, or until there is no more data to read, or until a zero-byte message block is encountered. read then returns the number of bytes read, and places the zero-byte message back on the stream to be retrieved by the next read or getmsg [see getmsg(2)]. In the two other modes, a zero-byte message returns a value of 0 and the message is removed from the stream. When a zero-byte message is read as the first message on a stream, a value of 0 is returned regardless of the read mode.

A read or readv from a STREAMS file returns the data in the message at the front of the stream head read queue, regardless of the priority band of the message.

Normally, a read from a STREAMS file can only process messages with data and without control information. The read fails if a message containing control information is encountered at the stream head. This default action can be changed by placing the stream in either control-data mode or control-discard mode with the I_SRDOPT ioctl(2). In control-data mode, control messages are converted to data messages by read. In control-discard mode, control messages are discarded by read, but any data associated with the control messages is returned to the user.

read and readv fail if one or more of the following are true:

EAGAIN	Mandatory file/record locking was set, O_NDELAY or O_NONBLOCK was set, and there was a blocking record lock.
EAGAIN	Total amount of system memory available when reading via raw I/O is temporarily insufficient.
EAGAIN	No data is waiting to be read on a file associated with a tty device and O_NONBLOCK was set.
EAGAIN	No message is waiting to be read on a stream and O_NDELAY or O_NONBLOCK was set.
EBADF	*fildes* is not a valid file descriptor open for reading.
EBADMSG	Message waiting to be read on a stream is not a data message.
EDEADLK	The read was going to go to sleep and cause a deadlock to occur.
EFAULT	*buf* points outside the allocated address space.
EINTR	A signal was caught during the read or readv system call.
EINVAL	Attempted to read from a stream linked to a multiplexor.
EIO	A physical I/O error has occurred, or the process is in a background process group and is attempting to read from its controlling terminal, and either the process is ignoring or blocking the SIGTTIN signal or the process group of the process is orphaned.
ENOLCK	The system record lock table was full, so the read or readv could not go to sleep until the blocking record lock was removed.

ENOLINK	*fildes* is on a remote machine and the link to that machine is no longer active.
ENXIO	The device associated with *fildes* is a block special or character special file and the value of the file pointer is out of range.

In addition, readv may return one of the following errors:

EFAULT	*iov* points outside the allocated address space.
EINVAL	*iovcnt* was less than or equal to 0 or greater than 16.
EINVAL	The sum of the `iov_len` values in the *iov* array overflowed a 32-bit integer.

A read from a STREAMS file also fails if an error message is received at the stream head. In this case, errno is set to the value returned in the error message. If a hangup occurs on the stream being read, read continues to operate normally until the stream head read queue is empty. Thereafter, it returns 0.

SEE ALSO
intro(2), creat(2), dup(2), fcntl(2), getmsg(2), ioctl(2), open(2), pipe(2)
streamio(7), termio(7) in the *System Administrator's Reference Manual*

DIAGNOSTICS
On success a non-negative integer is returned indicating the number of bytes actually read. Otherwise, a −1 is returned and errno is set to indicate the error.

readlink(2)

NAME
readlink – read the value of a symbolic link

SYNOPSIS
```
#include <unistd.h>

int readlink(const char *path, void *buf, size_t bufsiz);
```

DESCRIPTION
readlink places the contents of the symbolic link referred to by *path* in the buffer *buf*, which has size *bufsiz*. The contents of the link are not null-terminated when returned.

readlink fails and the buffer remains unchanged if:

EACCES	Search permission is denied for a component of the path prefix of *path*.
EFAULT	*path* or *buf* extends outside the allocated address space of the process.
EINVAL	The named file is not a symbolic link.
EIO	An I/O error occurs while reading from or writing to the file system.
ELOOP	Too many symbolic links are encountered in translating *path*.
ENAMETOOLONG	The length of the *path* argument exceeds {PATH_MAX}, or the length of a *path* component exceeds {NAME_MAX} while _POSIX_NO_TRUNC is in effect.
ENOENT	The named file does not exist.
ENOSYS	The file system does not support symbolic links.

DIAGNOSTICS
Upon successful completion readlink returns the number of characters placed in the buffer; otherwise, it returns −1 and places an error code in errno.

SEE ALSO
lstat(2), stat(2), symlink(2)

rename(2)

NAME
rename − change the name of a file

SYNOPSIS
    #include <stdio.h>

    int rename(const char *old, const char *new);

DESCRIPTION
rename renames a file. *old* is a pointer to the pathname of the file or directory to be renamed. *new* is a pointer to the new pathname of the file or directory. Both *old* and *new* must be of the same type (either both files, or both directories) and must reside on the same file system.

If *new* already exists, it is removed. Thus, if *new* names an existing directory, the directory must not have any entries other than, possibly, "." and "..". When renaming directories, the *new* pathname must not name a descendant of *old*. The implementation of rename ensures that upon successful completion a link named *new* will always exist.

If the final component of *old* is a symbolic link, the symbolic link is renamed, not the file or directory to which it points.

Write permission is required for both the directory containing *old* and the directory containing *new*.

rename fails, *old* is not changed, and no *new* file is created if one or more of the following are true:

EACCES	A component of either path prefix denies search permission; one of the directories containing *old* or *new* denies write permission; or one of the directories pointed to by *old* or *new* denies write permission.
EBUSY	*new* is a directory and the mount point for a mounted file system.
EDQUOT	The directory in which the entry for the new name is being placed cannot be extended because the user's quota of disk blocks on the file system containing the directory has been exhausted.
EEXIST	The link named by *new* is a directory containing entries other than "." and "..".
EFAULT	*old* or *new* points outside the process's allocated address space.
EINVAL	*old* is a parent directory of *new*, or an attempt is made to rename "." or "..".
EINTR	A signal was caught during execution of the rename system call.
EIO	An I/O error occurred while making or updating a directory entry.

EISDIR	*new* points to a directory but *old* points to a file that is not a directory.
ELOOP	Too many symbolic links were encountered in translating *old* or *new*.
EMULTIHOP	Components of pathnames require hopping to multiple remote machines and the file system type does not allow it.
ENAMETOOLONG	The length of the *old* or *new* argument exceeds {PATH_MAX}, or the length of a *old* or *new* component exceeds {NAME_MAX} while _POSIX_NO_TRUNC is in effect.
ENOENT	A component of either *old* or *new* does not exist, or the file referred to by either *old* or *new* does not exist.
ENOLINK	Pathnames point to a remote machine and the link to that machine is no longer active.
ENOSPC	The directory that would contain *new* is out of space.
ENOTDIR	A component of either path prefix is not a directory; or the *old* parameter names a directory and the *new* parameter names a file.
EROFS	The requested operation requires writing in a directory on a read-only file system.
EXDEV	The links named by *old* and *new* are on different file systems.

DIAGNOSTICS
Upon successful completion, a value of 0 is returned. Otherwise, a value of −1 is returned and errno is set to indicate the error.

NOTES
The system can deadlock if there is a loop in the file system graph. Such a loop takes the form of an entry in directory *a*, say *a/foo*, being a hard link to directory *b*, and an entry in directory *b*, say *b/bar*, being a hard link to directory *a*. When such a loop exists and two separate processes attempt to perform rename *a/foo b/bar* and rename *b/bar a/foo*, respectively, the system may deadlock attempting to lock both directories for modification. The system administrator should replace hard links to directories by symbolic links.

SEE ALSO
link(2), unlink(2)

NAME

rmdir – remove a directory

SYNOPSIS

    #include <unistd.h>

    int rmdir(const char *path);

DESCRIPTION

rmdir removes the directory named by the path name pointed to by *path*. The directory must not have any entries other than "." and "..".

If the directory's link count becomes zero and no process has the directory open, the space occupied by the directory is freed and the directory is no longer accessible. If one or more processes have the directory open when the last link is removed, the "." and ".." entries, if present, are removed before rmdir returns and no new entries may be created in the directory, but the directory is not removed until all references to the directory have been closed.

If *path* is a symbolic link, it is not followed.

Upon successful completion rmdir marks for update the st_ctime and st_mtime fields of the parent directory.

The named directory is removed unless one or more of the following are true:

EACCES	Search permission is denied for a component of the path prefix.
EACCES	Write permission is denied on the directory containing the directory to be removed.
EACCES	The parent directory has the sticky bit set and is not owned by the user; the directory is not owned by the user and is not writable by the user; the user is not a super-user.
EBUSY	The directory to be removed is the mount point for a mounted file system.
EEXIST	The directory contains entries other than those for "." and "..".
EFAULT	*path* points outside the process's allocated address space.
EINVAL	The directory to be removed is the current directory.
EINVAL	The directory to be removed is the "." entry of a directory.
EIO	An I/O error occurred while accessing the file system.
ELOOP	Too many symbolic links were encountered in translating *path*.
EMULTIHOP	Components of *path* require hopping to multiple remote machines and the file system does not allow it.
ENAMETOOLONG	The length of the *path* argument exceeds {PATH_MAX}, or the length of a *path* component exceeds {NAME_MAX} while _POSIX_NO_TRUNC is in effect.

ENOTDIR	A component of the path prefix is not a directory.
ENOENT	The named directory does not exist or is the null pathname.
EROFS	The directory entry to be removed is part of a read-only file system.
ENOLINK	*path* points to a remote machine, and the link to that machine is no longer active.

DIAGNOSTICS
Upon successful completion, a value of 0 is returned. Otherwise, a value of −1 is returned and errno is set to indicate the error.

SEE ALSO
mkdir(2)

rm(1), and mkdir(1) in the *User's Reference Manual*

NAME
sdenter, sdleave – synchronize access to a shared data segment

SYNOPSIS
cc [flag . . .] file . . . –lx

#include <sys/sd.h>

int sdenter(char *addr, int flags);

int sdleave(char *addr);

DESCRIPTION
sdenter is used to indicate that the current process is about to access the contents of a shared data segment. The actions performed depend on the value of *flags*. *flags* values are formed by OR-ing together entries from the following list:

SD_NOWAIT   If another process has called sdenter but not sdleave for the indicated segment, and the segment was not created with the SD_UNLOCK flag set, return an ENAVAIL error instead of waiting for the segment to become free.

SD_WRITE   Indicates that the process wants to write data to the shared data segment. A process that has attached to a shared data segment with the SD_RDONLY flag set will not be allowed to enter with the SD_WRITE flag set.

sdleave is used to indicate that the current process is done modifying the contents of a shared data segment.

Only changes made between invocations of sdenter and sdleave are guaranteed to be reflected in other processes. sdenter and sdleave are very fast; consequently, it is recommended that they be called frequently rather than leave sdenter in effect for any period of time. In particular, system calls should be avoided between sdenter and sdleave calls.

The fork system call is forbidden between calls to sdenter and sdleave if the segment was created without the SD_UNLOCK flag.

DIAGNOSTICS
Successful calls return 0. Unsuccessful calls return −1 and set errno to indicate the error. errno is set to EINVAL if a process does an sdenter with the SD_WRITE flag set and the segment is already attached with the SD_RDONLY flag set. errno is set to ENAVAIL if the SD_NOWAIT flag is set for sdenter and the shared data segment is not free.

SEE ALSO
sdget(2), sdgetv(2)

sdget(2) (Application Compatibility Package) sdget(2)

NAME
sdget, sdfree − attach and detach a shared data segment

SYNOPSIS
cc [*flag* . . .] *file* . . . −lx
#include <sys/sd.h>

char *sdget(char *path, int flags, /* long size, int mode */);

int sdfree(char *addr);

DESCRIPTION
sdget attaches a shared data segment to the data space of the current process. The actions performed are controlled by the value of *flags*. *flags* values are constructed by an OR of flags from the following list:

SD_RDONLY Attach the segment for reading only.

SD_WRITE   Attach the segment for both reading and writing.

SD_CREAT   If the segment named by *path* exists and is not in use (active), this flag will have the same effect as creating a segment from scratch. Otherwise, the segment is created according to the values of *size* and *mode*. Read and write access to the segment is granted to other processes based on the permissions passed in *mode*, and functions the same as those for regular files. Execute permission is meaningless. The segment is initialized to contain all zeroes.

SD_UNLOCK If the segment is created because of this call, the segment will be made so that more than one process can be between sdenter and sdleave calls.

sdfree detaches the current process from the shared data segment that is attached at the specified address. If the current process has done sdenter but not an sdleave for the specified segment, sdleave will be done before detaching the segment.

When no process remains attached to the segment, the contents of that segment disappear, and no process can attach to the segment without creating it by using the SD_CREAT flag in sdget. errno is set to EEXIST if a process tries to create a shared data segment that exists and is in use. errno is set to ENOTNAM if a process attempts an sdget on a file that exists but is not a shared data type.

DIAGNOSTICS
On successful completion, the address at which the segment was attached is returned. Otherwise, −1 is returned, and errno is set to indicate the error. errno is set to EINVAL if a process does an sdget on a shared data segment to which it is already attached. errno is set to EEXIST if a process tries to create a shared data segment that exists an is in use. errno is set to ENOTNAM if a process attempts an sdget on a file that exists but is not a shared data type.

The mode parameter must be included on the first call of the sdget function.

SEE ALSO
sdenter(2), sdgetv(2)

NAME

sdgetv — synchronize shared data access

SYNOPSIS

cc [*flag* . . .] *file* . . . −lx

#include <sys/sd.h>

int sdgetv(addr)

int sdwaitv(char *addr, int vnum);

DESCRIPTION

sdgetv and sdwaitv may be used to synchronize cooperating processes that are using shared data segments. The return value of both routines is the version number of the shared data segment attached to the process at address *addr*. The version number of a segment changes whenever some process does an sdleave for that segment.

sdgetv simply returns the version number of the indicated segment.

sdwaitv forces the current process to sleep until the version number for the indicated segment is no longer equal to *vnum*.

DIAGNOSTICS

Upon successful completion, both sdgetv and sdwaitv return a positive integer that is the current version number for the indicated shared data segment. Otherwise, a value of −1 is returned, and errno is set to indicate the error.

SEE ALSO

sdenter(2), sdget(2)

semctl(2)

NAME
semctl − semaphore control operations

SYNOPSIS
```
#include <sys/types.h>
#include <sys/ipc.h>
#include <sys/sem.h>

union semun {
     int val;
     struct semid_ds *buf;
     ushort *array;
};

int semctl(int semid, int semnum, int cmd, . . . /* union semun arg */);
```

DESCRIPTION
semctl provides a variety of semaphore control operations as specified by *cmd*.

The following *cmd*s are executed with respect to the semaphore specified by *semid* and *semnum*:

- GETVAL   Return the value of semval [see intro(2)]. {READ}
- SETVAL   Set the value of semval to *arg*.val. {ALTER}. When this command is successfully executed, the semadj value corresponding to the specified semaphore in all processes is cleared.
- GETPID   Return the value of (int) sempid. {READ}
- GETNCNT   Return the value of semncnt. {READ}
- GETZCNT   Return the value of semzcnt. {READ}

The following *cmd*s return and set, respectively, every semval in the set of semaphores.

- GETALL   Place semvals into array pointed to by *arg*.array. {READ}
- SETALL   Set semvals according to the array pointed to by *arg*.array. {ALTER}. When this cmd is successfully executed, the semadj values corresponding to each specified semaphore in all processes are cleared.

The following *cmd*s are also available:

- IPC_STAT   Place the current value of each member of the data structure associated with *semid* into the structure pointed to by *arg*.buf. The contents of this structure are defined in intro(2). {READ}
- IPC_SET   Set the value of the following members of the data structure associated with *semid* to the corresponding value found in the structure pointed to by *arg*.buf:

    sem_perm.uid
    sem_perm.gid
    sem_perm.mode /* only access permission bits */

semctl(2)

This command can be executed only by a process that has an effective user ID equal to either that of super-user, or to the value of sem_perm.cuid or sem_perm.uid in the data structure associated with *semid*.

IPC_RMID Remove the semaphore identifier specified by *semid* from the system and destroy the set of semaphores and data structure associated with it. This command only be executed only by a process that has an effective user ID equal to either that of super-user, or to the value of sem_perm.cuid or sem_perm.uid in the data structure associated with *semid*.

semctl fails if one or more of the following are true:

EACCES   Operation permission is denied to the calling process [see intro(2)].

EINVAL   *semid* is not a valid semaphore identifier.

EINVAL   *semnum* is less than 0 or greater than sem_nsems.

EINVAL   *cmd* is not a valid command.

EINVAL   *cmd* is IPC_SET and sem_perm.uid or sem_perm.gid is not valid.

EOVERFLOW   *cmd* is IPC_STAT and *uid* or *gid* is too large to be stored in the structure pointed to by *arg.buf*.

ERANGE   *cmd* is SETVAL or SETALL and the value to which semval is to be set is greater than the system imposed maximum.

EPERM   *cmd* is equal to IPC_RMID or IPC_SET and the effective user ID of the calling process is not equal to that of super-user, or to the value of sem_perm.cuid or sem_perm.uid in the data structure associated with *semid*.

EFAULT   *arg*.buf points to an illegal address.

SEE ALSO
intro(2), semget(2), semop(2)

DIAGNOSTICS
Upon successful completion, the value returned depends on *cmd* as follows:

        GETVAL   the value of semval
        GETPID   the value of (int) sempid
        GETNCNT   the value of semncnt
        GETZCNT   the value of semzcnt
        all others a value of 0

Otherwise, a value of −1 is returned and errno is set to indicate the error.

semget(2)

NAME
semget – get set of semaphores

SYNOPSIS
```
#include <sys/types.h>
#include <sys/ipc.h>
#include <sys/sem.h>

int semget(key_t key, int nsems, int semflg);
```

DESCRIPTION

semget returns the semaphore identifier associated with *key*.

A semaphore identifier and associated data structure and set containing *nsems* semaphores [see intro(2)] are created for *key* if one of the following is true:

  key is equal to IPC_PRIVATE.

  key does not already have a semaphore identifier associated with it, and (*semflg*&IPC_CREAT) is true.

On creation, the data structure associated with the new semaphore identifier is initialized as follows:

  sem_perm.cuid, sem_perm.uid, sem_perm.cgid, and sem_perm.gid are set equal to the effective user ID and effective group ID, respectively, of the calling process.

  The access permission bits of sem_perm.mode are set equal to the access permission bits of *semflg*.

  sem_nsems is set equal to the value of *nsems*.

  sem_otime is set equal to 0 and sem_ctime is set equal to the current time.

semget fails if one or more of the following are true:

EINVAL	*nsems* is either less than or equal to zero or greater than the system-imposed limit.
EACCES	A semaphore identifier exists for *key*, but operation permission [see intro(2)] as specified by the low-order 9 bits of *semflg* would not be granted.
EINVAL	A semaphore identifier exists for *key*, but the number of semaphores in the set associated with it is less than *nsems*, and *nsems* is not equal to zero.
ENOENT	A semaphore identifier does not exist for *key* and (*semflg*&IPC_CREAT) is false.
ENOSPC	A semaphore identifier is to be created but the system-imposed limit on the maximum number of allowed semaphore identifiers system wide would be exceeded.
ENOSPC	A semaphore identifier is to be created but the system-imposed limit on the maximum number of allowed semaphores system wide would be exceeded.

EEXIST   A semaphore identifier exists for *key* but both (*semflg*&IPC_CREAT) and (*semflg*&IPC_EXCL) are both true.

SEE ALSO
intro(2), semctl(2), semop(2), stdipc(3C)

DIAGNOSTICS
Upon successful completion, a non-negative integer, namely a semaphore identifier, is returned. Otherwise, a value of −1 is returned and errno is set to indicate the error.

semop(2)

NAME
semop − semaphore operations

SYNOPSIS
    #include <sys/types.h>
    #include <sys/ipc.h>
    #include <sys/sem.h>

int semop(int semid, struct sembuf *sops, size_t nsops);

DESCRIPTION
semop is used to perform atomically an array of semaphore operations on the set of semaphores associated with the semaphore identifier specified by *semid*. *sops* is a pointer to the array of semaphore-operation structures. *nsops* is the number of such structures in the array. The contents of each structure includes the following members:

    short   sem_num;   /* semaphore number */
    short   sem_op;   /* semaphore operation */
    short   sem_flg;   /* operation flags */

Each semaphore operation specified by *sem_op* is performed on the corresponding semaphore specified by *semid* and *sem_num*.

sem_op specifies one of three semaphore operations as follows, depending on whether its value is negative, positive, or zero:

If *sem_op* is a negative integer, one of the following occurs: {ALTER}

> If semval [see intro(2)] is greater than or equal to the absolute value of *sem_op*, the absolute value of *sem_op* is subtracted from semval. Also, if (*sem_flg*&SEM_UNDO) is true, the absolute value of *sem_op* is added to the calling process's semadj value [see exit(2)] for the specified semaphore.

> If semval is less than the absolute value of *sem_op* and (*sem_flg*&IPC_NOWAIT) is true, semop returns immediately.

> If semval is less than the absolute value of *sem_op* and (*sem_flg*&IPC_NOWAIT) is false, semop increments the semncnt associated with the specified semaphore and suspends execution of the calling process until one of the following conditions occur.

>> semval becomes greater than or equal to the absolute value of *sem_op*. When this occurs, the value of semncnt associated with the specified semaphore is decremented, the absolute value of *sem_op* is subtracted from semval and, if (*sem_flg*&SEM_UNDO) is true, the absolute value of *sem_op* is added to the calling process's semadj value for the specified semaphore.

>> The *semid* for which the calling process is awaiting action is removed from the system [see semctl(2)]. When this occurs, errno is set equal to EIDRM, and a value of −1 is returned.

>> The calling process receives a signal that is to be caught. When this occurs, the value of semncnt associated with the specified semaphore is decremented, and the calling process resumes execution in the manner prescribed in signal(2).

If *sem_op* is a positive integer, the value of *sem_op* is added to semval and, if (*sem_flg*&SEM_UNDO) is true, the value of *sem_op* is subtracted from the calling process's semadj value for the specified semaphore. {ALTER}

If *sem_op* is zero, one of the following occurs: {READ}

> If semval is zero, semop returns immediately.
>
> If semval is not equal to zero and (*sem_flg*&IPC_NOWAIT) is true, semop returns immediately.
>
> If semval is not equal to zero and (*sem_flg*&IPC_NOWAIT) is false, semop increments the semzcnt associated with the specified semaphore and suspends execution of the calling process until one of the following occurs:
>
>> Semval becomes zero, at which time the value of semzcnt associated with the specified semaphore is decremented.
>>
>> The *semid* for which the calling process is awaiting action is removed from the system. When this occurs, errno is set equal to EIDRM, and a value of −1 is returned.
>>
>> The calling process receives a signal that is to be caught. When this occurs, the value of semzcnt associated with the specified semaphore is decremented, and the calling process resumes execution in the manner prescribed in signal(2).

semop fails if one or more of the following are true for any of the semaphore operations specified by *sops*:

EINVAL	*semid* is not a valid semaphore identifier.
EFBIG	*sem_num* is less than zero or greater than or equal to the number of semaphores in the set associated with *semid*.
E2BIG	*nsops* is greater than the system-imposed maximum.
EACCES	Operation permission is denied to the calling process [see intro(2)].
EAGAIN	The operation would result in suspension of the calling process but (*sem_flg*&IPC_NOWAIT) is true.
ENOSPC	The limit on the number of individual processes requesting an SEM_UNDO would be exceeded.
EINVAL	The number of individual semaphores for which the calling process requests a SEM_UNDO would exceed the limit.
ERANGE	An operation would cause a semval to overflow the system-imposed limit.
ERANGE	An operation would cause a semadj value to overflow the system-imposed limit.
EFAULT	*sops* points to an illegal address.

Upon successful completion, the value of sempid for each semaphore specified in the array pointed to by *sops* is set equal to the process ID of the calling process.

semop(2) semop(2)

SEE ALSO
intro(2), exec(2), exit(2), fork(2), semctl(2), semget(2)

DIAGNOSTICS
If *semop* returns due to the receipt of a signal, a value of −1 is returned to the calling process and errno is set to EINTR. If it returns due to the removal of a *semid* from the system, a value of −1 is returned and errno is set to EIDRM.

Upon successful completion, a value of zero is returned. Otherwise, a value of −1 is returned and errno is set to indicate the error.

setpgid(2)

NAME
setpgid – set process group ID

SYNOPSIS
    #include <sys/types.h>
    #include <unistd.h>

    int setpgid(pid_t pid, pid_t pgid);

DESCRIPTION
setpgid sets the process group ID of the process with ID *pid* to *pgid*. If *pgid* is equal to *pid*, the process becomes a process group leader. If *pgid* is not equal to *pid*, the process becomes a member of an existing process group.

If *pid* is equal to 0, the process ID of the calling process is used. If *pgid* is equal to 0, the process specified by *pid* becomes a process group leader.

setpgid fails and returns an error if one or more of the following are true:

EACCES	*pid* matches the process ID of a child process of the calling process and the child process has successfully executed an exec(2) function.
EINVAL	*pgid* is less than (pid_t) 0, or greater than or equal to {PID_MAX}.
EINVAL	The calling process has a controlling terminal that does not support job control.
EPERM	The process indicated by the *pid* argument is a session leader.
EPERM	*pid* matches the process ID of a child process of the calling process and the child process is not in the same session as the calling process.
EPERM	*pgid* does not match the process ID of the process indicated by the *pid* argument and there is no process with a process group ID that matches *pgid* in the same session as the calling process.
ESRCH	*pid* does not match the process ID of the calling process or of a child process of the calling process.

SEE ALSO
exec(2), exit(2), fork(2), getpid(2), getpgid(2), setsid(2)

DIAGNOSTICS
Upon successful completion, setpgid returns a value of 0. Otherwise, a value of −1 is returned and errno is set to indicate the error.

NAME
setpgrp – set process group ID

SYNOPSIS
    #include <sys/types.h>
    #include <unistd.h>

    pid_t setpgrp (void);

DESCRIPTION
If the calling process is not already a session leader, setpgrp sets the process group ID and session ID of the calling process to the process ID of the calling process, and releases the calling process's controlling terminal.

SEE ALSO
intro(2), exec(2), fork(2), getpid(2), kill(2), setsid(2), signal(2)

DIAGNOSTICS
setpgrp returns the value of the new process group ID.

NOTES
setpgrp will be phased out in favor of the setsid(2) function.

setsid(2)

NAME
setsid – set session ID

SYNOPSIS
```
#include <sys/types.h>
#include <unistd.h>
```
pid_t setsid(void);

DESCRIPTION
If the calling process is not already a process group leader, setsid sets the process group ID and session ID of the calling process to the process ID of the calling process, and releases the process's controlling terminal.

setsid will fail and return an error if the following is true:

EPERM   The calling process is already a process group leader, or there are processes other than the calling process whose process group ID is equal to the process ID of the calling process.

SEE ALSO
intro(2), exec(2), exit(2), fork(2), getpid(2), getpgid(2), getsid(2), setpgid(2), setpgrp, signal(2), sigsend(2)

NOTES
If the calling process is the last member of a pipeline started by a job control shell, the shell may make the calling process a process group leader. The other processes of the pipeline become members of that process group. In this case, the call to setsid will fail. For this reason, a process that calls setsid and expects to be part of a pipeline should always first fork; the parent should exit and the child should call setsid, thereby insuring that the process will work reliably when started by both job control shells and non-job control shells.

DIAGNOSTICS
Upon successful completion, setsid returns the calling process's session ID. Otherwise, a value of -1 is returned and errno is set to indicate the error.

setuid(2)

NAME
setuid, setgid – set user and group IDs

SYNOPSIS
```
#include <sys/types.h>
#include <unistd.h>

int setuid(uid_t uid);

int setgid(gid_t gid);
```

DESCRIPTION
The setuid system call sets the real user ID, effective user ID, and saved user ID of the calling process. The setgid system call sets the real group ID, effective group ID, and saved group ID of the calling process.

At login time, the real user ID, effective user ID, and saved user ID of the login process are set to the login ID of the user responsible for the creation of the process. The same is true for the real, effective, and saved group IDs; they are set to the group ID of the user responsible for the creation of the process.

When a process calls exec(2) to execute a file (program), the user and/or group identifiers associated with the process can change. If the file executed is a set-user-ID file, the effective and saved user IDs of the process are set to the owner of the file executed. If the file executed is a set-group-ID file, the effective and saved group IDs of the process are set to the group of the file executed. If the file executed is not a set-user-ID or set-group-ID file, the effective user ID, saved user ID, effective group ID, and saved group ID are not changed.

The following subsections describe the behavior of setuid and setgid with respect to the three types of user and group IDs.

setuid
 If the effective user ID of the process calling setuid is the superuser, the real, effective, and saved user IDs are set to the *uid* parameter.

 If the effective user ID of the calling process is not the superuser, but *uid* is either the real user ID or the saved user ID of the calling process, the effective user ID is set to *uid*.

setgid
 If the effective user ID of the process calling setgid is the superuser, the real, effective, and saved group IDs are set to the *gid* parameter.

 If the effective user ID of the calling process is not the superuser, but *gid* is either the real group ID or the saved group ID of the calling process, the effective group ID is set to *gid*.

 setuid and setgid fail if one or more of the following is true:

 EPERM   For setuid, if the effective user ID is not the superuser, and the *uid* parameter does not match either the real or saved user IDs. For setgid, if the effective user ID is not the superuser, and the *gid* parameter does not match either the real or saved group IDs.

setuid(2)   setuid(2)

    EINVAL   The *uid* or *gid* is out of range.

DIAGNOSTICS

Upon successful completion, a value of 0 is returned. Otherwise, a value of −1 is returned and errno is set to indicate the error.

SEE ALSO

intro(2), exec(2), getgroups(2), getuid(2), stat(5)

shmctl(2)

NAME
shmctl – shared memory control operations

SYNOPSIS
    #include <sys/types.h>
    #include <sys/ipc.h>
    #include <sys/shm.h>

    int shmctl (int shmid, int cmd, struct shmid_ds *buf);

DESCRIPTION
shmctl provides a variety of shared memory control operations as specified by *cmd*. The following *cmd*s are available:

IPC_STAT Place the current value of each member of the data structure associated with *shmid* into the structure pointed to by *buf*. The contents of this structure are defined in intro(2). {READ}

IPC_SET Set the value of the following members of the data structure associated with *shmid* to the corresponding value found in the structure pointed to by *buf*:

    shm_perm.uid
    shm_perm.gid
    shm_perm.mode /* only access permission bits */

This command can be executed only by a process that has an effective user ID equal to that of super-user, or to the value of shm_perm.cuid or shm_perm.uid in the data structure associated with *shmid*.

IPC_RMID Remove the shared memory identifier specified by *shmid* from the system and destroy the shared memory segment and data structure associated with it. This command can be executed only by a process that has an effective user ID equal to that of super-user, or to the value of shm_perm.cuid or shm_perm.uid in the data structure associated with *shmid*.

SHM_LOCK Lock the shared memory segment specified by *shmid* in memory. This command can be executed only by a process that has an effective user ID equal to super-user.

SHM_UNLOCK Unlock the shared memory segment specified by *shmid*. This command can be executed only by a process that has an effective user ID equal to super-user.

shmctl fails if one or more of the following are true:

EACCES *cmd* is equal to IPC_STAT and {READ} operation permission is denied to the calling process [see intro(2)].

EINVAL *shmid* is not a valid shared memory identifier.

EINVAL *cmd* is not a valid command.

shmctl(2)

	EINVAL	*cmd* is IPC_SET and shm_perm.uid or shm_perm.gid is not valid.
	EOVERFLOW	*cmd* is IPC_STAT and *uid* or *gid* is too large to be stored in the structure pointed to by *buf*.
	EPERM	*cmd* is equal to IPC_RMID or IPC_SET and the effective user ID of the calling process is not equal to that of super-user, or to the value of shm_perm.cuid or shm_perm.uid in the data structure associated with *shmid*.
	EPERM	*cmd* is equal to SHM_LOCK or SHM_UNLOCK and the effective user ID of the calling process is not equal to that of super-user.
	EFAULT	*buf* points to an illegal address.
	ENOMEM	*cmd* is equal to SHM_LOCK and there is not enough memory.

SEE ALSO
shmget(2), shmop(2)

DIAGNOSTICS
Upon successful completion, a value of 0 is returned. Otherwise, a value of −1 is returned and errno is set to indicate the error.

NOTES
The user must explicitly remove shared memory segments after the last reference to them has been removed.

shmget(2)

NAME
shmget – get shared memory segment identifier

SYNOPSIS
```
#include <sys/types.h>
#include <sys/ipc.h>
#include <sys/shm.h>

int shmget(key_t key, int size, int shmflg);
```

DESCRIPTION
shmget returns the shared memory identifier associated with *key*.

A shared memory identifier and associated data structure and shared memory segment of at least *size* bytes [see intro(2)] are created for *key* if one of the following are true:

key is equal to IPC_PRIVATE.

key does not already have a shared memory identifier associated with it, and (*shmflg*&IPC_CREAT) is true.

Upon creation, the data structure associated with the new shared memory identifier is initialized as follows:

shm_perm.cuid, shm_perm.uid, shm_perm.cgid, and shm_perm.gid are set equal to the effective user ID and effective group ID, respectively, of the calling process.

The access permission bits of shm_perm.mode are set equal to the access permission bits of *shmflg*. shm_segsz is set equal to the value of *size*.

shm_lpid, shm_nattch shm_atime, and shm_dtime are set equal to 0.

shm_ctime is set equal to the current time.

shmget fails if one or more of the following are true:

EINVAL	*size* is less than the system-imposed minimum or greater than the system-imposed maximum.
EACCES	A shared memory identifier exists for *key* but operation permission [see intro(2)] as specified by the low-order 9 bits of *shmflg* would not be granted.
EINVAL	A shared memory identifier exists for *key* but the size of the segment associated with it is less than *size* and *size* is not equal to zero.
ENOENT	A shared memory identifier does not exist for *key* and (*shmflg*&IPC_CREAT) is false.
ENOSPC	A shared memory identifier is to be created but the system-imposed limit on the maximum number of allowed shared memory identifiers system wide would be exceeded.
ENOMEM	A shared memory identifier and associated shared memory segment are to be created but the amount of available memory is not sufficient to fill the request.

shmget(2)

EEXIST   A shared memory identifier exists for *key* but both (*shmflg*&IPC_CREAT) and (*shmflg*&IPC_EXCL) are true.

SEE ALSO
intro(2), shmctl(2), shmop(2), stdipc(3C)

DIAGNOSTICS
Upon successful completion, a non-negative integer, namely a shared memory identifier is returned. Otherwise, a value of −1 is returned and errno is set to indicate the error.

NOTES
The user must explicitly remove shared memory segments after the last reference to them has been removed.

shmop(2)

NAME
shmop: shmat, shmdt – shared memory operations

SYNOPSIS
#include <sys/types.h>
#include <sys/ipc.h>
#include <sys/shm.h>

void *shmat(int shmid, void *shmaddr, int shmflg);

int shmdt (void *shmaddr);

DESCRIPTION
shmat attaches the shared memory segment associated with the shared memory identifier specified by *shmid* to the data segment of the calling process. The segment is attached at the address specified by one of the following criteria:

If *shmaddr* is equal to (void *) 0, the segment is attached at the first available address as selected by the system.

If *shmaddr* is not equal to (void *) 0 and (*shmflg*&SHM_RND) is true, the segment is attached at the address given by (*shmaddr* – (*shmaddr* modulus SHMLBA)).

If *shmaddr* is not equal to (void *) 0 and (*shmflg*&SHM_RND) is false, the segment is attached at the address given by *shmaddr*.

shmdt detaches from the calling process's data segment the shared memory segment located at the address specified by *shmaddr*.

The segment is attached for reading if (*shmflg*&SHM_RDONLY) is true {READ}, otherwise it is attached for reading and writing {READ/WRITE}.

shmat fails and does not attach the shared memory segment if one or more of the following are true:

EINVAL	*shmid* is not a valid shared memory identifier.
EACCES	Operation permission is denied to the calling process [see intro(2)].
ENOMEM	The available data space is not large enough to accommodate the shared memory segment.
EINVAL	*shmaddr* is not equal to zero, and the value of (*shmaddr* – (*shmaddr* modulus SHMLBA)). is an illegal address.
EINVAL	*shmaddr* is not equal to zero, (*shmflg*&SHM_RND) is false, and the value of *shmaddr* is an illegal address.
EMFILE	The number of shared memory segments attached to the calling process would exceed the system-imposed limit.
EINVAL	shmdt fails and does not detach the shared memory segment if *shmaddr* is not the data segment start address of a shared memory segment.

shmop(2) shmop(2)

SEE ALSO
intro(2), exec(2), exit(2), fork(2), shmctl(2), shmget(2)

DIAGNOSTICS
Upon successful completion, the return value is as follows:

shmat returns the data segment start address of the attached shared memory segment.

shmdt returns a value of 0.

Otherwise, a value of −1 is returned and errno is set to indicate the error.

NOTES
The user must explicitly remove shared memory segments after the last reference to them has been removed.

sigaction(2)

NAME
sigaction – detailed signal management

SYNOPSIS
```
#include <signal.h>
```
```
int sigaction(int sig, const struct sigaction *act,
    struct sigaction *oact);
```

DESCRIPTION
sigaction allows the calling process to examine and/or specify the action to be taken on delivery of a specific signal. [See signal(5) for an explanation of general signal concepts.]

sig specifies the signal and can be assigned any of the signals specified in signal(5) except SIGKILL and SIGSTOP

If the argument *act* is not NULL, it points to a structure specifying the new action to be taken when delivering *sig*. If the argument *oact* is not NULL, it points to a structure where the action previously associated with *sig* is to be stored on return from sigaction.

The sigaction structure includes the following members:

```
void        (*sa_handler)();
sigset_t    sa_mask;
int         sa_flags;
```

sa_handler specifies the disposition of the signal and may take any of the values specified in signal(5).

sa_mask specifies a set of signals to be blocked while the signal handler is active. On entry to the signal handler, that set of signals is added to the set of signals already being blocked when the signal is delivered. In addition, the signal that caused the handler to be executed will also be blocked, unless the SA_NODEFER flag has been specified. SIGSTOP and SIGKILL cannot be blocked (the system silently enforces this restriction).

sa_flags specifies a set of flags used to modify the delivery of the signal. It is formed by a logical OR of any of the following values:

SA_ONSTACK   If set and the signal is caught and an alternate signal stack has been declared with sigaltstack(2), the signal is delivered to the calling process on that stack. Otherwise, the signal is delivered on the same stack as the main program.

SA_RESETHAND If set and the signal is caught, the disposition of the signal is reset to SIG_DFL and the signal will not be blocked on entry to the signal handler (SIGILL, SIGTRAP, and SIGPWR cannot be automatically reset when delivered; the system silently enforces this restriction).

SA_NODEFER   If set and the signal is caught, the signal will not be automatically blocked by the kernel while it is being caught.

SA_RESTART		If set and the signal is caught, a system call that is interrupted by the execution of this signal's handler is transparently restarted by the system. Otherwise, that system call returns an EINTR error.
SA_SIGINFO		If cleared and the signal is caught, *sig* is passed as the only argument to the signal-catching function. If set and the signal is caught, two additional arguments are passed to the signal-catching function. If the second argument is not equal to NULL, it points to a siginfo_t structure containing the reason why the signal was generated [see siginfo(5)]; the third argument points to a ucontext_t structure containing the receiving process's context when the signal was delivered [see ucontext(5)].
SA_NOCLDWAIT		If set and *sig* equals SIGCHLD, the system will not create zombie processes when children of the calling process exit. If the calling process subsequently issues a wait(2), it blocks until all of the calling process's child processes terminate, and then returns a value of −1 with errno set to ECHILD.
SA_NOCLDSTOP		If set and *sig* equals SIGCHLD, *sig* will not be sent to the calling process when its child processes stop or continue.

sigaction fails if any of the following is true:

EINVAL	The value of the *sig* argument is not a valid signal number or is equal to SIGKILL or SIGSTOP.
EFAULT	*act* or *oact* points outside the process's allocated address space.

DIAGNOSTICS

On success, sigaction returns zero. On failure, it returns −1 and sets errno to indicate the error.

SEE ALSO

intro(2), exit(2), kill(2), pause(2), sigaltstack(2), signal(2), sigprocmask(2), sigsend(2), sigsuspend(2), wait(2), sigsetops(3C), siginfo(5), signal(5), ucontext(5)

kill(1) in the *User's Reference Manual*

NOTES

If the system call is reading from or writing to a terminal and the terminal's NOFLSH bit is cleared, data may be flushed [see termio(7)].

sigaltstack(2)

NAME
sigaltstack – set or get signal alternate stack context

SYNOPSIS
#include <signal.h>

int sigaltstack(const stack_t *ss, stack_t *oss);

DESCRIPTION
sigaltstack allows users to define an alternate stack area on which signals are to be processed. If *ss* is non-zero, it specifies a pointer to, and the size of a stack area on which to deliver signals, and tells the system if the process is currently executing on that stack. When a signal's action indicates its handler should execute on the alternate signal stack [specified with a sigaction(2) call], the system checks to see if the process is currently executing on that stack. If the process is not currently executing on the signal stack, the system arranges a switch to the alternate signal stack for the duration of the signal handler's execution.

The structure sigaltstack includes the following members.

```
char    *ss_sp
int     ss_size
int     ss_flags
```

If *ss* is not NULL, it points to a structure specifying the alternate signal stack that will take effect upon return from sigaltstack. The ss_sp and ss_size fields specify the new base and size of the stack, which is automatically adjusted for direction of growth and alignment. The ss_flags field specifies the new stack state and may be set to the following:

SS_DISABLE The stack is to be disabled and ss_sp and ss_size are ignored. If SS_DISABLE is not set, the stack will be enabled.

If *oss* is not NULL, it points to a structure specifying the alternate signal stack that was in effect prior to the call to sigaltstack. The ss_sp and ss_size fields specify the base and size of that stack. The ss_flags field specifies the stack's state, and may contain the following values:

SS_ONSTACK The process is currently executing on the alternate signal stack. Attempts to modify the alternate signal stack while the process is executing on it will fail.

SS_DISABLE The alternate signal stack is currently disabled.

sigaltstack fails if any of the following is true:

EFAULT Either *ss* or *oss* points outside the process's allocated address space.

EINVAL An attempt was made to disable an active stack or the ss_flags field specifies invalid flags.

ENOMEM The size of the alternate stack area is less than MINSIGSTKSZ.

NOTES
The value SIGSTKSZ is defined to be the number of bytes that would be used to cover the usual case when allocating an alternate stack area. The value MINSIGSTKSZ is defined to be the minimum stack size for a signal handler. In

computing an alternate stack size, a program should add that amount to its stack requirements to allow for the operating system overhead.

The following code fragment is typically used to allocate an alternate stack.

```
if ((sigstk.ss_sp = (char *)malloc(SIGSTKSZ)) == NULL)
    /* error return */;

sigstk.ss_size = SIGSTKSZ;
sigstk.ss_flags = 0;
if (sigaltstack(&sigstk, (stack_t *)0) < 0)
    perror("sigaltstack");
```

SEE ALSO

getcontext(2), sigaction(2), sigsetjmp(3C), ucontext(5).

DIAGNOSTICS

On success, sigaltstack returns zero. On failure, it returns −1 and sets errno to indicate the error.

NAME

signal, sigset, sighold, sigrelse, sigignore, sigpause – simplified signal management

SYNOPSIS

#include <signal.h>

void (*signal(int sig, void (*disp)(int))) (int);

void (*sigset(int sig, void (*disp)(int))) (int);

int sighold(int sig);

int sigrelse(int sig);

int sigignore(int sig);

int sigpause(int sig);

DESCRIPTION

These functions provide simplified signal management for application processes. See signal(5) for an explanation of general signal concepts.

signal and sigset are used to modify signal dispositions. *sig* specifies the signal, which may be any signal except SIGKILL and SIGSTOP. *disp* specifies the signal's disposition, which may be SIG_DFL, SIG_IGN, or the address of a signal handler. If signal is used, *disp* is the address of a signal handler, and *sig* is not SIGILL, SIGTRAP, or SIGPWR, the system first sets the signal's disposition to SIG_DFL before executing the signal handler. If sigset is used and *disp* is the address of a signal handler, the system adds *sig* to the calling process's signal mask before executing the signal handler; when the signal handler returns, the system restores the calling process's signal mask to its state prior to the delivery of the signal. In addition, if sigset is used and *disp* is equal to SIG_HOLD, *sig* is added to the calling process's signal mask and the signal's disposition remains unchanged.

sighold adds *sig* to the calling process's signal mask.

sigrelse removes *sig* from the calling process's signal mask.

sigignore sets the disposition of *sig* to SIG_IGN.

sigpause removes *sig* from the calling process's signal mask and suspends the calling process until a signal is received.

These functions fail if any of the following are true.

EINVAL   The value of the *sig* argument is not a valid signal or is equal to SIGKILL or SIGSTOP.

EINTR   A signal was caught during the system call sigpause.

NOTES

sighold in conjunction with sigrelse or sigpause may be used to establish critical regions of code that require the delivery of a signal to be temporarily deferred.

If `signal` or `sigset` is used to set SIGCHLD's disposition to a signal handler, SIGCHLD will not be sent when the calling process's children are stopped or continued.

If any of the above functions are used to set SIGCHLD's disposition to SIG_IGN, the calling process's child processes will not create zombie processes when they terminate [see exit(2)]. If the calling process subsequently waits for its children, it blocks until all of its children terminate; it then returns a value of −1 with errno set to ECHILD [see wait(2), waitid(2)].

DIAGNOSTICS

On success, `signal` returns the signal's previous disposition. On failure, it returns SIG_ERR and sets errno to indicate the error.

On success, `sigset` returns SIG_HOLD if the signal had been blocked or the signal's previous disposition if it had not been blocked. On failure, it returns SIG_ERR and sets errno to indicate the error.

All other functions return zero on success. On failure, they return −1 and set errno to indicate the error.

SEE ALSO

kill(2), pause(2), sigaction(2), sigsend(2), wait(2), waitid(2), signal(5)

NAME

sigpending – examine signals that are blocked and pending

SYNOPSIS

#include <signal.h>

int sigpending(sigset_t *set);

DESCRIPTION

The sigpending function retrieves those signals that have been sent to the calling process but are being blocked from delivery by the calling process's signal mask. The signals are stored in the space pointed to by the argument *set*.

sigpending fails if the following is true:

EFAULT   The *set* argument points outside the process's allocated address space.

SEE ALSO

sigaction(2), sigprocmask(2), sigsetops(3C)

DIAGNOSTICS

On success, sigpending returns zero. On failure, it returns −1 and sets errno to indicate the error.

sigprocmask(2)

NAME
sigprocmask – change or examine signal mask

SYNOPSIS
#include <signal.h>

int sigprocmask(int how, const sigset_t *set, sigset_t *oset);

DESCRIPTION
The sigprocmask function is used to examine and/or change the calling process's signal mask. If the value is SIG_BLOCK, the set pointed to by the argument *set* is added to the current signal mask. If the value is SIG_UNBLOCK, the set pointed by the argument *set* is removed from the current signal mask. If the value is SIG_SETMASK, the current signal mask is replaced by the set pointed to by the argument *set*. If the argument *oset* is not NULL, the previous mask is stored in the space pointed to by *oset*. If the value of the argument *set* is NULL, the value *how* is not significant and the process's signal mask is unchanged; thus, the call can be used to enquire about currently blocked signals.

If there are any pending unblocked signals after the call to sigprocmask, at least one of those signals will be delivered before the call to sigprocmask returns.

It is not possible to block those signals that cannot be ignored [see sigaction(2)]; this restriction is silently imposed by the system.

If sigprocmask fails, the process's signal mask is not changed.

sigprocmask fails if any of the following is true:

EINVAL	The value of the *how* argument is not equal to one of the defined values.
EFAULT	The value of *set* or *oset* points outside the process's allocated address space.

SEE ALSO
sigaction(2), signal(2), sigsetopts(3C), signal(5)

DIAGNOSTICS
On success, sigprocmask returns zero. On failure, it returns −1 and sets errno to indicate the error.

sigsem(2) (Application Compatibility Package) sigsem(2)

NAME
sigsem – signal a process waiting on a semaphore

SYNOPSIS
cc [flag . . .] file . . . -lx
sigsem(int sem_num);

DESCRIPTION
sigsem signals a process that is waiting on the semaphore *sem_num* that it may proceed and use the resource governed by the semaphore. sigsem is used in conjunction with waitsem to allow synchronization of processes wishing to access a resource. One or more processes may waitsem on the given semaphore and will be put to sleep until the process which currently has access to the resource issues a sigsem call. If there are any waiting processes, sigsem causes the process which is next in line on the semaphore's queue to be rescheduled for execution. The semaphore's queue is organized in First In, First Out (FIFO) order.

DIAGNOSTICS
sigsem returns the value (int) −1 if an error occurs. If *sem_num* does not refer to a semaphore type file, errno is set to ENOTNAM. If *sem_num* has not been previously opened by opensem, errno is set to EBADF. If the process issuing a sigsem call is not the current "owner" of the semaphore (that is, if the process has not issued a waitsem call before the sigsem), errno is set to ENAVAIL.

SEE ALSO
creatsem(2), opensem(2), waitsem(2)

sigsend(2)

NAME
sigsend, sigsendset − send a signal to a process or a group of processes

SYNOPSIS
    #include <sys/types.h>
    #include <sys/signal.h>
    #include <sys/procset.h>

    int sigsend(idtype_t idtype, id_t id, int sig);

    int sigsendset(procset_t *psp, int sig);

DESCRIPTION
sigsend sends a signal to the process or group of processes specified by *id* and *idtype*. The signal to be sent is specified by *sig* and is either zero or one of the values listed in signal(5). If *sig* is zero (the null signal), error checking is performed but no signal is actually sent. This value can be used to check the validity of *id* and *idtype*.

The real or effective user ID of the sending process must match the real or effective user ID of the receiving process, unless the effective user ID of the sending process is super-user, or *sig* is SIGCONT and the sending process has the same session ID as the receiving process.

If *idtype* is P_PID, *sig* is sent to the process with process ID *id*.

If *idtype* is P_PGID, *sig* is sent to any process with process group ID *id*.

If *idtype* is P_SID, *sig* is sent to any process with session ID *id*.

If *idtype* is P_UID, *sig* is sent to any process with effective user ID *id*.

If *idtype* is P_GID, *sig* is sent to any process with effective group ID *id*.

If *idtype* is P_CID, *sig* is sent to any process with scheduler class ID *id* [see priocntl(2)].

If *idtype* is P_ALL, *sig* is sent to all processes and *id* is ignored.

If *id* is P_MYID, the value of *id* is taken from the calling process.

The process with a process ID of 0 is always excluded. The process with a process ID of 1 is excluded unless *idtype* is equal to P_PID.

sigsendset provides an alternate interface for sending signals to sets of processes. This function sends signals to the set of processes specified by *psp*. *psp* is a pointer to a structure of type procset_t, defined in sys/procset.h, which includes the following members:

          idop_t   p_op;
          idtype_t   p_lidtype;
          id_t   p_lid;
          idtype_t   p_ridtype;
          id_t   p_rid;

p_lidtype and p_lid specify the ID type and ID of one ("left") set of processes; p_ridtype and p_rid specify the ID type and ID of a second ("right") set of processes. ID types and IDs are specified just as for the *idtype* and *id* arguments to sigsend. p_op specifies the operation to be performed on the two sets of processes to get the set of processes the system call is to apply to. The valid values for p_op and the processes they specify are:

POP_DIFF   set difference: processes in left set and not in right set

POP_AND   set intersection: processes in both left and right sets

POP_OR   set union: processes in either left or right set or both

POP_XOR   set exclusive-or: processes in left or right set but not in both

sigsend and sigsendset fail if one or more of the following are true:

EINVAL   *sig* is not a valid signal number.

EINVAL   *idtype* is not a valid idtype field.

EINVAL   *sig* is SIGKILL, *idtype* is P_PID and *id* is 1 (proc1).

ESRCH   No process can be found corresponding to that specified by *id* and *idtype*.

EPERM   The user ID of the sending process is not super-user, and its real or effective user ID does not match the real or effective user ID of the receiving process, and the calling process is not sending SIGCONT to a process that shares the same session.

In addition, sigsendset fails if:

EFAULT   psp points outside the process's allocated address space.

SEE ALSO

getpid(2), getpgrp(2), kill(2), priocntl(2), setpid(2), signal(2), signal(5)

kill(1) in the *User's Reference Manual*

DIAGNOSTICS

On success, sigsend returns zero. On failure, it returns −1 and sets errno to indicate the error.

sigsuspend(2)

NAME
sigsuspend – install a signal mask and suspend process until signal

SYNOPSIS
#include <signal.h>

int sigsuspend(const sigset_t *set);

DESCRIPTION
sigsuspend replaces the process's signal mask with the set of signals pointed to by the argument *set* and then suspends the process until delivery of a signal whose action is either to execute a signal catching function or to terminate the process.

If the action is to terminate the process, sigsuspend does not return. If the action is to execute a signal catching function, sigsuspend returns after the signal catching function returns. On return, the signal mask is restored to the set that existed before the call to sigsuspend.

It is not possible to block those signals that cannot be ignored [see signal(5)]; this restriction is silently imposed by the system.

sigsuspend fails if either of the following is true:

EINTR   A signal is caught by the calling process and control is returned from the signal catching function.

EFAULT   The *set* argument points outside the process's allocated address space.

DIAGNOSTICS
Since sigsuspend suspends process execution indefinitely, there is no successful completion return value. On failure, it returns −1 and sets errno to indicate the error.

SEE ALSO
sigaction(2), sigprocmask(2), sigpause(2), sigsetops(3C), signal(5)

stat(2)   stat(2)

NAME
stat, lstat, fstat – get file status

SYNOPSIS
```
#include <sys/types.h>
#include <sys/stat.h>

int stat(const char *path, struct stat *buf);

int lstat(const char *path, struct stat *buf);

int fstat(int fildes, struct stat *buf);
```

DESCRIPTION
path points to a path name naming a file. Read, write, or execute permission of the named file is not required, but all directories listed in the path name leading to the file must be searchable. stat obtains information about the named file.

Note that in a Remote File Sharing environment, the information returned by stat depends on the user/group mapping set up between the local and remote computers. [See idload(1M).]

lstat obtains file attributes similar to stat, except when the named file is a symbolic link; in that case lstat returns information about the link, while stat returns information about the file the link references.

fstat obtains information about an open file known by the file descriptor *fildes*, obtained from a successful open, creat, dup, fcntl, pipe, or ioctl system call.

buf is a pointer to a stat structure into which information is placed concerning the file.

The contents of the structure pointed to by *buf* include the following members:

```
        mode_t   st_mode;     /* File mode [see mknod(2)] */
        ino_t    st_ino;      /* Inode number */
        dev_t    st_dev;      /* ID of device containing */
                              /* a directory entry for this file */
        dev_t    st_rdev;     /* ID of device */
                              /* This entry is defined only for */
                              /* char special or block special files */
        nlink_t  st_nlink;    /* Number of links */
        uid_t    st_uid;      /* User ID of the file's owner */
        gid_t    st_gid;      /* Group ID of the file's group */
        off_t    st_size;     /* File size in bytes */
        time_t   st_atime;    /* Time of last access */
        time_t   st_mtime;    /* Time of last data modification */
        time_t   st_ctime;    /* Time of last file status change */
                              /* Times measured in seconds since */
                              /* 00:00:00 UTC, Jan. 1, 1970 */
        long     st_blksize;  /* Preferred I/O block size */
        long     st_blocks;   /* Number st_blksize blocks allocated */
```

stat(2)   **stat(2)**

st_mode
: The mode of the file as described in mknod(2). In addition to the modes described in mknod(2), the mode of a file may also be S_IFLNK if the file is a symbolic link. (Note that S_IFLNK may only be returned by lstat.)

st_ino
: This field uniquely identifies the file in a given file system. The pair st_ino and st_dev uniquely identifies regular files.

st_dev
: This field uniquely identifies the file system that contains the file. Its value may be used as input to the ustat system call to determine more information about this file system. No other meaning is associated with this value.

st_rdev
: This field should be used only by administrative commands. It is valid only for block special or character special files and only has meaning on the system where the file was configured.

st_nlink
: This field should be used only by administrative commands.

st_uid
: The user ID of the file's owner.

st_gid
: The group ID of the file's group.

st_size
: For regular files, this is the address of the end of the file. For block special or character special, this is not defined. See also pipe(2).

st_atime
: Time when file data was last accessed. Changed by the following system calls: creat, mknod, pipe, utime, and read.

st_mtime
: Time when data was last modified. Changed by the following system calls: creat, mknod, pipe, utime, and write.

st_ctime
: Time when file status was last changed. Changed by the following system calls: chmod, chown, creat, link, mknod, pipe, unlink, utime, and write.

st_blksize
: A hint as to the "best" unit size for I/O operations. This field is not defined for block-special or character-special files.

st_blocks
: The total number of physical blocks of size 512 bytes actually allocated on disk. This field is not defined for block-special or character-special files.

stat and lstat fail if one or more of the following are true:

EACCES
: Search permission is denied for a component of the path prefix.

EFAULT
: *buf* or *path* points to an invalid address.

EINTR
: A signal was caught during the stat or lstat system call.

ELOOP
: Too many symbolic links were encountered in translating *path*.

stat(2)

EMULTIHOP	Components of *path* require hopping to multiple remote machines and the file system does not allow it.
ENAMETOOLONG	The length of the *path* argument exceeds {PATH_MAX}, or the length of a *path* component exceeds {NAME_MAX} while _POSIX_NO_TRUNC is in effect.
ENOENT	The named file does not exist or is the null pathname.
ENOTDIR	A component of the path prefix is not a directory.
ENOLINK	*path* points to a remote machine and the link to that machine is no longer active.
EOVERFLOW	A component is too large to store in the structure pointed to by *buf*.

fstat fails if one or more of the following are true:

EBADF	*fildes* is not a valid open file descriptor.
EFAULT	*buf* points to an invalid address.
EINTR	A signal was caught during the fstat system call.
ENOLINK	*fildes* points to a remote machine and the link to that machine is no longer active.
EOVERFLOW	A component is too large to store in the structure pointed to by *buf*.

SEE ALSO

chmod(2), chown(2), creat(2), link(2), mknod(2), pipe(2), read(2), time(2), unlink(2), utime(2), write(2), fattach(3C), stat(5)

DIAGNOSTICS

Upon successful completion a value of 0 is returned. Otherwise, a value of −1 is returned and errno is set to indicate the error.

stat(2) (Application Compatibility Package) stat(2)

NAME
stat, lstat, fstat – get file status

SYNOPSIS
cc [*flag* . . .] *file* . . . -lx

#include <sys/types.h>
#include <sys/stat.h>

int stat (const char *path, struct stat *buf);

int lstat (const char *path, struct stat *buf);

int fstat (int fildes, struct stat *buf);

DESCRIPTION
path points to a path name naming a file. Read, write, or execute permission of the named file is not required, but all directories listed in the path name leading to the file must be searchable. stat obtains information about the named file.

Note that in a Remote File Sharing environment, the information returned by stat depends on the user/group mapping set up between the local and remote computers. [See idload(1M).]

lstat obtains file attributes similar to stat, except when the named file is a symbolic link; in that case lstat returns information about the link, while stat returns information about the file the link references.

fstat obtains information about an open file known by the file descriptor *fildes*, obtained from a successful open, creat, dup, fcntl, or pipe system call.

buf is a pointer to a stat structure into which information is placed concerning the file.

The contents of the structure pointed to by *buf* include the following members:

```
      mode_t  st_mode;     /* File mode [see mknod(2)] */
      ino_t   st_ino;      /* Inode number */
      dev_t   st_dev;      /* ID of device containing */
                           /* a directory entry for this file */
      dev_t   st_rdev;     /* ID of device */
                           /* This entry is defined only for */
                           /* character special files */,
                           /* XENIX special named files or block */
                           /* special files */
      nlink_t st_nlink;    /* Number of links */
      uid_t   st_uid;      /* User ID of the file's owner */
      gid_t   st_gid;      /* Group ID of the file's group */
      off_t   st_size;     /* File size in bytes */
      time_t  st_atime;    /* Time of last access */
      time_t  st_mtime;    /* Time of last data modification */
      time_t  st_ctime;    /* Time of last file status change */
                           /* Times measured in seconds since */
                           /* 00:00:00 GMT, Jan. 1, 1970 */
```

st_mode   The mode of the file as described in mknod(2).

st_ino   This field uniquely identifies the file in a given file system. The pair st_ino and st_dev uniquely identifies regular files.

st_dev   This field uniquely identifies the file system that contains the file. Its value may be used as input to the ustat system call to determine more information about this file system. No other meaning is associated with this value.

st_rdev   This field should be used only by administrative commands. It is valid only for block special files or character special files or XENIX special named files. The st_rdev field for block special and character special files only has meaning on the system where the file was configured.

If the file is a XENIX special named file, it contains the type code [see stat(4) for the XENIX semaphore and shared data type code values S_INSEM and S_INSHD].

st_nlink   This field should be used only by administrative commands.

st_uid   The user ID of the file's owner.

st_gid   The group ID of the file's group.

st_size   For regular files, this is the address of the end of the file. For pipes or FIFOs, this is the count of the data currently in the file. For block special character special, or XENIX special named files. this is not defined.

st_atime   Time when file data was last accessed. Changed by the following system calls: creat, mknod, pipe, utime, read, creatsem, opensem, sigsem, waitsem, sdget and sdfree.

st_mtime   Time when data was last modified. Changed by the following system calls: creat, mknod, pipe, utime, write.

st_ctime   Time when file status was last changed. Changed by the following system calls: chmod, chown, creat, link, mknod, pipe, unlink, utime, write, creatsem, sdget and sdfree.

stat and lstat fail if one or more of the following are true:

EACCES   Search permission is denied for a component of the path prefix.

EBADF   *fildes* is not a valid open file descriptor.

EFAULT   *buf* or *path* points to an invalid address.

EINTR   A signal was caught during the stat system call.

ELOOP   Too many symbolic links were encountered in translating *path*.

EMULTIHOP   Components of *path* require hopping to multiple remote machines.

ENAMETOOLONG	The length of the *path* argument exceeds {PATH_MAX}, or the length of a *path* component exceeds {NAME_MAX} while (_POSIX_NO_TRUNC) is in effect.
ENOENT	The named file does not exist or is the null pathname.
ENOTDIR	A component of the path prefix is not a directory.
ENOLINK	*path* points to a remote machine and the link to that machine is no longer active.
EOVERFLOW	A component is too large to store in the structure pointed to by *buf*.

fstat fails if one or more of the following are true:

ENOLINK	*fildes* points to a remote machine and the link to that machine is no longer active.
EOVERFLOW	A component is too large to store in the structure pointed to by *buf*.

SEE ALSO

chmod(2), chown(2), creat(2), link(2), mknod(2), pipe(2), read(2), time(2), unlink(2), utime(2), write(2), stat(5)

DIAGNOSTICS

Upon successful completion a value of 0 is returned. Otherwise, a value of −1 is returned and errno is set to indicate the error.

NAME
statvfs, fstatvfs – get file system information

SYNOPSIS
```
#include <sys/types.h>
#include <sys/statvfs.h>

int statvfs (const char *path, struct statvfs *buf);

int fstatvfs (int fildes, struct statvfs *buf);
```

DESCRIPTION
statvfs returns a "generic superblock" describing a file system; it can be used to acquire information about mounted file systems. *buf* is a pointer to a structure (described below) that is filled by the system call.

path should name a file that resides on that file system. The file system type is known to the operating system. Read, write, or execute permission for the named file is not required, but all directories listed in the path name leading to the file must be searchable.

The statvfs structure pointed to by *buf* includes the following members:

```
ulong   f_bsize;        /* preferred file system block size */
ulong   f_frsize;       /* fundamental filesystem block size
                           (if supported) */
ulong   f_blocks;       /* total # of blocks on file system
                           in units of f_frsize */
ulong   f_bfree;        /* total # of free blocks */
ulong   f_bavail;       /* # of free blocks avail to
                           non-superuser */
ulong   f_files;        /* total # of file nodes (inodes) */
ulong   f_ffree;        /* total # of free file nodes */
ulong   f_favail;       /* # of inodes avail to
                           non-superuser*/
fsid_t  f_fsid;         /* file system id (dev for now) */
char    f_basetype[FSTYPSZ]; /*  target fs type name,
                           null-terminated */
ulong   f_flag;         /* bit mask of flags */
ulong   f_namemax;      /* maximum file name length */
char    f_fstr[32];     /* file system specific string */
ulong   f_filler[16];   /* reserved for future expansion */
```

f_basetype contains a null-terminated FSType name of the mounted target (for example, s5 mounted over rfs will contain s5).

The following flags can be returned in the f_flag field:

```
ST_RDONLY    0x01    /* read-only file system */
ST_NOSUID    0x02    /* does not support setuid/setgid
                        semantics */
ST_NOTRUNC   0x04    /* does not truncate file names
                        longer than {NAME_MAX}*/
```

fstatvfs is similar to statvfs, except that the file named by *path* in statvfs is instead identified by an open file descriptor *fildes* obtained from a successful open, creat, dup, fcntl, or pipe system call.

statvfs fails if one or more of the following are true:

EACCES	Search permission is denied on a component of the path prefix.
EFAULT	*path* or *buf* points outside the process's allocated address space.
EINTR	A signal was caught during statvfs execution.
EIO	An I/O error occurred while reading the file system.
ELOOP	Too many symbolic links were encountered in translating *path*.
EMULTIHOP	Components of *path* require hopping to multiple remote machines and file system type does not allow it.
ENAMETOOLONG	The length of a *path* component exceeds {NAME_MAX} characters, or the length of *path* exceeds {PATH_MAX} characters.
ENOENT	Either a component of the path prefix or the file referred to by *path* does not exist.
ENOLINK	*path* points to a remote machine and the link to that machine is no longer active.
ENOTDIR	A component of the path prefix of *path* is not a directory.

fstatvfs fails if one or more of the following are true:

EFAULT	*buf* points to an invalid address.
EBADF	*fildes* is not an open file descriptor.
EINTR	A signal was caught during fstatvfs execution.
EIO	An I/O error occurred while reading the file system.

DIAGNOSTICS

Upon successful completion a value of 0 is returned. Otherwise, a value of −1 is returned and errno is set to indicate the error.

SEE ALSO

chmod(2), chown(2), creat(2), link(2), mknod(2), pipe(2), read(2), time(2), unlink(2), utime(2), write(2).

NAME
stime – set time

SYNOPSIS
#include <unistd.h>

int stime(const time_t *tp);

DESCRIPTION
stime sets the system's idea of the time and date. *tp* points to the value of time as measured in seconds from 00:00:00 UTC January 1, 1970.

stime will fail if:

EPERM   the effective user ID of the calling process is not super-user.

SEE ALSO
time(2)

DIAGNOSTICS
Upon successful completion, a value of 0 is returned. Otherwise, a value of −1 is returned and errno is set to indicate the error.

swapctl(2)

NAME
swapctl – manage swap space

SYNOPSIS
    #include <sys/stat.h>
    #include <sys/swap.h>

    int swapctl(int cmd, void *arg);

DESCRIPTION
swapctl adds, deletes, or returns information about swap resources. *cmd* specifies one of the following options contained in sys/swap.h:

    SC_ADD   /* add a resource for swapping */
    SC_LIST   /* list the resources for swapping */
    SC_REMOVE   /* remove a resource for swapping */
    SC_GETNSWP   /* return number of swap resources */

When SC_ADD or SC_REMOVE is specified, *arg* is a pointer to a swapres structure containing the following members:

    char   *sr_name;   /* pathname of resource */
    off_t   sr_start;   /* offset to start of swap area */
    off_t   sr_length;   /* length of swap area */

sr_start and sr_length are specified in 512-byte blocks. When SC_LIST is specified, *arg* is a pointer to a swaptable structure containing the following members:

    int   swt_n;   /* number of swapents following */
    struct swapent swt_ent[];   /* array of swt_n swapents */

A swapent structure contains the following members:

    char   *ste_path;   /* name of the swap file */
    off_t   ste_start;   /* starting block for swapping */
    off_t   ste_length;   /* length of swap area */
    long   ste_pages;   /* number of pages for swapping */
    long   ste_free;   /* number of ste_pages free */
    long   ste_flags;   /* ST_INDEL bit set if swap file */
                            /* is now being deleted */

SC_LIST causes swapctl to return at most swt_n entries. The return value of swapctl is the number actually returned. The ST_INDEL bit is turned on in ste_flags if the swap file is in the process of being deleted. When SC_GETNSWP is specified, swapctl returns as its value the number of swap resources in use. *arg* is ignored for this operation. The SC_ADD and SC_REMOVE functions will fail if calling process does not have appropriate privileges.

RETURN VALUE
Upon successful completion, the function swapctl returns a value of 0 for SC_ADD or SC_REMOVE, the number of struct swapent entries actually returned for SC_LIST, or the number of swap resources in use for SC_GETNSWP. Upon failure, the function swapctl returns a value of −1 and sets errno to indicate an error.

ERRORS
Under the following conditions, the function swapctl fails and sets errno to:

EEXIST	Part of the range specified by sr_start and sr_length is already being used for swapping on the specified resource (SC_ADD).
EFAULT	*arg*, *sr_name*, or *ste_path* points outside the allocated address space.
EINVAL	The specified function value is not valid, the path specified is not a swap resource (SC_REMOVE), part of the range specified by sr_start and sr_length lies outside the resource specified (SC_ADD), or the specified swap area is less than one page (SC_ADD).
EISDIR	The path specified for SC_ADD is a directory.
ELOOP	Too many symbolic links were encountered in translating the pathname provided to SC_ADD or SC_REMOVE .
ENAMETOOLONG	The length of a component of the path specified for SC_ADD or SC_REMOVE exceeds {NAME_MAX} characters or the length of the path exceeds {PATH_MAX} characters and {_POSIX_NO_TRUNC} is in effect.
ENOENT	The pathname specified for SC_ADD or SC_REMOVE does not exist.
ENOMEM	An insufficient number of struct swapent structures were provided to SC_LIST, or there were insufficient system storage resources available during an SC_ADD or SC_REMOVE, or the system would not have enough swap space after an SC_REMOVE.
ENOSYS	The pathname specified for SC_ADD or SC_REMOVE is not a file or block special device.
ENOTDIR	Pathname provided to SC_ADD or SC_REMOVE contained a component in the path prefix that was not a directory.
EPERM	The process does not have appropriate privileges.
EROFS	The pathname specified for SC_ADD is a read-only file system.

symlink(2)

NAME
symlink – make a symbolic link to a file

SYNOPSIS
    #include <unistd.h> int symlink(const char *name1, const char *name2);

DESCRIPTION
symlink creates a symbolic link *name2* to the file *name1*. Either name may be an arbitrary pathname, the files need not be on the same file system, and *name1* may be nonexistent.

The file to which the symbolic link points is used when an open(2) operation is performed on the link. A stat(2) on a symbolic link returns the linked-to file, while an lstat returns information about the link itself. This can lead to surprising results when a symbolic link is made to a directory. To avoid confusion in programs, the readlink(2) call can be used to read the contents of a symbolic link.

If the file named by *name2* does not exist, it is created. The permission mode of *name2* is 777 [see creat(2)].

The symbolic link is made unless one or more of the following are true:

EACCES	Search permission is denied for a component of the path prefix of *name2*.
EDQUOT	The directory in which the entry for the new symbolic link is being placed cannot be extended because the user's quota of disk blocks on the file system containing the directory has been exhausted.
EDQUOT	The new symbolic link cannot be created because the user's quota of disk blocks on the file system which will contain the link has been exhausted.
EDQUOT	The user's quota of inodes on the file system on which the file is being created has been exhausted.
EEXIST	The file referred to by *name2* already exists.
EFAULT	*name1* or *name2* points outside the allocated address space for the process.
EIO	An I/O error occurs while reading from or writing to the file system.
ELOOP	Too many symbolic links are encountered in translating *name2*.
ENAMETOOLONG	The length of the *name1* or *name2* argument exceeds {PATH_MAX}, or the length of a *name1* or *name2* component exceeds {NAME_MAX} while (_POSIX_NO_TRUNC) is in effect.
ENOENT	A component of the path prefix of *name2* does not exist.

ENOSPC		The directory in which the entry for the new symbolic link is being placed cannot be extended because no space is left on the file system containing the directory.
ENOSPC		The new symbolic link cannot be created because no space is left on the file system which will contain the link.
ENOSPC		There are no free inodes on the file system on which the file is being created.
ENOSYS		The file system does not support symbolic links
ENOTDIR		A component of the path prefix of *name2* is not a directory.
EROFS		The file *name2* would reside on a read-only file system.

DIAGNOSTICS

Upon successful completion symlink returns a value of 0; otherwise, it returns −1 and places an error code in errno.

SEE ALSO

link(2), readlink(2), unlink(2). cp(1) in the *User's Reference Manual*

NAME

sync – update super block

SYNOPSIS

    #include <unistd.h>

    void sync(void);

DESCRIPTION

sync causes all information in memory that should be on disk to be written out. This includes modified super blocks, modified i-nodes, and delayed block I/O.

It should be used by programs that examine a file system, such as fsck(1M), df(1M), and so on. It is mandatory before a re-boot.

The writing, although scheduled, is not necessarily completed before sync returns. The fsync system call completes the writing before it returns.

SEE ALSO

fsync(2)

sysfs(2)

NAME
sysfs – get file system type information

SYNOPSIS
```
#include <sys/fstyp.h>
#include <sys/fsid.h>

int sysfs(int opcode, const char *fsname);

int sysfs(int opcode, int fs_index, char *buf);

int sysfs(int opcode);
```

DESCRIPTION
sysfs returns information about the file system types configured in the system. The number of arguments accepted by sysfs varies and depends on the *opcode*. The currently recognized *opcodes* and their functions are:

GETFSIND   Translate *fsname*, a null-terminated file-system type identifier, into a file-system type index.

GETFSTYP   Translate *fs_index*, a file-system type index, into a null-terminated file-system type identifier and write it into the buffer pointed to by *buf*; this buffer must be at least of size FSTYPSZ as defined in <sys/fstyp.h>.

GETNFSTYP   Return the total number of file system types configured in the system.

sysfs fails if one or more of the following are true:

EINVAL   *fsname* points to an invalid file-system identifier; *fs_index* is zero, or invalid; *opcode* is invalid.

EFAULT   *buf* or *fsname* points to an invalid user address.

DIAGNOSTICS
Upon successful completion, sysfs returns the file-system type index if the *opcode* is GETFSIND, a value of 0 if the *opcode* is GETFSTYP, or the number of file system types configured if the *opcode* is GETNFSTYP. Otherwise, a value of −1 is returned and errno is set to indicate the error.

sysi86(2)

NAME
sysi86 – machine specific functions

SYNOPSIS
    #include <sys/sysi86.h>

    int sysi86 (int cmd, . . .);

DESCRIPTION
The sysi86 system call implements machine specific functions. The *cmd* argument determines the function to be performed. The types of the arguments expected depend on the function.

Command RTODC
When *cmd* is RTODC, the expected argument is the address of a struct rtc_t (from the header file sys/rtc.h):

    struct rtc_t {
            char rtc_sec, rtc_asec, rtc_min, rtc_amin,
            rtc_hr, rtc_ahr, rtc_dow, rtc_dom,
            rtc_mon, rtc_yr, rtc_statusa,
            rtc_statusb, rtc_statusc, rtc_statusd;
    };

This function reads the hardware time-of-day clock and returns the data in the structure referenced by the argument. This command is only available to the *super-user*.

RDUBLK
This command reads the u-block (per process user information as defined by *structuser* in the sys/user header file) for a given process. When *cmd* is RDUBLK, sysi86 takes three additional arguments: the process ID, the address of a buffer, and the number of bytes to read; i.e.,

    sysi86(RDULBK, pid, buf, n)
        pid_t pid;
        char *buf;
        int n;

Command SI86FPHW
This command expects the address of an integer as its argument. After successful return from the system call, the integer specifies how floating-point computation is supported.

The low-order byte of the integer contains the value of "fpkind", a variable that specifies whether an 80287 or 80387 floating-point coprocessor is present, emulated in software, or not supported. The values are defined in the header file sys/fp.h.

FP_NO	no fp chip, no emulator (no fp support)
FP_SW	no fp chip, using software emulator
FP_HW	chip present bit
FP_287	80287 chip present
FP_387	80387 chip present

Command SETNAME
This command, which is only available to the super-user, expects an argument of type *char* * which points to a NULL terminated string of at most 7 characters. The command will change the running system's *sysname* and *nodename* [see uname(2)] to this string.

Command STIME
When *cmd* is STIME, an argument of type long is expected. This function sets the system time and date (not the hardware clock). The argument contains the time as measured in seconds from 00:00:00 GMT January 1, 1970. Note that this command is only available to the super-user.

Command SI86DSCR
This command sets a segment or gate descriptor in the kernel. The following descriptor types are accepted:

    executable and data segments in the LDT at DPL 3
    a call gate in the GDT at DPL 3 that points to a segment in the LDT

The argument is a pointer to a request structure that contains the values to be placed in the descriptor. The request structure is declared in the sys/sysi86.h header file.

Command SI86MEM
This command returns the size of available memory in bytes.

Command SI86SWPI
When *cmd* is SI86SWPI, individual swapping areas may be added, deleted or the current areas determined. The address of an appropriately primed swap buffer is passed as the only argument. (Refer to the sys/swap.h header file for details of loading the buffer.)

The format of the swap buffer is:

```
struct swapint {
    char   si_cmd;       /*command: SI_LIST, SI_ADD, SI_DEL*/
    char   *si_buf;      /*swap file path pointer*/
    int    si_swplo;     /*start block*/
    int    si_nblks;     /*swap size*/
}
```

Note that the add and delete options of the command may only be exercised by the super-user.

Typically, a swap area is added by a single call to sysi86. First, the swap buffer is primed with appropriate entries for the structure members. Then sysi86 is invoked.

```
#include <sys/sysi86.h>
#include <sys/swap.h>

struct swapint swapbuf;   /*swap into buffer ptr*/

sysi86(SI86SWPI, &swapbuf);
```

If this command succeeds, it returns 0 to the calling process. This command fails, returning -1, if one or more of the following is true:

[EFAULT]	*swapbuf* points to an invalid address
[EFAULT]	*swapbuf.si_buf* points to an invalid address
[ENOTBLK]	Swap area specified is not a block special device
[EEXIST]	Swap area specified has already been added
[ENOSPC]	Too many swap areas in use (if adding)
[ENOMEM]	Tried to delete last remaining swap area
[EINVAL]	Bad arguments
[ENOMEM]	No place to put swapped pages when deleting a swap area

SEE ALSO
uname(2)
swap(1M) in the *User's/System Administrator's Reference Manual*

DIAGNOSTICS
Upon successful completion, zero is returned; otherwise, −1 is returned, and errno is set to indicate the error. When the *cmd* is invalid, errno is set to EINVAL.

NAME
sysinfo – get and set system information strings

SYNOPSIS
#include <sys/systeminfo.h>

long sysinfo (int command, char *buf, long count);

DESCRIPTION
sysinfo copies information relating to the UNIX system on which the process is executing into the buffer pointed to by *buf*; sysinfo can also set certain information where appropriate commands are available. *count* is the size of the buffer.

The POSIX P1003.1 interface sysconf [see sysconf(2)] provides a similar class of configuration information, but returns an integer rather than a string.

The commands available are:

SI_SYSNAME
Copy into the array pointed to by *buf* the string that would be returned by uname [see uname(2)] in the *sysname* field. This is the name of the implementation of the operating system, for example, *System V* or *UTS*.

SI_HOSTNAME
Copy into the array pointed to by *buf* a string that names the present host machine. This is the string that would be returned by uname [see uname(2)] in the *nodename* field. This hostname or nodename is often the name the machine is known by locally.

The *hostname* is the name of this machine as a node in some network; different networks may have different names for the node, but presenting the nodename to the appropriate network Directory or name-to-address mapping service should produce a transport end point address. The name may not be fully qualified.

Internet host names may be up to 256 bytes in length (plus the terminating null).

SI_SET_HOSTNAME
Copy the null-terminated contents of the array pointed to by *buf* into the string maintained by the kernel whose value will be returned by succeeding calls to sysinfo with the command SI_HOSTNAME. This command requires that the effective-user-id be super-user.

SI_RELEASE
Copy into the array pointed to by *buf* the string that would be returned by uname [see uname(2)] in the *release* field. Typical values might be *4.0* or *3.2*.

SI_VERSION
Copy into the array pointed to by *buf* the string that would be returned by uname [see uname(2)] in the *version* field. The syntax and semantics of this string are defined by the system provider.

SI_MACHINE	Copy into the array pointed to by *buf* the string that would be returned by uname [see uname(2)] in the *machine* field, for example, *3b2* or *580*.
SI_ARCHITECTURE	Copy into the array pointed to by *buf* a string describing the instruction set architecture of the current system, for example, *mc68030*, *m32100*, or *i80486*. These names may not match predefined names in the C language compilation system.
SI_HW_PROVIDER	Copies the name of the hardware manufacturer into the array pointed to by *buf*.
SI_HW_SERIAL	Copy into the array pointed to by *buf* a string which is the ASCII representation of the hardware-specific serial number of the physical machine on which the system call is executed. Note that this may be implemented in Read-Only Memory, via software constants set when building the operating system, or by other means, and may contain non-numeric characters. It is anticipated that manufacturers will not issue the same "serial number" to more than one physical machine. The pair of strings returned by SI_HW_PROVIDER and SI_HW_SERIAL is likely to be unique across all vendor's System V implementations.
SI_SRPC_DOMAIN	Copies the Secure Remote Procedure Call domain name into the array pointed to by *buf*.
SI_SET_SRPC_DOMAIN	Set the string to be returned by sysinfo with the SI_SRPC_DOMAIN command to the value contained in the array pointed to by *buf*. This command requires that the effective-user-id be super-user.

sysinfo will fail if one or both of the following are true:

EPERM	The process does not have appropriate privilege for a SET commands.
EINVAL	*buf* does not point to a valid address, or the data for a SET command exceeds the limits established by the implementation.

DIAGNOSTICS

Upon successful completion, the value returned indicates the buffer size in bytes required to hold the complete value and the terminating null character. If this value is no greater than the value passed in *count*, the entire string was copied; if this value is greater than *count*, the string copied into *buf* has been truncated to *count*−1 bytes plus a terminating null character.

Otherwise, a value of −1 is returned and *errno* is set to indicate the error.

USAGE

There is in many cases no corresponding programmatic interface to set these values; such strings are typically settable only by the system administrator modifying entries in the master.d directory or the code provided by the particular

sysinfo(2)

OEM reading a serial number or code out of read-only memory, or hard-coded in the version of the operating system.

A good starting guess for *count* is 257, which is likely to cover all strings returned by this interface in typical installations.

SEE ALSO
uname(2), sysconf(3C)
BSD compatibility package interfaces gethostname(3), gethostid(3)

termios(2)

NAME
termios: tcgetattr, tcsetattr, tcsendbreak, tcdrain, tcflush, tcflow, cfgetospeed, cfgetispeed, cfsetispeed, cfsetospeed, tcgetpgrp, tcsetpgrp, tcgetsid – general terminal interface

SYNOPSIS
```
#include <termios.h>

int tcgetattr(int fildes, struct termios *termios_p);

int tcsetattr(int fildes, int optional_actions,
    const struct termios *termios_p);

int tcsendbreak(int fildes, int duration);

int tcdrain(int fildes);

int tcflush(int fildes, int queue_selector);

int tcflow(int fildes, int action);

speed_t cfgetospeed(struct termios *termios_p);

int cfsetospeed(const struct termios *termios_p, speed_t speed);

speed_t cfgetispeed(struct termios *termios_p);

int cfsetispeed(const struct termios *termios_p, speed_t speed);

#include <sys/types.h>
#include <termios.h>

pid_t tcgetpgrp(int fildes);

int tcsetpgrp(int fildes, pid_t pgid);

pid_t tcgetsid(int fildes);
```

DESCRIPTION
These functions describe a general terminal interface for controlling asynchronous communications ports. A more detailed overview of the terminal interface can be found in termio(7), which also describes an ioctl(2) interface that provides the same functionality. However, the function interface described here is the preferred user interface.

Many of the functions described here have a *termios_p* argument that is a pointer to a termios structure. This structure contains the following members:

```
tcflag_t    c_iflag;        /* input modes */
tcflag_t    c_oflag;        /* output modes */
tcflag_t    c_cflag;        /* control modes */
tcflag_t    c_lflag;        /* local modes */
cc_t        c_cc[NCCS];     /* control chars */
```

These structure members are described in detail in termio(7).

Get and Set Terminal Attributes
The tcgetattr function gets the parameters associated with the object referred by *fildes* and stores them in the termios structure referenced by *termios_p*. This

function may be invoked from a background process; however, the terminal attributes may be subsequently changed by a foreground process.

The `tcsetattr` function sets the parameters associated with the terminal (unless support is required from the underlying hardware that is not available) from the termios structure referenced by *termios_p* as follows:

>If *optional_actions* is TCSANOW, the change occurs immediately.

>If *optional_actions* is TCSADRAIN, the change occurs after all output written to *fildes* has been transmitted. This function should be used when changing parameters that affect output.

>If *optional_actions* is TCSAFLUSH, the change occurs after all output written to the object referred by *fildes* has been transmitted, and all input that has been received but not read is discarded before the change is made.

The symbolic constants for the values of *optional_actions* are defined in termios.h.

Line Control

If the terminal is using asynchronous serial data transmission, the `tcsendbreak` function causes transmission of a continuous stream of zero-valued bits for a specific duration. If *duration* is zero, it causes transmission of zero-valued bits for at least 0.25 seconds, and not more than 0.5 seconds. If *duration* is not zero, it behaves in a way similar to `tcdrain`.

If the terminal is not using asynchronous serial data transmission, the `tcsendbreak` function sends data to generate a break condition or returns without taking any action.

The `tcdrain` function waits until all output written to the object referred to by *fildes* has been transmitted.

The `tcflush` function discards data written to the object referred to by *fildes* but not transmitted, or data received but not read, depending on the value of *queue_selector*:

>If *queue_selector* is TCIFLUSH, it flushes data received but not read.

>If *queue_selector* is TCOFLUSH, it flushes data written but not transmitted.

>If *queue_selector* is TCIOFLUSH, it flushes both data received but not read, and data written but not transmitted.

The `tcflow` function suspends transmission or reception of data on the object referred to by *fildes*, depending on the value of *action*:

>If *action* is TCOOFF, it suspends output.

>If *action* is TCOON, it restarts suspended output.

>If *action* if TCIOFF, the system transmits a STOP character, which causes the terminal device to stop transmitting data to the system.

>If *action* is TCION, the system transmits a START character, which causes the terminal device to start transmitting data to the system.

Get and Set Baud Rate

The baud rate functions get and set the values of the input and output baud rates in the termios structure. The effects on the terminal device described below do not become effective until the tcsetattr function is successfully called.

The input and output baud rates are stored in the termios structure. The values shown in the table are supported. The names in this table are defined in termios.h.

Name	Description	Name	Description
B0	Hang up	B600	600 baud
B50	50 baud	B1200	1200 baud
B75	75 baud	B1800	1800 baud
B110	110 baud	B2400	2400 baud
B134	134.5 baud	B4800	4800 baud
B150	150 baud	B9600	9600 baud
B200	200 baud	B19200	19200 baud
B300	300 baud	B38400	38400 baud

cfgetospeed gets the output baud rate stored in the termios structure pointed to by *termios_p*.

cfsetospeed sets the output baud rate stored in the termios structure pointed to by *termios_p* to *speed*. The zero baud rate, B0, is used to terminate the connection. If B0 is specified, the modem control lines are no longer asserted. Normally, this disconnects the line.

cfgetispeed gets the input baud rate and stores it in the termios structure pointed to by *termios_p*.

cfsetispeed sets the input baud rate stored in the termios structure pointed to by *termios_p* to *speed*. If the input baud rate is set to zero, the input baud rate is specified by the value of the output baud rate. Both cfsetispeed and cfsetospeed return a value of zero if successful and −1 to indicate an error. Attempts to set unsupported baud rates are ignored. This refers both to changes to baud rates not supported by the hardware, and to changes setting the input and output baud rates to different values if the hardware does not support this.

Get and Set Terminal Foreground Process Group ID

tcsetpgrp sets the foreground process group ID of the terminal specified by *fildes* to *pgid*. The file associated with *fildes* must be the controlling terminal of the calling process and the controlling terminal must be currently associated with the session of the calling process. f2pgid *must match a process group ID of a process in the same session as the calling process.*

tcgetpgrp returns the foreground process group ID of the terminal specified by *fildes*. tcgetpgrp is allowed from a process that is a member of a background process group; however, the information may be subsequently changed by a process that is a member of a foreground process group.

Get Terminal Session ID

tcgetsid returns the session ID of the terminal specified by *fildes*.

DIAGNOSTICS

On success, tcgetpgrp returns the process group ID of the foreground process group associated with the specified terminal. Otherwise, it returns −1 and sets errno to indicate the error.

On success, tcgetsid returns the session ID associated with the specified terminal. Otherwise, it returns −1 and sets errno to indicate the error.

On success, cfgetispeed returns the input baud rate from the termios structure.

On success, cfgetospeed returns the output baud rate from the termios structure.

On success, all other functions return a value of 0. Otherwise, they return −1 and set errno to indicate the error.

All of the functions fail if one of more of the following is true:

EBADF   The *fildes* argument is not a valid file descriptor.

ENOTTY   The file associated with *fildes* is not a terminal.

tcsetattr also fails if the following is true:

EINVAL   The *optional_actions* argument is not a proper value, or an attempt was made to change an attribute represented in the termios structure to an unsupported value.

tcsendbreak also fails if the following is true:

EINVAL   The device does not support the tcsendbreak function.

tcdrain also fails if one or more of the following is true:

EINTR   A signal interrupted the tcdrain function.

EINVAL   The device does not support the tcdrain function.

tcflush also fails if the following is true:

EINVAL   The device does not support the tcflush function or the *queue_selector* argument is not a proper value.

tcflow also fails if the following is true:

EINVAL   The device does not support the tcflow function or the *action* argument is not a proper value.

tcgetpgrp also fails if the following is true:

ENOTTY   the calling process does not have a controlling terminal, or *fildes* does not refer to the controlling terminal.

tcsetpgrp also fails if the following is true:

EINVAL   *pgid* is not a valid process group ID.

ENOTTY   the calling process does not have a controlling terminal, or *fildes* does not refer to the controlling terminal, or the controlling terminal is no longer associated with the session of the calling process.

EPERM   *pgid* does not match the process group of an existing process in the same session as the calling process.

tcgetsid also fails if the following is true:

EACCES   *fildes* is a terminal that is not allocated to a session.

SEE ALSO
setsid(2), setpgid(2)

termio(7) in the *System Administrator's Reference Manual*

NAME
time – get time

SYNOPSIS
#include <sys/types.h>
#include <time.h>

time_t time(time_t *tloc);

DESCRIPTION
time returns the value of time in seconds since 00:00:00 UTC, January 1, 1970.

If *tloc* is non-zero, the return value is also stored in the location to which *tloc* points.

SEE ALSO
stime(2), ctime(3C)

NOTES
time fails and its actions are undefined if *tloc* points to an illegal address.

DIAGNOSTICS
Upon successful completion, time returns the value of time. Otherwise, a value of (time_t)−1 is returned and errno is set to indicate the error.

times(2)

NAME
times – get process and child process times

SYNOPSIS
```
#include <sys/types.h>
#include <sys/times.h>

clock_t times(struct tms *buffer);
```

DESCRIPTION
times fills the tms structure pointed to by *buffer* with time-accounting information. The tms structure is defined in sys/times.h as follows:

```
struct tms {
        clock_t    tms_utime;
        clock_t    tms_stime;
        clock_t    tms_cutime;
        clock_t    tms_cstime;
};
```

This information comes from the calling process and each of its terminated child processes for which it has executed a wait routine. All times are reported in clock ticks per second. Clock ticks are a system-dependent parameter. The specific value for an implementation is defined by the variable CLK_TCK, found in the include file limits.h. (On a 3B2 Computer clock ticks occur 100 times per second.)

tms_utime is the CPU time used while executing instructions in the user space of the calling process.

tms_stime is the CPU time used by the system on behalf of the calling process.

tms_cutime is the sum of the tms_utime and the tms_cutime of the child processes.

tms_cstime is the sum of the tms_stime and the tms_cstime of the child processes.

times fails if:

EFAULT   *buffer* points to an illegal address.

SEE ALSO
exec(2), fork(2), time(2), wait(2), waitid(2), waitpid(3C).
time(1), timex(1) in the *User's Reference Manual*.

DIAGNOSTICS
Upon successful completion, times returns the elapsed real time, in clock ticks per second, from an arbitrary point in the past (for example, system start-up time). This point does not change from one invocation of times to another. If times fails, a −1 is returned and errno is set to indicate the error.

NAME
uadmin – administrative control

SYNOPSIS
`#include <sys/uadmin.h>`

`int uadmin(int` *cmd*`, int` *fcn*`, int` *mdep*`);`

DESCRIPTION
uadmin provides control for basic administrative functions. This system call is tightly coupled to the system administrative procedures and is not intended for general use. The argument *mdep* is provided for machine-dependent use and is not defined here.

As specified by *cmd*, the following commands are available:

A_SHUTDOWN   The system is shut down. All user processes are killed, the buffer cache is flushed, and the root file system is unmounted. The action to be taken after the system has been shut down is specified by *fcn*. The functions are generic; the hardware capabilities vary on specific machines.

    AD_HALT   Halt the processor and turn off the power.

    AD_BOOT   Reboot the system, using /stand/unix.

    AD_IBOOT   Interactive reboot; the system goes to firmware mode and if the user strikes any key immediately after `Booting UNIX` is displayed, they are prompted for a bootable program name. If *fcn* is not supplied or is invalid, AD_IBOOT is used as the default.

A_REBOOT   The system stops immediately without any further processing. The action to be taken next is specified by *fcn* as above.

A_REMOUNT   The root file system is mounted again after having been fixed. This should be used only during the startup process.

uadmin fails if any of the following are true:

EPERM   The effective user ID is not super-user.

DIAGNOSTICS
Upon successful completion, the value returned depends on *cmd* as follows:

    A_SHUTDOWN   Never returns.
    A_REBOOT   Never returns.
    A_REMOUNT   0

Otherwise, a value of −1 is returned and `errno` is set to indicate the error.

SEE ALSO
sysi86(2)

ulimit(2)

NAME
ulimit – get and set user limits

SYNOPSIS
```
#include <ulimit.h>

long ulimit(int cmd, ... /* newlimit */ );
```

DESCRIPTION
This function provides for control over process limits. The *cmd* values available are:

UL_GETFSIZE   Get the regular file size limit of the process. The limit is in units of 512-byte blocks and is inherited by child processes. Files of any size can be read.

UL_SETFSIZE   Set the regular file size limit of the process to the value of *newlimit*, taken as a `long`. Any process may decrease this limit, but only a process with an effective user ID of super-user may increase the limit.

UL_GMEMLIM   Get the maximum possible break value [see brk(2)].

UL_GDESLIM   Get the current value of the maximum number of open files per process configured in the system.

The `getrlimit` system call provides a more general interface for controlling process limits.

ulimit fails if the following is true:

EINVAL   The *cmd* argument is not valid.

EPERM   A process with an effective user ID other than super user attempts to increase its file size limit.

SEE ALSO
brk(2), getrlimit(2), write(2)

NOTES
ulimit is effective in limiting the growth of regular files. Pipes are currently limited to {PIPE_MAX}.

DIAGNOSTICS
Upon successful completion, a non-negative value is returned. Otherwise, a value of −1 is returned and `errno` is set to indicate the error.

NAME

umask – set and get file creation mask

SYNOPSIS

```
#include <sys/types.h>
#include <sys/stat.h>

mode_t umask(mode_t cmask);
```

DESCRIPTION

umask sets the process's file mode creation mask to *cmask* and returns the previous value of the mask. Only the access permission bits of *cmask* and the file mode creation mask are used.

SEE ALSO

chmod(2), creat(2), mknod(2), open(2), stat(5)

mkdir(1), sh(1) in the *User's Reference Manual*

DIAGNOSTICS

The previous value of the file mode creation mask is returned.

umount(2)

NAME
umount – unmount a file system

SYNOPSIS
```
#include <sys/mount.h>

int umount(const char *file);
```

DESCRIPTION
umount requests that a previously mounted file system contained on the block special device or directory identified by *file* be unmounted. *file* is a pointer to a path name. After unmounting the file system, the directory upon which the file system was mounted reverts to its ordinary interpretation.

umount may be invoked only by the super-user.

umount will fail if one or more of the following are true:

EPERM	The process's effective user ID is not super-user.
EINVAL	*file* does not exist.
ELOOP	Too many symbolic links were encountered in translating the path pointed to by *file*.
ENAMETOOLONG	The length of the *file* argument exceeds {PATH_MAX}, or the length of a *file* component exceeds {NAME_MAX} while _POSIX_NO_TRUNC is in effect.
ENOTBLK	*file* is not a block special device.
EINVAL	*file* is not mounted.
EBUSY	A file on *file* is busy.
EFAULT	*file* points to an illegal address.
EREMOTE	*file* is remote.
ENOLINK	*file* is on a remote machine, and the link to that machine is no longer active.
EMULTIHOP	Components of the path pointed to by *file* require hopping to multiple remote machines.

SEE ALSO
mount(2)

DIAGNOSTICS
Upon successful completion a value of 0 is returned. Otherwise, a value of −1 is returned and errno is set to indicate the error.

NAME

uname – get name of current UNIX system

SYNOPSIS

```
#include <sys/utsname.h>

int uname(struct utsname *name);
```

DESCRIPTION

uname stores information identifying the current UNIX system in the structure pointed to by *name*.

uname uses the structure utsname defined in sys/utsname.h whose members are:

```
char sysname[SYS_NMLN];
char nodename[SYS_NMLN];
char release[SYS_NMLN];
char version[SYS_NMLN];
char machine[SYS_NMLN];
```

uname returns a null-terminated character string naming the current UNIX system in the character array *sysname*. Similarly, *nodename* contains the name that the system is known by on a communications network. *release* and *version* further identify the operating system. *machine* contains a standard name that identifies the hardware that the UNIX system is running on.

EFAULT   uname fails if *name* points to an invalid address.

SEE ALSO

uname(1) in the *User's Reference Manual*

DIAGNOSTICS

Upon successful completion, a non-negative value is returned. Otherwise, a value of −1 is returned and errno is set to indicate the error.

unlink(2)

NAME
unlink – remove directory entry

SYNOPSIS
```
#include <unistd.h>
```
int unlink(const char *path);

DESCRIPTION
unlink removes the directory entry named by the path name pointed to by *path*. and decrements the link count of the file referenced by the directory entry. When all links to a file have been removed and no process has the file open, the space occupied by the file is freed and the file ceases to exist. If one or more processes have the file open when the last link is removed, space occupied by the file is not released until all references to the file have been closed. If *path* is a symbolic link, the symbolic link is removed. *path* should not name a directory unless the process has appropriate privileges. Applications should use rmdir to remove directories.

Upon successful completion unlink marks for update the st_ctime and st_mtime fields of the parent directory. Also, if the file's link count is not zero, the st_ctime field of the file is marked for update.

The named file is unlinked unless one or more of the following are true:

EACCES	Search permission is denied for a component of the *path* prefix.
EACCES	Write permission is denied on the directory containing the link to be removed.
EACCES	The parent directory has the sticky bit set and the file is not writable by the user; the user does not own the parent directory and the user does not own the file;
EBUSY	The entry to be unlinked is the mount point for a mounted file system.
EFAULT	*path* points outside the process's allocated address space.
EINTR	A signal was caught during the unlink system call.
ELOOP	Too many symbolic links were encountered in translating *path*.
EMULTIHOP	Components of *path* require hopping to multiple remote machines and the file system does not allow it.
ENAMETOOLONG	The length of the *path* argument exceeds {PATH_MAX}, or the length of a *path* component exceeds {NAME_MAX} while _POSIX_NO_TRUNC is in effect.
ENOENT	The named file does not exist or is a null pathname. The user is not a super-user.
ENOTDIR	A component of the *path* prefix is not a directory.

EPERM		The named file is a directory and the effective user ID of the process is not super-user.
ETXTBSY		The entry to be unlinked is the last link to a pure procedure (shared text) file that is being executed.
EROFS		The directory entry to be unlinked is part of a read-only file system.
ENOLINK		*path* points to a remote machine and the link to that machine is no longer active.

SEE ALSO

close(2), link(2), open(2), rmdir(2)
rm(1) in the *User's Reference Manual*

DIAGNOSTICS

Upon successful completion, a value of 0 is returned. Otherwise, a value of −1 is returned and errno is set to indicate the error.

NAME
ustat – get file system statistics

SYNOPSIS
    #include <sys/types.h>
    #include <ustat.h>

    int ustat(dev_t dev, struct ustat *buf);

DESCRIPTION
ustat returns information about a mounted file system. *dev* is a device number identifying a device containing a mounted file system [see makedev(3C)]. *buf* is a pointer to a ustat structure that includes the following elements:

    daddr_t f_tfree;   /* Total free blocks */
    ino_t   f_tinode;   /* Number of free inodes */
    char   f_fname[6]; /* Filsys name */
    char   f_fpack[6]; /* Filsys pack name */

ustat fails if one or more of the following are true:

EINVAL	*dev* is not the device number of a device containing a mounted file system.
EFAULT	*buf* points outside the process's allocated address space.
EINTR	A signal was caught during a ustat system call.
ENOLINK	*dev* is on a remote machine and the link to that machine is no longer active.
ECOMM	*dev* is on a remote machine and the link to that machine is no longer active.

SEE ALSO
stat(2), statvfs(2), makedev(3C), fs(4)

NOTES
ustat will be phased out in favor of the statvfs function.

DIAGNOSTICS
Upon successful completion, a value of 0 is returned. Otherwise, a value of −1 is returned and errno is set to indicate the error.

NAME

utime – set file access and modification times

SYNOPSIS

```
#include <sys/types.h>
#include <utime.h>

int utime(const char *path, const struct utimbuf *times);
```

DESCRIPTION

path points to a path name naming a file. utime sets the access and modification times of the named file.

If *times* is NULL, the access and modification times of the file are set to the current time. A process must be the owner of the file or have write permission to use utime in this manner.

If *times* is not NULL, *times* is interpreted as a pointer to a utimbuf structure (defined in utime.h) and the access and modification times are set to the values contained in the designated structure. Only the owner of the file or the super-user may use utime this way.

The times in the following structure are measured in seconds since 00:00:00 UTC, Jan. 1, 1970.

```
struct utimbuf {
        time_t actime;      /* access time */
        time_t modtime;     /* modification time */
};
```

utime also causes the time of the last file status change (st_ctime) to be updated.

utime will fail if one or more of the following are true:

EACCES	Search permission is denied by a component of the *path* prefix.
EACCES	The effective user ID is not super-user and not the owner of the file and *times* is NULL and write access is denied.
EFAULT	*times* is not NULL and points outside the process's allocated address space.
EFAULT	*path* points outside the process's allocated address space.
EINTR	A signal was caught during the utime system call.
ELOOP	Too many symbolic links were encountered in translating *path*.
EMULTIHOP	Components of *path* require hopping to multiple remote machines and the file system does not allow it.
ENAMETOOLONG	The length of the *path* argument exceeds {PATH_MAX}, or the length of a *path* component exceeds {NAME_MAX} while _POSIX_NO_TRUNC is in effect.

ENOENT	The named file does not exist or is a null pathname.
ENOLINK	*path* points to a remote machine and the link to that machine is no longer active.
ENOTDIR	A component of the *path* prefix is not a directory.
EPERM	The effective user ID is not super-user and not the owner of the file and *times* is not NULL.
EROFS	The file system containing the file is mounted read-only.

SEE ALSO
    stat(2)

DIAGNOSTICS
Upon successful completion, a value of 0 is returned. Otherwise, a value of −1 is returned and errno is set to indicate the error.

vfork(2)

NAME
vfork – spawn new process in a virtual memory efficient way

SYNOPSIS
```
#include <unistd.h>
```
pid_t vfork (void);

DESCRIPTION
vfork can be used to create new processes without fully copying the address space of the old process. It is useful when the purpose of fork would have been to create a new system context for an execve. vfork differs from fork in that the child borrows the parent's memory and thread of control until a call to execve or an exit (either by a call to exit or abnormally.) The parent process is suspended while the child is using its resources.

vfork returns 0 in the child's context and (later) the process ID (PID of the child in the parent's context.

vfork can normally be used just like fork. It does not work, however, to return while running in the child's context from the procedure which called vfork since the eventual return from vfork would then return to a no longer existent stack frame. Be careful, also, to call _exit rather than exit if you cannot execve, since exit will flush and close standard I/O channels, and thereby mess up the parent processes standard I/O data structures. Even with fork it is wrong to call exit since buffered data would then be flushed twice.

DIAGNOSTICS
Upon successful completion, vfork returns a value of 0 to the child process and returns the process ID of the child process to the parent process. Otherwise, a value of −1 is returned to the parent process, no child process is created, and the global variable errno is set to indicate the error.

vfork will fail and no child process will be created if one or more of the following are true:

EAGAIN	The system-imposed limit on the total number of processes under execution would be exceeded. This limit is determined when the system is generated.
EAGAIN	The system-imposed limit on the total number of processes under execution by a single user would be exceeded. This limit is determined when the system is generated.
ENOMEM	There is insufficient swap space for the new process.

SEE ALSO
exec(2), exit(2), fork(2), ioctl(2), wait(2)

NOTES
This system call will be eliminated in a future release. System implementation changes are making the efficiency gain of vfork over fork smaller. The memory sharing semantics of vfork can be obtained through other mechanisms.

To avoid a possible deadlock situation, processes that are children in the middle of a `vfork` are never sent `SIGTTOU` or `SIGTTIN` signals; rather, output or `ioctls` are allowed and input attempts result in an EOF indication.

On some systems, the implementation of `vfork` causes the parent to inherit register values from the child. This can create problems for certain optimizing compilers if <unistd.h> is not included in the source calling `vfork`.

wait(2)

NAME
wait – wait for child process to stop or terminate

SYNOPSIS
```
#include <sys/types.h>
#include <sys/wait.h>

pid_t wait(int *stat_loc);
```

DESCRIPTION
wait suspends the calling process until one of its immediate children terminates or until a child that is being traced stops because it has received a signal. The wait system call will return prematurely if a signal is received. If all child processes stopped or terminated prior to the call on wait, return is immediate.

If wait returns because the status of a child process is available, it returns the process ID of the child process. If the calling process had specified a non-zero value for *stat_loc*, the status of the child process will be stored in the location pointed to by *stat_loc*. It may be evaluated with the macros described on wstat(5). In the following, *status* is the object pointed to by *stat_loc*:

> If the child process stopped, the high order 8 bits of *status* will contain the number of the signal that caused the process to stop and the low order 8 bits will be set equal to WSTOPFLG.

> If the child process terminated due to an exit call, the low order 8 bits of *status* will be 0 and the high order 8 bits will contain the low order 8 bits of the argument that the child process passed to exit; see exit(2).

> If the child process terminated due to a signal, the high order 8 bits of *status* will be 0 and the low order 8 bits will contain the number of the signal that caused the termination. In addition, if WCOREFLG is set, a "core image" will have been produced; see signal(2).

If wait returns because the status of a child process is available, then that status may be evaluated with the macros defined by wstat(5).

If a parent process terminates without waiting for its child processes to terminate, the parent process ID of each child process is set to 1. This means the initialization process inherits the child processes; see intro(2).

wait will fail if one or both of the following is true:

ECHILD   The calling process has no existing unwaited-for child processes.

EINTR   The function was interrupted by a signal.

SEE ALSO
exec(2), exit(2), fork(2), intro(2), pause(2), ptrace(2), signal(2), signal(5), wstat(5)

NOTES
See NOTES in signal(2).

If SIGCLD is held, then wait does not recognize death of children.

wait(2)

DIAGNOSTICS

If wait returns due to a stopped or terminated child process, the process ID of the child is returned to the calling process. Otherwise, a value of −1 is returned and errno is set to indicate the error.

waitid(2)

NAME
waitid – wait for child process to change state

SYNOPSIS
```
#include <sys/types.h>
#include <wait.h>

int waitid(idtype_t idtype, id_t id, siginfo_t *infop, int options);
```

DESCRIPTION
waitid suspends the calling process until one of its children changes state. It records the current state of a child in the structure pointed to by *infop*. If a child process changed state prior to the call to waitid, waitid returns immediately.

The *idtype* and *id* arguments specify which children waitid is to wait for.

> If *idtype* is P_PID, waitid waits for the child with a process ID equal to (pid_t) *id*.
>
> If *idtype* is P_PGID, waitid waits for any child with a process group ID equal to (pid_t) *id*.
>
> If *idtype* is P_ALL, waitid waits for any children and *id* is ignored.

The *options* argument is used to specify which state changes *waitid* is to wait for. It is formed by an OR of any of the following flags:

WEXITED	Wait for process(es) to exit.
WTRAPPED	Wait for traced process(es) to become trapped or reach a breakpoint [see ptrace(2)].
WSTOPPED	Wait for and return the process status of any child that has stopped upon receipt of a signal.
WCONTINUED	Return the status for any child that was stopped and has been continued.
WNOHANG	Return immediately.
WNOWAIT	Keep the process in a waitable state.

infop must point to a siginfo_t structure, as defined in siginfo(5). siginfo_t is filled in by the system with the status of the process being waited for.

waitid fails if one or more of the following is true.

EFAULT	*infop* points to an invalid address.
EINTR	waitid was interrupted due to the receipt of a signal by the calling process.
EINVAL	An invalid value was specified for *options*.
EINVAL	*idtype* and *id* specify an invalid set of processes.
ECHILD	The set of processes specified by *idtype* and *id* does not contain any unwaited-for processes.

DIAGNOSTICS

If `waitid` returns due to a change of state of one of its children, a value of 0 is returned. Otherwise, a value of −1 is returned and `errno` is set to indicate the error.

SEE ALSO

intro(2), exec(2), exit(2), fork(2), pause(2), ptrace(2), signal(2), sigaction(2), wait(2), siginfo(5)

waitpid(2) waitpid(2)

NAME
waitpid – wait for child process to change state

SYNOPSIS
    #include <sys/types.h>
    #include <sys/wait.h>

    pid_t waitpid (pid_t pid, int *stat_loc, int options);

DESCRIPTION
waitpid suspends the calling process until one of its children changes state; if a child process changed state prior to the call to waitpid, return is immediate. *pid* specifies a set of child processes for which status is requested.

If *pid* is equal to (pid_t)-1, status is requested for any child process.

If *pid* is greater than (pid_t)0, it specifies the process ID of the child process for which status is requested.

If *pid* is equal to (pid_t)0 status is requested for any child process whose process group ID is equal to that of the calling process.

If *pid* is less than (pid_t)-1, status is requested for any child process whose process group ID is equal to the absolute value of *pid*.

If waitpid returns because the status of a child process is available, then that status may be evaluated with the macros defined by wstat(5). If the calling process had specified a non-zero value of *stat_loc*, the status of the child process will be stored in the location pointed to by *stat_loc*.

The *options* argument is constructed from the bitwise inclusive OR of zero or more of the following flags, defined in the header file sys/wait.h:

WCONTINUED   the status of any continued child process specified by *pid*, whose status has not been reported since it continued, shall also be reported to the calling process.

WNOHANG   waitpid will not suspend execution of the calling process if status is not immediately available for one of the child processes specified by *pid*.

WNOWAIT   keep the process whose status is returned in *stat_loc* in a waitable state. The process may be waited for again with identical results.

WUNTRACED   the status of any child processes specified by *pid* that are stopped, and whose status has not yet been reported since they stopped, shall also be reported to the calling process.

waitpid with *options* equal to WUNTRACED and *pid* equal to (pid_t)-1 is identical to a call to wait(2).

waitpid will fail if one or more of the following is true:

EINTR   waitpid was interrupted due to the receipt of a signal sent by the calling process.

waitpid(2)   waitpid(2)

    EINVAL   An invalid value was specified for *options*.

    ECHILD   The process or process group specified by *pid* does not exist or is not a child of the calling process or can never be in the states specified by *options*.

SEE ALSO
exec(2), exit(2), fork(2), intro(2), pause(2), ptrace(2), signal(2), sigaction(2), siginfo(5), wstat(5)

DIAGNOSTICS
If waitpid returns because the status of a child process is available, this function shall return a value equal to the process ID of the child process for which status is reported. If waitpid returns due to the delivery of a signal to the calling process, a value of −1 shall be returned and errno shall be set to EINTR. If this function was invoked with WNOHANG set in *options*, it has at least one child process specified by *pid* for which status is not available, and status is not available for any process specified by *pid*, a value of 0 shall be returned. Otherwise, a value of −1 shall be returned, and errno shall be set to indicate the error.

NAME
waitsem, nbwaitsem – await and check access to a resource governed by a semaphore

SYNOPSIS
cc [*flag* . . .] *file* . . . -lx

waitsem(int sem_num);

nbwaitsem(int sem_num);

DESCRIPTION
waitsem gives the calling process access to the resource governed by the semaphore *sem_num*. If the resource is in use by another process, waitsem will put the process to sleep until the resource becomes available; nbwaitsem will return the error ENAVAIL. waitsem and nbwaitsem are used in conjunction with sigsem to allow synchronization of processes waiting to access a resource. One or more processes may waitsem on the given semaphore and will be put to sleep until the process which currently has access to the resource issues sigsem. sigsem causes the process which is next in line on the semaphore's queue to be rescheduled for execution. The semaphore's queue is organized in First In, First Out (FIFO) order.

DIAGNOSTICS
waitsem returns the value (*int*) −1 if an error occurs. If *sem_num* has not been previously opened by a call to opensem or creatsem, errno is set to EBADF. If *sem_num* does not refer to a semaphore type file, errno is set to ENOTNAM. All processes waiting (or attempting to wait) on the semaphore return with errno set to ENAVAIL when the process controlling the semaphore exits without relinquishing control (thereby leaving the resource in an undeterminate state). If a process does two waitsems in a row without doing a intervening sigsem, errno is set to EINVAL.

SEE ALSO
opensem(2), creatsem(2)

NAME

write, writev - write on a file

SYNOPSIS

    #include <unistd.h>
    int write(int fildes, const void *buf, unsigned nbyte);

    #include <sys/types.h>
    #include <sys/uio.h>

    int writev(int fildes, const struct iovec *iov, int iovcnt);

DESCRIPTION

write attempts to write *nbyte* bytes from the buffer pointed to by *buf* to the file associated with *fildes*. If *nbyte* is zero and the file is a regular file, write returns zero and has no other results. *fildes* is a file descriptor obtained from a creat, open, dup, fcntl, pipe, or ioctl system call.

writev performs the same action as write, but gathers the output data from the *iovcnt* buffers specified by the members of the *iov* array: *iov*[0], *iov*[1], ..., *iov*[*iovcnt* - 1]. The *iovcnt* is valid if greater than 0 and less than or equal to {IOV_MAX}.

For writev, the iovec structure contains the following members:

          caddr_t   iov_base;
          int   iov_len;

Each iovec entry specifies the base address and length of an area in memory from which data should be written. writev always writes a complete area before proceeding to the next.

On devices capable of seeking, the actual writing of data proceeds from the position in the file indicated by the file pointer. On return from write, the file pointer is incremented by the number of bytes actually written. On a regular file, if the incremented file pointer is greater than the length of the file, the length of the file is set to the new file pointer.

On devices incapable of seeking, writing always takes place starting at the current position. The value of a file pointer associated with such a device is undefined.

If the O_APPEND flag of the file status flags is set, the file pointer is set to the end of the file prior to each write.

For regular files, if the O_SYNC flag of the file status flags is set, write does not return until both the file data and file status have been physically updated. This function is for special applications that require extra reliability at the cost of performance. For block special files, if O_SYNC is set, write does not return until the data has been physically updated.

A write to a regular file is blocked if mandatory file/record locking is set [see chmod(2)], and there is a record lock owned by another process on the segment of the file to be written:

If O_NDELAY or O_NONBLOCK is set, write returns −1 and sets errno to EAGAIN.

If O_NDELAY and O_NONBLOCK are clear, write sleeps until all blocking locks are removed or the write is terminated by a signal.

If a write requests that more bytes be written than there is room for—for example, if the write would exceed the process file size limit [see getrlimit(2) and ulimit(2)], the system file size limit, or the free space on the device—only as many bytes as there is room for will be written. For example, suppose there is space for 20 bytes more in a file before reaching a limit. A write of 512-bytes returns 20. The next write of a non-zero number of bytes gives a failure return (except as noted for pipes and FIFO below).

Write requests to a pipe or FIFO are handled the same as a regular file with the following exceptions:

There is no file offset associated with a pipe, hence each write request appends to the end of the pipe.

Write requests of {PIPE_BUF} bytes or less are guaranteed not to be interleaved with data from other processes doing writes on the same pipe. Writes of greater than {PIPE_BUF} bytes may have data interleaved, on arbitrary boundaries, with writes by other processes, whether or not the O_NONBLOCK or O_NDELAY flags are set.

If O_NONBLOCK and O_NDELAY are clear, a write request may cause the process to block, but on normal completion it returns *nbyte*.

If O_NONBLOCK is set, write requests are handled in the following way: the write does not block the process; write requests for {PIPE_BUF} or fewer bytes either succeed completely and return *nbyte*, or return −1 and set errno to EAGAIN. A write request for greater than {PIPE_BUF} bytes either transfers what it can and returns the number of bytes written, or transfers no data and returns −1 with errno set to EAGAIN. Also, if a request is greater than {PIPE_BUF} bytes and all data previously written to the pipe has been read, write transfers at least {PIPE_BUF} bytes.

If O_NDELAY is set, write requests are handled in the following way: the write does not block the process; write requests for {PIPE_BUF} or fewer bytes either succeed completely and return *nbyte*, or return 0. A write request for greater than {PIPE_BUF} bytes either transfers what it can and returns the number of bytes written, or transfers no data and returns 0. Also, if a request is greater than {PIPE_BUF} bytes and all data previously written to the pipe has been read, write transfers at least {PIPE_BUF} bytes.

When attempting to write to a file descriptor (other than a pipe or FIFO) that supports nonblocking writes and cannot accept the data immediately:

If O_NONBLOCK and O_NDELAY are clear, write blocks until the data can be accepted.

If O_NONBLOCK or O_NDELAY is set, write does not block the process. If some data can be written without blocking the process, write writes what it can and returns the number of bytes written. Otherwise, if O_NONBLOCK is set, it returns −1 and sets errno to EAGAIN or if O_NDELAY is set, it returns 0.

For STREAMS files [see intro(2)], the operation of write is determined by the values of the minimum and maximum *nbyte* range ("packet size") accepted by the stream. These values are contained in the topmost stream module. Unless the user pushes the topmost module [see I_PUSH in streamio(7)], these values can not be set or tested from user level. If *nbyte* falls within the packet size range, *nbyte* bytes are written. If *nbyte* does not fall within the range and the minimum packet size value is zero, write breaks the buffer into maximum packet size segments prior to sending the data downstream (the last segment may be smaller than the maximum packet size). If *nbyte* does not fall within the range and the minimum value is non-zero, write fails and sets errno to ERANGE. Writing a zero-length buffer (*nbyte* is zero) to a STREAMS device sends a zero length message with zero returned. However, writing a zero-length buffer to a pipe or FIFO sends no message and zero is returned. The user program may issue the I_SWROPT ioctl(2) to enable zero-length messages to be sent across the pipe or FIFO [see streamio(7)].

When writing to a stream, data messages are created with a priority band of zero. When writing to a stream that is not a pipe or FIFO:

If O_NDELAY and O_NONBLOCK are not set, and the stream cannot accept data (the stream write queue is full due to internal flow control conditions), write blocks until data can be accepted.

If O_NDELAY or O_NONBLOCK is set and the stream cannot accept data, write returns −1 and sets errno to EAGAIN.

If O_NDELAY or O_NONBLOCK is set and part of the buffer has already been written when a condition occurs in which the stream cannot accept additional data, write terminates and returns the number of bytes written.

write and writev fail and the file pointer remains unchanged if one or more of the following are true:

EAGAIN	Mandatory file/record locking is set, O_NDELAY or O_NONBLOCK is set, and there is a blocking record lock.
EAGAIN	Total amount of system memory available when reading via raw I/O is temporarily insufficient.
EAGAIN	An attempt is made to write to a stream that can not accept data with the O_NDELAY or O_NONBLOCK flag set.
EAGAIN	If a write to a pipe or FIFO of {PIPE_BUF} bytes or less is requested and less than *nbytes* of free space is available.
EBADF	*fildes* is not a valid file descriptor open for writing.

EDEADLK	The write was going to go to sleep and cause a deadlock situation to occur.
EFAULT	*buf* points outside the process's allocated address space.
EFBIG	An attempt is made to write a file that exceeds the process's file size limit or the maximum file size [see getrlimit(2) and ulimit(2)].
EINTR	A signal was caught during the write system call.
EINVAL	An attempt is made to write to a stream linked below a multiplexor.
EIO	The process is in the background and is attempting to write to its controlling terminal whose TOSTOP flag is set; the process is neither ignoring nor blocking SIGTTOU signals, and the process group of the process is orphaned.
ENOLCK	The system record lock table was full, so the write could not go to sleep until the blocking record lock was removed.
ENOLINK	*fildes* is on a remote machine and the link to that machine is no longer active.
ENOSR	An attempt is made to write to a stream with insufficient STREAMS memory resources available in the system.
ENOSPC	During a write to an ordinary file, there is no free space left on the device.
ENXIO	A hangup occurred on the stream being written to.
EPIPE and SIGPIPE signal	An attempt is made to write to a pipe that is not open for reading by any process.
EPIPE	An attempt is made to write to a FIFO that is not open for reading by any process.
EPIPE	An attempt is made to write to a pipe that has only one end open.
ERANGE	An attempt is made to write to a stream with *nbyte* outside specified minimum and maximum write range, and the minimum value is non-zero.
ENOLCK	Enforced record locking was enabled and {LOCK_MAX} regions are already locked in the system.

In addition, writev may return one of the following errors:

EINVAL	*iovcnt* was less than or equal to 0, or greater than 16.
EINVAL	One of the iov_len values in the *iov* array was negative.
EINVAL	The sum of the iov_len values in the *iov* array overflowed a 32-bit integer.

A `write` to a STREAMS file can fail if an error message has been received at the stream head. In this case, `errno` is set to the value included in the error message.

Upon successful completion `write` and `writev` mark for update the `st_ctime` and `st_mtime` fields of the file.

SEE ALSO

intro(2), creat(2), dup(2), fcntl(2), getrlimit(2), lseek(2), open(2), pipe(2), ulimit(2)

DIAGNOSTICS

On success, `write` returns the number of bytes actually written. Otherwise, it returns −1 and sets `errno` to indicate the error.

Section 3 – Library Functions

intro(3)	introduction to functions and libraries
a64l, l64a(3C)	convert between long integer and base-64 ASCII string
abort(3C)	generate an abnormal termination signal
abs, labs(3C)	return integer absolute value
accept(3N)	accept a connection on a socket
addseverity(3C)	build a list of severity levels for an application for use with fmtmsg
alloca(3)	memory allocator
assert(3X)	verify program assertion
atexit(3C)	add program termination routine
basename(3G)	return the last element of a path name
bessel: j0, j1, jn, y0, y1, yn(3M)	Bessel functions
bgets(3G)	read stream up to next delimiter
bind(3N)	bind a name to a socket
bsearch(3C)	binary search a sorted table
bstring: bcopy, bcmp, bzero, ffs(3)	bit and byte string operations
bufsplit(3G)	split buffer into fields
byteorder, htonl, htons, ntohl, ntohs(3N)	convert values between host and network byte order
catgets(3C)	read a program message
catopen, catclose(3C)	open/close a message catalog
clock(3C)	report CPU time used
connect(3N)	initiate a connection on a socket
conv: toupper, tolower, _toupper, _tolower, toascii(3C)	translate characters
copylist(3G)	copy a file into memory
crypt, setkey, encrypt(3C)	generate encryption
crypt(3X)	password and file encryption functions
ctermid(3S)	generate file name for terminal
ctime, localtime, gmtime, asctime, tzset(3C)	convert date and time to string
ctype: isdigit, isxdigit, islower, isupper, isalpha, isalnum, isspace, iscntrl, ispunct, isprint, isgraph, isascii(3C)	character handling
curs_addch: addch, waddch, mvaddch, mvwaddch, echochar, wechochar(3X)	add a character (with attributes) to a curses window and advance cursor
curs_addchstr: addchstr, addchnstr, waddchstr, waddchnstr, mvaddchstr, mvaddchnstr, mvwaddchstr, mvwaddchnstr(3X)	add string of characters (and attributes) to a curses window
curs_addstr: addstr, addnstr, waddstr, waddnstr, mvaddstr, mvaddnstr, mvwaddstr, mvwaddnstr(3X)	add a string of characters to a curses window and advance cursor

Section 3 – Library Functions

curs_attr: attroff, wattroff, attron, wattron, attrset, wattrset, standend, wstandend,
    standout, wstandout(3X) .... curses character and window attribute control routines
curs_beep: beep, flash(3X) .... curses bell and screen flash routines
curs_bkgd: bkgdset, wbkgdset, bkgd, wbkgd(3X)
    .... curses window background manipulation routines
curs_border: border, wborder, box, hline, whline, vline, wvline(3X)
    .... create curses borders, horizontal and vertical lines
curs_clear: erase, werase, clear, wclear, clrtobot, wclrtobot, clrtoeol, wclrtoeol(3X)
    .... clear all or part of a curses window
curs_color: start_color, init_pair, init_color, has_colors, can_change_color,
    color_content, pair_content(3X) .... curses color manipulation routines
curs_delch: delch, wdelch, mvdelch, mvwdelch(3X)
    .... delete character under cursor in a curses window
curs_deleteln: deleteln, wdeleteln, insdelln, winsdelln, insertln, winsertln(3X)
    .... delete and insert lines in a curses window
curs_getch: getch, wgetch, mvgetch, mvwgetch, ungetch(3X)
    .... get (or push back) characters from curses terminal keyboard
curs_getstr: getstr, wgetstr, mvgetstr, mvwgetstr, wgetnstr(3X)
    .... get character strings from curses terminal keyboard
curs_getyx: getyx, getparyx, getbegyx, getmaxyx(3X)
    .... get curses cursor and window coordinates
curs_inch: inch, winch, mvinch, mvwinch(3X)
    .... get a character and its attributes from a curses window
curs_inchstr: inchstr, inchnstr, winchstr, winchnstr, mvinchstr, mvinchnstr,
    mvwinchstr, mvwinchnstr(3X)
    .... get a string of characters (and attributes) from a curses window
curs_initscr: initscr, newterm, endwin, isendwin, set_term, delscreen(3X)
    .... curses screen initialization and manipulation routines
curs_inopts: cbreak, nocbreak, echo, noecho, halfdelay, intrflush, keypad, meta,
    nodelay, notimeout, raw, noraw, noqiflush, qiflush, timeout, wtimeout,
    typeahead(3X) .... curses terminal input option control routines
curs_insch: insch, winsch, mvinsch, mvwinsch(3X)
    .... insert a character before the character under the cursor in a curses window
curs_instr: insstr, insnstr, winsstr, winsnstr, mvinsstr, mvinsnstr, mvwinsstr,
    mvwinsnstr(3X) .... insert string before character under the cursor in a curses window
curs_instr: instr, innstr, winstr, winnstr, mvinstr, mvinnstr, mvwinstr,
    mvwinnstr(3X) .... get a string of characters from a curses window
curs_kernel: def_prog_mode, def_shell_mode, reset_prog_mode, reset_shell_mode,
    resetty, savetty, getsyx, setsyx, ripoffline, curs_set, napms(3X)
    .... low-level curses routines

Section 3 – Library Functions

curs_move: move, wmove(3X) .... move curses window cursor
curs_outopts: clearok, idlok, idcok immedok, leaveok, setscrreg, wsetscrreg,
    scrollok, nl, nonl(3X) .... curses terminal output option control routines
curs_overlay: overlay, overwrite, copywin(3X)
    .... overlap and manipulate overlapped curses windows
curs_pad: newpad, subpad, prefresh, pnoutrefresh, pechochar(3X)
    .... create and display curses pads
curs_printw: printw, wprintw, mvprintw, mvwprintw, vwprintw(3X)
    .... print formatted output in curses windows
curs_refresh: refresh, wrefresh, wnoutrefresh, doupdate, redrawwin,
    wredrawln(3X) .... refresh curses windows and lines
curs_scanw: scanw, wscanw, mvscanw, mvwscanw, vwscanw(3X)
    .... convert formatted input from a curses widow
curs_scr_dump: scr_dump, scr_restore, scr_init, scr_set(3X)
    .... read (write) a curses screen from (to) a file
curs_scroll: scroll, srcl, wscrl(3X) .... scroll a curses window
curs_slk: slk_init, slk_set, slk_refresh, slk_noutrefresh, slk_label, slk_clear,
    slk_restore, slk_touch, slk_attron, slk_attrset, slk_attroff(3X)
    .... curses soft label routines
curs_termattrs: baudrate, erasechar, has_ic, has_il, killchar, longname, termattrs,
    termname(3X) .... curses environment query routines
curs_termcap: tgetent, tgetflag, tgetnum, tgetstr, tgoto, tputs(3X)
    .... curses interfaces (emulated) to the termcap library
curs_terminfo: setupterm, setterm, set_curterm, del_curterm, restartterm, tparm,
    tputs, putp, vidputs, vidattr, mvcur, tigetflag, tigetnum, tigetstr(3X)
    .... curses interfaces to terminfo database
curs_touch: touchwin, touchline, untouchwin, wtouchln, is_linetouched,
    is_wintouched(3X) .... curses refresh control routines
curs_util: unctrl, keyname, filter, use_env, putwin, getwin, delay_output,
    flushinp(3X) .... miscellaneous curses utility routines
curs_window: newwin, delwin, mvwin, subwin, derwin, mvderwin, dupwin,
    wsyncup, syncok, wcursyncup, wsyncdown(3X) .... create curses windows
curses(3X) .... CRT screen handling and optimization package
cuserid(3S) .... get character login name of the user
dbm: dbminit, dbmclose, fetch, store, delete, firstkey, nextkey(3) .... data base subroutines
decimal_to_floating: decimal_to_single, decimal_to_double, decimal_to_extended(3)
    .... convert decimal record to floating-point value
dial(3C) .... establish an outgoing terminal line connection
difftime(3C) .... computes the difference between two calendar times
directory: opendir, readdir, telldir, seekdir, rewinddir, closedir(3C) .... directory operations

Section 3 – Library Functions

directory: opendir, readdir, telldir, seekdir, rewinddir, closedir(3C) .... directory operations
dirname(3G) .... report the parent directory name of a file path name
div, ldiv(3C) .... compute the quotient and remainder
dlclose(3X) .... close a shared object
dlerror(3X) .... get diagnostic information
dlopen(3X) .... open a shared object
dlsym(3X) .... get the address of a symbol in shared object
doconfig(3N) .... execute a configuration script
drand48, erand48, lrand48, nrand48, mrand48, jrand48, srand48, seed48,
    lcong48(3C) .... generate uniformly distributed pseudo-random numbers
dup2(3C) .... duplicate an open file descriptor
econvert, fconvert, gconvert, seconvert, sfconvert, sgconvert(3) .... output conversion
ecvt, ecvtl, fcvt, fcvtl, gcvt, gcvtl(3C) .... convert floating-point number to string
elf(3E) .... object file access library
elf_begin(3E) .... make a file descriptor
elf_cntl(3E) .... control a file descriptor
elf_end(3E) .... finish using an object file
elf_errmsg, elf_errno(3E) .... error handling
elf_fill(3E) .... set fill byte
elf_flagdata, elf_flagehdr, elf_flagelf, elf_flagphdr, elf_flagscn, elf_flagshdr(3E)
    .... manipulate flags
elf_fsize: elf32_fsize(3E) .... return the size of an object file type
elf_getarhdr(3E) .... retrieve archive member header
elf_getarsym(3E) .... retrieve archive symbol table
elf_getbase(3E) .... get the base offset for an object file
elf_getdata, elf_newdata, elf_rawdata(3E) .... get section data
elf_getehdr: elf32_getehdr, elf32_newehdr(3E) .... retrieve class-dependent object file header
elf_getident(3E) .... retrieve file identification data
elf_getphdr: elf32_getphdr, elf32_newphdr(3E)
    .... retrieve class-dependent program header table
elf_getscn, elf_ndxscn, elf_newscn, elf_nextscn(3E) .... get section information
elf_getshdr: elf32_getshdr(3E) .... retrieve class-dependent section header
elf_hash(3E) .... compute hash value
elf_kind(3E) .... determine file type
elf_next(3E) .... sequential archive member access
elf_rand(3E) .... random archive member access
elf_rawfile(3E) .... retrieve uninterpreted file contents
elf_strptr(3E) .... make a string pointer
elf_update(3E) .... update an ELF descriptor
elf_version(3E) .... coordinate ELF library and application versions

Section 3 – Library Functions

elf_xlate: elf32_xlatetof, elf32_xlatetom (3E) .... class-dependent data translation
end, etext, edata (3C) .... last locations in program
erf, erfc (3M) .... error function and complementary error function
ethers (3N) .... Ethernet address mapping operations
exp, expf, cbrt, log, logf, log10, log10f, pow, powf, sqrt, sqrtf (3M)
.... exponential, logarithm, power, square root functions
fattach (3C)
.... attach a STREAMS-based file descriptor to an object in the file system name space
fclose, fflush (3S) .... close or flush a stream
fdetach (3C) .... detach a name from a STREAMS-based file descriptor
ferror, feof, clearerr, fileno (3S) .... stream status inquiries
ffs (3C) .... find first set bit
floatingpoint (3) .... IEEE floating point definitions
floor, floorf, ceil, ceilf, copysign, fmod, fmodf, fabs, fabsf, rint, remainder (3M)
.... floor, ceiling, remainder, absolute value functions
floating_to_decimal: single_to_decimal, double_to_decimal, extended_to_decimal (3)
.... convert floating-point value to decimal record
fmtmsg (3C) .... display a message on stderr or system console
fopen, freopen, fdopen (3S) .... open a stream
fopen, freopen, fdopen (3S) .... open a stream
form_cursor: pos_form_cursor (3X) .... position forms window cursor
form_data: data_ahead, data_behind (3X)
.... tell if forms field has off-screen data ahead or behind
form_driver (3X) .... command processor for the forms subsystem
form_field: set_form_fields, form_fields, field_count, move_field (3X) .. connect fields to forms
form_field_attributes: set_field_fore, field_fore, set_field_back, field_back,
        set_field_pad, field_pad (3X) .... format the general display attributes of forms
form_field_buffer: set_field_buffer, field_buffer, set_field_status, field_status,
        set_max_field (3X) .... set and get forms field attributes
form_field_info: field_info, dynamic_field_info (3X) .... get forms field characteristics
form_field_just: set_field_just, field_just (3X) .... format the general appearance of forms
form_field_new: new_field, dup_field, link_field, free_field, (3X)
.... create and destroy forms fields
form_field_opts: set_field_opts, field_opts_on, field_opts_off, field_opts (3X)
.... forms field option routines
form_field_userptr: set_field_userptr, field_userptr (3X)
.... associate application data with forms
form_field_validation: set_field_type, field_type, field_arg (3X)
.... forms field data type validation

Section 3 – Library Functions

form_fieldtype: new_fieldtype, free_fieldtype, set_fieldtype_arg,
    set_fieldtype_choice, link_fieldtype(3X) .... forms fieldtype routines
form_hook: set_form_init, form_init, set_form_term, form_term, set_field_init,
    field_init, set_field_term, field_term(3X)
    .... assign application-specific routines for invocation by forms
form_new: new_form, free_form(3X) .... create and destroy forms
form_new_page: set_new_page, new_page(3X) .... forms pagination
form_opts: set_form_opts, form_opts_on, form_opts_off, form_opts(3X)
    .... forms option routines
form_page: set_form_page, form_page, set_current_field, current_field,
    field_index(3X) .... set forms current page and field
form_post: post_form, unpost_form(3X) .... write or erase forms from associated subwindows
form_userptr: set_form_userptr, form_userptr(3X) .... associate application data with forms
form_win: set_form_win, form_win, set_form_sub, form_sub, scale_form(3X)
    .... forms window and subwindow association routines
forms(3X) .... character based forms package
fpgetround, fpsetround, fpgetmask, fpsetmask, fpgetsticky, fpsetsticky(3C)
    .... IEEE floating-point environment control
fread, fwrite(3S) .... binary input/output
frexp, frexpl, ldexp, ldexpl, logb, modf, modff, modfl, nextafter, scalb, scalbl(3C)
    .... manipulate parts of floating-point numbers
fseek, rewind, ftell(3S) .... reposition a file pointer in a stream
fsetpos, fgetpos(3C) .... reposition a file pointer in a stream
ftime(3C) .... get date and time
ftw, nftw(3C) .... walk a file tree
gamma, lgamma(3M) .... log gamma function
getc, getchar, fgetc, getw(3S) .... get character or word from a stream
getcwd(3C) .... get pathname of current working directory
getdate(3C) .... convert user format date and time
getdtablesize(3) .... get descriptor table size
getenv(3C) .... return value for environment name
getgrent, getgrgid, getgrnam, setgrent, endgrent, fgetgrent(3C) .... get group file entry
gethostent, gethostbyaddr, gethostbyname, sethostent, endhostent(3N)
    .... get network host entry
gethostid(3) .... get unique identifier of current host
gethostname, sethostname(3) .... get/set name of current host
getitimer, setitimer(3C) .... get/set value of interval timer
getlogin(3C) .... get login name
getmntent, getmntany(3C) .... get mnttab file entry
getnetconfig(3N) .... get network configuration database entry

Section 3 – Library Functions

getnetent, getnetbyaddr, getnetbyname, setnetent, endnetent(3N) .... get network entry
getnetpath(3N) .... get netconfig entry corresponding to NETPATH component
getopt(3C) .... get option letter from argument vector
getpagesize(3) .... get system page size
getpass(3C) .... read a password
getpeername(3N) .... get name of connected peer
getpriority, setpriority(3) .... get/set program scheduling priority
getprotoent, getprotobynumber, getprotobyname, setprotoent, endprotoent(3N)
 .... get protocol entry
getpw(3C) .... get name from UID
getpwent, getpwuid, getpwnam, setpwent, endpwent, fgetpwent(3C)
 .... manipulate password file entry
getrusage(3) .... get information about resource utilization
gets, fgets(3S) .... get a string from a stream
getservent, getservbyport, getservbyname, setservent, endservent(3N) .... get service entry
getsockname(3N) .... get socket name
getsockopt, setsockopt(3N) .... get and set options on sockets
getspent, getspnam, setspent, endspent, fgetspent, lckpwdf, ulckpwdf(3C)
 .... manipulate shadow password file entry
getsubopt(3C) .... parse suboptions from a string
gettimeofday, settimeofday(3C) .... get or set the date and time
gettimeofday, settimeofday(3) .... get or set the date and time
gettxt(3C) .... retrieve a text string
getusershell, setusershell, endusershell(3) .... get legal user shells
getut: getutent, getutid, getutline, pututline, setutent, endutent, utmpname(3C)
 .... access utmp file entry
getutx: getutxent, getutxid, getutxline, pututxline, setutxent, endutxent,
 utmpxname, getutmp, getutmpx, updwtmp, updwtmpx(3C) .... access utmpx file entry
getvfsent, getvfsfile, getvfsspec, getvfsany(3C) .... get vfstab file entry
getwd(3) .... get current working directory pathname
gmatch(3G) .... shell global pattern matching
grantpt(3C) .... grant access to the slave pseudo-terminal device
hsearch, hcreate, hdestroy(3C) .... manage hash search tables
hypot(3M) .... Euclidean distance function
ieee_functions, fp_class, isnan, copysign, scalbn(3M)
 .... miscellaneous functions for IEEE arithmetic
ieee_handler(3M) .... IEEE exception trap handler function
index, rindex(3) .... string operations

Section 3 – Library Functions

inet: inet_addr, inet_network, inet_makeaddr, inet_lnaof, inet_netof, inet_ntoa(3N)
.... Internet address manipulation
initgroups(3C) .... initialize the supplementary group access list
insque, remque(3C) .... insert/remove element from a queue
isastream(3C) .... test a file descriptor
isencrypt(3G) .... determine whether a character buffer is encrypted
isnan, isnand, isnanf, isnanl, finite, finitel, fpclass, fpclassl, unordered,
    unorderedl(3C) .... determine type of floating-point number
killpg(3) .... send signal to a process group
l3tol, ltol3(3C) .... convert between 3-byte integers and long integers
libwindows(3X) .... windowing terminal function library
listen(3N) .... listen for connections on a socket
localeconv(3C) .... get numeric formatting information
lockf(3C) .... record locking on files
lsearch, lfind(3C) .... linear search and update
maillock(3X) .... manage lockfile for user's mailbox
makecontext, swapcontext(3C) .... manipulate user contexts
makedev, major, minor(3C) .... manage a device number
malloc, free, realloc, calloc, memalign, valloc,(3C) .... memory allocator
malloc, free, realloc, calloc, mallopt, mallinfo(3X) .... memory allocator
matherr(3M) .... error-handling function
mbchar: mbtowc, mblen, wctomb(3C) .... multibyte character handling
mbstring: mbstowcs, wcstombs(3C) .... multibyte string functions
mctl(3) .... memory management control
memory: memccpy, memchr, memcmp, memcpy, memmove, memset(3C)
.... memory operations
menu_attributes: set_menu_fore, menu_fore, set_menu_back, menu_back,
    set_menu_grey, menu_grey, set_menu_pad, menu_pad(3X)
.... control menus display attributes
menu_cursor: pos_menu_cursor(3X) .... correctly position a menus cursor
menu_driver(3X) .... command processor for the menus subsystem
menu_format: set_menu_format, menu_format(3X)
.... set and get maximum numbers of rows and columns in menus
menu_hook: set_item_init, item_init, set_item_term, item_term, set_menu_init,
    menu_init, set_menu_term, menu_term(3X)
.... assign application-specific routines for automatic invocation by menus
menu_item_current: set_current_item, current_item, set_top_row, top_row,
    item_index(3X) .... set and get current menus items
menu_item_name: item_name, item_description(3X) .... get menus item name and description
menu_item_new: new_item, free_item(3X) .... create and destroy menus items

menu_item_opts: set_item_opts, item_opts_on, item_opts_off, item_opts(3X)
.... menus item option routines
menu_item_userptr: set_item_userptr, item_userptr(3X)
.... associate application data with menus items
menu_item_value: set_item_value, item_value(3X) .... set and get menus item values
menu_item_visible: item_visible(3X) .... tell if menus item is visible
menu_items: set_menu_items, menu_items, item_count(3X)
.... connect and disconnect items to and from menus
menu_mark: set_menu_mark, menu_mark(3X) .... menus mark string routines
menu_new: new_menu, free_menu(3X) .... create and destroy menus
menu_opts: set_menu_opts, menu_opts_on, menu_opts_off, menu_opts(3X)
.... menus option routines
menu_pattern: set_menu_pattern, menu_pattern(3X)
.... set and get menus pattern match buffer
menu_post: post_menu, unpost_menu(3X)
.... write or erase menus from associated subwindows
menu_userptr: set_menu_userptr, menu_userptr(3X) ... associate application data with menus
menu_win: set_menu_win, menu_win, set_menu_sub, menu_sub, scale_menu(3X)
.... menus window and subwindow association routines
menus(3X) .... character based menus package
mkdirp, rmdirp(3G) .... create, remove directories in a path
mkfifo(3C) .... create a new FIFO
mkstemp(3) .... make a unique file name
mktemp(3C) .... make a unique file name
mktime(3C) .... converts a tm structure to a calendar time
mlock, munlock(3C) .... lock (or unlock) pages in memory
mlockall, munlockall(3C) .... lock or unlock address space
monitor(3C) .... prepare execution profile
mp: madd, msub, mult, mdiv, mcmp, min, mout, pow, gcd, rpow, msqrt, sdiv,
    itom, xtom, mtox, mfree(3X) .... multiple precision integer arithmetic
msync(3C) .... synchronize memory with physical storage
ndbm: dbm_clearerr, dbm_close, dbm_delete, dbm_error, dbm_fetch, dbm_firstkey,
    dbm_nextkey, dbm_open, dbm_store(3) .... data base subroutines
netdir_getbyname, netdir_getbyaddr, netdir_free, netdir_mergeaddr, taddr2uaddr,
    uaddr2taddr, netdir_perror, netdir_sperror(3N)
.... generic transport name-to-address translation
nice(3C) .... change priority of a process
nl_langinfo(3C) .... language information
nlist(3E) .... get entries from name list
nlist(3) .... get entries from symbol table

Section 3 – Library Functions

nlsgetcall(3N) .... get client's data passed via the listener
nlsprovider(3N) .... get name of transport provider
nlsrequest(3N) .... format and send listener service request message
offsetof(3C) .... offset of structure member
p2open, p2close(3G) .... open, close pipes to and from a command
panel_above: panel_above, panel_below(3X) .... panels deck traversal primitives
panel_move: move_panel(3X) .... move a panels window on the virtual screen
panel_new: new_panel, del_panel(3X) .... create and destroy panels
panel_show: show_panel, hide_panel, panel_hidden(3X) .. panels deck manipulation routines
panel_top: top_panel, bottom_panel(3X) .... panels deck manipulation routines
panel_update: update_panels(3X) .... panels virtual screen refresh routine
panel_userptr: set_panel_userptr, panel_userptr(3X)
.... associate application data with a panels panel
panel_window: panel_window, replace_panel(3X)
.... get or set the current window of a panels panel
panels(3X) .... character based panels package
pathfind(3G) .... search for named file in named directories
perror(3C) .... print system error messages
popen, pclose(3S) .... initiate pipe to/from a process
printf, fprintf, sprintf(3S) .... print formatted output
printf, fprintf, sprintf, vprintf, vfprintf, vsprintf(3S) .... formatted output conversion
psignal, psiginfo(3C) .... system signal messages
psignal, sys_siglist(3) .... system signal messages
ptsname(3C) .... get name of the slave pseudo-terminal device
publickey: getpublickey, getsecretkey(3N) .... retrieve public or secret key
putc, putchar, fputc, putw(3S) .... put character or word on a stream
putenv(3C) .... change or add value to environment
putpwent(3C) .... write password file entry
puts, fputs(3S) .... put a string on a stream
putspent(3C) .... write shadow password file entry
qsort(3C) .... quicker sort
raise(3C) .... send signal to program
rand, srand(3C) .... simple random-number generator
rand, srand(3C) .... simple random number generator
random, srandom, initstate, setstate(3)
.... better random number generator; routines for changing generators
realpath(3C) .... returns the real file name
reboot(3) .... reboot system or halt processor
recv, recvfrom, recvmsg(3N) .... receive a message from a socket
regcmp, regex(3G) .... compile and execute regular expression

10 Programmer's Reference Manual: Operating System API

regex, re_comp, re_exec(3) .... regular expression handler
regexpr: compile, step, advance(3G) .... regular expression compile and match routines
remove(3C) .... remove file
resolver, res_mkquery, res_send, res_init, dn_comp, dn_expand(3N) .... resolver routines
rexec(3N) .... return stream to a remote command
rpc(3N) .... library routines for remote procedure calls
rpc_clnt_auth: auth_destroy, authnone_create, authsys_create,
    authsys_create_default(3N)
    .... library routines for client side remote procedure call authentication
rpc_clnt_calls: clnt_call, clnt_freeres, clnt_geterr, clnt_perrno, clnt_perror,
    clnt_sperrno, clnt_sperror, rpc_broadcast, rpc_call(3N)
    .... library routines for client side calls
rpc_clnt_create: clnt_control, clnt_create, clnt_destroy, clnt_dg_create,
    clnt_pcreateerror, clnt_raw_create, clnt_spcreateerror, clnt_tli_create,
    clnt_tp_create, clnt_vc_create(3N)
    .... library routines for dealing with creation and manipulation of CLIENT handles
rpc_svc_calls: rpc_reg, svc_reg, svc_unreg, xprt_register, xprt_unregister(3N)
    .... library routines for registering servers
rpc_svc_create: svc_create, svc_destroy, svc_dg_create, svc_fd_create,
    svc_raw_create, svc_tli_create, svc_tp_create, svc_vc_create(3N)
    .... library routines for dealing with the creation of server handles
rpc_svc_err: svcerr_auth, svcerr_decode, svcerr_noproc, svcerr_noprog,
    svcerr_progvers, svcerr_systemerr, svcerr_weakauth(3N)
    .... library routines for server side remote procedure call errors
rpc_svc_reg: svc_freeargs, svc_getargs, svc_getreqset, svc_getrpccaller, svc_run,
    svc_sendreply(3N) .... library routines for RPC servers
rpc_xdr: xdr_accepted_reply, xdr_authsys_parms, xdr_callhdr, xdr_callmsg,
    xdr_opaque_auth, xdr_rejected_reply, xdr_replymsg(3N)
    .... XDR library routines for remote procedure calls
rpcbind: rpcb_getmaps, rpcb_getaddr, rpcb_gettime, rpcb_rmtcall, rpcb_set,
    rpcb_unset(3N) .... library routines for RPC bind service
rusers(3N) .... return information about users on remote machines
rwall(3N) .... write to specified remote machines
scandir, alphasort(3) .... scan a directory
scanf, fscanf, sscanf(3S) .... convert formatted input
secure_rpc: authdes_seccreate, authdes_getucred, getnetname, host2netname,
    key_decryptsession, key_encryptsession, key_gendes, key_setsecret,
    netname2host, netname2user, user2netname(3N)
    .... library routines for secure remote procedure calls
select(3C) .... synchronous I/O multiplexing

Section 3 – Library Functions

send, sendto, sendmsg(3N) .... send a message from a socket
setbuf, setvbuf(3S) .... assign buffering to a stream
setbuf, setbuffer, setlinebuf, setvbuf(3S) .... assign buffering to a stream
setbuffer, setlinebuf(3S) .... assign buffering to a stream
setjmp, longjmp(3C) .... non-local goto
setjmp, longjmp, _setjmp, _longjmp, sigsetjmp, siglongjmp(3) .... non-local goto
setlocale(3C) .... modify and query a program's locale
setregid(3) .... set real and effective group IDs
setreuid(3) .... set real and effective user IDs
shutdown(3N) .... shut down part of a full-duplex connection
sigblock, sigmask(3) .... block signals
sigfpe(3) .... signal handling for specific SIGFPE codes
siginterrupt(3) .... allow signals to interrupt system calls
signal(3) .... simplified software signal facilities
sigpause(3) .... automically release blocked signals and wait for interrupt
sigsetjmp, siglongjmp(3C) .... a non-local goto with signal state
sigsetmask(3) .... set current signal mask
sigemptyset, sigfillset, sigaddset, sigdelset, sigismember(3C) .... manipulate sets of signals
sigstack(3) .... set and/or get signal stack context
sigvec(3) .... software signal facilities
sinh, sinhf, cosh, coshf, tanh, tanhf, asinh, acosh, atanh(3M) .... hyperbolic functions
sleep(3C) .... suspend execution for interval
sleep(3) .... suspend execution for interval
socket(3N) .... create an endpoint for communication
socketpair(3N) .... create a pair of connected sockets
spray(3N) .... scatter data in order to check the network
sputl, sgetl(3X) .... access long integer data in a machine-independent fashion
ssignal, gsignal(3C) .... software signals
stdio(3S) .... standard buffered input/output package
stdipc: ftok(3C) .... standard interprocess communication package
str: strfind, strrspn, strtrns(3G) .... string manipulations
strccpy: streadd, strcadd, strecpy(3G) .. copy strings, compressing or expanding escape codes
strcoll(3C) .... string collation
strerror(3C) .... get error message string
strftime, cftime, ascftime(3C) .... convert date and time to string
string: strcat, strdup, strncat, strcmp, strncmp, strcpy, strncpy, strlen, strchr,
 strrchr, strpbrk, strspn, strcspn, strtok, strstr(3C) .... string operations
string: strcasecmp, strncasecmp(3) .... string operations
strtod, strtold, atof(3C) .... convert string to double-precision number
strtol, strtoul, atol, atoi(3C) .... convert string to integer

12 Programmer's Reference Manual: Operating System API

strxfrm (3C)	string transformation
swab (3C)	swap bytes
syscall (3)	indirect system call
sysconf (3C)	retrieves configurable system variables
sysconf (3C)	retrieves configurable system variables
syslog, openlog, closelog, setlogmask (3)	control system log
system (3S)	issue a shell command
t_accept (3N)	accept a connect request
t_alloc (3N)	allocate a library structure
t_bind (3N)	bind an address to a transport endpoint
t_close (3N)	close a transport endpoint
t_connect (3N)	establish a connection with another transport user
t_error (3N)	produce error message
t_free (3N)	free a library structure
t_getinfo (3N)	get protocol-specific service information
t_getstate (3N)	get the current state
t_listen (3N)	listen for a connect request
t_look (3N)	look at the current event on a transport endpoint
t_open (3N)	establish a transport endpoint
t_optmgmt (3N)	manage options for a transport endpoint
t_rcv (3N)	receive data or expedited data sent over a connection
t_rcvconnect (3N)	receive the confirmation from a connect request
t_rcvdis (3N)	retrieve information from disconnect
t_rcvrel (3N)	acknowledge receipt of an orderly release indication
t_rcvudata (3N)	receive a data unit
t_rcvuderr (3N)	receive a unit data error indication
t_snd (3N)	send data or expedited data over a connection
t_snddis (3N)	send user-initiated disconnect request
t_sndrel (3N)	initiate an orderly release
t_sndudata (3N)	send a data unit
t_sync (3N)	synchronize transport library
t_unbind (3N)	disable a transport endpoint
tam (3X)	TAM transition libraries
tcsetpgrp (3C)	set terminal foreground process group id
times (3C)	get process times
timezone (3C)	get time zone name given offset from GMT
tmpfile (3S)	create a temporary file
tmpnam, tempnam (3S)	create a name for a temporary file

Section 3 - Library Functions

trig: sin, sinf, cos, cosf, tan, tanf, asin, asinf, acos, acosf, atan, atanf, atan2,
    atan2f(3M) .... trigonometric functions
truncate, ftruncate(3C) .... set a file to a specified length
tsearch, tfind, tdelete, twalk(3C) .... manage binary search trees
ttyname, isatty(3C) .... find name of a terminal
ttyslot(3C) .... find the slot in the utmp file of the current user
ualarm(3) .... schedule signal after interval in microseconds
ungetc(3S) .... push character back onto input stream
unlockpt(3C) .... unlock a pseudo-terminal master/slave pair
usleep(3) .... suspend execution for interval in microseconds
utimes(3) .... set file times
vprintf, vfprintf, vsprintf(3S) .... print formatted output of a variable argument list
wait, wait3, WIFSTOPPED, WIFSIGNALED, WIFEXITED(3)
    .... wait for process to terminate or stop
xdr(3N) .... library routines for external data representation
xdr_admin: xdr_getpos, xdr_inline, xdrrec_eof, xdr_setpos(3N)
    .... library routines for external data representation
xdr_complex: xdr_array, xdr_bytes, xdr_opaque, xdr_pointer, xdr_reference,
    xdr_string, xdr_union, xdr_vector, xdr_wrapstring(3N)
    .... library routines for external data representation
xdr_create: xdr_destroy, xdrmem_create, xdrrec_create, xdrstdio_create(3N)
    .... library routines for external data representation stream creation
xdr_simple: xdr_bool, xdr_char, xdr_double, xdr_enum, xdr_float, xdr_free,
    xdr_int, xdr_long, xdr_short, xdr_u_char, xdr_u_long, xdr_u_short,
    xdr_void(3N) .... library routines for external data representation
ypclnt, yp_get_default_domain, yp_bind, yp_unbind, yp_match, yp_first, yp_next,
    yp_all, yp_order, yp_master, yperr_string, ypprot_err(3N) .... NIS client interface
yp_update(3N) .... change NIS information

intro(3)

NAME
intro – introduction to functions and libraries

DESCRIPTION
This section describes functions found in various libraries, other than those functions that directly invoke UNIX system primitives, which are described in Section 2 of this volume. Function declarations can be obtained from the #include files indicated on each page. Certain major collections are identified by a letter after the section number:

- (3C) These functions, together with those of Section 2 and those marked (3S), constitute the standard C library, libc, which is automatically linked by the C compilation system. The standard C library is implemented as a shared object, libc.so, and an archive, libc.a. C programs are linked with the shared object version of the standard C library by default. Specify -dn on the cc command line to link with the archive version. [See cc(1) for other overrides, and the "C Compilation System" chapter of the *Programmer's Guide: ANSI C and Programming Support Tools* for a discussion.]

- (3S) These functions constitute the "standard I/O package" [see stdio(3S)].

- (3E) These functions constitute the ELF access library, libelf. This library is not implemented as a shared object, and is not automatically linked by the C compilation system. Specify -lelf on the cc command line to link with this library.

- (3G) These functions constitute the general-purpose library, libgen. This library is not implemented as a shared object, and is not automatically linked by the C compilation system. Specify -lgen on the cc command line to link with this library.

- (3M) These functions constitute the math library, libm. Declarations for these functions may be obtained from the #include file math.h. [See math(5).]

    libm is not automatically loaded by the C compilation system; use the -l option to cc to access the library.

    libm contains the full set of double-precision routines plus some single-precision routines (designated by the suffix f) that give better performance with less precision. Selected routines are hand-optimized for performance. The optimized routines include sin, cos, tan, atan, atan2, exp, log, log10, pow, and sqrt and their single-precision equivalents.

    This library is not implemented as a shared object, and is not automatically linked by the C compilation system. Specify -lm on the cc command line to link with this library.

- (3N) These functions are contained in three libraries: the Network Services library, libnsl; the Sockets Interface library, libsocket; and the Internet Domain Name Server library, libresolv.

    The following functions constitute the libnsl library:

cr1	cr1 authentication library
cs	Connection Server library interface
des	Data Encryption Standards library
netdir	Network Directory functions. This contains look-up functions and the access point to network directory libraries for various network transports.
netselect	Network Selection routines. These functions manipulate the /etc/netconfig file and return entries.
nsl	Transport Library Interface (TLI). These functions contain the implementation of X/OPEN's Transport Level Interface.
rexec	REXEC library interface
rpc	User-level Remote Procedure Call library
saf	Service Access Facility library
yp	Network Information Service functions

The libsocket library has two components: inet, containing the Inernet library routines, and socket, containing the Socket Interface routines. The libresolv library contains the resolver routines.

The standard networking libraries are implemented as a shared object (libnsl.so and libsocket.so) or archive file (libresolv.a). To link with these libraries, specify the cc command line with -lnsl, -lsocket, or -lresolv, respectively.

(3X) Specialized libraries. The files in which these libraries are found are given on the appropriate pages.

DEFINITIONS

A character is any bit pattern able to fit into a byte on the machine. The null character is a character with value 0, conventionally represented in the C language as \0. A character array is a sequence of characters. A null-terminated character array (a *string*) is a sequence of characters, the last of which is the null character. The null string is a character array containing only the terminating null character. A NULL pointer is the value that is obtained by casting 0 into a pointer. C guarantees that this value will not match that of any legitimate pointer, so many functions that return pointers return NULL to indicate an error. The macro NULL is defined in stdio.h. Types of the form size_t are defined in the appropriate header files.

In the Network Services library, netbuf is a structure used in various TLI functions to send and receive data and information. netbuf is defined in sys/tiuser.h, and includes the following members:

```
struct netbuf {
      unsigned int maxlen;  /* The physical size of the buffer */
      unsigned int len; /* The number of bytes in the buffer */
      char *buf;   /* Points to user input and/or output buffer */
};
```

If netbuf is used for output, the function will set the user value of *len* on return. *maxlen* generally has significance only when *buf* is used to receive output from the TLI function. In this case, it specifies the maximum value of *len* that can be set by the function. If *maxlen* is not large enough to hold the returned information, an TBUFOVFLW error will generally result. However, certain functions may return part of the data and not generate an error.

FILES

```
INCDIR              usually /usr/include
LIBDIR              usually /usr/ccs/lib
LIBDIR/libc.so
LIBDIR/libc.a
LIBDIR/libgen.a
LIBDIR/libm.a
LIBDIR/libnsl.so
LIBDIR/libresolv.a
LIBDIR/libsfm.sa
LIBDIR/libsocket.so
/usr/lib/libc.so.1
```

SEE ALSO

ar(1), cc(1), ld(1), lint(1), nm(1), intro(2), stdio(3S), math(5)

The "C Compilation System" chapter in the *Programmer's Guide: ANSI C and Programming Support Tools*

The "Floating Point Operations" chapter in the *Programmer's Guide: ANSI C and Programming Support Tools*

DIAGNOSTICS

Math Library (libm) Only

For functions that return floating-point values, error handling varies according to compilation mode. Under the −Xt (default) option to cc, these functions return the conventional values 0, ±HUGE, or NaN when the function is undefined for the given arguments or when the value is not representable. In the −Xa and −Xc compilation modes, ±HUGE_VAL is returned instead of ±HUGE. (HUGE_VAL and HUGE are defined in math.h to be infinity and the largest-magnitude single-precision number, respectively.) In every case, the external variable errno [see intro(2)] is set to the value EDOM or ERANGE, although the value may vary for a given error depending on compilation mode.

NOTES

None of the functions, external variables, or macros should be redefined in the user's programs. Any other name may be redefined without affecting the behavior of other library functions, but such redefinition may conflict with a declaration in an included header file.

The header files in *INCDIR* provide function prototypes (function declarations including the types of arguments) for most of the functions listed in this manual. Function prototypes allow the compiler to check for correct usage of these functions in the user's program. The lint program checker may also be used and will report discrepancies even if the header files are not included with #include statements. Definitions for Sections 2, 3C, and 3S are checked automatically.

Other definitions can be included by using the −l option to `lint`. (For example, −lm includes definitions for `libm`.) Use of `lint` is highly recommended.

Users should carefully note the difference between STREAMS and *stream*. STREAMS is a set of kernel mechanisms that support the development of network services and data communication drivers. It is composed of utility routines, kernel facilities, and a set of data structures. A *stream* is a file with its associated buffering. It is declared to be a pointer to a type `FILE` defined in `stdio.h`.

In detailed definitions of components, it is sometimes necessary to refer to symbolic names that are implementation-specific, but which are not necessarily expected to be accessible to an application program. Many of these symbolic names describe boundary conditions and system limits.

In this section, for readability, these implementation-specific values are given symbolic names. These names always appear enclosed in curly brackets to distinguish them from symbolic names of other implementation-specific constants that are accessible to application programs by header files. These names are not necessarily accessible to an application program through a header file, although they may be defined in the documentation for a particular system.

In general, a portable application program should not refer to these symbolic names in its code. For example, an application program would not be expected to test the length of an argument list given to a routine to determine if it was greater than {ARG_MAX}.

a64l(3C)   (C Development Set)   a64l(3C)

NAME
    a64l, l64a – convert between long integer and base-64 ASCII string

SYNOPSIS
    #include <stdlib.h>

    long a64l (const char *s);

    char *l64a (long l);

DESCRIPTION
    These functions are used to maintain numbers stored in base-64 ASCII characters. These characters define a notation by which long integers can be represented by up to six characters; each character represents a "digit" in a radix-64 notation.

    The characters used to represent "digits" are . for 0, / for 1, 0 through 9 for 2–11, A through Z for 12–37, and a through z for 38–63.

    a64l takes a pointer to a null-terminated base-64 representation and returns a corresponding long value. If the string pointed to by s contains more than six characters, a64l will use the first six.

    a64l scans the character string from left to right with the least significant digit on the left, decoding each character as a 6-bit radix-64 number.

    l64a takes a long argument and returns a pointer to the corresponding base-64 representation. If the argument is 0, l64a returns a pointer to a null string.

NOTES
    The value returned by l64a is a pointer into a static buffer, the contents of which are overwritten by each call.

NAME

abort – generate an abnormal termination signal

SYNOPSIS

`#include <stdlib.h>`

`void abort (void);`

DESCRIPTION

abort first closes all open files, stdio(3S) streams, directory streams and message catalogue descriptors, if possible, then causes the signal SIGABRT to be sent to the calling process.

SEE ALSO

sdb(1), exit(2), kill(2), signal(2), catopen(3C), stdio(3S)

sh(1) in the *User's Reference Manual*

DIAGNOSTICS

If SIGABRT is neither caught nor ignored, and the current directory is writable, a core dump is produced and the message `abort - core dumped` is written by the shell [see sh(1)].

NAME
abs, `labs` – return integer absolute value

SYNOPSIS
```
#include <stdlib.h>
```
```
int abs (int val);
```

```
long labs (long lval);
```

DESCRIPTION
`abs` returns the absolute value of its `int` operand. `labs` returns the absolute value of its `long` operand.

SEE ALSO
floor(3M)

NOTES
In 2's-complement representation, the absolute value of the largest magnitude negative integral value is undefined.

accept(3N)

NAME
accept – accept a connection on a socket

SYNOPSIS
#include <sys/types.h>

int accept(int s, caddr_t addr, int *addrlen);

DESCRIPTION
The argument *s* is a socket that has been created with socket and bound to an address with bind, and that is listening for connections after a call to listen. accept extracts the first connection on the queue of pending connections, creates a new socket with the properties of *s*, and allocates a new file descriptor, *ns*, for the socket. If no pending connections are present on the queue and the socket is not marked as non-blocking, accept blocks the caller until a connection is present. If the socket is marked as non-blocking and no pending connections are present on the queue, accept returns an error as described below. accept uses the netconfig file to determine the STREAMS device file name associated with *s*. This is the device on which the connect indication will be accepted. The accepted socket, *ns*, is used to read and write data to and from the socket that connected to *ns*; it is not used to accept more connections. The original socket (*s*) remains open for accepting further connections.

The argument *addr* is a result parameter that is filled in with the address of the connecting entity as it is known to the communications layer. The exact format of the *addr* parameter is determined by the domain in which the communication occurs.

addrlen is a value-result parameter. Initially, it contains the amount of space pointed to by *addr*; on return it contains the length in bytes of the address returned.

accept is used with connection-based socket types, currently with SOCK_STREAM.

It is possible to select a socket for the purpose of an accept by selecting it for read. However, this will only indicate when a connect indication is pending; it is still necessary to call accept.

RETURN VALUE
accept returns −1 on error. If it succeeds, it returns a non-negative integer that is a descriptor for the accepted socket.

ERRORS
accept will fail if:

EBADF	The descriptor is invalid.
ENOTSOCK	The descriptor does not reference a socket.
EOPNOTSUPP	The referenced socket is not of type SOCK_STREAM.
EWOULDBLOCK	The socket is marked as non-blocking and no connections are present to be accepted.
EPROTO	A protocol error has occurred; for example, the STREAMS protocol stack has not been initialized.

ENODEV	The protocol family and type corresponding to *s* could not be found in the netconfig file.
ENOMEM	There was insufficient user memory available to complete the operation.
ENOSR	There were insufficient STREAMS resources available to complete the operation.

SEE ALSO
bind(3N), connect(3N), listen(3N), socket(3N), netconfig(4)

NOTES
The type of address structure passed to accept depends on the address family. UNIX domain sockets (address family AF_UNIX) require a socketaddr_un structure as defined in sys/un.h; Internet domain sockets (address family AF_INET) require a sockaddr_in structure as defined in netinet/in.h. Other address families may require other structures. Use the structure appropriate to the address family; cast the structure address to a generic caddr_t in the call to accept and pass the size of the structure in the *addrlen* argument.

See the "The Sockets Interface" section in the *Programmer's Guide: Networking Interfaces* for details.

NAME

addseverity – build a list of severity levels for an application for use with fmtmsg

SYNOPSIS

#include <fmtmsg.h>

int addseverity(int severity, const char *string);

DESCRIPTION

The addseverity function builds a list of severity levels for an application to be used with the message formatting facility, fmtmsg. *severity* is an integer value indicating the seriousness of the condition, and *string* is a pointer to a string describing the condition (string is not limited to a specific size).

If addseverity is called with an integer value that has not been previously defined, the function adds that new severity value and print string to the existing set of standard severity levels.

If addseverity is called with an integer value that has been previously defined, the function redefines that value with the new print string. Previously defined severity levels may be removed by supplying the NULL string. If addseverity is called with a negative number or an integer value of 0, 1, 2, 3, or 4, the function fails and returns −1. The values 0–4 are reserved for the standard severity levels and cannot be modified. Identifiers for the standard levels of severity are:

MM_HALT	indicates that the application has encountered a severe fault and is halting. Produces the print string HALT.
MM_ERROR	indicates that the application has detected a fault. Produces the print string ERROR.
MM_WARNING	indicates a condition that is out of the ordinary, that might be a problem, and should be watched. Produces the print string WARNING.
MM_INFO	provides information about a condition that is not in error. Produces the print string INFO.
MM_NOSEV	indicates that no severity level is supplied for the message.

Severity levels may also be defined at run time using the SEV_LEVEL environment variable [see fmtmsg(3C)].

EXAMPLES

When the function addseverity is used as follows:

    addseverity(7,"ALERT")

the following call to fmtmsg:

    fmtmsg(MM_PRINT, "UX:cat", 7, "invalid syntax", "refer to manual", "UX:cat:001")

produces:

    UX:cat: ALERT: invalid syntax
    TO FIX: refer to manual UX:cat:001

addseverity(3C) (Essential Utilities) **addseverity(3C)**

SEE ALSO
fmtmsg(1M), fmtmsg(3C), gettxt(3C), printf(3S)

DIAGNOSTICS
addseverity returns MM_OK on success or MM_NOTOK on failure.

NAME
alloca – memory allocator

SYNOPSIS
cc [*flag*. . .] *file* . . . −lucb
#include <alloca.h>
char *alloca(size)
int size;

DESCRIPTION
alloca allocates *size* bytes of space in the stack frame of the caller, and returns a pointer to the allocated block. This temporary space is automatically freed when the caller returns. Note: if the allocated block is beyond the current stack limit, the resulting behavior is undefined.

SEE ALSO
sigstack(3), sigvec(3)

csh(1) in the *User's Reference Manual*

ld(1), brk(2), getrlimit(2), calloc(3), and malloc(3) in the *Programmer's Reference Manual*

Stephenson, C.J., *Fast Fits*, in *Proceedings of the ACM 9th Symposium on Operating Systems*, SIGOPS Operating Systems Review, vol. 17, no. 5, October 1983

Core Wars, in *Scientific American*, May 1984

NOTES
alloca is machine-, compiler-, and most of all, system-dependent. Its use is strongly discouraged.

NAME
assert – verify program assertion

SYNOPSIS
#include <assert.h>

void assert (int expression);

DESCRIPTION
This macro is useful for putting diagnostics into programs. When it is executed, if *expression* is false (zero), assert prints

Assertion failed: *expression*, file *xyz*, line *nnn*

on the standard error output and aborts. In the error message, *xyz* is the name of the source file and *nnn* the source line number of the assert statement. The latter are respectively the values of the preprocessor macros __FILE__ and __LINE__.

Compiling with the preprocessor option –DNDEBUG [see cc(1)], or with the preprocessor control statement #define NDEBUG ahead of the #include assert.h statement, will stop assertions from being compiled into the program.

SEE ALSO
cc(1), abort(3C)

NOTES
Since assert is implemented as a macro, the *expression* may not contain any string literals.

NAME
atexit – add program termination routine

SYNOPSIS
#include <stdlib.h>

int atexit (void (*func)(void));

DESCRIPTION
atexit adds the function *func* to a list of functions to be called without arguments on normal termination of the program. Normal termination occurs by either a call to the exit system call or a return from main. At most 32 functions may be registered by atexit; the functions will be called in the reverse order of their registration.

atexit returns 0 if the registration succeeds, nonzero if it fails.

SEE ALSO
exit(2)

NAME

basename – return the last element of a path name

SYNOPSIS

cc [*flag* . . .] *file* . . . −lgen [*library* . . .]

```
#include <libgen.h>
```

```
char *basename (char *path);
```

DESCRIPTION

Given a pointer to a null-terminated character string that contains a path name, basename returns a pointer to the last element of *path*. Trailing "/" characters are deleted.

If *path* or **path* is zero, pointer to a static constant "." is returned.

EXAMPLES

Input string	Output pointer
/usr/lib	lib
/usr/	usr
/	/

SEE ALSO

dirname(3G)

basename(1) in the *User's Reference Manual*

bessel(3M) (Math Libraries) bessel(3M)

NAME
bessel: j0, j1, jn, y0, y1, yn − Bessel functions

SYNOPSIS
cc [*flag* ...] *file* ... −lm [*library* ...]

#include <math.h>

double j0 (double x);

double j1 (double x);

double jn (int n, double x);

double y0 (double x);

double y1 (double x);

double yn (int n, double x);

DESCRIPTION
j0 and j1 return Bessel functions of x of the first kind of orders 0 and 1, respectively. jn returns the Bessel function of x of the first kind of order n.

y0 and y1 return Bessel functions of x of the second kind of orders 0 and 1, respectively. yn returns the Bessel function of x of the second kind of order n. The value of x must be positive.

SEE ALSO
matherr(3M)

DIAGNOSTICS
Non-positive arguments cause y0, y1, and yn to return the value −HUGE and to set errno to EDOM. In addition, a message indicating DOMAIN error is printed on the standard error output.

Arguments too large in magnitude cause j0, j1, y0, and y1 to return 0 and to set errno to ERANGE. In addition, a message indicating TLOSS error is printed on the standard error output.

Except when the −Xc compilation option is used, these error-handling procedures may be changed with the function matherr. When the −Xa or −Xc compilation options are used, HUGE_VAL is returned instead of HUGE and no error messages are printed.

NAME
bgets – read stream up to next delimiter

SYNOPSIS
cc [*flag* ...] *file* ... -lgen [*library* ...]

```
#include <libgen.h>
char *bgets (char *buffer, size_t *count, FILE *stream,
    const char *breakstring);
```

DESCRIPTION
bgets reads characters from *stream* into *buffer* until either *count* is exhausted or one of the characters in *breakstring* is encountered in the stream. The read data is terminated with a null byte ('\0') and a pointer to the trailing null is returned. If a *breakstring* character is encountered, the last non-null is the delimiter character that terminated the scan.

Note that, except for the fact that the returned value points to the end of the read string rather than to the beginning, the call

```
bgets (buffer, sizeof buffer, stream, "\n");
```

is identical to

```
fgets (buffer, sizeof buffer, stream);
```

There is always enough room reserved in the buffer for the trailing null.

If *breakstring* is a null pointer, the value of *breakstring* from the previous call is used. If *breakstring* is null at the first call, no characters will be used to delimit the string.

EXAMPLES
```
#include   <libgen.h>

char buffer[8];
/* read in first user name from /etc/passwd */
fp = fopen("/etc/passwd","r");
bgets(buffer, 8, fp, ":");
```

DIAGNOSTICS
NULL is returned on error or end-of-file. Reporting the condition is delayed to the next call if any characters were read but not yet returned.

SEE ALSO
gets(3S)

NAME
bind – bind a name to a socket

SYNOPSIS
#include <sys/types.h>

int bind(int s, caddr_t name, int namelen);

DESCRIPTION
bind assigns a name to an unnamed socket. When a socket is created with socket, it exists in a name space (address family) but has no name assigned. bind requests that the name pointed to by *name* be assigned to the socket.

RETURN VALUE
If the bind is successful, a 0 value is returned. A return value of −1 indicates an error, which is further specified in the global errno.

ERRORS
The bind call will fail if:

EBADF	*s* is not a valid descriptor.
ENOTSOCK	*s* is a descriptor for a file, not a socket.
EADDRNOTAVAIL	The specified address is not available on the local machine.
EADDRINUSE	The specified address is already in use.
EINVAL	*namelen* is not the size of a valid address for the specified address family.
EINVAL	The socket is already bound to an address.
EACCES	The requested address is protected and the current user has inadequate permission to access it.
ENOSR	There were insufficient STREAMS resources for the operation to complete.

The following errors are specific to binding names in the UNIX domain:

ENOTDIR	A component of the path prefix of the pathname in *name* is not a directory.
ENOENT	A component of the path prefix of the pathname in *name* does not exist.
EACCES	Search permission is denied for a component of the path prefix of the pathname in *name*.
ELOOP	Too many symbolic links were encountered in translating the pathname in *name*.
EIO	An I/O error occurred while making the directory entry or allocating the inode.
EROFS	The inode would reside on a read-only file system.
EISDIR	A null pathname was specified.

SEE ALSO
    unlink(2) in the *Programmer's Reference Manual*

NOTES
    Binding a name in the UNIX domain creates a socket in the file system that must be deleted by the caller when it is no longer needed [see unlink(2)].

    The rules used in name binding vary between communication domains.

    The type of address structure passed to bind depends on the address family. UNIX domain sockets (address family AF_UNIX) require a socketaddr_un structure as defined in sys/un.h; Internet domain sockets (address family AF_INET) require a sockaddr_in structure as defined in netinet/in.h. Other address families may require other structures. Use the structure appropriate to the address family; cast the structure address to a generic caddr_t in the call to bind and pass the size of the structure in the *namelen* argument.

bsearch(3C)

NAME
bsearch – binary search a sorted table

SYNOPSIS
#include <stdlib.h>

void *bsearch (const void *key, const void *base, size_t nel,
    size_t size, int (*compar)(const void *, const void *));

DESCRIPTION
bsearch is a binary search routine generalized from Knuth (6.2.1) Algorithm B. It returns a pointer into a table (an array) indicating where a datum may be found or a null pointer if the datum cannot be found. The table must be previously sorted in increasing order according to a comparison function pointed to by *compar*. *key* points to a datum instance to be sought in the table. *base* points to the element at the base of the table. *nel* is the number of elements in the table. *size* is the number of bytes in each element. The function pointed to by *compar* is called with two arguments that point to the elements being compared. The function must return an integer less than, equal to, or greater than 0 as accordingly the first argument is to be considered less than, equal to, or greater than the second.

EXAMPLE
The example below searches a table containing pointers to nodes consisting of a string and its length. The table is ordered alphabetically on the string in the node pointed to by each entry.

This program reads in strings and either finds the corresponding node and prints out the string and its length, or prints an error message.

```
#include <stdio.h>
#include <stdlib.h>
#include <string.h>

struct node {                  /* these are stored in the table */
      char *string;
      int length;
};
static struct node table[] =   /* table to be searched */
{
      { "asparagus", 10 },
      { "beans", 6 },
      { "tomato", 7 },
      { "watermelon", 11 },
};

main()
{
      struct node *node_ptr, node;
      /* routine to compare 2 nodes */
      static int node_compare(const void *, const void *);
      char str_space[20];    /* space to read string into */
```

```
            node.string = str_space;
            while (scanf("%20s", node.string) != EOF) {
                node_ptr = bsearch( &node,
                        table, sizeof(table)/sizeof(struct node),
                        sizeof(struct node), node_compare);
                if (node_ptr != NULL) {
                        (void) printf("string = %20s, length = %d\n",
                                node_ptr->string, node_ptr->length);
                } else {
                        (void)printf("not found: %20s\n", node.string);
                }
            }
            return(0);
    }

    /* routine to compare two nodes based on an  */
    /* alphabetical ordering of the string field */
    static int
    node_compare(const void *node1, const void *node2)
    {
            return (strcmp(
                    ((const struct node *)node1)->string,
                    ((const struct node *)node2)->string));
    }
```

SEE ALSO
hsearch(3C), lsearch(3C), qsort(3C), tsearch(3C)

DIAGNOSTICS
A null pointer is returned if the key cannot be found in the table.

NOTES
The pointers to the key and the element at the base of the table should be of type pointer-to-*element*.

The comparison function need not compare every byte, so arbitrary data may be contained in the elements in addition to the values being compared.

If the number of elements in the table is less than the size reserved for the table, *nel* should be the lower number.

bstring(3)   (BSD Compatibility Package)   bstring(3)

NAME
bstring: bcopy, bcmp, bzero, ffs – bit and byte string operations

SYNOPSIS
cc [*flag*...] *file* ... –lucb

bcopy(b1, b2, length)
char *b1, *b2;
int length;

int bcmp(b1, b2, length)
char *b1, *b2;
int length;

bzero(b, length)
char *b;
int length;

DESCRIPTION
The functions bcopy, bcmp, and bzero operate on variable length strings of bytes. They do not check for null bytes as the routines in string(3) do.

bcopy copies *length* bytes from string *b1* to the string *b2*. Overlapping strings are handled correctly.

bcmp compares byte string *b1* against byte string *b2*, returning zero if they are identical, 1 otherwise. Both strings are assumed to be *length* bytes long. bcmp of length zero bytes always returns zero.

bzero places *length* 0 bytes in the string *b*.

NOTES
The bcmp and bcopy routines take parameters backwards from strcmp and strcpy.

SEE ALSO
string(3C) in the *Programmer's Reference Manual*

bufsplit(3G)   (Enhanced Programming Library)   bufsplit(3G)

NAME
bufsplit – split buffer into fields

SYNOPSIS
cc [*flag* ...] *file* ... −lgen [*library* ...]

#include <libgen.h>

size_t bufsplit (char *buf, size_t n, char **a);

DESCRIPTION
bufsplit examines the buffer, *buf*, and assigns values to the pointer array, *a*, so that the pointers point to the first *n* fields in *buf* that are delimited by tabs or new-lines.

To change the characters used to separate fields, call bufsplit with *buf* pointing to the string of characters, and *n* and *a* set to zero. For example, to use ':', '.', and ',' as separators along with tab and new-line:

bufsplit (":.,\t\n", 0, (char**)0);

RETURN VALUE
The number of fields assigned in the array *a*. If *buf* is zero, the return value is zero and the array is unchanged. Otherwise the value is at least one. The remainder of the elements in the array are assigned the address of the null byte at the end of the buffer.

EXAMPLES
```
/*
 * set a[0] = "This", a[1] = "is", a[2] = "a",
 * a[3] = "test"
 */
bufsplit("This\tis\ta\ttest\n", 4, a);
```

NOTES
bufsplit changes the delimiters to null bytes in *buf*.

NAME
byteorder, htonl, htons, ntohl, ntohs – convert values between host and network byte order

SYNOPSIS
#include <sys/types.h>
#include <netinet/in.h>

u_long htonl(u_long hostlong);

u_short htons(u_short hostshort);

u_long ntohl(u_long netlong);

u_short ntohs(u_short netshort);

DESCRIPTION
These routines convert 16 and 32 bit quantities between network byte order and host byte order. On some architectures these routines are defined as NULL macros in the include file netinet/in.h. On other architectures, if their host byte order is different from network byte order, these routines are functional.

These routines are most often used in conjunction with Internet addresses and ports as returned by gethostent(3N) and getservent(3N).

SEE ALSO
gethostent(3N), getservent(3N)

catgets(3C)

NAME
catgets – read a program message

SYNOPSIS
    #include <nl_types.h>

    char *catgets (nl_catd catd, int set_num, int msg_num, char *s);

DESCRIPTION
catgets attempts to read message *msg_num*, in set *set_num*, from the message catalogue identified by *catd*. *catd* is a catalogue descriptor returned from an earlier call to catopen. *s* points to a default message string which will be returned by catgets if the identified message catalogue is not currently available.

SEE ALSO
catopen(3C)

DIAGNOSTICS
If the identified message is retrieved successfully, catgets returns a pointer to an internal buffer area containing the null terminated message string. If the call is unsuccessful because the message catalogue identified by *catd* is not currently available, a pointer to *s* is returned.

NAME

catopen, catclose – open/close a message catalog

SYNOPSIS

```
#include <nl_types.h>
```

nl_catd catopen (char *name, int oflag);

int catclose (nl_catd catd);

DESCRIPTION

catopen opens a message catalog and returns a catalog descriptor. *name* specifies the name of the message catalog to be opened. If *name* contains a "/" then *name* specifies a pathname for the message catalog. Otherwise, the environment variable NLSPATH is used. If NLSPATH does not exist in the environment, or if a message catalog cannot be opened in any of the paths specified by NLSPATH, then the default path is used [see nl_types(5)].

The names of message catalogs, and their location in the filestore, can vary from one system to another. Individual applications can choose to name or locate message catalogs according to their own special needs. A mechanism is therefore required to specify where the catalog resides.

The NLSPATH variable provides both the location of message catalogs, in the form of a search path, and the naming conventions associated with message catalog files. For example:

NLSPATH=/nlslib/%L/%N.cat:/nlslib/%N/%L

The metacharacter % introduces a substitution field, where %L substitutes the current setting of the LANG environment variable (see following section), and %N substitutes the value of the *name* parameter passed to catopen. Thus, in the above example, catopen will search in /nlslib/$LANG/*name*.cat, then in /nlslib/*name*/$LANG, for the required message catalog.

NLSPATH will normally be set up on a system wide basis (for example, in /etc/profile) and thus makes the location and naming conventions associated with message catalogs transparent to both programs and users.

The full set of metacharacters is:

%N   The value of the name parameter passed to catopen.
%L   The value of LANG.
%l   The value of the language element of LANG.
%t   The value of the territory element of LANG.
%c   The value of the codeset element of LANG.
%%   A single %.

The LANG environment variable provides the ability to specify the user's requirements for native languages, local customs and character set, as an ASCII string in the form

LANG=language[_territory[.codeset]]

A user who speaks German as it is spoken in Austria and has a terminal which operates in ISO 8859/1 codeset, would want the setting of the LANG variable to be

    LANG=De_A.88591

With this setting it should be possible for that user to find any relevant catalogs should they exist.

Should the LANG variable not be set then the value of LC_MESSAGES as returned by setlocale is used. If this is NULL then the default path as defined in nl_types is used.

oflag is reserved for future use and should be set to 0. The results of setting this field to any other value are undefined.

catclose closes the message catalog identified by *catd*.

SEE ALSO
catgets(3C), setlocale(3C), environ(5), nl_types(5)

DIAGNOSTICS
If successful, catopen returns a message catalog descriptor for use on subsequent calls to catgets and catclose. Otherwise catopen returns (nl_catd) −1.

catclose returns 0 if successful, otherwise −1.

clock(3C) (C Development Set) clock(3C)

NAME
clock – report CPU time used

SYNOPSIS
    #include <time.h>

    clock_t clock (void);

DESCRIPTION
clock returns the amount of CPU time (in microseconds) used since the first call to clock in the calling process. The time reported is the sum of the user and system times of the calling process and its terminated child processes for which it has executed the wait system call, the pclose function, or the system function.

Dividing the value returned by clock by the constant CLOCKS_PER_SEC, defined in the time.h header file, will give the time in seconds.

The resolution of the clock is defined by CLK_TCK in limits.h, and is typically 1/100 or 1/60 of a second.

SEE ALSO
times(2), wait(2), popen(3S), system(3S)

NOTES
The value returned by clock is defined in microseconds for compatibility with systems that have CPU clocks with much higher resolution. Because of this, the value returned will wrap around after accumulating only 2147 seconds of CPU time (about 36 minutes). If the process time used is not available or cannot be represented, clock returns the value (clock_t)−1.

connect (3N)

NAME
connect – initiate a connection on a socket

SYNOPSIS
#include <sys/types.h>

int connect(int s, addr_t name, int namelen);

DESCRIPTION
The parameter *s* is a socket. If it is of type SOCK_DGRAM, connect specifies the peer with which the socket is to be associated; this address is the address to which datagrams are to be sent if a receiver is not explicitly designated; it is the only address from which datagrams are to be received. If the socket *s* is of type SOCK_STREAM, connect attempts to make a connection to another socket. The other socket is specified by *name*. *name* is an address in the communications space of the socket. Each communications space interprets the *name* parameter in its own way. If *s* is not bound, then it will be bound to an address selected by the underlying transport provider. Generally, stream sockets may successfully connect only once; datagram sockets may use connect multiple times to change their association. Datagram sockets may dissolve the association by connecting to a null address.

RETURN VALUE
If the connection or binding succeeds, then 0 is returned. Otherwise a −1 is returned and a more specific error code is stored in errno.

ERRORS
The call fails if:

EBADF	*s* is not a valid descriptor.
ENOTSOCK	*s* is a descriptor for a file, not a socket.
EINVAL	*namelen* is not the size of a valid address for the specified address family.
EADDRNOTAVAIL	The specified address is not available on the remote machine.
EAFNOSUPPORT	Addresses in the specified address family cannot be used with this socket.
EISCONN	The socket is already connected.
ETIMEDOUT	Connection establishment timed out without establishing a connection.
ECONNREFUSED	The attempt to connect was forcefully rejected. The calling program should close the socket descriptor, and issue another socket call to obtain a new descriptor before attempting another connect call.
ENETUNREACH	The network is not reachable from this host.
EADDRINUSE	The address is already in use.

connect(3N)

EINPROGRESS	The socket is non-blocking and the connection cannot be completed immediately. It is possible to select for completion by selecting the socket for writing. However, this is only possible if the socket STREAMS module is the topmost module on the protocol stack with a write service procedure. This will be the normal case.
EALREADY	The socket is non-blocking and a previous connection attempt has not yet been completed.
EINTR	The connection attempt was interrupted before any data arrived by the delivery of a signal.
ENOTSOCK	The file referred to by *name* is not a socket.
EPROTOTYPE	The file referred to by *name* is a socket of a type other than type *s* (for example, *s* is a SOCK_DGRAM socket, while *name* refers to a SOCK_STREAM socket).
ENOSR	There were insufficient STREAMS resources available to complete the operation.

The following errors are specific to connecting names in the UNIX domain. These errors may not apply in future versions of the UNIX IPC domain.

ENOTDIR	A component of the path prefix of the pathname in *name* is not a directory.
ENOENT	A component of the path prefix of the pathname in *name* does not exist.
ENOENT	The socket referred to by the pathname in *name* does not exist.
EACCES	Search permission is denied for a component of the path prefix of the pathname in *name*.
ELOOP	Too many symbolic links were encountered in translating the pathname in *name*.
EIO	An I/O error occurred while reading from or writing to the file system.

SEE ALSO
accept(3N), connect(3N), getsockname(3N), socket(3N)
close(2) in the *Programmer's Reference Manual*

NOTES
The type of address structure passed to connect depends on the address family. UNIX domain sockets (address family AF_UNIX) require a socketaddr_un structure as defined in sys/un.h; Internet domain sockets (address family AF_INET) require a sockaddr_in structure as defined in netinet/in.h. Other address families may require other structures. Use the structure appropriate to the address family; cast the structure address to a generic caddr_t in the call to connect and pass the size of the structure in the *namelen* argument.

NAME
conv: toupper, tolower, _toupper, _tolower, toascii – translate characters

SYNOPSIS
#include <ctype.h>

int toupper (int c);

int tolower (int c);

int _toupper (int c);

int _tolower (int c);

int toascii (int c);

DESCRIPTION
toupper and tolower have as their domain the range of the function getc: all values represented in an unsigned char and the value of the macro EOF as defined in stdio.h. If the argument of toupper represents a lower-case letter, the result is the corresponding upper-case letter. If the argument of tolower represents an upper-case letter, the result is the corresponding lower-case letter. All other arguments in the domain are returned unchanged.

The macros _toupper and _tolower accomplish the same things as toupper and tolower, respectively, but have restricted domains and are faster. _toupper requires a lower-case letter as its argument; its result is the corresponding upper-case letter. _tolower requires an upper-case letter as its argument; its result is the corresponding lower-case letter. Arguments outside the domain cause undefined results.

toascii yields its argument with all bits turned off that are not part of a standard 7-bit ASCII character; it is intended for compatibility with other systems.

toupper, tolower, _toupper, and _tolower are affected by LC_CTYPE. In the C locale, or in a locale where shift information is not defined, these functions determine the case of characters according to the rules of the ASCII-coded character set. Characters outside the ASCII range of characters are returned unchanged.

SEE ALSO
ctype(3C), getc(3S), setlocale(3C), environ(5)

copylist(3G)

NAME
copylist – copy a file into memory

SYNOPSIS
cc [*flag* . . .] *file* . . . −lgen [*library* . . .]

#include <libgen.h>

char *copylist (const char *filenm, off_t *szptr);

DESCRIPTION
copylist copies a list of items from a file into freshly allocated memory, replacing new-lines with null characters. It expects two arguments: a pointer *filenm* to the name of the file to be copied, and a pointer *szptr* to a variable where the size of the file will be stored.

Upon success, copylist returns a pointer to the memory allocated. Otherwise it returns NULL if it has trouble finding the file, calling malloc, or opening the file.

EXAMPLES
```
/* read "file" into buf */
off_t size;
char *buf;
buf = copylist("file", &size);
for (i = 0; i < size; i++)
    if(buf[i])
        putchar(buf[i]);
    else
        putchar('\n');
```

SEE ALSO
malloc(3C)

NAME

crypt, setkey, encrypt – generate encryption

SYNOPSIS

```
#include <crypt.h>

char *crypt (const char *key, const char *salt);

void setkey (const char *key);

void encrypt (char *block, int edflag);
```

DESCRIPTION

crypt is the password encryption function. It is based on a one-way encryption algorithm with variations intended (among other things) to frustrate use of hardware implementations of a key search.

key is the input string to encrypt, for instance, a user's typed password. Only the first eight characters are used; the rest are ignored. *salt* is a two-character string chosen from the set a–zA–Z0–9./; this string is used to perturb the hashing algorithm in one of 4096 different ways, after which the input string is used as the key to encrypt repeatedly a constant string. The returned value points to the encrypted input string. The first two characters of the return value are the *salt* itself.

The setkey and encrypt functions provide (rather primitive) access to the actual hashing algorithm. The argument of setkey is a character array of length 64 containing only the characters with numerical value 0 and 1. This string is divided into groups of 8, the low-order bit in each group is ignored; this gives a 56-bit key that is set into the machine. This is the key that will be used with the hashing algorithm to encrypt the string *block* with the encrypt function.

The *block* argument of encrypt is a character array of length 64 containing only the characters with numerical value 0 and 1. The argument array is modified in place to a similar array representing the bits of the argument after having been subjected to the hashing algorithm using the key set by setkey. The argument *edflag*, indicating decryption rather than encryption, is ignored; use encrypt in libcrypt [see crypt(3X)] for decryption.

SEE ALSO

getpass(3C), crypt(3X), passwd(4)
login(1), passwd(1) in the *User's Reference Manual*

DIAGNOSTICS

If *edflag* is set to anything other than zero, errno will be set to ENOSYS.

NOTES

The return value for crypt points to static data that are overwritten by each call.

crypt(3X) (Encryption Utilities)

NAME
crypt – password and file encryption functions

SYNOPSIS
cc [*flag* ...] *file* ... -lcrypt [*library* ...]

#include <crypt.h>

char *crypt (const char *key, const char *salt);

void setkey (const char *key);

void encrypt (char *block, int flag);

char *des_crypt (const char *key, const char *salt);

void des_setkey (const char *key);

void des_encrypt (char *block, int flag);

int run_setkey (int *connection, const char *key);

int run_crypt (long offset, char *buffer, unsigned int count, int *connection);

int crypt_close(int *connection);

DESCRIPTION
des_crypt is the password encryption function. It is based on a one-way hashing encryption algorithm with variations intended (among other things) to frustrate use of hardware implementations of a key search.

key is a user's typed password. *salt* is a two-character string chosen from the set [a-zA-Z0-9./]; this string is used to perturb the hashing algorithm in one of 4096 different ways, after which the password is used as the key to encrypt repeatedly a constant string. The returned value points to the encrypted password. The first two characters are the salt itself.

The des_setkey and des_encrypt entries provide (rather primitive) access to the actual hashing algorithm. The argument of des_setkey is a character array of length 64 containing only the characters with numerical value 0 and 1. If this string is divided into groups of 8, the low-order bit in each group is ignored, thereby creating a 56-bit key that is set into the machine. This key is the key that will be used with the hashing algorithm to encrypt the string *block* with the function des_encrypt.

The argument to the des_encrypt entry is a character array of length 64 containing only the characters with numerical value 0 and 1. The argument array is modified in place to a similar array representing the bits of the argument after having been subjected to the hashing algorithm using the key set by des_setkey. If *flag* is zero, the argument is encrypted; if non-zero, it is decrypted.

Note that decryption is not provided in the international version of crypt. The international version is part of the C Development Set, and the domestic version is part of the Encryption Utilities. If decryption is attempted with the international version of des_encrypt, an error message is printed.

crypt, setkey, and encrypt are front-end routines that invoke *des_crypt*, *des_setkey*, and *des_encrypt* respectively.

The routines run_setkey and run_crypt are designed for use by applications that need cryptographic capabilities [such as ed(1) and vi(1)] that must be compatible with the crypt(1) user-level utility. run_setkey establishes a two-way pipe connection with the crypt utility, using *key* as the password argument. run_crypt takes a block of characters and transforms the cleartext or ciphertext into their ciphertext or cleartext using the crypt utility. *offset* is the relative byte position from the beginning of the file that the block of text provided in *buffer* is coming from. *count* is the number of characters in *buffer*, and *connection* is an array containing indices to a table of input and output file streams. When encryption is finished, crypt_close is used to terminate the connection with the crypt utility.

run_setkey returns −1 if a connection with the crypt utility cannot be established. This result will occur in international versions of the UNIX system in which the crypt utility is not available. If a null key is passed to run_setkey, 0 is returned. Otherwise, 1 is returned. run_crypt returns −1 if it cannot write output or read input from the pipe attached to crypt. Otherwise it returns 0.

The program must be linked with the object file access routine library libcrypt.a.

SEE ALSO
getpass(3C), passwd(4)
crypt(1), login(1), passwd(1) in the *User's Reference Manual*

DIAGNOSTICS
In the international version of crypt(3X), a flag argument of 1 to encrypt or des_encrypt is not accepted, and errno is set to ENOSYS to indicate that the functionality is not available.

NOTES
The return value in crypt points to static data that are overwritten by each call.

NAME
ctermid – generate file name for terminal

SYNOPSIS
    #include <stdio.h>

    char *ctermid (char *s);

DESCRIPTION
ctermid generates the path name of the controlling terminal for the current process, and stores it in a string.

If *s* is a NULL pointer, the string is stored in an internal static area, the contents of which are overwritten at the next call to ctermid, and the address of which is returned. Otherwise, *s* is assumed to point to a character array of at least L_ctermid elements; the path name is placed in this array and the value of *s* is returned. The constant L_ctermid is defined in the stdio.h header file.

SEE ALSO
ttyname(3C)

NOTES
The difference between ctermid and ttyname(3C) is that ttyname must be handed a file descriptor and returns the actual name of the terminal associated with that file descriptor, while ctermid returns a string (/dev/tty) that will refer to the terminal if used as a file name. Thus ttyname is useful only if the process already has at least one file open to a terminal.

ctime(3C)   (C Programming Language Utilities)   ctime(3C)

NAME
ctime, localtime, gmtime, asctime, tzset – convert date and time to string

SYNOPSIS
    #include <time.h>

    char *ctime (const time_t *clock);

    struct tm *localtime (const time_t *clock);

    struct tm *gmtime (const time_t *clock);

    char *asctime (const struct tm *tm);

    extern time_t timezone, altzone;

    extern int daylight;

    extern char *tzname[2];

    void tzset (void);

DESCRIPTION
ctime, localtime, and gmtime accept arguments of type time_t, pointed to by clock, representing the time in seconds since 00:00:00 UTC, January 1, 1970. ctime returns a pointer to a 26-character string as shown below. Time zone and daylight savings corrections are made before the string is generated. The fields are constant in width:

    Fri Sep 13 00:00:00 1986\n\0

localtime and gmtime return pointers to tm structures, described below. localtime corrects for the main time zone and possible alternate ("daylight savings") time zone; gmtime converts directly to Coordinated Universal Time (UTC), which is the time the UNIX system uses internally.

asctime converts a tm structure to a 26-character string, as shown in the above example, and returns a pointer to the string.

Declarations of all the functions and externals, and the tm structure, are in the time.h header file. The structure declaration is:

    struct   tm {
        int   tm_sec;   /* seconds after the minute – [0, 61] */
                         /* for leap seconds */
        int   tm_min;   /* minutes after the hour – [0, 59] */
        int   tm_hour;   /* hour since midnight – [0, 23] */
        int   tm_mday;   /* day of the month – [1, 31] */
        int   tm_mon;   /* months since January – [0, 11] */
        int   tm_year;   /* years since 1900 */
        int   tm_wday;   /* days since Sunday – [0, 6] */
        int   tm_yday;   /* days since January 1 – [0, 365] */
        int   tm_isdst; /* flag for alternate daylight */
                         /* savings time */
    };

The value of tm_isdst is positive if daylight savings time is in effect, zero if daylight savings time is not in effect, and negative if the information is not available. (Previously, the value of tm_isdst was defined as non-zero if daylight savings time was in effect.)

The external time_t variable altzone contains the difference, in seconds, between Coordinated Universal Time and the alternate time zone. The external variable timezone contains the difference, in seconds, between UTC and local standard time. The external variable daylight indicates whether time should reflect daylight savings time. Both timezone and altzone default to 0 (UTC). The external variable daylight is non-zero if an alternate time zone exists. The time zone names are contained in the external variable tzname, which by default is set to:

```
char *tzname[2] = { "GMT", "   " };
```

These functions know about the peculiarities of this conversion for various time periods for the U.S.A. (specifically, the years 1974, 1975, and 1987). They will handle the new daylight savings time starting with the first Sunday in April, 1987.

tzset uses the contents of the environment variable TZ to override the value of the different external variables. The function tzset is called by asctime and may also be called by the user. See environ(5) for a description of the TZ environment variable.

tzset scans the contents of the environment variable and assigns the different fields to the respective variable. For example, the most complete setting for New Jersey in 1986 could be

```
EST5EDT4,116/2:00:00,298/2:00:00
```

or simply

```
EST5EDT
```

An example of a southern hemisphere setting such as the Cook Islands could be

```
KDT9:30KST10:00,63/5:00,302/20:00
```

In the longer version of the New Jersey example of TZ, tzname[0] is EST, timezone will be set to 5*60*60, tzname[1] is EDT, altzone will be set to 4*60*60, the starting date of the alternate time zone is the 117th day at 2 AM, the ending date of the alternate time zone is the 299th day at 2 AM (using zero-based Julian days), and daylight will be set positive. Starting and ending times are relative to the alternate time zone. If the alternate time zone start and end dates and the time are not provided, the days for the United States that year will be used and the time will be 2 AM. If the start and end dates are provided but the time is not provided, the time will be 2 AM. The effects of tzset are thus to change the values of the external variables timezone, altzone, daylight, and tzname. ctime, localtime, mktime, and strftime will also update these external variables as if they had called tzset at the time specified by the time_t or struct tm value that they are converting.

Note that in most installations, TZ is set to the correct value by default when the user logs on, via the local /etc/profile file [see profile(4) and timezone(4)].

FILES

/usr/lib/locale/*language*/LC_TIME – file containing locale specific date and time information

SEE ALSO

time(2), getenv(3C), mktime(3C), putenv(3C), printf(3S), setlocale(3C), strftime(3C), cftime(4), profile(4), timezone(4), environ(5)

NOTES

The return values for ctime, localtime, and gmtime point to static data whose content is overwritten by each call.

Setting the time during the interval of change from timezone to altzone or vice versa can produce unpredictable results. The system administrator must change the Julian start and end days annually.

NAME

ctype: isdigit, isxdigit, islower, isupper, isalpha, isalnum, isspace, iscntrl, ispunct, isprint, isgraph, isascii – character handling

SYNOPSIS

    #include <ctype.h>

    int isalpha(int c);

    int isupper(int c);

    int islower(int c);

    int isdigit(int c);

    int isxdigit(int c);

    int isalnum(int c);

    int isspace(int c);

    int ispunct(int c);

    int isprint(int c);

    int isgraph(int c);

    int iscntrl(int c);

    int isascii(int c);

DESCRIPTION

These macros classify character-coded integer values. Each is a predicate returning non-zero for true, zero for false. The behavior of these macros, except isascii, is affected by the current locale [see setlocale(3C)]. To modify the behavior, change the LC_TYPE category in setlocale, that is, setlocale (LC_CTYPE, *newlocale*). In the C locale, or in a locale where character type information is not defined, characters are classified according to the rules of the US-ASCII 7-bit coded character set.

The macro isascii is defined on all integer values; the rest are defined only where the argument is an int, the value of which is representable as an unsigned char, or EOF, which is defined by the stdio.h header file and represents end-of-file.

isalpha   tests for any character for which isupper or islower is true, or any character that is one of an implementation-defined set of characters for which none of iscntrl, isdigit, ispunct, or isspace is true. In the C locale, isalpha returns true only for the characters for which isupper or islower is true.

isupper   tests for any character that is an upper-case letter or is one of an implementation-defined set of characters for which none of iscntrl, isdigit, ispunct, isspace, or islower is true. In the C locale, isupper returns true only for the characters defined as upper-case ASCII characters.

islower	tests for any character that is a lower-case letter or is one of an implementation-defined set of characters for which none of iscntrl, isdigit, ispunct, isspace, or isupper is true. In the C locale, islower returns true only for the characters defined as lower-case ASCII characters.
isdigit	tests for any decimal-digit character.
isxdigit	tests for any hexadecimal-digit character ([0-9], [A-F] or [a-f]).
isalnum	tests for any character for which isalpha or isdigit is true (letter or digit).
isspace	tests for any space, tab, carriage-return, newline, vertical-tab or form-feed (standard white-space characters) or for one of an implementation-defined set of characters for which isalnum is false. In the C locale, isspace returns true only for the standard white-space characters.
ispunct	tests for any printing character which is neither a space nor a character for which isalnum is true.
isprint	tests for any printing character, including space (" ").
isgraph	tests for any printing character, except space.
iscntrl	tests for any "control character" as defined by the character set.
isascii	tests for any ASCII character, code between 0 and 0177 inclusive.

All the character classification macros and the conversion functions and macros use a table lookup.

Functions exist for all the above defined macros. To get the function form, the macro name must be undefined (for example, #undef isdigit).

FILES
/usr/lib/locale/*locale*/LC_CTYPE

SEE ALSO
chrtbl(1M), setlocale(3C), stdio(3S), ascii(5), environ(5)

DIAGNOSTICS
If the argument to any of the character handling macros is not in the domain of the function, the result is undefined.

NAME

curs_addch: addch, waddch, mvaddch, mvwaddch, echochar, wechochar – add a character (with attributes) to a curses window and advance cursor

SYNOPSIS

#include <curses.h>

addch(chtype ch);

waddch(WINDOW *win, chtype ch);

mvaddch(int y, int x, chtype ch);

mvwaddch(WINDOW *win, int y, int x, chtype ch);

echochar(chtype ch);

wechochar(WINDOW *win, chtype ch);

DESCRIPTION

With the addch, waddch, mvaddch and mvwaddch routines, the character *ch* is put into the window at the current cursor position of the window and the position of the window cursor is advanced. Its function is similar to that of putchar. At the right margin, an automatic newline is performed. At the bottom of the scrolling region, if scrollok is enabled, the scrolling region is scrolled up one line.

If *ch* is a tab, newline, or backspace, the cursor is moved appropriately within the window. A newline also does a clrtoeol before moving. Tabs are considered to be at every eighth column. If *ch* is another control character, it is drawn in the ^X notation. Calling winch after adding a control character does not return the control character, but instead returns the representation of the control character.

Video attributes can be combined with a character by ORing them into the parameter. This results in these attributes also being set. (The intent here is that text, including attributes, can be copied from one place to another using inch and addch.) [see standout, predefined video attribute constants, on the curs_attr(3X) page].

The echochar and wechochar routines are functionally equivalent to a call to addch followed by a call to refresh, or a call to waddch followed by a call to wrefresh. The knowledge that only a single character is being output is taken into consideration and, for non-control characters, a considerable performance gain might be seen by using these routines instead of their equivalents.

Line Graphics

The following variables may be used to add line drawing characters to the screen with routines of the addch family. When variables are defined for the terminal, the A_ALTCHARSET bit is turned on [see curs_attr(3X)]. Otherwise, the default character listed below is stored in the variable. The names chosen are consistent with the VT100 nomenclature.

Name	Default	Glyph Description
ACS_ULCORNER	+	upper left-hand corner
ACS_LLCORNER	+	lower left-hand corner
ACS_URCORNER	+	upper right-hand corner
ACS_LRCORNER	+	lower right-hand corner
ACS_RTEE	+	right tee (−|)
ACS_LTEE	+	left tee (|−)
ACS_BTEE	+	bottom tee (⊥)
ACS_TTEE	+	top tee (⊤)
ACS_HLINE	−	horizontal line
ACS_VLINE	|	vertical line
ACS_PLUS	+	plus
ACS_S1	−	scan line 1
ACS_S9	_	scan line 9
ACS_DIAMOND	+	diamond
ACS_CKBOARD	:	checker board (stipple)
ACS_DEGREE	'	degree symbol
ACS_PLMINUS	#	plus/minus
ACS_BULLET	o	bullet
ACS_LARROW	<	arrow pointing left
ACS_RARROW	>	arrow pointing right
ACS_DARROW	v	arrow pointing down
ACS_UARROW	^	arrow pointing up
ACS_BOARD	#	board of squares
ACS_LANTERN	#	lantern symbol
ACS_BLOCK	#	solid square block

RETURN VALUE

All routines return the integer ERR upon failure and an integer value other than ERR upon successful completion, unless otherwise noted in the preceding routine descriptions.

NOTES

The header file curses.h automatically includes the header files stdio.h and unctrl.h.

Note that addch, mvaddch, mvwaddch, and echochar may be macros.

SEE ALSO

curses(3X), curs_attr(3X), curs_clear(3X), curs_inch(3X), curs_outopts(3X), curs_refresh(3X) putc(3S)

NAME

curs_addchstr: addchstr, addchnstr, waddchstr, waddchnstr, mvaddchstr, mvaddchnstr, mvwaddchstr, mvwaddchnstr − add string of characters (and attributes) to a curses window

SYNOPSIS

#include <curses.h>

int addchstr(chtype *chstr);

int addchnstr(chtype *chstr, int n);

int waddchstr(WINDOW *win, chtype *chstr);

int waddchnstr(WINDOW *win, chtype *chstr, int n);

int mvaddchstr(int y, int x, chtype *chstr);

int mvaddchnstr(int y, int x, chtype *chstr, int n);

int mvwaddchstr(WINDOW *win, int y, int x, chtype *chstr);

int mvwaddchnstr(WINDOW *win, int y, int x,
    chtype *chstr, int n);

DESCRIPTION

All of these routines copy *chstr* directly into the window image structure starting at the current cursor position. The four routines with *n* as the last argument copy at most *n* elements, but no more than will fit on the line. If n=−1 then the whole string is copied, to the maximum number that fit on the line.

The position of the window cursor is not advanced. These routines works faster than waddnstr because they merely copy *chstr* into the window image structure. On the other hand, care must be taken when using these functions because they don't perform any kind of checking (such as for the newline character), they don't advance the current cursor position, and they truncate the string, rather then wrapping it around to the new line.

RETURN VALUE

All routines return the integer ERR upon failure and an integer value other than ERR upon successful completion, unless otherwise noted in the preceding routine descriptions.

NOTES

The header file curses.h automatically includes the header files stdio.h and unctrl.h.

Note that all routines except waddchnstr may be macros.

SEE ALSO

curses(3X)

NAME

curs_addstr: addstr, addnstr, waddstr, waddnstr, mvaddstr, mvaddnstr, mvwaddstr, mvwaddnstr - add a string of characters to a curses window and advance cursor

SYNOPSIS

#include <curses.h>

int addstr(char *str);

int addnstr(char *str, int n);

int waddstr(WINDOW *win, char *str);

int waddnstr(WINDOW *win, char *str, int n);

int mvaddstr(y, int x, char *str);

int mvaddnstr(y, int x, char *str, int n);

int mvwaddstr(WINDOW *win, int y, int x, char *str);

int mvwaddnstr(WINDOW *win, int y, int x, char *str,
    int n);

DESCRIPTION

All of these routines write all the characters of the null terminated character string *str* on the given window. It is similar to calling waddch once for each character in the string. The four routines with *n* as the last argument write at most *n* characters. If *n* is negative, then the entire string will be added.

RETURN VALUE

All routines return the integer ERR upon failure and an integer value other than ERR upon successful completion.

NOTES

The header file curses.h automatically includes the header files stdio.h and unctrl.h.

Note that all of these routines except waddstr and waddnstr may be macros.

SEE ALSO

curses(3X), curs_addch(3X)

NAME

curs_attr: attroff, wattroff, attron, wattron, attrset, wattrset, standend, wstandend, standout, wstandout – curses character and window attribute control routines

SYNOPSIS

#include <curses.h>

int attroff(int attrs);

int wattroff(WINDOW *win, int attrs);

int attron(int attrs);

int wattron(WINDOW *win, int attrs);

int attrset(int attrs);

int wattrset(WINDOW *win, int attrs);

int standend(void);

int wstandend(WINDOW *win);

int standout(void);

int wstandout(WINDOW *win);

DESCRIPTION

All of these routines manipulate the current attributes of the named window. The current attributes of a window are applied to all characters that are written into the window with waddch, waddstr and wprintw. Attributes are a property of the character, and move with the character through any scrolling and insert/delete line/character operations. To the extent possible on the particular terminal, they are displayed as the graphic rendition of characters put on the screen.

The routine attrset sets the current attributes of the given window to *attrs*. The routine attroff turns off the named attributes without turning any other attributes on or off. The routine attron turns on the named attributes without affecting any others. The routine standout is the same as attron(A_STANDOUT). The routine standend is the same as attrset(0), that is, it turns off all attributes.

Attributes

The following video attributes, defined in <curses.h>, can be passed to the routines attron, attroff, and attrset, or ORed with the characters passed to addch.

A_STANDOUT	Best highlighting mode of the terminal.
A_UNDERLINE	Underlining
A_REVERSE	Reverse video
A_BLINK	Blinking
A_DIM	Half bright
A_BOLD	Extra bright or bold
A_ALTCHARSET	Alternate character set
A_CHARTEXT	Bit-mask to extract a character
COLOR_PAIR(*n*)	Color-pair number *n*

The following macro is the reverse of COLOR_PAIR(*n*):

    PAIR_NUMBER(*attrs*)   Returns the pair number associated with the COLOR_PAIR(*n*) attribute.

RETURN VALUE

These routines always return 1.

NOTES

The header file `curses.h` automatically includes the header files `stdio.h` and `unctrl.h`.

Note that `attroff`, `wattroff`, `attron`, `wattron`, `attrset`, `wattrset`, `standend` and `standout` may be macros.

SEE ALSO

curses(3X), curs_addch(3X), curs_addstr(3X), curs_printw(3X)

curs_beep(3X)

NAME
curs_beep: beep, flash – curses bell and screen flash routines

SYNOPSIS
#include <curses.h>

int beep(void);

int flash(void);

DESCRIPTION
The `beep` and `flash` routines are used to signal the terminal user. The routine `beep` sounds the audible alarm on the terminal, if possible; if that is not possible, it flashes the screen (visible bell), if that is possible. The routine `flash` flashes the screen, and if that is not possible, sounds the audible signal. If neither signal is possible, nothing happens. Nearly all terminals have an audible signal (bell or beep), but only some can flash the screen.

RETURN VALUE
These routines always return OK.

NOTES
The header file `curses.h` automatically includes the header files `stdio.h` and `unctrl.h`.

SEE ALSO
curses(3X)

NAME

curs_bkgd: bkgdset, wbkgdset, bkgd, wbkgd − curses window background manipulation routines

SYNOPSIS

#include <curses.h>

void bkgdset(chtype ch);

void wbkgdset(WINDOW *win, chtype ch);

int bkgd(chtype ch);

int wbkgd(WINDOW *win, chtype ch);

DESCRIPTION

The bkgdset and wbkgdset routines manipulate the background of the named window. Background is a chtype consisting of any combination of attributes and a character. The attribute part of the background is combined (ORed) with all non-blank characters that are written into the window with waddch. Both the character and attribute parts of the background are combined with the blank characters. The background becomes a property of the character and moves with the character through any scrolling and insert/delete line/character operations. To the extent possible on a particular terminal, the attribute part of the background is displayed as the graphic rendition of the character put on the screen.

The bkgd and wbkgd routines combine the new background with every position in the window. Background is any combination of attributes and a character. Only the attribute part is used to set the background of non-blank characters, while both character and attributes are used for blank positions. To the extent possible on a particular terminal, the attribute part of the background is displayed as the graphic rendition of the character put on the screen.

RETURN VALUE

bkgd and wbkgd return the integer OK, or a non-negative integer, if immedok is set.

NOTES

The header file curses.h automatically includes the header files stdio.h and unctrl.h.

Note that bkgdset and bkgd may be macros.

SEE ALSO

curses(3X), curs_addch(3X), curs_outopts(3X)

NAME

curs_border: border, wborder, box, hline, whline, vline, wvline - create curses borders, horizontal and vertical lines

SYNOPSIS

#include <curses.h>

int border(chtype ls, chtype rs, chtype ts, chtype bs,
    chtype tl, chtype tr, chtype bl, chtype br);
int wborder(WINDOW *win, chtype ls, chtype rs,
    chtype ts, chtype bs, chtype tl, chtype tr,
    chtype bl, chtype br);
int box(WINDOW *win, chtype verch, chtype horch);
int hline(chtype ch, int n);
int whline(WINDOW *win, chtype ch, int n);
int vline(chtype ch, int n);
int wvline(WINDOW *win, chtype ch, int n);

DESCRIPTION

With the border, wborder and box routines, a border is drawn around the edges of the window. The argument *ls* is a character and attributes used for the left side of the border, *rs* - right side, *ts* - top side, *bs* - bottom side, *tl* - top left-hand corner, *tr* - top right-hand corner, *bl* - bottom left-hand corner, and *br* - bottom right-hand corner. If any of these arguments is zero, then the following default values (defined in curses.h) are used instead: ACS_VLINE, ACS_VLINE, ACS_HLINE, ACS_HLINE, ACS_ULCORNER, ACS_URCORNER, ACS_BLCORNER, ACS_BRCORNER.

box(*win*, *verch*, *horch*) is a shorthand for the following call: wborder(*win*, *verch*, *verch*, *horch*, *horch*, 0, 0, 0, 0).

hline and whline draw a horizontal (left to right) line using *ch* starting at the current cursor position in the window. The current cursor position is not changed. The line is at most *n* characters long, or as many as fit into the window.

vline and wvline draw a vertical (top to bottom) line using *ch* starting at the current cursor position in the window. The current cursor position is not changed. The line is at most *n* characters long, or as many as fit into the window.

RETURN VALUE

All routines return the integer OK, or a non-negative integer if immedok is set.

NOTES

The header file curses.h automatically includes the header files stdio.h and unctrl.h.

Note that border and box may be macros.

SEE ALSO
curses(3X), curs_outopts(3X)

NAME

curs_clear: erase, werase, clear, wclear, clrtobot, wclrtobot, clrtoeol, wclrtoeol – clear all or part of a curses window

SYNOPSIS

include <curses.h>

int erase(void);

int werase(WINDOW *win);

int clear(void);

int wclear(WINDOW *win);

int clrtobot(void);

int wclrtobot(WINDOW *win);

int clrtoeol(void);

int wclrtoeol(WINDOW *win);

DESCRIPTION

The erase and werase routines copy blanks to every position in the window.

The clear and wclear routines are like erase and werase, but they also call clearok, so that the screen is cleared completely on the next call to wrefresh for that window and repainted from scratch.

The clrtobot and wclrtobot routines erase all lines below the cursor in the window. Also, the current line to the right of the cursor, inclusive, is erased.

The clrtoeol and wclrtoeol routines erase the current line to the right of the cursor, inclusive.

RETURN VALUE

All routines return the integer OK, or a non-negative integer if immedok is set.

NOTES

The header file curses.h automatically includes the header files stdio.h and unctrl.h.

Note that erase, werase, clear, wclear, clrtobot, and clrtoeol may be macros.

SEE ALSO

curses(3X), curs_outopts(3X), curs_refresh(3X)

curs_color(3X)

NAME
curs_color: start_color, init_pair, init_color, has_colors, can_change_color, color_content, pair_content – curses color manipulation routines

SYNOPSIS
\# include <curses.h>

int start_color(void);

int init_pair(short pair, short f, short b);

int init_color(short color, short r, short g, short b);

bool has_colors(void);

bool can_change_color(void);

int color_content(short color, short *r, short *g, short *b);

int pair_content(short pair, short *f, short *b);

DESCRIPTION
Overview
curses provides routines that manipulate color on color alphanumeric terminals. To use these routines start_color must be called, usually right after initscr. Colors are always used in pairs (referred to as color-pairs). A color-pair consists of a foreground color (for characters) and a background color (for the field on which the characters are displayed). A programmer initializes a color-pair with the routine init_pair. After it has been initialized, COLOR_PAIR(*n*), a macro defined in curses.h, can be used in the same ways other video attributes can be used. If a terminal is capable of redefining colors, the programmer can use the routine init_color to change the definition of a color. The routines has_colors and can_change_color return TRUE or FALSE, depending on whether the terminal has color capabilities and whether the programmer can change the colors. The routine color_content allows a programmer to identify the amounts of red, green, and blue components in an initialized color. The routine pair_content allows a programmer to find out how a given color-pair is currently defined.

Routine Descriptions
The start_color routine requires no arguments. It must be called if the programmer wants to use colors, and before any other color manipulation routine is called. It is good practice to call this routine right after initscr. start_color initializes eight basic colors (black, red, green, yellow, blue, magenta, cyan, and white), and two global variables, COLORS and COLOR_PAIRS (respectively defining the maximum number of colors and color-pairs the terminal can support). It also restores the colors on the terminal to the values they had when the terminal was just turned on.

The init_pair routine changes the definition of a color-pair. It takes three arguments: the number of the color-pair to be changed, the foreground color number, and the background color number. The value of the first argument must be between 1 and COLOR_PAIRS−1. The value of the second and third arguments must be between 0 and COLORS. If the color-pair was previously initialized, the screen is refreshed and all occurrences of that color-pair is changed to the new definition.

The `init_color` routine changes the definition of a color. It takes four arguments: the number of the color to be changed followed by three RGB values (for the amounts of red, green, and blue components). The value of the first argument must be between 0 and COLORS. (See the section **Colors** for the default color index.) Each of the last three arguments must be a value between 0 and 1000. When `init_color` is used, all occurrences of that color on the screen immediately change to the new definition.

The `has_colors` routine requires no arguments. It returns TRUE if the terminal can manipulate colors; otherwise, it returns FALSE. This routine facilitates writing terminal-independent programs. For example, a programmer can use it to decide whether to use color or some other video attribute.

The `can_change_color` routine requires no arguments. It returns TRUE if the terminal supports colors and can change their definitions; other, it returns FALSE. This routine facilitates writing terminal-independent programs.

The `color_content` routine gives users a way to find the intensity of the red, green, and blue (RGB) components in a color. It requires four arguments: the color number, and three addresses of shorts for storing the information about the amounts of red, green, and blue components in the given color. The value of the first argument must be between 0 and COLORS. The values that are stored at the addresses pointed to by the last three arguments are between 0 (no component) and 1000 (maximum amount of component).

The `pair_content` routine allows users to find out what colors a given color-pair consists of. It requires three arguments: the color-pair number, and two addresses of shorts for storing the foreground and the background color numbers. The value of the first argument must be between 1 and COLOR_PAIRS-1. The values that are stored at the addresses pointed to by the second and third arguments are between 0 and COLORS.

Colors

In curses.h the following macros are defined. These are the default colors. curses also assumes that COLOR_BLACK is the default background color for all terminals.

```
COLOR_BLACK
COLOR_RED
COLOR_GREEN
COLOR_YELLOW
COLOR_BLUE
COLOR_MAGENTA
COLOR_CYAN
COLOR_WHITE
```

RETURN VALUE

All routines that return an integer return ERR upon failure and OK upon successful completion.

NOTES
    The header file `curses.h` automatically includes the header files `stdio.h` and `unctrl.h`.

SEE ALSO
    curses(3X), curs_initscr(3X), curs_attr(3X)

curs_delch(3X)

NAME
curs_delch: delch, wdelch, mvdelch, mvwdelch – delete character under cursor in a curses window

SYNOPSIS
#include <curses.h>

int delch(void);

int wdelch(WINDOW *win);

int mvdelch(int y, int x);

int mvwdelch(WINDOW *win, int y, int x);

DESCRIPTION
With these routines the character under the cursor in the window is deleted; all characters to the right of the cursor on the same line are moved to the left one position and the last character on the line is filled with a blank. The cursor position does not change (after moving to y, x, if specified). (This does not imply use of the hardware delete character feature.)

RETURN VALUE
All routines return the integer ERR upon failure and an integer value other than ERR upon successful completion.

NOTES
The header file curses.h automatically includes the header files stdio.h and unctrl.h.

Note that delch, mvdelch, and mvwdelch may be macros.

SEE ALSO
curses(3X)

NAME

curs_deleteln: deleteln, wdeleteln, insdelln, winsdelln, insertln, winsertln - delete and insert lines in a curses window

SYNOPSIS

#include <curses.h>

int deleteln(void);

int wdeleteln(WINDOW *win);

int insdelln(int n);

int winsdelln(WINDOW *win, int n);

int insertln(void);

int winsertln(WINDOW *win);

DESCRIPTION

With the deleteln and wdeleteln routines, the line under the cursor in the window is deleted; all lines below the current line are moved up one line. The bottom line of the window is cleared. The cursor position does not change. (This does not imply use of a hardware delete line feature.)

With the insdelln and winsdelln routines, for positive n, insert n lines into the specified window above the current line. The n bottom lines are lost. For negative n, delete n lines (starting with the one under the cursor), and move the remaining lines up. The bottom n lines are cleared. The current cursor position remains the same.

With the insertln and insertln routines, a blank line is inserted above the current line and the bottom line is lost. (This does not imply use of a hardware insert line feature.)

RETURN VALUE

All routines return the integer ERR upon failure and an integer value other than ERR upon successful completion.

NOTES

The header file curses.h automatically includes the header files stdio.h and unctrl.h.

Note that all but winsdelln may be a macros.

SEE ALSO

curses(3X)

NAME

curs_getch: getch, wgetch, mvgetch, mvwgetch, ungetch − get (or push back) characters from curses terminal keyboard

SYNOPSIS

#include <curses.h>

int getch(void);

int wgetch(WINDOW *win);

int mvgetch(int y, int x);

int mvwgetch(WINDOW *win, int y, int x);

int ungetch(int ch);

DESCRIPTION

With the getch, wgetch, mvgetch and mvwgetch, routines a character is read from the terminal associated with the window. In no-delay mode, if no input is waiting, the value ERR is returned. In delay mode, the program waits until the system passes text through to the program. Depending on the setting of cbreak, this is after one character (cbreak mode), or after the first newline (nocbreak mode). In half-delay mode, the program waits until a character is typed or the specified timeout has been reached. Unless noecho has been set, the character will also be echoed into the designated window.

If the window is not a pad, and it has been moved or modified since the last call to wrefresh, wrefresh will be called before another character is read.

If keypad is TRUE, and a function key is pressed, the token for that function key is returned instead of the raw characters. Possible function keys are defined in curses.h with integers beginning with 0401, whose names begin with KEY_. If a character that could be the beginning of a function key (such as escape) is received, curses sets a timer. If the remainder of the sequence does not come in within the designated time, the character is passed through; otherwise, the function key value is returned. For this reason, many terminals experience a delay between the time a user presses the escape key and the escape is returned to the program. Since tokens returned by these routines are outside the ASCII range, they are not printable.

The ungetch routine places *ch* back onto the input queue to be returned by the next call to wgetch.

Function Keys

The following function keys, defined in curses.h, might be returned by getch if keypad has been enabled. Note that not all of these may be supported on a particular terminal if the terminal does not transmit a unique code when the key is pressed or if the definition for the key is not present in the *terminfo* database.

Name	Key name
KEY_BREAK	Break key
KEY_DOWN	The four arrow keys ...
KEY_UP	
KEY_LEFT	
KEY_RIGHT	
KEY_HOME	Home key (upward+left arrow)
KEY_BACKSPACE	Backspace
KEY_F0	Function keys; space for 64 keys is reserved.
KEY_F(n)	For $0 \le n \le 63$
KEY_DL	Delete line
KEY_IL	Insert line
KEY_DC	Delete character
KEY_IC	Insert char or enter insert mode
KEY_EIC	Exit insert char mode
KEY_CLEAR	Clear screen
KEY_EOS	Clear to end of screen
KEY_EOL	Clear to end of line
KEY_SF	Scroll 1 line forward
KEY_SR	Scroll 1 line backward (reverse)
KEY_NPAGE	Next page
KEY_PPAGE	Previous page
KEY_STAB	Set tab
KEY_CTAB	Clear tab
KEY_CATAB	Clear all tabs
KEY_ENTER	Enter or send
KEY_SRESET	Soft (partial) reset
KEY_RESET	Reset or hard reset
KEY_PRINT	Print or copy

KEY_LL	Home down or bottom (lower left). Keypad is arranged like this:
	    A1 up A3
	  left B2 right
	    C1 down C3

KEY_A1	Upper left of keypad
KEY_A3	Upper right of keypad
KEY_B2	Center of keypad
KEY_C1	Lower left of keypad
KEY_C3	Lower right of keypad
KEY_BTAB	Back tab key
KEY_BEG	Beg(inning) key
KEY_CANCEL	Cancel key
KEY_CLOSE	Close key
KEY_COMMAND	Cmd (command) key
KEY_COPY	Copy key
KEY_CREATE	Create key

Name	Key name
KEY_END	End key
KEY_EXIT	Exit key
KEY_FIND	Find key
KEY_HELP	Help key
KEY_MARK	Mark key
KEY_MESSAGE	Message key
KEY_MOVE	Move key
KEY_NEXT	Next object key
KEY_OPEN	Open key
KEY_OPTIONS	Options key
KEY_PREVIOUS	Previous object key
KEY_REDO	Redo key
KEY_REFERENCE	Ref(erence) key
KEY_REFRESH	Refresh key
KEY_REPLACE	Replace key
KEY_RESTART	Restart key
KEY_RESUME	Resume key
KEY_SAVE	Save key
KEY_SBEG	Shifted beginning key
KEY_SCANCEL	Shifted cancel key
KEY_SCOMMAND	Shifted command key
KEY_SCOPY	Shifted copy key
KEY_SCREATE	Shifted create key
KEY_SDC	Shifted delete char key
KEY_SDL	Shifted delete line key
KEY_SELECT	Select key
KEY_SEND	Shifted end key
KEY_SEOL	Shifted clear line key
KEY_SEXIT	Shifted exit key
KEY_SFIND	Shifted find key
KEY_SHELP	Shifted help key
KEY_SHOME	Shifted home key
KEY_SIC	Shifted input key
KEY_SLEFT	Shifted left arrow key
KEY_SMESSAGE	Shifted message key
KEY_SMOVE	Shifted move key
KEY_SNEXT	Shifted next key
KEY_SOPTIONS	Shifted options key
KEY_SPREVIOUS	Shifted prev key
KEY_SPRINT	Shifted print key
KEY_SREDO	Shifted redo key
KEY_SREPLACE	Shifted replace key
KEY_SRIGHT	Shifted right arrow
KEY_SRSUME	Shifted resume key
KEY_SSAVE	Shifted save key
KEY_SSUSPEND	Shifted suspend key

Name	Key name
KEY_SUNDO	Shifted undo key
KEY_SUSPEND	Suspend key
KEY_UNDO	Undo key

RETURN VALUE

All routines return the integer ERR upon failure and an integer value other than ERR upon successful completion.

NOTES

The header file `curses.h` automatically includes the header files `stdio.h` and `unctrl.h`.

Use of the escape key by a programmer for a single character function is discouraged.

When using `getch`, `wgetch`, `mvgetch`, or `mvwgetch`, nocbreak mode (nocbreak) and echo mode (echo) should not be used at the same time. Depending on the state of the tty driver when each character is typed, the program may produce undesirable results.

Note that `getch`, `mvgetch`, and `mvwgetch` may be macros.

SEE ALSO

curses(3X), curs_inopts(3X), curs_move(3X), curs_refresh(3X)

NAME

curs_getstr: getstr, wgetstr, mvgetstr, mvwgetstr, wgetnstr − get character strings from curses terminal keyboard

SYNOPSIS

#include <curses.h>

int getstr(char *str);

int wgetstr(WINDOW *win, char *str);

int mvgetstr(int y, int x, char *str);

int mvwgetstr(WINDOW *win, int y, int x, char *str);

int wgetnstr(WINDOW *win, char *str, int n);

DESCRIPTION

The effect of getstr is as though a series of calls to getch were made, until a newline and carriage return is received. The resulting value is placed in the area pointed to by the character pointer str. wgetnstr reads at most n characters, thus preventing a possible overflow of the input buffer. The user's erase and kill characters are interpreted, as well as any special keys (such as function keys, "home" key, "clear" key, and so on).

RETURN VALUE

All routines return the integer ERR upon failure and an integer value other than ERR upon successful completion.

NOTES

The header file curses.h automatically includes the header files stdio.h and unctrl.h.

Note that getstr, mvgetstr, and mvwgetstr may be macros.

SEE ALSO

curses(3X), curs_getch(3X)

NAME
curs_getyx: getyx, getparyx, getbegyx, getmaxyx − get curses cursor and window coordinates

SYNOPSIS
#include <curses.h>

void getyx(WINDOW *win, int y, int x);

void getparyx(WINDOW *win, int y, int x);

void getbegyx(WINDOW *win, int y, int x);

void getmaxyx(WINDOW *win, int y, int x);

DESCRIPTION
With the getyx macro, the cursor position of the window is placed in the two integer variables y and x.

With the getparyx macro, if *win* is a subwindow, the beginning coordinates of the subwindow relative to the parent window are placed into two integer variables, y and x. Otherwise, −1 is placed into y and x.

Like getyx, the getbegyx and getmaxyx macros store the current beginning coordinates and size of the specified window.

RETURN VALUE
The return values of these macros are undefined (that is, they should not be used as the right-hand side of assignment statements).

NOTES
The header file curses.h automatically includes the header files stdio.h and unctrl.h.

Note that all of these interfaces are macros and that "&" is not necessary before the variables y and x.

SEE ALSO
curses(3X)

curs_inch(3X)

NAME
curs_inch: inch, winch, mvinch, mvwinch - get a character and its attributes from a curses window

SYNOPSIS
#include <curses.h>

chtype inch(void);

chtype winch(WINDOW *win);

chtype mvinch(int y, int x);

chtype mvwinch(WINDOW *win, int y, int x);

DESCRIPTION
With these routines, the character, of type chtype, at the current position in the named window is returned. If any attributes are set for that position, their values are ORed into the value returned. Constants defined in <curses.h> can be used with the & (logical AND) operator to extract the character or attributes alone.

Attributes
The following bit-masks may be ANDed with characters returned by winch.

A_CHARTEXT	Bit-mask to extract character
A_ATTRIBUTES	Bit-mask to extract attributes
A_COLOR	Bit-mask to extract color-pair field information

NOTES
The header file curses.h automatically includes the header files stdio.h and unctrl.h.

Note that all of these routines may be macros.

SEE ALSO
curses(3X)

NAME

curs_inchstr: inchstr, inchnstr, winchstr, winchnstr, mvinchstr, mvinchnstr, mvwinchstr, mvwinchnstr – get a string of characters (and attributes) from a curses window

SYNOPSIS

#include <curses.h>

int inchstr(chtype *chstr);

int inchnstr(chtype *chstr, int n);

int winchstr(WINDOW *win, chtype *chstr);

int winchnstr(WINDOW *win, chtype *chstr, int n);

int mvinchstr(int y, int x, chtype *chstr);

int mvinchnstr(int y, int x, chtype *chstr, int n);

int mvwinchstr(WINDOW *win, int y, int x, chtype *chstr);

int mvwinchnstr(WINDOW *win, int y, int x, chtype *chstr, int n);

DESCRIPTION

With these routines, a string of type chtype, starting at the current cursor position in the named window and ending at the right margin of the window, is returned. The four functions with *n* as the last argument, return the string at most *n* characters long. Constants defined in curses.h can be used with the & (logical AND) operator to extract the character or the attribute alone from any position in the *chstr* [see curs_inch(3X)].

RETURN VALUE

All routines return the integer ERR upon failure and an integer value other than ERR upon successful completion.

NOTES

The header file curses.h automatically includes the header files stdio.h and unctrl.h.

Note that all routines except winchnstr may be macros.

SEE ALSO

curses(3X), curs_inch(3X)

NAME

curs_initscr: initscr, newterm, endwin, isendwin, set_term, delscreen − curses screen initialization and manipulation routines

SYNOPSIS

#include <curses.h>

WINDOW *initscr(void);

int endwin(void);

int isendwin(void);

SCREEN *newterm(char *type, FILE *outfd, FILE *infd);

SCREEN *set_term(SCREEN *new);

void delscreen(SCREEN* sp);

DESCRIPTION

initscr is almost always the first routine that should be called (the exceptions are slk_init, filter, ripoffline, use_env and, for multiple-terminal applications, newterm.) This determines the terminal type and initializes all curses data structures. initscr also causes the first call to refresh to clear the screen. If errors occur, initscr writes an appropriate error message to standard error and exits; otherwise, a pointer is returned to stdscr. If the program needs an indication of error conditions, newterm() should be used instead of initscr; initscr should only be called once per application.

A program that outputs to more than one terminal should use the newterm routine for each terminal instead of initscr. A program that needs an indication of error conditions, so it can continue to run in a line-oriented mode if the terminal cannot support a screen-oriented program, would also use this routine. The routine newterm should be called once for each terminal. It returns a variable of type SCREEN * which should be saved as a reference to that terminal. The arguments are the *type* of the terminal to be used in place of $TERM, a file pointer for output to the terminal, and another file pointer for input from the terminal (if *type* is NULL, $TERM will be used). The program must also call endwin for each terminal being used before exiting from curses. If newterm is called more than once for the same terminal, the first terminal referred to must be the last one for which endwin is called.

A program should always call endwin before exiting or escaping from curses mode temporarily. This routine restores tty modes, moves the cursor to the lower left-hand corner of the screen and resets the terminal into the proper non-visual mode. Calling refresh or doupdate after a temporary escape causes the program to resume visual mode.

The isendwin routine returns TRUE if endwin has been called without any subsequent calls to wrefresh, and FALSE otherwise.

The set_term routine is used to switch between different terminals. The screen reference new becomes the new current terminal. The previous terminal is returned by the routine. This is the only routine which manipulates SCREEN pointers; all other routines affect only the current terminal.

The delscreen routine frees storage associated with the SCREEN data structure. The endwin routine does not do this, so delscreen should be called after endwin if a particular SCREEN is no longer needed.

RETURN VALUE

endwin returns the integer ERR upon failure and OK upon successful completion.

Routines that return pointers always return NULL on error.

NOTES

The header file curses.h automatically includes the header files stdio.h and unctrl.h.

Note that initscr and newterm may be macros.

SEE ALSO

curses(3X), curs_kernel(3X), curs_refresh(3X), curs_slk(3X), curs_util(3X)

NAME

curs_inopts: cbreak, nocbreak, echo, noecho, halfdelay, intrflush, keypad, meta, nodelay, notimeout, raw, noraw, noqiflush, qiflush, timeout, wtimeout, typeahead – curses terminal input option control routines

SYNOPSIS

#include <curses.h>

int cbreak(void);

int nocbreak(void);

int echo(void);

int noecho(void);

int halfdelay(int tenths);

int intrflush(WINDOW *win, bool bf);

int keypad(WINDOW *win, bool bf);

int meta(WINDOW *win, bool bf);

int nodelay(WINDOW *win, bool bf);

int notimeout(WINDOW *win, bool bf);

int raw(void);

int noraw(void);

void noqiflush(void);

void qiflush(void);

void timeout(int delay);

void wtimeout(WINDOW *win, int delay);

int typeahead(int fd);

DESCRIPTION

The cbreak and nocbreak routines put the terminal into and out of cbreak mode, respectively. In this mode, characters typed by the user are immediately available to the program, and erase/kill character-processing is not performed. When out of this mode, the tty driver buffers the typed characters until a newline or carriage return is typed. Interrupt and flow control characters are unaffected by this mode. Initially the terminal may or may not be in cbreak mode, as the mode is inherited; therefore, a program should call cbreak or nocbreak explicitly. Most interactive programs using curses set the cbreak mode.

Note that cbreak overrides raw. [See curs_getch(3X) for a discussion of how these routines interact with echo and noecho.]

The echo and noecho routines control whether characters typed by the user are echoed by getch as they are typed. Echoing by the tty driver is always disabled, but initially getch is in echo mode, so characters typed are echoed. Authors of most interactive programs prefer to do their own echoing in a controlled area of the screen, or not to echo at all, so they disable echoing by calling noecho. [See curs_getch(3X) for a discussion of how these routines interact with cbreak and nocbreak.]

The halfdelay routine is used for half-delay mode, which is similar to cbreak mode in that characters typed by the user are immediately available to the program. However, after blocking for *tenths* tenths of seconds, ERR is returned if nothing has been typed. The value of tenths must be a number between 1 and 255. Use nocbreak to leave half-delay mode.

If the intrflush option is enabled, (*bf* is TRUE), when an interrupt key is pressed on the keyboard (interrupt, break, quit) all output in the tty driver queue will be flushed, giving the effect of faster response to the interrupt, but causing curses to have the wrong idea of what is on the screen. Disabling (*bf* is FALSE), the option prevents the flush. The default for the option is inherited from the tty driver settings. The window argument is ignored.

The keypad option enables the keypad of the user's terminal. If enabled (*bf* is TRUE), the user can press a function key (such as an arrow key) and wgetch returns a single value representing the function key, as in KEY_LEFT. If disabled (*bf* is FALSE), curses does not treat function keys specially and the program has to interpret the escape sequences itself. If the keypad in the terminal can be turned on (made to transmit) and off (made to work locally), turning on this option causes the terminal keypad to be turned on when wgetch is called. The default value for keypad is false.

Initially, whether the terminal returns 7 or 8 significant bits on input depends on the control mode of the tty driver [see termio(7)]. To force 8 bits to be returned, invoke meta(*win*, TRUE). To force 7 bits to be returned, invoke meta(*win*, FALSE). The window argument, *win*, is always ignored. If the terminfo capabilities smm (meta_on) and rmm (meta_off) are defined for the terminal, smm is sent to the terminal when meta(*win*, TRUE) is called and rmm is sent when meta(*win*, FALSE) is called.

The nodelay option causes getch to be a non-blocking call. If no input is ready, getch returns ERR. If disabled (*bf* is FALSE), getch waits until a key is pressed.

While interpreting an input escape sequence, wgetch sets a timer while waiting for the next character. If notimeout(*win*, TRUE) is called, then wgetch does not set a timer. The purpose of the timeout is to differentiate between sequences received from a function key and those typed by a user.

With the raw and noraw routines, the terminal is placed into or out of raw mode. Raw mode is similar to cbreak mode, in that characters typed are immediately passed through to the user program. The differences are that in raw mode, the interrupt, quit, suspend, and flow control characters are all passed through uninterpreted, instead of generating a signal. The behavior of the BREAK key depends on other bits in the tty driver that are not set by curses.

When the noqiflush routine is used, normal flush of input and output queues associated with the INTR, QUIT and SUSP characters will not be done [see termio(7)]. When qiflush is called, the queues will be flushed when these control characters are read.

The `timeout` and `wtimeout` routines set blocking or non-blocking read for a given window. If *delay* is negative, blocking read is used (that is, waits indefinitely for input). If *delay* is zero, then non-blocking read is used (that is, read returns ERR if no input is waiting). If *delay* is positive, then read blocks for *delay* milliseconds, and returns ERR if there is still no input. Hence, these routines provide the same functionality as `nodelay`, plus the additional capability of being able to block for only *delay* milliseconds (where *delay* is positive).

curses does "line-breakout optimization" by looking for typeahead periodically while updating the screen. If input is found, and it is coming from a tty, the current update is postponed until `refresh` or `doupdate` is called again. This allows faster response to commands typed in advance. Normally, the input FILE pointer passed to `newterm`, or `stdin` in the case that `initscr` was used, will be used to do this typeahead checking. The `typeahead` routine specifies that the file descriptor *fd* is to be used to check for typeahead instead. If *fd* is −1, then no typeahead checking is done.

RETURN VALUE
All routines that return an integer return ERR upon failure and an integer value other than ERR upon successful completion, unless otherwise noted in the preceding routine descriptions.

NOTES
The header file `curses.h` automatically includes the header files `stdio.h` and `unctrl.h`.

Note that echo, noecho, halfdelay, intrflush, meta, nodelay, notimeout, noqiflush, qiflush, timeout, and `wtimeout` may be macros.

SEE ALSO
curses(3X), curs_getch(3X), curs_initscr(3X), termio(7)

curs_insch(3X)

NAME
curs_insch: insch, winsch, mvinsch, mvwinsch – insert a character before the character under the cursor in a curses window

SYNOPSIS
#include <curses.h>

int insch(chtype ch);

int winsch(WINDOW *win, chtype ch);

int mvinsch(int y, int x, chtype ch);

int mvwinsch(WINDOW *win, int y, int x, chtype ch);

DESCRIPTION
With these routines, the character *ch* is inserted before the character under the cursor. All characters to the right of the cursor are moved one space to the right, with the possibility of the rightmost character on the line being lost. The cursor position does not change (after moving to *y*, *x*, if specified). (This does not imply use of the hardware insert character feature.)

RETURN VALUE
All routines return the integer ERR upon failure and an integer value other than ERR upon successful completion.

NOTES
The header file curses.h automatically includes the header files stdio.h and unctrl.h.

Note that insch, mvinsch, and mvwinsch may be macros.

SEE ALSO
curses(3X)

NAME

curs_instr: insstr, insnstr, winsstr, winsnstr, mvinsstr, mvinsnstr, mvwinsstr, mvwinsnstr – insert string before character under the cursor in a curses window

SYNOPSIS

#include <curses.h>

int insstr(char *str);
int insnstr(char *str, int n);
int winsstr(WINDOW *win, char *str);
int winsnstr(WINDOW *win, char *str, int n);
int mvinsstr(int y, int x, char *str);
int mvinsnstr(int y, int x, char *str, int n);
int mvwinsstr(WINDOW *win, int y, int x, char *str);
int mvwinsnstr(WINDOW *win, int y, int x, char *str, int n);

DESCRIPTION

With these routines, a character string (as many characters as will fit on the line) is inserted before the character under the cursor. All characters to the right of the cursor are moved to the right, with the possibility of the rightmost characters on the line being lost. The cursor position does not change (after moving to *y*, *x*, if specified). (This does not imply use of the hardware insert character feature.) The four routines with *n* as the last argument insert at most *n* characters. If $n<=0$, then the entire string is inserted.

If a character in *str* is a tab, newline, carriage return or backspace, the cursor is moved appropriately within the window. A newline also does a clrtoeol before moving. Tabs are considered to be at every eighth column. If a character in *str* is another control character, it is drawn in the ^X notation. Calling winch after adding a control character (and moving to it, if necessary) does not return the control character, but instead returns the representation of the control character.

RETURN VALUE

All routines return the integer ERR upon failure and an integer value other than ERR upon successful completion.

NOTES

The header file curses.h automatically includes the header files stdio.h and unctrl.h.

Note that all but winsnstr may be macros.

SEE ALSO

curses(3X), curs_clear(3X), curs_inch(3X)

NAME
curs_instr: instr, innstr, winstr, winnstr, mvinstr, mvinnstr, mvwinstr, mvwinnstr – get a string of characters from a curses window

SYNOPSIS
#include <curses.h>

int instr(char *str);

int innstr(char *str, int n);

int winstr(WINDOW *win, char *str);

int winnstr(WINDOW *win, char *str, int n);

int mvinstr(int y, int x, char *str);

int mvinnstr(int y, int x, char *str, int n);

int mvwinstr(WINDOW *win, int y, int x, char *str);

int mvwinnstr(WINDOW *win, int y, int x, char *str, int n);

DESCRIPTION
These routines return a string of characters in *str*, starting at the current cursor position in the named window and ending at the right margin of the window. Attributes are stripped from the characters. The four functions with *n* as the last argument return the string at most *n* characters long.

RETURN VALUE
All routines return the integer ERR upon failure and an integer value other than ERR upon successful completion.

NOTES
The header file curses.h automatically includes the header files stdio.h and unctrl.h.

Note that all routines except winnstr may be macros.

SEE ALSO
curses(3X)

curs_kernel(3X)

NAME
curs_kernel: def_prog_mode, def_shell_mode, reset_prog_mode, reset_shell_mode, resetty, savetty, getsyx, setsyx, ripoffline, curs_set, napms − low-level curses routines

SYNOPSIS
    #include <curses.h>

    int def_prog_mode(void);

    int def_shell_mode(void);

    int reset_prog_mode(void);

    int reset_shell_mode(void);

    int resetty(void);

    int savetty(void);

    int getsyx(int y, int x);

    int setsyx(int y, int x);

    int ripoffline(int line, int (*init)(WINDOW *, int));

    int curs_set(int visibility);

    int napms(int ms);

DESCRIPTION
The following routines give low-level access to various curses functionality. Theses routines typically are used inside library routines.

The def_prog_mode and def_shell_mode routines save the current terminal modes as the "program" (in curses) or "shell" (not in curses) state for use by the reset_prog_mode and reset_shell_mode routines. This is done automatically by initscr.

The reset_prog_mode and reset_shell_mode routines restore the terminal to "program" (in curses) or "shell" (out of curses) state. These are done automatically by endwin and, after an endwin, by doupdate, so they normally are not called.

The resetty and savetty routines save and restore the state of the terminal modes. savetty saves the current state in a buffer and resetty restores the state to what it was at the last call to savetty.

With the getsyx routine, the current coordinates of the virtual screen cursor are returned in y and x. If leaveok is currently TRUE, then −1,−1 is returned. If lines have been removed from the top of the screen, using ripoffline, y and x include these lines; therefore, y and x should be used only as arguments for setsyx.

With the setsyx routine, the virtual screen cursor is set to y, x. If y and x are both −1, then leaveok is set. The two routines getsyx and setsyx are designed to be used by a library routine, which manipulates curses windows but does not want to change the current position of the program's cursor. The library routine would call getsyx at the beginning, do its manipulation of its own windows, do a wnoutrefresh on its windows, call setsyx, and then call doupdate.

The ripoffline routine provides access to the same facility that slk_init [see curs_slk(3X)] uses to reduce the size of the screen. ripoffline must be called before initscr or newterm is called. If *line* is positive, a line is removed from the top of stdscr; if *line* is negative, a line is removed from the bottom. When this is done inside initscr, the routine init (supplied by the user) is called with two arguments: a window pointer to the one-line window that has been allocated and an integer with the number of columns in the window. Inside this initialization routine, the integer variables LINES and COLS (defined in curses.h) are not guaranteed to be accurate and wrefresh or doupdate must not be called. It is allowable to call wnoutrefresh during the initialization routine.

ripoffline can be called up to five times before calling initscr or newterm.

With the curs_set routine, the cursor state is set to invisible, normal, or very visible for visibility equal to 0, 1, or 2 respectively. If the terminal supports the *visibility* requested, the previous *cursor* state is returned; otherwise, ERR is returned.

The napms routine is used to sleep for *ms* milliseconds.

RETURN VALUE

Except for curs_set, these routines always return OK. curs_set returns the previous cursor state, or ERR if the requested *visibility* is not supported.

NOTES

The header file curses.h automatically includes the header files stdio.h and unctrl.h.

Note that getsyx is a macro, so & is not necessary before the variables *y* and *x*.

SEE ALSO

curses(3X), curs_initscr(3X), curs_outopts(3X), curs_refresh(3X), curs_scr_dump(3X), curs_slk(3X)

curs_move(3X)

NAME
curs_move: move, wmove – move curses window cursor

SYNOPSIS
#include <curses.h>

int move(int y, int x);

int wmove(WINDOW *win, int y, int x);

DESCRIPTION
With these routines, the cursor associated with the window is moved to line y and column x. This routine does not move the physical cursor of the terminal until refresh is called. The position specified is relative to the upper left-hand corner of the window, which is (0,0).

RETURN VALUE
These routines return the integer ERR upon failure and an integer value other than ERR upon successful completion.

NOTES
The header file curses.h automatically includes the header files stdio.h and unctrl.h.

Note that move may be a macro.

SEE ALSO
curses(3X), curs_refresh(3X)

curs_outopts(3X)

NAME

curs_outopts: clearok, idlok, idcok immedok, leaveok, setscrreg, wsetscrreg, scrollok, nl, nonl - curses terminal output option control routines

SYNOPSIS

```
#include <curses.h>

int clearok(WINDOW *win, bool bf);

int idlok(WINDOW *win, bool bf);

void idcok(WINDOW *win, bool bf);

void immedok(WINDOW *win, bool bf);

int leaveok(WINDOW *win, bool bf);

int setscrreg(int top, int bot);

int wsetscrreg(WINDOW *win, int top, int bot);

int scrollok(WINDOW *win, bool bf);

int nl(void);

int nonl(void);
```

DESCRIPTION

These routines set options that deal with output within curses. All options are initially FALSE, unless otherwise stated. It is not necessary to turn these options off before calling endwin.

With the clearok routine, if enabled (*bf* is TRUE), the next call to wrefresh with this window will clear the screen completely and redraw the entire screen from scratch. This is useful when the contents of the screen are uncertain, or in some cases for a more pleasing visual effect. If the *win* argument to clearok is the global variable curscr, the next call to wrefresh with any window causes the screen to be cleared and repainted from scratch.

With the idlok routine, if enabled (*bf* is TRUE), curses considers using the hardware insert/delete line feature of terminals so equipped. If disabled (*bf* is FALSE), curses very seldom uses this feature. (The insert/delete character feature is always considered.) This option should be enabled only if the application needs insert/delete line, for example, for a screen editor. It is disabled by default because insert/delete line tends to be visually annoying when used in applications where it isn't really needed. If insert/delete line cannot be used, curses redraws the changed portions of all lines.

With the idcok routine, if enabled (*bf* is TRUE), curses considers using the hardware insert/delete character feature of terminals so equipped. This is enabled by default.

With the immedok routine, if enabled (*bf* is TRUE), any change in the window image, such as the ones caused by waddch, wclrtobot, wscrl, and so on, automatically cause a call to wrefresh. However, it may degrade the performance considerably, due to repeated calls to wrefresh. It is disabled by default.

Normally, the hardware cursor is left at the location of the window cursor being refreshed. The leaveok option allows the cursor to be left wherever the update happens to leave it. It is useful for applications where the cursor is not used, since it reduces the need for cursor motions. If possible, the cursor is made invisible when this option is enabled.

The setscrreg and wsetscrreg routines allow the application programmer to set a software scrolling region in a window. *top* and *bot* are the line numbers of the top and bottom margin of the scrolling region. (Line 0 is the top line of the window.) If this option and scrollok are enabled, an attempt to move off the bottom margin line causes all lines in the scrolling region to scroll up one line. Only the text of the window is scrolled. (Note that this has nothing to do with the use of a physical scrolling region capability in the terminal, like that in the VT100. If idlok is enabled and the terminal has either a scrolling region or insert/delete line capability, they will probably be used by the output routines.)

The scrollok option controls what happens when the cursor of a window is moved off the edge of the window or scrolling region, either as a result of a newline action on the bottom line, or typing the last character of the last line. If disabled, (*bf* is FALSE), the cursor is left on the bottom line. If enabled, (*bf* is TRUE), wrefresh is called on the window, and the physical terminal and window are scrolled up one line. [Note that in order to get the physical scrolling effect on the terminal, it is also necessary to call idlok.]

The nl and nonl routines control whether newline is translated into carriage return and linefeed on output, and whether return is translated into newline on input. Initially, the translations do occur. By disabling these translations using nonl, curses is able to make better use of the linefeed capability, resulting in faster cursor motion.

RETURN VALUE

setscrreg and wsetscrreg return OK upon success and ERR upon failure. All other routines that return an integer always return OK.

NOTES

The header file curses.h automatically includes the header files stdio.h and unctrl.h.

Note that clearok, leaveok, scrollok, idcok, nl, nonl and setscrreg may be macros.

The immedok routine is useful for windows that are used as terminal emulators.

SEE ALSO

curses(3X), curs_addch(3X), curs_clear(3X), curs_initscr(3X), curs_scroll(3X), curs_refresh(3X).

NAME

curs_overlay: overlay, overwrite, copywin − overlap and manipulate overlapped curses windows

SYNOPSIS

#include <curses.h>

int overlay(WINDOW *srcwin, WINDOW *dstwin);

int overwrite(WINDOW *srcwin, WINDOW *dstwin);

int copywin(WINDOW *srcwin, WINDOW *dstwin, int sminrow,
      int smincol, int dminrow, int dmincol, int dmaxrow,
      int dmaxcol, int overlay);

DESCRIPTION

The overlay and overwrite routines overlay *srcwin* on top of *dstwin*. *scrwin* and *dstwin* are not required to be the same size; only text where the two windows overlap is copied. The difference is that overlay is non-destructive (blanks are not copied) whereas overwrite is destructive.

The copywin routine provides a finer granularity of control over the overlay and overwrite routines. Like in the prefresh routine, a rectangle is specified in the destination window, (*dminrow*, *dmincol*) and (*dmaxrow*, *dmaxcol*), and the upper-left-corner coordinates of the source window, (*sminrow*, *smincol*). If the argument *overlay* is true, then copying is non-destructive, as in overlay.

RETURN VALUE

Routines that return an integer return ERR upon failure and an integer value other than ERR upon successful completion.

NOTES

The header file curses.h automatically includes the header files stdio.h and unctrl.h.

Note that overlay and overwrite may be macros.

SEE ALSO

curses(3X), curs_pad(3X), curs_refresh(3X)

NAME

curs_pad: newpad, subpad, prefresh, pnoutrefresh, pechochar – create and display curses pads

SYNOPSIS

#include <curses.h>

WINDOW *newpad(int nlines, int ncols);

WINDOW *subpad(WINDOW *orig, int nlines, int ncols,
    int begin_y, int begin_x);

int prefresh(WINDOW *pad, int pminrow, int pmincol,
    int sminrow, int smincol, int smaxrow, int smaxcol);

int pnoutrefresh(WINDOW *pad, int pminrow, int pmincol,
    int sminrow, int smincol, int smaxrow, int smaxcol);

int pechochar(WINDOW *pad, chtype ch);

DESCRIPTION

The newpad routine creates and returns a pointer to a new pad data structure with the given number of lines, *nlines*, and columns, *ncols*. A pad is like a window, except that it is not restricted by the screen size, and is not necessarily associated with a particular part of the screen. Pads can be used when a large window is needed, and only a part of the window will be on the screen at one time. Automatic refreshes of pads (for example, from scrolling or echoing of input) do not occur. It is not legal to call wrefresh with a *pad* as an argument; the routines prefresh or pnoutrefresh should be called instead. Note that these routines require additional parameters to specify the part of the pad to be displayed and the location on the screen to be used for the display.

The subpad routine creates and returns a pointer to a subwindow within a pad with the given number of lines, *nlines*, and columns, *ncols*. Unlike subwin, which uses screen coordinates, the window is at position (*begin_x*, *begin_y*) on the pad. The window is made in the middle of the window *orig*, so that changes made to one window affect both windows. During the use of this routine, it will often be necessary to call touchwin or touchline on *orig* before calling prefresh.

The prefresh and pnoutrefresh routines are analogous to wrefresh and wnoutrefresh except that they relate to pads instead of windows. The additional parameters are needed to indicate what part of the pad and screen are involved. *pminrow* and *pmincol* specify the upper left-hand corner of the rectangle to be displayed in the pad. *sminrow*, *smincol*, *smaxrow*, and *smaxcol* specify the edges of the rectangle to be displayed on the screen. The lower right-hand corner of the rectangle to be displayed in the pad is calculated from the screen coordinates, since the rectangles must be the same size. Both rectangles must be entirely contained within their respective structures. Negative values of *pminrow*, *pmincol*, *sminrow*, or *smincol* are treated as if they were zero.

The pechochar routine is functionally equivalent to a call to addch followed by a call to refresh, a call to waddch followed by a call to wrefresh, or a call to waddch followed by a call to prefresh. The knowledge that only a single character is being output is taken into consideration and, for non-control characters, a considerable performance gain might be seen by using these routines instead of their equivalents. In the case of pechochar, the last location of the pad on the screen is reused for the arguments to prefresh.

RETURN VALUE

Routines that return an integer return ERR upon failure and an integer value other than ERR upon successful completion.

Routines that return pointers return NULL on error.

NOTES

The header file curses.h automatically includes the header files stdio.h and unctrl.h.

Note that pechochar may be a macro.

SEE ALSO

curses(3X), curs_refresh(3X), curs_touch(3X), curs_addch(3X)

NAME

curs_printw: printw, wprintw, mvprintw, mvwprintw, vwprintw - print formatted output in curses windows

SYNOPSIS

#include <curses.h>

int printw(char *fmt [, arg]...);

int wprintw(WINDOW *win, char *fmt [, arg]...);

int mvprintw(int y, int x, char *fmt [, arg]...);

int mvwprintw(WINDOW *win, int y, int x,
    char *fmt [, arg]...);

#include <varargs.h>

int vwprintw(WINDOW *win, char *fmt, varglist);

DESCRIPTION

The printw, wprintw, mvprintw and mvwprintw routines are analogous to printf [see printf(3S)]. In effect, the string that would be output by printf is output instead as though waddstr was used on the given window.

The vwprintw routine is analogous to vprintf [see vprintf(3S)] and performs a wprintw using a variable argument list. The third argument is a va_list, a pointer to a list of arguments, as defined in varargs.h.

RETURN VALUE

All routines return the integer ERR upon failure and an integer value other than ERR upon successful completion.

NOTES

The header file curses.h automatically includes the header files stdio.h and unctrl.h.

SEE ALSO

curses(3X), printf(3S), vprintf(3S)

NAME
curs_refresh: refresh, wrefresh, wnoutrefresh, doupdate, redrawwin, wredrawln – refresh curses windows and lines

SYNOPSIS
#include <curses.h>

int refresh(void);

int wrefresh(WINDOW *win);

int wnoutrefresh(WINDOW *win);

int doupdate(void);

int redrawwin(WINDOW *win);

int wredrawln(WINDOW *win, int beg_line, int num_lines);

DESCRIPTION
The refresh and wrefresh routines (or wnoutrefresh and doupdate) must be called to get any output on the terminal, as other routines merely manipulate data structures. The routine wrefresh copies the named window to the physical terminal screen, taking into account what is already there in order to do optimizations. The refresh routine is the same, using stdscr as the default window. Unless leaveok has been enabled, the physical cursor of the terminal is left at the location of the cursor for that window.

The wnoutrefresh and doupdate routines allow multiple updates with more efficiency than wrefresh alone. In addition to all the window structures, curses keeps two data structures representing the terminal screen: a physical screen, describing what is actually on the screen, and a virtual screen, describing what the programmer wants to have on the screen.

The routine wrefresh works by first calling wnoutrefresh, which copies the named window to the virtual screen, and then calling doupdate, which compares the virtual screen to the physical screen and does the actual update. If the programmer wishes to output several windows at once, a series of calls to wrefresh results in alternating calls to wnoutrefresh and doupdate, causing several bursts of output to the screen. By first calling wnoutrefresh for each window, it is then possible to call doupdate once, resulting in only one burst of output, with fewer total characters transmitted and less CPU time used. If the *win* argument to wrefresh is the global variable curscr, the screen is immediately cleared and repainted from scratch.

The redrawwin routine indicates to curses that some screen lines are corrupted and should be thrown away before anything is written over them. These routines could be used for programs such as editors, which want a command to redraw some part of the screen or the entire screen. The routine redrawln is preferred over redrawwin where a noisy communication line exists and redrawing the entire window could be subject to even more communication noise. Just redrawing several lines offers the possibility that they would show up unblemished.

RETURN VALUE
All routines return the integer ERR upon failure and an integer value other than ERR upon successful completion.

NOTES
The header file `curses.h` automatically includes the header files `stdio.h` and `unctrl.h`.

Note that `refresh` and `redrawwin` may be macros.

SEE ALSO
curses(3X), curs_outopts(3X)

NAME

curs_scanw: scanw, wscanw, mvscanw, mvwscanw, vwscanw − convert formatted input from a curses widow

SYNOPSIS

#include <curses.h>

int scanw(char *fmt [, arg] ...);

int wscanw(WINDOW *win, char *fmt [, arg] ...);

int mvscanw(int y, int x, char *fmt [, arg] ...);

int mvwscanw(WINDOW *win, int y, int x,
    char *fmt [, arg] ...);

int vwscanw(WINDOW *win, char *fmt, va_list varglist);

DESCRIPTION

The scanw, wscanw and mvscanw routines correspond to scanf [see scanf(3S)]. The effect of these routines is as though wgetstr were called on the window, and the resulting line used as input for the scan. Fields which do not map to a variable in the *fmt* field are lost.

The vwscanw routine is similar to vwprintw in that it performs a wscanw using a variable argument list. The third argument is a *va_list*, a pointer to a list of arguments, as defined in varargs.h.

RETURN VALUE

vwscanw returns ERR on failure and an integer equal to the number of fields scanned on success.

Applications may interrogate the return value from the scanw, wscanw, mvscanw and mvwscanw routines to determine the number of fields which were mapped in the call.

NOTES

The header file curses.h automatically includes the header files stdio.h and unctrl.h.

SEE ALSO

curses(3X), curs_getstr, curs_printw, scanf(3S)

NAME

curs_scr_dump: scr_dump, scr_restore, scr_init, scr_set – read (write) a curses screen from (to) a file

SYNOPSIS

#include <curses.h>

int scr_dump(char *filename);

int scr_restore(char *filename);

int scr_init(char *filename);

int scr_set(char *filename);

DESCRIPTION

With the scr_dump routine, the current contents of the virtual screen are written to the file *filename*.

With the scr_restore routine, the virtual screen is set to the contents of *filename*, which must have been written using scr_dump. The next call to doupdate restores the screen to the way it looked in the dump file.

With the scr_init routine, the contents of *filename* are read in and used to initialize the curses data structures about what the terminal currently has on its screen. If the data is determined to be valid, curses bases its next update of the screen on this information rather than clearing the screen and starting from scratch. scr_init is used after initscr or a system [see system(BA_LIB)] call to share the screen with another process which has done a scr_dump after its endwin call. The data is declared invalid if the time-stamp of the tty is old or the terminfo capabilities rmcup and nrrmc exist.

The scr_set routine is a combination of scr_restore and scr_init. It tells the program that the information in *filename* is what is currently on the screen, and also what the program wants on the screen. This can be thought of as a screen inheritance function.

To read (write) a window from (to) a file, use the getwin and putwin routines [see curs_util(3X)].

RETURN VALUE

All routines return the integer ERR upon failure and OK upon success.

NOTES

The header file curses.h automatically includes the header files stdio.h and unctrl.h.

Note that scr_init, scr_set, and scr_restore may be macros.

SEE ALSO

curses(3X), curs_initscr(3X), curs_refresh(3X), curs_util(3X), system(3S)

NAME
curs_scroll: scroll, srcl, wscrl – scroll a curses window

SYNOPSIS
#include <curses.h>

int scroll(WINDOW *win);

int scrl(int n);

int wscrl(WINDOW *win, int n);

DESCRIPTION
With the scroll routine, the window is scrolled up one line. This involves moving the lines in the window data structure. As an optimization, if the scrolling region of the window is the entire screen, the physical screen is scrolled at the same time.

With the scrl and wscrl routines, for positive *n* scroll the window up *n* lines (line *i+n* becomes *i*); otherwise scroll the window down *n* lines. This involves moving the lines in the window character image structure. The current cursor position is not changed.

For these functions to work, scrolling must be enabled via scrollok.

RETURN VALUE
All routines return the integer ERR upon failure and an integer value other than ERR upon successful completion.

NOTES
The header file curses.h automatically includes the header files stdio.h and unctrl.h.

Note that scrl and scroll may be macros.

SEE ALSO
curses(3X), curs_outopts(3X)

curs_slk(3X)

NAME
curs_slk: slk_init, slk_set, slk_refresh, slk_noutrefresh, slk_label, slk_clear, slk_restore, slk_touch, slk_attron, slk_attrset, slk_attroff – curses soft label routines

SYNOPSIS
#include <curses.h>

int slk_init(int fmt);

int slk_set(int labnum, char *label, int fmt);

int slk_refresh(void);

int slk_noutrefresh(void);

char *slk_label(int labnum);

int slk_clear(void);

int slk_restore(void);

int slk_touch(void);

int slk_attron(chtype attrs);

int slk_attrset(chtype attrs);

int slk_attroff(chtype attrs);

DESCRIPTION
curses manipulates the set of soft function-key labels that exist on many terminals. For those terminals that do not have soft labels, curses takes over the bottom line of stdscr, reducing the size of stdscr and the variable LINES. curses standardizes on eight labels of up to eight characters each.

To use soft labels, the slk_init routine must be called before initscr or newterm is called. If initscr eventually uses a line from stdscr to emulate the soft labels, then *fmt* determines how the labels are arranged on the screen. Setting *fmt* to 0 indicates a 3-2-3 arrangement of the labels; 1 indicates a 4-4 arrangement.

With the slk_set routine, *labnum* is the label number, from 1 to 8. *label* is the string to be put on the label, up to eight characters in length. A null string or a null pointer sets up a blank label. *fmt* is either 0, 1, or 2, indicating whether the label is to be left-justified, centered, or right-justified, respectively, within the label.

The slk_refresh and slk_noutrefresh routines correspond to the wrefresh and wnoutrefresh routines.

With the slk_label routine, the current label for label number *labnum* is returned with leading and trailing blanks stripped.

With the slk_clear routine, the soft labels are cleared from the screen.

With the `slk_restore` routine, the soft labels are restored to the screen after a `slk_clear` is performed.

With the `slk_touch` routine, all the soft labels are forced to be output the next time a `slk_noutrefresh` is performed.

The `slk_attron`, `slk_attrset` and `slk_attroff` routines correspond to `attron`, `attrset`, and `attroff`. They have an effect only if soft labels are simulated on the bottom line of the screen.

RETURN VALUE

Routines that return an integer return ERR upon failure and an integer value other than ERR upon successful completion.

`slk_label` returns NULL on error.

NOTES

The header file `curses.h` automatically includes the header files `stdio.h` and `unctrl.h`.

Most applications would use `slk_noutrefresh` because a `wrefresh` is likely to follow soon.

SEE ALSO

curses(3X), curs_attr(3X), curs_initscr(3X), curs_refresh(3X)

NAME

curs_termattrs: baudrate, erasechar, has_ic, has_il, killchar, longname, termattrs, termname − curses environment query routines

SYNOPSIS

#include <curses.h>

int baudrate(void);

char erasechar(void);

int has_ic(void);

int has_il(void);

char killchar(void);

char *longname(void);

chtype termattrs(void);

char *termname(void);

DESCRIPTION

The baudrate routine returns the output speed of the terminal. The number returned is in bits per second, for example 9600, and is an integer.

With the erasechar routine, the user's current erase character is returned.

The has_ic routine is true if the terminal has insert- and delete-character capabilities.

The has_il routine is true if the terminal has insert- and delete-line capabilities, or can simulate them using scrolling regions. This might be used to determine if it would be appropriate to turn on physical scrolling using scrollok.

With the killchar routine, the user's current line kill character is returned.

The longname routine returns a pointer to a static area containing a verbose description of the current terminal. The maximum length of a verbose description is 128 characters. It is defined only after the call to initscr or newterm. The area is overwritten by each call to newterm and is not restored by set_term, so the value should be saved between calls to newterm if longname is going to be used with multiple terminals.

If a given terminal doesn't support a video attribute that an application program is trying to use, curses may substitute a different video attribute for it. The termattrs function returns a logical OR of all video attributes supported by the terminal. This information is useful when a curses program needs complete control over the appearance of the screen.

The termname routine returns the value of the environmental variable TERM (truncated to 14 characters).

RETURN VALUE

longname and termname return NULL on error.

Routines that return an integer return ERR upon failure and an integer value other than ERR upon successful completion.

NOTES

The header file curses.h automatically includes the header files stdio.h and unctrl.h.

Note that termattrs may be a macro.

SEE ALSO

curses(3X), curs_initscr(3X), curs_outopts(3X)

NAME

curs_termcap: tgetent, tgetflag, tgetnum, tgetstr, tgoto, tputs − curses interfaces (emulated) to the termcap library

SYNOPSIS

#include <curses.h>
#include <term.h>

int tgetent(char *bp, char *name);

int tgetflag(char id[2]);

int tgetnum(char id[2]);

char *tgetstr(char id[2], char **area);

char *tgoto(char *cap, int col, int row);

int tputs(char *str, int affcnt, int (*putc)(void));

DESCRIPTION

These routines are included as a conversion aid for programs that use the *termcap* library. Their parameters are the same and the routines are emulated using the *terminfo* database. These routines are supported at Level 2 and should not be used in new applications.

The tgetent routine looks up the termcap entry for *name*. The emulation ignores the buffer pointer *bp*.

The tgetflag routine gets the boolean entry for *id*.

The tgetnum routine gets the numeric entry for *id*.

The tgetstr routine returns the string entry for *id*. Use tputs to output the returned string.

The tgoto routine instantiates the parameters into the given capability. The output from this routine is to be passed to tputs.

The tputs routine is described on the curs_terminfo(4) manual page.

RETURN VALUE

Routines that return an integer return ERR upon failure and an integer value other than ERR upon successful completion.

Routines that return pointers return NULL on error.

NOTES

The header file curses.h automatically includes the header files stdio.h and unctrl.h.

SEE ALSO

curses(3X), curs_terminfo(4), putc(3S)

NAME

curs_terminfo: setupterm, setterm, set_curterm, del_curterm, restartterm, tparm, tputs, putp, vidputs, vidattr, mvcur, tigetflag, tigetnum, tigetstr − curses interfaces to terminfo database

SYNOPSIS

```
#include <curses.h>
#include <term.h>
```

int setupterm(char *term, int fildes, int *errret);

int setterm(char *term);

int set_curterm(TERMINAL *nterm);

int del_curterm(TERMINAL *oterm);

int restartterm(char *term, int fildes, int *errret);

char *tparm(char *str, long int p1, long int p2, long int p3,
    long int p4, long int p5, long int p6, long int p7,
    long int p8, long int p9);

int tputs(char *str, int affcnt, int (*putc)(char));

int putp(char *str);

int vidputs(chtype attrs, int (*putc)(char));

int vidattr(chtype attrs);

int mvcur(int oldrow, int oldcol, int newrow, int newcol);

int tigetflag(char *capname);

int tigetnum(char *capname);

int tigetstr(char *capname);

DESCRIPTION

These low-level routines must be called by programs that have to deal directly with the terminfo database to handle certain terminal capabilities, such as programming function keys. For all other functionality, curses routines are more suitable and their use is recommended.

Initially, setupterm should be called. Note that setupterm is automatically called by initscr and newterm. This defines the set of terminal-dependent variables [listed in terminfo(4)]. The terminfo variables lines and columns are initialized by setupterm as follows: If use_env(FALSE) has been called, values for lines and columns specified in terminfo are used. Otherwise, if the environment variables LINES and COLUMNS exist, their values are used. If these environment variables do not exist and the program is running in a window, the current window size is used. Otherwise, if the environment variables do not exist, the values for lines and columns specified in the terminfo database are used.

The header files `curses.h` and `term.h` should be included (in this order) to get the definitions for these strings, numbers, and flags. Parameterized strings should be passed through `tparm` to instantiate them. All terminfo strings [including the output of `tparm`] should be printed with `tputs` or `putp`. Call the `reset_shell_mode` to restore the tty modes before exiting [see `curs_kernel`(3X)]. Programs which use cursor addressing should output `enter_ca_mode` upon startup and should output `exit_ca_mode` before exiting. Programs desiring shell escapes should call `reset_shell_mode` and output `exit_ca_mode` before the shell is called and should output `enter_ca_mode` and call `reset_prog_mode` after returning from the shell.

The `setupterm` routine reads in the `terminfo` database, initializing the `terminfo` structures, but does not set up the output virtualization structures used by `curses`. The terminal type is the character string *term*; if *term* is null, the environment variable TERM is used. All output is to file descriptor `fildes` which is initialized for output. If *errret* is not null, then `setupterm` returns OK or ERR and stores a status value in the integer pointed to by *errret*. A status of 1 in *errret* is normal, 0 means that the terminal could not be found, and −1 means that the `terminfo` database could not be found. If *errret* is null, `setupterm` prints an error message upon finding an error and exits. Thus, the simplest call is:

    setupterm((char *)0, 1, (int *)0);,

which uses all the defaults and sends the output to `stdout`.

The `setterm` routine is being replaced by `setupterm`. The call:

    setupterm(term, 1, (int *)0)

provides the same functionality as `setterm`(*term*). The `setterm` routine is included here for compatibility and is supported at Level 2.

The `set_curterm` routine sets the variable `cur_term` to *nterm*, and makes all of the `terminfo` boolean, numeric, and string variables use the values from *nterm*.

The `del_curterm` routine frees the space pointed to by *oterm* and makes it available for further use. If *oterm* is the same as `cur_term`, references to any of the `terminfo` boolean, numeric, and string variables thereafter may refer to invalid memory locations until another `setupterm` has been called.

The `restartterm` routine is similar to `setupterm` and `initscr`, except that it is called after restoring memory to a previous state. It assumes that the windows and the input and output options are the same as when memory was saved, but the terminal type and baud rate may be different.

The `tparm` routine instantiates the string *str* with parameters *pi*. A pointer is returned to the result of *str* with the parameters applied.

The `tputs` routine applies padding information to the string *str* and outputs it. The *str* must be a terminfo string variable or the return value from `tparm`, `tgetstr`, or `tgoto`. *affcnt* is the number of lines affected, or 1 if not applicable. *putc* is a `putchar`-like routine to which the characters are passed, one at a time.

The putp routine calls tputs(*str*, 1, putchar). Note that the output of putp always goes to stdout, not to the *fildes* specified in setupterm.

The vidputs routine displays the string on the terminal in the video attribute mode *attrs*, which is any combination of the attributes listed in curses(3X). The characters are passed to the putchar-like routine *putc*.

The vidattr routine is like the vidputs routine, except that it outputs through putchar.

The mvcur routine provides low-level cursor motion.

The tigetflag, tigetnum and tigetstr routines return the value of the capability corresponding to the terminfo *capname* passed to them, such as xenl.

With the tigetflag routine, the value −1 is returned if *capname* is not a boolean capability.

With the tigetnum routine, the value −2 is returned if *capname* is not a numeric capability.

With the tigetstr routine, the value (char *)−1 is returned if *capname* is not a string capability.

The *capname* for each capability is given in the table column entitled *capname* code in the capabilities section of terminfo(4).

```
char *boolnames, *boolcodes, *boolfnames
char *numnames, *numcodes, *numfnames
char *strnames, *strcodes, *strfnames
```

These null-terminated arrays contain the *capnames*, the termcap codes, and the full C names, for each of the terminfo variables.

RETURN VALUE

All routines return the integer ERR upon failure and an integer value other than ERR upon successful completion, unless otherwise noted in the preceding routine descriptions.

Routines that return pointers always return NULL on error.

NOTES

The header file curses.h automatically includes the header files stdio.h and unctrl.h.

The setupterm routine should be used in place of setterm.

Note that vidattr and vidputs may be macros.

SEE ALSO

curses(3X), curs_initscr(3X), curs_kernel(3X), curs_termcap(3X), putc(3S), terminfo(4)

curs_touch(3X)

NAME
curs_touch: touchwin, touchline, untouchwin, wtouchln, is_linetouched, is_wintouched – curses refresh control routines

SYNOPSIS
#include <curses.h>

int touchwin(WINDOW *win);

int touchline(WINDOW *win, int start, int count);

int untouchwin(WINDOW *win);

int wtouchln(WINDOW *win, int y, int n, int changed);

int is_linetouched(WINDOW *win, int line);

int is_wintouched(WINDOW *win);

DESCRIPTION
The touchwin and touchline routines throw away all optimization information about which parts of the window have been touched, by pretending that the entire window has been drawn on. This is sometimes necessary when using overlapping windows, since a change to one window affects the other window, but the records of which lines have been changed in the other window do not reflect the change. The routine touchline only pretends that *count* lines have been changed, beginning with line *start*.

The untouchwin routine marks all lines in the window as unchanged since the last call to wrefresh.

The wtouchln routine makes *n* lines in the window, starting at line *y*, look as if they have (*changed*=1) or have not (*changed*=0) been changed since the last call to wrefresh.

The is_linetouched and is_wintouched routines return TRUE if the specified line/window was modified since the last call to wrefresh; otherwise they return FALSE. In addition, is_linetouched returns ERR if *line* is not valid for the given window.

RETURN VALUE
All routines return the integer ERR upon failure and an integer value other than ERR upon successful completion, unless otherwise noted in the preceding routine descriptions.

NOTES
The header file curses.h automatically includes the header files stdio.h and unctrl.h.

Note that all routines except wtouchln may be macros.

SEE ALSO
curses(3X), curs_refresh(3X)

curs_util(3X)

NAME
curs_util: unctrl, keyname, filter, use_env, putwin, getwin, delay_output, flushinp – miscellaneous curses utility routines

SYNOPSIS
#include <curses.h>

char *unctrl(chtype c);

char *keyname(int c);

int filter(void);

void use_env(char bool);

int putwin(WINDOW *win, FILE *filep);

WINDOW *getwin(FILE *filep);

int delay_output(int ms);

int flushinp(void);

DESCRIPTION
The unctrl macro expands to a character string which is a printable representation of the character *c*. Control characters are displayed in the ^X notation. Printing characters are displayed as is.

With the keyname routine, a character string corresponding to the key *c* is returned.

The filter routine, if used, is called before initscr or newterm are called. It makes curses think that there is a one-line screen. curses does not use any terminal capabilities that assume that they know on what line of the screen the cursor is positioned.

The use_env routine, if used, is called before initscr or newterm are called. When called with FALSE as an argument, the values of lines and columns specified in the *terminfo* database will be used, even if environment variables LINES and COLUMNS (used by default) are set, or if curses is running in a window (in which case default behavior would be to use the window size if LINES and COLUMNS are not set).

With the putwin routine, all data associated with window *win* is written into the file to which *filep* points. This information can be later retrieved using the getwin function.

The getwin routine reads window related data stored in the file by putwin. The routine then creates and initializes a new window using that data. It returns a pointer to the new window.

The delay_output routine inserts an *ms* millisecond pause in output. This routine should not be used extensively because padding characters are used rather than a CPU pause.

The flushinp routine throws away any typeahead that has been typed by the user and has not yet been read by the program.

RETURN VALUE

Except for flushinp, routines that return an integer return ERR upon failure and an integer value other than ERR upon successful completion.

flushinp always returns OK.

Routines that return pointers return NULL on error.

NOTES

The header file curses.h automatically includes the header files stdio.h and unctrl.h.

Note that unctrl is a macro, which is defined in unctrl.h.

SEE ALSO

curses(3X), curs_initscr(3X), curs_scr_dump(3X)

NAME

curs_window: newwin, delwin, mvwin, subwin, derwin, mvderwin, dupwin, wsyncup, syncok, wcursyncup, wsyncdown − create curses windows

SYNOPSIS

#include <curses.h>

WINDOW *newwin(int nlines, int ncols, int begin_y,
    intbegin_x);

int delwin(WINDOW *win);

int mvwin(WINDOW *win, int y, int x);

WINDOW *subwin(WINDOW *orig, int nlines, int ncols,
    int begin_y, int begin_x);

WINDOW *derwin(WINDOW *orig, int nlines, int ncols,
    int begin_y, int begin_x);

int mvderwin(WINDOW *win, int par_y, int par_x);

WINDOW *dupwin(WINDOW *win);

void wsyncup(WINDOW *win);

int syncok(WINDOW *win, bool bf);

void wcursyncup(WINDOW *win);

void wsyncdown(WINDOW *win);

DESCRIPTION

The newwin routine creates and returns a pointer to a new window with the given number of lines, *nlines*, and columns, *ncols*. The upper left-hand corner of the window is at line *begin_y*, column *begin_x*. If either *nlines* or *ncols* is zero, they default to LINES − *begin_y* and COLS − *begin_x*. A new full-screen window is created by calling newwin(0,0,0,0).

The delwin routine deletes the named window, freeing all memory associated with it. Subwindows must be deleted before the main window can be deleted.

The mvwin routine moves the window so that the upper left-hand corner is at position (*x*, *y*). If the move would cause the window to be off the screen, it is an error and the window is not moved. Moving subwindows is allowed, but should be avoided.

The subwin routine creates and returns a pointer to a new window with the given number of lines, *nlines*, and columns, *ncols*. The window is at position (*begin_y*, *begin_x*) on the screen. (This position is relative to the screen, and not to the window *orig*.) The window is made in the middle of the window *orig*, so that changes made to one window will affect both windows. The subwindow shares memory with the window *orig*. When using this routine, it is necessary to call touchwin or touchline on *orig* before calling wrefresh on the subwindow.

The derwin routine is the same as subwin, except that *begin_y* and *begin_x* are relative to the origin of the window *orig* rather than the screen. There is no difference between the subwindows and the derived windows.

The mvderwin routine moves a derived window (or subwindow) inside its parent window. The screen-relative parameters of the window are not changed. This routine is used to display different parts of the parent window at the same physical position on the screen.

The dupwin routine creates an exact duplicate of the window *win*.

Each curses window maintains two data structures: the character image structure and the status structure. The character image structure is shared among all windows in the window hierarchy (that is, the window with all subwindows). The status structure, which contains information about individual line changes in the window, is private to each window. The routine wrefresh uses the status data structure when performing screen updating. Since status structures are not shared, changes made to one window in the hierarchy may not be properly reflected on the screen.

The routine wsyncup causes the changes in the status structure of a window to be reflected in the status structures of its ancestors. If syncok is called with second argument TRUE then wsyncup is called automatically whenever there is a change in the window.

The routine wcursyncup updates the current cursor position of all the ancestors of the window to reflect the current cursor position of the window.

The routine wsyncdown updates the status structure of the window to reflect the changes in the status structures of its ancestors. Applications seldom call this routine because it is called automatically by wrefresh.

RETURN VALUE

Routines that return an integer return the integer ERR upon failure and an integer value other than ERR upon successful completion.

delwin returns the integer ERR upon failure and OK upon successful completion.

Routines that return pointers return NULL on error.

NOTES

The header file curses.h automatically includes the header files stdio.h and unctrl.h.

If many small changes are made to the window, the wsyncup option could degrade performance.

Note that syncok may be a macro.

SEE ALSO

curses(3X), curs_refresh(3X), curs_touch(3X)

NAME
curses - CRT screen handling and optimization package

SYNOPSIS
#include <curses.h>

DESCRIPTION
The curses library routines give the user a terminal-independent method of updating character screens with reasonable optimization. A program using these routines must be compiled with the -lcurses option of cc.

The curses package allows: overall screen, window and pad manipulation; output to windows and pads; reading terminal input; control over terminal and curses input and output options; environment query routines; color manipulation; use of soft label keys; terminfo access; and access to low-level curses routines.

To initialize the routines, the routine initscr or newterm must be called before any of the other routines that deal with windows and screens are used. The routine endwin must be called before exiting. To get character-at-a-time input without echoing (most interactive, screen oriented programs want this), the following sequence should be used:
 initscr, cbreak, noecho;
Most programs would additionally use the sequence:
 nonl, intrflush(stdscr, FALSE), keypad(stdscr, TRUE);

Before a curses program is run, the tab stops of the terminal should be set and its initialization strings, if defined, must be output. This can be done by executing the tput init command after the shell environment variable TERM has been exported. [See terminfo(4) for further details.]

The curses library permits manipulation of data structures, called *windows*, which can be thought of as two-dimensional arrays of characters representing all or part of a CRT screen. A default window called stdscr, which is the size of the terminal screen, is supplied. Others may be created with newwin.

Windows are referred to by variables declared as WINDOW *. These data structures are manipulated with routines described on 3X paages (whose names begin "curs_"). Among which the most basic routines are move and addch. More general versions of these routines are included with names beginning with w, allowing the user to specify a window. The routines not beginning with w affect stdscr.)

After using routines to manipulate a window, refresh is called, telling curses to make the user's CRT screen look like stdscr. The characters in a window are actually of type chtype, (character and attribute data) so that other information about the character may also be stored with each character.

Special windows called *pads* may also be manipulated. These are windows which are not constrained to the size of the screen and whose contents need not be completely displayed. See curs_pad(3X) for more information.

In addition to drawing characters on the screen, video attributes and colors may be included, causing the characters to show up in such modes as underlined, in reverse video, or in color on terminals that support such display enhancements. Line drawing characters may be specified to be output. On input, curses is also able to translate arrow and function keys that transmit escape sequences into single values. The video attributes, line drawing characters, and input values use names, defined in curses.h, such as A_REVERSE, ACS_HLINE, and KEY_LEFT.

If the environment variables LINES and COLUMNS are set, or if the program is executing in a window environment, line and column information in the environment will override information read by *terminfo*. This would effect a program running in an AT&T 630 layer, for example, where the size of a screen is changeable.

If the environment variable TERMINFO is defined, any program using curses checks for a local terminal definition before checking in the standard place. For example, if TERM is set to att4424, then the compiled terminal definition is found in
    /usr/share/lib/terminfo/a/att4424.
(The a is copied from the first letter of att4424 to avoid creation of huge directories.) However, if TERMINFO is set to $HOME/myterms, curses first checks
    $HOME/myterms/a/att4424,
and if that fails, it then checks
    /usr/share/lib/terminfo/a/att4424.
This is useful for developing experimental definitions or when write permission in /usr/share/lib/terminfo is not available.

The integer variables LINES and COLS are defined in curses.h and will be filled in by initscr with the size of the screen. The constants TRUE and FALSE have the values 1 and 0, respectively.

The curses routines also define the WINDOW * variable curscr which is used for certain low-level operations like clearing and redrawing a screen containing garbage. The curscr can be used in only a few routines.

Routine and Argument Names

Many curses routines have two or more versions. The routines prefixed with w require a window argument. The routines prefixed with p require a pad argument. Those without a prefix generally use stdscr.

The routines prefixed with mv require an x and y coordinate to move to before performing the appropriate action. The mv routines imply a call to move before the call to the other routine. The coordinate y always refers to the row (of the window), and x always refers to the column. The upper left-hand corner is always (0,0), not (1,1).

The routines prefixed with mvw take both a window argument and x and y coordinates. The window argument is always specified before the coordinates.

In each case, *win* is the window affected, and *pad* is the pad affected; *win* and *pad* are always pointers to type WINDOW.

curses(3X) (Terminal Information Utilities) curses(3X)

Option setting routines require a Boolean flag *bf* with the value TRUE or FALSE; *bf* is always of type bool. The variables *ch* and *attrs* below are always of type chtype. The types WINDOW, SCREEN, bool, and chtype are defined in curses.h. The type TERMINAL is defined in term.h. All other arguments are integers.

Routine Name Index

The following table lists each curses routine and the name of the manual page on which it is described.

curses Routine Name	Manual Page Name
addch	curs_addch(3X)
addchnstr	curs_addchstr(3X)
addchstr	curs_addchstr(3X)
addnstr	curs_addstr(3X)
addstr	curs_addstr(3X)
attroff	curs_attr(3X)
attron	curs_attr(3X)
attrset	curs_attr(3X)
baudrate	curs_termattrs(3X)
beep	curs_beep(3X)
bkgd	curs_bkgd(3X)
bkgdset	curs_bkgd(3X)
border	curs_border(3X)
box	curs_border(3X)
can_change_color	curs_color(3X)
cbreak	curs_inopts(3X)
clear	curs_clear(3X)
clearok	curs_outopts(3X)
clrtobot	curs_clear(3X)
clrtoeol	curs_clear(3X)
color_content	curs_color(3X)
copywin	curs_overlay(3X)
curs_set	curs_kernel(3X)
def_prog_mode	curs_kernel(3X)
def_shell_mode	curs_kernel(3X)
del_curterm	curs_terminfo(4)
delay_output	curs_util(3X)
delch	curs_delch(3X)
deleteln	curs_deleteln(3X)
delscreen	curs_initscr(3X)
delwin	curs_window(3X)
derwin	curs_window(3X)
doupdate	curs_refresh(3X)
dupwin	curs_window(3X)
echo	curs_inopts(3X)
echochar	curs_addch(3X)
endwin	curs_initscr(3X)
erase	curs_clear(3X)

curses Routine Name	Manual Page Name
erasechar	curs_termattrs(3X)
filter	curs_util(3X)
flash	curs_beep(3X)
flushinp	curs_util(3X)
getbegyx	curs_getyx(3X)
getch	curs_getch(3X)
getmaxyx	curs_getyx(3X)
getparyx	curs_getyx(3X)
getstr	curs_getstr(3X)
getsyx	curs_kernel(3X)
getwin	curs_util(3X)
getyx	curs_getyx(3X)
halfdelay	curs_inopts(3X)
has_colors	curs_color(3X)
has_ic	curs_termattrs(3X)
has_il	curs_termattrs(3X)
hline	curs_border(3X)
idcok	curs_outopts(3X)
idlok	curs_outopts(3X)
immedok	curs_outopts(3X)
inch	curs_inch(3X)
inchnstr	curs_inchstr(3X)
inchstr	curs_inchstr(3X)
init_color	curs_color(3X)
init_pair	curs_color(3X)
initscr	curs_initscr(3X)
innstr	curs_instr(3X)
insch	curs_insch(3X)
insdelln	curs_deleteln(3X)
insertln	curs_deleteln(3X)
insnstr	curs_insstr(3X)
insstr	curs_insstr(3X)
instr	curs_instr(3X)
intrflush	curs_inopts(3X)
is_linetouched	curs_touch(3X)
is_wintouched	curs_touch(3X)
isendwin	curs_initscr(3X)
keyname	curs_util(3X)
keypad	curs_inopts(3X)
killchar	curs_termattrs(3X)
leaveok	curs_outopts(3X)
longname	curs_termattrs(3X)
meta	curs_inopts(3X)
move	curs_move(3X)
mvaddch	curs_addch(3X)
mvaddchnstr	curs_addchstr(3X)

curses Routine Name	Manual Page Name
mvaddchstr	curs_addchstr(3X)
mvaddnstr	curs_addstr(3X)
mvaddstr	curs_addstr(3X)
mvcur	curs_terminfo(4)
mvdelch	curs_delch(3X)
mvderwin	curs_window(3X)
mvgetch	curs_getch(3X)
mvgetstr	curs_getstr(3X)
mvinch	curs_inch(3X)
mvinchnstr	curs_inchstr(3X)
mvinchstr	curs_inchstr(3X)
mvinnstr	curs_instr(3X)
mvinsch	curs_insch(3X)
mvinsnstr	curs_insstr(3X)
mvinsstr	curs_insstr(3X)
mvinstr	curs_instr(3X)
mvprintw	curs_printw(3X)
mvscanw	curs_scanw(3X)
mvwaddch	curs_addch(3X)
mvwaddchnstr	curs_addchstr(3X)
mvwaddchstr	curs_addchstr(3X)
mvwaddnstr	curs_addstr(3X)
mvwaddstr	curs_addstr(3X)
mvwdelch	curs_delch(3X)
mvwgetch	curs_getch(3X)
mvwgetstr	curs_getstr(3X)
mvwin	curs_window(3X)
mvwinch	curs_inch(3X)
mvwinchnstr	curs_inchstr(3X)
mvwinchstr	curs_inchstr(3X)
mvwinnstr	curs_instr(3X)
mvwinsch	curs_insch(3X)
mvwinsnstr	curs_insstr(3X)
mvwinsstr	curs_insstr(3X)
mvwinstr	curs_instr(3X)
mvwprintw	curs_printw(3X)
mvwscanw	curs_scanw(3X)
napms	curs_kernel(3X)
newpad	curs_pad(3X)
newterm	curs_initscr(3X)
newwin	curs_window(3X)
nl	curs_outopts(3X)
nocbreak	curs_inopts(3X)
nodelay	curs_inopts(3X)
noecho	curs_inopts(3X)
nonl	curs_outopts(3X)

curses(3X) (Terminal Information Utilities) **curses(3X)**

curses Routine Name	Manual Page Name
noqiflush	curs_inopts(3X)
noraw	curs_inopts(3X)
notimeout	curs_inopts(3X)
overlay	curs_overlay(3X)
overwrite	curs_overlay(3X)
pair_content	curs_color(3X)
pechochar	curs_pad(3X)
pnoutrefresh	curs_pad(3X)
prefresh	curs_pad(3X)
printw	curs_printw(3X)
putp	curs_terminfo(4)
putwin	curs_util(3X)
qiflush	curs_inopts(3X)
raw	curs_inopts(3X)
redrawwin	curs_refresh(3X)
refresh	curs_refresh(3X)
reset_prog_mode	curs_kernel(3X)
reset_shell_mode	curs_kernel(3X)
resetty	curs_kernel(3X)
restartterm	curs_terminfo(4)
ripoffline	curs_kernel(3X)
savetty	curs_kernel(3X)
scanw	curs_scanw(3X)
scr_dump	curs_scr_dump(3X)
scr_init	curs_scr_dump(3X)
scr_restore	curs_scr_dump(3X)
scr_set	curs_scr_dump(3X)
scrl	curs_scroll(3X)
scroll	curs_scroll(3X)
scrollok	curs_outopts(3X)
set_curterm	curs_terminfo(4)
set_term	curs_initscr(3X)
setscrreg	curs_outopts(3X)
setsyx	curs_kernel(3X)
setterm	curs_terminfo(4)
setupterm	curs_terminfo(4)
slk_attroff	curs_slk(3X)
slk_attron	curs_slk(3X)
slk_attrset	curs_slk(3X)
slk_clear	curs_slk(3X)
slk_init	curs_slk(3X)
slk_label	curs_slk(3X)
slk_noutrefresh	curs_slk(3X)
slk_refresh	curs_slk(3X)
slk_restore	curs_slk(3X)
slk_set	curs_slk(3X)

curses Routine Name	Manual Page Name
slk_touch	curs_slk(3X)
standend	curs_attr(3X)
standout	curs_attr(3X)
start_color	curs_color(3X)
subpad	curs_pad(3X)
subwin	curs_window(3X)
syncok	curs_window(3X)
termattrs	curs_termattrs(3X)
termname	curs_termattrs(3X)
tgetent	curs_termcap(3X)
tgetflag	curs_termcap(3X)
tgetnum	curs_termcap(3X)
tgetstr	curs_termcap(3X)
tgoto	curs_termcap(3X)
tigetflag	curs_terminfo(4)
tigetnum	curs_terminfo(4)
tigetstr	curs_terminfo(4)
timeout	curs_inopts(3X)
touchline	curs_touch(3X)
touchwin	curs_touch(3X)
tparm	curs_terminfo(4)
tputs	curs_termcap(3X)
tputs	curs_terminfo(4)
typeahead	curs_inopts(3X)
unctrl	curs_util(3X)
ungetch	curs_getch(3X)
untouchwin	curs_touch(3X)
use_env	curs_util(3X)
vidattr	curs_terminfo(4)
vidputs	curs_terminfo(4)
vline	curs_border(3X)
vwprintw	curs_printw(3X)
vwscanw	curs_scanw(3X)
waddch	curs_addch(3X)
waddchnstr	curs_addchstr(3X)
waddchstr	curs_addchstr(3X)
waddnstr	curs_addstr(3X)
waddstr	curs_addstr(3X)
wattroff	curs_attr(3X)
wattron	curs_attr(3X)
wattrset	curs_attr(3X)
wbkgd	curs_bkgd(3X)
wbkgdset	curs_bkgd(3X)
wborder	curs_border(3X)
wclear	curs_clear(3X)
wclrtobot	curs_clear(3X)

curses Routine Name	Manual Page Name
wclrtoeol	curs_clear(3X)
wcursyncup	curs_window(3X)
wdelch	curs_delch(3X)
wdeleteln	curs_deleteln(3X)
wechochar	curs_addch(3X)
werase	curs_clear(3X)
wgetch	curs_getch(3X)
wgetnstr	curs_getstr(3X)
wgetstr	curs_getstr(3X)
whline	curs_border(3X)
winch	curs_inch(3X)
winchnstr	curs_inchstr(3X)
winchstr	curs_inchstr(3X)
winnstr	curs_instr(3X)
winsch	curs_insch(3X)
winsdelln	curs_deleteln(3X)
winsertln	curs_deleteln(3X)
winsnstr	curs_insstr(3X)
winsstr	curs_insstr(3X)
winstr	curs_instr(3X)
wmove	curs_move(3X)
wnoutrefresh	curs_refresh(3X)
wprintw	curs_printw(3X)
wredrawln	curs_refresh(3X)
wrefresh	curs_refresh(3X)
wscanw	curs_scanw(3X)
wscrl	curs_scroll(3X)
wsetscrreg	curs_outopts(3X)
wstandend	curs_attr(3X)
wstandout	curs_attr(3X)
wsyncdown	curs_window(3X)
wsyncup	curs_window(3X)
wtimeout	curs_inopts(3X)
wtouchln	curs_touch(3X)
wvline	curs_border(3X)

RETURN VALUE

Routines that return an integer return ERR upon failure and an integer value other than ERR upon successful completion, unless otherwise noted in the routine descriptions.

All macros return the value of the w version, except setscrreg, wsetscrreg, getyx, getbegyx, getmaxyx. The return values of setscrreg, wsetscrreg, getyx, getbegyx, and getmaxyx are undefined (that is, these should not be used as the right-hand side of assignment statements).

Routines that return pointers return NULL on error.

SEE ALSO
    terminfo(4) and 3X pages whose names begin "curs_" for detailed routine descriptions.

NOTES
    The header file `curs.h` automatically includes the header files `stdio.h` and `unctrl.h`.

NAME

cuserid – get character login name of the user

SYNOPSIS

#include <stdio.h>

char *cuserid (char *s);

DESCRIPTION

cuserid generates a character-string representation of the login name that the owner of the current process is logged in under. If s is a NULL pointer, this representation is generated in an internal static area, the address of which is returned. Otherwise, s is assumed to point to an array of at least L_cuserid characters; the representation is left in this array. The constant L_cuserid is defined in the stdio.h header file.

SEE ALSO

getlogin(3C), getpwent(3C)

DIAGNOSTICS

If the login name cannot be found, cuserid returns a NULL pointer; if s is not a NULL pointer, a null character `\0´ will be placed at s[0].

dbm(3) (BSD Compatibility Package) dbm(3)

NAME
dbm: dbminit, dbmclose, fetch, store, delete, firstkey, nextkey – data base subroutines

SYNOPSIS
cc [*flag*. . .] *file* . . . −ldbm

#include <dbm.h>

typedef struct {
char *dptr;
int dsize;
} datum;

dbminit(file)
char *file;

dbmclose

datum fetch(key)
datum key;

store(key, content)
datum key, content;

delete(key)
datum key;

datum firstkey

datum nextkey(key)
datum key;

DESCRIPTION
Note: the dbm library has been superceded by ndbm(3), and is now implemented using ndbm.

These functions maintain key/content pairs in a data base. The functions will handle very large (a billion blocks) databases and will access a keyed item in one or two file system accesses. The functions are obtained with the loader option −libdbm.

*key*s and *content*s are described by the datum typedef. A datum specifies a string of *dsize* bytes pointed to by *dptr*. Arbitrary binary data, as well as normal ASCII strings, are allowed. The data base is stored in two files. One file is a directory containing a bit map and has .dir as its suffix. The second file contains all data and has .pag as its suffix.

Before a database can be accessed, it must be opened by dbminit. At the time of this call, the files *file*.dir and *file*.pag must exist. An empty database is created by creating zero-length .dir and .pag files.

A database may be closed by calling dbmclose. You must close a database before opening a new one.

Once open, the data stored under a key is accessed by fetch and data is placed under a key by store. A key (and its associated contents) is deleted by delete. A linear pass through all keys in a database may be made, in an (apparently) random order, by use of firstkey and nextkey. firstkey will return the first key in the database. With any key nextkey will return the next key in the database. This code will traverse the data base:

```
for (key = firstkey; key.dptr != NULL; key = nextkey(key))
```

SEE ALSO
ndbm(3)

RETURN VALUE
All functions that return an `int` indicate errors with negative values. A zero return indicates no error. Routines that return a `datum` indicate errors with a NULL (0) *dptr*.

NOTES
The `.pag` file will contain holes so that its apparent size is about four times its actual content. Older versions of the UNIX operating system may create real file blocks for these holes when touched. These files cannot be copied by normal means (cp(1), cat(1), tar(1), ar(1)) without filling in the holes.

dptr pointers returned by these subroutines point into static storage that is changed by subsequent calls.

The sum of the sizes of a key/content pair must not exceed the internal block size (currently 1024 bytes). Moreover all key/content pairs that hash together must fit on a single block. `store` will return an error in the event that a disk block fills with inseparable data.

`delete` does not physically reclaim file space, although it does make it available for reuse.

The order of keys presented by `firstkey` and `nextkey` depends on a hashing function, not on anything interesting.

There are no interlocks and no reliable cache flushing; thus concurrent updating and reading is risky.

NAME

decimal_to_floating: decimal_to_single, decimal_to_double, decimal_to_extended – convert decimal record to floating-point value

SYNOPSIS

cc [*flag*...] *file*... -lucb

#include <floatingpoint.h>

void decimal_to_single(px, pm, pd, ps)
single *px ;
decimal_mode *pm;
decimal_record *pd;
fp_exception_field_type *ps;

void decimal_to_double(px, pm, pd, ps)
double *px ;
decimal_mode *pm;
decimal_record *pd;
fp_exception_field_type *ps;

void decimal_to_extended(px, pm, pd, ps)
extended *px ;
decimal_mode *pm;
decimal_record *pd;
fp_exception_field_type *ps;

DESCRIPTION

The decimal_to_floating functions convert the decimal record at *pd* into a floating-point value at *px*, observing the modes specified in *pm* and setting exceptions in *ps*. If there are no IEEE exceptions, *ps* will be zero.

pd->sign and *pd->fpclass* are always taken into account. *pd->exponent* and *pd->ds* are used when *pd->fpclass* is *fp_normal* or *fp_subnormal*. In these cases *pd->ds* must contain one or more ASCII digits followed by a NULL. *px* is set to a correctly rounded approximation to

$$(pd\text{->}sign) * (pd\text{->}ds) * 10^{**} (pd\text{->}exponent)$$

Thus if *pd->exponent* == −2 and *pd->ds* == "1234", *px* will get 12.34 rounded to storage precision. *pd->ds* cannot have more than DECIMAL_STRING_LENGTH−1 significant digits because one character is used to terminate the string with a NULL. If *pd->more!=0* on input then additional nonzero digits follow those in *pd->ds*; *fp_inexact* is set accordingly on output in *ps*.

px is correctly rounded according to the IEEE rounding modes in *pm->rd*. *ps* is set to contain *fp_inexact*, *fp_underflow*, or *fp_overflow* if any of these arise.

pd->ndigits, *pm->df*, and *pm->ndigits* are not used.

strtod(3C), scanf(3S), fscanf(), and sscanf() all use decimal_to_double.

SEE ALSO

scanf(3S), strtod(3C) in the *Programmer's Reference Manual*

dial(3C) (C Programming Language Utilities) dial(3C)

NAME
dial – establish an outgoing terminal line connection

SYNOPSIS
#include <dial.h>

int dial(CALL call);

void undial(int fd);

DESCRIPTION
dial returns a file-descriptor for a terminal line open for read/write. The argument to dial is a CALL structure (defined in the dial.h header file).

When finished with the terminal line, the calling program must invoke undial to release the semaphore that has been set during the allocation of the terminal device.

The definition of CALL in the dial.h header file is:

```
typedef struct {
        struct termio  *attr;    /* pointer to termio attribute struct */
        int            baud;     /* transmission data rate */
        int            speed;    /* 212A modem: low=300, high=1200 */
        char           *line;    /* device name for out-going line */
        char           *telno;   /* pointer to tel-no digits string */
        int            modem;    /* specify modem control for direct lines */
        char           *device;  /* unused */
        int            dev_len;  /* unused */
} CALL;
```

The CALL element speed is intended only for use with an outgoing dialed call, in which case its value should be either 300 or 1200 to identify the 113A modem, or the high- or low-speed setting on the 212A modem. Note that the 113A modem or the low-speed setting of the 212A modem will transmit at any rate between 0 and 300 bits per second. However, the high-speed setting of the 212A modem transmits and receives at 1200 bits per second only. The CALL element baud is for the desired transmission baud rate. For example, one might set baud to 110 and speed to 300 (or 1200). However, if speed is set to 1200, baud must be set to high (1200).

If the desired terminal line is a direct line, a string pointer to its device-name should be placed in the line element in the CALL structure. Legal values for such terminal device names are kept in the Devices file. In this case, the value of the baud element should be set to -1. This value will cause dial to determine the correct value from the Devices file.

The telno element is for a pointer to a character string representing the telephone number to be dialed. Such numbers may consist only of these characters:

    0-9   dial 0-9
    *   dial *
    #   dial #
    =   wait for secondary dial tone
    −   delay for approximately 4 seconds

The CALL element modem is used to specify modem control for direct lines. This element should be non-zero if modem control is required. The CALL element attr is a pointer to a termio structure, as defined in the termio.h header file. A NULL value for this pointer element may be passed to the dial function, but if such a structure is included, the elements specified in it will be set for the outgoing terminal line before the connection is established. This setting is often important for certain attributes such as parity and baud-rate.

The CALL elements device and dev_len are no longer used. They are retained in the CALL structure for compatibility reasons.

FILES

/etc/uucp/Devices
/etc/uucp/Systems
/var/spool/uucp/LCK..*tty-device*

SEE ALSO

alarm(2), read(2), write(2).

termio(7) in the *System Administrator's Reference Manual*.

uucp(1C) in the *User's Reference Manual*.

DIAGNOSTICS

On failure, a negative value indicating the reason for the failure will be returned. Mnemonics for these negative indices as listed here are defined in the dial.h header file.

```
INTRPT      -1     /* interrupt occurred */
D_HUNG      -2     /* dialer hung (no return from write) */
NO_ANS      -3     /* no answer within 10 seconds */
ILL_BD      -4     /* illegal baud-rate */
A_PROB      -5     /* acu problem (open() failure) */
L_PROB      -6     /* line problem (open() failure) */
NO_Ldv      -7     /* can't open Devices file */
DV_NT_A     -8     /* requested device not available */
DV_NT_K     -9     /* requested device not known */
NO_BD_A    -10     /* no device available at requested baud */
NO_BD_K    -11     /* no device known at requested baud */
DV_NT_E    -12     /* requested speed does not match */
BAD_SYS    -13     /* system not in Systems file*/
```

NOTES

Including the dial.h header file automatically includes the termio.h header file.

An alarm(2) system call for 3600 seconds is made (and caught) within the dial module for the purpose of "touching" the LCK.. file and constitutes the device allocation semaphore for the terminal device. Otherwise, uucp(1C) may simply delete the LCK.. entry on its 90-minute clean-up rounds. The alarm may go off while the user program is in a read(2) or write(2) system call, causing an apparent error return. If the user program expects to be around for an hour or more, error returns from reads should be checked for (errno==EINTR), and the read possibly reissued.

NAME

difftime – computes the difference between two calendar times

SYNOPSIS

#include <time.h>

double difftime (time_t time1, time_t time0);

DESCRIPTION

difftime computes the difference between two calendar times. f4difftime returns the difference *(time1-time0)* expressed in seconds as a double. This function is provided because there are no general arithmetic properties defined for type time_t.

SEE ALSO

ctime(3C)

NAME
directory: opendir, readdir, telldir, seekdir, rewinddir, closedir – directory operations

SYNOPSIS
#include <dirent.h>

DIR *opendir (const char *filename);

struct dirent *readdir (DIR *dirp);

long telldir (DIR *dirp);

void seekdir (DIR *dirp, long loc);

void rewinddir (DIR *dirp);

int closedir (DIR *dirp);

DESCRIPTION
opendir opens the directory named by *filename* and associates a directory stream with it. opendir returns a pointer to be used to identify the directory stream in subsequent operations. The directory stream is positioned at the first entry. A null pointer is returned if *filename* cannot be accessed or is not a directory, or if it cannot malloc(3C) enough memory to hold a DIR structure or a buffer for the directory entries.

readdir returns a pointer to the next active directory entry and positions the directory stream at the next entry. No inactive entries are returned. It returns NULL upon reaching the end of the directory or upon detecting an invalid location in the directory. readdir buffers several directory entries per actual read operation; readdir marks for update the st_atime field of the directory each time the directory is actually read.

telldir returns the current location associated with the named directory stream.

seekdir sets the position of the next readdir operation on the directory stream. The new position reverts to the position associated with the directory stream at the time the telldir operation that provides *loc* was performed. Values returned by telldir are valid only if the directory has not changed because of compaction or expansion. This situation is not a problem with System V, but it may be a problem with some file system types.

rewinddir resets the position of the named directory stream to the beginning of the directory. It also causes the directory stream to refer to the current state of the corresponding directory, as a call to opendir would.

closedir closes the named directory stream and frees the DIR structure.

The following errors can occur as a result of these operations.

opendir returns NULL on failure and sets errno to one of the following values:

ENOTDIR	A component of *filename* is not a directory.
EACCES	A component of *filename* denies search permission.

EACCES	Read permission is denied on the specified directory.
EMFILE	The maximum number of file descriptors are currently open.
ENFILE	The system file table is full.
EFAULT	*filename* points outside the allocated address space.
ELOOP	Too many symbolic links were encountered in translating *filename*.
ENAMETOOLONG	The length of the *filename* argument exceeds {PATH_MAX}, or the length of a *filename* component exceeds {NAME_MAX} while {_POSIX_NO_TRUNC} is in effect.
ENOENT	A component of *filename* does not exist or is a null pathname.

`readdir` returns NULL on failure and sets `errno` to one of the following values:

ENOENT	The current file pointer for the directory is not located at a valid entry.
EBADF	The file descriptor determined by the DIR stream is no longer valid. This result occurs if the DIR stream has been closed.

`telldir`, `seekdir`, and `closedir` return −1 on failure and set `errno` to the following value:

EBADF	The file descriptor determined by the DIR stream is no longer valid. This results if the DIR stream has been closed.

EXAMPLE

Here is a sample program that prints the names of all the files in the current directory:

```
#include <stdio.h>
#include <dirent.h>

main()
{
      DIR *dirp;
      struct dirent *direntp;

      dirp = opendir( "." );
      while ( (direntp = readdir( dirp )) != NULL )
            (void)printf( "%s\n", direntp->d_name );
      closedir( dirp );
      return (0);
}
```

directory(3C)

SEE ALSO
getdents(2), dirent(4), mkdir(2), rmdir(2)

NOTES
rewinddir is implemented as a macro, so its function address cannot be taken.

These functions overwrite the buffer as needed, so applications should copy data to preserve it.

NAME

directory: opendir, readdir, telldir, seekdir, rewinddir, closedir − directory operations

SYNOPSIS

#include <dirent.h>

DIR *opendir (const char *filename);

struct dirent *readdir (DIR *dirp);

long telldir (DIR *dirp);

void seekdir (DIR *dirp, long loc);

void rewinddir (DIR *dirp);

int closedir (DIR *dirp);

DESCRIPTION

opendir opens the directory named by *filename* and associates a directory stream with it. opendir returns a pointer to be used to identify the directory stream in subsequent operations. The directory stream is positioned at the first entry. A null pointer is returned if *filename* cannot be accessed or is not a directory, or if it cannot malloc enough memory to hold a DIR structure or a buffer for the directory entries.

readdir returns a pointer to the next active directory entry and positions the directory stream at the next entry. No inactive entries are returned. It returns NULL upon reaching the end of the directory or upon detecting an invalid location in the directory. readdir buffers several directory entries per actual read operation; readdir marks for update the st_atime field of the directory each time the directory is actually read.

telldir returns the current location associated with the named directory stream.

seekdir sets the position of the next readdir operation on the directory stream. The new position reverts to the position associated with the directory stream at the time the telldir operation that provides *loc* was performed. Values returned by telldir are valid only if the directory has not changed because of compaction or expansion. This situation is not a problem with System V, but it may be a problem with some file system types.

rewinddir resets the position of the named directory stream to the beginning of the directory. It also causes the directory stream to refer to the current state of the corresponding directory, as a call to opendir would.

closedir closes the named directory stream and frees the DIR structure.

The following errors can occur as a result of these operations.

opendir returns NULL on failure and sets errno to one of the following values:

ENOTDIR	A component of *filename* is not a directory.
EACCES	A component of *filename* denies search permission.

EACCES	Read permission is denied on the specified directory.
EMFILE	The maximum number of file descriptors are currently open.
ENFILE	The system file table is full.
EFAULT	*filename* points outside the allocated address space.
ELOOP	Too many symbolic links were encountered in translating *filename*.
ENAMETOOLONG	The length of the *filename* argument exceeds {PATH_MAX}, or the length of a *filename* component exceeds {NAME_MAX} while {_POSIX_NO_TRUNC} is in effect.
ENOENT	A component of *filename* does not exist or is a null pathname.

readdir returns NULL on failure and sets errno to one of the following values:

ENOENT	The current file pointer for the directory is not located at a valid entry.
EBADF	The file descriptor determined by the DIR stream is no longer valid. This result occurs if the DIR stream has been closed.

telldir, seekdir, and closedir return −1 on failure and set errno to the following value:

EBADF	The file descriptor determined by the DIR stream is no longer valid. This results if the DIR stream has been closed.

EXAMPLE

Here is a sample program that prints the names of all the files in the current directory:

```
#include <stdio.h>
#include <dirent.h>

main()
{
    DIR *dirp;
    struct dirent *direntp;

    dirp = opendir( "." );
    while ( (direntp = readdir( dirp )) != NULL )
        (void)printf( "%s\n", direntp->d_name );
    closedir( dirp );
    return (0);
}
```

directory(3C)　　　　　　(BSD Compatibility Package)　　　　　　directory(3C)

SEE ALSO

getdents(2), dirent(4).

NOTES

rewinddir is implemented as a macro, so its function address cannot be taken.

dirname(3G)

NAME
dirname – report the parent directory name of a file path name

SYNOPSIS
cc [*flag* ...] *file* ... −lgen [*library* ...]

```
#include <libgen.h>

char *dirname (char *path);
```

DESCRIPTION
Given a pointer to a null-terminated character string that contains a file system path name, dirname returns a pointer to a static constant string that is the parent directory of that file. In doing this, it sometimes places a null byte in the path name after the next to last element, so the content of *path* must be disposable. Trailing "/" characters in the path are not counted as part of the path.

If *path* or *path* is zero, a pointer to a static constant "." is returned.

dirname and basename together yield a complete path name. dirname (*path*) is the directory where basename (*path*) is found.

EXAMPLES
A simple file name and the strings "." and ".." all have "." as their return value.

Input string	Output pointer
/usr/lib	/usr
/usr/	/
usr	.
/	/
.	.
..	.

The following code reads a path name, changes directory to the appropriate directory [see chdir(2)], and opens the file.

```
char path[100], *pathcopy;
int fd;
gets (path);
pathcopy = strdup (path);
chdir (dirname (pathcopy) );
fd = open (basename (path), O_RDONLY);
```

SEE ALSO
chdir(2), basename(3G).
basename(1) in the *User's Reference Manual*.

NAME

div, ldiv – compute the quotient and remainder

SYNOPSIS

    #include <stdlib.h>

    div_t div (int numer, int denom);

    ldiv_t ldiv (long int numer, long int denom);

DESCRIPTION

div computes the quotient and remainder of the division of the numerator *numer* by the denominator *denom*. This function provides a well-defined semantics for the signed integral division and remainder operations, unlike the implementation-defined semantics of the built-in operations. The sign of the resulting quotient is that of the algebraic quotient, and, if the division is inexact, the magnitude of the resulting quotient is the largest integer less than the magnitude of the algebraic quotient. If the result cannot be represented, the behavior is undefined; otherwise, *quotient * denom + remainder* will equal *numer*.

div returns a structure of type div_t, comprising both the quotient and remainder:

    typedef struct div_t {
        int   quot; /*quotient*/
        int   rem; /*remainder*/
    } div_t;

ldiv is similar to div, except that the arguments and the members of the returned structure (which has type ldiv_t) all have type long int.

NAME
dlclose – close a shared object

SYNOPSIS
cc [*flag* ...] *file* ... -ldl [*library* ...]

```
#include <dlfcn.h>

int dlclose(void *handle);
```

DESCRIPTION
dlclose disassociates a shared object previously opened by dlopen from the current process. Once an object has been closed using dlclose, its symbols are no longer available to dlsym. All objects loaded automatically as a result of invoking dlopen on the referenced object [see dlopen(3X)] are also closed. *handle* is the value returned by a previous invocation of dlopen.

SEE ALSO
dlerror(3X), dlopen(3X), dlsym(3X).

DIAGNOSTICS
If the referenced object was successfully closed, dlclose returns 0. If the object could not be closed, or if *handle* does not refer to an open object, dlclose returns a non-0 value. More detailed diagnostic information is available through dlerror.

NOTES
A successful invocation of dlclose does not guarantee that the objects associated with *handle* have actually been removed from the address space of the process. Objects loaded by one invocation of dlopen may also be loaded by another invocation of dlopen. The same object may also be opened multiple times. An object is not removed from the address space until all references to that object through an explicit dlopen invocation have been closed and all other objects implicitly referencing that object have also been closed.

Once an object has been closed by dlclose, referencing symbols contained in that object can cause undefined behavior.

NAME
dlerror – get diagnostic information

SYNOPSIS
cc [*flag* ...] *file* ... -ldl [*library* ...]

#include <dlfcn.h>

char *dlerror(void);

DESCRIPTION
dlerror returns a null-terminated character string (with no trailing newline) that describes the last error that occurred during dynamic linking processing. If no dynamic linking errors have occurred since the last invocation of dlerror, dlerror returns NULL. Thus, invoking dlerror a second time, immediately following a prior invocation, results in NULL being returned.

SEE ALSO
dlclose(3X), dlopen(3X), dlsym(3X).

NOTES
The messages returned by dlerror may reside in a static buffer that is overwritten on each call to dlerror. Application code should not write to this buffer. Programs wishing to preserve an error message should make their own copies of that message.

NAME
dlopen – open a shared object

SYNOPSIS
cc [*flag* ...] *file* ... -ldl [*library* ...]

#include <dlfcn.h>

void *dlopen(char *pathname, int mode);

DESCRIPTION
dlopen is one of a family of routines that give the user direct access to the dynamic linking facilities. (See "C Compilation System" in the *Programmer's Guide: ANSI C and Programming Support Tools*). These routines are available in a library that is loaded if the option -ldl is used with cc or ld.

dlopen makes a shared object available to a running process. dlopen returns to the process a *handle* the process may use on subsequent calls to dlsym and dlclose. This value should not be interpreted in any way by the process. *pathname* is the path name of the object to be opened; it may be an absolute path or relative to the current directory. If the value of *pathname* is 0, dlopen makes the symbols contained in the original a.out, and all of the objects that were loaded at program startup with the a.out, available through dlsym.

When a shared object is brought into the address space of a process, it may contain references to symbols whose addresses are not known until the object is loaded. These references must be relocated before the symbols can be accessed. The *mode* parameter governs when these relocations take place and may have the following values:

RTLD_LAZY
Under this *mode*, only references to data symbols are relocated when the object is loaded. References to functions are not relocated until a given function is invoked for the first time. This *mode* should result in better performance, since a process may not reference all of the functions in any given shared object.

RTLD_NOW
Under this *mode*, all necessary relocations are performed when the object is first loaded. This may result in some wasted effort, if relocations are performed for functions that are never referenced, but is useful for applications that need to know as soon as an object is loaded that all symbols referenced during execution will be available.

SEE ALSO
cc(1), ld(1), sh(1), exec(2), dlclose(3X), dlerror(3X), dlsym(3X).

The "C Compilation System" chapter in the *Programmer's Guide: ANSI C and Programming Support Tools*.

DIAGNOSTICS
If *pathname* cannot be found, cannot be opened for reading, is not a shared object, or if an error occurs during the process of loading *pathname* or relocating its symbolic references, dlopen returns NULL. More detailed diagnostic information is available through dlerror.

NOTES

If other shared objects were link edited with *pathname* when *pathname* was built, those objects are automatically loaded by dlopen. The directory search path to be used to find both *pathname* and the other *needed* objects may be specified by setting the environment variable LD_LIBRARY_PATH. This environment variable should contain a colon-separated list of directories, in the same format as the PATH variable [see sh(1)]. LD_LIBRARY_PATH is ignored if the process is running setuid or setgid [see exec(2)] or if the name specified is not a simple file name (that is, contains a / character). Objects whose names resolve to the same absolute or relative path name may be opened any number of times using dlopen, however, the object referenced is loaded only once into the address space of the current process. The same object referenced by two different path names, however, may be loaded multiple times. For example, given the object /usr/home/me/mylibs/mylib.so, and assuming the current working directory is /usr/home/me/workdir,

```
. . .
void *handle1;
void *handle2;

handle1 = dlopen("../mylibs/mylib.so", RTLD_LAZY);
handle2 = dlopen("/usr/home/me/mylibs/mylib.so", RTLD_LAZY);
. . .
```

results in mylibs.so being loaded twice for the current process. On the other hand, given the same object and current working directory, if LD_LIBRARY_PATH=/usr/home/me/mylibs, then

```
. . .
void *handle1;
void *handle2;

handle1 = dlopen("mylib.so", RTLD_LAZY);
handle2 = dlopen("/usr/home/me/mylibs/mylib.so", RTLD_LAZY);
. . .
```

results in mylibs.so being loaded only once.

Objects loaded by a single invocation of dlopen may import symbols from one another or from any object loaded automatically during program startup, but objects loaded by one dlopen invocation may not directly reference symbols from objects loaded by a different dlopen invocation. Those symbols may, however, be referenced indirectly using dlsym.

Users who wish to gain access to the symbol table of the a.out itself using dlsym(0, *mode*) should be aware that some symbols defined in the a.out may not be available to the dynamic linker. The symbol table created by ld for use by the dynamic linker might contain only a subset of the symbols defined in the a.out: specifically those referenced by the shared objects with which the a.out is linked.

NAME

dlsym – get the address of a symbol in shared object

SYNOPSIS

cc [*flag* ...] *file* ... -ldl [*library* ...]

```
#include <dlfcn.h>

void *dlsym(void *handle, char *name);
```

DESCRIPTION

dlsym allows a process to obtain the address of a symbol defined within a shared object previously opened by dlopen. *handle* is a value returned by a call to dlopen; the corresponding shared object must not have been closed using dlclose. *name* is the symbol's name as a character string. dlsym searches for the named symbol in all shared objects loaded automatically as a result of loading the object referenced by *handle* [see dlopen(3X)].

EXAMPLES

The following example shows how one can use dlopen and dlsym to access either function or data objects. For simplicity, error checking has been omitted.

```
void *handle;
int i, *iptr;
int (*fptr)(int);

/* open the needed object */
handle = dlopen("/usr/mydir/libx.so", RTLD_LAZY);

/* find address of function and data objects */
fptr = (int (*)(int))dlsym(handle, "some_function");

iptr = (int *)dlsym(handle, "int_object");

/* invoke function, passing value of integer as a parameter */

i = (*fptr)(*iptr);
```

SEE ALSO

dlclose(3X), dlerror(3X), dlopen(3X).

DIAGNOSTICS

If *handle* does not refer to a valid object opened by dlopen, or if the named symbol cannot be found within any of the objects associated with *handle*, dlsym returns NULL. More detailed diagnostic information is available through dlerror.

doconfig(3N) (Networking Support Utilities) doconfig(3N)

NAME
     doconfig - execute a configuration script

SYNOPSIS
     # include <sac.h>

     int doconfig(int fd, char *script, long rflag);

DESCRIPTION
     doconfig is a Service Access Facility library function that interprets the configuration scripts contained in the files /etc/saf/*pmtag*/_config, /etc/saf/_sysconfig, and /etc/saf/*pmtag*/*svctag*.

     script is the name of the configuration script; *fd* is a file descriptor that designates the stream to which stream manipulation operations are to be applied; *rflag* is a bitmask that indicates the mode in which script is to be interpreted. *rflag* may take two values, NORUN and NOASSIGN, which may be or'd. If *rflag* is zero, all commands in the configuration script are eligible to be interpreted. If *rflag* has the NOASSIGN bit set, the assign command is considered illegal and will generate an error return. If *rflag* has the NORUN bit set, the run and runwait commands are considered illegal and will generate error returns.

     The configuration language in which script is written consists of a sequence of commands, each of which is interpreted separately. The following reserved keywords are defined: assign, push, pop, runwait, and run. The comment character is #; when a # occurs on a line, everything from that point to the end of the line is ignored. Blank lines are not significant. No line in a command script may exceed 1024 characters.

     assign *variable=value*
          Used to define environment variables. *variable* is the name of the environment variable and *value* is the value to be assigned to it. The value assigned must be a string constant; no form of parameter substitution is available. *value* may be quoted. The quoting rules are those used by the shell for defining environment variables. assign will fail if space cannot be allocated for the new variable or if any part of the specification is invalid.

     push *module1*[, *module2*, *module3*, ...]
          Used to push STREAMS modules onto the stream designated by *fd*. *module1* is the name of the first module to be pushed, *module2* is the name of the second module to be pushed, etc. The command will fail if any of the named modules cannot be pushed. If a module cannot be pushed, the subsequent modules on the same command line will be ignored and modules that have already been pushed will be popped.

     pop [*module*]
          Used to pop STREAMS modules off the designated stream. If pop is invoked with no arguments, the top module on the stream is popped. If an argument is given, modules will be popped one at a time until the named module is at the top of the stream. If the named module is not on the designated stream, the stream is left as it was and the command fails. If *module* is the special keyword ALL, then all modules on the

stream will be popped. Note that only modules above the topmost driver are affected.

runwait *command*
: The runwait command runs a command and waits for it to complete. *command* is the pathname of the command to be run. The command is run with /usr/bin/sh -c prepended to it; shell scripts may thus be executed from configuration scripts. The runwait command will fail if *command* cannot be found or cannot be executed, or if *command* exits with a non-zero status.

run *command*
: The run command is identical to runwait except that it does not wait for *command* to complete. *command* is the pathname of the command to be run. run will not fail unless it is unable to create a child process to execute the command.

Although they are syntactically indistinguishable, some of the commands available to run and runwait are interpreter built-in commands. Interpreter built-ins are used when it is necessary to alter the state of a process within the context of that process. The doconfig interpreter built-in commands are similar to the shell special commands and, like these, they do not spawn another process for execution. See sh(1). The initial set of built-in commands is:

```
cd
ulimit
umask
```

DIAGNOSTICS

doconfig returns 0 if the script was interpreted successfully. If a command in the script fails, the interpretation of the script ceases at that point and a positive number is returned; this number indicates which line in the script failed. If a system error occurs, a value of −1 is returned. When a script fails, the process whose environment was being established should not be started.

SEE ALSO

pmadm(1M) and sacadm(1M) in the *System Administrator's Reference Manual*
sh(1) in the *User's Reference Manual*

NAME

drand48, erand48, lrand48, nrand48, mrand48, jrand48, srand48, seed48, lcong48 − generate uniformly distributed pseudo-random numbers

SYNOPSIS

```
#include <stdlib.h>
```

double drand48 (void);

double erand48 (unsigned short xsubi[3]);

long lrand48 (void);

long nrand48 (unsigned short xsubi[3]);

long mrand48 (void);

long jrand48 (unsigned short xsubi[3]);

void srand48 (long seedval);

unsigned short *seed48 (unsigned short seed16v[3]);

void lcong48 (unsigned short param[7]);

DESCRIPTION

This family of functions generates pseudo-random numbers using the well-known linear congruential algorithm and 48-bit integer arithmetic.

Functions `drand48` and `erand48` return non-negative double-precision floating-point values uniformly distributed over the interval [0.0, 1.0).

Functions `lrand48` and `nrand48` return non-negative long integers uniformly distributed over the interval [0, 2^{31}).

Functions `mrand48` and `jrand48` return signed long integers uniformly distributed over the interval [−2^{31}, 2^{31}).

Functions `srand48`, `seed48`, and `lcong48` are initialization entry points, one of which should be invoked before either `drand48`, `lrand48`, or `mrand48` is called. (Although it is not recommended practice, constant default initializer values will be supplied automatically if `drand48`, `lrand48`, or `mrand48` is called without a prior call to an initialization entry point.) Functions `erand48`, `nrand48`, and `jrand48` do not require an initialization entry point to be called first.

All the routines work by generating a sequence of 48-bit integer values, X_i, according to the linear congruential formula

$$X_{n+1} = (aX_n + c)_{\bmod m} \qquad n \geq 0.$$

The parameter $m = 2^{48}$; hence 48-bit integer arithmetic is performed. Unless `lcong48` has been invoked, the multiplier value a and the addend value c are given by

$$a = 5\text{DEECE66D}_{16} = 273673163155_8$$
$$c = \text{B}_{16} = 13_8.$$

The value returned by any of the functions drand48, erand48, lrand48, nrand48, mrand48, or jrand48 is computed by first generating the next 48-bit X_i in the sequence. Then the appropriate number of bits, according to the type of data item to be returned, are copied from the high-order (leftmost) bits of X_i and transformed into the returned value.

The functions drand48, lrand48, and mrand48 store the last 48-bit X_i generated in an internal buffer. X_i must be initialized prior to being invoked. The functions erand48, nrand48, and jrand48 require the calling program to provide storage for the successive X_i values in the array specified as an argument when the functions are invoked. These routines do not have to be initialized; the calling program must place the desired initial value of X_i into the array and pass it as an argument. By using different arguments, functions erand48, nrand48, and jrand48 allow separate modules of a large program to generate several independent streams of pseudo-random numbers, that is, the sequence of numbers in each stream will not depend upon how many times the routines have been called to generate numbers for the other streams.

The initializer function srand48 sets the high-order 32 bits of X_i to the 32 bits contained in its argument. The low-order 16 bits of X_i are set to the arbitrary value $330E_{16}$.

The initializer function seed48 sets the value of X_i to the 48-bit value specified in the argument array. In addition, the previous value of X_i is copied into a 48-bit internal buffer, used only by seed48, and a pointer to this buffer is the value returned by seed48. This returned pointer, which can just be ignored if not needed, is useful if a program is to be restarted from a given point at some future time — use the pointer to get at and store the last X_i value, and then use this value to reinitialize via seed48 when the program is restarted.

The initialization function lcong48 allows the user to specify the initial X_i, the multiplier value a, and the addend value c. Argument array elements *param[0-2]* specify X_i, *param[3-5]* specify the multiplier a, and *param[6]* specifies the 16-bit addend c. After lcong48 has been called, a subsequent call to either srand48 or seed48 will restore the "standard" multiplier and addend values, a and c, specified on the previous page.

SEE ALSO
rand(3C).

dup2(3C)

NAME
dup2 – duplicate an open file descriptor

SYNOPSIS
#include <unistd.h>

int dup2 (int fildes, int fildes2);

DESCRIPTION
fildes is a file descriptor referring to an open file, and *fildes2* is a non-negative integer less than {OPEN_MAX} (the maximum number of open files). dup2 causes *fildes2* to refer to the same file as *fildes*. If *fildes2* already referred to an open file, not *fildes*, it is closed first. If *fildes2* refers to *fildes*, or if *fildes* is not a valid open file descriptor, *fildes2* will not be closed first.

dup2 will fail if one or more of the following are true:

EBADF	*fildes* is not a valid open file descriptor.
EBADF	*fildes2* is negative or greater than or equal to {OPEN_MAX}.
EINTR	a signal was caught during the dup2 call.
EMFILE	{OPEN_MAX} file descriptors are currently open.

SEE ALSO
creat(2), close(2), exec(2), fcntl(2), open(2), pipe(2), lockf(3C), limits(4).

DIAGNOSTICS
Upon successful completion a non-negative integer, namely, the file descriptor, is returned. Otherwise, a value of −1 is returned and errno is set to indicate the error.

econvert(3)   (BSD Compatibility Package)   econvert(3)

NAME
econvert, fconvert, gconvert, seconvert, sfconvert, sgconvert – output conversion

SYNOPSIS
cc [*flag*...] *file* ... -lucb

#include <floatingpoint.h>

char *econvert(value, ndigit, decpt, sign, buf)
double value;
int ndigit, *decpt, *sign;
char *buf;

char *fconvert(value, ndigit, decpt, sign, buf)
double value;
int ndigit, *decpt, *sign;
char *buf;

char *gconvert(value, ndigit, trailing, buf)
double value;
int ndigit;
int trailing;
char *buf;

char *seconvert(value, ndigit, decpt, sign, buf)
single *value;
int ndigit, *decpt, *sign;
char *buf;

char *sfconvert(value, ndigit, decpt, sign, buf)
single *value;
int ndigit, *decpt, *sign;
char *buf;

char *sgconvert(value, ndigit, trailing, buf)
single *value;
int ndigit;
int trailing;
char *buf;

DESCRIPTION
econvert converts the *value* to a NULL-terminated string of *ndigit* ASCII digits in *buf* and returns a pointer to *buf*. *buf* should contain at least *ndigit*+1 characters. The position of the decimal point relative to the beginning of the string is stored indirectly through *decpt*. Thus *buf* == "314" and *decpt* == 1 corresponds to the numerical value 3.14, while *buf* == "314" and *decpt* == -1 corresponds to the numerical value .0314. If the sign of the result is negative, the word pointed to by *sign* is nonzero; otherwise it is zero. The least significant digit is rounded.

fconvert works much like econvert, except that the correct digit has been rounded as if for sprintf(%w.nf) output with n=*ndigit* digits to the right of the decimal point. *ndigit* can be negative to indicate rounding to the left of the decimal point. The return value is a pointer to *buf*. *buf* should contain at least 310+*max*(0,*ndigit*) characters to accommodate any double-precision *value*.

gconvert converts the *value* to a NULL-terminated ASCII string in *buf* and returns a pointer to *buf*. It produces *ndigit* significant digits in fixed-decimal format, like sprintf(%w.nf), if possible, and otherwise in floating-decimal format, like sprintf(%w.ne); in either case *buf* is ready for printing, with sign and exponent. The result corresponds to that obtained by

> (void) sprintf(buf,``%w.ng'',value) ;

If *trailing*= 0, trailing zeros and a trailing point are suppressed, as in sprintf(%g). If *trailing*!= 0, trailing zeros and a trailing point are retained, as in sprintf(%#g).

seconvert, sfconvert, and sgconvert are single-precision versions of these functions, and are more efficient than the corresponding double-precision versions. A pointer rather than the value itself is passed to avoid C's usual conversion of single-precision arguments to double.

IEEE Infinities and NaNs are treated similarly by these functions. "NaN" is returned for NaN, and "Inf" or "Infinity" for Infinity. The longer form is produced when $ndigit \geq 8$.

SEE ALSO

sprintf(3S) in the *Programmer's Reference Manual*

NAME

ecvt, ecvtl, fcvt, fcvtl, gcvt, gcvtl – convert floating-point number to string

SYNOPSIS

```
#include <stdlib.h>

char *ecvt (double value, int ndigit, int *decpt, int *sign);

char *ecvtl (long double value, int ndigit, int *decpt, int *sign);

char *fcvt (double value, int ndigit, int *decpt, int *sign);

char *fcvtl (long double value, int ndigit, int *decpt, int *sign);

char *gcvt (double value, int ndigit, char *buf);

char *gcvtl (long double value, int ndigit, char *buf);
```

DESCRIPTION

ecvt and ecvtl convert *value* to a null-terminated string of *ndigit* digits and return a pointer thereto. The high-order digit is non-zero, unless the value is zero. The low-order digit is rounded. The position of the decimal point relative to the beginning of the string is stored indirectly through *decpt* (negative means to the left of the returned digits). The decimal point is not included in the returned string. If the sign of the result is negative, the word pointed to by *sign* is non-zero, otherwise it is zero.

fcvt and fcvtl are identical to ecvt and ecvtl, except that the correct digit has been rounded for printf %f output of the number of digits specified by *ndigit*.

gcvt and gcvtl convert the *value* to a null-terminated string in the array pointed to by *buf* and return *buf*. They attempt to produce *ndigit* significant digits in %f format if possible, otherwise %e format (scientific notation), ready for printing. A minus sign, if there is one, or a decimal point will be included as part of the returned string. Trailing zeros are suppressed.

SEE ALSO

printf(3S).

NOTES

The values returned by ecvt, ecvtl, fcvt, and fcvtl point to a single static data array whose content is overwritten by each call.

elf(3E) (ELF Library)

NAME
elf - object file access library

SYNOPSIS
cc [*flag* ...] *file* ... -lelf [*library* ...]

#include <libelf.h>

DESCRIPTION
Functions in the ELF access library let a program manipulate ELF (Executable and Linking Format) object files, archive files, and archive members. The header file provides type and function declarations for all library services.

Programs communicate with many of the higher-level routines using an *ELF descriptor*. That is, when the program starts working with a file, elf_begin creates an ELF descriptor through which the program manipulates the structures and information in the file. These ELF descriptors can be used both to read and to write files. After the program establishes an ELF descriptor for a file, it may then obtain *section descriptors* to manipulate the sections of the file [see elf_getscn(3E)]. Sections hold the bulk of an object file's real information, such as text, data, the symbol table, and so on. A section descriptor "belongs" to a particular ELF descriptor, just as a section belongs to a file. Finally, *data descriptors* are available through section descriptors, allowing the program to manipulate the information associated with a section. A data descriptor "belongs" to a section descriptor.

Descriptors provide private handles to a file and its pieces. In other words, a data descriptor is associated with one section descriptor, which is associated with one ELF descriptor, which is associated with one file. Although descriptors are private, they give access to data that may be shared. Consider programs that combine input files, using incoming data to create or update another file. Such a program might get data descriptors for an input and an output section. It then could update the output descriptor to reuse the input descriptor's data. That is, the descriptors are distinct, but they could share the associated data bytes. This sharing avoids the space overhead for duplicate buffers and the performance overhead for copying data unnecessarily.

FILE CLASSES
ELF provides a framework in which to define a family of object files, supporting multiple processors and architectures. An important distinction among object files is the *class*, or capacity, of the file. The 32-bit class supports architectures in which a 32-bit object can represent addresses, file sizes, etc., as in the following.

Name	Purpose
Elf32_Addr	Unsigned address
Elf32_Half	Unsigned medium integer
Elf32_Off	Unsigned file offset
Elf32_Sword	Signed large integer
Elf32_Word	Unsigned large integer
unsigned char	Unsigned small integer

Other classes will be defined as necessary, to support larger (or smaller) machines. Some library services deal only with data objects for a specific class, while others are class-independent. To make this distinction clear, library function names reflect their status, as described below.

DATA REPRESENTATIONS

Conceptually, two parallel sets of objects support cross compilation environments. One set corresponds to file contents, while the other set corresponds to the native memory image of the program manipulating the file. Type definitions supplied by the header files work on the native machine, which may have different data encodings (size, byte order, etc.) than the target machine. Although native memory objects should be at least as big as the file objects (to avoid information loss), they may be bigger if that is more natural for the host machine.

Translation facilities exist to convert between file and memory representations. Some library routines convert data automatically, while others leave conversion as the program's responsibility. Either way, programs that create object files must write file-typed objects to those files; programs that read object files must take a similar view. See elf_xlate(3E) and elf_fsize(3E) for more information.

Programs may translate data explicitly, taking full control over the object file layout and semantics. If the program prefers not to have and exercise complete control, the library provides a higher-level interface that hides many object file details. elf_begin and related functions let a program deal with the native memory types, converting between memory objects and their file equivalents automatically when reading or writing an object file.

ELF VERSIONS

Object file versions allow ELF to adapt to new requirements. Three—independent—versions can be important to a program. First, an application program knows about a particular version by virtue of being compiled with certain header files. Second, the access library similarly is compiled with header files that control what versions it understands. Third, an ELF object file holds a value identifying its version, determined by the ELF version known by the file's creator. Ideally, all three versions would be the same, but they may differ.

> If a program's version is newer than the access library, the program might use information unknown to the library. Translation routines might not work properly, leading to undefined behavior. This condition merits installing a new library.
>
> The library's version might be newer than the program's and the file's. The library understands old versions, thus avoiding compatibility problems in this case.
>
> Finally, a file's version might be newer than either the program or the library understands. The program might or might not be able to process the file properly, depending on whether the file has extra information and whether that information can be safely ignored. Again, the safe alternative is to install a new library that understands the file's version.

To accommodate these differences, a program must use `elf_version` to pass its version to the library, thus establishing the *working version* for the process. Using this, the library accepts data from and presents data to the program in the proper representations. When the library reads object files, it uses each file's version to interpret the data. When writing files or converting memory types to the file equivalents, the library uses the program's working version for the file data.

SYSTEM SERVICES

As mentioned above, `elf_begin` and related routines provide a higher-level interface to ELF files, performing input and output on behalf of the application program. These routines assume a program can hold entire files in memory, without explicitly using temporary files. When reading a file, the library routines bring the data into memory and perform subsequent operations on the memory copy. Programs that wish to read or write large object files with this model must execute on a machine with a large process virtual address space. If the underlying operating system limits the number of open files, a program can use `elf_cntl` to retrieve all necessary data from the file, allowing the program to close the file descriptor and reuse it.

Although the `elf_begin` interfaces are convenient and efficient for many programs, they might be inappropriate for some. In those cases, an application may invoke the `elf_xlate` data translation routines directly. These routines perform no input or output, leaving that as the application's responsibility. By assuming a larger share of the job, an application controls its input and output model.

LIBRARY NAMES

Names associated with the library take several forms.

`elf_`*name*	These class-independent names perform some service, *name*, for the program.
`elf32_`*name*	Service names with an embedded class, 32 here, indicate they work only for the designated class of files.
`Elf_`*Type*	Data types can be class-independent as well, distinguished by *Type*.
`Elf32_`*Type*	Class-dependent data types have an embedded class name, 32 here.
`ELF_C_`*CMD*	Several functions take commands that control their actions. These values are members of the `Elf_Cmd` enumeration; they range from zero through `ELF_C_NUM-1`.
`ELF_F_`*FLAG*	Several functions take flags that control library status and/or actions. Flags are bits that may be combined.
`ELF32_FSZ_`*TYPE*	These constants give the file sizes in bytes of the basic ELF types for the 32-bit class of files. See `elf_fsize` for more information.
`ELF_K_`*KIND*	The function `elf_kind` identifies the *KIND* of file associated with an ELF descriptor. These values are members of the `Elf_Kind` enumeration; they range from zero through `ELF_K_NUM-1`.

elf(3E) (ELF Library) elf(3E)

ELF_T_*TYPE*   When a service function, such as elf_xlate, deals with multiple types, names of this form specify the desired *TYPE*. Thus, for example, ELF_T_EHDR is directly related to Elf32_Ehdr. These values are members of the Elf_Type enumeration; they range from zero through ELF_T_NUM-1.

SEE ALSO

cof2elf(1), elf_begin(3E), elf_cntl(3E), elf_end(3E), elf_error(3E), elf_fill(3E), elf_flag(3E), elf_fsize(3E), elf_getarhdr(3E), elf_getarsym(3E), elf_getbase(3E), elf_getdata(3E), elf_getehdr(3E), elf_getident(3E), elf_getphdr(3E), elf_getscn(3E), elf_getshdr(3E), elf_hash(3E), elf_kind(3E), elf_next(3E), elf_rand(3E), elf_rawfile(3E), elf_strptr(3E), elf_update(3E), elf_version(3E), elf_xlate(3E), a.out(4), ar(4)

The "Object Files" in the chapter *Programmer's Guide: ANSI C and Programming Support Tools*.

NOTES

Information in the ELF header files is separated into common parts and processor-specific parts. A program can make a processor's information available by including the appropriate header file: <sys/elf_*NAME*.h> where *NAME* matches the processor name as used in the ELF file header.

Symbol	Processor
M32	AT&T WE 32100
SPARC	SPARC
386	Intel 80386
486	Intel 80486
860	Intel 80860
68K	Motorola 68000
88K	Motorola 88000

Other processors will be added to the table as necessary. To illustrate, a program could use the following code to "see" the processor-specific information for the WE 32100.

```
#include <libelf.h>
#include <sys/elf_M32.h>
```

Without the <sys/elf_M32.h> definition, only the common ELF information would be visible.

NAME

elf_begin – make a file descriptor

SYNOPSIS

cc [*flag* ...] *file* ... -lelf [*library* ...]

#include <libelf.h>

Elf *elf_begin(int fildes, Elf_Cmd cmd, Elf *ref);

DESCRIPTION

elf_begin, elf_next, elf_rand, and elf_end work together to process ELF object files, either individually or as members of archives. After obtaining an ELF descriptor from elf_begin, the program may read an existing file, update an existing file, or create a new file. *fildes* is an open file descriptor that elf_begin uses for reading or writing. The initial file offset [see lseek(2)] is unconstrained, and the resulting file offset is undefined.

cmd may have the following values.

ELF_C_NULL   When a program sets *cmd* to this value, elf_begin returns a null pointer, without opening a new descriptor. *ref* is ignored for this command. See elf_next(3E) and the examples below for more information.

ELF_C_READ   When a program wishes to examine the contents of an existing file, it should set *cmd* to this value. Depending on the value of *ref*, this command examines archive members or entire files. Three cases can occur.

First, if *ref* is a null pointer, elf_begin allocates a new ELF descriptor and prepares to process the entire file. If the file being read is an archive, elf_begin also prepares the resulting descriptor to examine the initial archive member on the next call to elf_begin, as if the program had used elf_next or elf_rand to "move" to the initial member.

Second, if *ref* is a non-null descriptor associated with an archive file, elf_begin lets a program obtain a separate ELF descriptor associated with an individual member. The program should have used elf_next or elf_rand to position *ref* appropriately (except for the initial member, which elf_begin prepares; see the example below). In this case, *fildes* should be the same file descriptor used for the parent archive.

Finally, if *ref* is a non-null ELF descriptor that is not an archive, elf_begin increments the number of activations for the descriptor and returns *ref*, without allocating a new descriptor and without changing the descriptor's read/write permissions. To terminate the descriptor for *ref*, the program must call elf_end once for each activation. See elf_next(3E) and the examples below for more information.

ELF_C_RDWR		This command duplicates the actions of ELF_C_READ and additionally allows the program to update the file image [see elf_update(3E)]. That is, using ELF_C_READ gives a read-only view of the file, while ELF_C_RDWR lets the program read *and* write the file. ELF_C_RDWR is not valid for archive members. If *ref* is non-null, it must have been created with the ELF_C_RDWR command.
ELF_C_WRITE		If the program wishes to ignore previous file contents, presumably to create a new file, it should set *cmd* to this value. *ref* is ignored for this command.

elf_begin "works" on all files (including files with zero bytes), providing it can allocate memory for its internal structures and read any necessary information from the file. Programs reading object files thus may call elf_kind or elf_getehdr to determine the file type (only object files have an ELF header). If the file is an archive with no more members to process, or an error occurs, elf_begin returns a null pointer. Otherwise, the return value is a non-null ELF descriptor.

Before the first call to elf_begin, a program must call elf_version to coordinate versions.

SYSTEM SERVICES

When processing a file, the library decides when to read or write the file, depending on the program's requests. Normally, the library assumes the file descriptor remains usable for the life of the ELF descriptor. If, however, a program must process many files simultaneously and the underlying operating system limits the number of open files, the program can use elf_cntl to let it reuse file descriptors. After calling elf_cntl with appropriate arguments, the program may close the file descriptor without interfering with the library.

All data associated with an ELF descriptor remain allocated until elf_end terminates the descriptor's last activation. After the descriptors have been terminated, the storage is released; attempting to reference such data gives undefined behavior. Consequently, a program that deals with multiple input (or output) files must keep the ELF descriptors active until it finishes with them.

EXAMPLES

A prototype for reading a file appears below. If the file is a simple object file, the program executes the loop one time, receiving a null descriptor in the second iteration. In this case, both elf and arf will have the same value, the activation count will be two, and the program calls elf_end twice to terminate the descriptor. If the file is an archive, the loop processes each archive member in turn, ignoring those that are not object files.

```
if (elf_version(EV_CURRENT) == EV_NONE)
{
        /* library out of date */
        /* recover from error */
}
cmd = ELF_C_READ;
arf = elf_begin(fildes, cmd, (Elf *)0);
while ((elf = elf_begin(fildes, cmd, arf)) != 0)
{
        if ((ehdr = elf32_getehdr(elf)) != 0)
        {
                /* process the file ... */
        }
        cmd = elf_next(elf);
        elf_end(elf);
}
elf_end(arf);
```

Alternatively, the next example illustrates random archive processing. After identifying the file as an archive, the program repeatedly processes archive members of interest. For clarity, this example omits error checking and ignores simple object files. Additionally, this fragment preserves the ELF descriptors for all archive members, because it does not call elf_end to terminate them.

```
elf_version(EV_CURRENT);
arf = elf_begin(fildes, ELF_C_READ, (Elf *)0);
if (elf_kind(arf) != ELF_K_AR)
{
        /* not an archive */
}
/* initial processing */
/* set offset = ... for desired member header */
while (elf_rand(arf, offset) == offset)
{
        if ((elf = elf_begin(fildes, ELF_C_READ, arf)) == 0)
                break;
        if ((ehdr = elf32_getehdr(elf)) != 0)
        {
                /* process archive member ... */
        }
        /* set offset = ... for desired member header */
}
```

The following outline shows how one might create a new ELF file. This example is simplified to show the overall flow.

```
elf_version(EV_CURRENT);
fildes = open("path/name", O_RDWR|O_TRUNC|O_CREAT, 0666);
if ((elf = elf_begin(fildes, ELF_C_WRITE, (Elf *)0)) == 0)
        return;
ehdr = elf32_newehdr(elf);
phdr = elf32_newphdr(elf, count);
scn = elf_newscn(elf);
shdr = elf32_getshdr(scn);
data = elf_newdata(scn);
elf_update(elf, ELF_C_WRITE);
elf_end(elf);
```

Finally, the following outline shows how one might update an existing ELF file. Again, this example is simplified to show the overall flow.

```
elf_version(EV_CURRENT);
fildes = open("path/name", O_RDWR);
elf = elf_begin(fildes, ELF_C_RDWR, (Elf *)0);

/* add new or delete old information ... */

close(creat("path/name", 0666));
elf_update(elf, ELF_C_WRITE);
elf_end(elf);
```

In the example above, the call to creat truncates the file, thus ensuring the resulting file will have the "right" size. Without truncation, the updated file might be as big as the original, even if information were deleted. The library truncates the file, if it can, with ftruncate [see truncate(2)]. Some systems, however, do not support ftruncate, and the call to creat protects against this.

Notice that both file creation examples open the file with write *and* read permissions. On systems that support mmap, the library uses it to enhance performance, and mmap requires a readable file descriptor. Although the library can use a write-only file descriptor, the application will not obtain the performance advantages of mmap.

SEE ALSO

cof2elf(1), creat(2), lseek(2), mmap(2), open(2), truncate(2), elf(3E), elf_cntl(3E), elf_end(3E), elf_getarhdr(3E), elf_getbase(3E), elf_getdata(3E), elf_getehdr(3E), elf_getphdr(3E), elf_getscn(3E), elf_kind(3E), elf_next(3E), elf_rand(3E), elf_rawfile(3E), elf_update(3E), elf_version(3E), ar(4)

NOTES

COFF is an object file format that preceded ELF. When a program calls elf_begin on a COFF file, the library translates COFF structures to their ELF equivalents, allowing programs to read (but not to write) a COFF file as if it were ELF. This conversion happens only to the memory image and not to the file itself. After the initial elf_begin, file offsets and addresses in the ELF header, the program headers, and the section headers retain the original COFF values [see elf_getehdr, elf_getphdr, and elf_getshdr]. A program may call elf_update to adjust these values (without writing the file), and the library will then present a consistent, ELF view of the file. Data obtained through `elf_getdata` are translated (the COFF symbol table is presented as ELF, and so on). Data viewed through `elf_rawdata` undergo no conversion, allowing the program to view the bytes from the file itself.

Some COFF debugging information is not translated, though this does not affect the semantics of a running program.

Although the ELF library supports COFF, programmers are strongly encouraged to recompile their programs, obtaining ELF object files.

NAME
elf_cntl - control a file descriptor

SYNOPSIS
cc [*flag* ...] *file* ... -lelf [*library* ...]

#include <libelf.h>

int elf_cntl(Elf *elf, Elf_Cmd cmd);

DESCRIPTION
elf_cntl instructs the library to modify its behavior with respect to an ELF descriptor, *elf*. As elf_begin(3E) describes, an ELF descriptor can have multiple activations, and multiple ELF descriptors may share a single file descriptor. Generally, elf_cntl commands apply to all activations of *elf*. Moreover, if the ELF descriptor is associated with an archive file, descriptors for members within the archive will also be affected as described below. Unless stated otherwise, operations on archive members do not affect the descriptor for the containing archive.

The *cmd* argument tells what actions to take and may have the following values.

ELF_C_FDDONE
> This value tells the library not to use the file descriptor associated with *elf*. A program should use this command when it has requested all the information it cares to use and wishes to avoid the overhead of reading the rest of the file. The memory for all completed operations remains valid, but later file operations, such as the initial elf_getdata for a section, will fail if the data are not in memory already.

ELF_C_FDREAD
> This command is similar to ELF_C_FDDONE, except it forces the library to read the rest of the file. A program should use this command when it must close the file descriptor but has not yet read everything it needs from the file. After elf_cntl completes the ELF_C_FDREAD command, future operations, such as elf_getdata, will use the memory version of the file without needing to use the file descriptor.

If elf_cntl succeeds, it returns zero. Otherwise *elf* was null or an error occurred, and the function returns -1.

SEE ALSO
elf(3E), elf_begin(3E), elf_getdata(3E), elf_rawfile(3E)

NOTE
If the program wishes to use the "raw" operations [see elf_rawdata, which elf_getdata(3E) describes, and elf_rawfile(3E)] after disabling the file descriptor with ELF_C_FDDONE or ELF_C_FDREAD, it must execute the raw operations explicitly beforehand. Otherwise, the raw file operations will fail. Calling elf_rawfile makes the entire image available, thus supporting subsequent elf_rawdata calls.

elf_end(3E) (ELF Library) elf_end(3E)

NAME
elf_end – finish using an object file

SYNOPSIS
cc [*flag* ...] *file* ... -lelf [*library* ...]

#include <libelf.h>

int elf_end(Elf *elf);

DESCRIPTION
A program uses `elf_end` to terminate an ELF descriptor, *elf*, and to deallocate data associated with the descriptor. Until the program terminates a descriptor, the data remain allocated. *elf* should be a value previously returned by `elf_begin`; a null pointer is allowed as an argument, to simplify error handling. If the program wishes to write data associated with the ELF descriptor to the file, it must use `elf_update` before calling `elf_end`.

As `elf_begin`(3E) explains, a descriptor can have more than one activation. Calling `elf_end` removes one activation and returns the remaining activation count. The library does not terminate the descriptor until the activation count reaches zero. Consequently, a zero return value indicates the ELF descriptor is no longer valid.

SEE ALSO
elf(3E), elf_begin(3E), elf_update(3E)

NAME
elf_errmsg, elf_errno – error handling

SYNOPSIS
cc [*flag* ...] *file* ... -lelf [*library* ...]

#include <libelf.h>

const char *elf_errmsg(int err);
int elf_errno(void);

DESCRIPTION
If an ELF library function fails, a program may call elf_errno to retrieve the library's internal error number. As a side effect, this function resets the internal error number to zero, which indicates no error.

elf_errmsg takes an error number, *err*, and returns a null-terminated error message (with no trailing new-line) that describes the problem. A zero *err* retrieves a message for the most recent error. If no error has occurred, the return value is a null pointer (not a pointer to the null string). Using *err* of −1 also retrieves the most recent error, except it guarantees a non-null return value, even when no error has occurred. If no message is available for the given number, elf_errmsg returns a pointer to an appropriate message. This function does not have the side effect of clearing the internal error number.

EXAMPLE
The following fragment clears the internal error number and checks it later for errors. Unless an error occurs after the first call to elf_errno, the next call will return zero.

```
        (void)elf_errno();
        while (more_to_do)
        {
                /* processing ... */
                if ((err = elf_errno()) != 0)
                {
                        msg = elf_errmsg(err);
                        /* print msg */
                }
        }
```

SEE ALSO
elf(3E), elf_version(3E)

NAME
elf_fill − set fill byte

SYNOPSIS
cc [*flag* ...] *file* ... −lelf [*library* ...]

#include <libelf.h>

void elf_fill(int fill);

DESCRIPTION
Alignment constraints for ELF files sometimes require the presence of "holes." For example, if the data for one section are required to begin on an eight-byte boundary, but the preceding section is too "short," the library must fill the intervening bytes. These bytes are set to the *fill* character. The library uses zero bytes unless the application supplies a value. See elf_getdata(3E) for more information about these holes.

SEE ALSO
elf(3E), elf_getdata(3E), elf_flag(3E), elf_update(3E)

NOTE
An application can assume control of the object file organization by setting the ELF_F_LAYOUT bit [see elf_flag(3E)]. When this is done, the library does not fill holes.

NAME

elf_flagdata, elf_flagehdr, elf_flagelf, elf_flagphdr, elf_flagscn, elf_flagshdr — manipulate flags

SYNOPSIS

cc [*flag* ...] *file* ... -lelf [*library* ...]

#include <libelf.h>

unsigned elf_flagdata(Elf_Data *data, Elf_Cmd cmd, unsigned flags);

unsigned elf_flagehdr(Elf *elf, Elf_Cmd cmd, unsigned flags);

unsigned elf_flagelf(Elf *elf, Elf_Cmd cmd, unsigned flags);

unsigned elf_flagphdr(Elf *elf, Elf_Cmd cmd, unsigned flags);

unsigned elf_flagscn(Elf_Scn *scn, Elf_Cmd cmd, unsigned flags);

unsigned elf_flagshdr(Elf_Scn *scn, Elf_Cmd cmd, unsigned flags);

DESCRIPTION

These functions manipulate the flags associated with various structures of an ELF file. Given an ELF descriptor (*elf*), a data descriptor (*data*), or a section descriptor (*scn*), the functions may set or clear the associated status bits, returning the updated bits. A null descriptor is allowed, to simplify error handling; all functions return zero for this degenerate case.

cmd may have the following values.

ELF_C_CLR   The functions clear the bits that are asserted in *flags*. Only the non-zero bits in *flags* are cleared; zero bits do not change the status of the descriptor.

ELF_C_SET   The functions set the bits that are asserted in *flags*. Only the non-zero bits in *flags* are set; zero bits do not change the status of the descriptor.

Descriptions of the defined *flags* bits appear below.

ELF_F_DIRTY   When the program intends to write an ELF file, this flag asserts the associated information needs to be written to the file. Thus, for example, a program that wished to update the ELF header of an existing file would call elf_flagehdr with this bit set in *flags* and *cmd* equal to ELF_C_SET. A later call to elf_update would write the marked header to the file.

ELF_F_LAYOUT   Normally, the library decides how to arrange an output file. That is, it automatically decides where to place sections, how to align them in the file, etc. If this bit is set for an ELF descriptor, the program assumes responsibility for determining all file positions. This bit is meaningful only for elf_flagelf and applies to the entire file associated with the descriptor.

elf_flag(3E) (ELF Library) elf_flag(3E)

When a flag bit is set for an item, it affects all the subitems as well. Thus, for example, if the program sets the ELF_F_DIRTY bit with elf_flagelf, the entire logical file is "dirty."

EXAMPLE

The following fragment shows how one might mark the ELF header to be written to the output file.

```
ehdr = elf32_getehdr(elf);
/* dirty ehdr ... */
elf_flagehdr(elf, ELF_C_SET, ELF_F_DIRTY);
```

SEE ALSO

elf(3E), elf_end(3E), elf_getdata(3E), elf_getehdr(3E), elf_update(3E)

NAME
elf_fsize: elf32_fsize − return the size of an object file type

SYNOPSIS
cc [*flag* ...] *file* ... −lelf [*library* ...]

#include <libelf.h>

size_t elf32_fsize(Elf_Type type, size_t count, unsigned ver);

DESCRIPTION
elf32_fsize gives the size in bytes of the 32-bit file representation of *count* data objects with the given *type*. The library uses version *ver* to calculate the size [see elf(3E) and elf_version(3E)].

Constant values are available for the sizes of fundamental types.

Elf_Type	File Size	Memory Size
ELF_T_ADDR	ELF32_FSZ_ADDR	sizeof(Elf32_Addr)
ELF_T_BYTE	1	sizeof(unsigned char)
ELF_T_HALF	ELF32_FSZ_HALF	sizeof(Elf32_Half)
ELT_T_OFF	ELF32_FSZ_OFF	sizeof(Elf32_Off)
ELF_T_SWORD	ELF32_FSZ_SWORD	sizeof(Elf32_Sword)
ELF_T_WORD	ELF32_FSZ_WORD	sizeof(Elf32_Word)

elf32_fsize returns zero if the value of *type* or *ver* is unknown. See elf_xlate(3E) for a list of the *type* values.

SEE ALSO
elf(3E), elf_version(3E), elf_xlate(3E)

NAME
elf_getarhdr - retrieve archive member header

SYNOPSIS
cc [flag ...] file ... -lelf [library ...]

#include <libelf.h>

Elf_Arhdr *elf_getarhdr(Elf *elf);

DESCRIPTION
elf_getarhdr returns a pointer to an archive member header, if one is available for the ELF descriptor elf. Otherwise, no archive member header exists, an error occurred, or elf was null; elf_getarhdr then returns a null value. The header includes the following members.

```
char           *ar_name;
time_t         ar_date;
long           ar_uid;
long           ar_gid;
unsigned long  ar_mode;
off_t          ar_size;
char           *ar_rawname;
```

An archive member name, available through ar_name, is a null-terminated string, with the ar format control characters removed. The ar_rawname member holds a null-terminated string that represents the original name bytes in the file, including the terminating slash and trailing blanks as specified in the archive format.

In addition to "regular" archive members, the archive format defines some special members. All special member names begin with a slash (/), distinguishing them from regular members (whose names may not contain a slash). These special members have the names (ar_name) defined below.

/   This is the archive symbol table. If present, it will be the first archive member. A program may access the archive symbol table through elf_getarsym. The information in the symbol table is useful for random archive processing [see elf_rand(3E)].

//   This member, if present, holds a string table for long archive member names. An archive member's header contains a 16-byte area for the name, which may be exceeded in some file systems. The library automatically retrieves long member names from the string table, setting ar_name to the appropriate value.

Under some error conditions, a member's name might not be available. Although this causes the library to set ar_name to a null pointer, the ar_rawname member will be set as usual.

SEE ALSO
elf(3E), elf_begin(3E), elf_getarsym(3E), elf_rand(3E), ar(4)

NAME
elf_getarsym – retrieve archive symbol table

SYNOPSIS
cc [*flag* ...] *file* ... -lelf [*library* ...]

#include <libelf.h>

Elf_Arsym *elf_getarsym(Elf *elf, size_t *ptr);

DESCRIPTION
elf_getarsym returns a pointer to the archive symbol table, if one is available for the ELF descriptor *elf*. Otherwise, the archive doesn't have a symbol table, an error occurred, or *elf* was null; elf_getarsym then returns a null value. The symbol table is an array of structures that include the following members.

```
char         *as_name;
size_t        as_off;
unsigned long as_hash;
```

These members have the following semantics.

as_name   A pointer to a null-terminated symbol name resides here.

as_off   This value is a byte offset from the beginning of the archive to the member's header. The archive member residing at the given offset defines the associated symbol. Values in as_off may be passed as arguments to elf_rand to access the desired archive member.

as_hash   This is a hash value for the name, as computed by elf_hash.

If *ptr* is non-null, the library stores the number of table entries in the location to which *ptr* points. This value is set to zero when the return value is null. The table's last entry, which is included in the count, has a null as_name, a zero value for as_off, and ~0UL for as_hash.

SEE ALSO
elf(3E), elf_getarhdr(3E), elf_hash(3E), elf_rand(3E), ar(4)

elf_getbase(3E)　　　　　　　　　　(ELF Library)　　　　　　　　　　elf_getbase(3E)

NAME
　　elf_getbase – get the base offset for an object file

SYNOPSIS
　　cc [*flag* ...] *file* ... -lelf [*library* ...]

　　#include <libelf.h>

　　off_t elf_getbase(Elf *elf);

DESCRIPTION
　　elf_getbase returns the file offset of the first byte of the file or archive member associated with *elf*, if it is known or obtainable, and −1 otherwise. A null *elf* is allowed, to simplify error handling; the return value in this case is −1. The base offset of an archive member is the beginning of the member's information, not the beginning of the archive member header.

SEE ALSO
　　elf(3E), elf_begin(3E), ar(4).

NAME
elf_getdata, elf_newdata, elf_rawdata – get section data

SYNOPSIS
cc [*flag* ...] *file* ... -lelf [*library* ...]

#include <libelf.h>

Elf_Data *elf_getdata(Elf_Scn *scn, Elf_Data *data);

Elf_Data *elf_newdata(Elf_Scn *scn);

Elf_Data *elf_rawdata(Elf_Scn *scn, Elf_Data *data);

DESCRIPTION
These functions access and manipulate the data associated with a section descriptor, *scn*. When reading an existing file, a section will have a single data buffer associated with it. A program may build a new section in pieces, however, composing the new data from multiple data buffers. For this reason, "the" data for a section should be viewed as a list of buffers, each of which is available through a data descriptor.

elf_getdata lets a program step through a section's data list. If the incoming data descriptor, *data*, is null, the function returns the first buffer associated with the section. Otherwise, *data* should be a data descriptor associated with *scn*, and the function gives the program access to the next data element for the section. If *scn* is null or an error occurs, elf_getdata returns a null pointer.

elf_getdata translates the data from file representations into memory representations [see elf_xlate(3E)] and presents objects with memory data types to the program, based on the file's *class* [see elf(3E)]. The working library version [see elf_version(3E)] specifies what version of the memory structures the program wishes elf_getdata to present.

elf_newdata creates a new data descriptor for a section, appending it to any data elements already associated with the section. As described below, the new data descriptor appears empty, indicating the element holds no data. For convenience, the descriptor's type (d_type below) is set to ELF_T_BYTE, and the version (d_version below) is set to the working version. The program is responsible for setting (or changing) the descriptor members as needed. This function implicitly sets the ELF_F_DIRTY bit for the section's data [see elf_flag(3E)]. If *scn* is null or an error occurs, elf_newdata returns a null pointer.

elf_rawdata differs from elf_getdata by returning only uninterpreted bytes, regardless of the section type. This function typically should be used only to retrieve a section image from a file being read, and then only when a program must avoid the automatic data translation described below. Moreover, a program may not close or disable [see elf_cntl(3E)] the file descriptor associated with *elf* before the initial raw operation, because elf_rawdata might read the data from the file to ensure it doesn't interfere with elf_getdata. See elf_rawfile(3E) for a related facility that applies to the entire file. When elf_getdata provides the right translation, its use is recommended over elf_rawdata. If *scn* is null or an error occurs, elf_rawdata returns a null pointer.

The `Elf_Data` structure includes the following members.

```
void         *d_buf;
Elf_Type     d_type;
size_t       d_size;
off_t        d_off;
size_t       d_align;
unsigned     d_version;
```

These members are available for direct manipulation by the program. Descriptions appear below.

d_buf   A pointer to the data buffer resides here. A data element with no data has a null pointer.

d_type This member's value specifies the type of the data to which `d_buf` points. A section's type determines how to interpret the section contents, as summarized below.

d_size This member holds the total size, in bytes, of the memory occupied by the data. This may differ from the size as represented in the file. The size will be zero if no data exist. [See the discussion of SHT_NOBITS below for more information.]

d_off   This member gives the offset, within the section, at which the buffer resides. This offset is relative to the file's section, not the memory object's.

d_align This member holds the buffer's required alignment, from the beginning of the section. That is, `d_off` will be a multiple of this member's value. For example, if this member's value is four, the beginning of the buffer will be four-byte aligned within the section. Moreover, the entire section will be aligned to the maximum of its constituents, thus ensuring appropriate alignment for a buffer within the section and within the file.

d_version This member holds the version number of the objects in the buffer. When the library originally read the data from the object file, it used the working version to control the translation to memory objects.

DATA ALIGNMENT

As mentioned above, data buffers within a section have explicit alignment constraints. Consequently, adjacent buffers sometimes will not abut, causing "holes" within a section. Programs that create output files have two ways of dealing with these holes.

First, the program can use `elf_fill` to tell the library how to set the intervening bytes. When the library must generate gaps in the file, it uses the fill byte to initialize the data there. The library's initial fill value is zero, and `elf_fill` lets the application change that.

Second, the application can generate its own data buffers to occupy the gaps, filling the gaps with values appropriate for the section being created. A program might even use different fill values for different sections. For example, it could set text sections' bytes to no-operation instructions, while filling data section holes with zero. Using this technique, the library finds no holes to fill, because the application eliminated them.

SECTION AND MEMORY TYPES

`elf_getdata` interprets sections' data according to the section type, as noted in the section header available through `elf_getshdr`. The following table shows the section types and how the library represents them with memory data types for the 32-bit file class. Other classes would have similar tables. By implication, the memory data types control translation by `elf_xlate`.

Section Type	Elf_Type	32-Bit Type
SHT_DYNAMIC	ELF_T_DYN	Elf32_Dyn
SHT_DYNSYM	ELF_T_SYM	Elf32_Sym
SHT_HASH	ELF_T_WORD	Elf32_Word
SHT_NOBITS	ELF_T_BYTE	unsigned char
SHT_NOTE	ELF_T_BYTE	unsigned char
SHT_NULL	none	none
SHT_PROGBITS	ELF_T_BYTE	unsigned char
SHT_REL	ELF_T_REL	Elf32_Rel
SHT_RELA	ELF_T_RELA	Elf32_Rela
SHT_STRTAB	ELF_T_BYTE	unsigned char
SHT_SYMTAB	ELF_T_SYM	Elf32_Sym
other	ELF_T_BYTE	unsigned char

`elf_rawdata` creates a buffer with type ELF_T_BYTE.

As mentioned above, the program's working version controls what structures the library creates for the application. The library similarly interprets section types according to the versions. If a section type "belongs" to a version newer than the application's working version, the library does not translate the section data. Because the application cannot know the data format in this case, the library presents an untranslated buffer of type ELF_T_BYTE, just as it would for an unrecognized section type.

A section with a special type, SHT_NOBITS, occupies no space in an object file, even when the section header indicates a non-zero size. `elf_getdata` and `elf_rawdata` "work" on such a section, setting the *data* structure to have a null buffer pointer and the type indicated above. Although no data are present, the d_size value is set to the size from the section header. When a program is creating a new section of type SHT_NOBITS, it should use `elf_newdata` to add data buffers to the section. These "empty" data buffers should have the d_size members set to the desired size and the d_buf members set to null.

EXAMPLE

The following fragment obtains the string table that holds section names (ignoring error checking). See `elf_strptr`(3E) for a variation of string table handling.

elf_getdata (3E) (ELF Library) elf_getdata (3E)

```
        ehdr = elf32_getehdr(elf);
        scn = elf_getscn(elf, (size_t)ehdr->e_shstrndx);
        shdr = elf32_getshdr(scn);
        if (shdr->sh_type != SHT_STRTAB)
        {
                /* not a string table */
        }
        data = 0;
        if ((data = elf_getdata(scn, data)) == 0 || data->d_size == 0)
        {
                /* error or no data */
        }
```

The e_shstrndx member in an ELF header holds the section table index of the string table. The program gets a section descriptor for that section, verifies it is a string table, and then retrieves the data. When this fragment finishes, data->d_buf points at the first byte of the string table, and data->d_size holds the string table's size in bytes.

SEE ALSO

elf(3E), elf_cntl(3E), elf_fill(3E), elf_flag(3E), elf_getehdr(3E), elf_getscn(3E), elf_getshdr(3E), elf_rawfile(3E), elf_version(3E), elf_xlate(3E)

NAME
elf_getehdr: elf32_getehdr, elf32_newehdr – retrieve class-dependent object file header

SYNOPSIS
cc [*flag* ...] *file* ... −lelf [*library* ...]

#include <libelf.h>

Elf32_Ehdr *elf32_getehdr(Elf *elf);

Elf32_Ehdr *elf32_newehdr(Elf *elf);

DESCRIPTION
For a 32-bit class file, elf32_getehdr returns a pointer to an ELF header, if one is available for the ELF descriptor *elf*. If no header exists for the descriptor, elf32_newehdr allocates a "clean" one, but it otherwise behaves the same as elf32_getehdr. It does not allocate a new header if one exists already. If no header exists (for elf_getehdr), one cannot be created (for elf_newehdr), a system error occurs, the file is not a 32-bit class file, or *elf* is null, both functions return a null pointer.

The header includes the following members.

```
unsigned char   e_ident[EI_NIDENT];
Elf32_Half      e_type;
Elf32_Half      e_machine;
Elf32_Word      e_version;
Elf32_Addr      e_entry;
Elf32_Off       e_phoff;
Elf32_Off       e_shoff;
Elf32_Word      e_flags;
Elf32_Half      e_ehsize;
Elf32_Half      e_phentsize;
Elf32_Half      e_phnum;
Elf32_Half      e_shentsize;
Elf32_Half      e_shnum;
Elf32_Half      e_shstrndx;
```

elf32_newehdr automatically sets the ELF_F_DIRTY bit [see elf_flag(3E)]. A program may use elf_getident to inspect the identification bytes from a file.

SEE ALSO
elf(3E), elf_begin(3E), elf_flag(3E), elf_getident(3E)

NAME
elf_getident − retrieve file identification data

SYNOPSIS
cc [flag ...] file ... −lelf [library ...]

#include <libelf.h>

char *elf_getident(Elf *elf, size_t *ptr);

DESCRIPTION
As elf(3E) explains, ELF provides a framework for various classes of files, where basic objects may have 32 bits, 64 bits, etc. To accommodate these differences, without forcing the larger sizes on smaller machines, the initial bytes in an ELF file hold identification information common to all file classes. Every ELF header's e_ident has EI_NIDENT bytes with the following interpretation.

e_ident Index	Value	Purpose
EI_MAG0	ELFMAG0	File identification
EI_MAG1	ELFMAG1	
EI_MAG2	ELFMAG2	
EI_MAG3	ELFMAG3	
EI_CLASS	ELFCLASSNONE	File class
	ELFCLASS32	
	ELFCLASS64	
EI_DATA	ELFDATANONE	Data encoding
	ELFDATA2LSB	
	ELFDATA2MSB	
EI_VERSION	EV_CURRENT	File version
7−15	0	Unused, set to zero

Other kinds of files [see elf_kind(3E)] also may have identification data, though they would not conform to e_ident.

elf_getident returns a pointer to the file's "initial bytes." If the library recognizes the file, a conversion from the file image to the memory image may occur. In any case, the identification bytes are guaranteed not to have been modified, though the size of the unmodified area depends on the file type. If *ptr* is non-null, the library stores the number of identification bytes in the location to which *ptr* points. If no data are present, *elf* is null, or an error occurs, the return value is a null pointer, with zero optionally stored through *ptr*.

SEE ALSO
elf(3E), elf_begin(3E), elf_getehdr(3E), elf_kind(3E), elf_rawfile(3E)

elf_getphdr(3E) (ELF Library) elf_getphdr(3E)

NAME
elf_getphdr: elf32_getphdr, elf32_newphdr – retrieve class-dependent program header table

SYNOPSIS
cc [*flag* ...] *file* ... -lelf [*library* ...]

#include <libelf.h>

Elf32_Phdr *elf32_getphdr(Elf *elf);

Elf32_Phdr *elf32_newphdr(Elf *elf, size_t count);

DESCRIPTION
For a 32-bit class file, elf32_getphdr returns a pointer to the program execution header table, if one is available for the ELF descriptor *elf*.

elf32_newphdr allocates a new table with *count* entries, regardless of whether one existed previously, and sets the ELF_F_DIRTY bit for the table [see elf_flag(3E)]. Specifying a zero *count* deletes an existing table. Note this behavior differs from that of elf32_newehdr [see elf32_getehdr(3E)], allowing a program to replace or delete the program header table, changing its size if necessary.

If no program header table exists, the file is not a 32-bit class file, an error occurs, or *elf* is null, both functions return a null pointer. Additionally, elf32_newphdr returns a null pointer if *count* is zero.

The table is an array of Elf32_Phdr structures, each of which includes the following members.

```
Elf32_Word    p_type;
Elf32_Off     p_offset;
Elf32_Addr    p_vaddr;
Elf32_Addr    p_paddr;
Elf32_Word    p_filesz;
Elf32_Word    p_memsz;
Elf32_Word    p_flags;
Elf32_Word    p_align;
```

The ELF header's e_phnum member tells how many entries the program header table has [see elf_getehdr(3E)]. A program may inspect this value to determine the size of an existing table; elf32_newphdr automatically sets the member's value to *count*. If the program is building a new file, it is responsible for creating the file's ELF header before creating the program header table.

SEE ALSO
elf(3E), elf_begin(3E), elf_flag(3E), elf_getehdr(3E).

NAME

elf_getscn, elf_ndxscn, elf_newscn, elf_nextscn − get section information

SYNOPSIS

cc [*flag* ...] *file* ... −lelf [*library* ...]

```
#include <libelf.h>

Elf_Scn *elf_getscn(Elf *elf, size_t index);

size_t elf_ndxscn(Elf_Scn *scn);

Elf_Scn *elf_newscn(Elf *elf);

Elf_Scn *elf_nextscn(Elf *elf, Elf_Scn *scn);
```

DESCRIPTION

These functions provide indexed and sequential access to the sections associated with the ELF descriptor *elf*. If the program is building a new file, it is responsible for creating the file's ELF header before creating sections; see elf_getehdr(3E).

elf_getscn returns a section descriptor, given an *index* into the file's section header table. Note the first "real" section has index 1. Although a program can get a section descriptor for the section whose *index* is 0 (SHN_UNDEF, the undefined section), the section has no data and the section header is "empty" (though present). If the specified section does not exist, an error occurs, or *elf* is null, elf_getscn returns a null pointer.

elf_newscn creates a new section and appends it to the list for *elf*. Because the SHN_UNDEF section is required and not "interesting" to applications, the library creates it automatically. Thus the first call to elf_newscn for an ELF descriptor with no existing sections returns a descriptor for section 1. If an error occurs or *elf* is null, elf_newscn returns a null pointer.

After creating a new section descriptor, the program can use elf_getshdr to retrieve the newly created, "clean" section header. The new section descriptor will have no associated data [see elf_getdata(3E)]. When creating a new section in this way, the library updates the e_shnum member of the ELF header and sets the ELF_F_DIRTY bit for the section [see elf_flag(3E)]. If the program is building a new file, it is responsible for creating the file's ELF header [see elf_getehdr(3E)] before creating new sections.

elf_nextscn takes an existing section descriptor, *scn*, and returns a section descriptor for the next higher section. One may use a null *scn* to obtain a section descriptor for the section whose index is 1 (skipping the section whose index is SHN_UNDEF). If no further sections are present or an error occurs, elf_nextscn returns a null pointer.

elf_ndxscn takes an existing section descriptor, *scn*, and returns its section table index. If *scn* is null or an error occurs, elf_ndxscn returns SHN_UNDEF.

EXAMPLE

An example of sequential access appears below. Each pass through the loop processes the next section in the file; the loop terminates when all sections have been processed.

```
            scn = 0;
            while ((scn = elf_nextscn(elf, scn)) != 0)
            {
                    /* process section */
            }
```
SEE ALSO
    elf(3E), elf_begin(3E), elf_flag(3E), elf_getdata(3E), elf_getehdr(3E), elf_getshdr(3E)

elf_getshdr(3E) (ELF Library) elf_getshdr(3E)

NAME
elf_getshdr: elf32_getshdr – retrieve class-dependent section header

SYNOPSIS
cc [*flag* ...] *file* ... -lelf [*library* ...]

#include <libelf.h>

Elf32_Shdr *elf32_getshdr(Elf_Scn *scn);

DESCRIPTION
For a 32-bit class file, elf32_getshdr returns a pointer to a section header for the section descriptor *scn*. Otherwise, the file is not a 32-bit class file, *scn* was null, or an error occurred; elf32_getshdr then returns NULL.

The header includes the following members.

```
        Elf32_Word      sh_name;
        Elf32_Word      sh_type;
        Elf32_Word      sh_flags;
        Elf32_Addr      sh_addr;
        Elf32_Off       sh_offset;
        Elf32_Word      sh_size;
        Elf32_Word      sh_link;
        Elf32_Word      sh_info;
        Elf32_Word      sh_addralign;
        Elf32_Word      sh_entsize;
```

If the program is building a new file, it is responsible for creating the file's ELF header before creating sections.

SEE ALSO
elf(3E), elf_flag(3E), elf_getscn(3E), f4elf_strptr(3E).

elf_hash(3E) (ELF Library) elf_hash(3E)

NAME
elf_hash – compute hash value

SYNOPSIS
cc [*flag* ...] *file* ... -lelf [*library* ...]

#include <libelf.h>

unsigned long elf_hash(const char *name);

DESCRIPTION
elf_hash computes a hash value, given a null terminated string, *name*. The returned hash value, *h*, can be used as a bucket index, typically after computing *h* mod *x* to ensure appropriate bounds.

Hash tables may be built on one machine and used on another because elf_hash uses unsigned arithmetic to avoid possible differences in various machines' signed arithmetic. Although *name* is shown as char* above, elf_hash treats it as unsigned char* to avoid sign extension differences. Using char* eliminates type conflicts with expressions such as elf_hash("name").

ELF files' symbol hash tables are computed using this function [see elf_getdata(3E) and elf_xlate(3E)]. The hash value returned is guaranteed not to be the bit pattern of all ones (~0UL).

SEE ALSO
elf(3E), elf_getdata(3E), elf_xlate(3E)

NAME
elf_kind - determine file type

SYNOPSIS
cc [*flag* ...] *file* ... -lelf [*library* ...]

#include <libelf.h>

Elf_Kind elf_kind(Elf *elf);

DESCRIPTION
This function returns a value identifying the kind of file associated with an ELF descriptor (*elf*). Currently defined values appear below.

ELF_K_AR   The file is an archive [see ar(4)]. An ELF descriptor may also be associated with an archive *member*, not the archive itself, and then elf_kind identifies the member's type.

ELF_K_COFF   The file is a COFF object file. elf_begin(3E) describes the library's handling for COFF files.

ELF_K_ELF   The file is an ELF file. The program may use elf_getident to determine the class. Other functions, such as elf_getehdr, are available to retrieve other file information.

ELF_K_NONE   This indicates a kind of file unknown to the library.

Other values are reserved, to be assigned as needed to new kinds of files. *elf* should be a value previously returned by elf_begin. A null pointer is allowed, to simplify error handling, and causes elf_kind to return ELF_K_NONE.

SEE ALSO
elf(3E), elf_begin(3E), elf_getehdr(3E), elf_getident(3E), ar(4)

NAME
elf_next – sequential archive member access

SYNOPSIS
cc [*flag* ...] *file* ... -lelf [*library* ...]

#include <libelf.h>

Elf_Cmd elf_next(Elf *elf);

DESCRIPTION
elf_next, elf_rand, and elf_begin manipulate simple object files and archives. *elf* is an ELF descriptor previously returned from elf_begin.

elf_next provides sequential access to the next archive member. That is, having an ELF descriptor, *elf*, associated with an archive member, elf_next prepares the containing archive to access the following member when the program calls elf_begin. After successfully positioning an archive for the next member, elf_next returns the value ELF_C_READ. Otherwise, the open file was not an archive, *elf* was null, or an error occurred, and the return value is ELF_C_NULL. In either case, the return value may be passed as an argument to elf_begin, specifying the appropriate action.

SEE ALSO
elf(3E), elf_begin(3E), elf_getarsym(3E), elf_rand(3E), ar(4)

elf_rand(3E) (ELF Library)

NAME
elf_rand – random archive member access

SYNOPSIS
cc [*flag* ...] *file* ... -lelf [*library* ...]

#include <libelf.h>

size_t elf_rand(Elf *elf, size_t offset);

DESCRIPTION
elf_rand, elf_next, and elf_begin manipulate simple object files and archives. *elf* is an ELF descriptor previously returned from elf_begin.

elf_rand provides random archive processing, preparing *elf* to access an arbitrary archive member. *elf* must be a descriptor for the archive itself, not a member within the archive. *offset* gives the byte offset from the beginning of the archive to the archive header of the desired member. See elf_getarsym(3E) for more information about archive member offsets. When elf_rand works, it returns *offset*. Otherwise it returns 0, because an error occurred, *elf* was null, or the file was not an archive (no archive member can have a zero offset). A program may mix random and sequential archive processing.

EXAMPLE
An archive starts with a "magic string" that has SARMAG bytes; the initial archive member follows immediately. An application could thus provide the following function to rewind an archive (the function returns −1 for errors and 0 otherwise).

```
#include <ar.h>
#include <libelf.h>

int
rewindelf(Elf *elf)
{
        if (elf_rand(elf, (size_t)SARMAG) == SARMAG)
                return 0;
        return -1;
}
```

SEE ALSO
elf(3E), elf_begin(3E), elf_getarsym(3E), elf_next(3E), ar(4)

NAME
elf_rawfile - retrieve uninterpreted file contents

SYNOPSIS
cc [*flag* ...] *file* ... -lelf [*library* ...]

```
#include <libelf.h>
```

char *elf_rawfile(Elf *elf, size_t *ptr);

DESCRIPTION
elf_rawfile returns a pointer to an uninterpreted byte image of the file. This function should be used only to retrieve a file being read. For example, a program might use elf_rawfile to retrieve the bytes for an archive member.

A program may not close or disable [see elf_cntl(3E)] the file descriptor associated with *elf* before the initial call to elf_rawfile, because elf_rawfile might have to read the data from the file if it does not already have the original bytes in memory. Generally, this function is more efficient for unknown file types than for object files. The library implicitly translates object files in memory, while it leaves unknown files unmodified. Thus asking for the uninterpreted image of an object file may create a duplicate copy in memory.

elf_rawdata [see elf_getdata(3E)] is a related function, providing access to sections within a file.

If *ptr* is non-null, the library also stores the file's size, in bytes, in the location to which *ptr* points. If no data are present, *elf* is null, or an error occurs, the return value is a null pointer, with zero optionally stored through *ptr*.

SEE ALSO
elf(3E), elf_begin(3E), elf_cntl(3E), elf_getdata(3E), elf_getehdr(3E), elf_getident(3E), elf_kind(3E)

NOTE
A program that uses elf_rawfile and that also interprets the same file as an object file potentially has two copies of the bytes in memory. If such a program requests the raw image first, before it asks for translated information (through such functions as elf_getehdr, elf_getdata, and so on), the library "freezes" its original memory copy for the raw image. It then uses this frozen copy as the source for creating translated objects, without reading the file again. Consequently, the application should view the raw file image returned by elf_rawfile as a read-only buffer, unless it wants to alter its own view of data subsequently translated. In any case, the application may alter the translated objects without changing bytes visible in the raw image.

Multiple calls to elf_rawfile with the same ELF descriptor return the same value; the library does not create duplicate copies of the file.

NAME

elf_strptr - make a string pointer

SYNOPSIS

cc [flag ...] file ... -lelf [library ...]

#include <libelf.h>

char *elf_strptr(Elf *elf, size_t section, size_t offset);

DESCRIPTION

This function converts a string section *offset* to a string pointer. *elf* identifies the file in which the string section resides, and *section* gives the section table index for the strings. elf_strptr normally returns a pointer to a string, but it returns a null pointer when *elf* is null, *section* is invalid or is not a section of type SHT_STRTAB, the section data cannot be obtained, *offset* is invalid, or an error occurs.

EXAMPLE

A prototype for retrieving section names appears below. The file header specifies the section name string table in the e_shstrndx member. The following code loops through the sections, printing their names.

```
if ((ehdr = elf32_getehdr(elf)) == 0)
{
        /* handle the error */
        return;
}
ndx = ehdr->e_shstrndx;
scn = 0;
while ((scn = elf_nextscn(elf, scn)) != 0)
{
        char    *name = 0;
        if ((shdr = elf32_getshdr(scn)) != 0)
          name = elf_strptr(elf, ndx, (size_t)shdr->sh_name);
        printf("'%s'\n", name? name: "(null)");
}
```

SEE ALSO

elf(3E), elf_getdata(3E), elf_getshdr(3E), elf_xlate(3E)

NOTE

A program may call elf_getdata to retrieve an entire string table section. For some applications, that would be both more efficient and more convenient than using elf_strptr.

NAME
elf_update – update an ELF descriptor

SYNOPSIS
cc [*flag* ...] *file* ... -lelf [*library* ...]

#include <libelf.h>

off_t elf_update(Elf *elf, Elf_Cmd cmd);

DESCRIPTION
elf_update causes the library to examine the information associated with an ELF descriptor, *elf*, and to recalculate the structural data needed to generate the file's image.

cmd may have the following values.

ELF_C_NULL This value tells elf_update to recalculate various values, updating only the ELF descriptor's memory structures. Any modified structures are flagged with the ELF_F_DIRTY bit. A program thus can update the structural information and then reexamine them without changing the file associated with the ELF descriptor. Because this does not change the file, the ELF descriptor may allow reading, writing, or both reading and writing [see elf_begin(3E)].

ELF_C_WRITE If *cmd* has this value, elf_update duplicates its ELF_C_NULL actions and also writes any "dirty" information associated with the ELF descriptor to the file. That is, when a program has used elf_getdata or the elf_flag facilities to supply new (or update existing) information for an ELF descriptor, those data will be examined, coordinated, translated if necessary [see elf_xlate(3E)], and written to the file. When portions of the file are written, any ELF_F_DIRTY bits are reset, indicating those items no longer need to be written to the file [see elf_flag(3E)]. The sections' data are written in the order of their section header entries, and the section header table is written to the end of the file.

When the ELF descriptor was created with elf_begin, it must have allowed writing the file. That is, the elf_begin command must have been either ELF_C_RDWR or ELF_C_WRITE.

If elf_update succeeds, it returns the total size of the file image (not the memory image), in bytes. Otherwise an error occurred, and the function returns −1.

When updating the internal structures, elf_update sets some members itself. Members listed below are the application's responsibility and retain the values given by the program.

ELF Header

Member	Notes
e_ident[EI_DATA]	Library controls other e_ident values
e_type	
e_machine	
e_version	
e_entry	
e_phoff	Only when ELF_F_LAYOUT asserted
e_shoff	Only when ELF_F_LAYOUT asserted
e_flags	
e_shstrndx	

Program Header

Member	Notes
p_type	The application controls all program header entries
p_offset	
p_vaddr	
p_paddr	
p_filesz	
p_memsz	
p_flags	
p_align	

Section Header

Member	Notes
sh_name	
sh_type	
sh_flags	
sh_addr	
sh_offset	Only when ELF_F_LAYOUT asserted
sh_size	Only when ELF_F_LAYOUT asserted
sh_link	
sh_info	
sh_addralign	Only when ELF_F_LAYOUT asserted
sh_entsize	

	Member	Notes
Data Descriptor	d_buf d_type d_size d_off d_align d_version	Only when ELF_F_LAYOUT asserted

Note the program is responsible for two particularly important members (among others) in the ELF header. The e_version member controls the version of data structures written to the file. If the version is EV_NONE, the library uses its own internal version. The e_ident[EI_DATA] entry controls the data encoding used in the file. As a special case, the value may be ELFDATANONE to request the native data encoding for the host machine. An error occurs in this case if the native encoding doesn't match a file encoding known by the library.

Further note that the program is responsible for the sh_entsize section header member. Although the library sets it for sections with known types, it cannot reliably know the correct value for all sections. Consequently, the library relies on the program to provide the values for unknown section type. If the entry size is unknown or not applicable, the value should be set to zero.

When deciding how to build the output file, elf_update obeys the alignments of individual data buffers to create output sections. A section's most strictly aligned data buffer controls the section's alignment. The library also inserts padding between buffers, as necessary, to ensure the proper alignment of each buffer.

SEE ALSO

elf(3E), elf_begin(3E), elf_flag(3E), elf_fsize(3E), elf_getdata(3E), elf_getehdr(3E), elf_getshdr(3E), elf_xlate(3E)

NOTE

As mentioned above, the ELF_C_WRITE command translates data as necessary, before writing them to the file. This translation is not always transparent to the application program. If a program has obtained pointers to data associated with a file [for example, see elf_getehdr(3E) and elf_getdata(3E)], the program should reestablish the pointers after calling elf_update.

As elf_begin(3E) describes, a program may "update" a COFF file to make the image consistent for ELF . The ELF_C_NULL command updates only the memory image; one can use the ELF_C_WRITE command to modify the file as well. Absolute executable files (a.out files) require special alignment, which cannot normally be preserved between COFF and ELF . Consequently, one may not update an executable COFF file with the ELF_C_WRITE command (though ELF_C_NULL is allowed).

elf_version(3E) (ELF Library)

NAME
elf_version – coordinate ELF library and application versions

SYNOPSIS
cc [*flag* ...] *file* ... -lelf [*library* ...]

#include <libelf.h>

unsigned elf_version(unsigned ver);

DESCRIPTION
As elf(3E) explains, the program, the library, and an object file have independent notions of the "latest" ELF version. elf_version lets a program determine the ELF library's *internal version*. It further lets the program specify what memory types it uses by giving its own *working version*, *ver*, to the library. Every program that uses the ELF library must coordinate versions as described below.

The header file <libelf.h> supplies the version to the program with the macro EV_CURRENT. If the library's internal version (the highest version known to the library) is lower than that known by the program itself, the library may lack semantic knowledge assumed by the program. Accordingly, elf_version will not accept a working version unknown to the library.

Passing *ver* equal to EV_NONE causes elf_version to return the library's internal version, without altering the working version. If *ver* is a version known to the library, elf_version returns the previous (or initial) working version number. Otherwise, the working version remains unchanged and elf_version returns EV_NONE.

EXAMPLE
The following excerpt from an application program protects itself from using an older library.

```
if (elf_version(EV_CURRENT) == EV_NONE)
{
        /* library out of date */
        /* recover from error */
}
```

NOTES
The working version should be the same for all operations on a particular elf descriptor. Changing the version between operations on a descriptor will probably not give the expected results.

SEE ALSO
elf(3E), elf_begin(3E), elf_xlate(3E)

elf_xlate(3E)

NAME

elf_xlate: elf32_xlatetof, elf32_xlatetom — class-dependent data translation

SYNOPSIS

cc [*flag* ...] *file* ... -lelf [*library* ...]

#include <libelf.h>

Elf_Data *elf32_xlatetof(Elf_Data *dst, const Elf_Data *src,
    unsigned encode);

Elf_Data *elf32_xlatetom(Elf_Data *dst, const Elf_Data *src,
    unsigned encode);

DESCRIPTION

elf32_xlatetom translates various data structures from their 32-bit class file representations to their memory representations; elf32_xlatetof provides the inverse. This conversion is particularly important for cross development environments. *src* is a pointer to the source buffer that holds the original data; *dst* is a pointer to a destination buffer that will hold the translated copy. *encode* gives the byte encoding in which the file objects are (to be) represented and must have one of the encoding values defined for the ELF header's e_ident[EI_DATA] entry [see elf_getident(3E)]. If the data can be translated, the functions return *dst*. Otherwise, they return null because an error occurred, such as incompatible types, destination buffer overflow, etc.

elf_getdata(3E) describes the Elf_Data descriptor, which the translation routines use as follows.

d_buf   Both the source and destination must have valid buffer pointers.

d_type   This member's value specifies the type of the data to which d_buf points and the type of data to be created in the destination. The program supplies a d_type value in the source; the library sets the destination's d_type to the same value. These values are summarized below.

d_size   This member holds the total size, in bytes, of the memory occupied by the source data and the size allocated for the destination data. If the destination buffer is not large enough, the routines do not change its original contents. The translation routines reset the destination's d_size member to the actual size required, after the translation occurs. The source and destination sizes may differ.

d_version   This member holds version number of the objects (desired) in the buffer. The source and destination versions are independent.

Translation routines allow the source and destination buffers to coincide. That is, dst->d_buf may equal src->d_buf. Other cases where the source and destination buffers overlap give undefined behavior.

Elf_Type	32-Bit Memory Type
ELF_T_ADDR	Elf32_Addr
ELF_T_BYTE	unsigned char
ELF_T_DYN	Elf32_Dyn
ELF_T_EHDR	Elf32_Ehdr
ELF_T_HALF	Elf32_Half
ELT_T_OFF	Elf32_Off
ELF_T_PHDR	Elf32_Phdr
ELF_T_REL	Elf32_Rel
ELF_T_RELA	Elf32_Rela
ELF_T_SHDR	Elf32_Shdr
ELF_T_SWORD	Elf32_Sword
ELF_T_SYM	Elf32_Sym
ELF_T_WORD	Elf32_Word

"Translating" buffers of type ELF_T_BYTE does not change the byte order.

SEE ALSO
elf(3E), elf_fsize(3E), elf_getdata(3E), elf_getident(3E)

NAME

end, etext, edata – last locations in program

SYNOPSIS

extern etext;

extern edata;

extern end;

DESCRIPTION

These names refer neither to routines nor to locations with interesting contents; only their addresses are meaningful.

etext The address of etext is the first address above the program text.

edata The address of edata is the first address above the initialized data region.

end   The address of end is the first address above the uninitialized data region.

SEE ALSO

cc(1), brk(2), malloc(3C), stdio(3S).

NOTE

When execution begins, the program break (the first location beyond the data) coincides with end, but the program break may be reset by the routines brk, malloc, the standard input/output library [see stdio(3S)], by the profile (–p) option of cc, and so on. Thus, the current value of the program break should be determined by sbrk (0) [see brk(2)].

erf(3M) (Math Libraries) erf(3M)

NAME
    erf, erfc – error function and complementary error function

SYNOPSIS
    cc [*flag* ...] *file* ... −lm [*library* ...]

    #include <math.h>

    double erf (double x);

    double erfc (double x);

DESCRIPTION
    erf returns the error function of *x*, defined as

$$\frac{2}{\sqrt{\pi}} \int_0^x e^{-t^2} dt$$

   erfc, which returns 1.0 − erf(x), is provided because of the extreme loss of relative accuracy if erf(x) is called for large *x* and the result subtracted from 1.0 (for example, for *x* = 5, 12 places are lost).

SEE ALSO
    exp(3M).

NAME
ethers – Ethernet address mapping operations

SYNOPSIS
```
#include <sys/types.h>
#include <sys/socket.h>
#include <net/if.h>
#include <netinet/in.h>
#include <netinet/if_ether.h>
```

char *ether_ntoa(struct ether_addr *e);

struct ether_addr *ether_aton(char *s);

int ether_ntohost(char *hostname, struct ether_addr *e);

int ether_hostton(char *hostname, struct ether_addr *e);

int ether_line(char *l, struct ether_addr *e, char *hostname);

DESCRIPTION
These routines are useful for mapping 48 bit Ethernet numbers to their ASCII representations or their corresponding host names, and vice versa.

The function ether_ntoa converts a 48 bit Ethernet number pointed to by e to its standard ASCII representation; it returns a pointer to the ASCII string. The representation is of the form $x:x:x:x:x:x$ where x is a hexadecimal number between 0 and ff. The function ether_aton converts an ASCII string in the standard representation back to a 48 bit Ethernet number; the function returns NULL if the string cannot be scanned successfully.

The function ether_ntohost maps an Ethernet number (pointed to by e) to its associated hostname. The string pointed to by hostname must be long enough to hold the hostname and a NULL character. The function returns zero upon success and non-zero upon failure. Inversely, the function ether_hostton maps a hostname string to its corresponding Ethernet number; the function modifies the Ethernet number pointed to by e. The function also returns zero upon success and non-zero upon failure. The function ether_line scans a line (pointed to by l) and sets the hostname and the Ethernet number (pointed to by e). The string pointed to by hostname must be long enough to hold the hostname and a NULL character. The function returns zero upon success and non-zero upon failure. The format of the scanned line is described by ethers(4).

FILES
/etc/ethers

SEE ALSO
ethers(4)

NAME

exp, expf, cbrt, log, logf, log10, log10f, pow, powf, sqrt, sqrtf – exponential, logarithm, power, square root functions

SYNOPSIS

cc [flag ...] file ... −lm [library ...]

cc −O −Ksd [flag ...] file ... −J sfm [library ...]

#include <math.h>

double exp (double x);

float expf (float x);

double cbrt (double x);

double log (double x);

float logf (float x);

double log10 (double x);

float log10f (float x);

double pow (double x, double y);

float powf (float x, float y);

double sqrt (double x);

float sqrtf (float x);

DESCRIPTION

exp and expf return e^x.

cbrt returns the cube root of x.

log and logf return the natural logarithm of x. The value of x must be positive.

log10 and log10f return the base ten logarithm of x. The value of x must be positive.

pow and powf return x^y. If x is 0, y must be positive. If x is negative, y must be an integer.

sqrt and sqrtf return the non-negative square root of x. The value of x may not be negative.

SEE ALSO

hypot(3M), matherr(3M), sinh(3M)

DIAGNOSTICS

exp and expf return HUGE when the correct value would overflow, or 0 when the correct value would underflow, and set errno to ERANGE.

log, logf, log10, and log10f return −HUGE and set errno to EDOM when x is non-positive. A message indicating DOMAIN error is printed on standard error.

pow and powf return 0 and set errno to EDOM when x is 0 and y is non-positive, or when x is negative and y is not an integer. In these cases, a message indicating DOMAIN error is printed on standard error. When the correct value for pow or powf would overflow or underflow, these functions return ±HUGE or 0, respectively, and set errno to ERANGE.

sqrt and sqrtf return 0 and set errno to EDOM when x is negative. A message indicating DOMAIN error is printed on the standard error output.

Except when the −Xc compilation option is used, these error-handling procedures may be changed with the function matherr. When the −Xa or −Xc compilation options are used, HUGE_VAL is returned instead of HUGE and no error messages are printed. In these compilation modes, pow and powf return 1, with no error, when both x and y are 0; when x is 0 and y is negative, they return −HUGE_VAL and set errno to EDOM. Under −Xc, log and logf return −HUGE_VAL and set errno to ERANGE when x is 0. Under −Xc, sqrt and sqrtf return NaN when x is negative.

fattach(3C)

NAME
fattach – attach a STREAMS-based file descriptor to an object in the file system name space

SYNOPSIS
     int fattach(int fildes, const char *path);

DESCRIPTION
The fattach routine attaches a STREAMS-based file descriptor to an object in the file system name space, effectively associating a name with *fildes*. *fildes* must be a valid open file descriptor representing a STREAMS file. *path* is a path name of an existing object and the user must have appropriate privileges or be the owner of the file and have write permissions. All subsequent operations on *path* will operate on the STREAMS file until the STREAMS file is detached from the node. *fildes* can be attached to more than one *path*, that is, a stream can have several names associated with it.

The attributes of the named stream [see stat(2)], are initialized as follows: the permissions, user ID, group ID, and times are set to those of *path*, the number of links is set to 1, and the size and device identifier are set to those of the streams device associated with *fildes*. If any attributes of the named stream are subsequently changed [e.g., chmod(2)], the attributes of the underlying object are not affected.

RETURN VALUE
If successful, fattach returns 0; otherwise it returns -1 and sets errno to indicate an error.

ERRORS
Under the following conditions, the function fattach fails and sets errno to:

EACCES	The user is the owner of *path* but does not have write permissions on *path* or *fildes* is locked.
EBADF	*fildes* is not a valid open file descriptor.
ENOENT	*path* does not exist.
ENOTDIR	A component of a path prefix is not a directory.
EINVAL	*fildes* does not represent a STREAMS file.
EPERM	The effective user ID is not the owner of *path* or a user with the appropriate privileges.
EBUSY	*path* is currently a mount point or has a STREAMS file descriptor attached it.
ENAMETOOLONG	The size of *path* exceeds {PATH_MAX}, or the component of a path name is longer than {NAME_MAX} while {_POSIX_NO_TRUNC} is in effect.
ELOOP	Too many symbolic links were encountered in translating *path*.
EREMOTE	*path* is a file in a remotely mounted directory.

fattach (3C)

SEE ALSO

fdetach(1M), fdetach(3C), isastream(3C), streamio(7)
in the *Programmer's Guide: STREAMS*

NAME
fclose, fflush – close or flush a stream

SYNOPSIS
```
#include <stdio.h>

int fclose (FILE *stream);

int fflush (FILE *stream);
```

DESCRIPTION
fclose causes any buffered data waiting to be written for the named *stream* [see intro(3)] to be written out, and the *stream* to be closed. If the underlying file pointer is not already at end of file, and the file is one capable of seeking, the file pointer is adjusted so that the next operation on the open file pointer deals with the byte after the last one read from or written to the file being closed.

fclose is performed automatically for all open files upon calling exit.

If *stream* points to an output stream or an update stream on which the most recent operation was not input, fflush causes any buffered data waiting to be written for the named *stream* to be written to that file. Any unread data buffered in *stream* is discarded. The *stream* remains open. If *stream* is open for reading, the underlying file pointer is not already at end of file, and the file is one capable of seeking, the file pointer is adjusted so that the next operation on the open file pointer deals with the byte after the last one read from or written to the stream.

When calling fflush, if *stream* is a null pointer, all files open for writing are flushed.

SEE ALSO
close(2), exit(2), intro(3), fopen(3S), setbuf(3S), stdio(3S).

DIAGNOSTICS
Upon successful completion these functions return a value of zero. Otherwise EOF is returned.

fdetach(3C)

NAME
fdetach – detach a name from a STREAMS-based file descriptor

SYNOPSIS
    int fdetach(const char *path);

DESCRIPTION
The fdetach routine detaches a STREAMS-based file descriptor from a name in the file system. *path* is the path name of the object in the file system name space, which was previously attached [see fattach(3C)]. The user must be the owner of the file or a user with the appropriate privileges. All subsequent operations on *path* will operate on the file system node and not on the STREAMS file. The permissions and status of the node are restored to the state the node was in before the STREAMS file was attached to it.

RETURN VALUE
If successful, fdetach returns 0; otherwise it returns -1 and sets errno to indicate an error.

ERRORS
Under the following conditions, the function fdetach fails and sets errno to:

EPERM The effective user ID is not the owner of *path* or is not a user with appropriate permissions.

ENOTDIR A component of the path prefix is not a directory.

ENOENT *path* does not exist.

EINVAL *path* is not attached to a STREAMS file.

ENAMETOOLONG The size of *path* exceeds {PATH_MAX}, or a path name component is longer than {NAME_MAX} while {_POSIX_NO_TRUNC} is in effect.

ELOOP Too many symbolic links were encountered in translating *path*.

SEE ALSO
fdetach(1M), fattach(3C), streamio(7)
in the *Programmer's Guide: STREAMS*

NAME
ferror, feof, clearerr, fileno – stream status inquiries

SYNOPSIS
#include <stdio.h>

int ferror (FILE *stream);

int feof (FILE *stream);

void clearerr (FILE *stream);

int fileno (FILE *stream);

DESCRIPTION
ferror returns non-zero when an error has previously occurred reading from or writing to the named *stream* [see intro(3)], otherwise zero.

feof returns non-zero when EOF has previously been detected reading the named input *stream*, otherwise zero.

clearerr resets the error indicator and EOF indicator to zero on the named *stream*.

fileno returns the integer file descriptor associated with the named *stream* [see open(2)].

SEE ALSO
open(2), fopen(3S), stdio(3S).

ffs(3C) (C Development Set)

NAME
 ffs – find first set bit

SYNOPSIS
 #include <string.h>

 int ffs(const int i);

DESCRIPTION
 ffs finds the first bit set in the argument passed it and returns the index of that bit. Bits are numbered starting at 1 from the low order bit. A return value of zero indicates that the value passed is zero.

floatingpoint(3)   (BSD Compatibility Package)   **floatingpoint(3)**

NAME
floatingpoint – IEEE floating point definitions

SYNOPSIS
cc [*flag*...] *file*... -lucb

#include <sys/ieeefp.h>
#include <fp.h>

DESCRIPTION
This file defines constants, types, variables, and functions used to implement standard floating point according to ANSI/IEEE Std 754-1985. The variables and functions are implemented in libucb.a. The included file <sys/ieeefp.h> defines certain types of interest to the kernel.

IEEE Rounding Modes:

fp_direction_type	The type of the IEEE rounding direction mode. Note: the order of enumeration varies according to hardware.
fp_direction	The IEEE rounding direction mode currently in force. This is a global variable that is intended to reflect the hardware state, so it should only be written indirectly through a function that also sets the hardware state.
fp_precision_type	The type of the IEEE rounding precision mode, which only applies on systems that support extended precision.
fp_precision	The IEEE rounding precision mode currently in force. This is a global variable that is intended to reflect the hardware state on systems with extended precision, so it should only be written indirectly.

SIGFPE Handling:

sigfpe_code_type	The type of a SIGFPE code.
sigfpe_handler_type	The type of a user-definable SIGFPE exception handler called to handle a particular SIGFPE code.
SIGFPE_DEFAULT	A macro indicating the default SIGFPE exception handling, namely to perform the exception handling specified by calls to ieee_handler(3M), if any, and otherwise to dump core using abort(3).
SIGFPE_IGNORE	A macro indicating an alternate SIGFPE exception handling, namely to ignore and continue execution.
SIGFPE_ABORT	A macro indicating an alternate SIGFPE exception handling, namely to abort with a core dump.

IEEE Exception Handling:

N_IEEE_EXCEPTION
: The number of distinct IEEE floating-point exceptions.

fp_exception_type
: The type of the N_IEEE_EXCEPTION exceptions. Each exception is given a bit number.

fp_exception_field_type
: The type intended to hold at least N_IEEE_EXCEPTION bits corresponding to the IEEE exceptions numbered by fp_exception_type. Thus fp_inexact corresponds to the least significant bit and fp_invalid to the fifth least significant bit. Note: some operations may set more than one exception.

fp_accrued_exceptions
: The IEEE exceptions between the time this global variable was last cleared, and the last time a function was called to update the variable by obtaining the hardware state.

ieee_handlers
: An array of user-specifiable signal handlers for use by the standard SIGFPE handler for IEEE arithmetic-related SIGFPE codes. Since IEEE trapping modes correspond to hardware modes, elements of this array should only be modified with a function like ieee_handler(3M) that performs the appropriate hardware mode update. If no sigfpe_handler has been declared for a particular IEEE-related SIGFPE code, then the related ieee_handlers will be invoked.

IEEE Formats and Classification:

single; extended
: Definitions of IEEE formats.

fp_class_type
: An enumeration of the various classes of IEEE values and symbols.

IEEE Base Conversion:

The functions described under floating_to_decimal(3) and decimal_to_floating(3) not only satisfy the IEEE Standard, but also the stricter requirements of correct rounding for all arguments.

DECIMAL_STRING_LENGTH
: The length of a decimal_string.

decimal_string
: The digit buffer in a decimal_record.

decimal_record
: The canonical form for representing an unpacked decimal floating-point number.

decimal_form
: The type used to specify fixed or floating binary to decimal conversion.

decimal_mode	A struct that contains specifications for conversion between binary and decimal.
decimal_string_form	An enumeration of possible valid character strings representing floating-point numbers, infinities, or NaNs.

FILES

/usr/include/sys/ieeefp.h
/usr/include/fp.h
/usr/ucblib/libucb.a

SEE ALSO

decimal_to_floating(3), econvert(3), floating_to_decimal(3), ieee_handler(3M), sigfpe(3)

abort(3), strtod(3) in the *Programmer's Reference Manual*

floor(3M) (Math Libraries)

NAME
floor, floorf, ceil, ceilf, copysign, fmod, fmodf, fabs, fabsf, rint, remainder – floor, ceiling, remainder, absolute value functions

SYNOPSIS
cc [*flag* ...] *file* ... -lm [*library* ...]

#include <math.h>

double floor (double x);

float floorf (float x);

double ceil (double x);

float ceilf (float x);

double copysign (double x, double y);

double fmod (double x, double y);

float fmodf (float x, float y);

double fabs (double x);

float fabsf (float x);

double rint (double x);

double remainder (double x, double y);

DESCRIPTION
floor and floorf return the largest integer not greater than x. ceil and ceilf return the smallest integer not less than x.

copysign returns x but with the sign of y.

fmod and fmodf return the floating point remainder of the division of x by y. More precisely, they return the number f with the same sign as x, such that $x = iy + f$ for some integer i, and $|f| < |y|$.

fabs and fabsf return the absolute value of x, $|x|$.

rint returns the nearest integer value to its floating point argument x as a double-precision floating point number. The returned value is rounded according to the currently set machine rounding mode. If round-to-nearest (the default mode) is set and the difference between the function argument and the rounded result is exactly 0.5, then the result will be rounded to the nearest even integer.

remainder returns the floating point remainder of the division of x by y. More precisely, it returns the value $r = x - yn$, where n is the integer nearest the exact value x/y. Whenever $|n - x/y| = \frac{1}{2}$, then n is even.

SEE ALSO
abs(3C), matherr(3M)

DIAGNOSTICS
fmod and fmodf return x when y is 0 and set errno to EDOM. remainder returns NaN when y is 0 and sets errno to EDOM. In both cases, except in compilation modes -Xa or -Xc, a message indicating DOMAIN error is printed on the standard error output. Except under -Xc, these error-handling procedures may be changed with the function matherr.

floating_to_decimal(3)   (BSD Compatibility Package)   floating_to_decimal(3)

NAME
floating_to_decimal: single_to_decimal, double_to_decimal, extended_to_decimal – convert floating-point value to decimal record

SYNOPSIS
cc [*flag*...] *file*... -lucb

#include <floatingpoint.h>

void single_to_decimal(px, pm, pd, ps)
single *px ;
decimal_mode *pm;
decimal_record *pd;
fp_exception_field_type *ps;

void double_to_decimal(px, pm, pd, ps)
double *px ;
decimal_mode *pm;
decimal_record *pd;
fp_exception_field_type *ps;

void extended_to_decimal(px, pm, pd, ps)
extended *px ;
decimal_mode *pm;
decimal_record *pd;
fp_exception_field_type *ps;

DESCRIPTION
The floating_to_decimal functions convert the floating-point value at *px into a decimal record at *pd, observing the modes specified in *pm and setting exceptions in *ps. If there are no IEEE exceptions, *ps will be zero.

If *px is zero, infinity, or NaN, then only pd->sign and pd->fpclass are set. Otherwise pd->exponent and pd->ds are also set so that

(pd->sign) * (pd->ds) *10** (pd->exponent)

is a correctly rounded approximation to *px. pd->ds has at least one and no more than DECIMAL_STRING_LENGTH−1 significant digits because one character is used to terminate the string with a NULL.

pd->ds is correctly rounded according to the IEEE rounding modes in pm->rd. *ps has fp_inexact set if the result was inexact, and has fp_overflow set if the string result does not fit in pd->ds because of the limitation DECIMAL_STRING_LENGTH.

If pm->df==floating_form, then pd->ds always contains pm->ndigits significant digits. Thus if *px == 12.34 and pm->ndigits == 8, then pd->ds will contain 12340000 and pd->exponent will contain −6.

If pm->df==fixed_form and pm->ndigits >= 0, then pd->ds always contains pm->ndigits after the point and as many digits as necessary before the point. Since the latter is not known in advance, the total number of digits required is returned in pd->ndigits; if that number >= DECIMAL_STRING_LENGTH, then ds is undefined. pd->exponent always gets −pm->ndigits. Thus if *px == 12.34 and pm->ndigits == 1, then pd->ds gets 123, pd->exponent gets −1, and pd->ndigits gets 3.

floating_to_decimal(3) (BSD Compatibility Package)

If *pm->df==fixed_form* and *pm->ndigits* < 0, then *pm->ds* always contains −*pm->ndigits* trailing zeros; in other words, rounding occurs −*pm->ndigits* to the left of the decimal point, but the digits rounded away are retained as zeros. The total number of digits required is in *pd->ndigits*. *pd->exponent* always gets 0. Thus if **px* == 12.34 and *pm->ndigits* == −1, then *pd->ds* gets 10, *pd->exponent* gets 0, and *pd->ndigits* gets 2.

pd->more is not used.

econvert(3), fconvert, gconvert, printf(3S), and sprintf, all use double_to_decimal.

SEE ALSO

econvert(3)
printf(3S) in the *Programmer's Reference Manual*

fmtmsg(3C) (Essential Utilities) fmtmsg(3C)

NAME
fmtmsg – display a message on stderr or system console

SYNOPSIS
```
#include <fmtmsg.h>

int fmtmsg(long classification, const char *label, int severity,
     const char *text, const char *action, const char *tag);
```

DESCRIPTION
Based on a message's classification component, fmtmsg writes a formatted message to stderr, to the console, or to both.

fmtmsg can be used instead of the traditional printf interface to display messages to stderr. fmtmsg, in conjunction with gettxt, provides a simple interface for producing language-independent applications.

A formatted message consists of up to five standard components as defined below. The component, *classification*, is not part of the standard message displayed to the user, but rather defines the source of the message and directs the display of the formatted message.

classification
Contains identifiers from the following groups of major classifications and subclassifications. Any one identifier from a subclass may be used in combination by ORing the values together with a single identifier from a different subclass. Two or more identifiers from the same subclass should not be used together, with the exception of identifiers from the display subclass. (Both display subclass identifiers may be used so that messages can be displayed to both stderr and the system console).

"Major classifications" identify the source of the condition. Identifiers are: MM_HARD (hardware), MM_SOFT (software), and MM_FIRM (firmware).

"Message source subclassifications" identify the type of software in which the problem is spotted. Identifiers are: MM_APPL (application), MM_UTIL (utility), and MM_OPSYS (operating system).

"Display subclassifications" indicate where the message is to be displayed. Identifiers are: MM_PRINT to display the message on the standard error stream, MM_CONSOLE to display the message on the system console. Neither, either, or both identifiers may be used.

"Status subclassifications" indicate whether the application will recover from the condition. Identifiers are: MM_RECOVER (recoverable) and MM_NRECOV (non-recoverable).

An additional identifier, MM_NULLMC, indicates that no classification component is supplied for the message.

label Identifies the source of the message. The format of this component is two fields separated by a colon. The first field is up to 10 characters long; the second is up to 14 characters. Suggested usage is that *label* identifies the package in which the application resides as well as the program or application name. For example, the *label* UX:cat indicates the UNIX System V package and the cat application.

severity
Indicates the seriousness of the condition. Identifiers for the standard levels of *severity* are:

MM_HALT indicates that the application has encountered a severe fault and is halting. Produces the print string HALT.

MM_ERROR indicates that the application has detected a fault. Produces the print string ERROR.

MM_WARNING indicates a condition out of the ordinary that might be a problem and should be watched. Produces the print string WARNING.

MM_INFO provides information about a condition that is not in error. Produces the print string INFO.

MM_NOSEV indicates that no severity level is supplied for the message.

Other severity levels may be added by using the addseverity routine.

text Describes the condition that produced the message. The *text* string is not limited to a specific size.

action Describes the first step to be taken in the error recovery process. fmtmsg precedes each action string with the prefix: TO FIX:. The *action* string is not limited to a specific size.

tag An identifier which references on-line documentation for the message. Suggested usage is that *tag* includes the *label* and a unique identifying number. A sample *tag* is UX:cat:146.

Environment Variables

There are two environment variables that control the behavior of fmtmsg: MSGVERB and SEV_LEVEL.

MSGVERB tells fmtmsg which message components it is to select when writing messages to stderr. The value of MSGVERB is a colon-separated list of optional keywords. MSGVERB can be set as follows:

MSGVERB=[*keyword*[:*keyword*[:...]]]
export MSGVERB

Valid *keywords* are: label, severity, text, action, and tag. If MSGVERB contains a keyword for a component and the component's value is not the component's null value, fmtmsg includes that component in the message when writing the message to stderr. If MSGVERB does not include a keyword for a message component, that component is not included in the display of the message. The keywords may appear in any order. If MSGVERB is not defined, if its value is the null-string, if its value is not of the correct format, or if it contains keywords other than the valid ones listed above, fmtmsg selects all components.

The first time fmtmsg is called, it examines the MSGVERB environment variable to see which message components it is to select when generating a message to write to the standard error stream, stderr. The values accepted on the initial call are saved for future calls.

MSGVERB affects only which components are selected for display to the standard error stream. All message components are included in console messages.

SEV_LEVEL defines severity levels and associates print strings with them for use by fmtmsg. The standard severity levels shown below cannot be modified. Additional severity levels can also be defined, redefined, and removed using addseverity [see addseverity(3C)]. If the same severity level is defined by both SEV_LEVEL and addseverity, the definition by addseverity is controlling.

```
0    (no severity is used)
1    HALT
2    ERROR
3    WARNING
4    INFO
```

SEV_LEVEL can be set as follows:

SEV_LEVEL=[description[:description[:...]]]
export SEV_LEVEL

description is a comma-separated list containing three fields:

description=severity_keyword,level,printstring

severity_keyword is a character string that is used as the keyword on the −s *severity* option to the fmtmsg command. (This field is not used by the fmtmsg function.)

level is a character string that evaluates to a positive integer (other than 0, 1, 2, 3, or 4, which are reserved for the standard severity levels). If the keyword *severity_keyword* is used, *level* is the severity value passed on to the fmtmsg function.

printstring is the character string used by fmtmsg in the standard message format whenever the severity value *level* is used.

If a *description* in the colon list is not a three-field comma list, or, if the second field of a comma list does not evaluate to a positive integer, that *description* in the colon list is ignored.

The first time fmtmsg is called, it examines the SEV_LEVEL environment variable, if defined, to see whether the environment expands the levels of severity beyond the five standard levels and those defined using addseverity. The values accepted on the initial call are saved for future calls.

Use in Applications

One or more message components may be systematically omitted from messages generated by an application by using the null value of the argument for that component.

The table below indicates the null values and identifiers for fmtmsg arguments.

Argument	Type	Null-Value	Identifier
label	char*	(char*) NULL	MM_NULLLBL
severity	int	0	MM_NULLSEV
class	long	0L	MM_NULLMC
text	char*	(char*) NULL	MM_NULLTXT
action	char*	(char*) NULL	MM_NULLACT
tag	char*	(char*) NULL	MM_NULLTAG

Another means of systematically omitting a component is by omitting the component keyword(s) when defining the MSGVERB environment variable (see the "Environment Variables" section).

EXAMPLES

Example 1:

The following example of fmtmsg:

```
fmtmsg(MM_PRINT, "UX:cat", MM_ERROR, "invalid syntax", "refer
to manual", "UX:cat:001")
```

produces a complete message in the standard message format:

```
UX:cat: ERROR: invalid syntax
        TO FIX: refer to manual   UX:cat:001
```

Example 2:

When the environment variable MSGVERB is set as follows:

```
MSGVERB=severity:text:action
```

and the Example 1 is used, fmtmsg produces:

```
ERROR: invalid syntax
TO FIX: refer to manual
```

Example 3:

When the environment variable SEV_LEVEL is set as follows:

```
SEV_LEVEL=note,5,NOTE
```

the following call to fmtmsg:

```
fmtmsg(MM_UTIL | MM_PRINT, "UX:cat", 5, "invalid syntax",
"refer to manual", "UX:cat:001")
```

produces:

```
UX:cat: NOTE: invalid syntax
        TO FIX: refer to manual   UX:cat:001
```

SEE ALSO

addseverity(3C), gettxt(3C), printf(3S).
fmtmsg(1) in the *User's Reference Manual*.

DIAGNOSTICS

The exit codes for fmtmsg are the following:

MM_OK	The function succeeded.
MM_NOTOK	The function failed completely.
MM_NOMSG	The function was unable to generate a message on the standard error stream, but otherwise succeeded.
MM_NOCON	The function was unable to generate a console message, but otherwise succeeded.

fopen(3S)

(C Development Set)

fopen(3S)

NAME
fopen, freopen, fdopen – open a stream

SYNOPSIS
```
#include <stdio.h>
```
FILE *fopen (const char *filename, const char *type);

FILE *freopen (const char *filename, const char *type, FILE *stream);

FILE *fdopen (int fildes, const char *type);

DESCRIPTION
fopen opens the file named by *filename* and associates a *stream* with it. fopen returns a pointer to the FILE structure associated with the *stream*.

filename points to a character string that contains the name of the file to be opened.

type is a character string beginning with one of the following sequences:

    "r" or "rb"   open for reading

    "w" or "wb"   truncate to zero length or create for writing

    "a" or "ab"   append; open for writing at end of file, or create for writing

    "r+", "r+b" or "rb+"
        open for update (reading and writing)

    "w+", "w+b" or "wb+"
        truncate or create for update

    "a+", "a+b" or "ab+"
        append; open or create for update at end-of-file

The "b" is ignored in the above *types*. The "b" exists to distinguish binary files from text files. However, there is no distinction between these types of files on a UNIX system.

freopen substitutes the named file in place of the open *stream*. A flush is first attempted, and then the original *stream* is closed, regardless of whether the open ultimately succeeds. Failure to flush or close *stream* successfully is ignored. freopen returns a pointer to the FILE structure associated with *stream*.

freopen is typically used to attach the preopened *streams* associated with stdin, stdout, and stderr to other files. stderr is by default unbuffered, but the use of freopen will cause it to become buffered or line-buffered.

fdopen associates a *stream* with a file descriptor. File descriptors are obtained from open, dup, creat, or pipe, which open files but do not return pointers to a FILE structure *stream*. Streams are necessary input for almost all of the Section 3S library routines. The *type* of *stream* must agree with the mode of the open file. The file position indicator associated with *stream* is set to the position indicated by the file offset associated with *fildes*.

When a file is opened for update, both input and output may be done on the resulting *stream*. However, output may not be directly followed by input without an intervening `fflush`, `fseek`, `fsetpos`, or `rewind`, and input may not be directly followed by output without an intervening `fseek`, `fsetpos`, or `rewind`, or an input operation that encounters end-of-file.

When a file is opened for append (i.e., when *type* is "a", "ab", "a+", or "ab+"), it is impossible to overwrite information already in the file. `fseek` may be used to reposition the file pointer to any position in the file, but when output is written to the file, the current file pointer is disregarded. All output is written at the end of the file and causes the file pointer to be repositioned at the end of the output. If two separate processes open the same file for append, each process may write freely to the file without fear of destroying output being written by the other. The output from the two processes will be intermixed in the file in the order in which it is written.

When opened, a *stream* is fully buffered if and only if it can be determined not to refer to an interactive device. The error and end-of-file indicators are cleared for the *stream*.

SEE ALSO

close(2), creat(2), dup(2), open(2), pipe(2), write(2), fclose(3S), fseek(3S), setbuf(3S), stdio(3S).

DIAGNOSTICS

The functions `fopen` and `freopen` return a null pointer if *path* cannot be accessed, or if *type* is invalid, or if the file cannot be opened.

The function `fdopen` returns a null pointer if *fildes* is not an open file descriptor, or if *type* is invalid, or if the file cannot be opened.

The functions `fopen` or `fdopen` may fail and not set `errno` if there are no free stdio streams.

File descriptors used by `fdopen` must be less than 255.

fopen(3S) (BSD Compatibility Package) fopen(3S)

NAME
fopen, freopen, fdopen – open a stream

SYNOPSIS
cc [*flag*...] *file* ... -lucb

#include <stdio.h>

FILE *fopen(filename, type)
char *filename, *type;

FILE *freopen(filename, type, stream)
char *filename, *type;
FILE *stream;

FILE *fdopen(fildes, type)
int fildes;
char *type;

DESCRIPTION
fopen opens the file named by *filename* and associates a stream with it. If the open succeeds, fopen returns a pointer to be used to identify the stream in subsequent operations.

filename points to a character string that contains the name of the file to be opened.

type is a character string having one of the following values:

- r   open for reading
- w   truncate or create for writing
- a   append: open for writing at end of file, or create for writing
- r+   open for update (reading and writing)
- w+   truncate or create for update
- a+   append; open or create for update at EOF

freopen opens the file named by *filename* and associates the stream pointed to by *stream* with it. The *type* argument is used just as in fopen. The original stream is closed, regardless of whether the open ultimately succeeds. If the open succeeds, freopen returns the original value of *stream*.

freopen is typically used to attach the preopened streams associated with stdin, stdout, and stderr to other files.

fdopen associates a stream with the file descriptor *fildes*. File descriptors are obtained from calls like open, dup, creat, or pipe(2), which open files but do not return streams. Streams are necessary input for many of the Section 3S library routines. The *type* of the stream must agree with the mode of the open file.

When a file is opened for update, both input and output may be done on the resulting stream. However, output may not be directly followed by input without an intervening fseek or rewind, and input may not be directly followed by output without an intervening fseek, rewind, or an input operation which encounters EOF.

SEE ALSO

open(2), pipe(2), fclose(3S), fseek(3S), fopen(3S), malloc(3C) in the *Programmer's Reference Manual*

RETURN VALUE

fopen, freopen, and fdopen return a NULL pointer on failure.

NOTES

fopen differs from the library routine of the same name in the base system only in interface.

In order to support the same number of open files that the system does, fopen must allocate additional memory for data structures using calloc [see malloc(3)] after 64 files have been opened. This confuses some programs which use their own memory allocators.

NAME
form_cursor: pos_form_cursor – position forms window cursor

SYNOPSIS
#include <form.h>

int pos_form_cursor(FORM *form);

DESCRIPTION
pos_form_cursor moves the form window cursor to the location required by the form driver to resume form processing. This may be needed after the application calls a curses library I/O routine.

RETURN VALUE
pos_form_cursor returns one of the following:

E_OK	– The function returned successfully.
E_SYSTEM_ERROR	– System error.
E_BAD_ARGUMENT	– An argument is incorrect.
E_NOT_POSTED	– The form is not posted.

NOTES
The header file <form.h> automatically includes the header files <eti.h> and <curses.h>.

SEE ALSO
curses(3X), forms(3X)

form_data(3X)

NAME
form_data: data_ahead, data_behind - tell if forms field has off-screen data ahead or behind

SYNOPSIS
#include <form.h>

int data_ahead(FORM *form);

int data_behind(FORM *form);

DESCRIPTION
data_ahead returns TRUE (1) if the current field has more off-screen data ahead; otherwise it returns FALSE (0).

data_behind returns TRUE (1) if the current field has more off-screen data behind; otherwise it returns FALSE (0).

NOTES
The header file <form.h> automatically includes the header files <eti.h> and <curses.h>.

SEE ALSO
curses(3X), forms(3X)

NAME
form_driver – command processor for the forms subsystem

SYNOPSIS
#include <form.h>

int form_driver(FORM *form, int c);

DESCRIPTION
form_driver is the workhorse of the forms subsystem; it checks to determine whether the character c is a forms request or data. If it is a request, the form driver executes the request and reports the result. If it is data (a printable ASCII character), it enters the data into the current position in the current field. If it is not recognized, the form driver assumes it is an application-defined command and returns E_UNKNOWN_COMMAND. Application defined commands should be defined relative to MAX_COMMAND, the maximum value of a request listed below.

Form driver requests:

REQ_NEXT_PAGE	Move to the next page.
REQ_PREV_PAGE	Move to the previous page.
REQ_FIRST_PAGE	Move to the first page.
REQ_LAST_PAGE	Move to the last page.
REQ_NEXT_FIELD	Move to the next field.
REQ_PREV_FIELD	Move to the previous field.
REQ_FIRST_FIELD	Move to the first field.
REQ_LAST_FIELD	Move to the last field.
REQ_SNEXT_FIELD	Move to the sorted next field.
REQ_SPREV_FIELD	Move to the sorted prev field.
REQ_SFIRST_FIELD	Move to the sorted first field.
REQ_SLAST_FIELD	Move to the sorted last field.
REQ_LEFT_FIELD	Move left to field.
REQ_RIGHT_FIELD	Move right to field.
REQ_UP_FIELD	Move up to field.
REQ_DOWN_FIELD	Move down to field.
REQ_NEXT_CHAR	Move to the next character in the field.
REQ_PREV_CHAR	Move to the previous character in the field.
REQ_NEXT_LINE	Move to the next line in the field.
REQ_PREV_LINE	Move to the previous line in the field.
REQ_NEXT_WORD	Move to the next word in the field.
REQ_PREV_WORD	Move to the previous word in the field.
REQ_BEG_FIELD	Move to the first char in the field.
REQ_END_FIELD	Move after the last char in the field.
REQ_BEG_LINE	Move to the beginning of the line.
REQ_END_LINE	Move after the last char in the line.
REQ_LEFT_CHAR	Move left in the field.
REQ_RIGHT_CHAR	Move right in the field.
REQ_UP_CHAR	Move up in the field.
REQ_DOWN_CHAR	Move down in the field.

form_driver(3X)

REQ_NEW_LINE	Insert/overlay a new line.
REQ_INS_CHAR	Insert the blank character at the cursor.
REQ_INS_LINE	Insert a blank line at the cursor.
REQ_DEL_CHAR	Delete the character at the cursor.
REQ_DEL_PREV	Delete the character before the cursor.
REQ_DEL_LINE	Delete the line at the cursor.
REQ_DEL_WORD	Delete the word at the cursor.
REQ_CLR_EOL	Clear to the end of the line.
REQ_CLR_EOF	Clear to the end of the field.
REQ_CLR_FIELD	Clear the entire field.
REQ_OVL_MODE	Enter overlay mode.
REQ_INS_MODE	Enter insert mode.
REQ_SCR_FLINE	Scroll the field forward a line.
REQ_SCR_BLINE	Scroll the field backward a line.
REQ_SCR_FPAGE	Scroll the field forward a page.
REQ_SCR_BPAGE	Scroll the field backward a page.
REQ_SCR_FHPAGE	Scroll the field forward half a page.
REQ_SCR_BHPAGE	Scroll the field backward half a page.
REQ_SCR_FCHAR	Horizontal scroll forward a character.
REQ_SCR_BCHAR	Horizontal scroll backward a character.
REQ_SCR_HFLINE	Horizontal scroll forward a line.
REQ_SCR_HBLINE	Horizontal scroll backward a line.
REQ_SCR_HFHALF	Horizontal scroll forward half a line.
REQ_SCR_HBHALF	Horizontal scroll backward half a line.
REQ_VALIDATION	Validate field.
REQ_PREV_CHOICE	Display the previous field choice.
REQ_NEXT_CHOICE	Display the next field choice.

RETURN VALUE

form_driver returns one of the following:

E_OK	– The function returned successfully.
E_SYSTEM_ERROR	– System error.
E_BAD_ARGUMENT	– An argument is incorrect.
E_NOT_POSTED	– The form is not posted.
E_INVALID_FIELD	– The field contents are invalid.
E_BAD_STATE	– The routine was called from an initialization or termination function.
E_REQUEST_DENIED	– The form driver request failed.
E_UNKNOWN_COMMAND	– An unknown request was passed to the the form driver.

NOTES

The header file <form.h> automatically includes the header files <eti.h> and <curses.h>.

SEE ALSO
    curses(3X), forms(3X)

form_field(3X)

NAME
form_field: set_form_fields, form_fields, field_count, move_field – connect fields to forms

SYNOPSIS
#include <form.h>

int set_form_fields(FORM *form, FIELD **field);

FIELD **form_fields(FORM *form);

int field_count(FORM *form);

int move_field(FIELD *field, int frow, int fcol);

DESCRIPTION
set_form_fields changes the fields connected to *form* to *fields*. The original fields are disconnected.

form_fields returns a pointer to the field pointer array connected to *form*.

field_count returns the number of fields connected to *form*.

move_field moves the disconnected *field* to the location *frow*, *fcol* in the forms subwindow.

RETURN VALUE
form_fields returns NULL on error.

field_count returns −1 on error.

set_form_fields and move_field return one of the following:

E_OK	– The function returned successfully.
E_CONNECTED	– The field is already connected to a form.
E_SYSTEM_ERROR	– System error.
E_BAD_ARGUMENT	– An argument is incorrect.
E_POSTED	– The form is posted.

NOTES
The header file <form.h> automatically includes the header files <eti.h> and <curses.h>.

SEE ALSO
curses(3X), forms(3X)

form_field_attributes(3X)

NAME
form_field_attributes: set_field_fore, field_fore, set_field_back, field_back, set_field_pad, field_pad – format the general display attributes of forms

SYNOPSIS
#include <form.h>

int set_field_fore(FIELD *field, chtype attr);
chtype field_fore(FIELD *field);

int set_field_back(FIELD *field, chtype attr);
chtype field_back(FIELD *field);

int set_field_pad(FIELD *field, int pad);
int field_pad(FIELD *field);

DESCRIPTION
set_field_fore sets the foreground attribute of *field*. The foreground attribute is the low-level curses display attribute used to display the field contents. field_fore returns the foreground attribute of *field*.

set_field_back sets the background attribute of *field*. The background attribute is the low-level curses display attribute used to display the extent of the field. field_back returns the background attribute of *field*.

set_field_pad sets the pad character of *field* to *pad*. The pad character is the character used to fill within the field. field_pad returns the pad character of *field*.

RETURN VALUE
field_fore, field_back and field_pad return default values if *field* is NULL. If *field* is not NULL and is not a valid FIELD pointer, the return value from these routines is undefined.

set_field_fore, set_field_back and set_field_pad return one of the following:

E_OK	– The function returned successfully.
E_SYSTEM_ERROR	– System error.
E_BAD_ARGUMENT	– An argument is incorrect.

NOTES
The header file <form.h> automatically includes the header files <eti.h> and <curses.h>.

SEE ALSO
curses(3X), forms(3X)

NAME

form_field_buffer: set_field_buffer, field_buffer, set_field_status, field_status, set_max_field – set and get forms field attributes

SYNOPSIS

```
#include <form.h>

int set_field_buffer(FIELD *field, int buf, char *value);
char *field_buffer(FIELD *field, int buf);

int set_field_status(FIELD *field, int status);
int field_status(FIELD *field);

int set_max_field(FIELD *field, int max);
```

DESCRIPTION

set_field_buffer sets buffer *buf* of *field* to *value*. Buffer 0 stores the displayed contents of the field. Buffers other than 0 are application specific and not used by the forms library routines. field_buffer returns the value of *field* buffer *buf*.

Every field has an associated status flag that is set whenever the contents of field buffer 0 changes. set_field_status sets the status flag of *field* to *status*. field_status returns the status of *field*.

set_max_field sets a maximum growth on a dynamic field, or if *max*=0 turns off any maximum growth.

RETURN VALUE

field_buffer returns NULL on error.

field_status returns TRUE or FALSE.

set_field_buffer, set_field_status and set_max_field return one of the following:

E_OK	– The function returned successfully.
E_SYSTEM_ERROR	– System error.
E_BAD_ARGUMENT	– An argument is incorrect.

NOTES

The header file <form.h> automatically includes the header files <eti.h> and <curses.h>.

SEE ALSO

curses(3X), forms(3X)

form_field_info(3X)

NAME
form_field_info: field_info, dynamic_field_info - get forms field characteristics

SYNOPSIS
#include <form.h>

int field_info(FIELD *field, int *rows, int *cols,
    int *frow, int *fcol, int *nrow, int *nbuf);

int dynamic_field_info(FIELD *field, int *drows, int *dcols,
    int *max);

DESCRIPTION
field_info returns the size, position, and other named field characteristics, as defined in the original call to new_field, to the locations pointed to by the arguments *rows, cols, frow, fcol, nrow,* and *nbuf.*

dynamic_field_info returns the actual size of the *field* in the pointer arguments *drows, dcols* and returns the maximum growth allowed for *field* in *max*. If no maximum growth limit is specified for *field, max* will contain 0. A field can be made dynamic by turning off the field option O_STATIC.

RETURN VALUE
These routines return one of the following:

E_OK	- The function returned successfully.
E_SYSTEM_ERROR	- System error.
E_BAD_ARGUMENT	- An argument is incorrect.

NOTES
The header file <form.h> automatically includes the header files <eti.h> and <curses.h>.

SEE ALSO
curses(3X), forms(3X)

form_field_just(3X)

NAME
form_field_just: set_field_just, field_just – format the general appearance of forms

SYNOPSIS
#include <form.h>

int set_field_just(FIELD *field, int justification);

int field_just(FIELD *field);

DESCRIPTION
set_field_just sets the justification for *field*. Justification may be one of:
NO_JUSTIFICATION, JUSTIFY_RIGHT, JUSTIFY_LEFT, or JUSTIFY_CENTER.

The field justification will be ignored if *field* is a dynamic field.

field_just returns the type of justification assigned to *field*.

RETURN VALUE
field_just returns the one of:
NO_JUSTIFICATION, JUSTIFY_RIGHT, JUSTIFY_LEFT, or JUSTIFY_CENTER.

set_field_just returns one of the following:

E_OK	– The function returned successfully.
E_SYSTEM_ERROR	– System error.
E_BAD_ARGUMENT	– An argument is incorrect.

NOTES
The header file <form.h> automatically includes the header files <eti.h> and <curses.h>.

SEE ALSO
curses(3X), forms(3X)

NAME

form_field_new: new_field, dup_field, link_field, free_field, – create and destroy forms fields

SYNOPSIS

#include <form.h>

FIELD *new_field(int r, int c, int frow, int fcol,
    int nrow, int ncol);

FIELD *dup_field(FIELD *field, int frow, int fcol);

FIELD *link_field(FIELD *field, int frow, int fcol);

int free_field(FIELD *field);

DESCRIPTION

new_field creates a new field with *r* rows and *c* columns, starting at *frow, fcol*, in the subwindow of a form. *nrow* is the number of off-screen rows and *nbuf* is the number of additional working buffers. This routine returns a pointer to the new field.

dup_field duplicates *field* at the specified location. All field attributes are duplicated, including the current contents of the field buffers.

link_field also duplicates *field* at the specified location. However, unlike dup_field, the new field shares the field buffers with the original field. After creation, the attributes of the new field can be changed without affecting the original field.

free_field frees the storage allocated for *field*.

RETURN VALUE

Routines that return pointers return NULL on error. free_field returns one of the following:

E_OK	– The function returned successfully.
E_CONNECTED	– The field is already connected to a form.
E_SYSTEM_ERROR	– System error.
E_BAD_ARGUMENT	– An argument is incorrect.

NOTES

The header file <form.h> automatically includes the header files <eti.h> and <curses.h>.

SEE ALSO

forms(3X)

form_field_opts(3X)

NAME
form_field_opts: set_field_opts, field_opts_on, field_opts_off, field_opts – forms field option routines

SYNOPSIS
#include <form.h>

int set_field_opts(FIELD *field, OPTIONS opts);
int field_opts_on(FIELD *field, OPTIONS opts);
int field_opts_off(FIELD *field, OPTIONS opts);
OPTIONS field_opts(FIELD *field);

DESCRIPTION
set_field_opts turns on the named options of *field* and turns off all remaining options. Options are boolean values that can be OR-ed together.

field_opts_on turns on the named options; no other options are changed.

field_opts_off turns off the named options; no other options are changed.

field_opts returns the options set for *field*.

Field Options:

O_VISIBLE	The field is displayed.
O_ACTIVE	The field is visited during processing.
O_PUBLIC	The field contents are displayed as data is entered.
O_EDIT	The field can be edited.
O_WRAP	Words not fitting on a line are wrapped to the next line.
O_BLANK	The whole field is cleared if a character is entered in the first position.
O_AUTOSKIP	Skip to the next field when the current field becomes full.
O_NULLOK	A blank field is considered valid.
O_STATIC	The field buffers are fixed in size.
O_PASSOK	Validate field only if modified by user.

RETURN VALUE
set_field_opts, field_opts_on and field_opts_off return one of the following:

E_OK	– The function returned successfully.
E_SYSTEM_ERROR	– System error.
E_CURRENT	– The field is the current field.

NOTES
The header file <form.h> automatically includes the header files <eti.h> and <curses.h>.

SEE ALSO
curses(3X), forms(3X)

form_field_userptr (3X)

NAME
form_field_userptr: set_field_userptr, field_userptr – associate application data with forms

SYNOPSIS
#include <form.h>

int set_field_userptr(FIELD *field, char *ptr);
char *field_userptr(FIELD *field);

DESCRIPTION
Every field has an associated user pointer that can be used to store pertinent data. set_field_userptr sets the user pointer of *field*. field_userptr returns the user pointer of *field*.

RETURN VALUE
field_userptr returns NULL on error. set_field_userptr returns one of the following:

E_OK   – The function returned successfully.
E_SYSTEM_ERROR   – System error.

NOTES
The header file <form.h> automatically includes the header files <eti.h> and <curses.h>.

SEE ALSO
curses(3X), forms(3X)

NAME
form_field_validation: set_field_type, field_type, field_arg - forms field data type validation

SYNOPSIS
#include <form.h>

int set_field_type(FIELD *field, FIELDTYPE *type,...);

FIELDTYPE *field_type(FIELD *field);

char *field_arg(FIELD *field);

DESCRIPTION
set_field_type associates the specified field type with *field*. Certain field types take additional arguments. TYPE_ALNUM, for instance, requires one, the minimum width specification for the field. The other predefined field types are: TYPE_ALPHA, TYPE_ENUM, TYPE_INTEGER, TYPE_NUMERIC, TYPE_REGEXP.

field_type returns a pointer to the field type of *field*. NULL is returned if no field type is assigned.

field_arg returns a pointer to the field arguments associated with the field type of *field*. NULL is returned if no field type is assigned.

RETURN VALUE
field_type and field_arg return NULL on error.

set_field_type returns one of the following:

E_OK	- The function returned successfully.
E_SYSTEM_ERROR	- System error.

NOTES
The header file <form.h> automatically includes the header files <eti.h> and <curses.h>.

SEE ALSO
curses(3X), forms(3X)

form_fieldtype(3X)

NAME
form_fieldtype: new_fieldtype, free_fieldtype, set_fieldtype_arg, set_fieldtype_choice, link_fieldtype - forms fieldtype routines

SYNOPSIS
#include <form.h>

FIELDTYPE *new_fieldtype(int (* field_check)(FIELD *, char *),
    int (* char_check)(int, char *));

int free_fieldtype(FIELDTYPE *fieldtype);

int set_fieldtype_arg(FIELDTYPE *fieldtype,
    char *(* mak_arg)(va_list *),
    char *(* copy_arg)(char *), void (* free_arg)(char *));

int set_fieldtype_choice(FIELDTYPE *fieldtype,
    int (* next_choice)(FIELD *, char *),
    int (* prev_choice)(FIELD *, char *));

FIELDTYPE *link_fieldtype(FIELDTYPE *type1, FIELDTYPE *type2);

DESCRIPTION
new_fieldtype creates a new field type. The application programmer must write the function *field_check*, which validates the field value, and the function *char_check*, which validates each character. free_fieldtype frees the space allocated for the field type.

By associating function pointers with a field type, set_fieldtype_arg connects to the field type additional arguments necessary for a set_field_type call. Function *mak_arg* allocates a structure for the field specific parameters to set_field_type and returns a pointer to the saved data. Function *copy_arg* duplicates the structure created by *make_arg*. Function *free_arg* frees any storage allocated by *make_arg* or *copy_arg*.

The form_driver requests REQ_NEXT_CHOICE and REQ_PREV_CHOICE let the user request the next or previous value of a field type comprising an ordered set of values. set_fieldtype_choice allows the application programmer to implement these requests for the given field type. It associates with the given field type those application-defined functions that return pointers to the next or previous choice for the field.

link_fieldtype returns a pointer to the field type built from the two given types. The constituent types may be any application-defined or pre-defined types.

RETURN VALUE
Routines that return pointers always return NULL on error. Routines that return an integer return one of the following:

E_OK	– The function returned successfully.
E_SYSTEM_ERROR	– System error.
E_BAD_ARGUMENT	– An argument is incorrect.
E_CONNECTED	– Type is connected to one or more fields.

NOTES

The header file <form.h> automatically includes the header files <eti.h> and <curses.h>.

SEE ALSO

curses(3X), forms(3X)

form_hook(3X)

NAME
form_hook: set_form_init, form_init, set_form_term, form_term, set_field_init, field_init, set_field_term, field_term – assign application-specific routines for invocation by forms

SYNOPSIS
```
#include <form.h>

int set_form_init(FORM *form, void (*func)(FORM *));
void (*)(FORM *) form_init(FORM *form);

int set_form_term(FORM *form, void (*func)(FORM *));
void (*)(FORM *) form_term(FORM *form);

int set_field_init(FORM *form, void (*func)(FORM *));
void (*)(FORM *) field_init(FORM *form);

int set_field_term(FORM *form, void (*func)(FORM *));
void (*)(FORM *) field_term(FORM *form);
```

DESCRIPTION
These routines allow the programmer to assign application specific routines to be executed automatically at initialization and termination points in the forms application. The user need not specify any application-defined initialization or termination routines at all, but they may be helpful for displaying messages or page numbers and other chores.

set_form_init assigns an application-defined initialization function to be called when the *form* is posted and just after a page change. form_init returns a pointer to the initialization function, if any.

set_form_term assigns an application-defined function to be called when the *form* is unposted and just before a page change. form_term returns a pointer to the function, if any.

set_field_init assigns an application-defined function to be called when the *form* is posted and just after the current field changes. field_init returns a pointer to the function, if any.

set_field_term assigns an application-defined function to be called when the *form* is unposted and just before the current field changes. field_term returns a pointer to the function, if any.

RETURN VALUE
Routines that return pointers always return NULL on error. Routines that return an integer return one of the following:

E_OK   – The function returned successfully.
E_SYSTEM_ERROR – System error.

NOTES
The header file form.h automatically includes the header files eti.h and curses.h.

SEE ALSO
curses(3X), forms(3X)

NAME
form_new: new_form, free_form – create and destroy forms

SYNOPSIS
#include <form.h>

FORM *new_form(FIELD **fields);

int free_form(FORM *form);

DESCRIPTION
new_form creates a new form connected to the designated fields and returns a pointer to the form.

free_form disconnects the *form* from its associated field pointer array and deallocates the space for the form.

RETURN VALUE
new_form always returns NULL on error. free_form returns one of the following:

E_OK	– The function returned successfully.
E_BAD_ARGUMENT	– An argument is incorrect.
E_POSTED	– The form is posted.

NOTES
The header file <form.h> automatically includes the header files <eti.h> and <curses.h>.

SEE ALSO
curses(3X), forms(3X)

form_new_page(3X)

NAME
form_new_page: set_new_page, new_page – forms pagination

SYNOPSIS
#include <form.h>

int set_new_page(FIELD *field, int bool);

int new_page(FIELD *field);

DESCRIPTION
set_new_page marks *field* as the beginning of a new page on the form.

new_page returns a boolean value indicating whether or not *field* begins a new page of the form.

RETURN VALUE
new_page returns TRUE or FALSE.

set_new_page returns one of the following:

E_OK	– The function returned successfully.
E_CONNECTED	– The field is already connected to a form.
E_SYSTEM_ERROR	– System error.

NOTES
The header file <form.h> automatically includes the header files <eti.h> and <curses.h>.

SEE ALSO
curses(3X), forms(3X)

form_opts(3X)

NAME
form_opts: set_form_opts, form_opts_on, form_opts_off, form_opts – forms option routines

SYNOPSIS
#include <form.h>

int set_form_opts(FORM *form, OPTIONS opts);
int form_opts_on(FORM *form, OPTIONS opts);
int form_opts_off(FORM *form, OPTIONS opts);
OPTIONS form_opts(FORM *form);

DESCRIPTION
set_form_opts turns on the named options for *form* and turns off all remaining options. Options are boolean values which can be OR-ed together.

form_opts_on turns on the named options; no other options are changed.

form_opts_off turns off the named options; no other options are changed.

form_opts returns the options set for *form*.

Form Options:

O_NL_OVERLOAD	Overload the REQ_NEW_LINE form driver request.
O_BS_OVERLOAD	Overload the REQ_DEL_PREV form driver request.

RETURN VALUE
set_form_opts, form_opts_on and form_opts_off return one of the following:

E_OK	– The function returned successfully.
E_SYSTEM_ERROR	– System error.

NOTES
The header file <form.h> automatically includes the header files <eti.h> and <curses.h>.

SEE ALSO
curses(3X), forms(3X)

form_page(3X)

NAME
form_page: set_form_page, form_page, set_current_field, current_field, field_index — set forms current page and field

SYNOPSIS
```
#include <form.h>

int set_form_page(FORM *form, int page);
int form_page(FORM *form);

int set_current_field(FORM *form, FIELD *field);
FIELD *current_field(FORM *form);

int field_index(FIELD *field);
```

DESCRIPTION
set_form_page sets the page number of *form* to *page*. form_page returns the current page number of *form*.

set_current_field sets the current field of *form* to *field*. current_field returns a pointer to the current field of *form*.

field_index returns the index in the field pointer array of *field*.

RETURN VALUE
form_page returns −1 on error.

current_field returns NULL on error.

field_index returns −1 on error.

set_form_page and set_current_field return one of the following:

E_OK	− The function returned successfully.
E_SYSTEM_ERROR	− System error.
E_BAD_ARGUMENT	− An argument is incorrect.
E_BAD_STATE	− The routine was called from an initialization or termination function.
E_INVALID_FIELD	− The field contents are invalid.
E_REQUEST_DENIED	− The form driver request failed.

NOTES
The header file <form.h> automatically includes the header files <eti.h> and <curses.h>.

SEE ALSO
curses(3X), forms(3X)

form_post(3X)

NAME
form_post: post_form, unpost_form — write or erase forms from associated subwindows

SYNOPSIS
#include <form.h>

int post_form(FORM *form);

int unpost_form(FORM *form);

DESCRIPTION
post_form writes *form* into its associated subwindow. The application programmer must use curses library routines to display the form on the physical screen or call update_panels if the panels library is being used.

unpost_form erases *form* from its associated subwindow.

RETURN VALUE
These routines return one of the following:

E_OK	– The function returned successfully.
E_SYSTEM_ERROR	– System error.
E_BAD_ARGUMENT	– An argument is incorrect.
E_POSTED	– The form is posted.
E_NOT_POSTED	– The form is not posted.
E_NO_ROOM	– The form does not fit in the subwindow.
E_BAD_STATE	– The routine was called from an initialization or termination function.
E_NOT_CONNECTED	– The field is not connected to a form.

NOTES
The header file <form.h> automatically includes the header files <eti.h> and <curses.h>.

SEE ALSO
curses(3X), forms(3X), panels(3X), panel_update(3X)

form_userptr(3X)

NAME
form_userptr: set_form_userptr, form_userptr – associate application data with forms

SYNOPSIS
#include <form.h>

int set_form_userptr(FORM *form, char *ptr);
char *form_userptr(FORM *form);

DESCRIPTION
Every form has an associated user pointer that can be used to store pertinent data. set_form_userptr sets the user pointer of *form*. form_userptr returns the user pointer of *form*.

RETURN VALUE
form_userptr returns NULL on error. set_form_userptr returns one of the following:

E_OK   – The function returned successfully.
E_SYSTEM_ERROR – System error.

NOTES
The header file <form.h> automatically includes the header files <eti.h> and <curses.h>.

SEE ALSO
curses(3X), forms(3X)

form_win(3X)

NAME
form_win: set_form_win, form_win, set_form_sub, form_sub, scale_form – forms window and subwindow association routines

SYNOPSIS
#include <form.h>

int set_form_win(FORM *form, WINDOW *win);
WINDOW *form_win(FORM *form);

int set_form_sub(FORM *form, WINDOW *sub);
WINDOW *form_sub(FORM *form);

int scale_form(FORM *form, int *rows, int *cols);

DESCRIPTION
set_form_win sets the window of *form* to *win*. form_win returns a pointer to the window associated with *form*.

set_form_sub sets the subwindow of *form* to *sub*. form_sub returns a pointer to the subwindow associated with *form*.

scale_form returns the smallest window size necessary for the subwindow of *form*. *rows* and *cols* are pointers to the locations used to return the number of rows and columns for the form.

RETURN VALUE
Routines that return pointers always return NULL on error. Routines that return an integer return one of the following:

E_OK	– The function returned successfully.
E_SYSTEM_ERROR	– System error.
E_BAD_ARGUMENT	– An argument is incorrect.
E_NOT_CONNECTED	– The field is not connected to a form.
E_POSTED	– The form is posted.

NOTES
The header file <form.h> automatically includes the header files <eti.h> and <curses.h>.

SEE ALSO
curses(3X), forms(3X)

forms(3X)

NAME
forms – character based forms package

SYNOPSIS
#include <form.h>

DESCRIPTION
The form library is built using the curses library, and any program using forms routines must call one of the curses initialization routines such as initscr. A program using these routines must be compiled with -lform and -lcurses on the cc command line.

The forms package gives the applications programmer a terminal-independent method of creating and customizing forms for user-interaction. The forms package includes: field routines, which are used to create and customize fields, link fields and assign field types; fieldtype routines, which are used to create new field types for validating fields; and form routines, which are used to create and customize forms, assign pre/post processing functions, and display and interact with forms.

Current Default Values for Field Attributes
The forms package establishes initial current default values for field attributes. During field initialization, each field attribute is assigned the current default value for that attribute. An application can change or retrieve a current default attribute value by calling the appropriate set or retrieve routine with a NULL field pointer. If an application changes a current default field attribute value, subsequent fields created using new_field will have the new default attribute value. (The attributes of previously created fields are not changed if a current default attribute value is changed.)

Routine Name Index
The following table lists each forms routine and the name of the manual page on which it is described.

forms Routine Name	Manual Page Name
current_field	form_page(3X)
data_ahead	form_data(3X)
data_behind	form_data(3X)
dup_field	form_field_new(3X)
dynamic_field_info	form_field_info(3X)
field_arg	form_field_validation(3X)
field_back	form_field_attributes(3X)
field_buffer	form_field_buffer(3X)
field_count	form_field(3X)
field_fore	form_field_attributes(3X)
field_index	form_page(3X)
field_info	form_field_info(3X)
field_init	form_hook(3X)
field_just	form_field_just(3X)
field_opts	form_field_opts(3X)

forms Routine Name	Manual Page Name
field_opts_off	form_field_opts(3X)
field_opts_on	form_field_opts(3X)
field_pad	form_field_attributes(3X)
field_status	form_field_buffer(3X)
field_term	form_hook(3X)
field_type	form_field_validation(3X)
field_userptr	form_field_userptr(3X)
form_driver	form_driver(3X)
form_fields	form_field(3X)
form_init	form_hook(3X)
form_opts	form_opts(3X)
form_opts_off	form_opts(3X)
form_opts_on	form_opts(3X)
form_page	form_page(3X)
form_sub	form_win(3X)
form_term	form_hook(3X)
form_userptr	form_userptr(3X)
form_win	form_win(3X)
free_field	form_field_new(3X)
free_fieldtype	form_fieldtype(3X)
free_form	form_new(3X)
link_field	form_field_new(3X)
link_fieldtype	form_fieldtype(3X)
move_field	form_field(3X)
new_field	form_field_new(3X)
new_fieldtype	form_fieldtype(3X)
new_form	form_new(3X)
new_page	form_new_page(3X)
pos_form_cursor	form_cursor(3X)
post_form	form_post(3X)
scale_form	form_win(3X)
set_current_field	form_page(3X)
set_field_back	form_field_attributes(3X)
set_field_buffer	form_field_buffer(3X)
set_field_fore	form_field_attributes(3X)
set_field_init	form_hook(3X)
set_field_just	form_field_just(3X)
set_field_opts	form_field_opts(3X)
set_field_pad	form_field_attributes(3X)
set_field_status	form_field_buffer(3X)
set_field_term	form_hook(3X)
set_field_type	form_field_validation(3X)
set_field_userptr	form_field_userptr(3X)
set_fieldtype_arg	form_fieldtype(3X)
set_fieldtype_choice	form_fieldtype(3X)
set_form_fields	form_field(3X)

forms Routine Name	Manual Page Name
set_form_init	form_hook(3X)
set_form_opts	form_opts(3X)
set_form_page	form_page(3X)
set_form_sub	form_win(3X)
set_form_term	form_hook(3X)
set_form_userptr	form_userptr(3X)
set_form_win	form_win(3X)
set_max_field	form_field_buffer(3X)
set_new_page	form_new_page(3X)
unpost_form	form_post(3X)

RETURN VALUE

Routines that return a pointer always return NULL on error. Routines that return an integer return one of the following:

E_OK	- The function returned successfully.
E_CONNECTED	- The field is already connected to a form.
E_SYSTEM_ERROR	- System error.
E_BAD_ARGUMENT	- An argument is incorrect.
E_CURRENT	- The field is the current field.
E_POSTED	- The form is posted.
E_NOT_POSTED	- The form is not posted.
E_INVALID_FIELD	- The field contents are invalid.
E_NOT_CONNECTED	- The field is not connected to a form.
E_NO_ROOM	- The form does not fit in the subwindow.
E_BAD_STATE	- The routine was called from an initialization or termination function.
E_REQUEST_DENIED	- The form driver request failed.
E_UNKNOWN_COMMAND	- An unknown request was passed to the the form driver.

NOTES

The header file <form.h> automatically includes the header files <eti.h> and <curses.h>.

SEE ALSO

curses(3X), and 3X pages whose names begin "form_" for detailed routine descriptions.

fpgetround(3C)

NAME
fpgetround, fpsetround, fpgetmask, fpsetmask, fpgetsticky, fpsetsticky – IEEE floating-point environment control

SYNOPSIS
```
#include <ieeefp.h>
```
fp_rnd fpgetround (void);

fp_rnd fpsetround (fp_rnd rnd_dir);

fp_except fpgetmask (void);

fp_except fpsetmask (fp_except mask);

fp_except fpgetsticky (void);

fp_except fpsetsticky (fp_except sticky);

DESCRIPTION
There are five floating-point exceptions: divide-by-zero, overflow, underflow, imprecise (inexact) result, and invalid operation. When a floating-point exception occurs, the corresponding sticky bit is set (1), and if the mask bit is enabled (1), the trap takes place. These routines let the user change the behavior on occurrence of any of these exceptions, as well as change the rounding mode for floating-point operations.

```
FP_X_INV     /* invalid operation exception */
FP_X_OFL     /* overflow exception */
FP_X_UFL     /* underflow exception */
FP_X_DZ      /* divide-by-zero exception */
FP_X_IMP     /* imprecise (loss of precision) */
FP_RN        /* round to nearest representative number */
FP_RP        /* round to plus infinity */
FP_RM        /* round to minus infinity */
FP_RZ        /* round to zero (truncate) */
```

fpgetround returns the current rounding mode.

fpsetround sets the rounding mode and returns the previous rounding mode.

fpgetmask returns the current exception masks.

fpsetmask sets the exception masks and returns the previous setting.

fpgetsticky returns the current exception sticky flags.

fpsetsticky sets (clears) the exception sticky flags and returns the previous setting.

The default environment is rounding mode set to nearest (FP_RN) and all traps disabled.

Individual bits may be examined using the constants defined in ieeefp.h.

SEE ALSO
isnan(3C)

NOTES

fpsetsticky modifies all sticky flags. fpsetmask changes all mask bits. fpsetmask clears the sticky bit corresponding to any exception being enabled.

C requires truncation (round to zero) for floating point to integral conversions. The current rounding mode has no effect on these conversions.

One must clear the sticky bit to recover from the trap and to proceed. If the sticky bit is not cleared before the next trap occurs, a wrong exception type may be signaled.

NAME
fread, fwrite − binary input/output

SYNOPSIS
```
#include <stdio.h>

size_t fread (void *ptr, size_t size, size_t nitems, FILE *stream);

size_t fwrite (const void *ptr, size_t size, size_t nitems, FILE
    *stream);
```

DESCRIPTION
fread reads into an array pointed to by *ptr* up to *nitems* items of data from *stream*, where an item of data is a sequence of bytes (not necessarily terminated by a null byte) of length *size*. fread stops reading bytes if an end-of-file or error condition is encountered while reading *stream*, or if *nitems* items have been read. fread increments the data pointer in *stream* to point to the byte following the last byte read if there is one. fread does not change the contents of *stream*. fread returns the number of items read.

fwrite writes to the named output *stream* at most *nitems* items of data from the array pointed to by *ptr*, where an item of data is a sequence of bytes (not necessarily terminated by a null byte) of length *size*. fwrite stops writing when it has written *nitems* items of data or if an error condition is encountered on *stream*. fwrite does not change the contents of the array pointed to by *ptr*. fwrite increments the data-pointer in *stream* by the number of bytes written. fwrite returns the number of items written.

If *size* or *nitems* is zero, then fread and fwrite return a value of 0 and do not effect the state of *stream*.

The ferror or feof routines must be used to distinguish between an error condition and end-of-file condition.

SEE ALSO
exit(2), lseek(2), read(2), write(2), abort(3C), fclose(3S), fopen(3S), getc(3S), gets(3S), printf(3S), putc(3S), puts(3S), scanf(3S), stdio(3S).

DIAGNOSTICS
If an error occurs, the error indicator for *stream* is set.

frexp(3C) (C Programming Language Utilities) frexp(3C)

NAME
frexp, frexpl, ldexp, ldexpl, logb, modf, modff, modfl, nextafter, scalb, scalbl — manipulate parts of floating-point numbers

SYNOPSIS
#include <math.h>

double frexp (double value, int *eptr);

long double frexpl (long double value, int *eptr);

double ldexp (double value, int exp);

long double ldexpl (long double value, int exp);

double logb (double value);

double nextafter (double value1, double value2);

double scalb (double value, double exp);

long double scalbl (long double value, double exp);

double modf (double value, double *iptr);

float modff (float value, float *iptr);

long double modfl (long double value, long double *iptr);

DESCRIPTION
Every non-zero number can be written uniquely as $x * 2^n$, where the "mantissa" x is in the range $0.5 \leq |x| < 1.0$, and the "exponent" n is an integer. frexp returns the mantissa of a double *value* and stores the exponent indirectly in the location pointed to by *eptr*. If *value* is zero, both results returned by frexp are zero. frexpl returns the mantissa of a long double *value*.

ldexp, ldexpl, scalb, and scalbl return the quantity $value * 2^{exp}$. The only difference is that scalb and scalbl of a signaling NaN will result in the invalid operation exception being raised.

logb returns the unbiased exponent of its floating-point argument as a double-precision floating-point value.

modf, modff (single-precision version), and modfl (long double version) return the signed fractional part of *value* and store the integral part indirectly in the location pointed to by *iptr*.

nextafter returns the next representable double-precision floating-point value following *value1* in the direction of *value2*. Thus, if *value2* is less than *value1*, nextafter returns the largest representable floating-point number less than *value1*.

SEE ALSO
cc(1), intro(3M).

DIAGNOSTICS
If ldexp or ldexpl would cause overflow, ±HUGE (defined in math.h) is returned (according to the sign of *value*), and errno is set to ERANGE. If ldexp or ldexpl would cause underflow, zero is returned and errno is set to ERANGE. If the input *value* to ldexp or ldexpl is NaN or infinity, that input is returned and errno is set to EDOM. The same error conditions apply to scalb and scalbl except that a

signaling NaN as input will result in the raising of the invalid operation exception.

logb of NaN returns that NaN, logb of infinity returns positive infinity, and logb of zero returns negative infinity and results in the raising of the divide by zero exception. In each of these conditions errno is set to EDOM.

If input *value1* to nextafter is positive or negative infinity, that input is returned and errno is set to EDOM. The overflow and inexact exceptions are signalled when input *value1* is finite, but nextafter(*value1*, *value2*) is not. The underflow and inexact exceptions are signalled when nextafter(*value1*, *value2*) lies strictly between $\pm 2^{-1022}$. In both cases errno is set to ERANGE.

When the program is compiled with the cc options -Xc or -Xa, HUGE_VAL is returned instead of HUGE.

fseek(3S)

NAME
fseek, rewind, ftell – reposition a file pointer in a stream

SYNOPSIS
#include <stdio.h>

int fseek (FILE *stream, long offset, int ptrname);

void rewind (FILE *stream);

long ftell (FILE *stream);

DESCRIPTION
fseek sets the position of the next input or output operation on the *stream* [see intro(3)]. The new position is at the signed distance *offset* bytes from the beginning, from the current position, or from the end of the file, according to a *ptrname* value of SEEK_SET, SEEK_CUR, or SEEK_END (defined in stdio.h) as follows:

SEEK_SET   set position equal to *offset* bytes.

SEEK_CUR   set position to current location plus *offset*.

SEEK_END   set position to EOF plus *offset*.

fseek allows the file position indicator to be set beyond the end of the existing data in the file. If data is later written at this point, subsequent reads of data in the gap will return zero until data is actually written into the gap. fseek, by itself, does not extend the size of the file.

rewind (stream) is equivalent to:

    (void) fseek (stream, 0L, SEEK_SET);

except that rewind also clears the error indicator on *stream*.

fseek and rewind clear the EOF indicator and undo any effects of ungetc on *stream*. After fseek or rewind, the next operation on a file opened for update may be either input or output.

If *stream* is writable and buffered data has not been written to the underlying file, fseek and rewind cause the unwritten data to be written to the file.

ftell returns the offset of the current byte relative to the beginning of the file associated with the named *stream*.

SEE ALSO
lseek(2), write(2), fopen(3S), popen(3S), stdio(3S), ungetc(3S)

DIAGNOSTICS
fseek returns −1 for improper seeks, otherwise zero. An improper seek can be, for example, an fseek done on a file that has not been opened via fopen; in particular, fseek may not be used on a terminal or on a file opened via popen. After a stream is closed, no further operations are defined on that stream.

NOTES
Although on the UNIX system an offset returned by ftell is measured in bytes, and it is permissible to seek to positions relative to that offset, portability to non-UNIX systems requires that an offset be used by fseek directly. Arithmetic may not meaningfully be performed on such an offset, which is not necessarily measured in bytes.

fsetpos(3C) (C Development Set) fsetpos(3C)

NAME
fsetpos, fgetpos – reposition a file pointer in a stream

SYNOPSIS
```
#include <stdio.h>

int fsetpos (FILE *stream, const fpos_t *pos);

int fgetpos (FILE *stream, fpos_t *pos);
```

DESCRIPTION
fsetpos sets the position of the next input or output operation on the *stream* according to the value of the object pointed to by *pos*. The object pointed to by *pos* must be a value returned by an earlier call to fgetpos on the same stream.

fsetpos clears the end-of-file indicator for the stream and undoes any effects of the ungetc function on the same stream. After fsetpos, the next operation on a file opened for update may be either input or output.

fgetpos stores the current value of the file position indicator for *stream* in the object pointed to by *pos*. The value stored contains information usable by fsetpos for repositioning the stream to its position at the time of the call to fgetpos.

If successful, both fsetpos and fgetpos return zero. Otherwise, they both return nonzero.

SEE ALSO
fseek(3S), lseek(2) ungetc(3S)

ftime(3C) (BSD Compatibility Package) ftime(3C)

NAME
ftime – get date and time

SYNOPSIS
cc [*flag*...] *file*... -lucb

```
#include <sys/types.h>
#include <sys/timeb.h>

ftime(tp)
struct timeb *tp;
```

DESCRIPTION
The ftime entry fills in a structure pointed to by its argument, as defined by <sys/timeb.h>:

```
struct timeb
{
        time_t  time;
        unsigned short millitm;
        short   timezone;
        short   dstflag;
};
```

The structure contains the time since the epoch in seconds, up to 1000 milliseconds of more-precise interval, the local time zone (measured in minutes of time westward from Greenwich), and a flag that, if nonzero, indicates that Daylight Saving time applies locally during the appropriate part of the year.

SEE ALSO
date(1) in the *User's Reference Manual*
gettimeofday(2), ctime(3) in the *Programmer's Reference Manual*

ftw(3C)

NAME
ftw, nftw – walk a file tree

SYNOPSIS
```
#include <ftw.h>

int ftw (const char *path, int (*fn) (const char *, const struct
    stat *, int), int depth);

int nftw (const char *path, int (*fn) (const char *, const struct
    stat *, int, struct FTW*), int depth, int flags);
```

DESCRIPTION
ftw recursively descends the directory hierarchy rooted in *path*. For each object in the hierarchy, ftw calls the user-defined function *fn*, passing it a pointer to a null-terminated character string containing the name of the object, a pointer to a stat structure (see stat(2)) containing information about the object, and an integer. Possible values of the integer, defined in the ftw.h header file, are:

FTW_F   The object is a file.

FTW_D   The object is a directory.

FTW_DNR   The object is a directory that cannot be read. Descendants of the directory will not be processed.

FTW_NS   stat failed on the object because of lack of appropriate permission or the object is a symbolic link that points to a non-existent file. The stat buffer passed to *fn* is undefined.

ftw visits a directory before visiting any of its descendants.

The tree traversal continues until the tree is exhausted, an invocation of *fn* returns a nonzero value, or some error is detected within ftw (such as an I/O error). If the tree is exhausted, ftw returns zero. If *fn* returns a nonzero value, ftw stops its tree traversal and returns whatever value was returned by *fn*. If ftw detects an error other than EACCES, it returns −1, and sets the error type in errno.

The function nftw is similar to ftw except that it takes an additional argument, *flags*. The *flags* field is used to specify:

FTW_PHYS   Physical walk, does not follow symbolic links. Otherwise, nftw will follow links but will not walk down any path that crosses itself.

FTW_MOUNT The walk will not cross a mount point.

FTW_DEPTH All subdirectories will be visited before the directory itself.

FTW_CHDIR The walk will change to each directory before reading it.

The function nftw calls *fn* with four arguments at each file and directory. The first argument is the pathname of the object, the second is a pointer to the stat buffer, the third is an integer giving additional information, and the fourth is a struct FTW that contains the following members:

```
int base;
int level;
```

base is the offset into the pathname of the base name of the object. level indicates the depth relative to the rest of the walk, where the root level is zero.

The values of the third argument are as follows:

FTW_F   The object is a file.

FTW_D   The object is a directory.

FTW_DP   The object is a directory and subdirectories have been visited.

FTW_SLN The object is a symbolic link that points to a non-existent file.

FTW_DNR The object is a directory that cannot be read. *fn* will not be called for any of its descendants.

FTW_NS   stat failed on the object because of lack of appropriate permission. The stat buffer passed to *fn* is undefined. stat failure other than lack of appropriate permission (EACCES) is considered an error and nftw will return −1.

Both ftw and nftw use one file descriptor for each level in the tree. The *depth* argument limits the number of file descriptors so used. If *depth* is zero or negative, the effect is the same as if it were 1. *depth* must not be greater than the number of file descriptors currently available for use. ftw will run faster if *depth* is at least as large as the number of levels in the tree. When ftw and nftw return, they close any file descriptors they have opened; they do not close any file descriptors that may have been opened by *fn*.

SEE ALSO
stat(2), malloc(3C)

NOTES
Because ftw is recursive, it is possible for it to terminate with a memory fault when applied to very deep file structures.

ftw uses malloc(3C) to allocate dynamic storage during its operation. If ftw is forcibly terminated, such as by longjmp being executed by *fn* or an interrupt routine, ftw will not have a chance to free that storage, so it will remain permanently allocated. A safe way to handle interrupts is to store the fact that an interrupt has occurred, and arrange to have *fn* return a nonzero value at its next invocation.

gamma (3M) (Math Libraries) gamma (3M)

NAME
gamma, lgamma – log gamma function

SYNOPSIS
cc [*flag* ...] *file* ... −lm [*library* ...]

```
#include <math.h>

double gamma (double x);

double lgamma (double x);

extern int signgam;
```

DESCRIPTION
gamma and lgamma return

$$\ln(|\Gamma(x)|)$$

where $\Gamma(x)$ is defined as

$$\int_0^\infty e^{-t} t^{x-1} dt$$

The sign of $\Gamma(x)$ is returned in the external integer signgam. The argument x may not be a non-positive integer.

The following C program fragment might be used to calculate Γ:

```
if ((y = gamma(x)) > LN_MAXDOUBLE)
    error();
y = signgam * exp(y);
```

where LN_MAXDOUBLE is the least value that causes exp to return a range error, and is defined in the values.h header file.

SEE ALSO
exp(3M), matherr(3M), values(5)

DIAGNOSTICS
For non-positive integer arguments HUGE is returned and errno is set to EDOM. A message indicating SING error is printed on the standard error output.

If the correct value would overflow, gamma and lgamma return HUGE and set errno to ERANGE.

Except when the −Xc compilation option is used, these error-handling procedures may be changed with the function matherr. When the −Xa or −Xc compilation options are used, HUGE_VAL is returned instead of HUGE and no error messages are printed.

NAME
getc, getchar, fgetc, getw – get character or word from a stream

SYNOPSIS
#include <stdio.h>

int getc (FILE *stream);

int getchar (void);

int fgetc (FILE *stream);

int getw (FILE *stream);

DESCRIPTION
getc returns the next character (that is, byte) from the named input *stream* [see intro(3)] as an unsigned char converted to an int. It also moves the file pointer, if defined, ahead one character in *stream*. getchar is defined as getc(stdin). getc and getchar are macros.

fgetc behaves like getc, but is a function rather than a macro. fgetc runs more slowly than getc, but it takes less space per invocation and its name can be passed as an argument to a function.

getw returns the next word (that is, integer) from the named input *stream*. getw increments the associated file pointer, if defined, to point to the next word. The size of a word is the size of an integer and varies from machine to machine. getw assumes no special alignment in the file.

SEE ALSO
fclose(3S), ferror(3S), fopen(3S), fread(3S), gets(3S), putc(3S), scanf(3S), stdio(3S), ungetc(3S)

DIAGNOSTICS
These functions return the constant EOF at end-of-file or upon an error and set the EOF or error indicator of *stream*, respectively. Because EOF is a valid integer, ferror should be used to detect getw errors.

NOTES
If the integer value returned by getc, getchar, or fgetc is stored into a character variable and then compared against the integer constant EOF, the comparison may never succeed, because sign-extension of a character on widening to integer is implementation dependent.

The macro version of getc evaluates a *stream* argument more than once and may treat side effects incorrectly. In particular, getc(*f++) does not work sensibly. Use fgetc instead.

Because of possible differences in word length and byte ordering, files written using putw are implementation dependent, and may not be read using getw on a different processor.

Functions exist for all the above-defined macros. To get the function form, the macro name must be undefined (for example, #undef getc).

getcwd(3C)

NAME
getcwd – get pathname of current working directory

SYNOPSIS
```
#include <unistd.h>

char *getcwd (char *buf, int size);
```

DESCRIPTION
getcwd returns a pointer to the current directory pathname. The value of *size* must be at least one greater than the length of the pathname to be returned.

If *buf* is not NULL, the pathname will be stored in the space pointed to by *buf*.

If *buf* is a NULL pointer, getcwd will obtain *size* bytes of space using malloc(3C). In this case, the pointer returned by getcwd may be used as the argument in a subsequent call to free.

getcwd will fail if one or more of the following are true:

EACCES   A parent directory cannot be read to get its name.

EINVAL   *size* is equal to 0.

ERANGE   *size* is less than 0 or is greater than 0 and less than the length of the pathname plus 1.

EXAMPLE
Here is a program that prints the current working directory.

```
#include <unistd.h>
#include <stdio.h>

main()
{
    char *cwd;
    if ((cwd = getcwd(NULL, 64)) == NULL)
    {
        perror("pwd");
        exit(2);
    }
    (void)printf("%s\n", cwd);
    return(0);
}
```

SEE ALSO
malloc(3C)

DIAGNOSTICS
Returns NULL with errno set if *size* is not large enough, or if an error occurs in a lower-level function.

getdate (3C)   (C Programming Language Utilities)   getdate (3C)

NAME
getdate – convert user format date and time

SYNOPSIS
#include <time.h>

struct tm *getdate (const char *string);

extern int getdate_err;

DESCRIPTION
getdate converts user-definable date and/or time specifications pointed to by *string* into a tm structure. The structure declaration is in the time.h header file [see also ctime(3C)].

User-supplied templates are used to parse and interpret the input string. The templates are text files created by the user and identified via the environment variable DATEMSK. Each line in the template represents an acceptable date and/or time specification using some of the same field descriptors as the ones used by the date command. The first line in the template that matches the input specification is used for interpretation and conversion into the internal time format. If successful, the function getdate returns a pointer to a tm structure; otherwise, it returns NULL and sets the global variable getdate_err to indicate the error.

The following field descriptors are supported:

%%	same as %
%a	abbreviated weekday name
%A	full weekday name
%b	abbreviated month name
%B	full month name
%c	locale's appropriate date and time representation
%d	day of month (01-31; the leading 0 is optional)
%e	same as %d
%D	date as %m/%d/%y
%h	abbreviated month name
%H	hour (00-23)
%I	hour (01-12)
%m	month number (01-12)
%M	minute (00-59)
%n	same as \n
%p	locale's equivalent of either AM or PM
%r	time as %I:%M:%S %p
%R	time as %H:%M
%S	seconds (00-59)
%t	insert a tab
%T	time as %H:%M:%S
%w	weekday number (0-6; Sunday = 0)
%x	locale's appropriate date representation

%X   locale's appropriate time representation
%y   year within century (00-99)
%Y   year as ccyy (for example, 1986)
%Z   time zone name or no characters if no time zone exists

The month and weekday names can consist of any combination of upper and lower case letters. The user can request that the input date or time specification be in a specific language by setting the categories LC_TIME and LC_CTYPE of setlocale.

The following example shows the possible contents of a template:

```
%m
%A %B %d %Y, %H:%M:%S
%A
%B
%m/%d/%y %I %p
%d,%m,%Y %H:%M
at %A the %dst of %B in %Y
run job at %I %p,%B %dnd
%A den %d. %B %Y %H.%M Uhr
```

The following are examples of valid input specifications for the above template:

```
getdate("10/1/87 4 PM")
getdate("Friday")
getdate("Friday September 19 1987, 10:30:30")
getdate("24,9,1986 10:30")
getdate("at monday the 1st of december in 1986")
getdate("run job at 3 PM, december %2nd")
```

If the LANG environment variable is set to german, the following is valid:

```
getdate("freitag den 10. oktober 1986 10.30 Uhr")
```

Local time and date specification are also supported. The following examples show how local date and time specification can be defined in the template.

Invocation	Line in Template
getdate("11/27/86")	%m/%d/%y
getdate("27.11.86")	%d.%m.%y
getdate("86-11-27")	%y-%m-%d
getdate("Friday 12:00:00")	%A %H:%M:%S

The following rules are applied for converting the input specification into the internal format:

If only the weekday is given, today is assumed if the given day is equal to the current day and next week if it is less.

If only the month is given, the current month is assumed if the given month is equal to the current month and next year if it is less and no year is given. (The first day of month is assumed if no day is given.)

If no hour, minute, and second are given, the current hour, minute, and second are assumed.

If no date is given, today is assumed if the given hour is greater than the current hour and tomorrow is assumed if it is less.

The following examples illustrate the above rules. Assume that the current date is Mon Sep 22 12:19:47 EDT 1986 and the LANG environment variable is not set.

Input	Line in Template	Date
Mon	%a	Mon Sep 22 12:19:48 EDT 1986
Sun	%a	Sun Sep 28 12:19:49 EDT 1986
Fri	%a	Fri Sep 26 12:19:49 EDT 1986
September	%B	Mon Sep 1 12:19:49 EDT 1986
January	%B	Thu Jan 1 12:19:49 EST 1987
December	%B	Mon Dec 1 12:19:49 EST 1986
Sep Mon	%b %a	Mon Sep 1 12:19:50 EDT 1986
Jan Fri	%b %a	Fri Jan 2 12:19:50 EST 1987
Dec Mon	%b %a	Mon Dec 1 12:19:50 EST 1986
Jan Wed 1989	%b %a %Y	Wed Jan 4 12:19:51 EST 1989
Fri 9	%a %H	Fri Sep 26 09:00:00 EDT 1986
Feb 10:30	%b %H:%S	Sun Feb 1 10:00:30 EST 1987
10:30	%H:%M	Tue Sep 23 10:30:00 EDT 1986
13:30	%H:%M	Mon Sep 22 13:30:00 EDT 1986

FILES

/usr/lib/locale/<locale>/LC_TIME   language specific printable files
/usr/lib/locale/<locale>/LC_CTYPE code set specific printable files

SEE ALSO

setlocale(3C), ctype(3C), environ(5)

DIAGNOSTICS

On failure getdate returns NULL and sets the variable getdate_err to indicate the error.

The following is a complete list of the getdate_err settings and their meanings.

1   The DATEMSK environment variable is null or undefined.
2   The template file cannot be opened for reading.
3   Failed to get file status information.
4   The template file is not a regular file.
5   An error is encountered while reading the template file.
6   malloc failed (not enough memory is available).
7   There is no line in the template that matches the input.
8   The input specification is invalid (for example, February 31).

NOTES

Subsequent calls to getdate alter the contents of getdate_err.

Dates before 1970 and after 2037 are illegal.

getdate makes explicit use of macros described in ctype(3C).

Previous implementations of getdate may return char *.

NAME
getdtablesize – get descriptor table size

SYNOPSIS
cc [*flag*...] *file* ... -lucb

long getdtablesize()

DESCRIPTION
Each process has a descriptor table which is guaranteed to have at least 20 slots. The entries in the descriptor table are numbered with small integers starting at 0. The call getdtablesize returns the current maximum size of this table by calling the getrlimit system call.

SEE ALSO
close(2), dup(2), getrlimit(2), and open(2) in the *Programmer's Reference Manual*

NAME
getenv – return value for environment name

SYNOPSIS
#include <stdlib.h>

char *getenv (const char *name);

DESCRIPTION
getenv searches the environment list [see environ(5)] for a string of the form *name=value* and, if the string is present, returns a pointer to the *value* in the current environment. Otherwise, it returns a null pointer.

SEE ALSO
exec(2), putenv(3C), environ(5)

getgrent(3C)   (C Programming Language Utilities)   **getgrent(3C)**

NAME
getgrent, getgrgid, getgrnam, setgrent, endgrent, fgetgrent – get group file entry

SYNOPSIS
#include <grp.h>

struct group *getgrent (void);

struct group *getgrgid (gid_t gid);

struct group *getgrnam (const char *name);

void setgrent (void);

void endgrent (void);

struct group *fgetgrent (FILE *f);

DESCRIPTION
getgrent, getgrgid, and getgrnam each return pointers to an object containing the broken-out fields of a line in the /etc/group file. Each line contains a "group" structure, defined in the grp.h header file with the following members:

```
char  *gr_name;    /* the name of the group */
char  *gr_passwd;  /* the encrypted group password */
gid_t gr_gid;      /* the numerical group ID */
char  **gr_mem;    /* vector of pointers to member names */
```

When first called, getgrent returns a pointer to the first group structure in the file; thereafter, it returns a pointer to the next group structure in the file; so, successive calls may be used to search the entire file. getgrgid searches from the beginning of the file until a numerical group id matching *gid* is found and returns a pointer to the particular structure in which it was found.

getgrnam searches from the beginning of the file until a group name matching *name* is found and returns a pointer to the particular structure in which it was found. If an end-of-file or an error is encountered on reading, these functions return a null pointer.

A call to setgrent has the effect of rewinding the group file to allow repeated searches. endgrent may be called to close the group file when processing is complete.

fgetgrent returns a pointer to the next group structure in the stream *f*, which matches the format of /etc/group.

FILES
/etc/group

SEE ALSO
getlogin(3C), getpwent(3C)
group(4) in the *System Administrator's Reference Manual*.

DIAGNOSTICS
getgrent, getgrid, getgrnam, and fgetgrent return a null pointer on EOF or error.

NOTES
All information is contained in a static area, so it must be copied if it is to be saved.

gethostent(3N)

NAME
gethostent, gethostbyaddr, gethostbyname, sethostent, endhostent − get network host entry

SYNOPSIS
```
#include <sys/types.h>
#include <sys/socket.h>
#include <netdb.h>
```

struct hostent *gethostent(void);

struct hostent *gethostbyaddr(char *addr, int len, int type);

struct hostent *gethostbyname(char *name);

int sethostent(int stayopen);

int endhostent(void);

DESCRIPTION
gethostent, gethostbyaddr, and gethostbyname each return a pointer to an object with the following structure containing the broken-out fields of a line in the network host data base, /etc/hosts. In the case of gethostbyaddr, *addr* is a pointer to the binary format address of length *len* (not a character string).

The hostent structure has the following members:

```
char  *h_name;       /* official name of host */
char  **h_aliases;   /* alias list */
int   h_addrtype;    /* host address type */
int   h_length;      /* length of address */
char  **h_addr_list; /* list of addresses from name server */
```

The members of this structure are:

h_name   Official name of the host.

h_aliases   A zero terminated array of alternate names for the host.

h_addrtype   The type of address being returned; currently always AF_INET.

h_length   The length, in bytes, of the address.

h_addr_list A pointer to a list of network addresses for the named host. Host addresses are returned in network byte order.

gethostent reads the next line of the file, opening the file if necessary.

sethostent opens and rewinds the file. If the *stayopen* flag is non-zero, the host data base will not be closed after each call to gethostent (either directly, or indirectly through one of the other gethost calls).

endhostent closes the file.

gethostbyname and gethostbyaddr sequentially search from the beginning of the file until a matching host name or host address is found, or until an EOF is encountered. Host addresses are supplied in network order.

gethostbyaddr takes a pointer to an address structure. This structure is unique to each type of address. For address of type AF_INET this is an in_addr structure. See netinet/in.h for the in_addr structure definition.

FILES
/etc/hosts

SEE ALSO
hosts(4)

DIAGNOSTICS
A NULL pointer is returned on an EOF or error.

NOTES
All information is contained in a static area so it must be copied if it is to be saved. Only the Internet address format is currently understood.

gethostid(3)   (BSD Compatibility Package)   gethostid(3)

NAME
    gethostid – get unique identifier of current host

SYNOPSIS
    cc [*flag*. . .] *file* . . . -lucb

    gethostid()

DESCRIPTION
    gethostid returns the 32-bit identifier for the current host, which should be unique across all hosts. This number is usually taken from the CPU board's ID PROM.

    This routine resides in libucb.

SEE ALSO
    hostid(1)
    sysinfo(2) in the *Programmer's Reference Manual*

NAME
gethostname, sethostname – get/set name of current host

SYNOPSIS
cc [*flag*...] *file* ... -lucb

```
int gethostname(name, namelen)
char *name;
int namelen;

int sethostname(name, namelen)
char *name;
int namelen;
```

DESCRIPTION
gethostname returns the standard host name for the current processor, as previously set by sethostname. The parameter *namelen* specifies the size of the array pointed to by *name*. The returned name is null-terminated unless insufficient space is provided.

sethostname sets the name of the host machine to be *name*, which has length *namelen*. This call is restricted to the privileged user and is normally used only when the system is bootstrapped.

RETURN VALUE
If the call succeeds a value of 0 is returned. If the call fails, then a value of -1 is returned and an error code is placed in the global location errno.

ERRORS
The following error may be returned by these calls:

EFAULT   The *name* or *namelen* parameter gave an invalid address.

EPERM   The caller was not the privileged user. Note: this error only applies to sethostname.

SEE ALSO
gethostid(3)

uname(2) in the *Programmer's Reference Manual*

NOTES
Host names are limited to MAXHOSTNAMELEN characters, currently 256. (See the param.h header file.)

getitimer(3C)

NAME
getitimer, setitimer - get/set value of interval timer

SYNOPSIS
```
#include <sys/time.h>
int getitimer(int which, struct itimerval *value);
int setitimer(int which, struct itimerval *value, struct itimerval
    *ovalue);
```

DESCRIPTION
The system provides each process with three interval timers, defined in sys/time.h. The getitimer call stores the current value of the timer specified by *which* into the structure pointed to by *value*. The setitimer call sets the value of the timer specified by *which* to the value specified in the structure pointed to by *value*, and if *ovalue* is not NULL, stores the previous value of the timer in the structure pointed to by *ovalue*.

A timer value is defined by the itimerval structure [see gettimeofday(3C) for the definition of timeval], which includes the following members:

```
struct timeval   it_interval;   /* timer interval */
struct timeval   it_value;      /* current value */
```

If it_value is non-zero, it indicates the time to the next timer expiration. If it_interval is non-zero, it specifies a value to be used in reloading it_value when the timer expires. Setting it_value to zero disables a timer, regardless of the value of it_interval. Setting it_interval to zero disables a timer after its next expiration (assuming it_value is non-zero).

Time values smaller than the resolution of the system clock are rounded up to this resolution.

The three timers are:

ITIMER_REAL   Decrements in real time. A SIGALRM signal is delivered when this timer expires.

ITIMER_VIRTUAL Decrements in process virtual time. It runs only when the process is executing. A SIGVTALRM signal is delivered when it expires.

ITIMER_PROF   Decrements both in process virtual time and when the system is running on behalf of the process. It is designed to be used by interpreters in statistically profiling the execution of interpreted programs. Each time the ITIMER_PROF timer expires, the SIGPROF signal is delivered. Because this signal may interrupt in-progress system calls, programs using this timer must be prepared to restart interrupted system calls.

SEE ALSO
alarm(2), gettimeofday(3C)

DIAGNOSTICS
If the calls succeed, a value of 0 is returned. If an error occurs, the value -1 is returned, and an error code is placed in the global variable errno.

Under the following conditions, the functions getitimer and setitimer fail and set errno to:

EINVAL   The specified number of seconds is greater than 100,000,000, the number of microseconds is greater than or equal to 1,000,000, or the *which* parameter is unrecognized.

NOTES

The microseconds field should not be equal to or greater than one second.

setitimer is independent of the alarm system call.

Do not use setitimer with the sleep routine. A sleep following a setitimer wipes out knowledge of the user signal handler.

getlogin(3C) (C Development Set) **getlogin(3C)**

NAME
getlogin – get login name

SYNOPSIS
#include <stdlib.h>

char *getlogin (void);

DESCRIPTION
getlogin returns a pointer to the login name as found in /var/adm/utmp. It may be used in conjunction with getpwnam to locate the correct password file entry when the same user id is shared by several login names.

If getlogin is called within a process that is not attached to a terminal, it returns a null pointer. The correct procedure for determining the login name is to call cuserid, or to call getlogin and if it fails to call getpwuid.

FILES
/var/adm/utmp

SEE ALSO
cuserid(3S), getgrent(3C), getpwent(3C), utmp(4)

DIAGNOSTICS
Returns a null pointer if the login name is not found.

NOTES
The return values point to static data whose content is overwritten by each call.

getmntent(3C)

NAME
getmntent, getmntany – get mnttab file entry

SYNOPSIS
#include <stdio.h>
#include <sys/mnttab.h>

int getmntent (FILE *fp, struct mnttab *mp);

int getmntany (FILE *fp, struct mnttab *mp, struct mnttab *mpref);

DESCRIPTION
getmntent and getmntany each fill in the structure pointed to by *mp* with the broken-out fields of a line in the /etc/mnttab file. Each line in the file contains a mnttab structure, declared in the sys/mnttab.h header file:

```
struct mnttab {
    char *mnt_special;
    char *mnt_mountp;
    char *mnt_fstype;
    char *mnt_mntopts;
    char *mnt_time;
};
```

The fields have meanings described in mnttab(4).

getmntent returns a pointer to the next mnttab structure in the file; so successive calls can be used to search the entire file. getmntany searches the file referenced by *fp* until a match is found between a line in the file and *mpref*. *mpref* matches the line if all non-null entries in *mpref* match the corresponding fields in the file. Note that these routines do not open, close, or rewind the file.

FILES
/etc/mnttab

SEE ALSO
mnttab(4)

DIAGNOSTICS
If the next entry is successfully read by getmntent or a match is found with getmntany, 0 is returned. If an end-of-file is encountered on reading, these functions return −1. If an error is encountered, a value greater than 0 is returned. The possible error values are:

MNT_TOOLONG	A line in the file exceeded the internal buffer size of MNT_LINE_MAX.
MNT_TOOMANY	A line in the file contains too many fields.
MNT_TOOFEW	A line in the file contains too few fields.

NOTES
The members of the mnttab structure point to information contained in a static area, so it must be copied if it is to be saved.

NAME

getnetconfig – get network configuration database entry

SYNOPSIS

```
#include <netconfig.h>
```

void *setnetconfig(void);

struct netconfig *getnetconfig(void *handlep);

int endnetconfig(void *handlep);

struct netconfig *getnetconfigent(char *netid);

void freenetconfigent(struct netconfig *netconfigp);

DESCRIPTION

The five library routines described on this page are part of the UNIX System V Network Selection component. They provide application access to the system network configuration database, /etc/netconfig. In addition to the netconfig database and the routines for accessing it, Network Selection includes the environment variable NETPATH [see environ(5)] and the NETPATH access routines described in getnetpath(3N).

A call to setnetconfig has the effect of "binding" or "rewinding" the netconfig database. setnetconfig must be called before the first call to getnetconfig and may be called at any other time. setnetconfig need *not* be called before a call to getnetconfigent. setnetconfig returns a unique handle to be used by getnetconfig.

When first called, getnetconfig returns a pointer to the current entry in the netconfig database, formatted as a netconfig structure. getnetconfig can thus be used to search the entire netconfig file. getnetconfig returns NULL at end of file.

endnetconfig should be called when processing is complete to release resources for reuse. Programmers should be aware, however, that the last call to endnetconfig frees all memory allocated by getnetconfig for the struct netconfig data structure. endnetconfig may not be called before setnetconfig. endnetconfig returns 0 on success and −1 on failure (for example, if setnetconfig was not called previously).

getnetconfigent returns a pointer to the netconfig structure corresponding to *netid*. It returns NULL if *netid* is invalid (that is, does not name an entry in the netconfig database). It returns NULL and sets errno in case of failure (for example, if setnetconfig was not called previously).

freenetconfigent frees the netconfig structure pointed to by *netconfigp*, previously returned by getnetconfigent.

SEE ALSO

netconfig(4), getnetpath(3N)
environ(5) in the *Programmer's Reference Manual*
Programmer's Guide: Networking Interfaces
System Administrator's Guide

NAME
getnetent, getnetbyaddr, getnetbyname, setnetent, endnetent – get network entry

SYNOPSIS
#include <netdb.h>

struct netent *getnetent(void);

struct netent *getnetbyname(char *name);

struct netent *getnetbyaddr(long net, int type);

int setnetent(int stayopen);

int endnetent(void);

DESCRIPTION
getnetent, getnetbyname, and getnetbyaddr each return a pointer to an object with the following structure containing the broken-out fields of a line in the network data base, /etc/networks.

The structure netent include the following members:

```
char     *n_name;          /* official name of net */
char     **n_aliases;      /* alias list */
int      n_addrtype;       /* net type */
unsigned long n_net;       /* network number */
```

The members of this structure are:

n_name   The official name of the network.

n_aliases   A zero terminated list of alternate names for the network.

n_addrtype   The type of the network number returned; currently only AF_INET.

n_net   The network number. Network numbers are returned in machine byte order.

getnetent reads the next line of the file, opening the file if necessary.

setnetent opens and rewinds the file. If the *stayopen* flag is non-zero, the net data base will not be closed after each call to getnetent (either directly, or indirectly through one of the other getnet calls).

endnetent closes the file.

getnetbyname and getnetbyaddr sequentially search from the beginning of the file until a matching net name or net address and type is found, or until EOF is encountered. Network numbers are supplied in host order.

FILES
/etc/networks

SEE ALSO
networks(4)

DIAGNOSTICS

A NULL pointer is returned on EOF or error.

NOTES

All information is contained in a static area so it must be copied if it is to be saved. Only Internet network numbers are currently understood.

NAME

getnetpath – get netconfig entry corresponding to NETPATH component

SYNOPSIS

```
#include <netconfig.h>

void *setnetpath(void);
struct netconfig *getnetpath(void *handlep);
int endnetpath(void *handlep);
```

DESCRIPTION

The three routines described on this page are part of the UNIX System V Network Selection component. They provide application access to the system network configuration database, /etc/netconfig, as it is "filtered" by the NETPATH environment variable [see environ(5)]. Network Selection also includes routines that access the network configuration database directly [see getnetconfig(3N)].

A call to setnetpath "binds" or "rewinds" NETPATH. setnetpath must be called before the first call to getnetpath and may be called at any other time. It returns a handle that is used by getnetpath. setnetpath will fail if the netconfig database is not present. If NETPATH is unset, setnetpath returns the number of "visible" networks in the netconfig file. The set of visible networks constitutes a default NETPATH.

When first called, getnetpath returns a pointer to the netconfig database entry corresponding to the first valid NETPATH component. The netconfig entry is formatted as a netconfig structure. On each subsequent call, getnetpath returns a pointer to the netconfig entry that corresponds to the next valid NETPATH component. getnetpath can thus be used to search the netconfig database for all networks included in the NETPATH variable. When NETPATH has been exhausted, getnetpath returns NULL.

getnetpath silently ignores invalid NETPATH components. A NETPATH component is invalid if there is no corresponding entry in the netconfig database.

If the NETPATH variable is unset, getnetpath behaves as if NETPATH were set to the sequence of "default" or "visible" networks in the netconfig database, in the order in which they are listed.

endnetpath may be called to "unbind" NETPATH when processing is complete, releasing resources for reuse. Programmer's should be aware, however, that endnetpath frees all memory allocated by setnetpath. endnetpath returns 0 on success and –1 on failure (for example, if setnetpath was not called previously).

SEE ALSO

netconfig(4), getnetconfig(3N)
environ(5) in the *Programmer's Reference Manual*
Programmer's Guide: Networking Interfaces
System Administrator's Guide

getopt(3C) (C Programming Language Utilities) getopt(3C)

NAME
getopt – get option letter from argument vector

SYNOPSIS
#include <stdlib.h>

int getopt (int argc, char * const *argv, const char *optstring);

extern char *optarg;

extern int optind, opterr, optopt;

DESCRIPTION
getopt returns the next option letter in *argv* that matches a letter in *optstring*. It supports all the rules of the command syntax standard [see intro(1)]. Since all new commands are intended to adhere to the command syntax standard, they should use getopts(1), getopt(3C), or getsubopts(3C) to parse positional parameters and check for options that are legal for that command.

optstring must contain the option letters the command using getopt will recognize; if a letter is followed by a colon, the option is expected to have an argument, or group of arguments, which may be separated from it by white space. *optarg* is set to point to the start of the option argument on return from getopt.

getopt places in *optind* the *argv* index of the next argument to be processed. *optind* is external and is initialized to 1 before the first call to getopt. When all options have been processed (that is, up to the first non-option argument), getopt returns EOF. The special option "--" (two hyphens) may be used to delimit the end of the options; when it is encountered, EOF is returned and "--" is skipped. This is useful in delimiting non-option arguments that begin with "-" (hyphen).

EXAMPLE
The following code fragment shows how one might process the arguments for a command that can take the mutually exclusive options a and b, and the option o, which requires an argument:

```
#include <stdlib.h>
#include <stdio.h>

main (int argc, char **argv)
{
    int c;
    extern char *optarg;
    extern int optind;
    int aflg = 0;
    int bflg = 0;
    int errflg = 0;
    char *ofile = NULL;

    while ((c = getopt(argc, argv, "abo:")) != EOF)
        switch (c) {
        case 'a':
            if (bflg)
                errflg++;
```

```
                        else
                                aflg++;
                        break;
                case 'b':
                        if (aflg)
                                errflg++;
                        else
                                bflg++;
                        break;
                case 'o':
                        ofile = optarg;
                        (void)printf("ofile = %s\n", ofile);
                        break;
                case '?':
                        errflg++;
                }
        if (errflg) {
                (void)fprintf(stderr,
                        "usage: cmd [-a|-b] [-o<file>] files...\n");
                exit (2);
        }
        for ( ; optind < argc; optind++)
                (void)printf("%s\n", argv[optind]);
        return 0;
}
```

SEE ALSO

getsubopt(3C)
getopts(1), intro(1) in the *User's Reference Manual*

DIAGNOSTICS

getopt prints an error message on the standard error and returns a "?" (question mark) when it encounters an option letter not included in *optstring* or no argument after an option that expects one. This error message may be disabled by setting opterr to 0. The value of the character that caused the error is in optopt.

NOTES

The library routine getopt does not fully check for mandatory arguments. That is, given an option string a:b and the input -a -b, getopt assumes that -b is the mandatory argument to the option -a and not that -a is missing a mandatory argument.

It is a violation of the command syntax standard [see intro(1)] for options with arguments to be grouped with other options, as in cmd -aboxxx file, where a and b are options, o is an option that requires an argument, and xxx is the argument to o. Although this syntax is permitted in the current implementation, it should not be used because it may not be supported in future releases. The correct syntax is cmd -ab -oxxx file.

getpagesize(3)   (BSD Compatibility Package)   **getpagesize(3)**

NAME
    getpagesize – get system page size

SYNOPSIS
    cc [*flag*. . .] *file* . . . -lucb

    int getpagesize(VOID);

DESCRIPTION
    getpagesize returns the number of bytes in a page. Page granularity is the granularity of many of the memory management calls.

    The page size is a system page size and need not be the same as the underlying hardware page size.

SEE ALSO
    pagesize(1)
    brk(2) in the *Programmer's Reference Manual*

NAME

getpass – read a password

SYNOPSIS

```
#include <stdlib.h>

char *getpass (const char *prompt);
```

DESCRIPTION

getpass reads up to a newline or EOF from the file /dev/tty, after prompting on the standard error output with the null-terminated string *prompt* and disabling echoing. A pointer is returned to a null-terminated string of at most 8 characters. If /dev/tty cannot be opened, a null pointer is returned. An interrupt will terminate input and send an interrupt signal to the calling program before returning.

FILES

/dev/tty

NOTE

The return value points to static data whose content is overwritten by each call.

getpeername(3N)

NAME
getpeername – get name of connected peer

SYNOPSIS
    int getpeername(int s, caddr_t name, int *namelen);

DESCRIPTION
getpeername returns the name of the peer connected to socket *s*. The int pointed to by the *namelen* parameter should be initialized to indicate the amount of space pointed to by *name*. On return it contains the actual size of the name returned (in bytes). The name is truncated if the buffer provided is too small.

RETURN VALUE
0 is returned if the call succeeds, −1 if it fails.

ERRORS
The call succeeds unless:

EBADF	The argument *s* is not a valid descriptor.
ENOTSOCK	The argument *s* is a file, not a socket.
ENOTCONN	The socket is not connected.
ENOMEM	There was insufficient user memory for the operation to complete.
ENOSR	There were insufficient STREAMS resources available for the operation to complete.

SEE ALSO
accept(3N), bind(3N), getsockname(3N), socket(3N)

NOTES
The type of address structure passed to accept depends on the address family. UNIX domain sockets (address family AF_UNIX) require a socketaddr_un structure as defined in sys/un.h; Internet domain sockets (address family AF_INET) require a sockaddr_in structure as defined in netinet/in.h. Other address families may require other structures. Use the structure appropriate to the address family; cast the structure address to a generic caddr_t in the call to getpeername and pass the size of the structure in the *namelen* argument.

See "The Sockets Interface" section in the *Programmer's Guide: Networking Interfaces* for details.

NAME
getpriority, setpriority – get/set program scheduling priority

SYNOPSIS
cc [*flag*. . .] *file* . . . -lucb

#include <sys/time.h>
#include <sys/resource.h>

int getpriority(*which, who*)
int *which, who;*

int setpriority(*which, who, prio*)
int *which, who, prio;*

DESCRIPTION
The scheduling priority of the process, process group, or user, as indicated by *which* and *who* is obtained with getpriority and set with setpriority The default priority is 0; lower priorities cause more favorable scheduling.

which is one of PRIO_PROCESS, PRIO_PGRP, or PRIO_USER, and *who* is interpreted relative to *which* (a process identifier for PRIO_PROCESS, process group identifier for PRIO_PGRP, and a user ID for PRIO_USER). A zero value of *who* denotes the current process, process group, or user.

getpriority returns the highest priority (lowest numerical value) enjoyed by any of the specified processes. setpriority sets the priorities of all of the specified processes to the value specified by *prio*. If *prio* is less than −20, a value of −20 is used; if it is greater than 20, a value of 20 is used. Only the privileged user may lower priorities.

RETURN VALUE
Since getpriority can legitimately return the value −1, it is necessary to clear the external variable errno prior to the call, then check it afterward to determine if a −1 is an error or a legitimate value. The setpriority call returns 0 if there is no error, or −1 if there is.

ERRORS
getpriority and setpriority may return one of the following errors:

ESRCH   No process was located using the *which* and *who* values specified.

EINVAL *which* was not one of PRIO_PROCESS, PRIO_PGRP, or PRIO_USER.

In addition to the errors indicated above, setpriority may fail with one of the following errors returned:

EPERM   A process was located, but one of the following is true:

- Neither its effective nor real user ID matched the effective user ID of the caller, and neither the effective nor the real user ID of the process executing the setpriority was the privileged user.
- The call to getpriority would have changed a process' priority to a value lower than its current value, and the effective user ID of the process executing the call was not that of the privileged user.

SEE ALSO
>renice(1M)
>
>nice(1) in the *User's Reference Manual*
>fork(2) in the *Programmer's Reference Manual*

NOTES
>It is not possible for the process executing setpriority to lower any other process down to its current priority, without requiring privileged user privileges.

NAME

getprotoent, getprotobynumber, getprotobyname, setprotoent, endprotoent – get protocol entry

SYNOPSIS

```
#include <netdb.h>
```

struct protoent *getprotoent(void);

struct protoent *getprotobyname(char *name);

struct protoent *getprotobynumber(int proto);

int setprotoent(int stayopen);

int endprotoent(void);

DESCRIPTION

getprotoent, getprotobyname, and getprotobynumber each return a pointer to an object with the following structure containing the broken-out fields of a line in the network protocol data base, /etc/protocols.

The protoent structure include the following members:

```
char    *p_name;        /* official name of protocol */
char    **p_aliases;    /* alias list */
int     p_proto;        /* protocol number */
```

The members of this structure are:

> *p_name*   the official name of the protocol
>
> *p_aliases*   a zero terminated list of alternate names for the protocol
>
> *p_proto*   the protocol number

getprotoent reads the next line of the file, opening the file if necessary.

setprotoent opens and rewinds the file. If the *stayopen* flag is non-zero, the net data base will not be closed after each call to getprotoent (either directly, or indirectly through one of the other getproto calls).

endprotoent closes the file.

getprotobyname and getprotobynumber sequentially search from the beginning of the file until a matching protocol name or protocol number is found, or until an EOF is encountered.

FILES

/etc/protocols

SEE ALSO

protocols(4)

DIAGNOSTICS

A NULL pointer is returned on an EOF or error.

All information is contained in a static area so it must be copied if it is to be saved. Only the Internet protocols are currently understood.

getpw(3C) (C Development Set) **getpw(3C)**

NAME
getpw – get name from UID

SYNOPSIS
#include <stdlib.h>

int getpw (uid_t uid, char *buf);

DESCRIPTION
getpw searches the password file for a user id number that equals *uid*, copies the line of the password file in which *uid* was found into the array pointed to by *buf*, and returns 0. getpw returns non-zero if *uid* cannot be found.

This routine is included only for compatibility with prior systems and should not be used; see getpwent(3C) for routines to use instead.

FILES
/etc/passwd

SEE ALSO
getpwent(3C)
passwd(4) in the *System Administrator's Reference Manual*

DIAGNOSTICS
getpw returns non-zero on error.

getpwent(3C)

NAME
getpwent, getpwuid, getpwnam, setpwent, endpwent, fgetpwent – manipulate password file entry

SYNOPSIS
```
#include <pwd.h>
```
struct passwd *getpwent (void);

struct passwd *getpwuid (uid_t uid);

struct passwd *getpwnam (const char *name);

void setpwent (void);

void endpwent (void);

struct passwd *fgetpwent (FILE *f);

DESCRIPTION
getpwent, getpwuid, and getpwnam each returns a pointer to an object with the following structure containing the broken-out fields of a line in the /etc/passwd file. Each line in the file contains a passwd structure, declared in the pwd.h header file:

```
struct passwd {
        char    *pw_name;
        char    *pw_passwd;
        uid_t pw_uid;
        gid_t pw_gid;
        char    *pw_age;
        char    *pw_comment;
        char    *pw_gecos;
        char    *pw_dir;
        char    *pw_shell;
};
```

getpwent when first called returns a pointer to the first passwd structure in the file; thereafter, it returns a pointer to the next passwd structure in the file; so successive calls can be used to search the entire file. getpwuid searches from the beginning of the file until a numerical user id matching *uid* is found and returns a pointer to the particular structure in which it was found. getpwnam searches from the beginning of the file until a login name matching *name* is found, and returns a pointer to the particular structure in which it was found. If an end-of-file or an error is encountered on reading, these functions return a null pointer.

A call to setpwent has the effect of rewinding the password file to allow repeated searches. endpwent may be called to close the password file when processing is complete.

fgetpwent returns a pointer to the next passwd structure in the stream *f*, which matches the format of /etc/passwd.

FILES
/etc/passwd

SEE ALSO
getlogin(3C), getgrent(3C)
passwd(4) in the *System Administrator's Reference Manual*

DIAGNOSTICS
getpwent, getpwnid, getpwnam, and fgetpwent return a null pointer on EOF or error.

NOTES
All information is contained in a static area, so it must be copied if it is to be saved.

NAME

getrusage – get information about resource utilization

SYNOPSIS

cc [*flag*. . .] *file* . . . -lucb

#include <sys/time.h>
#include <sys/resource.h>

getrusage(who, rusage)
int who;
struct rusage *rusage;

DESCRIPTION

getrusage returns information about the resources utilized by the current process, or all its terminated child processes. The interpretation for some values reported, such as ru_idrss, are dependent on the clock tick interval. This interval is an implementation dependent value.

The who parameter is one of RUSAGE_SELF or RUSAGE_CHILDREN. The buffer to which *rusage* points will be filled in with the following structure:

```
struct      rusage {
    struct timeval ru_utime;    /* user time used */
    struct timeval ru_stime;    /* system time used */
    int     ru_maxrss;          /* maximum resident set size */
    int     ru_ixrss;           /* currently 0 */
    int     ru_idrss;           /* integral resident set size */
    int     ru_isrss;           /* currently 0 */
    int     ru_minflt;          /* page faults not requiring physical I/O */
    int     ru_majflt;          /* page faults requiring physical I/O */
    int     ru_nswap;           /* swaps */
    int     ru_inblock;         /* block input operations */
    int     ru_oublock;         /* block output operations */
    int     ru_msgsnd;          /* messages sent */
    int     ru_msgrcv;          /* messages received */
    int     ru_nsignals;        /* signals received */
    int     ru_nvcsw;           /* voluntary context switches */
    int     ru_nivcsw;          /* involuntary context switches */
};
```

The fields are interpreted as follows:

ru_utime   The total amount of time spent executing in user mode. Time is given in seconds and microseconds.

ru_stime   The total amount of time spent executing in system mode. Time is given in seconds and microseconds.

ru_maxrss   The maximum resident set size. Size is given in pages (the size of a page, in bytes, is given by the getpagesize(3) system call). Also, see NOTES.

ru_ixrss	Currently returns 0.
ru_idrss	An integral value indicating the amount of memory in use by a process while the process is running. This value is the sum of the resident set sizes of the process running when a clock tick occurs. The value is given in pages times clock ticks. Note: it does not take sharing into account. Also, see NOTES.
ru_isrss	Currently returns 0.
ru_minflt	The number of page faults serviced which did not require any physical I/O activity. Also, see NOTES.
ru_majflt	The number of page faults serviced which required physical I/O activity. This could include page ahead operations by the kernel. Also, see NOTES.
ru_nswap	The number of times a process was swapped out of main memory.
ru_inblock	The number of times the file system had to perform input in servicing a read(2) request.
ru_oublock	The number of times the file system had to perform output in servicing a write(2) request.
ru_msgsnd	The number of messages sent over sockets.
ru_msgrcv	The number of messages received from sockets.
ru_nsignals	The number of signals delivered.
ru_nvcsw	The number of times a context switch resulted due to a process voluntarily giving up the processor before its time slice was completed (usually to await availability of a resource).
ru_nivcsw	The number of times a context switch resulted due to a higher priority process becoming runnable or because the current process exceeded its time slice.

RETURN VALUE

If successful, the value of the appropriate structure is filled in, and 0 is returned. If the call fails, a −1 is returned.

ERRORS

getrusage will fail if:

EINVAL	The who parameter is not a valid value.
EFAULT	The address specified by the rusage argument is not in a valid portion of the process's address space.

SEE ALSO

sar(1M) in the *System Administrator's Reference Manual*
gettimeofday(3), read(2), times(2), wait(3), write(2) in the *Programmer's Reference Manual*

NOTES

Only the *timeval* fields of struct rusage are supported in this implementation.

The numbers ru_inblock and ru_oublock account only for real I/O, and are approximate measures at best. Data supplied by the caching mechanism is charged only to the first process to read and the last process to write the data.

The way resident set size is calculated is an approximation, and could misrepresent the true resident set size.

Page faults can be generated from a variety of sources and for a variety of reasons. The customary cause for a page fault is a direct reference by the program to a page which is not in memory. Now, however, the kernel can generate page faults on behalf of the user, for example, servicing read(2) and write(2) system calls. Also, a page fault can be caused by an absent hardware translation to a page, even though the page is in physical memory.

In addition to hardware detected page faults, the kernel may cause pseudo page faults in order to perform some housekeeping. For example, the kernel may generate page faults, even if the pages exist in physical memory, in order to lock down pages involved in a raw I/O request.

By definition, *major* page faults require physical I/O, while *minor* page faults do not require physical I/O. For example, reclaiming the page from the free list would avoid I/O and generate a minor page fault. More commonly, minor page faults occur during process startup as references to pages which are already in memory. For example, if an address space faults on some hot executable or shared library, this results in a minor page fault for the address space. Also, any one doing a read(2) or write(2) to something that is in the page cache will get a minor page fault(s) as well.

There is no way to obtain information about a child process which has not yet terminated.

NAME

gets, fgets – get a string from a stream

SYNOPSIS

#include <stdio.h>

char *gets (char *s);

char *fgets (char *s, int n, FILE *stream);

DESCRIPTION

gets reads characters from the standard input stream [see intro(3)], stdin, into the array pointed to by *s*, until a newline character is read or an end-of-file condition is encountered. The newline character is discarded and the string is terminated with a null character.

fgets reads characters from the *stream* into the array pointed to by *s*, until $n-1$ characters are read, or a newline character is read and transferred to *s*, or an end-of-file condition is encountered. The string is then terminated with a null character.

When using gets, if the length of an input line exceeds the size of *s*, indeterminate behavior may result. For this reason, it is strongly recommended that gets be avoided in favor of fgets.

SEE ALSO

lseek(2), read(2), ferror(3S), fopen(3S), fread(3S), getc(3S), scanf(3S), stdio(3S), ungetc(3S)

DIAGNOSTICS

If end-of-file is encountered and no characters have been read, no characters are transferred to *s* and a null pointer is returned. If a read error occurs, such as trying to use these functions on a file that has not been opened for reading, a null pointer is returned and the error indicator for the stream is set. If end-of-file is encountered, the EOF indicator for the stream is set. Otherwise *s* is returned.

getservent(3N)   **getservent(3N)**

NAME
getservent, getservbyport, getservbyname, setservent, endservent – get service entry

SYNOPSIS
#include <netdb.h>

struct servent *getservent(void);

struct servent *getservbyname(char *name, char *proto);

struct servent *getservbyport(int port, char *proto);

int setservent(int stayopen);

int endservent(void);

DESCRIPTION
getservent, *getservbyname*, and *getservbyport* each return a pointer to an object with the following structure containing the broken-out fields of a line in the network services data base, /etc/services.

The servent structure includes the following members:

```
char    *s_name;        /* official name of service */
char    **s_aliases;    /* alias list */
int     s_port;         /* port service resides at */
char    *s_proto;       /* protocol to use */
```

The members of this structure are:

s_name   The official name of the service.

s_aliases A zero terminated list of alternate names for the service.

s_port   The port number at which the service resides. Port numbers are returned in network short byte order.

s_proto   The name of the protocol to use when contacting the service.

getservent reads the next line of the file, opening the file if necessary.

setservent opens and rewinds the file. If the *stayopen* flag is non-zero, the net data base will not be closed after each call to getservent (either directly, or indirectly through one of the other getserv calls).

endservent closes the file.

getservbyname and getservbyport sequentially search from the beginning of the file until a matching protocol name or port number is found, or until EOF is encountered. If a protocol name is also supplied (non-NULL), searches must also match the protocol.

FILES
/etc/services

SEE ALSO
getprotoent(3N), services(4)

getservent(3N) getservent(3N)

DIAGNOSTICS
A NULL pointer is returned on EOF or error.

All information is contained in a static area so it must be copied if it is to be saved. Expecting port numbers to fit in a 32 bit quantity is probably naive.

NAME

getsockname – get socket name

SYNOPSIS

    int getsockname(int s, caddr_t name, int *namelen);

DESCRIPTION

getsockname returns the current *name* for socket *s*. The *namelen* parameter should be initialized to indicate the amount of space pointed to by *name*. On return it contains the actual size of the *name* returned (in bytes).

RETURN VALUE

0 is returned if the call succeeds; −1 if it fails.

ERRORS

The call succeeds unless:

EBADF	The argument *s* is not a valid descriptor.
ENOTSOCK	The argument *s* is a file, not a socket.
ENOMEM	There was insufficient user memory for the operation to complete.
ENOSR	There were insufficient STREAMS resources available for the operation to complete.

SEE ALSO

bind(3N), getpeername(3N), socket(3N)

NOTES

The type of address structure passed to accept depends on the address family. UNIX domain sockets (address family AF_UNIX) require a socketaddr_un structure as defined in sys/un.h; Internet domain sockets (address family AF_INET) require a sockaddr_in structure as defined in netinet/in.h. Other address families may require other structures. Use the structure appropriate to the address family; cast the structure address to a generic caddr_t in the call to getsockname and pass the size of the structure in the *namelen* argument.

See "The Sockets Interface" section in the *Programmer's Guide: Networking Interfaces* for details.

The functionality of getsockname is provided by t_getname in TLI. t_getname will be replaced in the next release of System V.

The syntax for t_getname is as follows:

    t_getname(int fd, struct netbuf *name, register int type);

If *type* is equal to LOCALNAME, then the address of the local side of the connection is returned; otherwise, the address of the remote side is returned.

NAME

getsockopt, setsockopt – get and set options on sockets

SYNOPSIS

#include <sys/types.h>
#include <sys/socket.h>

int getsockopt(int s, int level, int optname, char *optval,
    int *optlen);

int setsockopt(int s, int level, int optname, char *optval,
    int optlen);

DESCRIPTION

getsockopt and setsockopt manipulate *options* associated with a socket. Options may exist at multiple protocol levels; they are always present at the uppermost socket level.

When manipulating socket options, the level at which the option resides and the name of the option must be specified. To manipulate options at the socket level, *level* is specified as SOL_SOCKET. To manipulate options at any other level, *level* is the protocol number of the protocol that controls the option. For example, to indicate that an option is to be interpreted by the TCP protocol, *level* is set to the TCP protocol number [see getprotoent(3N)].

The parameters *optval* and *optlen* are used to access option values for setsockopt. For getsockopt, they identify a buffer in which the value(s) for the requested option(s) are to be returned. For getsockopt, *optlen* is a value-result parameter, initially containing the size of the buffer pointed to by *optval*, and modified on return to indicate the actual size of the value returned. If no option value is to be supplied or returned, a 0 *optval* may be supplied.

optname and any specified options are passed uninterpreted to the appropriate protocol module for interpretation. The include file sys/socket.h contains definitions for the socket-level options described below. Options at other protocol levels vary in format and name.

Most socket-level options take an int for *optval*. For setsockopt, the *optval* parameter should be non-zero to enable a boolean option, or zero if the option is to be disabled. SO_LINGER uses a struct linger parameter that specifies the desired state of the option and the linger interval (see below). struct linger is defined in /usr/include/sys/socket.h.

The following options are recognized at the socket level. Except as noted, each may be examined with getsockopt and set with setsockopt.

SO_DEBUG	toggle recording of debugging information
SO_REUSEADDR	toggle local address reuse
SO_KEEPALIVE	toggle keep connections alive
SO_DONTROUTE	toggle routing bypass for outgoing messages
SO_LINGER	linger on close if data is present
SO_BROADCAST	toggle permission to transmit broadcast messages

SO_OOBINLINE	toggle reception of out-of-band data in band
SO_SNDBUF	set buffer size for output
SO_RCVBUF	set buffer size for input
SO_TYPE	get the type of the socket (get only)
SO_ERROR	get and clear error on the socket (get only)

SO_DEBUG enables debugging in the underlying protocol modules. SO_REUSEADDR indicates that the rules used in validating addresses supplied in a bind call should allow reuse of local addresses. SO_KEEPALIVE enables the periodic transmission of messages on a connected socket. If the connected party fails to respond to these messages, the connection is considered broken and processes using the socket are notified using a SIGPIPE signal. SO_DONTROUTE indicates that outgoing messages should bypass the standard routing facilities. Instead, messages are directed to the appropriate network interface according to the network portion of the destination address.

SO_LINGER controls the action taken when unsent messages are queued on a socket and a close is performed. If the socket promises reliable delivery of data and SO_LINGER is set, the system will block the process on the close attempt until it is able to transmit the data or until it decides it is unable to deliver the information (a timeout period, termed the linger interval, is specified in the setsockopt call when SO_LINGER is requested). If SO_LINGER is disabled and a close is issued, the system will process the close() in a manner that allows the process to continue as quickly as possible.

The option SO_BROADCAST requests permission to send broadcast datagrams on the socket. With protocols that support out-of-band data, the SO_OOBINLINE option requests that out-of-band data be placed in the normal data input queue as received; it will then be accessible with recv or read calls without the MSG_OOB flag. SO_SNDBUF and SO_RCVBUF are options that adjust the normal buffer sizes allocated for output and input buffers, respectively. The buffer size may be increased for high-volume connections or may be decreased to limit the possible backlog of incoming data. The system places an absolute limit on these values. Finally, SO_TYPE and SO_ERROR are options used only with getsockopt. SO_TYPE returns the type of the socket (for example, SOCK_STREAM). It is useful for servers that inherit sockets on startup. SO_ERROR returns any pending error on the socket and clears the error status. It may be used to check for asynchronous errors on connected datagram sockets or for other asynchronous errors.

RETURN VALUE
A 0 is returned if the call succeeds, -1 if it fails.

ERRORS
The call succeeds unless:

EBADF	The argument s is not a valid descriptor.
ENOTSOCK	The argument s is a file, not a socket.
ENOPROTOOPT	The option is unknown at the level indicated.
ENOMEM	There was insufficient user memory available for the operation to complete.

getsockopt(3N)

ENOSR   There were insufficient STREAMS resources available for the operation to complete.

SEE ALSO
socket(3N), getprotoent(3N)
close(2), ioctl(2), read(2) in the *Programmer's Reference Manual*

getspent(3C)

NAME
getspent, getspnam, setspent, endspent, fgetspent, lckpwdf, ulckpwdf – manipulate shadow password file entry

SYNOPSIS
```
#include <shadow.h>
```
struct spwd *getspent (void);

struct spwd *getspnam (const char *name);

int lckpwdf (void);

int ulckpwdf (void);

void setspent (void);

void endspent (void);

struct spwd *fgetspent (FILE *fp);

DESCRIPTION
The getspent and getspnam routines each return a pointer to an object with the following structure containing the broken-out fields of a line in the /etc/shadow file. Each line in the file contains a "shadow password" structure, declared in the shadow.h header file:

```
struct spwd{
    char *sp_namp;
    char *sp_pwdp;
    long sp_lstchg;
    long sp_min;
    long sp_max;
    long sp_warn;
    long sp_inact;
    long sp_expire;
    unsigned long   sp_flag;
};
```

The getspent routine when first called returns a pointer to the first spwd structure in the file; thereafter, it returns a pointer to the next spwd structure in the file; so successive calls can be used to search the entire file. The getspnam routine searches from the beginning of the file until a login name matching *name* is found, and returns a pointer to the particular structure in which it was found. The getspent and getspnam routines populate the sp_min, sp_max, sp_lstchg, sp_warn, sp_inact, sp_expire, or sp_flag field with −1 if the corresponding field in /etc/shadow is empty. If an end-of-file or an error is encountered on reading, or there is a format error in the file, these functions return a null pointer and set errno to EINVAL.

/etc/.pwd.lock is the lock file. It is used to coordinate modification access to the password files /etc/passwd and /etc/shadow. lckpwdf and ulckpwdf are routines that are used to gain modification access to the password files, through the lock file. A process first uses lckpwdf to lock the lock file, thereby gaining exclusive rights to modify the /etc/passwd or /etc/shadow password file. Upon completing modifications, a process should release the lock on the lock file via `ulckpwdf`. This mechanism prevents simultaneous modification of the password files.

`lckpwdf` attempts to lock the file /etc/.pwd.lock within 15 seconds. If unsuccessful, for example, /etc/.pwd.lock is already locked, it returns −1. If successful, a return code other than −1 is returned.

`ulckpwdf` attempts to unlock the file /etc/.pwd.lock. If unsuccessful, for example, /etc/.pwd.lock is already unlocked, it returns −1. If successful, it returns 0.

A call to the `setspent` routine has the effect of rewinding the shadow password file to allow repeated searches. The `endspent` routine may be called to close the shadow password file when processing is complete.

The `fgetspent` routine returns a pointer to the next `spwd` structure in the stream *fp*, which matches the format of /etc/shadow.

FILES
/etc/shadow
/etc/passwd
/etc/.pwd.lock

SEE ALSO
getpwent(3C), putpwent(3C), putspent(3C)

DIAGNOSTICS
`getspent`, `getspnam`, `lckpwdf`, `ulckpwdf`, and `fgetspent` return a null pointer on EOF or error.

NOTES
This routine is for internal use only; compatibility is not guaranteed.

All information is contained in a static area, so it must be copied if it is to be saved.

getsubopt(3C)

NAME
getsubopt – parse suboptions from a string

SYNOPSIS
    #include <stdlib.h>

    int getsubopt (char **optionp, char * const *tokens, char **valuep);

DESCRIPTION
getsubopt parses suboptions in a flag argument that was initially parsed by getopt. These suboptions are separated by commas and may consist of either a single token or a token-value pair separated by an equal sign. Since commas delimit suboptions in the option string, they are not allowed to be part of the suboption or the value of a suboption. A command that uses this syntax is mount(1M), which allows the user to specify mount parameters with the -o option as follows:

    mount -o rw,hard,bg,wsize=1024 speed:/usr /usr

In this example there are four suboptions: rw, hard, bg, and wsize, the last of which has an associated value of 1024.

getsubopt takes the address of a pointer to the option string, a vector of possible tokens, and the address of a value string pointer. It returns the index of the token that matched the suboption in the input string or -1 if there was no match. If the option string at *optionp* contains only one subobtion, getsubopt updates *optionp* to point to the null character at the end of the string; otherwise it isolates the suboption by replacing the comma separator with a null character, and updates *optionp* to point to the start of the next suboption. If the suboption has an associated value, getsubopt updates *valuep* to point to the value's first character. Otherwise it sets *valuep* to NULL.

The token vector is organized as a series of pointers to null strings. The end of the token vector is identified by a null pointer.

When getsubopt returns, if *valuep* is not NULL, then the suboption processed included a value. The calling program may use this information to determine if the presence or lack of a value for this subobtion is an error.

Additionally, when getsubopt fails to match the suboption with the tokens in the *tokens* array, the calling program should decide if this is an error, or if the unrecognized option should be passed to another program.

EXAMPLE
The following code fragment shows how to process options to the mount command using getsubopt.

    #include <stdlib.h>

    char *myopts[] = {
    #define READONLY   0
                "ro",
    #define READWRITE   1
                "rw",

getsubopt(3C)

```
            #define WRITESIZE   2
                        "wsize",
            #define READSIZE    3
                        "rsize",
                        NULL};

    main(argc, argv)
            int   argc;
            char **argv;
    {
            int sc, c, errflag;
            char *options, *value;
            extern char *optarg;
            extern int optind;
            .
            .
            .
            while((c = getopt(argc, argv, "abf:o:")) != -1) {
                switch (c) {
                case 'a': /* process a option */
                        break;
                case 'b': /* process b option */
                        break;
                case 'f':
                        ofile = optarg;
                        break;
                case '?':
                        errflag++;
                        break;
                case 'o':
                        options = optarg;
                        while (*options != '\0') {
                            switch(getsubopt(&options,myopts,&value) {
                            case READONLY : /* process ro option */
                                    break;
                            case READWRITE : /* process rw option */
                                    break;
                            case WRITESIZE : /* process wsize option */
                                    if (value == NULL) {
                                        error_no_arg();
                                        errflag++;
                                    } else
                                        write_size = atoi(value);
                                    break;
                            case READSIZE : /* process rsize option */
                                    if (value == NULL) {
                                        error_no_arg();
                                        errflag++;
                                    } else
```

```
                            read_size = atoi(value);
                        break;
                    default :
                        /* process unknown token */
                        error_bad_token(value);
                        errflag++;
                        break;
                }
            }
            break;
        }
    }
    if (errflag) {
        /* print usage instructions etc. */
    }
    for (; optind<argc; optind++) {
        /* process remaining arguments */
    }
    .
    .
    .
}
```

SEE ALSO

getopt(3C)

DIAGNOSTICS

getsubopt returns −1 when the token it is scanning is not in the token vector. The variable addressed by *valuep* contains a pointer to the first character of the token that was not recognized rather than a pointer to a value for that token.

The variable addressed by *optionp* points to the next option to be parsed, or a null character if there are no more options.

NOTES

During parsing, commas in the option input string are changed to null characters. White space in tokens or token-value pairs must be protected from the shell by quotes.

gettimeofday(3C)

NAME
gettimeofday, settimeofday – get or set the date and time

SYNOPSIS
```
#include <sys/time.h>

int gettimeofday (struct timeval *tp);

int settimeofday (struct timeval *tp);
```

DESCRIPTION
`gettimeofday` gets and `settimeofday` sets the system's notion of the current time. The current time is expressed in elapsed seconds and microseconds since 00:00 Universal Coordinated Time, January 1, 1970. The resolution of the system clock is hardware dependent; the time may be updated continuously or in clock ticks.

tp points to a `timeval` structure, which includes the following members:

```
long    tv_sec;     /* seconds since Jan. 1, 1970 */
long    tv_usec;    /* and microseconds */
```

If *tp* is a null pointer, the current time information is not returned or set.

The `TZ` environment variable holds time zone information. See `timezone`(4).

Only the privileged user may set the time of day.

SEE ALSO
adjtime(2), ctime(3C), timezone(4)

DIAGNOSTICS
A −1 return value indicates that an error occurred and `errno` has been set. The following error codes may be set in `errno`:

EINVAL   *tp* specifies an invalid time.

EPERM   A user other than the privileged user attempted to set the time or time zone.

NOTES
The implementation of `settimeofday` ignores the `tv_usec` field of `tp`. If the time needs to be set with better than one second accuracy, call `settimeofday` for the seconds and then `adjtime` for finer accuracy.

gettimeofday(3)   (BSD Compatibility Package)   gettimeofday(3)

NAME
gettimeofday, settimeofday – get or set the date and time

SYNOPSIS
cc [*flag*. . .] *file* . . . -lucb

#include <sys/time.h>

int gettimeofday(tp, tzp)
struct timeval *tp;
struct timezone *tzp;   /* obsolete */

int settimeofday(tp, tzp)
struct timeval *tp;
struct timezone *tzp;   /* obsolete */

DESCRIPTION
The system's notion of the current Greenwich time is obtained with the gettimeofday call, and set with the settimeofday call. The current time is expressed in elapsed seconds and microseconds since 00:00 GMT, January 1, 1970 (zero hour). The resolution of the system clock is hardware dependent; the time may be updated continuously, or in "ticks."

tp points to a timeval structure, which includes the following members:

        long tv_sec;   /* seconds since Jan. 1, 1970 */
        long tv_usec;   /* and microseconds */

If *tp* is a NULL pointer, the current time information is not returned or set.

tzp is an obsolete pointer formerly used to get and set timezone information. *tzp* is now ignored. Timezone information is now handled using the TZ environment variable; see timezone(4).

Only the privileged user may set the time of day.

RETURN VALUE
A −1 return value indicates an error occurred; in this case an error code is stored in the global variable errno.

ERRORS
The following error codes may be set in errno:

EINVAL   *tp* specifies an invalid time.

EPERM   A user other than the privileged user attempted to set the time.

SEE ALSO
date(1) in the *User's Reference Manual*
adjtime(2), ctime(3C), gettimeofday(3C), timezone(4) in the *Programmer's Reference Manual*

NOTES
Time is never correct enough to believe the microsecond values.

tzp is ignored.

NAME

gettxt – retrieve a text string

SYNOPSIS

```
#include <unistd.h>

char *gettxt (const char *msgid, const char *dflt_str);
```

DESCRIPTION

gettxt retrieves a text string from a message file. The arguments to the function are a message identification *msgid* and a default string *dflt_str* to be used if the retrieval fails.

The text strings are in files created by the mkmsgs utility [see mkmsgs(1)] and installed in directories in /usr/lib/locale/<*locale*>/LC_MESSAGES.

The directory <*locale*> can be viewed as the language in which the text strings are written. The user can request that messages be displayed in a specific language by setting the environment variable LC_MESSAGES. If LC_MESSAGES is not set, the environment variable LANG will be used. If LANG is not set, the files containing the strings are in /usr/lib/locale/C/LC_MESSAGES/*.

The user can also change the language in which the messages are displayed by invoking the setlocale function with the appropriate arguments.

If gettxt fails to retrieve a message in a specific language it will try to retrieve the same message in U.S. English. On failure, the processing depends on what the second argument *dflt_str* points to. A pointer to the second argument is returned if the second argument is not the null string. If *dflt_str* points to the null string, a pointer to the U.S. English text string "Message not found!!\n" is returned.

The following depicts the acceptable syntax of *msgid* for a call to gettxt.

<*msgid*> = <*msgfilename*>:<*msgnumber*>

The first field is used to indicate the file that contains the text strings and must be limited to 14 characters. These characters must be selected from the set of all character values excluding \0 (null) and the ASCII code for / (slash) and : (colon). The names of message files must be the same as the names of files created by mkmsgs and installed in /usr/lib/locale/<*locale*>/LC_MESSAGES/*. The numeric field indicates the sequence number of the string in the file. The strings are numbered from *1* to *n* where *n* is the number of strings in the file.

On failure to pass the correct msgid or a valid message number to gettxt a pointer to the text string "Message not found!!\n" is returned.

EXAMPLE

```
gettxt("UX:10", "hello world\n")
gettxt("UX:10", "")
```

UX is the name of the file that contains the messages. 10 is the message number.

FILES

/usr/lib/locale/C/LC_MESSAGES/*   contains default message files created by mkmsgs

/usr/lib/locale/*locale*/LC_MESSAGES/* contains message files for different languages created by mkmsgs

SEE ALSO
fmtmsg(3C), setlocale(3C), environ(5)
exstr(1), mkmsgs(1), srchtxt(1) in the *User's Reference Manual*

getusershell(3) (BSD Compatibility Package) getusershell(3)

NAME
getusershell, setusershell, endusershell – get legal user shells

SYNOPSIS
cc [*flag*...] *file* ... –lucb

char *getusershell()

setusershell()
endusershell()

DESCRIPTION
getusershell returns a pointer to a legal user shell as defined by the system manager in the file /etc/shells. If /etc/shells does not exist, the locations of the standard system shells, /usr/bin/csh, /usr/bin/sh, and /usr/bin/ksh are returned.

getusershell reads the next line (opening the file if necessary); setusershell rewinds the file; endusershell closes it.

FILES
/etc/shells
/usr/bin/csh
/usr/bin/ksh
/usr/bin/sh

RETURN VALUE
The routine getusershell returns a NULL pointer (0) on EOF or error.

NOTES
All information is contained in a static area so it must be copied if it is to be saved.

NAME

getut: getutent, getutid, getutline, pututline, setutent, endutent, utmpname - access utmp file entry

SYNOPSIS

```
#include <utmp.h>
```

struct utmp *getutent (void);

struct utmp *getutid (const struct utmp *id);

struct utmp *getutline (const struct utmp *line);

struct utmp *pututline (const struct utmp *utmp);

void setutent (void);

void endutent (void);

int utmpname (const char *file);

DESCRIPTION

getutent, getutid, getutline, and pututline each return a pointer to a structure with the following members:

```
char      ut_user[8];     /* user login name */
char      ut_id[4];       /* /etc/inittab id (usually line #) */
char      ut_line[12];    /* device name (console, lnxx) */
short     ut_pid;         /* process id ~*/
short     ut_type;        /* type of entry */
struct    exit_status {
} ut_exit;                /* exit status of a process */
                          /* marked as DEAD_PROCESS */
time_t    ut_time;        /* time entry was made */
```

The structure exit status includes the following members:

```
short   e_termination;    /* termination status */
short   e_exit;           /* exit status */
```

getutent reads in the next entry from a utmp-like file. If the file is not already open, it opens it. If it reaches the end of the file, it fails.

getutid searches forward from the current point in the utmp file until it finds an entry with a ut_type matching id->ut_type if the type specified is RUN_LVL, BOOT_TIME, OLD_TIME, or NEW_TIME. If the type specified in id is INIT_PROCESS, LOGIN_PROCESS, USER_PROCESS, or DEAD_PROCESS, then getutid will return a pointer to the first entry whose type is one of these four and whose ut_id field matches id->ut_id . If the end of file is reached without a match, it fails.

getutline searches forward from the current point in the utmp file until it finds an entry of the type LOGIN_PROCESS or USER_PROCESS that also has a ut_line string matching the line->ut_line string. If the end of file is reached without a match, it fails.

pututline writes out the supplied utmp structure into the utmp file. It uses getutid to search forward for the proper place if it finds that it is not already at the proper place. It is expected that normally the user of pututline will have searched for the proper entry using one of the getut routines. If so, pututline will not search. If pututline does not find a matching slot for the new entry, it will add a new entry to the end of the file. It returns a pointer to the utmp structure.

setutent resets the input stream to the beginning of the file. This reset should be done before each search for a new entry if it is desired that the entire file be examined.

endutent closes the currently open file.

utmpname allows the user to change the name of the file examined, from /var/adm/utmp to any other file. It is most often expected that this other file will be /var/adm/wtmp. If the file does not exist, this will not be apparent until the first attempt to reference the file is made. utmpname does not open the file. It just closes the old file if it is currently open and saves the new file name. If the file name given is longer than 79 characters, utmpname returns 0. Otherwise, it will return 1.

FILES
/var/adm/utmp
/var/adm/wtmp

SEE ALSO
ttyslot(3C), utmp(4)

DIAGNOSTICS
A null pointer is returned upon failure to read, whether for permissions or having reached the end of file, or upon failure to write.

NOTES
The most current entry is saved in a static structure. Multiple accesses require that it be copied before further accesses are made. On each call to either getutid or getutline, the routine examines the static structure before performing more I/O. If the contents of the static structure match what it is searching for, it looks no further. For this reason, to use getutline to search for multiple occurrences, it would be necessary to zero out the static area after each success, or getutline would just return the same structure over and over again. There is one exception to the rule about emptying the structure before further reads are done. The implicit read done by pututline (if it finds that it is not already at the correct place in the file) will not hurt the contents of the static structure returned by the getutent, getutid or getutline routines, if the user has just modified those contents and passed the pointer back to pututline.

These routines use buffered standard I/O for input, but pututline uses an unbuffered non-standard write to avoid race conditions between processes trying to modify the utmp and wtmp files.

getutx(3C)

NAME
getutx: getutxent, getutxid, getutxline, pututxline, setutxent, endutxent, utmpxname, getutmp, getutmpx, updwtmp, updwtmpx – access utmpx file entry

SYNOPSIS
```
#include <utmpx.h>
struct utmpx *getutxent (void);
struct utmpx *getutxid (const struct utmpx *id);
struct utmpx *getutxline (const struct utmpx *line);
struct utmpx *pututxline (const struct utmpx *utmpx);
void setutxent (void);
void endutxent (void);
int utmpxname (const char *file);
void getutmp (struct utmpx *utmpx, struct utmp *utmp);
void getutmpx (struct utmp *utmp, struct utmpx *utmpx);
void updwtmp (char *wfile, struct utmp *utmp);
void updwtmpx (char *wfilex, struct utmpx *utmpx);
```

DESCRIPTION
getutxent, getutxid, and getutxline each return a pointer to a structure of the following type:

```
struct      utmpx {
    char      ut_user[32];           /* user login name */
    char      ut_id[4];              /* /etc/inittab id (usually */
                                     /* line #) */
    char      ut_line[32];           /* device name (console, lnxx) */
    pid_t     ut_pid;                /* process id */
    short     ut_type;               /* type of entry */
    struct    exit_status {
        short     e_termination;     /* termination status */
        short     e_exit;            /* exit status */
    } ut_exit;                       /* exit status of a process */
                                     /* marked as DEAD_PROCESS */
    struct timeval    ut_tv;         /* time entry was made */
    short ut_syslen;                 /* significant length of ut_host */
                                     /* including terminating null */
    char      ut_host[257];          /* host name, if remote */
};
```

getutxent reads in the next entry from a utmpx-like file. If the file is not already open, it opens it. If it reaches the end of the file, it fails.

getutxid searches forward from the current point in the utmpx file until it finds an entry with a ut_type matching *id*->ut_type if the type specified is RUN_LVL, BOOT_TIME, OLD_TIME, or NEW_TIME. If the type specified in *id* is INIT_PROCESS, LOGIN_PROCESS, USER_PROCESS, or DEAD_PROCESS, then getutxid will return a pointer to the first entry whose type is one of these four and whose *ut_id* field matches *id*->ut_id. If the end of file is reached without a match, it fails.

getutxline searches forward from the current point in the utmpx file until it finds an entry of the type LOGIN_PROCESS or USER_PROCESS which also has a *ut_line* string matching the *line*->ut_line string. If the end of file is reached without a match, it fails.

pututxline writes out the supplied utmpx structure into the utmpx file. It uses getutxid to search forward for the proper place if it finds that it is not already at the proper place. It is expected that normally the user of pututxline will have searched for the proper entry using one of the getutx routines. If so, pututxline will not search. If pututxline does not find a matching slot for the new entry, it will add a new entry to the end of the file. It returns a pointer to the utmpx structure.

setutxent resets the input stream to the beginning of the file. This should be done before each search for a new entry if it is desired that the entire file be examined.

endutxent closes the currently open file.

utmpxname allows the user to change the name of the file examined, from /var/adm/utmpx to any other file. It is most often expected that this other file will be /var/adm/wtmpx. If the file does not exist, this will not be apparent until the first attempt to reference the file is made. utmpxname does not open the file. It just closes the old file if it is currently open and saves the new file name. The new file name must end with the "x" character to allow the name of the corresponding utmp file to be easily obtainable (otherwise an error code of 1 is returned).

getutmp copies the information stored in the fields of the utmpx structure to the corresponding fields of the utmp structure. If the information in any field of utmpx does not fit in the corresponding utmp field, the data is truncated.

getutmpx copies the information stored in the fields of the utmp structure to the corresponding fields of the utmpx structure.

updwtmp checks the existence of *wfile* and its parallel file, whose name is obtained by appending an "x" to *wfile*. If only one of them exists, the second one is created and initialized to reflect the state of the existing file. utmp is written to *wfile* and the corresponding utmpx structure is written to the parallel file.

updwtmpx checks the existence of *wfilex* and its parallel file, whose name is obtained by truncating the final "x" from *wfilex*. If only one of them exists, the second one is created and initialized to reflect the state of the existing file. utmpx is written to *wfilex*, and the corresponding utmp structure is written to the parallel file.

FILES

/var/adm/utmp, /var/adm/utmpx
/var/adm/wtmp, /var/adm/wtmpx

SEE ALSO

ttyslot(3C), utmp(4), utmpx(4)

DIAGNOSTICS

A null pointer is returned upon failure to read, whether for permissions or having reached the end of file, or upon failure to write.

NOTES

The most current entry is saved in a static structure. Multiple accesses require that it be copied before further accesses are made. On each call to either getutxid or getutxline, the routine examines the static structure before performing more I/O. If the contents of the static structure match what it is searching for, it looks no further. For this reason, to use getutxline to search for multiple occurrences it would be necessary to zero out the static after each success, or getutxline would just return the same structure over and over again. There is one exception to the rule about emptying the structure before further reads are done. The implicit read done by pututxline (if it finds that it is not already at the correct place in the file) will not hurt the contents of the static structure returned by the getutxent, getutxid, or getutxline routines, if the user has just modified those contents and passed the pointer back to pututxline.

These routines use buffered standard I/O for input, but pututxline uses an unbuffered write to avoid race conditions between processes trying to modify the utmpx and wtmpx files.

getvfsent(3C)

NAME
getvfsent, getvfsfile, getvfsspec, getvfsany – get vfstab file entry

SYNOPSIS
    #include <stdio.h>
    #include <sys/vfstab.h>

    int getvfsent (FILE *fp, struct vfstab *vp);

    int getvfsfile (FILE *fp, struct vfstab *vp, char *file);

    int getvfsspec (FILE *fp, struct vfstab *vp, char *spec);

    int getvfsany (FILE *fp, struct vfstab *vp, struct vfstab *vref);

DESCRIPTION
getvfsent, getvfsfile, getvfsspec, and getvfsany each fill in the structure pointed to by *vp* with the broken-out fields of a line in the file *fp*. Each line in the file contains a vfstab structure, declared in the sys/vfstab.h header file:

              char *vfs_special;
              char *vfs_fsckdev;
              char *vfs_mountp;
              char *vfs_fstype;
              char *vfs_fsckpass;
              char *vfs_automnt;
              char *vfs_mntopts;

The fields have meanings described in vfstab(4).

getvfsent fills *vp* with the next vfstab structure in *fp* so successive calls can be used to search the entire file. getvfsfile searches the file referenced by *fp* until a mount point matching *file* is found and fills *vp* with the fields from the line in the file. getvfsspec searches the file referenced by *fp* until a special device matching *spec* is found and fills *vp* with the fields from the line in the file. *spec* will try to match on device type (block or character special) and major and minor device numbers. If it cannot match in this manner, then it compares the strings. getvfsany searches the file referenced by *fp* until a match is found between a line in the file and *vref*. *vref* matches the line if all non-null entries in *vref* match the corresponding fields in the file.

Note that these routines do not open, close, or rewind the file.

FILES
/etc/vfstab

DIAGNOSTICS
If the next entry is successfully read by getvfsent or a match is found with getvfsfile, getvfsspec, or getvfsany, 0 is returned. If an end-of-file is encountered on reading, these functions return −1. If an error is encountered, a value greater than 0 is returned. The possible error values are:

VFS_TOOLONG		A line in the file exceeded the internal buffer size of VFS_LINE_MAX.
VFS_TOOMANY		A line in the file contains too many fields.
VFS_TOOFEW		A line in the file contains too few fields.

NOTES

The members of the vfstab structure point to information contained in a static area, so it must be copied if it is to be saved.

NAME

getwd – get current working directory pathname

SYNOPSIS

cc [*flag*...] *file* ... -lucb

#include <sys/param.h>

char *getwd(pathname)
char pathname[MAXPATHLEN];

DESCRIPTION

getwd copies the absolute pathname of the current working directory to *pathname* and returns a pointer to the result.

RETURN VALUE

getwd returns zero and places a message in *pathname* if an error occurs.

SEE ALSO

getcwd(3C) in the *Programmer's Reference Manual*

gmatch(3G) (Enhanced Programming Library) gmatch(3G)

NAME
    gmatch – shell global pattern matching

SYNOPSIS
    cc [*flag* ...] *file* ... −lgen [*library* ...]

    #include <libgen.h>

    int gmatch (const char *str, const char *pattern);

DESCRIPTION
    gmatch checks whether the null-terminated string *str* matches the null-terminated pattern string *pattern*. See the sh(1) section "File Name Generation" for a discussion of pattern matching. gmatch returns non-zero if the pattern matches the string, zero if the pattern doesn't. A backslash ('\') is used as an escape character in pattern strings.

EXAMPLE
        char *s;

        gmatch (s, "*[a\-]")

    gmatch returns non-zero (true) for all strings with 'a' or '−' as their last character.

SEE ALSO
    sh(1) in the *User's Reference Manual*

NAME

grantpt – grant access to the slave pseudo-terminal device

SYNOPSIS

    int grantpt(int fildes);

DESCRIPTION

The function grantpt changes the mode and ownership of the slave pseudo-terminal device associated with its master pseudo-terminal counter part. *fildes* is the file descriptor returned from a successful open of the master pseudo-terminal device. A setuid root program [see setuid(2)] is invoked to change the permissions. The user ID of the slave is set to the effective owner of the calling process and the group ID is set to a reserved group. The permission mode of the slave pseudo-terminal is set to readable, writeable by the owner and writeable by the group.

RETURN VALUE

Upon successful completion, the function grantpt returns 0; otherwise it returns −1. Failure could occur if *fildes* is not an open file descriptor, if *fildes* is not associated with a master pseudo-terminal device, or if the corresponding slave device could not be accessed.

SEE ALSO

open(2), setuid(2)

ptsname(3C), unlockpt(3C) in the *Programmer's Guide: STREAMS*

hsearch(3C) (C Development Set) hsearch(3C)

NAME
hsearch, hcreate, hdestroy – manage hash search tables

SYNOPSIS
```
#include <search.h>
```

ENTRY *hsearch (ENTRY item, ACTION action);

int hcreate (size_t nel);

void hdestroy (void);

DESCRIPTION
hsearch is a hash-table search routine generalized from Knuth (6.4) Algorithm D. It returns a pointer into a hash table indicating the location at which an entry can be found. The comparison function used by hsearch is strcmp [see string(3C)]. *item* is a structure of type ENTRY (defined in the search.h header file) containing two pointers: *item.key* points to the comparison key, and *item.data* points to any other data to be associated with that key. (Pointers to types other than void should be cast to pointer-to-void.) *action* is a member of an enumeration type ACTION (defined in search.h) indicating the disposition of the entry if it cannot be found in the table. ENTER indicates that the item should be inserted in the table at an appropriate point. Given a duplicate of an existing item, the new item is not entered and hsearch returns a pointer to the existing item. FIND indicates that no entry should be made. Unsuccessful resolution is indicated by the return of a null pointer.

hcreate allocates sufficient space for the table, and must be called before hsearch is used. *nel* is an estimate of the maximum number of entries that the table will contain. This number may be adjusted upward by the algorithm in order to obtain certain mathematically favorable circumstances.

hdestroy destroys the search table, and may be followed by another call to hcreate.

EXAMPLE
The following example will read in strings followed by two numbers and store them in a hash table, discarding duplicates. It will then read in strings and find the matching entry in the hash table and print it out.

```
#include <stdio.h>
#include <search.h>
#include <string.h>
#include <stdlib.h>

struct info {           /* this is the info stored in table */
      int age, room;    /* other than the key */
};

#define NUM_EMPL   5000    /* # of elements in search table */

main( )
{
      /* space to store strings */
```

```
        char string_space[NUM_EMPL*20];
        /* space to store employee info */
        struct info info_space[NUM_EMPL];
        /* next avail space in string_space */
        char *str_ptr = string_space;
        /* next avail space in info_space */
        struct info *info_ptr = info_space;
        ENTRY item, *found_item;
        /* name to look for in table */
        char name_to_find[30];
        int i = 0;

        /* create table */
        (void) hcreate(NUM_EMPL);
        while (scanf("%s%d%d", str_ptr, &info_ptr->age,
              &info_ptr->room) != EOF && i++ < NUM_EMPL) {
            /* put info in structure, and structure in item */
            item.key = str_ptr;
            item.data = (void *)info_ptr;
            str_ptr += strlen(str_ptr) + 1;
            info_ptr++;
            /* put item into table */
            (void) hsearch(item, ENTER);
        }

        /* access table */
        item.key = name_to_find;
        while (scanf("%s", item.key) != EOF) {
            if ((found_item = hsearch(item, FIND)) != NULL) {
            /* if item is in the table */
            (void)printf("found %s, age = %d, room = %d\n",
                  found_item->key,
                  ((struct info *)found_item->data)->age,
                  ((struct info *)found_item->data)->room);
          } else {
            (void)printf("no such employee %s\n",
                  name_to_find)
          }
        }
        return 0;
}
```

SEE ALSO

bsearch(3C), lsearch(3C), malloc(3C), malloc(3X), string(3C), tsearch(3C)

DIAGNOSTICS

hsearch returns a null pointer if either the action is FIND and the item could not be found or the action is ENTER and the table is full.

hcreate returns zero if it cannot allocate sufficient space for the table.

NOTES

hsearch and hcreate use malloc(3C) to allocate space.

Only one hash search table may be active at any given time.

hypot(3M) (Math Libraries) hypot(3M)

NAME
hypot – Euclidean distance function

SYNOPSIS
cc [*flag* ...] *file* ... -lm [*library* ...]

#include <math.h>

double hypot (double x, double y);

DESCRIPTION
hypot returns

sqrt (x * x + y * y)

taking precautions against unwarranted overflows.

SEE ALSO
matherr(3M).

DIAGNOSTICS
When the correct value would overflow, hypot returns HUGE and sets errno to ERANGE.

Except when the -Xc compilation option is used, these error-handling procedures may be changed with the function matherr. When the -Xa or -Xc compilation options are used, HUGE_VAL is returned instead of HUGE.

ieee_functions(3M) (BSD Compatibility Package) ieee_functions(3M)

NAME
ieee_functions, fp_class, isnan, copysign, scalbn – miscellaneous functions for IEEE arithmetic

SYNOPSIS
cc [*flag*...] *file* ... −lucb

```
#include <fp.h>
#include <math.h>
#include <stdio.h>
```

enum fp_class_type fp_class(x)
double x;

int isnan(x)
double x;

double copysign(x,y)
double x, y;

double scalbn(x,n)
double x; int n;

DESCRIPTION
Most of these functions provide capabilities required by ANSI/IEEE Std 754-1985 or suggested in its appendix.

fp_class(*x*) corresponds to the IEEE's class() and classifies *x* as zero, subnormal, normal, ∞, or quiet or signaling *NaN*; /usr/ucbinclude/sys/ieeefp.h defines enum fp_class_type. The following function returns 0 if the indicated condition is not satisfied:

   isnan(*x*)   returns 1 if *x* is *NaN*

copysign(*x*,*y*) returns *x* with *y*'s sign bit.

scalbn(*x*,*n*) returns *x*∗ 2∗∗n computed by exponent manipulation rather than by actually performing an exponentiation or a multiplication. Thus

$$1 \leq \text{scalbn}(\text{fabs}(x), -\text{ilogb}(x)) < 2$$

for every *x* except 0, ∞, and *NaN*.

FILES
/usr/ucbinclude/sys/ieeefp.h
/usr/ucbinclude/math.h
/usr/include/values.h

ieee_handler(3M) (BSD Compatibility Package) ieee_handler(3M)

NAME
ieee_handler – IEEE exception trap handler function

SYNOPSIS
cc [flag. . .] file . . . -lucb

#include <fp.h>

int ieee_handler(action,exception,hdl)
char action[], exception[];
sigfpe_handler_type hdl;

DESCRIPTION
This function provides easy exception handling to exploit ANSI/IEEE Std 754-1985 arithmetic in a C program. All arguments are pointers to strings. Results arising from invalid arguments and invalid combinations are undefined for efficiency.

There are three types of *action* : get, set, and clear. There are five types of *exception* :

inexact	
division	division by zero exception
underflow	
overflow	
invalid	
all	all five exceptions above
common	invalid, overflow, and division exceptions

Note: all and common only make sense with set or clear

hdl contains the address of a signal-handling routine. <fp.h> defines *sigfpe_handler_type*.

get will get the location of the current handler routine for *exception* in hdl . set will set the routine pointed at by hdl to be the handler routine and at the same time enable the trap on *exception*, except when hdl == SIGFPE_DEFAULT or SIGFPE_IGNORE; then ieee_handler will disable the trap on *exception*. When hdl == SIGFPE_ABORT, any trap on *exception* will dump core using abort(3). clear all disables trapping on all five exceptions.

Two steps are required to intercept an IEEE-related SIGFPE code with ieee_handler:

1) Set up a handler with ieee_handler.

2) Perform a floating-point operation that generates the intended IEEE exception.

Unlike sigfpe(3), ieee_handler also adjusts floating-point hardware mode bits affecting IEEE trapping. For clear, set SIGFPE_DEFAULT, or set SIGFPE_IGNORE, the hardware trap is disabled. For any other set, the hardware trap is enabled.

SIGFPE signals can be handled using sigvec(2), signal(3), signal(3F), sigfpe(3), or ieee_handler(3M). In a particular program, to avoid confusion, use only one of these interfaces to handle SIGFPE signals.

ieee_handler(3M) (BSD Compatibility Package) **ieee_handler(3M)**

RETURN VALUE

ieee_handler normally returns 0. In the case of set, 1 will be returned if the action is not available (for instance, not supported in hardware).

EXAMPLE

A user-specified signal handler might look like this:

```
void sample_handler( sig, code, scp, addr)
int sig ;                /* sig == SIGFPE always */
int code ;
struct sigcontext *scp ;
char *addr ;
{
    /*
       Sample user-written sigfpe code handler.
       Prints a message and continues.
        struct sigcontext is defined in <signal.h>.
    */
    printf("ieee exception code %x occurred at pc %X \n",
      code,scp->sc_pc);
}
```

and it might be set up like this:

```
extern void sample_handler;
main
{
    sigfpe_handler_type hdl, old_handler1, old_handler2;
/*
 * save current overflow and invalid handlers
 */
    ieee_handler("get","overflow",old_handler1);
    ieee_handler("get","invalid", old_handler2);
/*
 * set new overflow handler to sample_handler and set new
 * invalid handler to SIGFPE_ABORT (abort on invalid)
 */
    hdl = (sigfpe_handler_type) sample_handler;
    if(ieee_handler("set","overflow",hdl) != 0)
        printf("ieee_handler can't set overflow \n");
    if(ieee_handler("set","invalid",SIGFPE_ABORT) != 0)
        printf("ieee_handler can't set invalid \n");
    ...
/*
 * restore old overflow and invalid handlers
 */
    ieee_handler("set","overflow", old_handler1);
    ieee_handler("set","invalid", old_handler2);
}
```

FILES
/usr/include/fp.h
/usr/include/signal.h

SEE ALSO
floatingpoint(3), ieee_handler(3), sigfpe(3), signal(3) sigvec(3), signal(2), abort(3C) in the *Programmer's Reference Manual*

NAME

index, rindex − string operations

SYNOPSIS

#include <string.h>

char *index(s, c)
char *s, c;

char *rindex(s, c)
char *s, c;

DESCRIPTION

These functions operate on NULL-terminated strings. They do not check for overflow of any receiving string.

index and rindex returns a pointer to the first (last) occurrence of character c in string s, or a NULL pointer if c does not occur in the string. The NULL character terminating a string is considered to be part of the string.

SEE ALSO

bstring(3), strings(3)

malloc(3C) in the *Programmer's Reference Manual*

NOTES

For user convenience, these functions are declared in the optional <strings.h> header file.

On the Sun processor, as well as on many other machines, you can *not* use a NULL pointer to indicate a NULL string. A NULL pointer is an error and results in an abort of the program. If you wish to indicate a NULL string, you must have a pointer that points to an explicit NULL string. On some implementations of the C language on some machines, a NULL pointer, if dereferenced, would yield a NULL string; this highly non-portable trick was used in some programs. Programmers using a NULL pointer to represent an empty string should be aware of this portability issue; even on machines where dereferencing a NULL pointer does not cause an abort of the program, it does not necessarily yield a NULL string.

Character movement is performed differently in different implementations. Thus overlapping moves may yield surprises.

inet(3N) (User Environment Utilities) inet(3N)

NAME
inet: inet_addr, inet_network, inet_makeaddr, inet_lnaof, inet_netof, inet_ntoa − Internet address manipulation

SYNOPSIS
```
#include <sys/types.h>
#include <sys/socket.h>
#include <netinet/in.h>
#include <arpa/inet.h>

unsigned long inet_addr(char *cp);

unsigned long inet_network(char *cp);

struct in_addr inet_makeaddr(int net, int lna);

int inet_lnaof(struct in_addr in);

int inet_netof(struct in_addr in);

char *inet_ntoa(struct in_addr in);
```

DESCRIPTION
The routines inet_addr and inet_network each interpret character strings representing numbers expressed in the Internet standard '.' notation, returning numbers suitable for use as Internet addresses and Internet network numbers, respectively. The routine inet_makeaddr takes an Internet network number and a local network address and constructs an Internet address from it. The routines inet_netof and inet_lnaof break apart Internet host addresses, returning the network number and local network address part, respectively.

The routine inet_ntoa returns a pointer to a string in the base 256 notation *d.d.d.d* described below.

All Internet addresses are returned in network order (bytes ordered from left to right). All network numbers and local address parts are returned as machine format integer values.

INTERNET ADDRESSES
Values specified using the '.' notation take one of the following forms:

            a.b.c.d
            a.b.c
            a.b
            a

When four parts are specified, each is interpreted as a byte of data and assigned, from left to right, to the four bytes of an Internet address.

When a three part address is specified, the last part is interpreted as a 16-bit quantity and placed in the right most two bytes of the network address. This makes the three part address format convenient for specifying Class B network addresses as 128.net.host.

When a two part address is supplied, the last part is interpreted as a 24-bit quantity and placed in the right most three bytes of the network address. This makes the two part address format convenient for specifying Class A network addresses as net.host.

When only one part is given, the value is stored directly in the network address without any byte rearrangement.

All numbers supplied as parts in a '.' notation may be decimal, octal, or hexadecimal, as specified in the C language (that is, a leading 0x or 0X implies hexadecimal; otherwise, a leading 0 implies octal; otherwise, the number is interpreted as decimal).

SEE ALSO
gethostent(3N), getnetent(3N), hosts(4), networks(4)

DIAGNOSTICS
The value -1 is returned by `inet_addr` and `inet_network` for malformed requests.

NOTES
The problem of host byte ordering versus network byte ordering is confusing. A simple way to specify Class C network addresses in a manner similar to that for Class B and Class A is needed.

The return value from `inet_ntoa` points to static information which is overwritten in each call.

NAME
initgroups – initialize the supplementary group access list

SYNOPSIS
```
#include <grp.h>
#include <sys/types.h>
```
int initgroups (const char *name, gid_t basegid)

DESCRIPTION
initgroups reads the group file, using getgrent, to get the group membership for the user specified by *name* and then initializes the supplementary group access list of the calling process using setgroups. The *basegid* group ID is also included in the supplementary group access list. This is typically the real group ID from the password file.

While scanning the group file, if the number of groups, including the *basegid* entry, exceeds {NGROUPS_MAX}, subsequent group entries are ignored.

initgroups will fail and not change the supplementary group access list if:

EPERM   The effective user ID is not superuser.

SEE ALSO
setgroups(2), getgrent(3C)

DIAGNOSTICS
Upon successful completion, a value of 0 is returned. Otherwise, a value of −1 is returned and errno is set to indicate the error.

NAME

insque, remque – insert/remove element from a queue

SYNOPSIS

include <search.h>

void insque(struct qelem *elem, struct qelem *pred);

void remque(struct qelem *elem);

DESCRIPTION

insque and remque manipulate queues built from doubly linked lists. Each element in the queue must be in the following form:

```
struct qelem {
    struct    qelem *q_forw;
    struct    qelem *q_back;
    char  q_data[];
};
```

insque inserts *elem* in a queue immediately after *pred*. remque removes an entry *elem* from a queue.

isastream(3C)

NAME
isastream – test a file descriptor

SYNOPSIS
    int isastream(int fildes);

DESCRIPTION
The function isastream() determines if a file descriptor represents a STREAMS file. *fildes* refers to an open file.

RETURN VALUE
If successful, isastream() returns 1 if *fildes* represents a STREAMS file, and 0 if not. On failure, isastream() returns -1 with errno set to indicate an error.

ERRORS
Under the following conditions, isastream() fails and sets errno to:

EBADF   *fildes* is not a valid open file.

SEE ALSO
streamio(7) in the *Programmer's Guide: STREAMS*

isencrypt(3G)

NAME
isencrypt – determine whether a character buffer is encrypted

SYNOPSIS
cc [*flag* ...] *file* ... -lgen [*library* ...]

#include <libgen.h>

int isencrypt (const char *fbuf, size_t ninbuf);

DESCRIPTION
isencrypt uses heuristics to determine whether a buffer of characters is encrypted. It requires two arguments: a pointer to an array of characters and the number of characters in the buffer.

isencrypt assumes that the file is not encrypted if all the characters in the first block are ASCII characters. If there are non-ASCII characters in the first *ninbuf* characters, isencrypt assumes that the buffer is encrypted if the setlocale LC_CTYPE category is set to C or ascii.

If the LC_CTYPE category is set to a value other than C or ascii, then isencrypt uses a combination of heuristics to determine if the buffer is encrypted. If *ninbuf* has at least 64 characters, a chi-square test is used to determine if the bytes in the buffer have a uniform distribution; and isencrypt assumes the buffer is encrypted if it does. If the buffer has less than 64 characters, a check is made for null characters and a terminating new-line to determine whether the buffer is encrypted.

DIAGNOSTICS
If the buffer is encrypted, 1 is returned; otherwise zero is returned.

SEE ALSO
setlocale(3C).

isnan(3C)

NAME
isnan, isnand, isnanf, isnanl, finite, finitel, fpclass, fpclassl, unordered, unorderedl – determine type of floating-point number

SYNOPSIS
#include <ieeefp.h>

int isnand (double dsrc);

int isnanf (float fsrc);

int isnanl (long double dsrc);

int finite (double dsrc);

int finitel (long double dsrc);

fpclass_t fpclass (double dsrc);

fpclass_t fpclassl (long double dsrc);

int unordered (double dsrc1, double dsrc2);

int unorderedl (long double dsrc1, long double dsrc2);

#include <math.h>

int isnan (double dsrc);

DESCRIPTION
isnan, isnand, isnanf, and isnanl return true (1) if the argument *dsrc* or *fsrc* is a NaN; otherwise they return false (0). The functionality of isnan is identical to that of isnand.

isnanf is implemented as a macro included in the ieeefp.h header file.

fpclass and fpclassl return the class the *dsrc* belongs to. The 10 possible classes are as follows:

```
FP_SNAN        signaling NaN
FP_QNAN        quiet NaN
FP_NINF        negative infinity
FP_PINF        positive infinity
FP_NDENORM     negative denormalized non-zero
FP_PDENORM     positive denormalized non-zero
FP_NZERO       negative zero
FP_PZERO       positive zero
FP_NNORM       negative normalized non-zero
FP_PNORM       positive normalized non-zero
```

finite and finitel return true (1) if the argument *dsrc* is neither infinity nor NaN; otherwise they return false (0).

unordered and unorderedl return true (1) if one of the two arguments is unordered with respect to the other argument. This is equivalent to reporting whether either argument is NaN. If neither of the arguments is NaN, false (0) is returned.

None of these routines generate any exception, even for signaling NaNs.

SEE ALSO

fpgetround(3C), intro(3M).

killpg(3) (BSD Compatibility Package) killpg(3)

NAME
killpg – send signal to a process group

SYNOPSIS
cc [flag. . .] file . . . -lucb

int killpg(pgrp, sig)
int pgrp, sig;

DESCRIPTION
killpg sends the signal *sig* to the process group *pgrp*. See sigvec(3) for a list of signals.

The real or effective user ID of the sending process must match the real or saved set-user ID of the receiving process, unless the effective user ID of the sending process is the privileged user. A single exception is the signal SIGCONT, which may always be sent to any descendant of the current process.

RETURN VALUE
Upon successful completion, a value of 0 is returned. Otherwise, a value of −1 is returned and the global variable errno is set to indicate the error.

ERRORS
killpg will fail and no signal will be sent if any of the following occur:

EINVAL   *sig* is not a valid signal number.

ESRCH   No processes were found in the specified process group.

EPERM   The effective user ID of the sending process is not privileged user, and neither its real nor effective user ID matches the real or saved set-user ID of one or more of the target processes.

SEE ALSO
sigvec(3)

kill(2), setpgrp(2), sigaction(2) in the *Programmer's Reference Manual*

l3tol(3C) (C Development Set) l3tol(3C)

NAME
      l3tol, ltol3 – convert between 3-byte integers and long integers

SYNOPSIS
      #include <stdlib.h>

      void l3tol (long *lp, const char *cp, int n);

      void ltol3 (char *cp, const long *lp, int n);

DESCRIPTION
      l3tol converts a list of *n* three-byte integers packed into a character string pointed to by *cp* into a list of long integers pointed to by *lp*.

      ltol3 performs the reverse conversion from long integers (*lp*) to three-byte integers (*cp*).

      These functions are useful for file-system maintenance where the block numbers are three bytes long.

SEE ALSO
      fs(4).

NOTES
      Because of possible differences in byte ordering, the numerical values of the long integers are machine-dependent.

libwindows(3X) (Layers Windowing Utilities) libwindows(3X)

NAME
libwindows − windowing terminal function library

SYNOPSIS
cc [*flag* ...] *file* ... −lwindows [*library* ...]

int openagent (void);

int New (int cntlfd, int origin_x, int origin_y,
  int corner_x, int corner_y);

int Newlayer (int cntlfd, int origin_x, int origin_y,
  int corner_x, int corner_y);

int openchan (int chan);

int Runlayer (int chan, char *command);

int Current (int cntlfd, int chan);

int Delete (int cntlfd, int chan);

int Top (int cntlfd, int chan);

int Bottom (int cntlfd, int chan);

int Move (int cntlfd, int chan, int origin_x, int origin_y);

int Reshape (int cntlfd, int chan, int origin_x, int origin_y,
  int corner_x, int corner_y);

int Exit (int cntlfd);

DESCRIPTION
This library of routines enables a program running on a host UNIX system to perform windowing terminal functions [see layers(1)].

The openagent routine opens the control channel of the xt(7) channel group to which the calling process belongs. Upon successful completion, openagent returns a file descriptor that can be passed to any of the other libwindows routines except openchan and Runlayer. (The file descriptor can also be passed to the close system call.) Otherwise, the value −1 is returned.

The New routine creates a new layer with a separate shell. The *origin_x, origin_y, corner_x,* and *corner_y* arguments are the coordinates of the layer rectangle. If all the coordinate arguments are 0, the user must define the layer's rectangle interactively. The layer appears on top of any overlapping layers. The layer is not made current (that is, the keyboard is not attached to the new layer). Upon successful completion, New returns the xt(7) channel number associated with the layer. Otherwise, the value −1 is returned.

The Newlayer routine creates a new layer without executing a separate shell. Otherwise it is identical to New, described above.

The openchan routine opens the channel argument *chan* which is obtained from the New or Newlayer routine. Upon successful completion, openchan returns a file descriptor that can be used as input to write(2) or close(2). Otherwise, the value −1 is returned.

The Runlayer routine runs the specified *command* in the layer associated with the channel argument *chan*. This layer is usually a layer previously created with Newlayer. Any processes currently attached to this layer will be killed, and the new process will have the environment of the layers process.

The Current routine makes the layer associated with the channel argument *chan* current (that is, attached to the keyboard).

The Delete routine deletes the layer associated with the channel argument *chan* and kills all host processes associated with the layer.

The Top routine makes the layer associated with the channel argument *chan* appear on top of all overlapping layers.

The Bottom routine puts the layer associated with the channel argument *chan* under all overlapping layers.

The Move routine moves the layer associated with the channel argument *chan* from its current screen location to a new screen location at the origin point (*origin_x, origin_y*). The size and contents of the layer are maintained.

The Reshape routine reshapes the layer associated with the channel argument *chan*. The arguments *origin_x, origin_y, corner_x,* and *corner_y* are the new coordinates of the layer rectangle. If all the coordinate arguments are 0, the user is allowed to define the layer's rectangle interactively.

The Exit routine causes the layers program to exit, killing all processes associated with it.

FILES

ULIBDIR/libwindows.a   windowing terminal function library
ULIBDIR   usually /usr/lib

SEE ALSO

close(2), write(2), jagent(5).
layers(1) in the *User's Reference Manual.*

DIAGNOSTICS

Upon successful completion, Runlayer, Current, Delete, Top, Bottom, Move, Reshape, and Exit return 0, while openagent, New, Newlayer, and openchan return values as described above under each routine. If an error occurs, −1 is returned.

NOTES

The values of layer rectangle coordinates are dependent on the type of terminal. This dependency affects the routines that pass layer rectangle coordinates: Move, New, Newlayer, and Reshape. Some terminals will expect these numbers to be passed as character positions (bytes); others will expect the information to be in pixels (bits).

For example, for a terminal with `New`, `Newlayer`, and `Reshape` minimum values of 8 (pixels) for *origin_x* and *origin_y* and maximum values of 792 (pixels) for *corner_x* and 1016 (pixels) for *corner_y*, the minimum layer size is 28 by 28 pixels and the maximum layer size is 784 by 1008 pixels.

It is recommended that applications use `/dev/xt/??[0-7]` instead of `/dev/xt??[0-7]` when accessing the `xt` driver.

listen(3N)

NAME
listen – listen for connections on a socket

SYNOPSIS
    int listen(int s, int backlog);

DESCRIPTION
To accept connections, a socket is first created with socket, a backlog for incoming connections is specified with listen and then the connections are accepted with accept. The listen call applies only to sockets of type SOCK_STREAM or SOCK_SEQPACKET.

The *backlog* parameter defines the maximum length the queue of pending connections may grow to. If a connection request arrives with the queue full, the client will receive an error with an indication of ECONNREFUSED.

RETURN VALUE
A 0 return value indicates success; −1 indicates an error.

ERRORS
The call fails if:

EBADF	The argument s is not a valid descriptor.
ENOTSOCK	The argument s is not a socket.
EOPNOTSUPP	The socket is not of a type that supports the operation listen.

NOTES
There is currently no *backlog* limit.

NAME

localeconv – get numeric formatting information

SYNOPSIS

```
#include <locale.h>

struct lconv *localeconv (void);
```

DESCRIPTION

localeconv sets the components of an object with type struct lconv (defined in locale.h) with the values appropriate for the formatting of numeric quantities (monetary and otherwise) according to the rules of the current locale [see setlocale(3C)]. The definition of struct lconv is given below (the values for the fields in the C locale are given in comments):

```
char *decimal_point;         /* "." */
char *thousands_sep;         /* "" (zero length string) */
char *grouping;              /* "" */
char *int_curr_symbol;       /* "" */
char *currency_symbol;       /* "" */
char *mon_decimal_point;     /* "" */
char *mon_thousands_sep;     /* "" */
char *mon_grouping;          /* "" */
char *positive_sign;         /* "" */
char *negative_sign;         /* "" */
char int_frac_digits;        /* CHAR_MAX */
char frac_digits;            /* CHAR_MAX */
char p_cs_precedes;          /* CHAR_MAX */
char p_sep_by_space;         /* CHAR_MAX */
char n_cs_precedes;          /* CHAR_MAX */
char n_sep_by_space;         /* CHAR_MAX */
char p_sign_posn;            /* CHAR_MAX */
char n_sign_posn;            /* CHAR_MAX */
```

The members of the structure with type char * are strings, any of which (except decimal_point) can point to "", to indicate that the value is not available in the current locale or is of zero length. The members with type char are nonnegative numbers, any of which can be CHAR_MAX (defined in the limits.h header file) to indicate that the value is not available in the current locale. The members are the following:

char *decimal_point
: The decimal-point character used to format non-monetary quantities.

char *thousands_sep
: The character used to separate groups of digits to the left of the decimal-point character in formatted non-monetary quantities.

char *grouping
: A string in which each element is taken as an integer that indicates the number of digits that comprise the current group in a formatted non-monetary quantity. The elements of grouping are interpreted according to the following:

CHAR-MAX   No further grouping is to be performed.

0   The previous element is to be repeatedly used for the remainder of the digits.

other   The value is the number of digits that comprise the current group. The next element is examined to determine the size of the next group of digits to the left of the current group.

`char *int_curr_symbol`
The international currency symbol applicable to the current locale, left-justified within a four-character space-padded field. The character sequences should match with those specified in: *ISO 4217 Codes for the Representation of Currency and Funds*.

`char *currency_symbol`
The local currency symbol applicable to the current locale.

`char *mon_decimal_point`
The decimal point used to format monetary quantities.

`char *mon_thousands_sep`
The separator for groups of digits to the left of the decimal point in formatted monetary quantities.

`char *mon_grouping`
A string in which each element is taken as an integer that indicates the number of digits that comprise the current group in a formatted monetary quantity. The elements of `mon_grouping` are interpreted according to the rules described under `grouping`.

`char *positive_sign`
The string used to indicate a nonnegative-valued formatted monetary quantity.

`char *negative_sign`
The string used to indicate a negative-valued formatted monetary quantity.

`char int_frac_digits`
The number of fractional digits (those to the right of the decimal point) to be displayed in an internationally formatted monetary quantity.

`char frac_digits`
The number of fractional digits (those to the right of the decimal point) to be displayed in a formatted monetary quantity.

`char p_cs_precedes`
Set to 1 or 0 if the `currency_symbol` respectively precedes or succeeds the value for a nonnegative formatted monetary quantity.

`char p_sep_by_space`
Set to 1 or 0 if the `currency_symbol` respectively is or is not separated by a space from the value for a nonnegative formatted monetary quantity.

localeconv(3C) (C Programming Language Utilities) localeconv(3C)

    `char n_cs_precedes`
        Set to 1 or 0 if the `currency_symbol` respectively precedes or succeeds the value for a negative formatted monetary quantity.

    `char n_sep_by_space`
        Set to 1 or 0 if the `currency_symbol` respectively is or is not separated by a space from the value for a negative formatted monetary quantity.

    `char p_sign_posn`
        Set to a value indicating the positioning of the `positive_sign` for a non-negative formatted monetary quantity. The value of `p_sign_posn` is interpreted according to the following:

        0   Parentheses surround the quantity and `currency_symbol`.
        1   The sign string precedes the quantity and `currency_symbol`.
        2   The sign string succeeds the quantity and `currency_symbol`.
        3   The sign string immediately precedes the `currency_symbol`.
        4   The sign string immediately succeeds the `currency_symbol`.

    `char n_sign_posn`
        Set to a value indicating the positioning of the `negative_sign` for a negative formatted monetary quantity. The value of `n_sign_posn` is interpreted according to the rules described under `p_sign_posn`.

RETURNS
`localeconv` returns a pointer to the filled-in object. The structure pointed to by the return value may be overwritten by a subsequent call to `localeconv`.

EXAMPLES
The following table illustrates the rules used by four countries to format monetary quantities.

Country	Positive format	Negative format	International format
Italy	L.1.234	-L.1.234	ITL.1.234
Netherlands	F 1.234,56	F -1.234,56	NLG 1.234,56
Norway	kr1.234,56	kr1.234,56-	NOK 1.234,56
Switzerland	SFrs.1,234.56	SFrs.1,234.56C	CHF 1,234.56

For these four countries, the respective values for the monetary members of the structure returned by `localeconv` are as follows:

	Italy	Netherlands	Norway	Switzerland
`int_curr_symbol`	"ITL."	"NLG "	"NOK "	"CHF "
`currency_symbol`	"L."	"F"	"kr"	"SFrs."
`mon_decimal_point`	""	","	","	"."
`mon_thousands_sep`	"."	"."	"."	","
`mon_grouping`	"\3"	"\3"	"\3"	"\3"
`positive_sign`	""	""	""	""
`negative_sign`	"-"	"-"	"-"	"C"
`int_frac_digits`	0	2	2	2
`frac_digits`	0	2	2	2

p_cs_precedes	1	1	1	1
p_sep_by_space	0	1	0	0
n_cs_precedes	1	1	1	1
n_sep_by_space	0	1	0	0
p_sign_posn	1	1	1	1
n_sign_posn	1	4	2	2

FILES

/usr/lib/locale/*locale*/LC_MONETARY   LC_MONETARY database for *locale*
/usr/lib/locale/*locale*/LC_NUMERIC   LC_NUMERIC database for *locale*

SEE ALSO

setlocale(3C).
chrtbl(1M), montbl(1M) in the *System Administrator's Reference Manual*.

lockf(3C)

NAME
lockf – record locking on files

SYNOPSIS
#include <unistd.h>

int lockf (int fildes, int function, long size);

DESCRIPTION
lockf locks sections of a file. Advisory or mandatory write locks depend on the mode bits of the file; see chmod(2). Other processes that try to lock the locked file section either get an error or go to sleep until the resource becomes unlocked. All the locks for a process are removed when the process terminates. See fcntl(2) for more information about record locking.

fildes is an open file descriptor. The file descriptor must have O_WRONLY or O_RDWR permission in order to establish locks with this function call.

function is a control value that specifies the action to be taken. The permissible values for *function* are defined in unistd.h as follows:

```
#define F_ULOCK  0  /* unlock previously locked section */
#define F_LOCK   1  /* lock section for exclusive use */
#define F_TLOCK  2  /* test & lock section for exclusive use */
#define F_TEST   3  /* test section for other locks */
```

All other values of *function* are reserved for future extensions and will result in an error return if not implemented.

F_TEST is used to detect if a lock by another process is present on the specified section. F_LOCK and F_TLOCK both lock a section of a file if the section is available. F_ULOCK removes locks from a section of the file.

size is the number of contiguous bytes to be locked or unlocked. The resource to be locked or unlocked starts at the current offset in the file and extends forward for a positive size and backward for a negative size (the preceding bytes up to but not including the current offset). If *size* is zero, the section from the current offset through the largest file offset is locked (that is, from the current offset through the present or any future end-of-file). An area need not be allocated to the file in order to be locked as such locks may exist past the end-of-file.

The sections locked with F_LOCK or F_TLOCK may, in whole or in part, contain or be contained by a previously locked section for the same process. Locked sections will be unlocked starting at the the point of the offset through *size* bytes or to the end of file if *size* is (off_t) 0. When this situation occurs, or if this situation occurs in adjacent sections, the sections are combined into a single section. If the request requires that a new element be added to the table of active locks and this table is already full, an error is returned, and the new section is not locked.

F_LOCK and F_TLOCK requests differ only by the action taken if the resource is not available. F_LOCK will cause the calling process to sleep until the resource is available. F_TLOCK will cause the function to return a −1 and set errno to EACCES if the section is already locked by another process.

F_ULOCK requests may, in whole or in part, release one or more locked sections controlled by the process. When sections are not fully released, the remaining sections are still locked by the process. Releasing the center section of a locked section requires an additional element in the table of active locks. If this table is full, an errno is set to ENOLCK and the requested section is not released.

A potential for deadlock occurs if a process controlling a locked resource is put to sleep by requesting another process's locked resource. Thus calls to lockf or fcntl scan for a deadlock prior to sleeping on a locked resource. An error return is made if sleeping on the locked resource would cause a deadlock.

Sleeping on a resource is interrupted with any signal. The alarm system call may be used to provide a timeout facility in applications that require this facility.

lockf will fail if one or more of the following are true:

EBADF   *fildes* is not a valid open descriptor.

EAGAIN *cmd* is F_TLOCK or F_TEST and the section is already locked by another process.

EDEADLK *cmd* is F_LOCK and a deadlock would occur.

ENOLCK *cmd* is F_LOCK, F_TLOCK, or F_ULOCK and the number of entries in the lock table would exceed the number allocated on the system.

ECOMM   *fildes* is on a remote machine and the link to that machine is no longer active.

SEE ALSO
intro(2), alarm(2), chmod(2), close(2), creat(2), fcntl(2), open(2), read(2), write(2)

DIAGNOSTICS
On success, lockf returns 0. On failure, lockf returns −1 and sets errno to indicate the error.

NOTES
Unexpected results may occur in processes that do buffering in the user address space. The process may later read/write data that is/was locked. The standard I/O package is the most common source of unexpected buffering.

Because in the future the variable errno will be set to EAGAIN rather than EACCES when a section of a file is already locked by another process, portable application programs should expect and test for either value.

lsearch(3C) (C Development Set) lsearch(3C)

NAME
lsearch, lfind – linear search and update

SYNOPSIS
#include <search.h>

void *lsearch (const void *key, void * base, size_t *nelp,
    size_t width, int (*compar) (const void *, const void *));

void *lfind (const void *key, const void *base, size_t *nelp,
    size_t width, int (*compar)(const void *, const void *));

DESCRIPTION
lsearch is a linear search routine generalized from Knuth (6.1) Algorithm S. It returns a pointer into a table indicating where a datum may be found. If the datum does not occur, it is added at the end of the table. *key* points to the datum to be sought in the table. *base* points to the first element in the table. *nelp* points to an integer containing the current number of elements in the table. The integer is incremented if the datum is added to the table. *width* is the size of an element in bytes. *compar* is a pointer to the comparison function that the user must supply (strcmp, for example). It is called with two arguments that point to the elements being compared. The function must return zero if the elements are equal and non-zero otherwise.

lfind is the same as lsearch except that if the datum is not found, it is not added to the table. Instead, a null pointer is returned.

NOTES
The pointers to the key and the element at the base of the table may be pointers to any type.

The comparison function need not compare every byte, so arbitrary data may be contained in the elements in addition to the values being compared.

The value returned should be cast into type pointer-to-element.

EXAMPLE
This program will read in less than TABSIZE strings of length less than ELSIZE and store them in a table, eliminating duplicates, and then will print each entry.

```
#include <search.h>
#include <string.h>
#include <stdlib.h>
#include <stdio.h>

#define TABSIZE 50
#define ELSIZE 120

main()
{
        char line[ELSIZE];         /* buffer to hold input string */
        char tab[TABSIZE][ELSIZE]; /* table of strings */
        size_t nel = 0;            /* number of entries in tab */
        int i;
```

```
        while (fgets(line, ELSIZE, stdin) != NULL &&
            nel < TABSIZE)
            (void) lsearch(line, tab, &nel, ELSIZE, mycmp);
        for( i = 0; i < nel; i++ )
            (void) fputs(tab[i], stdout);
        return 0;
    }
```

SEE ALSO

bsearch(3C), hsearch(3C), string(3C), tsearch(3C).

NOTES

If the searched-for datum is found, both lsearch and lfind return a pointer to it. Otherwise, lfind returns NULL and lsearch returns a pointer to the newly added element.

Undefined results can occur if there is not enough room in the table to add a new item.

maillock(3X)

NAME
maillock – manage lockfile for user's mailbox

SYNOPSIS
cc [flag ...] file ... -lmail [library ...]

#include <maillock.h>

int maillock (const char *user, int retrycnt);

int mailunlock (void);

DESCRIPTION
The maillock function attempts to create a lockfile for the user's mailfile. If a lockfile already exists, maillock assumes the contents of the file is the process ID (as a null-terminated ASCII string) of the process that created the lockfile (presumably with a call to maillock). If the process that created the lockfile is still alive, maillock will sleep and try again *retrycnt* times before returning with an error indication. The sleep algorithm is to sleep for 5 seconds times the attempt number. That is, the first sleep will be for 5 seconds, the next sleep will be for 10 seconds, etc. until the number of attempts reaches *retrycnt*. When the lockfile is no longer needed, it should be removed by calling mailunlock.

user is the login name of the user for whose mailbox the lockfile will be created. maillock assumes that users' mailfiles are in the "standard" place as defined in maillock.h.

RETURN VALUE
The following return code definitions are contained in maillock.h. Only L_SUCCESS is returned for mailunlock.

```
#define   L_SUCCESS    0   /* Lockfile created or removed */
#define   L_NAMELEN    1   /* Recipient name > 13 chars */
#define   L_TMPLOCK    2   /* Can't create tmp file */
#define   L_TMPWRITE   3   /* Can't write pid into lockfile */
#define   L_MAXTRYS    4   /* Failed after retrycnt attempts */
#define   L_ERROR      5   /* Check errno for reason */
```

FILES
LIBDIR/llib-mail.ln
LIBDIR/mail.a
/var/mail/*
/var/mail/*.lock

NOTES
mailunlock will only remove the lockfile created from the most previous call to maillock. Calling maillock for different users without intervening calls to mailunlock will cause the initially created lockfile(s) to remain, potentially blocking subsequent message delivery until the current process finally terminates.

makecontext(3C)

NAME
makecontext, swapcontext – manipulate user contexts

SYNOPSIS
#include <ucontext.h>

void makecontext (ucontext_t *ucp, (void(*)())func, int argc, ...);

int swapcontext (ucontext_t *oucp, ucontext_t *ucp);

DESCRIPTION
These functions are useful for implementing user-level context switching between multiple threads of control within a process.

makecontext modifies the context specified by ucp, which has been initialized using getcontext; when this context is resumed using swapcontext or setcontext [see getcontext(2)], program execution continues by calling the function func, passing it the arguments that follow argc in the makecontext call. Before a call is made to makecontext, the context being modified should have a stack allocated for it. The integer value of argc must match the number of arguments that follow argc. Otherwise the behavior is undefined.

The uc_link field is used to determine the context that will be resumed when the context being modified by makecontext returns. The uc_link field should be initialized prior to the call to makecontext.

swapcontext saves the current context in the context structure pointed to by oucp and sets the context to the context structure pointed to by ucp.

These functions will fail if either of the following is true:

ENOMEM ucp does not have enough stack left to complete the operation.

EFAULT ucp or oucp points to an invalid address.

SEE ALSO
exit(2), getcontext(2), sigaction(2), sigprocmask(2), ucontext(5).

DIAGNOSTICS
On successful completion, swapcontext return a value of zero. Otherwise, a value of −1 is returned and errno is set to indicate the error.

NOTES
The size of the ucontext_t structure may change in future releases. To remain binary compatible, users of these features must always use makecontext or getcontext to create new instances of them.

makedev(3C)

NAME
makedev, major, minor – manage a device number

SYNOPSIS
    #include <sys/types.h>
    #include <sys/mkdev.h>

    dev_t makedev(major_t maj, minor_t min);

    major_t major(dev_t device);

    minor_t minor(dev_t device);

DESCRIPTION
The makedev routine returns a formatted device number on success and NODEV on failure. *maj* is the major number. *min* is the minor number. makedev can be used to create a device number for input to mknod(2).

The major routine returns the major number component from *device*.

The minor routine returns the minor number component from *device*.

makedev will fail if one or more of the following are true:

      EINVAL One or both of the arguments *maj* and *min* is too large.

      EINVAL The *device* number created from *maj* and *min* is NODEV.

major will fail if one or more of the following are true:

      EINVAL The *device* argument is NODEV.

      EINVAL The major number component of *device* is too large.

minor will fail if the following is true:

      EINVAL The *device* argument is NODEV.

SEE ALSO
stat(2), mknod(2).

DIAGNOSTICS
On failure, NODEV is returned and errno is set to indicate the error.

NAME

malloc, free, realloc, calloc, memalign, valloc, – memory allocator

SYNOPSIS

#include <stdlib.h>

void *malloc (size_t size);

void free (void *ptr);

void *realloc (void *ptr, size_t size);

void *calloc (size_t nelem, size_t elsize);

void *memalign(size_t alignment, size_t size);

void *valloc(size_t size);

DESCRIPTION

malloc and free provide a simple general-purpose memory allocation package. malloc returns a pointer to a block of at least *size* bytes suitably aligned for any use.

The argument to free is a pointer to a block previously allocated by malloc, calloc or realloc. After free is performed this space is made available for further allocation. If *ptr* is a NULL pointer, no action occurs.

Undefined results will occur if the space assigned by malloc is overrun or if some random number is handed to free.

realloc changes the size of the block pointed to by *ptr* to *size* bytes and returns a pointer to the (possibly moved) block. The contents will be unchanged up to the lesser of the new and old sizes. If *ptr* is NULL, realloc behaves like malloc for the specified size. If *size* is zero and *ptr* is not a null pointer, the object pointed to is freed.

calloc allocates space for an array of *nelem* elements of size *elsize*. The space is initialized to zeros.

memalign allocates *size* bytes on a specified alignment boundary, and returns a pointer to the allocated block. The value of the returned address is guaranteed to be an even multiple of *alignment*. Note: the value of *alignment* must be a power of two, and must be greater than or equal to the size of a word.

valloc(size) is equivalent to memalign(sysconf(_SC_PAGESIZE),size).

Each of the allocation routines returns a pointer to space suitably aligned (after possible pointer coercion) for storage of any type of object.

malloc, realloc, calloc, memalign, and valloc will fail if there is not enough available memory.

SEE ALSO

malloc(3X).

DIAGNOSTICS

If there is no available memory, malloc, realloc, memalign, valloc, and calloc return a null pointer. When realloc returns NULL, the block pointed to by *ptr* is left intact. If *size*, *nelem*, or *elsize* is 0, a unique pointer to the arena is returned.

malloc(3X) (Specialized Libraries) malloc(3X)

NAME
malloc, free, realloc, calloc, mallopt, mallinfo – memory allocator

SYNOPSIS
cc [*flag* ...] *file* ... −lmalloc [*library* ...]

#include <stdlib.h>

void *malloc (size_t size);

void free (void *ptr);

void *realloc (void *ptr, size_t size);

void *calloc (size_t nelem, size_t elsize);

#include <malloc.h>

int mallopt (int cmd, int value);

struct mallinfo mallinfo (void);

DESCRIPTION
malloc and free provide a simple general-purpose memory allocation package.

malloc returns a pointer to a block of at least *size* bytes suitably aligned for any use.

The argument to free is a pointer to a block previously allocated by malloc; after free is performed this space is made available for further allocation, and its contents have been destroyed (but see mallopt below for a way to change this behavior). If *ptr* is a null pointer, no action occurs.

Undefined results occur if the space assigned by malloc is overrun or if some random number is handed to free.

realloc changes the size of the block pointed to by *ptr* to *size* bytes and returns a pointer to the (possibly moved) block. The contents are unchanged up to the lesser of the new and old sizes. If *ptr* is a null pointer, realloc behaves like malloc for the specified size. If *size* is zero and *ptr* is not a null pointer, the object it points to is freed.

calloc allocates space for an array of *nelem* elements of size *elsize*. The space is initialized to zeros.

mallopt provides for control over the allocation algorithm.. The available values for *cmd* are:

- M_MXFAST   Set *maxfast* to *value*. The algorithm allocates all blocks below the size of *maxfast* in large groups and then doles them out very quickly. The default value for *maxfast* is 24.

- M_NLBLKS   Set *numlblks* to *value*. The above mentioned "large groups" each contain *numlblks* blocks. *numlblks* must be greater than 0. The default value for *numlblks* is 100.

- M_GRAIN   Set *grain* to *value*. The sizes of all blocks smaller than *maxfast* are considered to be rounded up to the nearest multiple of *grain*. *grain* must be greater than 0. The default value of *grain* is the smallest number of bytes that will allow alignment of any data type. Value will be rounded up to a multiple of the default when *grain* is set.

M_KEEP   Preserve data in a freed block until the next malloc, realloc, or calloc. This option is provided only for compatibility with the old version of malloc and is not recommended.

These values are defined in the malloc.h header file.

mallopt may be called repeatedly, but may not be called after the first small block is allocated.

mallinfo provides instrumentation describing space usage. It returns the structure:

```
struct mallinfo {
    int arena;       /* total space in arena */
    int ordblks;     /* number of ordinary blocks */
    int smblks;      /* number of small blocks */
    int hblkhd;      /* space in holding block headers */
    int hblks;       /* number of holding blocks */
    int usmblks;     /* space in small blocks in use */
    int fsmblks;     /* space in free small blocks */
    int uordblks;    /* space in ordinary blocks in use */
    int fordblks;    /* space in free ordinary blocks */
    int keepcost;    /* space penalty if keep option */
                     /* is used */
}
```

This structure is defined in the malloc.h header file.

Each of the allocation routines returns a pointer to space suitably aligned (after possible pointer coercion) for storage of any type of object.

SEE ALSO
brk(2), malloc(3C)

DIAGNOSTICS
malloc, realloc, and calloc return a NULL pointer if there is not enough available memory. When realloc returns NULL, the block pointed to by *ptr* is left intact. If mallopt is called after any allocation or if *cmd* or *value* are invalid, non-zero is returned. Otherwise, it returns zero.

NOTES
Note that unlike malloc(3C), this package does not preserve the contents of a block when it is freed, unless the M_KEEP option of mallopt is used.

Undocumented features of malloc(3C) have not been duplicated.

Function prototypes for malloc, realloc, calloc and free are also defined in the <malloc.h> header file for compatibility with old applications. New applications should include <stdlib.h> to access the prototypes for these functions.

matherr(3M) (Math Libraries) matherr(3M)

NAME
matherr – error-handling function

SYNOPSIS
cc [*flag* ...] *file* ... −lm [*library* ...]

#include <math.h>

int matherr (struct exception *x);

DESCRIPTION
matherr is invoked by functions in the math libraries when errors are detected. Note that matherr is not invoked when the −Xc compilation option is used. Users may define their own procedures for handling errors, by including a function named matherr in their programs. matherr must be of the form described above. When an error occurs, a pointer to the exception structure x will be passed to the user-supplied matherr function. This structure, which is defined in the math.h header file, is as follows:

```
struct exception {
        int type;
        char *name;
        double arg1, arg2, retval;
};
```

The element type is an integer describing the type of error that has occurred, from the following list of constants (defined in the header file):

DOMAIN	argument domain error
SING	argument singularity
OVERFLOW	overflow range error
UNDERFLOW	underflow range error
TLOSS	total loss of significance
PLOSS	partial loss of significance

The element name points to a string containing the name of the function that incurred the error. The variables arg1 and arg2 are the arguments with which the function was invoked. retval is set to the default value that will be returned by the function unless the user's matherr sets it to a different value.

If the user's matherr function returns non-zero, no error message will be printed, and errno will not be set.

If matherr is not supplied by the user, the default error-handling procedures, described with the math functions involved, will be invoked upon error. These procedures are also summarized in the table below. In every case, errno is set to EDOM or ERANGE and the program continues.

	Default Error Handling Procedures					
	Types of Errors					
type	DOMAIN	SING	OVERFLOW	UNDERFLOW	TLOSS	PLOSS
errno	EDOM	EDOM	ERANGE	ERANGE	ERANGE	ERANGE
BESSEL: y0, y1, yn (arg ≤ 0)	– M, –H	– –	– –	– –	M, 0 –	– –
EXP, EXPF:	–	–	H	0	–	–
LOG, LOG10: LOGF, LOG10F: (arg < 0) (arg = 0)	M, –H M, –H	– –	– –	– –	– –	– –
POW, POWF: neg ** non-int 0 ** non-pos	– M, 0 M, 0	– – –	±H – –	0 – –	– – –	– – –
SQRT, SQRTF:	M, 0	–	–	–	–	–
FMOD, FMODF: (arg2 = 0)	M, X	–	–	–	–	–
REMAINDER: (arg2 = 0)	M, N	–	–	–	–	–
GAMMA, LGAMMA:	–	M, H	H	–	–	–
HYPOT:	–	–	H	–	–	–
SINH, SINHF:	–	–	±H	–	–	–
COSH, COSHF:	–	–	H	–	–	–
ASIN, ACOS, ATAN2: ASINF, ACOSF, ATAN2F:	M, 0	–	–	–	–	–
ACOSH:	M, N	–	–	–	–	–
ATANH: (|arg| > 1) (|arg| = 1)	M, N –	– M, N	– –	– –	– –	– –

Abbreviations	
M	Message is printed (not with the −Xa or −Xc options).
H	HUGE is returned (HUGE_VAL with the −Xa or −Xc options).
−H	−HUGE is returned (−HUGE_VAL with the −Xa or −Xc options).
±H	HUGE or −HUGE is returned.
	(HUGE_VAL or −HUGE_VAL with the −Xa or −Xc options).
0	0 is returned.
X	*arg1* is returned.
N	NaN is returned.

EXAMPLE

```
#include <math.h>
#include <stdio.h>
#include <stdlib.h>
#include <string.h>

int
matherr(register struct exception *x);
{
        switch (x->type) {
        case DOMAIN:
                /* change sqrt to return sqrt(-arg1), not 0 */
                if (!strcmp(x->name, "sqrt")) {
                        x->retval = sqrt(-x->arg1);
                        return (0); /* print message and set errno */
                }
        case SING:
                /* all other domain or sing errors, print message */
                /* and abort */
                fprintf(stderr, "domain error in %s\n", x->name);
                abort( );
        case PLOSS:
                /* print detailed error message */
                fprintf(stderr, "loss of significance in %s(%g)=%g\n",
                        x->name, x->arg1, x->retval);
                return (1); /* take no other action */
        }
        return (0); /* all other errors, execute default procedure */
}
```

NOTES

Error handling in −Xa and −Xt modes [see cc(1)] is described more completely on individual math library pages.

NAME

mbchar: mbtowc, mblen, wctomb – multibyte character handling

SYNOPSIS

```
#include <stdlib.h>

int mbtowc (wchar_t *pwc, const char *s, size_t n);

int mblen (const char *s, size_t n);

int wctomb (char *s, wchar_t wchar);
```

DESCRIPTION

Multibyte characters are used to represent characters in an extended character set. This is needed for locales where 8 bits are not enough to represent all the characters in the character set.

The multibyte character handling functions provide the means of translating multibyte characters into wide characters and back again. Wide characters have type wchar_t (defined in stdlib.h), which is an integral type whose range of values can represent distinct codes for all members of the largest extended character set specified among the supported locales.

A maximum of 3 extended character sets are supported for each locale. The number of bytes in an extended character set is defined by the LC_CTYPE category of the locale [see setlocale(3C)]. However, the maximum number of bytes in any multibyte character will never be greater than MB_LEN_MAX. which is defined in stdlib.h. The maximum number of bytes in a character in an extended character set in the current locale is given by the macro, MB_CUR_MAX, also defined in stdlib.h.

mbtowc determines the number of bytes that comprise the multibyte character pointed to by s. Also, if *pwc* is not a null pointer, mbtowc converts the multibyte character to a wide character and places the result in the object pointed to by *pwc*. (The value of the wide character corresponding to the null character is zero.) At most *n* characters will be examined, starting at the character pointed to by s.

If s is a null pointer, mbtowc simply returns 0. If s is not a null pointer, then, if s points to the null character, mbtowc returns 0; if the next *n* or fewer bytes form a valid multibyte character, mbtowc returns the number of bytes that comprise the converted multibyte character; otherwise, s does not point to a valid multibyte character and mbtowc returns −1.

mblen determines the number of bytes comprising the multibyte character pointed to by s. It is equivalent to

```
mbtowc ((wchar_t *)0, s, n);
```

wctomb determines the number of bytes needed to represent the multibyte character corresponding to the code whose value is *wchar*, and, if s is not a null pointer, stores the multibyte character representation in the array pointed to by s. At most MB_CUR_MAX characters are stored.

If s is a null pointer, wctomb simply returns 0. If s is not a null pointer, wctomb returns −1 if the value of *wchar* does not correspond to a valid multibyte character; otherwise it returns the number of bytes that comprise the multibyte character corresponding to the value of *wchar*.

SEE ALSO
   mbstring(3C), setlocale(3C), environ(5).
   chrtbl(1M) in the *System Administrator's Reference Manual*.

NAME
mbstring: mbstowcs, wcstombs – multibyte string functions

SYNOPSIS
    #include <stdlib.h>

    size_t mbstowcs (wchar_t *pwcs, const char *s, size_t n);

    size_t wcstombs (char *s, const wchar_t *pwcs, size_t n);

DESCRIPTION
mbstowcs converts a sequence of multibyte characters from the array pointed to by *s* into a sequence of corresponding wide character codes and stores these codes into the array pointed to by *pwcs*, stopping after *n* codes are stored or a code with value zero (a converted null character) is stored. If an invalid multibyte character is encountered, mbstowcs returns (size_t)−1. Otherwise, mbstowcs returns the number of array elements modified, not including the terminating zero code, if any.

wcstombs converts a sequence of wide character codes from the array pointed to by *pwcs* into a sequence of multibyte characters and stores these multibyte characters into the array pointed to by *s*, stopping if a multibyte character would exceed the limit of *n* total bytes or if a null character is stored. If a wide character code is encountered that does not correspond to a valid multibyte character, wcstombs returns (size_t)−1. Otherwise, wcstombs returns the number of bytes modified, not including a terminating null character, if any.

SEE ALSO
mbchar(3C), setlocale(3C), environ(5).
chrtbl(1M) in the *System Administrator's Reference Manual*.

NAME

mctl – memory management control

SYNOPSIS

cc [*flag*. . .] *file* . . . -lucb

#include <sys/types.h>
#include <sys/mman.h>

mctl(caddr_t addr, size_t len, int function, void *arg);

DESCRIPTION

mctl applies a variety of control functions over pages identified by the mappings established for the address range [*addr, addr + len*). The function to be performed is identified by the argument *function*. Valid functions are defined in mman.h as follows.

MC_LOCK

Lock the pages in the range in memory. This function is used to support mlock. See mlock(3) for semantics and usage. *arg* is ignored.

MC_LOCKAS

Lock the pages in the address space in memory. This function is used to support mlockall. See mlockall(3) for semantics and usage. *addr* and *len* are ignored. *arg* is an integer built from the flags:

MCL_CURRENT	Lock current mappings
MCL_FUTURE	Lock future mappings

MC_SYNC

Synchronize the pages in the range with their backing storage. Optionally invalidate cache copies. This function is used to support msync. See msync(3) for semantics and usage. *arg* is used to represent the *flags* argument to msync. It is constructed from an OR of the following values:

MS_SYNC	Synchronized write
MS_ASYNC	Return immediately
MS_INVALIDATE	Invalidate mappings

MS_ASYNC returns after all I/O operations are scheduled. MS_SYNC does not return until all I/O operations are complete. Specify exactly one of MS_ASYNC or MS_SYNC. MS_INVALIDATE invalidates all cached copies of data from memory, requiring them to be re-obtained from the object's permanent storage location upon the next reference.

MC_UNLOCK

Unlock the pages in the range. This function is used to support munlock. See munlock(3) for semantics and usage. *arg* is ignored.

MC_UNLOCKAS

Remove address space memory lock, and locks on all current mappings. This function is used to support munlockall(3). *addr* and *len* must have the value 0. *arg* is ignored.

RETURN VALUE

mctl returns 0 on success, −1 on failure.

ERRORS

mctl fails if:

EAGAIN	Some or all of the memory identified by the operation could not be locked due to insufficient system resources.
EBUSY	MS_INVALIDATE was specified and one or more of the pages is locked in memory.
EINVAL	*addr* is not a multiple of the page size as returned by getpagesize.
EINVAL	*addr* and/or *len* do not have the value 0 when MC_LOCKAS or MC_UNLOCKAS are specified.
EINVAL	*arg* is not valid for the function specified.
EIO	An I/O error occurred while reading from or writing to the file system.
ENOMEM	Addresses in the range [*addr*, *addr* + *len*) are invalid for the address space of a process, or specify one or more pages which are not mapped.
EPERM	The process's effective user ID is not super-user and one of MC_LOCK, MC_LOCKAS, MC_UNLOCK, or MC_UNLOCKAS was specified.

SEE ALSO

getpagesize(3)

mmap(2), mlock(3C), mlockall(3C), msync(3C) in the *Programmer's Reference Manual*

NAME

memory: memccpy, memchr, memcmp, memcpy, memmove, memset – memory operations

SYNOPSIS

```
#include <string.h>

void *memccpy (void *s1, const void *s2, int c, size_t n);

void *memchr (const void *s, int c, size_t n);

int memcmp (const void *s1, const void *s2, size_t n);

void *memcpy (void *s1, const void *s2, size_t n);

void *memmove (void *s1, const void *s2, size_t n);

void *memset (void *s, int c, size_t n);
```

DESCRIPTION

These functions operate as efficiently as possible on memory areas (arrays of bytes bounded by a count, not terminated by a null character). They do not check for the overflow of any receiving memory area.

memccpy copies bytes from memory area s2 into s1, stopping after the first occurrence of c (converted to an unsigned char) has been copied, or after n bytes have been copied, whichever comes first. It returns a pointer to the byte after the copy of c in s1, or a null pointer if c was not found in the first n bytes of s2.

memchr returns a pointer to the first occurrence of c (converted to an unsigned char) in the first n bytes (each interpreted as an unsigned char) of memory area s, or a null pointer if c does not occur.

memcmp compares its arguments, looking at the first n bytes (each interpreted as an unsigned char), and returns an integer less than, equal to, or greater than 0, according as s1 is lexicographically less than, equal to, or greater than s2 when taken to be unsigned characters.

memcpy copies n bytes from memory area s2 to s1. It returns s1.

memmove copies n bytes from memory areas s2 to s1. Copying between objects that overlap will take place correctly. It returns s1.

memset sets the first n bytes in memory area s to the value of c (converted to an unsigned char). It returns s.

SEE ALSO

string(3C).

menu_attributes(3X)

NAME
menu_attributes: set_menu_fore, menu_fore, set_menu_back, menu_back, set_menu_grey, menu_grey, set_menu_pad, menu_pad − control menus display attributes

SYNOPSIS
```
#include <menu.h>
int set_menu_fore(MENU *menu, chtype attr);
chtype menu_fore(MENU *menu);
int set_menu_back(MENU *menu, chtype attr);
chtype menu_back(MENU *menu);
int set_menu_grey(MENU *menu, chtype attr);
chtype menu_grey(MENU *menu);
int set_menu_pad(MENU *menu, int pad);
int menu_pad(MENU *menu);
```

DESCRIPTION
set_menu_fore sets the foreground attribute of *menu* — the display attribute for the current item (if selectable) on single-valued menus and for selected items on multi-valued menus. This display attribute is a curses library visual attribute. menu_fore returns the foreground attribute of *menu*.

set_menu_back sets the background attribute of menu — the display attribute for unselected, yet selectable, items. This display attribute is a curses library visual attribute.

set_menu_grey sets the grey attribute of *menu* — the display attribute for non-selectable items in multi-valued menus. This display attribute is a curses library visual attribute. menu_grey returns the grey attribute of *menu*.

The pad character is the character that fills the space between the name and description of an item. set_menu_pad sets the pad character for *menu* to *pad*. menu_pad returns the pad character of *menu*.

RETURN VALUE
These routines return one of the following:

E_OK   − The routine returned successfully.
E_SYSTEM_ERROR − System error.
E_BAD_ARGUMENT − An incorrect argument was passed to the routine.

NOTES
The header file <menu.h> automatically includes the header files <eti.h> and <curses.h>.

SEE ALSO
curses(3X), menus(3X)

NAME

menu_cursor: pos_menu_cursor – correctly position a menus cursor

SYNOPSIS

#include <menu.h>

int pos_menu_cursor(MENU *menu);

DESCRIPTION

pos_menu_cursor moves the cursor in the window of *menu* to the correct position to resume menu processing. This is needed after the application calls a curses library I/O routine.

RETURN VALUE

This routine returns one of the following:

E_OK	– The routine returned successfully.
E_SYSTEM_ERROR	– System error.
E_BAD_ARGUMENT	– An incorrect argument was passed to the routine.
E_NOT_POSTED	– The menu has not been posted.

NOTES

The header file <menu.h> automatically includes the header files <eti.h> and <curses.h>.

SEE ALSO

curses(3X), menus(3X), panels(3X), panel_update(3X)

NAME
menu_driver − command processor for the menus subsystem

SYNOPSIS
#include <menu.h>

int menu_driver(MENU *menu, int c);

DESCRIPTION
menu_driver is the workhorse of the menus subsystem. It checks to determine whether the character c is a menu request or data. If c is a request, the menu driver executes the request and reports the result. If c is data (a printable ASCII character), it enters the data into the pattern buffer and tries to find a matching item. If no match is found, the menu driver deletes the character from the pattern buffer and returns E_NO_MATCH. If the character is not recognized, the menu driver assumes it is an application-defined command and returns E_UNKNOWN_COMMAND.

Menu driver requests:

REQ_LEFT_ITEM	Move left to an item.
REQ_RIGHT_ITEM	Move right to an item.
REQ_UP_ITEM	Move up to an item.
REQ_DOWN_ITEM	Move down to an item.
REQ_SCR_ULINE	Scroll up a line.
REQ_SCR_DLINE	Scroll down a line.
REQ_SCR_DPAGE	Scroll up a page.
REQ_SCR_UPAGE	Scroll down a page.
REQ_FIRST_ITEM	Move to the first item.
REQ_LAST_ITEM	Move to the last item.
REQ_NEXT_ITEM	Move to the next item.
REQ_PREV_ITEM	Move to the previous item.
REQ_TOGGLE_ITEM	Select/de-select an item.
REQ_CLEAR_PATTERN	Clear the menu pattern buffer.
REQ_BACK_PATTERN	Delete the previous character from pattern buffer.
REQ_NEXT_MATCH	Move the next matching item.
REQ_PREV_MATCH	Move to the previous matching item.

RETURN VALUE
menu_driver returns one of the following:

E_OK	− The routine returned successfully.
E_SYSTEM_ERROR	− System error.
E_BAD_ARGUMENT	− An incorrect argument was passed to the routine.
E_BAD_STATE	− The routine was called from an initialization or termination function.
E_NOT_POSTED	− The menu has not been posted.

E_UNKNOWN_COMMAND	– An unknown request was passed to the menu driver.
E_NO_MATCH	– The character failed to match.
E_NOT_SELECTABLE	– The item cannot be selected.
E_REQUEST_DENIED	– The menu driver could not process the request.

NOTES

Application defined commands should be defined relative to (greater than) MAX_COMMAND, the maximum value of a request listed above.

The header file <menu.h> automatically includes the header files <eti.h> and <curses.h>.

SEE ALSO

curses(3X), menus(3X)

menu_format(3X)

NAME
menu_format: set_menu_format, menu_format – set and get maximum numbers of rows and columns in menus

SYNOPSIS
#include <menu.h>

int set_menu_format(MENU *menu, int rows, int cols);

void menu_format(MENU *menu, int *rows, int *cols);

DESCRIPTION
set_menu_format sets the maximum number of rows and columns of items that may be displayed at one time on a menu. If the menu contains more items than can be displayed at once, the menu will be scrollable.

menu_format returns the maximum number of rows and columns that may be displayed at one time on *menu*. *rows* and *cols* are pointers to the variables used to return these values.

RETURN VALUE
set_menu_format returns one of the following:

E_OK	– The routine returned successfully.
E_SYSTEM_ERROR	– System error.
E_BAD_ARGUMENT	– An incorrect argument was passed to the routine.
E_POSTED	– The menu is already posted.

NOTES
The header file <menu.h> automatically includes the header files <eti.h> and <curses.h>.

SEE ALSO
curses(3X), menus(3X)

menu_hook(3X)

NAME
menu_hook: set_item_init, item_init, set_item_term, item_term, set_menu_init, menu_init, set_menu_term, menu_term – assign application-specific routines for automatic invocation by menus

SYNOPSIS
#include <menu.h>

int set_item_init(MENU *menu, void (*func)(MENU *));
void (*)(MENU *) item_init(MENU *menu);

int set_item_term(MENU *menu, void (*func)(MENU *));
void (*)(MENU *) item_term(MENU *menu);

int set_menu_init(MENU *menu, void (*func)(MENU *));
void (*)(MENU *) menu_init(MENU *menu);

int set_menu_term(MENU *menu, void (*func)(MENU *));
void (*)(MENU *) menu_term(MENU *menu);

DESCRIPTION
set_item_init assigns the application-defined function to be called when the *menu* is posted and just after the current item changes. item_init returns a pointer to the item initialization routine, if any, called when the *menu* is posted and just after the current item changes.

set_item_term assigns an application-defined function to be called when the *menu* is unposted and just before the current item changes. item_term returns a pointer to the termination function, if any, called when the *menu* is unposted and just before the current item changes.

set_menu_init assigns an application-defined function to be called when the *menu* is posted and just after the top row changes on a posted menu. menu_init returns a pointer to the menu initialization routine, if any, called when the *menu* is posted and just after the top row changes on a posted menu.

set_menu_term assigns an application-defined function to be called when the *menu* is unposted and just before the top row changes on a posted menu. menu_term returns a pointer to the menu termination routine, if any, called when the *menu* is unposted and just before the top row changes on a posted menu.

RETURN VALUE
Routines that return pointers always return NULL on error. Routines that return an integer return one of the following:

E_OK   – The routine returned successfully.
E_SYSTEM_ERROR – System error.

NOTES
The header file <menu.h> automatically includes the header files <eti.h> and <curses.h>.

menu_hook(3X) menu_hook(3X)

SEE ALSO
curses(3X), menus(3X), menu_control(3X), menu_hook(3X)

NAME

menu_item_current: set_current_item, current_item, set_top_row, top_row, item_index – set and get current menus items

SYNOPSIS

```
#include <menu.h>

int set_current_item(MENU *menu, ITEM *item);
ITEM *current_item(MENU *menu);

int set_top_row(MENU *menu, int row);
int top_row(MENU *menu);

int item_index(ITEM *item);
```

DESCRIPTION

The current item of a menu is the item where the cursor is currently positioned. set_current_item sets the current item of *menu* to *item*. current_item returns a pointer to the the current item in *menu*.

set_top_row sets the top row of *menu* to *row*. The left-most item on the new top row becomes the current item. top_row returns the number of the menu row currently displayed at the top of *menu*.

item_index returns the index to the *item* in the item pointer array. The value of this index ranges from 0 through *N*–1, where *N* is the total number of items connected to the menu.

RETURN VALUE

current_item returns NULL on error.

top_row and index_item return –1 on error.

set_current_item and set_top_row return one of the following:

E_OK	– The routine returned successfully.
E_SYSTEM_ERROR	– System error.
E_BAD_ARGUMENT	– An incorrect argument was passed to the routine.
E_BAD_STATE	– The routine was called from an initialization or termination function.
E_NOT_CONNECTED	– No items are connected to the menu.

NOTES

The header file <menu.h> automatically includes the header files <eti.h> and <curses.h>.

SEE ALSO

curses(3X), menus(3X)

NAME

menu_item_name: item_name, item_description – get menus item name and description

SYNOPSIS

#include <menu.h>

char *item_name(ITEM *item);

char *item_description(ITEM *item);

DESCRIPTION

item_name returns a pointer to the name of *item*.

item_description returns a pointer to the description of *item*.

RETURN VALUE

These routines return NULL on error.

NOTES

The header file <menu.h> automatically includes the header files <eti.h> and <curses.h>.

SEE ALSO

curses(3X), menus(3X), menu_new(3X)

NAME
menu_item_new: new_item, free_item – create and destroy menus items

SYNOPSIS
#include <menu.h>

ITEM *new_item(char *name, char *desc);

int free_item(ITEM *item);

DESCRIPTION
new_item creates a new item from *name* and *description*, and returns a pointer to the new item.

free_item frees the storage allocated for *item*. Once an item is freed, the user can no longer connect it to a menu.

RETURN VALUE
new_item returns NULL on error.

free_item returns one of the following:

E_OK	– The routine returned successfully.
E_SYSTEM_ERROR	– System error.
E_BAD_ARGUMENT	– An incorrect argument was passed to the routine.
E_CONNECTED	– One or more items are already connected to another menu.

NOTES
The header file <menu.h> automatically includes the header files <eti.h> and <curses.h>.

SEE ALSO
curses(3X), menus(3X)

menu_item_opts(3X)

NAME
menu_item_opts: set_item_opts, item_opts_on, item_opts_off, item_opts – menus item option routines

SYNOPSIS
```
#include <menu.h>

int set_item_opts(ITEM *item, OPTIONS opts);
int item_opts_on(ITEM *item, OPTIONS opts);
int item_opts_off(ITEM *item, OPTIONS opts);
OPTIONS item_opts(ITEM *item);
```

DESCRIPTION
set_item_opts turns on the named options for *item* and turns off all other options. Options are boolean values that can be OR-ed together.

item_opts_on turns on the named options for *item*; no other option is changed.

item_opts_off turns off the named options for *item*; no other option is changed.

item_opts returns the current options of *item*.

Item Options:

    O_SELECTABLE   The item can be selected during menu processing.

RETURN VALUE
Except for item_opts, these routines return one of the following:

E_OK   – The routine returned successfully.
E_SYSTEM_ERROR – System error.

NOTES
The header file <menu.h> automatically includes the header files <eti.h> and <curses.h>.

SEE ALSO
curses(3X), menus(3X)

NAME

menu_item_userptr: set_item_userptr, item_userptr – associate application data with menus items

SYNOPSIS

     #include <menu.h>

     int set_item_userptr(ITEM *item, char *userptr);

     char *item_userptr(ITEM *item);

DESCRIPTION

Every item has an associated user pointer that can be used to store relevant information. set_item_userptr sets the user pointer of *item*. item_userptr returns the user pointer of *item*.

RETURN VALUE

item_userptr returns NULL on error. set_item_userptr returns one of the following:

     E_OK   – The routine returned successfully.
     E_SYSTEM_ERROR   – System error.

NOTES

The header file <menu.h> automatically includes the header files <eti.h> and <curses.h>.

SEE ALSO

curses(3X), menus(3X)

NAME
menu_item_value: set_item_value, item_value – set and get menus item values

SYNOPSIS
#include <menu.h>

int set_item_value(ITEM *item, int bool);

int item_value(ITEM *item);

DESCRIPTION
Unlike single-valued menus, multi-valued menus enable the end-user to select one or more items from a menu. set_item_value sets the selected value of the *item* — TRUE (selected) or FALSE (not selected). set_item_value may be used only with multi-valued menus. To make a menu multi-valued, use set_menu_opts or menu_opts_off to turn off the option O_ONEVALUE. [see menu_opts(3X)].

item_value returns the select value of *item*, either TRUE (selected) or FALSE (unselected).

RETURN VALUE
set_item_value returns one of the following:

E_OK	– The routine returned successfully.
E_SYSTEM_ERROR	– System error.
E_REQUEST_DENIED	– The menu driver could not process the request.

NOTES
The header file <menu.h> automatically includes the header files <eti.h> and <curses.h>.

SEE ALSO
curses(3X), menus(3X), menu_opts(3X)

NAME
menu_item_visible: item_visible – tell if menus item is visible

SYNOPSIS
#include <menu.h>

int item_visible(ITEM *item);

DESCRIPTION
A menu item is visible if it currently appears in the subwindow of a posted menu. item_visible returns TRUE if *item* is visible, otherwise it returns FALSE.

NOTES
The header file <menu.h> automatically includes the header files <eti.h> and <curses.h>.

SEE ALSO
curses(3X), menus(3X), menu_new(3X)

menu_items(3X)

NAME
menu_items: set_menu_items, menu_items, item_count − connect and disconnect items to and from menus

SYNOPSIS
#include <menu.h>

int set_menu_items(MENU *menu, ITEM **items);

ITEM **menu_items(MENU *menu);

int item_count(MENU *menu);

DESCRIPTION
set_menu_items changes the item pointer array connected to *menu* to the item pointer array *items*.

menu_items returns a pointer to the item pointer array connected to *menu*.

item_count returns the number of items in *menu*.

RETURN VALUE
menu_items returns NULL on error.

item_count returns -1 on error.

set_menu_items returns one of the following:

E_OK	− The routine returned successfully.
E_SYSTEM_ERROR	− System error.
E_BAD_ARGUMENT	− An incorrect argument was passed to the routine.
E_POSTED	− The menu is already posted.
E_CONNECTED	− One or more items are already connected to another menu.

NOTES
The header file <menu.h> automatically includes the header files <eti.h> and <curses.h>.

SEE ALSO
curses(3X), menus(3X)

menu_mark(3X)

NAME
menu_mark: set_menu_mark, menu_mark – menus mark string routines

SYNOPSIS
#include <menu.h>

int set_menu_mark(MENU *menu, char *mark);

char *menu_mark(MENU *menu);

DESCRIPTION
menus displays mark strings to distinguish selected items in a menu (or the current item in a single-valued menu). set_menu_mark sets the mark string of *menu* to *mark*. menu_mark returns a pointer to the mark string of *menu*.

RETURN VALUE
menu_mark returns NULL on error. set_menu_mark returns one of the following:

E_OK	– The routine returned successfully.
E_SYSTEM_ERROR	– System error.
E_BAD_ARGUMENT	– An incorrect argument was passed to the routine.

NOTES
The header file <menu.h> automatically includes the header files <eti.h> and <curses.h>.

SEE ALSO
curses(3X), menus(3X)

menu_new(3X)

NAME
menu_new: new_menu, free_menu – create and destroy menus

SYNOPSIS
#include <menu.h>

MENU *new_menu(ITEM **items);

int free_menu(MENU *menu);

DESCRIPTION
new_menu creates a new menu connected to the item pointer array *items* and returns a pointer to the new menu.

free_menu disconnects *menu* from its associated item pointer array and frees the storage allocated for the menu.

RETURN VALUE
new_menu returns NULL on error.

free_menu returns one of the following:

E_OK	– The routine returned successfully.
E_SYSTEM_ERROR	– System error.
E_BAD_ARGUMENT	– An incorrect argument was passed to the routine.
E_POSTED	– The menu is already posted.

NOTES
The header file <menu.h> automatically includes the header files <eti.h> and <curses.h>.

SEE ALSO
curses(3X), menus(3X)

NAME

menu_opts: set_menu_opts, menu_opts_on, menu_opts_off, menu_opts – menus option routines

SYNOPSIS

#include <menu.h>

int set_menu_opts(MENU *menu, OPTIONS opts);
int menu_opts_on(MENU *menu, OPTIONS opts);
int menu_opts_off(MENU *menu, OPTIONS opts);
OPTIONS menu_opts(MENU *menu);

DESCRIPTION

Menu Options

set_menu_opts turns on the named options for *menu* and turns off all other options. Options are boolean values that can be OR-ed together.

menu_opts_on turns on the named options for *menu*; no other option is changed.

menu_opts_off turns off the named options for *menu*; no other option is changed.

menu_opts returns the current options of *menu*.

Menu Options:

O_ONEVALUE	Only one item can be selected from the menu.
O_SHOWDESC	Display the description of the items.
O_ROWMAJOR	Display the menu in row major order.
O_IGNORECASE	Ignore the case when pattern matching.
O_SHOWMATCH	Place the cursor within the item name when pattern matching.
O_NONCYCLIC	Make certain menu driver requests non-cyclic.

RETURN VALUE

Except for menu_opts, these routines return one of the following:

E_OK	– The routine returned successfully.
E_SYSTEM_ERROR	– System error.
E_POSTED	– The menu is already posted.

NOTES

The header file <menu.h> automatically includes the header files <eti.h> and <curses.h>.

SEE ALSO

curses(3X), menus(3X)

menu_pattern(3X)

NAME
menu_pattern: set_menu_pattern, menu_pattern – set and get menus pattern match buffer

SYNOPSIS
#include <menu.h>

int set_menu_pattern(MENU *menu, char *pat);

char *menu_pattern(MENU *menu);

DESCRIPTION
Every menu has a pattern buffer to match entered data with menu items. set_menu_pattern sets the pattern buffer to *pat* and tries to find the first item that matches the pattern. If it does, the matching item becomes the current item. If not, the current item does not change. menu_pattern returns the string in the pattern buffer of *menu*.

RETURN VALUE
menu_pattern returns NULL on error. set_menu_pattern returns one of the following:

E_OK	– The routine returned successfully.
E_SYSTEM_ERROR	– System error.
E_BAD_ARGUMENT	– An incorrect argument was passed to the routine.
E_NO_MATCH	– The character failed to match.

NOTES
The header file <menu.h> automatically includes the header files <eti.h> and <curses.h>.

SEE ALSO
curses(3X), menus(3X)

menu_post(3X)

NAME
menu_post: post_menu, unpost_menu – write or erase menus from associated subwindows

SYNOPSIS
#include <menu.h>

int post_menu(MENU *menu);

int unpost_menu(MENU *menu);

DESCRIPTION
post_menu writes *menu* to the subwindow. The application programmer must use curses library routines to display the menu on the physical screen or call update_panels if the panels library is being used.

unpost_menu erases *menu* from its associated subwindow.

RETURN VALUE
These routines return one of the following:

E_OK	– The routine returned successfully.
E_SYSTEM_ERROR	– System error.
E_BAD_ARGUMENT	– An incorrect argument was passed to the routine.
E_POSTED	– The menu is already posted.
E_BAD_STATE	– The routine was called from an initialization or termination function.
E_NO_ROOM	– The menu does not fit within its subwindow.
E_NOT_POSTED	– The menu has not been posted.
E_NOT_CONNECTED	– No items are connected to the menu.

NOTES
The header file <menu.h> automatically includes the header files <eti.h> and <curses.h>.

SEE ALSO
curses(3X), menus(3X), panels(3X)

menu_userptr(3X)

NAME
menu_userptr: set_menu_userptr, menu_userptr − associate application data with menus

SYNOPSIS
```
#include <menu.h>

int set_menu_userptr(MENU *menu, char *userptr);
char *menu_userptr(MENU *menu);
```

DESCRIPTION
Every menu has an associated user pointer that can be used to store relevant information. set_menu_userptr sets the user pointer of *menu*. menu_userptr returns the user pointer of *menu*.

RETURN VALUE
menu_userptr returns NULL on error.

set_menu_userptr returns one of the following:

E_OK	− The routine returned successfully.
E_SYSTEM_ERROR	− System error.

NOTES
The header file <menu.h> automatically includes the header files <eti.h> and <curses.h>.

SEE ALSO
curses(3X), menus(3X)

NAME

menu_win: set_menu_win, menu_win, set_menu_sub, menu_sub, scale_menu – menus window and subwindow association routines

SYNOPSIS

#include <menu.h>

int set_menu_win(MENU *menu, WINDOW *win);
WINDOW *menu_win(MENU *menu);

int set_menu_sub(MENU *menu, WINDOW *sub);
WINDOW *menu_sub(MENU *menu);

int scale_window(MENU *menu, int *rows, int *cols);

DESCRIPTION

set_menu_win sets the window of *menu* to *win*. menu_win returns a pointer to the window of *menu*.

set_menu_sub sets the subwindow of *menu* to *sub*. menu_sub returns a pointer to the subwindow of *menu*.

scale_window returns the minimum window size necessary for the subwindow of *menu*. *rows* and *cols* are pointers to the locations used to return the values.

RETURN VALUE

Routines that return pointers always return NULL on error. Routines that return an integer return one of the following:

E_OK	– The routine returned successfully.
E_SYSTEM_ERROR	– System error.
E_BAD_ARGUMENT	– An incorrect argument was passed to the routine.
E_POSTED	– The menu is already posted.
E_NOT_CONNECTED	– No items are connected to the menu.

NOTES

The header file <menu.h> automatically includes the header files <eti.h> and <curses.h>.

SEE ALSO

curses(3X), menus(3X)

NAME
menus – character based menus package

SYNOPSIS
`#include <menu.h>`

DESCRIPTION
The menu library is built using the curses library, and any program using menus routines must call one of the curses initialization routines, such as initscr. A program using these routines must be compiled with -lmenu and -lcurses on the cc command line.

The menus package gives the applications programmer a terminal-independent method of creating and customizing menus for user interaction. The menus package includes: item routines, which are used to create and customize menu items; and menu routines, which are used to create and customize menus, assign pre- and post-processing routines, and display and interact with menus.

Current Default Values for Item Attributes
The menus package establishes initial current default values for item attributes. During item initialization, each item attribute is assigned the current default value for that attribute. An application can change or retrieve a current default attribute value by calling the appropriate set or retrieve routine with a NULL item pointer. If an application changes a current default item attribute value, subsequent items created using new_item will have the new default attribute value. (The attributes of previously created items are not changed if a current default attribute value is changed.)

Routine Name Index
The following table lists each menus routine and the name of the manual page on which it is described.

menus Routine Name	Manual Page Name
current_item	menu_item_current(3X)
free_item	menu_item_new(3X)
free_menu	menu_new(3X)
item_count	menu_items(3X)
item_description	menu_item_name(3X)
item_index	menu_item_current(3X)
item_init	menu_hook(3X)
item_name	menu_item_name(3X)
item_opts	menu_item_opts(3X)
item_opts_off	menu_item_opts(3X)
item_opts_on	menu_item_opts(3X)
item_term	menu_hook(3X)
item_userptr	menu_item_userptr(3X)
item_value	menu_item_value(3X)
item_visible	menu_item_visible(3X)
menu_back	menu_attributes(3X)
menu_driver	menu_driver(3X)

menus Routine Name	Manual Page Name
menu_fore	menu_attributes(3X)
menu_format	menu_format(3X)
menu_grey	menu_attributes(3X)
menu_init	menu_hook(3X)
menu_items	menu_items(3X)
menu_mark	menu_mark(3X)
menu_opts	menu_opts(3X)
menu_opts_off	menu_opts(3X)
menu_opts_on	menu_opts(3X)
menu_pad	menu_attributes(3X)
menu_pattern	menu_pattern(3X)
menu_sub	menu_win(3X)
menu_term	menu_hook(3X)
menu_userptr	menu_userptr(3X)
menu_win	menu_win(3X)
new_item	menu_item_new(3X)
new_menu	menu_new(3X)
pos_menu_cursor	menu_cursor(3X)
post_menu	menu_post(3X)
scale_menu	menu_win(3X)
set_current_item	menu_item_current(3X)
set_item_init	menu_hook(3X)
set_item_opts	menu_item_opts(3X)
set_item_term	menu_hook(3X)
set_item_userptr	menu_item_userptr(3X)
set_item_value	menu_item_value(3X)
set_menu_back	menu_attributes(3X)
set_menu_fore	menu_attributes(3X)
set_menu_format	menu_format(3X)
set_menu_grey	menu_attributes(3X)
set_menu_init	menu_hook(3X)
set_menu_items	menu_items(3X)
set_menu_mark	menu_mark(3X)
set_menu_opts	menu_opts(3X)
set_menu_pad	menu_attributes(3X)
set_menu_pattern	menu_pattern(3X)
set_menu_sub	menu_win(3X)
set_menu_term	menu_hook(3X)
set_menu_userptr	menu_userptr(3X)
set_menu_win	menu_win(3X)
set_top_row	menu_item_current(3X)
top_row	menu_item_current(3X)
unpost_menu	menu_post(3X)

RETURN VALUE

Routines that return pointers always return NULL on error. Routines that return an integer return one of the following:

E_OK	– The routine returned successfully.
E_SYSTEM_ERROR	– System error.
E_BAD_ARGUMENT	– An incorrect argument was passed to the routine.
E_POSTED	– The menu is already posted.
E_CONNECTED	– One or more items are already connected to another menu.
E_BAD_STATE	– The routine was called from an initialization or termination function.
E_NO_ROOM	– The menu does not fit within its subwindow.
E_NOT_POSTED	– The menu has not been posted.
E_UNKNOWN_COMMAND	– An unknown request was passed to the menu driver.
E_NO_MATCH	– The character failed to match.
E_NOT_SELECTABLE	– The item cannot be selected.
E_NOT_CONNECTED	– No items are connected to the menu.
E_REQUEST_DENIED	– The menu driver could not process the request.

NOTES

The header file <menu.h> automatically includes the header files <eti.h> and <curses.h>.

SEE ALSO

curses(3X), and 3X pages whose names begin "menu_" for detailed routine descriptions.

mkdirp(3G)

NAME
mkdirp, rmdirp – create, remove directories in a path

SYNOPSIS
cc [*flag* ...] *file* ... -lgen [*library* ...]

#include <libgen.h>

int mkdirp (const char *path, mode_t mode);

int rmdirp (char *d, char *d1);

DESCRIPTION
mkdirp creates all the missing directories in the given *path* with the given *mode*. [See chmod(2) for the values of *mode*.] The protection part of the *mode* argument is modified by the process's file creation mask [see umask(2)].

rmdirp removes directories in path *d*. This removal starts at the end of the path and moves back toward the root as far as possible. If an error occurs, the remaining path is stored in *d1*. rmdirp returns a 0 only if it is able to remove every directory in the path.

EXAMPLES
```
/* create scratch directories */
if (mkdirp("/tmp/sub1/sub2/sub3", 0755) == -1) {
    fprintf(stderr, "cannot create directory");
    exit(1);
}
chdir("/tmp/sub1/sub2/sub3");
 .
 .
 .
/* cleanup */
chdir("/tmp");
rmdirp("sub1/sub2/sub3");
```

DIAGNOSTICS
If a needed directory cannot be created, mkdirp returns -1 and sets errno to one of the mkdir error numbers. If all the directories are created, or existed to begin with, it returns zero.

NOTES
mkdirp uses malloc to allocate temporary space for the string.

rmdirp returns -2 if a "." or ".." is in the path and -3 if an attempt is made to remove the current directory. If an error occurs other than one of the above, -1 is returned.

SEE ALSO
mkdir(2), rmdir(2), umask(2).

NAME

mkfifo – create a new FIFO

SYNOPSIS

```
#include <sys/types.h>
#include <sys/stat.h>

int mkfifo (const char *path, mode_t mode);
```

DESCRIPTION

The mkfifo routine creates a new FIFO special file named by the pathname pointed to by *path*. The mode of the new FIFO is initialized from *mode*. The file permission bits of the *mode* argument are modified by the process's file creation mask [see umask(2)].

The FIFO's owner ID is set to the process's effective user ID. The FIFO's group ID is set to the process's effective group ID, or if the S_ISGID bit is set in the parent directory then the group ID of the FIFO is inherited from the parent.

mkfifo calls the system call mknod to make the file.

SEE ALSO

chmod(2), exec(2), mknod(2), umask(2), fs(4), stat(5).
mkdir(1) in the *User's Reference Manual*.

DIAGNOSTICS

Upon successful completion a value of 0 is returned. Otherwise, a value of −1 is returned and errno is set to indicate the error.

NOTES

Bits other than the file permission bits in *mode* are ignored.

NAME

mkstemp – make a unique file name

SYNOPSIS

cc [*flag*...] *file*... -lucb

mkstemp(template)
char *template;

DESCRIPTION

mkstemp creates a unique file name, typically in a temporary filesystem, by replacing *template* with a unique file name, and returns a file descriptor for the template file open for reading and writing. The string in *template* should contain a file name with six trailing Xs; mkstemp replaces the Xs with a letter and the current process ID. The letter will be chosen so that the resulting name does not duplicate an existing file. mkstemp avoids the race between testing whether the file exists and opening it for use.

SEE ALSO

getpid(2), open(2), tmpfile(3S), tmpnam(3S) in the *Programmer's Reference Manual*

RETURN VALUE

mkstemp returns −1 if no suitable file could be created.

NOTES

It is possible to run out of letters.

mkstemp actually changes the template string which you pass; this means that you cannot use the same template string more than once — you need a fresh template for every unique file you want to open.

When mkstemp is creating a new unique filename it checks for the prior existence of a file with that name. This means that if you are creating more than one unique filename, it is bad practice to use the same root template for multiple invocations of mkstemp.

NAME
mktemp – make a unique file name

SYNOPSIS
`#include <stdlib.h>`

`char *mktemp(char *template);`

DESCRIPTION
mktemp replaces the contents of the string pointed to by *template* with a unique file name, and returns *template*. The string in *template* should look like a file name with six trailing Xs; mktemp will replace the Xs with a character string that can be used to create a unique file name.

SEE ALSO
tmpfile(3S), tmpnam(3S).

DIAGNOSTIC
mktemp will assign to *template* the empty string if it cannot create a unique name.

NOTES
mktemp can create only 26 unique file names per process for each unique *template*.

mktime(3C)

NAME
mktime – converts a tm structure to a calendar time

SYNOPSIS
```
#include <time.h>

time_t mktime (struct tm *timeptr);
```

DESCRIPTION
mktime converts the time represented by the tm structure pointed to by *timeptr* into a calendar time (the number of seconds since 00:00:00 UTC, January 1, 1970).

The tm structure has the following format.

```
struct      tm {
    int     tm_sec;     /* seconds after the minute [0, 61] */
    int     tm_min;     /* minutes after the hour [0, 59] */
    int     tm_hour;    /* hour since midnight [0, 23] */
    int     tm_mday;    /* day of the month [1, 31] */
    int     tm_mon;     /* months since January [0, 11] */
    int     tm_year;    /* years since 1900 */
    int     tm_wday;    /* days since Sunday [0, 6] */
    int     tm_yday;    /* days since January 1 [0, 365] */
    int     tm_isdst;   /* flag for daylight savings time */
};
```

In addition to computing the calendar time, mktime normalizes the supplied tm structure. The original values of the tm_wday and tm_yday components of the structure are ignored, and the original values of the other components are not restricted to the ranges indicated in the definition of the structure. On successful completion, the values of the tm_wday and tm_yday components are set appropriately, and the other components are set to represent the specified calendar time, but with their values forced to be within the appropriate ranges. The final value of tm_mday is not set until tm_mon and tm_year are determined.

The original values of the components may be either greater than or less than the specified range. For example, a tm_hour of −1 means 1 hour before midnight, tm_mday of 0 means the day preceding the current month, and tm_mon of −2 means 2 months before January of tm_year.

If tm_isdst is positive, the original values are assumed to be in the alternate timezone. If it turns out that the alternate timezone is not valid for the computed calendar time, then the components are adjusted to the main timezone. Likewise, if tm_isdst is zero, the original values are assumed to be in the main timezone and are converted to the alternate timezone if the main timezone is not valid. If tm_isdst is negative, the correct timezone is determined and the components are not adjusted.

Local timezone information is used as if mktime had called tzset.

mktime returns the specified calendar time. If the calendar time cannot be represented, the function returns the value (time_t)−1.

EXAMPLE
What day of the week is July 4, 2001?

```
#include <stdio.h>
#include <time.h>

static char *const wday[] = {
    "Sunday", "Monday", "Tuesday", "Wednesday",
    "Thursday", "Friday", "Saturday", "-unknown-"
};
struct tm time_str;
/*...*/
time_str.tm_year= 2001 - 1900;
time_str.tm_mon = 7 - 1;
time_str.tm_mday= 4;
time_str.tm_hour= 0;
time_str.tm_min = 0;
time_str.tm_sec     = 1;
time_str.tm_isdst   = -1;
if (mktime(&time_str) == -1)
    time_str.tm_wday=7;
printf("%s\n", wday[time_str.tm_wday]);
```

SEE ALSO
ctime(3C), getenv(3C), timezone(4).

NOTES
tm_year of the tm structure must be for year 1970 or later. Calendar times before 00:00:00 UTC, January 1, 1970 or after 03:14:07 UTC, January 19, 2038 cannot be represented.

mlock(3C)

NAME
mlock, munlock – lock (or unlock) pages in memory

SYNOPSIS
#include <sys/types.h>

int mlock(caddr_t addr, size_t len);

int munlock(caddr_t addr, size_t len);

DESCRIPTION
The function mlock uses the mappings established for the address range [*addr*, *addr* + *len*) to identify pages to be locked in memory. The effect of mlock (*addr*, *len*) is equivalent to memcntl (*addr*, *len*, MC_LOCK, 0, 0, 0).

munlock removes locks established with mlock. The effect of munlock (*addr*, *len*) is equivalent to memcntl (*addr*, *len*, MC_UNLOCK, 0, 0, 0).

Locks established with mlock are not inherited by a child process after a fork and are not nested.

SEE ALSO
fork(2), memcntl(2), mmap(2), mlockall(3C), plock(2), sysconf(3C).

DIAGNOSTICS
Upon successful completion, the functions mlock and munlock return 0; otherwise, they return −1 and set errno to indicate the error.

NOTES
Use of mlock and munlock requires that the user have appropriate privileges.

mlockall(3C)

NAME
mlockall, munlockall – lock or unlock address space

SYNOPSIS
```
#include <sys/mman.h>

int mlockall(int flags);

int munlockall(void);
```

DESCRIPTION
The function mlockall causes all pages mapped by an address space to be locked in memory. The effect of mlockall (*flags*) is equivalent to:

    memcntl(0, 0, MC_LOCKAS, *flags*, 0, 0)

The value of *flags* determines whether the pages to be locked are those currently mapped by the address space, those that will be mapped in the future, or both:

    MCL_CURRENT   Lock current mappings
    MCL_FUTURE   Lock future mappings

The function munlockall removes address space locks and locks on mappings in the address space. The effect of munlockall is equivalent to:

    memcntl(0, 0, MC_UNLOCKAS, 0, 0, 0)

Locks established with mlockall are not inherited by a child process after a fork and are not nested.

SEE ALSO
fork(2), memcntl(2), mlock(3C), mmap(2), plock(2), sysconf(3C).

DIAGNOSTICS
Upon successful completion, the functions mlockall and munlockall return 0; otherwise, they return −1 and set errno to indicate the error.

NOTES
Use of mlockall and munlockall requires that the user have appropriate privileges.

monitor(3C) (C Development Set) monitor(3C)

NAME
monitor – prepare execution profile

SYNOPSIS
#include <mon.h>

void monitor (int (*lowpc)(), int (*highpc)(), WORD *buffer,
    size_t bufsize, size_t nfunc);

DESCRIPTION
monitor is an interface to profil, and is called automatically with default parameters by any program created by cc -p. Except to establish further control over profiling activity, it is not necessary to explicitly call monitor.

When used, monitor is called at least at the beginning and the end of a program. The first call to monitor initiates the recording of two different kinds of execution-profile information: execution-time distribution and function call count. Execution-time distribution data is generated by profil and the function call counts are generated by code supplied to the object file (or files) by cc -p. Both types of information are collected as a program executes. The last call to monitor writes this collected data to the output file mon.out.

lowpc and *highpc* are the beginning and ending addresses of the region to be profiled.

buffer is the address of a user-supplied array of WORD (WORD is defined in the header file mon.h). *buffer* is used by monitor to store the histogram generated by profil and the call counts.

bufsize identifies the number of array elements in *buffer*.

nfunc is the number of call count cells that have been reserved in *buffer*. Additional call count cells will be allocated automatically as they are needed.

bufsize should be computed using the following formula:

```
size_of_buffer =
    sizeof(struct hdr) +
    nfunc * sizeof(struct cnt) +
    ((highpc-lowpc)/BARSIZE) * sizeof(WORD) +
    sizeof(WORD) - 1 ;
bufsize = (size_of_buffer / sizeof(WORD)) ;
```

where:

lowpc, highpc, nfunc are the same as the arguments to monitor;

BARSIZE is the number of program bytes that correspond to each histogram bar, or cell, of the profil buffer;

the hdr and cnt structures and the type WORD are defined in the header file mon.h.

The default call to monitor is shown below:

    monitor (&eprol, &etext, wbuf, wbufsz, 600);

where:

eprol is the beginning of the user's program when linked with cc -p [see end(3C)];

etext is the end of the user's program [see end(3C)];

wbuf is an array of WORD with *wbufsz* elements;

wbufsz is computed using the *bufsize* formula shown above with *BARSIZE* of 8;

600 is the number of call count cells that have been reserved in *buffer*.

These parameter settings establish the computation of an execution-time distribution histogram that uses profil for the entire program, initially reserves room for 600 call count cells in *buffer*, and provides for enough histogram cells to generate significant distribution-measurement results. [For more information on the effects of *bufsize* on execution-distribution measurements, see profil(2).]

To stop execution monitoring and write the results to a file, use the following:

    monitor((int (*)( ))0, (int (*)( ))0, (WORD *)0, 0, 0);

Use prof to examine the results.

FILES

mon.out

SEE ALSO

cc(1), prof(1), profil(2), end(3C).

NOTE

Additional calls to monitor after main has been called and before exit has been called will add to the function-call count capacity, but such calls will also replace and restart the profil histogram computation.

The name of the file written by monitor is controlled by the environment variable PROFDIR. If PROFDIR does not exist, the file mon.out is created in the current directory. If PROFDIR exists but has no value, monitor does no profiling and creates no output file. If PROFDIR is *dirname*, and monitor is called automatically by compilation with cc -p, the file created is *dirname/pid.progname* where *progname* is the name of the program.

mp(3X) (BSD Compatibility Package) mp(3X)

NAME
mp: madd, msub, mult, mdiv, mcmp, min, mout, pow, gcd, rpow, msqrt, sdiv, itom, xtom, mtox, mfree – multiple precision integer arithmetic

SYNOPSIS
cc [*flag*. . .] *file* . . . −lmp

#include <mp.h>

madd(a, b, c)
MINT *a, *b, *c;

msub(a, b, c)
MINT *a, *b, *c;

mult(a, b, c)
MINT *a, *b, *c;

mdiv(a, b, q, r)
MINT *a, *b, *q, *r;

mcmp(a,b)
MINT *a, *b;

min(a)
MINT *a;

mout(a)
MINT *a;

pow(a, b, c, d)
MINT *a, *b, *c, *d;

gcd(a, b, c)
MINT *a, *b, *c;

rpow(a, n, b)
MINT *a, *b;
short n;

msqrt(a, b, r)
MINT *a, *b, *r;

sdiv(a, n, q, r)
MINT *a, *q;
short n, *r;

MINT *itom(n)
short n;

MINT *xtom(s)
char *s;

char *mtox(a)
MINT *a;

void mfree(a)
MINT *a;

DESCRIPTION

These routines perform arithmetic on integers of arbitrary length. The integers are stored using the defined type MINT. Pointers to a MINT should be initialized using the function itom, which sets the initial value to n. Alternatively, xtom may be used to initialize a MINT from a string of hexadecimal digits. mfree may be used to release the storage allocated by the itom and xtom routines.

madd, msub and mult assign to their third arguments the sum, difference, and product, respectively, of their first two arguments. mdiv assigns the quotient and remainder, respectively, to its third and fourth arguments. sdiv is like mdiv except that the divisor is an ordinary integer. msqrt produces the square root and remainder of its first argument. mcmp compares the values of its arguments and returns 0 if the two values are equal, >0 if the first argument is greater than the second, and <0 if the second argument is greater than the first. rpow calculates a raised to the power b, while pow calculates this reduced modulo m. min and mout do decimal input and output. gcd finds the greatest common divisor of the first two arguments, returning it in the third argument. mtox provides the inverse of xtom. To release the storage allocated by mtox, use free [see malloc(3)].

Use the −libmp loader option to obtain access to these functions.

RETURN VALUE

Illegal operations and running out of memory produce messages and core images.

FILES

/usr/ucblib/libmp.a

SEE ALSO

malloc(3) in the *Programmer's Reference Manual*

NAME

msync – synchronize memory with physical storage

SYNOPSIS

```
#include <sys/types.h>
#include <sys/mman.h>

int msync(caddr_t addr, size_t len, int flags);
```

DESCRIPTION

The function msync writes all modified copies of pages over the range [*addr, addr + len*) to their backing storage locations. msync optionally invalidates any copies so that further references to the pages will be obtained by the system from their backing storage locations. The backing storage for a modified MAP_SHARED mapping is the file the page is mapped to; the backing storage for a modified MAP_PRIVATE mapping is its swap area.

flags is a bit pattern built from the following values:

MS_ASYNC	perform asynchronous writes
MS_SYNC	perform synchronous writes
MS_INVALIDATE	invalidate mappings

If MS_ASYNC is set, msync returns immediately once all write operations are scheduled; if MS_SYNC is set, msync does not return until all write operations are completed.

MS_INVALIDATE invalidates all cached copies of data in memory, so that further references to the pages will be obtained by the system from their backing storage locations.

The effect of msync (*addr, len, flags*) is equivalent to:

memcntl (*addr, len*, MC_SYNC, *flags*, 0, 0)

SEE ALSO

memcntl(2), mmap(2), sysconf(3C).

DIAGNOSTICS

Upon successful completion, the function msync returns 0; otherwise, it returns −1 and sets errno to indicate the error.

NOTES

msync should be used by programs that require a memory object to be in a known state, for example, in building transaction facilities.

NAME

ndbm: dbm_clearerr, dbm_close, dbm_delete, dbm_error, dbm_fetch, dbm_firstkey, dbm_nextkey, dbm_open, dbm_store − data base subroutines

SYNOPSIS

cc [*flag*. . .] *file* . . . −ldbm

#include <ndbm.h>

typedef struct {
    char *dptr;
    int dsize;
} datum;

int dbm_clearerr(db)
DBM *db;

void dbm_close (db)
DBM *db;

int dbm_delete(db, key)
DBM *db;
datum key;

int dbm_error(db)
DBM *db;

datum dbm_fetch(db, key)
DBM *db;
datum key;

datum dbm_firstkey(db)
DBM *db;

datum dbm_nextkey(db)
DBM *db;

DBM *dbm_open(file, flags, mode)
char *file;
int flags, mode;

int dbm_store(db, key, content, flags)
DBM *db;
datum key, content;
int flags;

DESCRIPTION

These functions maintain *key/content* pairs in a data base. The functions will handle very large (a billion blocks) data base and will access a keyed item in one or two file system accesses. This package replaces the earlier dbm(3X) library, which managed only a single data base.

*key*s and *content*s are described by the datum typedef. A datum specifies a string of *dsize* bytes pointed to by *dptr*. Arbitrary binary data, as well as normal ASCII strings, are allowed. The data base is stored in two files. One file is a directory containing a bit map and has .dir as its suffix. The second file contains all data and has .pag as its suffix.

Before a data base can be accessed, it must be opened by dbm_open. This will open and/or create the files *file*.dir and *file*.pag depending on the flags parameter (see open(2V)).

A data base is closed by calling dbm_close.

Once open, the data stored under a key is accessed by dbm_fetch and data is placed under a key by dbm_store. The *flags* field can be either DBM_INSERT or DBM_REPLACE. DBM_INSERT will only insert new entries into the data base and will not change an existing entry with the same key. DBM_REPLACE will replace an existing entry if it has the same key. A key (and its associated contents) is deleted by dbm_delete. A linear pass through all keys in a data base may be made, in an (apparently) random order, by use of dbm_firstkey and dbm_nextkey. dbm_firstkey will return the first key in the data base. dbm_nextkey will return the next key in the data base. This code will traverse the data base:

for (key = dbm_firstkey(db); key.dptr != NULL; key = dbm_nextkey(db))

dbm_error returns non-zero when an error has occurred reading or writing the data base. dbm_clearerr resets the error condition on the named data base.

SEE ALSO

open(2), dbm(3X) in the *Programmer's Reference Manual*

RETURN VALUE

All functions that return an int indicate errors with negative values. A zero return indicates no error. Routines that return a datum indicate errors with a NULL (0) *dptr*. If dbm_store is called with a *flags* value of DBM_INSERT and finds an existing entry with the same key, it returns 1.

NOTES

The .pag file will contain holes so that its apparent size is about four times its actual content. Older versions of the UNIX operating system may create real file blocks for these holes when touched. These files cannot be copied by normal means (cp(1), cat(1), tar(1), ar(1)) without filling in the holes.

dptr pointers returned by these subroutines point into static storage that is changed by subsequent calls.

The sum of the sizes of a *key/content* pair must not exceed the internal block size (currently 4096 bytes). Moreover all *key/content* pairs that hash together must fit on a single block. dbm_store will return an error in the event that a disk block fills with inseparable data.

dbm_delete does not physically reclaim file space, although it does make it available for reuse.

The order of keys presented by dbm_firstkey and dbm_nextkey depends on a hashing function.

There are no interlocks and no reliable cache flushing; thus concurrent updating and reading is risky.

NAME

netdir_getbyname, netdir_getbyaddr, netdir_free, netdir_mergeaddr, taddr2uaddr, uaddr2taddr, netdir_perror, netdir_sperror − generic transport name-to-address translation

SYNOPSIS

```
#include <netdir.h>

int netdir_getbyname(struct netconfig *config, struct nd_hostserv
    *service, struct nd_addrlist *addrs);

int netdir_getbyaddr(struct netconfig *config, struct
    nd_hostservlist **service, struct netbuf *netaddr);

void netdir_free(void *ptr, int ident);

int netdir_mergeaddr(struct netconfig *config, char *mrg_uaddr,
    char *s_uaddr, char *c_uaddr);

char *taddr2uaddr(struct netconfig *config, struct netbuf *addr);

struct netbuf *uaddr2taddr(struct netconfig *config, char *uaddr);

int netdir_options(struct netconfig *netconfig, int option, int fd,
    char *pointer_to_args);

void netdir_perror(char *s);

char *netdir_sperror(void);
```

DESCRIPTION

These routines provide a generic interface for name-to-address mapping that will work with all transport protocols. This interface provides a generic way for programs to convert transport specific addresses into common structures and back again.

The netdir_getbyname routine maps the machine name and service name in the nd_hostserv structure to a collection of addresses of the type understood by the transport identified in the netconfig structure. This routine returns all addresses that are valid for that transport in the nd_addrlist structure. The netconfig structure is described on the netconfig(4) manual page. The nd_hostserv and nd_addrlist structures have the following elements.

```
         nd_addrlist structure:
              int            n_cnt;      /* number of netbufs */
              struct netbuf  *n_addrs;   /* the netbufs */

         nd_hostserv structure:
              char *h_host;   /* the host name */
              char *h_serv;   /* the service name */
```

netdir_getbyname accepts some special-case host names. These host names are hints to the underlying mapping routines that define the intent of the request. This information is required for some transport provider developers to provide the correct information back to the caller. The host names are defined in netdir.h. The currently defined host names are:

HOST_SELF   Represents the address to which local programs will bind their endpoints. HOST_SELF differs from the host name provided by gethostname(), which represents the address to which *remote* programs will bind their endpoints.

HOST_ANY   Represents any host accessible by this transport provider. HOST_ANY allows applications to specify a required service without specifying a particular host name.

HOST_BROADCAST
            Represents the address for all hosts accessible by this transport provider. Network requests to this address will be received by all machines.

All fields of the nd_hostserv structure must be initialized.

To find all available transports, call the netdir_getbyname routine with each netconfig structure returned by the getnetpath call.

The netdir_getbyaddr routine maps addresses to service names. This routine returns a list of host and service pairs that would yield this address. If more than one tuple of host and service name is returned then the first tuple contains the preferred host and service names. The nd_hostservlist structure contains the following members:

```
      int      h_cnt;              /* the number of nd_hostservs */
      struct hostserv  *h_hostservs;   /* the entries */
```

The netdir_free structure is used to free the structures allocated by the name to address translation routines.

The netdir_mergeaddr routine is used by a network service to return an optimized network addresses to a client. This routine takes the universal address of the endpoint that the service has bound to, which is pointed to by the *s_uaddr* parameter, and the address of the endpoint that a request came in on, which is pointed to by the *c_uaddr* paramter, to create an optimized address for communication with the service. The service address should be an address returned by the netdir_getbyname call, specified with the special host name HOST_SELF.

The taddr2uaddr and uaddr2taddr routines support translation between universal addresses and TLI type netbufs. They take and return character string pointers. The taddr2uaddr routine returns a pointer to a string that contains the universal address and returns NULL if the conversion is not possible. This is not a fatal condition as some transports may not support a universal address form.

option, *fd*, and *pointer_to_args* are passed to the netdir_options routine for the transport specified in netconfigp. There are four values for *option*:

      ND_SET_BROADCAST
      ND_SET_RESERVEDPORT

ND_CHECK_RESERVEDPORT
ND_MERGEADDR

If a transport provider does not support an option, `netdir_options` returns -1 and sets `_nderror` to ND_NOCTRL.

The specific actions of each option follow.

ND_SET_BROADCAST   Sets the transport provider up to allow broadcast, if the transport supports broadcast. *fd* is a file descriptor into the transport (that is, the result of a t_open of /dev/udp). *pointer_to_args* is not used. If this completes, broadcast operations may be performed on file descriptor *fd*.

ND_SET_RESERVEDPORT   Allows the application to bind to a reserved port, if that concept exists for the transport provider. *fd* is a file descriptor into the transport (it must not be bound to an address). If *pointer_to_args* is NULL, *fd* will be bound to a reserved port. If *pointer_to_args* is a pointer to a netbuf structure, an attempt will be made to bind to a reserved port on the specified address.

ND_CHECK_RESERVEDPORT   Used to verify that an address corresponds to a reserved port, if that concept exists for the transport provider. *fd* is not used. *pointer_to_args* is a pointer to a netbuf structure that contains an address. This option returns 0 only if the address specified in *pointer_to_args* is reserved.

ND_MERGEADDR   Used to take a "local address" (like the 0.0.0.0 address that TCP uses) and return a "real address" that client machines can connect to. *fd* is not used. *pointer_to_args* is a pointer to a struct nd_mergearg, which has the following members:

```
char *s_uaddr; /* server's universal address */
char *c_uaddr; /* client's universal address */
char *m_uaddr; /* merged universal address */
```

s_uaddr is something like 0.0.0.0.1.12, and, if the call is successful, m_uaddr will be set to something like 192.11.109.89.1.12. For most transports, m_uaddr is exactly what s_uaddr is.

The `netdir_perror()` routine prints an error message on the standard output stating why one of the name-to-address mapping routines failed. The error message is preceded by the string given as an argument.

The `netdir_sperror` routine returns a string containing an error message stating why one of the name-to-address mapping routines failed.

SEE ALSO
getnetpath(3N)

nice(3C) (BSD Compatibility Package)

NAME
nice – change priority of a process

SYNOPSIS
cc [*flag*. . .] *file* . . . -lucb

int nice(incr)
int incr;

DESCRIPTION
The scheduling priority of the process is augmented by *incr*. Positive priorities get less service than normal. Priority 10 is recommended to users who wish to execute long-running programs without undue impact on system performance.

Negative increments are illegal, except when specified by the privileged user. The priority is limited to the range −20 (most urgent) to 20 (least). Requests for values above or below these limits result in the scheduling priority being set to the corresponding limit.

The priority of a process is passed to a child process by fork(2). For a privileged process to return to normal priority from an unknown state, nice should be called successively with arguments −40 (goes to priority −20 because of truncation), 20 (to get to 0), then 0 (to maintain compatibility with previous versions of this call).

RETURN VALUE
Upon successful completion, nice returns 0. Otherwise, a value of −1 is returned and errno is set to indicate the error.

ERRORS
The priority is not changed if:

EACCES   The value of *incr* specified was negative, and the effective user ID is not the privileged user.

SEE ALSO
renice(1M)

nice(1), priocntl(2) in the *User's Reference Manual*
fork(2), getpriority(2), priocntl(2) in the *Programmer's Reference Manual*

nl_langinfo(3C)

NAME
nl_langinfo – language information

SYNOPSIS
```
#include <nl_types.h>
#include <langinfo.h>
```

char *nl_langinfo (nl_item item);

DESCRIPTION
nl_langinfo returns a pointer to a null-terminated string containing information relevant to a particular language or cultural area defined in the programs locale. The manifest constant names and values of *item* are defined by langinfo.h.

For example:

nl_langinfo (ABDAY_1);

would return a pointer to the string "Dim" if the identified language was French and a French locale was correctly installed; or "Sun" if the identified language was English.

SEE ALSO
gettxt(3C), localeconv(3C), setlocale(3C), strftime(3C), langinfo(5), nl_types(5)

DIAGNOSTICS
If setlocale has not been called successfully, or if langinfo data for a supported language is either not available or *item* is not defined therein, then nl_langinfo returns a pointer to the corresponding string in the C locale. In all locales, nl_langinfo returns a pointer to an empty string if *item* contains an invalid setting.

NOTES
The array pointed to by the return value should not be modified by the program. Subsequent calls to nl_langinfo may overwrite the array.

The nl_langinfo function is built upon the functions localeconv, strftime, and gettxt [see langinfo(5)]. Where possible users are advised to use these interfaces to the required data instead of using calls to nl_langinfo.

nlist(3E)   (ELF Library)   nlist(3E)

NAME
nlist – get entries from name list

SYNOPSIS
cc [*flag* ...] *file* ... -lelf [*library* ...]

#include <nlist.h>

int nlist (const char *filename, struct nlist *nl);

DESCRIPTION
nlist examines the name list in the executable file whose name is pointed to by *filename*, and selectively extracts a list of values and puts them in the array of nlist structures pointed to by *nl*. The name list *nl* consists of an array of structures containing names of variables, types, and values. The list is terminated with a null name, that is, a null string is in the name position of the structure. Each variable name is looked up in the name list of the file. If the name is found, the type, value, storage class, and section number of the name are inserted in the other fields. The type field may be set to 0 if the file was not compiled with the -g option to cc(1). nlist will always return the information for an external symbol of a given name if the name exists in the file. If an external symbol does not exist, and there is more than one symbol with the specified name in the file (such as static symbols defined in separate files), the values returned will be for the last occurrence of that name in the file. If the name is not found, all fields in the structure except n_name are set to 0.

This function is useful for examining the system name list kept in the file /stand/unix. In this way programs can obtain system addresses that are up to date.

SEE ALSO
a.out(4)

DIAGNOSTICS
All value entries are set to 0 if the file cannot be read or if it does not contain a valid name list.

nlist returns 0 on success, -1 on error.

NAME

nlist – get entries from symbol table

SYNOPSIS

cc [*flag*. . .] *file* . . . -lucb

#include <nlist.h>

int nlist(filename, nl)
char *filename;
struct nlist *nl;

DESCRIPTION

nlist examines the symbol table from the executable image whose name is pointed to by *filename*, and selectively extracts a list of values and puts them in the array of nlist structures pointed to by *nl*. The name list pointed to by nl consists of an array of structures containing names, types and values. The n_name field of each such structure is taken to be a pointer to a character string representing a symbol name. The list is terminated by an entry with a NULL pointer (or a pointer to a NULL string) in the n_name field. For each entry in *nl*, if the named symbol is present in the executable image's symbol table, its value and type are placed in the n_value and n_type fields. If a symbol cannot be located, the corresponding n_type field of nl is set to zero.

RETURN VALUE

Upon normal completion, nlist returns the number of symbols that were not located in the symbol table. If an error occurs, nlist returns −1 and sets all of the n_type fields in members of the array pointed to by nl to zero.

SEE ALSO

a.out(4) in the *Programmer's Reference Manual*

NAME
nlsgetcall – get client's data passed via the listener

SYNOPSIS
    #include <sys/tiuser.h>

    struct t_call *nlsgetcall (int fd);

DESCRIPTION
nlsgetcall allows server processes started by the listener process to access the client's t_call structure, that is, the *sndcall* argument of t_connect(3N).

The t_call structure returned by nlsgetcall can be released using t_free(3N).

nlsgetcall returns the address of an allocated t_call structure or NULL if a t_call structure cannot be allocated. If the t_alloc succeeds, undefined environment variables are indicated by a negative *len* field in the appropriate netbuf structure. A *len* field of zero in the netbuf structure is valid and means that the original buffer in the listener's t_call structure was NULL.

NOTES
The *len* field in the netbuf structure is defined as being unsigned. In order to check for error returns, it should first be cast to an int.

The listener process limits the amount of user data (*udata*) and options data (*opt*) to 128 bytes each. Address data *addr* is limited to 64 bytes. If the original data was longer, no indication of overflow is given.

Server processes must call t_sync(3N) before calling this routine.

DIAGNOSTICS
A NULL pointer is returned if a t_call structure cannot be allocated by t_alloc. t_errno can be inspected for further error information. Undefined environment variables are indicated by a negative length field (*len*) in the appropriate netbuf structure.

FILES
    /usr/lib/libnsl_s.a
    /usr/lib/libnls.a

SEE ALSO
nlsadmin(1),   getenv(3),   t_connect(3N),   t_alloc(3N),   t_free(3N), t_error(3N).

NAME
nlsprovider - get name of transport provider

SYNOPSIS
char *nlsprovider();

DESCRIPTION
nlsprovider returns a pointer to a null terminated character string which contains the name of the transport provider as placed in the environment by the listener process. If the variable is not defined in the environment, a NULL pointer is returned.

The environment variable is only available to server processes started by the listener process.

SEE ALSO
nlsadmin(1M)

DIAGNOSTICS
If the variable is not defined in the environment, a NULL pointer is returned.

FILES
/usr/lib/libnls.a
/usr/lib/libnsl_s.a

NAME

nlsrequest – format and send listener service request message

SYNOPSIS

```
#include <listen.h>

int nlsrequest (int fd, char *service_code);

extern int _nlslog, t_errno;
extern char *_nlsrmsg;
```

DESCRIPTION

Given a virtual circuit to a listener process (*fd*) and a service code of a server process, nlsrequest formats and sends a *service request message* to the remote listener process requesting that it start the given service. nlsrequest waits for the remote listener process to return a *service request response message*, which is made available to the caller in the static, null terminated data buffer pointed to by _nlsrmsg. The *service request response message* includes a success or failure code and a text message. The entire message is printable.

SEE ALSO

nlsadmin(1), t_error(3).

FILES

/usr/lib/libnls.a
/usr/lib/libnsl_s.a

DIAGNOSTICS

The success or failure code is the integer return code from nlsrequest. Zero indicates success, other negative values indicate nlsrequest failures as follows:

-1: Error encountered by nlsrequest, see t_errno.

Postive values are error return codes from the *listener* process. Mnemonics for these codes are defined in <listen.h>.

2: Request message not interpretable.
3: Request service code unknown.
4: Service code known, but currently disabled.

If non-null, _nlsrmsg contains a pointer to a static, null terminated character buffer containing the *service request response message*. Note that both _nlsrmsg and the data buffer are overwritten by each call to nlsrequest.

If _nlslog is non-zero, nlsrequest prints error messages on stderr. Initially, _nlslog is zero.

NOTES

nlsrequest cannot always be certain that the remote server process has been successfully started. In this case, nlsrequest returns with no indication of an error and the caller will receive notification of a disconnect event via a T_LOOK error before or during the first t_snd or t_rcv call.

offsetof(3C) (C Development Set) offsetof(3C)

NAME
offsetof – offset of structure member

SYNOPSIS
#include <stddef.h>

size_t offsetof (type, member-designator);

DESCRIPTION
offsetof is a macro defined in stddef.h which expands to an integral constant expression that has type size_t, the value of which is the offset in bytes, to the structure member (designated by *member-designator*), from the beginning of its structure (designated by *type*).

p2open(3G)

NAME
p2open, p2close – open, close pipes to and from a command

SYNOPSIS
cc [*flag* ...] *file* ... −lgen [*library* ...]

```
#include <libgen.h>

int p2open (const char *cmd, FILE *fp[2]);

int p2close (FILE *fp[2]);
```

DESCRIPTION
p2open forks and execs a shell running the command line pointed to by *cmd*. On return, fp[0] points to a FILE pointer to write the command's standard input and fp[1] points to a FILE pointer to read from the command's standard output. In this way the program has control over the input and output of the command.

The function returns 0 if successful; otherwise it returns −1.

p2close is used to close the file pointers that p2open opened. It waits for the process to terminate and returns the process status. It returns 0 if successful; otherwise it returns −1.

EXAMPLES
```
#include <stdio.h>
#include <libgen.h>

main(argc,argv)
int argc;
char **argv;
{
        FILE *fp[2];
        pid_t pid;
        char buf[16];

        pid=p2open("/usr/bin/cat", fp);
        if ( pid == 0 ) {
                fprintf(stderr, "p2open failed\n");
                exit(1);
        }
        write(fileno(fp[0]),"This is a test\n", 16);
        if(read(fileno(fp[1]), buf, 16) <=0)
                fprintf(stderr, "p2open failed\n");
        else
                write(1, buf, 16);
        (void)p2close(fp);
}
```

SEE ALSO
fclose(3S), popen(3S), setbuf(3S).

DIAGNOSTICS
A common problem is having too few file descriptors. p2close returns −1 if the two file pointers are not from the same p2open.

NOTES

Buffered writes on `fp[0]` can make it appear that the command is not listening. Judiciously placed `fflush` calls or unbuffering `fp[0]` can be a big help; see fclose(3S).

Many commands use buffered output when connected to a pipe. That, too, can make it appear as if things are not working.

Usage is not the same as for popen, although it is closely related.

panel_above(3X)   panel_above(3X)

NAME
panel_above: panel_above, panel_below − panels deck traversal primitives

SYNOPSIS
#include <panel.h>

PANEL *panel_above(PANEL *panel);

PANEL *panel_below(PANEL *panel);

DESCRIPTION
panel_above returns a pointer to the panel just above *panel*, or NULL if *panel* is the top panel. panel_below returns a pointer to the panel just below *panel*, or NULL if *panel* is the bottom panel.

If NULL is passed for *panel*, panel_above returns a pointer to the bottom panel in the deck, and panel_below returns a pointer to the top panel in the deck.

RETURN VALUE
NULL is returned if an error occurs.

NOTES
These routines allow traversal of the deck of currently visible panels.

The header file <panel.h> automatically includes the header file <curses.h>.

SEE ALSO
curses(3X), panels(3X)

NAME
panel_move: move_panel – move a panels window on the virtual screen

SYNOPSIS
#include <panel.h>

int move_panel(PANEL *panel, int starty, int startx);

DESCRIPTION
move_panel moves the curses window associated with *panel* so that its upper left-hand corner is at *starty*, *startx*. See usage note, below.

RETURN VALUE
OK is returned if the routine completes successfully, otherwise ERR is returned.

NOTES
For panels windows, use move_panel instead of the mvwin curses routine. Otherwise, update_panels will not properly update the virtual screen.

The header file <panel.h> automatically includes the header file <curses.h>.

SEE ALSO
curses(3X), panels(3X), panel_update(3X)

panel_new(3X)   panel_new(3X)

NAME
panel_new: new_panel, del_panel − create and destroy panels

SYNOPSIS
#include <panel.h>

PANEL *new_panel(WINDOW *win);

int del_panel(PANEL *panel);

DESCRIPTION
new_panel creates a new panel associated with *win* and returns the panel pointer. The new panel is placed on top of the panel deck.

del_panel destroys *panel*, but not its associated window.

RETURN VALUE
new_panel returns NULL if an error occurs.

del_win returns OK if successful, ERR otherwise.

NOTES
The header file <panel.h> automatically includes the header file <curses.h>.

SEE ALSO
curses(3X), panels(3X), panel_update(3X)

panel_show(3X)

NAME
panel_show: show_panel, hide_panel, panel_hidden – panels deck manipulation routines

SYNOPSIS
#include <panel.h>

int show_panel(PANEL *panel);

int hide_panel(PANEL *panel);

int panel_hidden(PANEL *panel);

DESCRIPTION
show_panel makes *panel*, previously hidden, visible and places it on top of the deck of panels.

hide_panel removes *panel* from the panel deck and, thus, hides it from view. The internal data structure of the panel is retained.

panel_hidden returns TRUE (1) or FALSE (0) indicating whether or not *panel* is in the deck of panels.

RETURN VALUE
show_panel and hide_panel return the integer OK upon successful completion or ERR upon error.

NOTES
The header file <panel.h> automatically includes the header file <curses.h>.

SEE ALSO
curses(3X), panels(3X), panel_update(3X)

panel_top(3X)

NAME
panel_top: top_panel, bottom_panel − panels deck manipulation routines

SYNOPSIS
#include <panel.h>

int top_panel(PANEL *panel);

int bottom_panel(PANEL *panel);

DESCRIPTION
top_panel pulls *panel* to the top of the desk of panels. It leaves the size, location, and contents of its associated window unchanged.

bottom_panel puts *panel* at the bottom of the deck of panels. It leaves the size, location, and contents of its associated window unchanged.

RETURN VALUE
All of these routines return the integer OK upon successful completion or ERR upon error.

NOTES
The header file <panel.h> automatically includes the header file <curses.h>.

SEE ALSO
curses(3X), panels(3X), panel_update(3X)

NAME
panel_update: update_panels – panels virtual screen refresh routine

SYNOPSIS
#include <panel.h>

void update_panels(void);

DESCRIPTION
update_panels refreshes the virtual screen to reflect the depth relationships between the panels in the deck. The user must use the curses library call doupdate [see curs_refresh(3X)] to refresh the physical screen.

NOTES
The header file <panel.h> automatically includes the header file <curses.h>.

SEE ALSO
curses(3X), panels(3X), curs_refresh(3X)

panel_userptr(3X)   **panel_userptr(3X)**

NAME
panel_userptr: set_panel_userptr, panel_userptr – associate application data with a panels panel

SYNOPSIS
#include <panel.h>

int set_panel_userptr(PANEL *panel, char *ptr);

char * panel_userptr(PANEL *panel);

DESCRIPTION
Each panel has a user pointer available for maintaining relevant information.

set_panel_userptr sets the user pointer of *panel* to *ptr*.

panel_userptr returns the user pointer of *panel*.

RETURN VALUE
set_panel_userptr returns OK if successful, ERR otherwise.

panel_userptr returns NULL if there is no user pointer assigned to *panel*.

NOTES
The header file <panel.h> automatically includes the header file <curses.h>.

SEE ALSO
curses(3X), panels(3X)

panel_window(3X)

NAME
panel_window: panel_window, replace_panel – get or set the current window of a panels panel

SYNOPSIS
#include <panel.h>

WINDOW *panel_window(PANEL *panel);

int replace_panel(PANEL *panel, WINDOW *win);

DESCRIPTION
panel_window returns a pointer to the window of *panel*.

replace_panel replaces the current window of *panel* with *win*.

RETURN VALUE
panel_window returns NULL on failure.

replace_panel returns OK on successful completion, ERR otherwise.

NOTES
The header file <panel.h> automatically includes the header file <curses.h>.

SEE ALSO
curses(3X), panels(3X)

panels(3X)

NAME
panels – character based panels package

SYNOPSIS
#include <panel.h>

DESCRIPTION
The panel library is built using the curses library, and any program using panels routines must call one of the curses initialization routines such as initscr. A program using these routines must be compiled with -lpanel and -lcurses on the cc command line.

The panels package gives the applications programmer a way to have depth relationships between curses windows; a curses window is associated with every panel. The panels routines allow curses windows to overlap without making visible the overlapped portions of underlying windows. The initial curses window, stdscr, lies beneath all panels. The set of currently visible panels is the *deck* of panels.

The panels package allows the applications programmer to create panels, fetch and set their associated windows, shuffle panels in the deck, and manipulate panels in other ways.

Routine Name Index
The following table lists each panels routine and the name of the manual page on which it is described.

panels Routine Name	Manual Page Name
bottom_panel	panel_top(3X)
del_panel	panel_new(3X)
hide_panel	panel_show(3X)
move_panel	panel_move(3X)
new_panel	panel_new(3X)
panel_above	panel_above(3X)
panel_below	panel_above(3X)
panel_hidden	panel_show(3X)
panel_userptr	panel_userptr(3X)
panel_window	panel_window(3X)
replace_panel	panel_window(3X)
set_panel_userptr	panel_userptr(3X)
show_panel	panel_show(3X)
top_panel	panel_top(3X)
update_panels	panel_update(3X)

RETURN VALUE
Each panels routine that returns a pointer to an object returns NULL if an error occurs. Each panel routine that returns an integer, returns OK if it executes successfully and ERR if it does not.

NOTES
   The header file <panel.h> automatically includes the header file <curses.h>.

SEE ALSO
   curses(3X), and 3X pages whose names begin with panel_, for detailed routine descriptions.

pathfind(3G)

NAME
pathfind – search for named file in named directories

SYNOPSIS
cc [*flag* ...] *file* ... -lgen [*library* ...]

```
#include <libgen.h>
```

char *pathfind (const char *path, const char *name, const char *mode);

DESCRIPTION
pathfind searches the directories named in *path* for the file *name*. The directories named in *path* are separated by semicolons. *mode* is a string of option letters chosen from the set rwxfbcdpugks:

Letter	Meaning
r	readable
w	writable
x	executable
f	normal file
b	block special
c	character special
d	directory
p	FIFO (pipe)
u	set user ID bit
g	set group ID bit
k	sticky bit
s	size nonzero

Options read, write, and execute are checked relative to the real (not the effective) user ID and group ID of the current process.

If the file *name*, with all the characteristics specified by *mode*, is found in any of the directories specified by *path*, then pathfind returns a pointer to a string containing the member of *path*, followed by a slash character (/), followed by *name*.

If *name* begins with a slash, it is treated as an absolute path name, and *path* is ignored.

An empty *path* member is treated as the current directory. ./ is not prepended at the occurrence of the first match; rather, the unadorned *name* is returned.

EXAMPLES
To find the ls command using the PATH environment variable:

   pathfind (getenv ("PATH"), "ls", "rx")

SEE ALSO
access(2), mknod(2), stat(2), getenv(3C).

sh(1), test(1) in the *User's Reference Manual*.

DIAGNOSTICS
If no match is found, pathname returns a null pointer, ((char *) 0).

NOTES
The string pointed to by the returned pointer is stored in a static area that is reused on subsequent calls to pathfind.

perror(3C) (C Development Set) **perror(3C)**

NAME
    perror – print system error messages

SYNOPSIS
    #include <stdio.h>

    void perror (const char *s);

DESCRIPTION
    perror produces a message on the standard error output (file descriptor 2), describing the last error encountered during a call to a system or library function. The argument string s is printed first, then a colon and a blank, then the message and a newline. (However, if s is a null pointer or points to a null string, the colon is not printed.) To be of most use, the argument string should include the name of the program that incurred the error. The error number is taken from the external variable errno, which is set when errors occur but not cleared when non-erroneous calls are made.

SEE ALSO
    intro(2), fmtmsg(3C), strerror(3C).

NAME

popen, pclose – initiate pipe to/from a process

SYNOPSIS

```
#include <stdio.h>

FILE *popen (const char *command, const char *type);

int pclose (FILE *stream);
```

DESCRIPTION

popen creates a pipe between the calling program and the command to be executed. The arguments to popen are pointers to null-terminated strings. *command* consists of a shell command line. *type* is an I/O mode, either r for reading or w for writing. The value returned is a stream pointer such that one can write to the standard input of the command, if the I/O mode is w, by writing to the file *stream* [see intro(3)]; and one can read from the standard output of the command, if the I/O mode is r, by reading from the file *stream*.

A stream opened by popen should be closed by pclose, which waits for the associated process to terminate and returns the exit status of the command.

Because open files are shared, a type r command may be used as an input filter and a type w as an output filter.

EXAMPLE

Here is an example of a typical call:

```
#include <stdio.h>
#include <stdlib.h>

main()
{
        char *cmd = "/usr/bin/ls *.c";
        char buf[BUFSIZ];
        FILE *ptr;

        if ((ptr = popen(cmd, "r")) != NULL)
                while (fgets(buf, BUFSIZ, ptr) != NULL)
                        (void) printf("%s", buf);
        return 0;
}
```

This program will print on the standard output [see stdio(3S)] all the file names in the current directory that have a .c suffix.

SEE ALSO

pipe(2), wait(2), fclose(3S), fopen(3S), stdio(3S), system(3S).

DIAGNOSTICS

popen returns a null pointer if files or processes cannot be created.

pclose returns −1 if *stream* is not associated with a popened command.

NOTES

If the original and popened processes concurrently read or write a common file, neither should use buffered I/O. Problems with an output filter may be forestalled by careful buffer flushing, e.g., with fflush [see fclose(3S)].

A security hole exists through the IFS and PATH environment variables. Full pathnames should be used (or PATH reset) and IFS should be set to space and tab (" \t").

printf(3S)

NAME
printf, fprintf, sprintf – print formatted output

SYNOPSIS
#include <stdio.h>

int printf(const char *format, .../* args */);

int fprintf(FILE *strm, const char *format, .../* args */);

int sprintf(char *s, const char *format, .../* args */);

DESCRIPTION
printf places output on the standard output stream stdout.

fprintf places output on *strm*.

sprintf places output, followed by the null character (\0), in consecutive bytes starting at *s*. It is the user's responsibility to ensure that enough storage is available. Each function returns the number of characters transmitted (not including the \0 in the case of sprintf) or a negative value if an output error was encountered.

Each of these functions converts, formats, and prints its *args* under control of the *format*. The *format* is a character string that contains three types of objects defined below:

1. plain characters that are simply copied to the output stream;
2. escape sequences that represent non-graphic characters;
3. conversion specifications.

The following escape sequences produce the associated action on display devices capable of the action:

\a   Alert. Ring the bell.

\b   Backspace. Move the printing position to one character before the current position, unless the current position is the start of a line.

\f   Form feed. Move the printing position to the initial printing position of the next logical page.

\n   Newline. Move the printing position to the start of the next line.

\r   Carriage return. Move the printing position to the start of the current line.

\t   Horizontal tab. Move the printing position to the next implementation-defined horizontal tab position on the current line.

\v   Vertical tab. Move the printing position to the start of the next implementation-defined vertical tab position.

All forms of the printf functions allow for the insertion of a language-dependent decimal-point character. The decimal-point character is defined by the program's locale (category LC_NUMERIC). In the C locale, or in a locale where the decimal-point character is not defined, the decimal-point character defaults to a period (.).

Each conversion specification is introduced by the character %. After the character %, the following appear in sequence:

> An optional field, consisting of a decimal digit string followed by a $, specifying the next *args* to be converted. If this field is not provided, the *args* following the last *args* converted will be used.

> Zero or more *flags*, which modify the meaning of the conversion specification.

> An optional string of decimal digits to specify a minimum *field width*. If the converted value has fewer characters than the field width, it will be padded on the left (or right, if the left-adjustment flag (−), described below, has been given) to the field width.

> An optional precision that gives the minimum number of digits to appear for the d, i, o, u, x, or X conversions (the field is padded with leading zeros), the number of digits to appear after the decimal-point character for the e, E, and f conversions, the maximum number of significant digits for the g and G conversions, or the maximum number of characters to be printed from a string in s conversion. The precision takes the form of a period (.) followed by a decimal digit string; a null digit string is treated as zero. Padding specified by the precision overrides the padding specified by the field width.

> An optional h specifies that a following d, i, o, u, x, or X conversion specifier applies to a short int or unsigned short int argument (the argument will be promoted according to the integral promotions and its value converted to short int or unsigned short int before printing); an optional h specifies that a following n conversion specifier applies to a pointer to a short int argument. An optional l (ell) specifies that a following d, i, o, u, x, or X conversion specifier applies to a long int or unsigned long int argument; an optional l (ell) specifies that a following n conversion specifier applies to a pointer to long int argument. An optional L specifies that a following e, E, f, g, or G conversion specifier applies to a long double argument. If an h, l, or L appears before any other conversion specifier, the behavior is undefined.

> A conversion character (see below) that indicates the type of conversion to be applied.

A field width or precision may be indicated by an asterisk (*) instead of a digit string. In this case, an integer *args* supplies the field width or precision. The *args* that is actually converted is not fetched until the conversion letter is seen, so the *args* specifying field width or precision must appear before the *args* (if any) to be converted. If the *precision* argument is negative, it will be changed to zero. A negative field width argument is taken as a − flag, followed by a positive field width.

In format strings containing the *digits$ form of a conversion specification, a field width or precision may also be indicated by the sequence *digits$, giving the position in the argument list of an integer *args* containing the field width or precision.

When numbered argument specifications are used, specifying the Nth argument requires that all the leading arguments, from the first to the (N−1)th, be specified in the format string.

The *flag* characters and their meanings are:

-     The result of the conversion will be left-justified within the field. (It will be right-justified if this flag is not specified.)

+   The result of a signed conversion will always begin with a sign (+ or −). (It will begin with a sign only when a negative value is converted if this flag is not specified.)

space   If the first character of a signed conversion is not a sign, a space will be placed before the result. This means that if the space and + flags both appear, the space flag will be ignored.

The value is to be converted to an alternate form. For c, d, i, s, and u conversions, the flag has no effect. For an o conversion, it increases the precision to force the first digit of the result to be a zero. For x (or X) conversion, a non-zero result will have 0x (or 0X) prepended to it. For e, E, f, g, and G conversions, the result will always contain a decimal-point character, even if no digits follow the point (normally, a decimal point appears in the result of these conversions only if a digit follows it). For g and G conversions, trailing zeros will not be removed from the result as they normally are.

0   For d, i, o, u, x, X, e, E, f, g, and G conversions, leading zeros (following any indication of sign or base) are used to pad to the field width; no space padding is performed. If the 0 and − flags both appear, the 0 flag will be ignored. For d, i, o, u, x, and X conversions, if a precision is specified, the 0 flag will be ignored. For other conversions, the behavior is undefined.

Each conversion character results in fetching zero or more *args*. The results are undefined if there are insufficient *args* for the format. If the format is exhausted while *args* remain, the excess *args* are ignored.

The conversion characters and their meanings are:

d,i,o,u,x,X   The integer *arg* is converted to signed decimal (d or i), (unsigned octal (o), unsigned decimal (u), or unsigned hexadecimal notation (x and X). The x conversion uses the letters abcdef and the X conversion uses the letters ABCDEF. The precision specifies the minimum number of digits to appear. If the value being converted can be represented in fewer digits than the specified minimum, it will be expanded with leading zeros. The default precision is 1. The result of converting a zero value with a precision of zero is no characters.

f   The double *args* is converted to decimal notation in the style [−]*ddd.ddd*, where the number of digits after the decimal-point character [see setlocale(3C)] is equal to the precision specification. If the precision is omitted from *arg*, six digits are output; if the precision is explicitly zero and the # flag is not specified, no decimal-point character appears. If a decimal-point

	character appears, at least 1 digit appears before it. The value is rounded to the appropriate number of digits.
e,E	The double *args* is converted to the style [-]*d.ddd*e±*dd*, where there is one digit before the decimal-point character (which is non-zero if the argument is non-zero) and the number of digits after it is equal to the precision. When the precision is missing, six digits are produced; if the precision is zero and the # flag is not specified, no decimal-point character appears. The E conversion character will produce a number with E instead of e introducing the exponent. The exponent always contains at least two digits. The value is rounded to the appropriate number of digits.
g,G	The double *args* is printed in style f or e (or in style E in the case of a G conversion character), with the precision specifying the number of significant digits. If the precision is zero, it is taken as one. The style used depends on the value converted: style e (or E) will be used only if the exponent resulting from the conversion is less than −4 or greater than or equal to the precision. Trailing zeros are removed from the fractional part of the result. A decimal-point character appears only if it is followed by a digit.
c	The int *args* is converted to an unsigned char, and the resulting character is printed.
s	The *args* is taken to be a string (character pointer) and characters from the string are written up to (but not including) a terminating null character; if the precision is specified, no more than that many characters are written. If the precision is not specified, it is taken to be infinite, so all characters up to the first null character are printed. A NULL value for *args* will yield undefined results.
p	The *args* should be a pointer to void. The value of the pointer is converted to an implementation-defined set of sequences of printable characters, which should be the same as the set of sequences that are matched by the %p conversion of the scanf function.
n	The argument should be a pointer to an integer into which is written the number of characters written to the output standard I/O stream so far by this call to printf, fprintf, or sprintf. No argument is converted.
%	Print a %; no argument is converted.

If the character after the % or %*digits*$ sequence is not a valid conversion character, the results of the conversion are undefined.

If a floating-point value is the internal representation for infinity, the output is [±]*inf*, where *inf* is either inf or INF, depending on the conversion character. Printing of the sign follows the rules described above.

If a floating-point value is the internal representation for "not-a-number," the output is [±]*nan*0*xm*. Depending on the conversion character, *nan* is either nan or NAN. Additionally, 0*xm* represents the most significant part of the mantissa. Again depending on the conversion character, *x* will be x or X, and *m* will use the letters abcdef or ABCDEF. Printing of the sign follows the rules described above.

In no case does a non-existent or small field width cause truncation of a field; if the result of a conversion is wider than the field width, the field is simply expanded to contain the conversion result. Characters generated by printf and fprintf are printed as if the putc routine had been called.

EXAMPLE

To print a date and time in the form Sunday, July 3, 10:02, where weekday and month are pointers to null-terminated strings:

```
printf("%s, %s %i, %d:%.2d",
       weekday, month, day, hour, min);
```

To print π to 5 decimal places:

```
printf("pi = %.5f", 4 * atan(1.0));
```

SEE ALSO

exit(2), lseek(2), write(2), abort(3C), ecvt(3C), putc(3S), scanf(3S), setlocale(3C), stdio(3S).

DIAGNOSTICS

printf, fprintf, and sprintf return the number of characters transmitted, or return a negative value if an error was encountered.

printf(3S) (BSD Compatibility Package) printf(3S)

NAME
printf, fprintf, sprintf, vprintf, vfprintf, vsprintf – formatted output conversion

SYNOPSIS
cc [*flag*...] *file* ... -lucb

```
#include <stdio.h>
int printf(format [ , arg ] ... )
char *format;

int fprintf(stream, format [ , arg ] ... )
FILE *stream;
char *format;

char *sprintf(s, format [ , arg ] ... )
char *s, *format;

int vprintf(format, ap)
char *format;
va_list ap;

int vfprintf(stream, format, ap)
FILE *stream;
char *format;
va_list ap;

char *vsprintf(s, format, ap)
char *s, *format;
va_list ap;
```

DESCRIPTION
printf places output on the standard output stream stdout. fprintf places output on the named output *stream*. sprintf places "output," followed by the NULL character (\0), in consecutive bytes starting at *s; it is the user's responsibility to ensure that enough storage is available.

vprintf, vfprintf, and vsprintf are the same as printf, fprintf, and sprintf respectively, except that instead of being called with a variable number of arguments, they are called with an argument list as defined by varargs(5).

Each of these functions converts, formats, and prints its *arg*s under control of the *format*. The *format* is a character string which contains two types of objects: plain characters, which are simply copied to the output stream, and conversion specifications, each of which causes conversion and printing of zero or more *arg*s. The results are undefined if there are insufficient *arg*s for the format. If the format is exhausted while *arg*s remain, the excess *arg*s are simply ignored.

Each conversion specification is introduced by the character %. After the %, the following appear in sequence:

> Zero or more *flags*, which modify the meaning of the conversion specification.

An optional decimal digit string specifying a minimum *field width*. If the converted value has fewer characters than the field width, it will be padded on the left (or right, if the left-adjustment flag '−', described below, has been given) to the field width. The padding is with blanks unless the field width digit string starts with a zero, in which case the padding is with zeros.

A *precision* that gives the minimum number of digits to appear for the d, i, o, u, x, or X conversions, the number of digits to appear after the decimal point for the e, E, and f conversions, the maximum number of significant digits for the g and G conversion, or the maximum number of characters to be printed from a string in s conversion. The precision takes the form of a period (.) followed by a decimal digit string; a NULL digit string is treated as zero. Padding specified by the precision overrides the padding specified by the field width.

An optional l (ell) specifying that a following d, i, o, u, x, or X conversion character applies to a long integer *arg*. An l before any other conversion character is ignored.

A character that indicates the type of conversion to be applied.

A field width or precision or both may be indicated by an asterisk (*) instead of a digit string. In this case, an integer *arg* supplies the field width or precision. The *arg* that is actually converted is not fetched until the conversion letter is seen, so the *arg*s specifying field width or precision must appear *before* the *arg* (if any) to be converted. A negative field width argument is taken as a '−' flag followed by a positive field width. If the precision argument is negative, it will be changed to zero.

The flag characters and their meanings are:

−   The result of the conversion will be left-justified within the field.

+   The result of a signed conversion will always begin with a sign (+ or −).

blank   If the first character of a signed conversion is not a sign, a blank will be prefixed to the result. This implies that if the blank and + flags both appear, the blank flag will be ignored.

This flag specifies that the value is to be converted to an "alternate form."For c, d, i, s, and u conversions, the flag has no effect. For o conversion, it increases the precision to force the first digit of the result to be a zero. For x or X conversion, a non-zero result will have 0x or 0X prefixed to it. For e, E, f, g, and G conversions, the result will always contain a decimal point, even if no digits follow the point (normally, a decimal point appears in the result of these conversions only if a digit follows it). For g and G conversions, trailing zeroes will *not* be removed from the result (which they normally are).

The conversion characters and their meanings are:

d,i,o,u,x,X   The integer *arg* is converted to signed decimal (d or i), unsigned octal (o), unsigned decimal (u), or unsigned hexadecimal notation (x and X), respectively; the letters abcdef are used for x conversion and the letters ABCDEF for X conversion. The precision specifies the minimum number of digits to appear; if the value being converted can be represented in fewer digits, it will be expanded with leading zeroes. (For compatibility with older versions, padding with leading zeroes may alternatively be specified by prepending a zero to the field width. This does not imply an octal value for the field width.) The default precision is 1. The result of converting a zero value with a precision of zero is a NULL string.

f   The float or double *arg* is converted to decimal notation in the style [−]*ddd.ddd* where the number of digits after the decimal point is equal to the precision specification. If the precision is missing, 6 digits are given; if the precision is explicitly 0, no digits and no decimal point are printed.

e,E   The float or double *arg* is converted in the style [−]*d.ddd*e±*ddd*, where there is one digit before the decimal point and the number of digits after it is equal to the precision; when the precision is missing, 6 digits are produced; if the precision is zero, no decimal point appears. The E format code will produce a number with E instead of e introducing the exponent. The exponent always contains at least two digits.

g,G   The float or double *arg* is printed in style f or e (or in style E in the case of a G format code), with the precision specifying the number of significant digits. The style used depends on the value converted: style e or E will be used only if the exponent resulting from the conversion is less than −4 or greater than the precision. Trailing zeroes are removed from the result; a decimal point appears only if it is followed by a digit.

The e, E, f, g, and G formats print IEEE indeterminate values (infinity or not-a-number) as "Infinity" or "NaN" respectively.

c   The character *arg* is printed.

s   The *arg* is taken to be a string (character pointer) and characters from the string are printed until a NULL character (\0) is encountered or until the number of characters indicated by the precision specification is reached. If the precision is missing, it is taken to be infinite, so all characters up to the first NULL character are printed. A NULL value for *arg* will yield undefined results.

%   Print a %; no argument is converted.

In no case does a non-existent or small field width cause truncation of a field; if the result of a conversion is wider than the field width, the field is simply expanded to contain the conversion result. Padding takes place only if the specified field width exceeds the actual width. Characters generated by printf and fprintf are printed as if putc(3S) had been called.

RETURN VALUE

Upon success, printf and fprintf return the number of characters transmitted, excluding the null character. vprintf and vfprintf return the number of characters transmitted. sprintf and vsprintf always return s. If an output error is encountered, printf, fprint, vprintf, and vfprintf, return EOF.

EXAMPLE

To print a date and time in the form "Sunday, July 3, 10:02," where *weekday* and *month* are pointers to NULL-terminated strings:

```
printf("%s, %s %i, %d:%.2d", weekday, month, day, hour, min);
```

To print π to 5 decimal places:

```
printf("pi = %.5f", 4 * atan(1. 0));
```

SEE ALSO

econvert(3)

putc(3S), scanf(3S), varargs(5), vprintf(3S) in the *Programmer's Reference Manual*

NOTES

Very wide fields (>128 characters) fail.

psignal(3C)

NAME
psignal, psiginfo – system signal messages

SYNOPSIS
#include <siginfo.h>

void psignal (int sig, const char *s);

void psiginfo (siginfo_t *pinfo, char *s);

DESCRIPTION
psignal and psiginfo produce messages on the standard error output describing a signal. *sig* is a signal that may have been passed as the first argument to a signal handler. *pinfo* is a pointer to a siginfo structure that may have been passed as the second argument to an enhanced signal handler [see sigaction(2)]. The argument string *s* is printed first, then a colon and a blank, then the message and a newline.

SEE ALSO
sigaction(2), perror(3), siginfo(5), signal(5).

NAME
psignal, sys_siglist − system signal messages

SYNOPSIS
cc [*flag*...] *file* ... −lucb

psignal(sig, s)
unsigned sig;
char *s;

char *sys_siglist[ ];

DESCRIPTION
psignal produces a short message on the standard error file describing the indicated signal. First the argument string *s* is printed, then a colon, then the name of the signal and a NEWLINE. Most usefully, the argument string is the name of the program which incurred the signal. The signal number should be from among those found in <signal.h>.

To simplify variant formatting of signal names, the vector of message strings sys_siglist is provided; the signal number can be used as an index in this table to get the signal name without the newline. The define NSIG defined in <signal.h> is the number of messages provided for in the table; it should be checked because new signals may be added to the system before they are added to the table.

SEE ALSO
signal(3)

perror(3C) in the *Programmer's Reference Manual*

ptsname(3C)

NAME
ptsname – get name of the slave pseudo-terminal device

SYNOPSIS
#include <stdio.h>

char *ptsname(int *fildes*);

DESCRIPTION
The function ptsname() returns the name of the slave pseudo-terminal device associated with a master pseudo-terminal device. *fildes* is a file descriptor returned from a successful open of the master device. ptsname() returns a pointer to a string containing the null-terminated path name of the slave device of the form /dev/pts/N, where N is an integer between 0 and 255.

RETURN VALUE
Upon successful completion, the function ptsname() returns a pointer to a string which is the name of the pseudo-terminal slave device. This value points to a static data area that is overwritten by each call to ptsname(). Upon failure, ptsname() returns NULL. This could occur if *fildes* is an invalid file descriptor or if the slave device name does not exist in the file system.

SEE ALSO
open(2), grantpt(3C), ttyname(3C), unlockpt(3C)
Programmer's Guide: STREAMS

NAME

publickey: getpublickey, getsecretkey - retrieve public or secret key

SYNOPSIS

    #include <rpc/rpc.h>
    #include <rpc/key_prot.h>

    getpublickey(const char netname[MAXNETNAMELEN],
        char publickey[HEXKEYBYTES]);

    getsecretkey(const char netname[MAXNETNAMELEN],
        char secretkey[HEXKEYBYTES], const char *passwd);

DESCRIPTION

getpublickey and getsecretkey get public and secret keys for *netname* from the publickey(4) database.

getsecretkey has an extra argument, *passwd*, used to decrypt the encrypted secret key stored in the database.

Both routines return 1 if they are successful in finding the key, 0 otherwise. The keys are returned as NULL-terminated, hexadecimal strings. If the password supplied to getsecretkey fails to decrypt the secret key, the routine will return 1 but the *secretkey* argument will be a NULL string.

SEE ALSO

publickey(4)

NAME

putc, putchar, fputc, putw – put character or word on a stream

SYNOPSIS

#include <stdio.h>

int putc (int c, FILE *stream);

int putchar (int c);

int fputc (int c, FILE *stream);

int putw (int w, FILE *stream);

DESCRIPTION

putc writes c (converted to an unsigned char) onto the output *stream* [see intro(3)] at the position where the file pointer (if defined) is pointing, and advances the file pointer appropriately. If the file cannot support positioning requests, or *stream* was opened with append mode, the character is appended to the output *stream*. putchar(c) is defined as putc(c, stdout). putc and putchar are macros.

fputc behaves like putc, but is a function rather than a macro. fputc runs more slowly than putc, but it takes less space per invocation and its name can be passed as an argument to a function.

putw writes the word (that is, integer) w to the output *stream* (where the file pointer, if defined, is pointing). The size of a word is the size of an integer and varies from machine to machine. putw neither assumes nor causes special alignment in the file.

SEE ALSO

exit(2), lseek(2), write(2), abort(3C), fclose(3S), ferror(3S), fopen(3S), fread(3S), printf(3S), puts(3S), setbuf(3S), stdio(3S).

DIAGNOSTICS

On success, these functions (with the exception of putw) each return the value they have written. putw returns ferror *(stream)*. On failure, they return the constant EOF. This result will occur, for example, if the file *stream* is not open for writing or if the output file cannot grow.

NOTES

Because it is implemented as a macro, putc evaluates a *stream* argument more than once. In particular, putc(c, *f++); doesn't work sensibly. fputc should be used instead.

Because of possible differences in word length and byte ordering, files written using putw are machine-dependent, and may not be read using getw on a different processor.

Functions exist for all the above defined macros. To get the function form, the macro name must be undefined (for example, #undef putc).

putenv(3C)

NAME
putenv – change or add value to environment

SYNOPSIS
#include <stdlib.h>

int putenv (char *string);

DESCRIPTION
string points to a string of the form *"name=value."* putenv makes the value of the environment variable *name* equal to *value* by altering an existing variable or creating a new one. In either case, the string pointed to by *string* becomes part of the environment, so altering the string will change the environment. The space used by *string* is no longer used once a new string-defining *name* is passed to putenv. Because of this limitation, *string* should be declared static if it is declared within a function.

SEE ALSO
exec(2), getenv(3C), malloc(3C), environ(5).

DIAGNOSTICS
putenv returns non-zero if it was unable to obtain enough space via malloc for an expanded environment, otherwise zero.

NOTES
putenv manipulates the environment pointed to by *environ*, and can be used in conjunction with getenv. However, *envp* (the third argument to *main*) is not changed.

This routine uses malloc(3C) to enlarge the environment.

After putenv is called, environmental variables are not in alphabetical order. A potential error is to call the function putenv with a pointer to an automatic variable as the argument and to then exit the calling function while *string* is still part of the environment.

NAME
putpwent – write password file entry

SYNOPSIS
#include <pwd.h>

int putpwent (const struct passwd *p, FILE *f);

DESCRIPTION
putpwent is the inverse of getpwent(3C). Given a pointer to a passwd structure created by getpwent (or getpwuid or getpwnam), putpwent writes a line on the stream f, which matches the format of /etc/passwd.

SEE ALSO
getpwent(3C).

DIAGNOSTICS
putpwent returns non-zero if an error was detected during its operation, otherwise zero.

NAME

puts, fputs – put a string on a stream

SYNOPSIS

#include <stdio.h>

int puts (const char *s);

int fputs (const char *s, FILE *stream);

DESCRIPTION

puts writes the string pointed to by s, followed by a new-line character, to the standard output stream stdout [see intro(3)].

fputs writes the null-terminated string pointed to by s to the named output stream.

Neither function writes the terminating null character.

SEE ALSO

exit(2), lseek(2), write(2), abort(3C), fclose(3S), ferror(3S), fopen(3S), fread(3S), printf(3S), putc(3S), stdio(3S).

DIAGNOSTICS

On success both routines return the number of characters written; otherwise they return EOF.

NOTES

puts appends a new-line character while fputs does not.

putspent(3C)

NAME
putspent − write shadow password file entry

SYNOPSIS
    #include <shadow.h>

    int putspent (const struct spwd *p, FILE *fp);

DESCRIPTION
The putspent routine is the inverse of getspent. Given a pointer to a spwd structure created by the getspent routine (or the getspnam routine), the putspent routine writes a line on the stream *fp*, which matches the format of /etc/shadow.

If the sp_min, sp_max, sp_lstchg, sp_warn, sp_inact, or sp_expire field of the spwd structure is −1, or if sp_flag is 0, the corresponding /etc/shadow field is cleared.

SEE ALSO
getspent(3C), getpwent(3C), putpwent(3C).

DIAGNOSTICS
The putspent routine returns non-zero if an error was detected during its operation, otherwise zero.

NOTES
This routine is for internal use only, compatibility is not guaranteed.

qsort(3C)

NAME
qsort – quicker sort

SYNOPSIS
```
#include <stdlib.h>
```

```
void qsort (void* base, size_t nel, size_t width, int (*compar)
    (const void *, const void *));
```

DESCRIPTION
qsort is an implementation of the quicker-sort algorithm. It sorts a table of data in place. The contents of the table are sorted in ascending order according to the user-supplied comparison function.

base points to the element at the base of the table. *nel* is the number of elements in the table. *width* specifies the size of each element in bytes. *compar* is the name of the comparison function, which is called with two arguments that point to the elements being compared. The function must return an integer less than, equal to, or greater than zero to indicate if the first argument is to be considered less than, equal to, or greater than the second.

The contents of the table are sorted in ascending order according to the user supplied comparison function.

SEE ALSO
bsearch(3C), lsearch(3C), string(3C).
sort(1) in the *User's Reference Manual*.

NOTES
The comparison function need not compare every byte, so arbitrary data may be contained in the elements in addition to the values being compared.

The relative order in the output of two items that compare as equal is unpredictable.

NAME
raise – send signal to program

SYNOPSIS
#include <signal.h>

int raise (int sig);

DESCRIPTION
raise sends the signal *sig* to the executing program.

raise returns zero if the operation succeeds. Otherwise, raise returns −1 and errno is set to indicate the error. raise uses kill to send the signal to the executing program:

kill(getpid(), sig);

See kill(2) for a detailed list of failure conditions. See signal(2) for a list of signals.

SEE ALSO
getpid(2), kill(2), signal(2).

NAME
rand, srand – simple random-number generator

SYNOPSIS
#include <stdlib.h>

int rand (void);

void srand (unsigned int seed);

DESCRIPTION
rand uses a multiplicative congruent random-number generator with period 2^{32} that returns successive pseudo-random numbers in the range from 0 to RAND_MAX (defined in stdlib.h).

The function srand uses the argument *seed* as a seed for a new sequence of pseudo-random numbers to be returned by subsequent calls to the function rand. If the function srand is then called with the same *seed* value, the sequence of pseudo-random numbers will be repeated. If the function rand is called before any calls to srand have been made, the same sequence will be generated as when srand is first called with a *seed* value of 1.

NOTES
The spectral properties of rand are limited. drand48(3C) provides a much better, though more elaborate, random-number generator.

SEE ALSO
drand48(3C).

rand(3C)　　　　　　(BSD Compatibility Package)　　　　　　rand(3C)

NAME
rand, srand – simple random number generator

SYNOPSIS
cc [*flag*. . .] *file* . . . −lucb

srand(seed)
int seed;

rand()

DESCRIPTION
rand uses a multiplicative congruential random number generator with period 2^{32} to return successive pseudo-random numbers in the range from 0 to $2^{31}-1$.

srand can be called at any time to reset the random-number generator to a random starting point. The generator is initially seeded with a value of 1.

SEE ALSO
random(3)

drand48(2), drand(3C), rand(3C), srand(3C) in the *Programmer's Reference Manual*

NOTES
The spectral properties of rand leave a great deal to be desired. drand48(2) and random(3) provide much better, though more elaborate, random-number generators.

The low bits of the numbers generated are not very random; use the middle bits. In particular the lowest bit alternates between 0 and 1.

random(3)　　　　　　　(BSD Compatibility Package)　　　　　　　random(3)

NAME
    random, srandom, initstate, setstate − better random number generator; routines for changing generators

SYNOPSIS
    cc [*flag*...] *file* ... −lucb

    long　random()

    srandom(seed)
    int　seed;

    char　*initstate(seed, state, n)
    unsigned　seed;
    char　*state;
    int　n;

    char　*setstate(state)
    char　*state;

DESCRIPTION
    random uses a non-linear additive feedback random number generator employing a default table of size 31 long integers to return successive pseudo-random numbers in the range from 0 to $2^{31}-1$. The period of this random number generator is very large, approximately $16 \times (2^{31}-1)$.

    random/srandom have (almost) the same calling sequence and initialization properties as rand/srand [see rand(3C)]. The difference is that rand(3C) produces a much less random sequence—in fact, the low dozen bits generated by rand go through a cyclic pattern. All the bits generated by random are usable. For example,

        random()&01

    will produce a random binary value.

    Unlike srand, srandom does not return the old seed because the amount of state information used is much more than a single word. Two other routines are provided to deal with restarting/changing random number generators. Like rand(3C), however, random will, by default, produce a sequence of numbers that can be duplicated by calling srandom with 1 as the seed.

    The initstate routine allows a state array, passed in as an argument, to be initialized for future use. *n* specifies the size of *state* in bytes. initstate uses *n* to decide how sophisticated a random number generator it should use—the more state, the better the random numbers will be. Current "optimal" values for the amount of state information are 8, 32, 64, 128, and 256 bytes; other amounts will be rounded down to the nearest known amount. Using less than 8 bytes will cause an error. The seed for the initialization (which specifies a starting point for the random number sequence, and provides for restarting at the same point) is also an argument. initstate returns a pointer to the previous state information array.

Once a state has been initialized, the setstate routine provides for rapid switching between states. setstate returns a pointer to the previous state array; its argument state array is used for further random number generation until the next call to initstate or setstate.

Once a state array has been initialized, it may be restarted at a different point either by calling initstate (with the desired seed, the state array, and its size) or by calling both setstate (with the state array) and srandom (with the desired seed). The advantage of calling both setstate and srandom is that the size of the state array does not have to be remembered after it is initialized.

With 256 bytes of state information, the period of the random number generator is greater than 2^{69}, which should be sufficient for most purposes.

EXAMPLE

```
/* Initialize an array and pass it in to initstate. */
static long state1[32] = {
    3,
    0x9a319039, 0x32d9c024, 0x9b663182, 0x5da1f342,
    0x7449e56b, 0xbeb1dbb0, 0xab5c5918, 0x946554fd,
    0x8c2e680f, 0xeb3d799f, 0xb11ee0b7, 0x2d436b86,
    0xda672e2a, 0x1588ca88, 0xe369735d, 0x904f35f7,
    0xd7158fd6, 0x6fa6f051, 0x616e6b96, 0xac94efdc,
    0xde3b81e0, 0xdf0a6fb5, 0xf103bc02, 0x48f340fb,
    0x36413f93, 0xc622c298, 0xf5a42ab8, 0x8a88d77b,
    0xf5ad9d0e, 0x8999220b, 0x27fb47b9
};
main()
{
    unsigned seed;
    int n;

    seed = 1;
    n = 128;
    initstate(seed, state1, n);
    setstate(state1);
    printf("%d0,random());
}
```

SEE ALSO
rand(3C)

drand48(2), drand(3C), rand(3C), srand(3C) in the *Programmer's Reference Manual*

RETURN VALUE
If initstate is called with less than 8 bytes of state information, or if setstate detects that the state information has been garbled, error messages are printed on the standard error output.

NOTES
About two-thirds the speed of rand(3C).

realpath(3C) (C Programming Language Utilities) realpath(3C)

NAME
realpath − returns the real file name

SYNOPSIS
#include <stdlib.h>
#include <sys/param.h>

char *realpath (char * *file_name*, char * *resolved_name*);

DESCRIPTION
realpath resolves all links and references to "." and ".." in *file_name* and stores it in *resolved_name*.

It can handle both relative and absolute path names. For absolute path names and the relative names whose resolved name cannot be expressed relatively (for example, ../../reldir), it returns the *resolved absolute* name. For the other relative path names, it returns the *resolved relative* name.

resolved_name must be big enough (MAXPATHLEN) to contain the fully resolved path name.

SEE ALSO
getcwd(3C).

DIAGNOSTICS
If there is no error, realpath returns a pointer to the *resolved_name*. Otherwise it returns a null pointer and places the name of the offending file in *resolved_name*. The global variable errno is set to indicate the error.

NOTES
realpath operates on null-terminated strings.

One should have execute permission on all the directories in the given and the resolved path.

realpath may fail to return to the current directory if an error occurs.

reboot(3)   (BSD Compatibility Package)   reboot(3)

NAME
reboot – reboot system or halt processor

SYNOPSIS
cc [flag...] file ... -lucb

#include <sys/reboot.h>

reboot(howto, [bootargs])
int howto;
char *bootargs;

DESCRIPTION
reboot reboots the system, and is invoked automatically in the event of unrecoverable system failures. howto is a mask of options passed to the bootstrap program. The system call interface permits only RB_HALT or RB_AUTOBOOT to be passed to the reboot program; the other flags are used in scripts stored on the console storage media, or used in manual bootstrap procedures. When none of these options (for instance RB_AUTOBOOT) is given, the system is rebooted from file /stand/unix. An automatic consistency check of the disks is then normally performed.

The bits of howto that are used are:

RB_HALT   the processor is simply halted; no reboot takes place. RB_HALT should be used with caution.

RB_ASKNAME   Interpreted by the bootstrap program itself, causing it to inquire as to what file should be booted. Normally, the system is booted from the file /stand/unix without asking.

RETURN VALUE
If successful, this call never returns. Otherwise, a −1 is returned and an error is returned in the global variable errno.

ERRORS
EPERM   The caller is not the super-user.

FILES
/vmunix

SEE ALSO
halt(1M) init(1M) reboot(1M)

intro(1M), crash(1M) in the *System Administrator's Reference Manual*

NOTES
Any other howto argument causes /stand/unix to boot.

Only the super-user may reboot a machine.

recv(3N)

NAME
recv, recvfrom, recvmsg – receive a message from a socket

SYNOPSIS
#include <sys/types.h>

int recv(int *s*, char *buf, int *len*, int *flags*);

int recvfrom(int *s*, char *buf, int *len*, int *flags*, caddr_t *from*, int *fromlen);

int recvmsg(int *s*, struct msghdr *msg, int *flags*);

DESCRIPTION
s is a socket created with socket. recv, recvfrom, and recvmsg are used to receive messages from another socket. recv may be used only on a *connected* socket [see connect(3N)], while recvfrom and recvmsg may be used to receive data on a socket whether it is in a connected state or not.

If *from* is not a NULL pointer, the source address of the message is filled in. *fromlen* is a value-result parameter, initialized to the size of the buffer associated with *from*, and modified on return to indicate the actual size of the address stored there. The length of the message is returned. If a message is too long to fit in the supplied buffer, excess bytes may be discarded depending on the type of socket the message is received from [see socket(3N)].

If no messages are available at the socket, the receive call waits for a message to arrive, unless the socket is nonblocking [see fcntl(2)] in which case −1 is returned with the external variable errno set to EWOULDBLOCK.

The select call may be used to determine when more data arrives.

The *flags* parameter is formed by ORing one or more of the following:

MSG_OOB   Read any out-of-band data present on the socket rather than the regular in-band data.

MSG_PEEK   Peek at the data present on the socket; the data is returned, but not consumed, so that a subsequent receive operation will see the same data.

The recvmsg() call uses a msghdr structure to minimize the number of directly supplied parameters. This structure is defined in sys/socket.h and includes the following members:

```
caddr_t       msg_name;           /* optional address */
int           msg_namelen;        /* size of address */
struct iovec  *msg_iov;           /* scatter/gather array */
int           msg_iovlen;         /* # elements in msg_iov */
caddr_t       msg_accrights;      /* access rights sent/received */
int           msg_accrightslen;
```

Here msg_name and msg_namelen specify the destination address if the socket is unconnected; msg_name may be given as a NULL pointer if no names are desired or required. The msg_iov and msg_iovlen describe the scatter-gather locations, as described in read. A buffer to receive any access rights sent along with the message is specified in msg_accrights, which has length msg_accrightslen.

RETURN VALUE

These calls return the number of bytes received, or −1 if an error occurred.

ERRORS

The calls fail if:

EBADF	*s* is an invalid descriptor.
ENOTSOCK	*s* is a descriptor for a file, not a socket.
EINTR	The operation was interrupted by delivery of a signal before any data was available to be received.
EWOULDBLOCK	The socket is marked non-blocking and the requested operation would block.
ENOMEM	There was insufficient user memory available for the operation to complete.
ENOSR	There were insufficient STREAMS resouces available for the operation to complete.

SEE ALSO

connect(3N), getsockopt(3N), send(3N), socket(3N).

fcntl(2), ioctl(2), read(2) in the *Programmer's Reference Manual*.

NOTES

The type of address structure passed to recv depends on the address family. UNIX domain sockets (address family AF_UNIX) require a socketaddr_un structure as defined in sys/un.h; Internet domain sockets (address family AF_INET) require a sockaddr_in structure as defined in netinet/in.h. Other address families may require other structures. Use the structure appropriate to the address family; cast the structure address to a generic caddr_t in the call to recv and pass the size of the structure in the *fromlen* argument.

See "The Sockets Interface" section in the *Programmer's Guide: Networking Interfaces* for details.

NAME

regcmp, regex – compile and execute regular expression

SYNOPSIS

    #include <libgen.h>

cc [*flag* ...] *file* ... −lgen [*library* ...]

    char *regcmp (const char *string1 [, char *string2, ...],
        (char *)0);

    char *regex (const char *re, const char *subject
        [, char *ret0, ...]);

    extern char *__loc1;

DESCRIPTION

regcmp compiles a regular expression (consisting of the concatenated arguments) and returns a pointer to the compiled form. malloc(3C) is used to create space for the compiled form. It is the user's responsibility to free unneeded space so allocated. A NULL return from regcmp indicates an incorrect argument. regcmp(1) has been written to generally preclude the need for this routine at execution time. regcmp is located in library libform.

regex executes a compiled pattern against the subject string. Additional arguments are passed to receive values back. regex returns NULL on failure or a pointer to the next unmatched character on success. A global character pointer __loc1 points to where the match began. regcmp and regex were mostly borrowed from the editor, ed(1); however, the syntax and semantics have been changed slightly. The following are the valid symbols and associated meanings.

[ ] * . ^   These symbols retain their meaning in ed(1).

$ Matches the end of the string; \n matches a newline.

−   Within brackets the minus means through. For example, [a−z] is equivalent to [abcd...xyz]. The − can appear as itself only if used as the first or last character. For example, the character class expression []−] matches the characters] and −.

+   A regular expression followed by + means one or more times. For example, [0−9]+ is equivalent to [0−9][0−9]*.

{m} {m,} {m,u}
Integer values enclosed in { } indicate the number of times the preceding regular expression is to be applied. The value m is the minimum number and u is a number, less than 256, which is the maximum. If only m is present (that is, {m}), it indicates the exact number of times the regular expression is to be applied. The value {m,} is analogous to {m,infinity}. The plus (+) and star (*) operations are equivalent to {1,} and {0,} respectively.

(...)$n
The value of the enclosed regular expression is to be returned. The value will be stored in the (n+1)th argument following the subject argument. At most, ten enclosed regular expressions are allowed. regex makes its assignments unconditionally.

(...)   Parentheses are used for grouping. An operator, for example, *, +,
{ }, can work on a single character or a regular expression enclosed in
parentheses. For example, (a*(cb+)*)$0.

By necessity, all the above defined symbols are special. They must, therefore, be escaped with a \ (backslash) to be used as themselves.

EXAMPLES

The following example matches a leading newline in the subject string pointed at by cursor.

```
char *cursor, *newcursor, *ptr;
   . . .
newcursor = regex((ptr = regcmp("^\n", (char *)0)), cursor);
free(ptr);
```

The following example matches through the string Testing3 and returns the address of the character after the last matched character (the "4"). The string Testing3 is copied to the character array ret0.

```
char ret0[9];
char *newcursor, *name;
   . . .
name = regcmp("([A-Za-z][A-za-z0-9]{0,7})$0", (char *)0);
newcursor = regex(name, "012Testing345", ret0);
```

The following example applies a precompiled regular expression in file.i [see regcmp(1)] against *string*.

```
#include "file.i"
char *string, *newcursor;
   . . .
newcursor = regex(name, string);
```

SEE ALSO

regcmp(1), malloc(3C).
ed(1) in the *User's Reference Manual*.

NOTES

The user program may run out of memory if regcmp is called iteratively without freeing the vectors no longer required.

NAME

regex, re_comp, re_exec – regular expression handler

SYNOPSIS

cc [*flag*...] *file* ... -lucb

```
char *re_comp(s)
char *s;

re_exec(s)
char *s;
```

DESCRIPTION

re_comp compiles a string into an internal form suitable for pattern matching. re_exec checks the argument string against the last string passed to re_comp.

re_comp returns a NULL pointer if the string *s* was compiled successfully; otherwise a string containing an error message is returned. If re_comp is passed 0 or a NULL string, it returns without changing the currently compiled regular expression.

re_exec returns 1 if the string *s* matches the last compiled regular expression, 0 if the string *s* failed to match the last compiled regular expression, and −1 if the compiled regular expression was invalid (indicating an internal error).

The strings passed to both re_comp and re_exec may have trailing or embedded NEWLINE characters; they are terminated by NULL characters. The regular expressions recognized are described in the manual page entry for ed(1), given the above difference.

SEE ALSO

ed(1), ex(1), grep(1) in the *User's Reference Manual*

regcmp(1), regexpr(3G), regcmp(3X), regexpr(5) in the *Programmer's Reference Manual*

RETURN VALUE

re_exec returns −1 for an internal error.

re_comp returns one of the following strings if an error occurs:

```
No previous regular expression
Regular expression too long
unmatched \(
missing ]
too many \(\) pairs
unmatched \)
```

regexpr(3G)

NAME
regexpr: compile, step, advance – regular expression compile and match routines

SYNOPSIS
cc [*flag* ...] *file* ... -lgen [*library* ...]

#include <regexpr.h>

char *compile (const char *instring*, char *expbuf*, char *endbuf*);

int step (const char *string*, char *expbuf*);

int advance (const char *string*, char *expbuf*);

extern char *loc1, *loc2, *locs;

extern int nbra, regerrno, reglength;

extern char *braslist[], *braelist[];

DESCRIPTION
These routines are used to compile regular expressions and match the compiled expressions against lines. The regular expressions compiled are in the form used by ed.

The syntax of the compile routine is as follows:

    compile (*instring*, *expbuf*, *endbuf*)

The parameter *instring* is a null-terminated string representing the regular expression.

The parameter *expbuf* points to the place where the compiled regular expression is to be placed. If *expbuf* is NULL, compile uses malloc to allocate the space for the compiled regular expression. If an error occurs, this space is freed. It is the user's responsibility to free unneeded space after the compiled regular expression is no longer needed.

The parameter *endbuf* is one more than the highest address where the compiled regular expression may be placed. This argument is ignored if *expbuf* is NULL. If the compiled expression cannot fit in (*endbuf*–*expbuf*) bytes, compile returns NULL and regerrno (see below) is set to 50.

If compile succeeds, it returns a non-NULL pointer whose value depends on *expbuf*. If *expbuf* is non-NULL, compile returns a pointer to the byte after the last byte in the compiled regular expression. The length of the compiled regular expression is stored in reglength. Otherwise, compile returns a pointer to the space allocated by malloc.

If an error is detected when compiling the regular expression, a NULL pointer is returned from compile and regerrno is set to one of the non-zero error numbers indicated below:

ERROR	MEANING
11	Range endpoint too large.
16	Bad number.
25	''*digit*'' out of range.
36	Illegal or missing delimiter.
41	No remembered search string.
42	\\(\\) imbalance.
43	Too many \\(.
44	More than 2 numbers given in \\{ \\}.
45	} expected after \\.
46	First number exceeds second in \\{ \\}.
49	[ ] imbalance.
50	Regular expression overflow.

The call to step is as follows:

    step (string, expbuf)

The first parameter to step is a pointer to a string of characters to be checked for a match. This string should be null-terminated.

The parameter *expbuf* is the compiled regular expression obtained by a call of the function compile.

The function step returns non-zero if the given string matches the regular expression, and zero if the expressions do not match. If there is a match, two external character pointers are set as a side effect to the call to step. The variable set in step is loc1. loc1 is a pointer to the first character that matched the regular expression. The variable loc2 points to the character after the last character that matches the regular expression. Thus if the regular expression matches the entire line, loc1 points to the first character of *string* and loc2 points to the null at the end of *string*.

The purpose of step is to step through the *string* argument until a match is found or until the end of *string* is reached. If the regular expression begins with ^, step tries to match the regular expression at the beginning of the string only.

The function advance has the same arguments and side effects as step, but it always restricts matches to the beginning of the string.

If one is looking for successive matches in the same string of characters, locs should be set equal to loc2, and step should be called with *string* equal to loc2. locs is used by commands like ed and sed so that global substitutions like s/y*//g do not loop forever, and is NULL by default.

The external variable nbra is used to determine the number of subexpressions in the compiled regular expression. braslist and braelist are arrays of character pointers that point to the start and end of the nbra subexpressions in the matched string. For example, after calling step or advance with string sabcdefg and regular expression \\(abcdef\\), braslist[0] will point at a and braelist[0] will point at g. These arrays are used by commands like ed and sed for substitute replacement patterns that contain the \\n notation for subexpressions.

Note that it isn't necessary to use the external variables `regerrno`, `nbra`, `loc1`, `loc2` `locs`, `braelist`, and `braslist` if one is only checking whether or not a string matches a regular expression.

EXAMPLES
The following is similar to the regular expression code from `grep`:

```
#include <regexpr.h>
 . . .
if(compile(*argv, (char *)0, (char *)0) == (char *)0)
    regerr(regerrno);
 . . .
if (step(linebuf, expbuf))
    succeed();
```

SEE ALSO
regexp(5).
ed(1), grep(1), sed(1) in the *User's Reference Manual*.

NAME
remove – remove file

SYNOPSIS
#include <stdio.h>

int remove(const char *path);

DESCRIPTION
remove causes the file or empty directory whose name is the string pointed to by *path* to be no longer accessible by that name. A subsequent attempt to open that file using that name will fail, unless the file is created anew.

For files, remove is identical to unlink. For directories, remove is identical to rmdir.

See rmdir(2) and unlink(2) for a detailed list of failure conditions.

SEE ALSO
rmdir(2), unlink(2).

RETURN VALUE
Upon successful completion, remove returns a value of 0; otherwise, it returns a value of −1 and sets errno to indicate an error.

NAME

resolver, res_mkquery, res_send, res_init, dn_comp, dn_expand – resolver routines

SYNOPSIS

```
#include <sys/types.h>
#include <netinet/in.h>
#include <arpa/nameser.h>
#include <resolv.h>
```

int res_mkquery(int *op*, char **dname*, int *class*, int *type*, char **data*, int *datalen*, struct rrec **newrr*, char **buf*, int *buflen*);

int res_send(char **msg*, int *msglen*, char **answer*, int *anslen*);

void res_init(void);

int dn_comp(char **exp_dn*, char **comp_dn*, int *length*, char ***dnptrs*, char ***lastdnptr*);

int dn_expand(char **msg*, char **eomorig*, char **comp_dn*, char **exp_dn*, int *length*);

DESCRIPTION

These routines are used for making, sending and interpreting packets to Internet domain name servers. Global information that is used by the resolver routines is kept in the variable _res. Most of the values have reasonable defaults and can be ignored. Options are a simple bit mask and are OR'ed in to enable. Options stored in _res.options are defined in resolv.h and are as follows.

RES_INIT	True if the initial name server address and default domain name are initialized (that is, res_init has been called).
RES_DEBUG	Print debugging messages.
RES_AAONLY	Accept authoritative answers only. res_send will continue until it finds an authoritative answer or finds an error. Currently this is not implemented.
RES_USEVC	Use TCP connections for queries instead of UDP.
RES_STAYOPEN	Used with RES_USEVC to keep the TCP connection open between queries. This is useful only in programs that regularly do many queries. UDP should be the normal mode used.
RES_IGNTC	Unused currently (ignore truncation errors, that is, do not retry with TCP).
RES_RECURSE	Set the recursion desired bit in queries. This is the default. res_send does not do iterative queries and expects the name server to handle recursion.
RES_DEFNAMES	Append the default domain name to single label queries. This is the default.

res_init reads the initialization file to get the default domain name and the Internet address of the initial hosts running the name server. If this line does not exist, the host running the resolver is tried. res_mkquery makes a standard query message and places it in *buf*. res_mkquery will return the size of the query or −1 if the query is larger than *buflen*. *op* is usually QUERY but can be any of the query types defined in arpa/nameser.h. *dname* is the domain name. If *dname* consists of a single label and the RES_DEFNAMES flag is enabled (the default), *dname* will be appended with the current domain name. The current domain name is defined in a system file and can be overridden by the environment variable LOCALDOMAIN. *newrr* is currently unused but is intended for making update messages.

res_send sends a query to name servers and returns an answer. It will call res_init if RES_INIT is not set, send the query to the local name server, and handle timeouts and retries. The length of the message is returned or −1 if there were errors.

dn_expand expands the compressed domain name *comp_dn* to a full domain name. Expanded names are converted to upper case. *msg* is a pointer to the beginning of the message, *eomorig* is a pointer to the first memory location after the message, *exp_dn* is a pointer to a buffer of size *length* for the result. The size of the compressed name is returned or −1 if there was an error.

dn_comp compresses the domain name *exp_dn* and stores it in *comp_dn*. The size of the compressed name is returned or −1 if there were errors. *length* is the size of the array pointed to by *comp_dn*. *dnptrs* is a list of pointers to previously compressed names in the current message. The first pointer points to to the beginning of the message and the list ends with NULL. *lastdnptr* is a pointer to the end of the array pointed to *dnptrs*. A side effect is to update the list of pointers for labels inserted into the message by dn_comp as the name is compressed. If *dnptr* is NULL, do not try to compress names. If *lastdnptr* is NULL, do not update the list.

FILES
/usr/include/arpa/nameserv.h
/usr/include/netinet/in.h
/usr/include/resolv.h
/usr/include/sys/types.h
/etc/resolv.conf
/usr/lib/libresolv.a

SEE ALSO
named(1M), resolv.conf(4)

NOTES
/usr/lib/libresolv.a is necessary for compiling programs.

Programs must be loaded with the option −lresolv.

NAME
rexec – return stream to a remote command

SYNOPSIS
```
int rexec(char **ahost, u_short inport, char *user, char *passwd,
    char *cmd, int *fd2p);
```

DESCRIPTION
rexec looks up the host *ahost* using gethostbyname [see gethostent(3N)], returning −1 if the host does not exist. Otherwise *ahost* is set to the standard name of the host. If a username and password are both specified, then these are used to authenticate to the foreign host; otherwise, the user's .netrc file in his or her home directory is searched for appropriate information. If this fails, the user is prompted for the information.

The port inport specifies which well-known DARPA Internet port to use for the connection. The protocol for connection is described in detail in rexecd.

If the call succeeds, a socket of type SOCK_STREAM is returned to the caller, and given to the remote command as its standard input and standard output. If *fd2p* is non-zero, then a auxiliary channel to a control process will be setup, and a descriptor for it will be placed in *fd2p*. The control process will return diagnostic output from the command (unit 2) on this channel, and will also accept bytes on this channel as signal numbers, to be forwarded to the process group of the command. If *fd2p* is 0, then the standard error (unit 2 of the remote command) will be made the same as its standard output and no provision is made for sending arbitrary signals to the remote process, although you may be able to get its attention by using out-of-band data.

SEE ALSO
rexecd(1M) gethostent(3N), getservent(3N), rcmd(3N)

NOTES
There is no way to specify options to the socket call that rexec makes.

rpc(3N)

NAME
rpc – library routines for remote procedure calls

DESCRIPTION
RPC routines allow C language programs to make procedure calls on other machines across a network. First, the client calls a procedure to send a data packet to the server. On receipt of the packet, the server calls a dispatch routine to perform the requested service, and then sends back a reply.

The following sections describe data objects use by the RPC package.

Nettype
Some of the high-level RPC interface routines take a *nettype* string as one of the parameters [for example, clnt_create, svc_create, rpc_reg, rpc_call]. This string defines a class of transports which can be used for a particular application. The transports are tried in left to right order in the NETPATH variable or in top to down order in the /etc/netconfig file.

nettype can be one of the following:

netpath	Choose from the transports which have been indicated by their token names in the NETPATH variable. If NETPATH is unset or NULL, it defaults to visible. netpath is the default *nettype*.
visible	Choose the transports which have the visible flag (v) set in the /etc/netconfig file.
circuit_v	This is same as visible except that it chooses only the connection oriented transports from the entries in /etc/netconfig file.
datagram_v	This is same as visible except that it chooses only the connectionless datagram transports from the entries in /etc/netconfig file.
circuit_n	This is same as netpath except that it chooses only the connection oriented datagram transports
datagram_n	This is same as netpath except that it chooses only the connectionless datagram transports.
udp	It refers to Internet UDP.
tcp	It refers to Internet TCP.
raw	This is for memory based RPC, mainly for performance evaluation.

If *nettype* is NULL, it defaults to netpath.

Data Structures
Some of the data structures used by the RPC package are shown below.
The AUTH Structure
```
union des_block {
    struct {
        u_int32 high;
        u_int32 low;
    } key;
    char c[8];
};
typedef union des_block des_block;
extern bool_t xdr_des_block();

/*
 * Authentication info. Opaque to client.
 */
struct opaque_auth {
    enum_t  oa_flavor;  /* flavor of auth */
    caddr_t oa_base;    /* address of more auth stuff */
    u_int   oa_length;  /* not to exceed MAX_AUTH_BYTES */
};

/*
 * Auth handle, interface to client side authenticators.
 */
typedef struct {
    struct opaque_auth ah_cred;
    struct opaque_auth ah_verf;
    union  des_block   ah_key;
    struct auth_ops {
        void (*ah_nextverf)();
        int  (*ah_marshal)();   /* nextverf & serialize */
        int  (*ah_validate)();  /* validate varifier */
        int  (*ah_refresh)();   /* refresh credentials */
        void (*ah_destroy)();   /* destroy this structure */
    } *ah_ops;
    caddr_t ah_private;
} AUTH;
```
The CLIENT Structure
```
/*
 * Client rpc handle.
 * Created by individual implementations
 * Client is responsible for initializing auth, see e.g. auth_none.c.
 */
typedef struct {
    AUTH            *cl_auth;               /* authenticator */
    struct clnt_ops {
        enum clnt_stat  (*cl_call)();       /* call remote procedure */
        void            (*cl_abort)();      /* abort a call */
        void            (*cl_geterr)();     /* get specific error code */
        bool_t          (*cl_freeres)();    /* frees results */
        void            (*cl_destroy)();    /* destroy this structure */
        bool_t          (*cl_control)();    /* the ioctl() of rpc */
```

rpc(3N)

```
        } *cl_ops;
        caddr_t         cl_private;     /* private stuff */
        char            *cl_netid;      /* network token */
        char            *cl_tp;         /* device name */
} CLIENT;
```

The SVCXPRT Structure

```
enum xprt_stat {
    XPRT_DIED,
    XPRT_MOREREQS,
    XPRT_IDLE
};

/*
 * Server side transport handle
 */
typedef struct {
        int             xp_fd;
#define xp_sock         xp_fd
#endif
        u_short         xp_port;        /* associated port number.
                                         * Obsolete, but still used to
                                         * specify whether rendezvouser
                                         * or normal connection
                                         */
        struct xp_ops {
            bool_t          (*xp_recv)();       /* receive incoming requests */
            enum xprt_stat  (*xp_stat)();       /* get transport status */
            bool_t          (*xp_getargs)();    /* get arguments */
            bool_t          (*xp_reply)();      /* send reply */
            bool_t          (*xp_freeargs)();   /* free mem allocated for args */
            void            (*xp_destroy)();    /* destroy this struct */
        } *xp_ops;
        int             xp_addrlen;     /* length of remote addr. Obsolete */
        char            *xp_tp;         /* transport provider device name */
        char            *xp_netid;      /* network token */
        struct netbuf   xp_ltaddr;      /* local transport address */
        struct netbuf   xp_rtaddr;      /* remote transport address */
        char            xp_raddr[16];   /* remote address. Obsolete */
        struct opaque_auth xp_verf;     /* raw response verifier */
        caddr_t         xp_p1;          /* private: for use by svc ops */
        caddr_t         xp_p2;          /* private: for use by svc ops */
        caddr_t         xp_p3;          /* private: for use by svc lib */
} SVCXPRT;
```

The XDR Structure

```
/*
 * Xdr operations. XDR_ENCODE causes the type to be encoded into the
 * stream.  XDR_DECODE causes the type to be extracted from the stream.
 * XDR_FREE can be used to release the space allocated by an XDR_DECODE
 * request.
 */
enum xdr_op {
    XDR_ENCODE=0,
    XDR_DECODE=1,
```

```
        XDR_FREE=2
};

/*
 * This is the number of bytes per unit of external data.
 */
#define BYTES_PER_XDR_UNIT      (4)
#define RNDUP(x)  ((((x) + BYTES_PER_XDR_UNIT - 1) / BYTES_PER_XDR_UNIT) \
            * BYTES_PER_XDR_UNIT)

/*
 * A xdrproc_t exists for each data type which is to be encoded or decoded.
 *
 * The second argument to the xdrproc_t is a pointer to an opaque pointer.
 * The opaque pointer generally points to a structure of the data type
 * to be decoded.  If this pointer is 0, then the type routines should
 * allocate dynamic storage of the appropriate size and return it.
 * bool_t   (*xdrproc_t)(XDR *, caddr_t *);
 */
typedef     bool_t (*xdrproc_t)();

/*
 * The XDR handle.
 * Contains operation which is being applied to the stream,
 * an operations vector for the particular implementation (for example,
 * see xdr_mem.c), and two private fields for the use of the
 * particular impelementation.
 */
typedef struct {
    enum xdr_op x_op;           /* operation; fast additional param */
    struct xdr_ops {
        bool_t  (*x_getlong)();     /* get a long from underlying stream */
        bool_t  (*x_putlong)();     /* put a long to " */
        bool_t  (*x_getbytes)();    /* get some bytes from " */
        bool_t  (*x_putbytes)();    /* put some bytes to " */
        u_int   (*x_getpostn)();    /* returns bytes off from beginning */
        bool_t  (*x_setpostn)();    /* lets you reposition the stream */
        long *  (*x_inline)();      /* buf quick ptr to buffered data */
        void    (*x_destroy)();     /* free privates of this xdr_stream */
    } *x_ops;
    caddr_t     x_public;       /* users' data */
    caddr_t     x_private;      /* pointer to private data */
    caddr_t     x_base;         /* private used for position info */
    int         x_handy;        /* extra private word */
} XDR;
```

Index to Routines

The following table lists RPC routines and the manual reference pages on which they are described:

RPC Routine	Manual Reference Page
auth_destroy	rpc_clnt_auth(3N)
authdes_getucred	secure_rpc(3N)
authdes_seccreate	secure_rpc(3N)
authnone_create	rpc_clnt_auth(3N)
authsys_create	rpc_clnt_auth(3N)
authsys_create_default	rpc_clnt_auth(3N)
clnt_call	rpc_clnt_calls(3N)
clnt_control	rpc_clnt_create(3N)
clnt_create	rpc_clnt_create(3N)
clnt_destroy	rpc_clnt_create(3N)
clnt_dg_create	rpc_clnt_create(3N)
clnt_freeres	rpc_clnt_calls(3N)
clnt_geterr	rpc_clnt_calls(3N)
clnt_pcreateerror	rpc_clnt_create(3N)
clnt_perrno	rpc_clnt_calls(3N)
clnt_perror	rpc_clnt_calls(3N)
clnt_raw_create	rpc_clnt_create(3N)
clnt_spcreateerror	rpc_clnt_create(3N)
clnt_sperrno	rpc_clnt_calls(3N)
clnt_sperror	rpc_clnt_calls(3N)
clnt_tli_create	rpc_clnt_create(3N)
clnt_tp_create	rpc_clnt_create(3N)
clnt_vc_create	rpc_clnt_create(3N)
getnetname	secure_rpc(3N)
host2netname	secure_rpc(3N)
key_decryptsession	secure_rpc(3N)
key_encryptsession	secure_rpc(3N)
key_gendes	secure_rpc(3N)
key_setsecret	secure_rpc(3N)
netname2host	secure_rpc(3N)
netname2user	secure_rpc(3N)
rpc_broadcast	rpc_clnt_calls(3N)
rpc_call	rpc_clnt_calls(3N)
rpc_reg	rpc_svc_calls(3N)
svc_create	rpc_svc_create(3N)
svc_destroy	rpc_svc_create(3N)
svc_dg_create	rpc_svc_create(3N)
svc_fd_create	rpc_svc_create(3N)
svc_freeargs	rpc_svc_reg(3N)
svc_getargs	rpc_svc_reg(3N)
svc_getreqset	rpc_svc_reg(3N)
svc_getrpccaller	rpc_svc_reg(3N)
svc_raw_create	rpc_svc_create(3N)
svc_reg	rpc_svc_calls(3N)
svc_run	rpc_svc_reg(3N)
svc_sendreply	rpc_svc_reg(3N)

RPC Routine	Manual Reference Page
svc_tli_create	rpc_svc_create(3N)
svc_tp_create	rpc_svc_create(3N)
svc_unreg	rpc_svc_calls(3N)
svc_vc_create	rpc_svc_create(3N)
svcerr_auth	rpc_svc_err(3N)
svcerr_decode	rpc_svc_err(3N)
svcerr_noproc	rpc_svc_err(3N)
svcerr_noprog	rpc_svc_err(3N)
svcerr_progvers	rpc_svc_err(3N)
svcerr_systemerr	rpc_svc_err(3N)
svcerr_weakauth	rpc_svc_err(3N)
user2netname	secure_rpc(3N)
xdr_accepted_reply	rpc_xdr(3N)
xdr_authsys_parms	rpc_xdr(3N)
xdr_callhdr	rpc_xdr(3N)
xdr_callmsg	rpc_xdr(3N)
xdr_opaque_auth	rpc_xdr(3N)
xdr_rejected_reply	rpc_xdr(3N)
xdr_replymsg	rpc_xdr(3N)
xprt_register	rpc_svc_calls(3N)
xprt_unregister	rpc_svc_calls(3N)

FILES

/etc/netconfig

SEE ALSO

environ(5), getnetconfig(3N), getnetpath(3N), rpc_clnt_auth(3N), rpc_clnt_calls(3N), rpc_clnt_create(3N), rpc_svc_calls(3N), rpc_svc_create(3N), rpc_svc_err(3N), rpc_svc_reg(3N), rpc_xdr(3N), rpcbind(3N), secure_rpc(3N), xdr(3N), netconfig(4)

NAME

rpc_clnt_auth: auth_destroy, authnone_create, authsys_create, authsys_create_default – library routines for client side remote procedure call authentication

DESCRIPTION

These routines are part of the RPC library that allows C language programs to make procedure calls on other machines across the network, with desired authentication. First, the client calls a procedure to send a data packet to the server. Upon receipt of the packet, the server calls a dispatch routine to perform the requested service, and then sends back a reply.

These routines are normally called after creating the CLIENT handle. The client's authentication information is passed to the server when the RPC call is made.

Routines

The following routines require that the header rpc.h be included [see rpc(3N) for the definition of the AUTH data structure].

```
#include <rpc/rpc.h>

void
auth_destroy(AUTH *auth);
```

A function macro that destroys the authentication information associated with *auth*. Destruction usually involves deallocation of private data structures. The use of *auth* is undefined after calling auth_destroy.

```
AUTH *
authnone_create(void);
```

Create and return an RPC authentication handle that passes nonusable authentication information with each remote procedure call. This is the default authentication used by RPC.

```
AUTH *
authsys_create(const char *host, const uid_t uid, const gid_t gid,
     const int len, const gid_t *aup_gids);
```

Create and return an RPC authentication handle that contains AUTH_SYS authentication information. The parameter *host* is the name of the machine on which the information was created; *uid* is the user's user ID; *gid* is the user's current group ID; *len* and *aup_gids* refer to a counted array of groups to which the user belongs.

```
AUTH *
authsys_create_default(void);
```

Call authsys_create with the appropriate parameters.

SEE ALSO

rpc(3N), rpc_clnt_create(3N), rpc_clnt_calls(3N)

NAME

rpc_clnt_calls: clnt_call, clnt_freeres, clnt_geterr, clnt_perrno, clnt_perror, clnt_sperrno, clnt_sperror, rpc_broadcast, rpc_call − library routines for client side calls

DESCRIPTION

RPC library routines allow C language programs to make procedure calls on other machines across the network. First, the client calls a procedure to send a data packet to the server. Upon receipt of the packet, the server calls a dispatch routine to perform the requested service, and then sends back a reply.

The clnt_call, rpc_call and rpc_broadcast routines handle the client side of the procedure call. The remaining routines deal with error handling in the case of errors.

Routines

See rpc(3N) for the definition of the CLIENT data structure.

```
#include <rpc/rpc.h>
```

enum clnt_stat
clnt_call(CLIENT *clnt, const u_long procnum, const xdrproc_t inproc,
     caddr_t in, const xdrproc_t outproc, caddr_t out,
     const struct timeval tout);

> A function macro that calls the remote procedure *procnum* associated with the client handle, *clnt*, which is obtained with an RPC client creation routine such as clnt_create [see rpc_clnt_create(3N)]. The parameter *in* is the address of the procedure's argument(s), and *out* is the address of where to place the result(s); *inproc* is used to encode the procedure's parameters, and *outproc* is used to decode the procedure's results; *tout* is the time allowed for results to be returned.
>
> If the remote call succeeds, the status is returned in RPC_SUCCESS, otherwise an appropriate status is returned.

int clnt_freeres(CLIENT *clnt, const xdrproc_t outproc, caddr_t out);

> A function macro that frees any data allocated by the RPC/XDR system when it decoded the results of an RPC call. The parameter *out* is the address of the results, and *outproc* is the XDR routine describing the results. This routine returns 1 if the results were successfully freed, and 0 otherwise.

void
clnt_geterr(const CLIENT *clnt, struct rpc_err *errp);

> A function macro that copies the error structure out of the client handle to the structure at address *errp*.

```
void
clnt_perrno(const enum clnt_stat stat);
```

> Print a message to standard error corresponding to the condition indicated by *stat*. A newline is appended at the end of the message. Normally used after a procedure call fails, for instance rpc_call.

```
void
clnt_perror(const CLIENT *clnt, const char *s);
```

> Print a message to standard error indicating why an RPC call failed; *clnt* is the handle used to do the call. The message is prepended with string s and a colon. A newline is appended at the end of the message. Normally used after a procedure call fails, for instance clnt_call.

```
char *
clnt_sperrno(const enum clnt_stat stat);
```

> Take the same arguments as clnt_perrno, but instead of sending a message to the standard error indicating why an RPC call failed, return a pointer to a string which contains the message.
>
> clnt_sperrno is normally used instead of clnt_perrno when the program does not have a standard error (as a program running as a server quite likely does not), or if the programmer does not want the message to be output with printf [see printf(3S)], or if a message format different than that supported by clnt_perrno is to be used. Note: unlike clnt_sperror and clnt_spcreaterror [see rpc_clnt_create(3N)], clnt_sperrno does not return pointer to static data so the result will not get overwritten on each call.

```
char *
clnt_sperror(const CLIENT *clnt, const char *s);
```

> Like clnt_perror, except that (like clnt_sperrno) it returns a string instead of printing to standard error. However, clnt_sperror does not append a newline at the end of the message.
>
> Note: returns pointer to static data that is overwritten on each call.

```
enum clnt_stat
rpc_broadcast(const u_long prognum, const u_long versnum,
     const u_long procnum, const xdrproc_t inproc, caddr_t in,
     const xdrproc_t outproc, caddr_t out, const resultproc_t eachresult,
     const char *nettype);
```

Like rpc_call, except the call message is broadcast to the connectionless network specified by *nettype*. If *nettype* is NULL, it defaults to netpath. Each time it receives a response, this routine calls eachresult, whose form is:

```
bool_t
eachresult(const caddr_t out, const struct netbuf *addr,
     struct netconfig *netconf);
```

where *out* is the same as *out* passed to rpc_broadcast, except that the remote procedure's output is decoded there; *addr* points to the address of the machine that sent the results, and *netconf* is the netconfig structure of the transport on which the remote server responded. If eachresult returns 0, rpc_broadcast waits for more replies; otherwise it returns with appropriate status.

Note: broadcast file descriptors are limited in size to the maximum transfer size of that transport. For Ethernet, this value is 1500 bytes.

```
enum clnt_stat
rpc_call(const char *host, const u_long prognum,
     const u_long versnum, const u_long procnum,
     const xdrproc_t inproc, const xdrproc_t outproc,
     const char *in, char *out, const char *nettype);
```

Call the remote procedure associated with *prognum, versnum,* and *procnum* on the machine, *host*. The parameter *in* is the address of the procedure's argument(s), and *out* is the address of where to place the result(s); *inproc* is used to encode the procedure's parameters, and *outproc* is used to decode the procedure's results. *nettype* can be any of the values listed on rpc(3N). If *nettype* is NULL, it defaults to netpath. This routine returns 0 if it succeeds, or the value of enum clnt_stat cast to an integer if it fails. Use the clnt_perrno routine to translate failure statuses into messages.

Note: rpc_call uses the first available transport belonging to the class *nettype,* on which it can create a connection. You do not have control of timeouts or authentication using this routine. There is also no way to destroy the client handle.

SEE ALSO

printf(3S), rpc(3N), rpc_clnt_auth(3N), rpc_clnt_create(3N)

NAME

rpc_clnt_create: clnt_control, clnt_create, clnt_destroy, clnt_dg_create, clnt_pcreateerror, clnt_raw_create, clnt_spcreateerror, clnt_tli_create, clnt_tp_create, clnt_vc_create − library routines for dealing with creation and manipulation of CLIENT handles

DESCRIPTION

RPC library routines allow C language programs to make procedure calls on other machines across the network. First a CLIENT handle is created and then the client calls a procedure to send a data packet to the server. Upon receipt of the packet, the server calls a dispatch routine to perform the requested service, and then sends back a reply.

Routines

See rpc(3N) for the definition of the CLIENT data structure.

```
#include <rpc/rpc.h>

bool_t
clnt_control(CLIENT *clnt, const u_int req, char *info);
```

A function macro used to change or retrieve various information about a client object. *req* indicates the type of operation, and *info* is a pointer to the information. For both connectionless and connection-oriented transports, the supported values of *req* and their argument types and what they do are:

CLSET_TIMEOUT	struct timeval	set total timeout
CLGET_TIMEOUT	struct timeval	get total timeout

Note: if you set the timeout using clnt_control, the timeout parameter passed to clnt_call will be ignored in all future calls.

CLGET_FD	int	get the associated file descriptor
CLGET_SVC_ADDR	struct netbuf	get servers address
CLSET_FD_CLOSE	int	close the file descriptor when destroying the client handle [see clnt_destroy]
CLSET_FD_NCLOSE	int	do not close the file descriptor when destroying the client handle

The following operations are valid for connectionless transports only:

CLSET_RETRY_TIMEOUT	struct timeval	set the retry timeout
CLGET_RETRY_TIMEOUT	struct timeval	get the retry timeout

The retry timeout is the time that RPC waits for the server to reply before retransmitting the request.

clnt_control returns 1 on success and 0 on failure.

```
CLIENT *
clnt_create(const char *host, const u_long prognum,
     const u_long versnum, const char *nettype);
```

  Generic client creation routine for program *prognum* and version *versnum*. *host* identifies the name of the remote host where the server is located. *nettype* indicates the class of transport protocol to use. The transports are tried in left to right order in NETPATH variable or in top to down order in the netconfig database.

  clnt_create tries all the transports of the *nettype* class available from the NETPATH environment variable and the the netconfig database, and chooses the first successful one. Default timeouts are set, but can be modified using clnt_control.

```
void
clnt_destroy(CLIENT *clnt);
```

  A function macro that destroys the client's RPC handle. Destruction usually involves deallocation of private data structures, including *clnt* itself. Use of *clnt* is undefined after calling clnt_destroy. If the RPC library opened the associated file descriptor, or CLSET_FD_CLOSE was set using clnt_control, it will be closed.

```
CLIENT *
clnt_dg_create(const int fd, const struct netbuf *svcaddr,
     const u_long prognum, const u_long versnum,
     const u_int sendsz, const u_int recvsz);
```

  This routine creates an RPC client for the remote program *prognum* and version *versnum*; the client uses a connectionless transport. The remote program is located at address *svcaddr*. The parameter *fd* is an open and bound file descriptor. This routine will resend the call message in intervals of 15 seconds until a response is received or until the call times out. The total time for the call to time out is specified by clnt_call [see clnt_call in rpc_clnt_calls(3N)]. This routine returns NULL if it fails. The retry time out and the total time out periods can be changed using clnt_control. The user may set the size of the send and receive buffers with the parameters *sendsz* and *recvsz*; values of 0 choose suitable defaults.

```
void
clnt_pcreateerror(const char *s);
```

  Print a message to standard error indicating why a client RPC handle could not be created. The message is prepended with the string *s* and a colon, and appended with a newline.

```
CLIENT *
clnt_raw_create(const u_long prognum, const u_long versnum);
```
>   This routine creates a toy RPC client for the remote program *prognum* and version *versnum*. The transport used to pass messages to the service is a buffer within the process's address space, so the corresponding RPC server should live in the same address space; [see svc_raw_create in rpc_clnt_calls(3N)]. This allows simulation of RPC and acquisition of RPC overheads, such as round trip times, without any kernel interference. This routine returns NULL if it fails. clnt_raw_create should be called after svc_raw_create.

```
char *
clnt_spcreateerror(const char *s);
```
>   Like clnt_pcreateerror, except that it returns a string instead of printing to the standard error. A newline is not appended to the message in this case.
>
>   Note: returns a pointer to static data that is overwritten on each call.

```
CLIENT *
clnt_tli_create(const int fd, const struct netconfig *netconf,
    const struct netbuf *svcaddr, u const_long prognum,
    const u_long versnum, const u_int sendsz,
    const u_int recvsz);
```
>   This routine creates an RPC client handle for the remote program *prognum* and version *versnum*. The remote program is located at address *svcaddr*. If *svcaddr* is NULL and it is connection-oriented, it is assumed that the file descriptor is connected. For connectionless transports, if *svcaddr* is NULL, RPC_UNKNOWNADDR error is set. *fd* is a file descriptor which may be open, bound and connected. If it is RPC_ANYFD, it opens a file descriptor on the transport specified by *netconf*. If *netconf* is NULL, a RPC_UNKNOWNPROTO error is set. If *fd* is unbound, then it will attempt to bind the descriptor. The user may specify the size of the buffers with the parameters *sendsz* and *recvsz*; values of 0 choose suitable defaults. Depending upon the type of the transport (connection-oriented or connectionless), clnt_tli_create calls appropriate client creation routines. This routine returns NULL if it fails. The clnt_pcreaterror routine can be used to print the reason for failure. The remote rpcbind service [see rpcbind(1M)] will not be consulted for the address of the remote service.

```
CLIENT *
clnt_tp_create(const char *host, const u_long prognum,
    const u_long versnum, const struct netconfig *netconf);
```
>   clnt_tp_create creates a client handle for the transport specified by *netconf*. Default options are set, which can be changed using clnt_control calls. The remote rpcbind service on the host *host* is consulted for the address of the remote service. This routine returns NULL if it fails. The clnt_pcreaterror routine can be used to print the reason for failure.

```
CLIENT *
clnt_vc_create(const int fd, const struct netbuf *svcaddr,
     const u_long prognum, const u_long versnum,
     const u_int sendsz, const u_int recvsz);
```

This routine creates an RPC client for the remote program *prognum* and version *versnum*; the client uses a connection-oriented transport. The remote program is located at address *svcaddr*. The parameter *fd* is an open and bound file descriptor. The user may specify the size of the send and receive buffers with the parameters *sendsz* and *recvsz*; values of 0 choose suitable defaults. This routine returns NULL if it fails.

The address *svcaddr* should not be NULL and should point to the actual address of the remote program. clnt_vc_create will not consult the remote rpcbind service for this information.

SEE ALSO

rpcbind(1M), rpc(3N), rpc_clnt_auth(3N), rpc_clnt_calls(3N)

rpc_svc_calls(3N)

NAME
rpc_svc_calls: rpc_reg, svc_reg, svc_unreg, xprt_register, xprt_unregister – library routines for registering servers

DESCRIPTION
These routines are a part of the RPC library which allows the RPC servers to register themselves with rpcbind [see rpcbind(1M)], and it associates the given program and version number with the dispatch function.

Routines
See rpc(3N) for the definition of the SVCXPRT data structure.

```
#include <rpc/rpc.h>

int
rpc_reg(const u_long prognum, const u_long versnum,
       const u_long procnum, const char *(*procname),
       const xdrproc_t inproc, const xdrproc_t outproc,
       const char *nettype);
```

> Register program *prognum*, procedure *procname*, and version *versnum* with the RPC service package. If a request arrives for program *prognum*, version *versnum*, and procedure *procnum*, *procname* is called with a pointer to its parameter(s); *procname* should return a pointer to its static result(s); *inproc* is used to decode the parameters while *outproc* is used to encode the results. Procedures are registered on all available transports of the class *nettype*. *nettype* defines a class of transports which can be used for a particular application. If *nettype* is NULL, it defaults to netpath. This routine returns 0 if the registration succeeded, −1 otherwise.

```
int
svc_reg(const SVCXPRT *xprt, const u_long prognum, const u_long versnum,
       const void (*dispatch), const struct netconfig *netconf);
```

> Associates *prognum* and *versnum* with the service dispatch procedure, *dispatch*. If *netconf* is NULL, the service is not registered with the rpcbind service. If *netconf* is non-zero, then a mapping of the triple [*prognum, versnum, netconf->nc_netid*] to *xprt->xp_ltaddr* is established with the local rpcbind service.
>
> The svc_reg routine returns 1 if it succeeds, and 0 otherwise

```
void
svc_unreg(const u_long prognum, const u_long versnum);
```

> Remove, from the rpcbind service, all mappings of the double [*prognum, versnum*] to dispatch routines, and of the triple [*prognum, versnum, **] to network address.

```
void
xprt_register(const SVCXPRT *xprt);
```
      After RPC service transport handle *xprt* is created, it is registered with the RPC service package. This routine modifies the global variable `svc_fds`. Service implementors usually do not need this routine.

```
void
xprt_unregister(const SVCXPRT *xprt);
```
      Before an RPC service transport handle *xprt* is destroyed, it unregisters itself with the RPC service package. This routine modifies the global variable `svc_fds`. Service implementors usually do not need this routine.

SEE ALSO

rpcbind(1M), rpcbind(3N), rpc(3N), rpc_svc_err(3N), rpc_svc_create(3N), rpc_svc_reg(3N)

NAME

rpc_svc_create: svc_create, svc_destroy, svc_dg_create, svc_fd_create, svc_raw_create, svc_tli_create, svc_tp_create, svc_vc_create – library routines for dealing with the creation of server handles

DESCRIPTION

These routines are part of the RPC library which allows C language programs to make procedure calls on servers across the network. These routines deal with the creation of service handles. Once the handle is created, the server can be invoked by calling svc_run.

Routines

See rpc(3N) for the definition of the SVCXPRT data structure.

```
#include <rpc/rpc.h>

int
svc_create(
    const void (*dispatch) (const struct svc_req *, const SVCXPRT *),
    const u_long prognum, const u_long versnum,
    const char *nettype);
```

svc_create creates server handles for all the transports belonging to the class *nettype*.

nettype defines a class of transports which can be used for a particular application. The transports are tried in left to right order in NETPATH variable or in top to down order in the netconfig database.

If *nettype* is NULL, it defaults to netpath. svc_create registers itself with the rpcbind service [see rpcbind(1M)]. *dispatch* is called when there is a remote procedure call for the given *prognum* and *versnum*; this requires calling svc_run [see svc_run in rpc_svc_reg(3N)]. If it succeeds, svc_create returns the number of server handles it created, otherwise it returns 0 and the error message is logged.

```
void
svc_destroy(SVCXPRT *xprt);
```

A function macro that destroys the RPC service transport handle *xprt*. Destruction usually involves deallocation of private data structures, including *xprt* itself. Use of *xprt* is undefined after calling this routine.

```
SVCXPRT *
svc_dg_create(const int fd, const u_int sendsz, const u_int recvsz);
```

This routine creates a connectionless RPC service handle, and returns a pointer to it. This routine returns NULL if it fails, and an error message is logged. *sendsz* and *recvsz* are parameters used to specify the size of the buffers. If they are 0, suitable defaults are chosen. The file descriptor *fd* should be open and bound.

Note: since connectionless-based RPC messages can only hold limited amount of encoded data, this transport cannot be used for procedures that take large arguments or return huge results.

```
SVCXPRT *
svc_fd_create(const int fd, const u_int sendsz, const u_int recvsz);
```
This routine creates a service on top of any open and bound descriptor, and returns the handle to it. Typically, this descriptor is a connected file descriptor for a connection-oriented transport. *sendsz* and *recvsz* indicate sizes for the send and receive buffers. If they are 0, a reasonable default is chosen. This routine returns NULL, if it fails, and an error message is logged.

```
SVCXPRT *
svc_raw_create(void);
```
This routine creates a toy RPC service transport, to which it returns a pointer. The transport is really a buffer within the process's address space, so the corresponding RPC client should live in the same address space; [see clnt_raw_create in rpc_clnt_create]. This routine allows simulation of RPC and acquisition of RPC overheads (such as round trip times), without any kernel interference. This routine returns NULL if it fails, and an error message is logged.

```
SVCXPRT *
svc_tli_create(const int fd, const struct netconfig *netconf,
     const struct t_bind *bindaddr, const u_int sendsz,
     const u_int recvsz);
```
This routine creates an RPC server handle, and returns a pointer to it. *fd* is the file descriptor on which the service is listening. If *fd* is RPC_ANYFD, it opens a file descriptor on the transport specified by *netconf*. If the file descriptor is unbound, it is bound to the address specified by *bindaddr*, if *bindaddr* is non-null, otherwise it is bound to a default address chosen by the transport. In the case where the default address is chosen, the number of outstanding connect requests is set to 8 for connection-oriented transports. The user may specify the size of the send and receive buffers with the parameters *sendsz* and *recvsz*; values of 0 choose suitable defaults. This routine returns NULL if it fails, and an error message is logged.

```
SVCPRT *
svc_tp_create(const void (*dispatch)(const RQSTP *, const SVCXPRT *),
     const u_long prognum, const u_long versnum,
     const struct netconfig *netconf);
```
svc_tp_create creates a server handle for the network specified by *netconf*, and registers itself with the rpcbind service. *dispatch* is called when there is a remote procedure call for the given *prognum* and *versnum*; this requires calling svc_run. svc_tp_create returns the service handle if it succeeds, otherwise a NULL is returned, and an error message is logged.

```
SVCXPRT *
svc_vc_create(const int fd, const u_int sendsz, const u_int recvsz);
```
This routine creates a connection-oriented RPC service and returns a pointer to it. This routine returns NULL if it fails, and an error message is logged. The users may specify the size of the send and receive buffers with the parameters *sendsz* and *recvsz*; values of 0 choose suitable defaults. The file descriptor *fd* should be open and bound.

SEE ALSO
rpcbind(1M), rpc(3N), rpc_svc_calls(3N), rpc_svc_err(3N), rpc_svc_reg(3N)

NAME

rpc_svc_err: svcerr_auth, svcerr_decode, svcerr_noproc, svcerr_noprog, svcerr_progvers, svcerr_systemerr, svcerr_weakauth – library routines for server side remote procedure call errors

DESCRIPTION

These routines are part of the RPC library which allows C language programs to make procedure calls on other machines across the network.

These routines can be called by the server side dispatch function if there is any error in the transaction with the client.

Routines

See rpc(3N) for the definition of the SVCXPRT data structure.

```
#include <rpc/rpc.h>
```

```
void
svcerr_auth(const SVCXPRT *xprt, const enum auth_stat why);
```

> Called by a service dispatch routine that refuses to perform a remote procedure call due to an authentication error.

```
void
svcerr_decode(const SVCXPRT *xprt);
```

> Called by a service dispatch routine that cannot successfully decode the remote parameters [see svc_getargs in rpc_svc_reg(3N)].

```
void
svcerr_noproc(const SVCXPRT *xprt);
```

> Called by a service dispatch routine that does not implement the procedure number that the caller requests.

```
void
svcerr_noprog(const SVCXPRT *xprt);
```

> Called when the desired program is not registered with the RPC package. Service implementors usually do not need this routine.

```
void
svcerr_progvers(const SVCXPRT *xprt);
```

> Called when the desired version of a program is not registered with the RPC package. Service implementors usually do not need this routine.

```
void
svcerr_systemerr(const SVCXPRT *xprt);
```

> Called by a service dispatch routine when it detects a system error not covered by any particular protocol. For example, if a service can no longer allocate storage, it may call this routine.

rpc_svc_err(3N)

```
void
svcerr_weakauth(const SVCXPRT *xprt);
```
Called by a service dispatch routine that refuses to perform a remote procedure call due to insufficient (but correct) authentication parameters. The routine calls svcerr_auth(xprt, AUTH_TOOWEAK).

SEE ALSO

rpc(3N), rpc_svc_calls(3N), rpc_svc_create(3N), rpc_svc_reg(3N)

NAME

rpc_svc_reg: svc_freeargs, svc_getargs, svc_getreqset, svc_getrpccaller, svc_run, svc_sendreply – library routines for RPC servers

DESCRIPTION

These routines are part of the RPC library which allows C language programs to make procedure calls on other machines across the network.

These routines are associated with the server side of the RPC mechanism. Some of them are called by the server side dispatch function, while others [such as svc_run] are called when the server is initiated.

Routines

```
#include <rpc/rpc.h>

int
svc_freeargs(const SVCXPRT *xprt, const xdrproc_t inproc, char *in);
```

>   A function macro that frees any data allocated by the RPC/XDR system when it decoded the arguments to a service procedure using svc_getargs. This routine returns 1 if the results were successfully freed, and 0 otherwise.

```
int
svc_getargs(const SVCXPRT *xprt, const xdrproc_t inproc, caddr_t *in);
```

>   A function macro that decodes the arguments of an RPC request associated with the RPC service transport handle *xprt*. The parameter *in* is the address where the arguments will be placed; *inproc* is the XDR routine used to decode the arguments. This routine returns 1 if decoding succeeds, and 0 otherwise.

```
void
svc_getreqset(fd_set *rdfds);
```

>   This routine is only of interest if a service implementor does not call svc_run, but instead implements custom asynchronous event processing. It is called when poll has determined that an RPC request has arrived on some RPC file descriptors; *rdfds* is the resultant read file descriptor bit mask. The routine returns when all file descriptors associated with the value of *rdfds* have been serviced

```
struct netbuf *
svc_getrpccaller(const SVCXPRT *xprt);
```

>   The approved way of getting the network address of the caller of a procedure associated with the RPC service transport handle *xprt*.

```
void
svc_run(void);
```

>   This routine never returns. It waits for RPC requests to arrive, and calls the appropriate service procedure using svc_getreqset when one arrives. This procedure is usually waiting for a poll library call to return.

```
int
svc_sendreply(const SVCXPRT *xprt, const xdrproc_t outproc,
    const caddr_t *out);
```
Called by an RPC service's dispatch routine to send the results of a remote procedure call. The parameter *xprt* is the request's associated transport handle; *outproc* is the XDR routine which is used to encode the results; and *out* is the address of the results. This routine returns 1 if it succeeds, 0 otherwise.

SEE ALSO

poll(2), rpc(3N), rpc_svc_calls(3N), rpc_svc_create(3N), rpc_svc_err(3N)

rpc_xdr(3N)

NAME
rpc_xdr: xdr_accepted_reply, xdr_authsys_parms, xdr_callhdr, xdr_callmsg, xdr_opaque_auth, xdr_rejected_reply, xdr_replymsg − XDR library routines for remote procedure calls

DESCRIPTION
These routines are used for describing the RPC messages in XDR language. They should normally be used by those who do not want to use the RPC package.

Routines
See rpc(3N) for the definition of the XDR data structure.

```
#include <rpc/rpc.h>

bool_t
xdr_accepted_reply(XDR *xdrs, const struct accepted_reply *ar);
```
    Used for encoding RPC reply messages. It encodes the status of the RPC call in the XDR language format, and in the case of success, it encodes the call results also.

```
bool_t
xdr_authsys_parms(XDR *xdrs, const struct authsys_parms *aupp);
```
    Used for describing operating system credentials. It includes machine-name, uid, gid list, etc.

```
void
xdr_callhdr(XDR *xdrs, const struct rpc_msg *chdr);
```
    Used for describing RPC call header messages. It encodes the static part of the call message header in the XDR language format. It includes information such as transaction ID, RPC version number, program and version number.

```
bool_t
xdr_callmsg(XDR *xdrs, const struct rpc_msg *cmsg);
```
    Used for describing RPC call messages. This includes all the RPC call information such as transaction ID, RPC version number, program number, version number, authentication information, etc. This is normally used by servers to determine information about the client RPC call.

```
bool_t
xdr_opaque_auth(XDR *xdrs, const struct opaque_auth *ap);
```
    Used for describing RPC opaque authentication information messages.

```
bool_t
xdr_rejected_reply(XDR *xdrs, const struct rejected_reply *rr);
```
    Used for describing RPC reply messages. It encodes the rejected RPC message in the XDR language format. The message could be rejected either because of version number mis-match or because of authentication errors.

```
bool_t
xdr_replymsg(XDR *xdrs, const struct rpc_msg *rmsg);
```
Used for describing RPC reply messages. It encodes all the RPC reply message in the XDR language format This reply could be either an acceptance, rejection or NULL.

SEE ALSO
rpc(3N)

NAME
rpcbind: rpcb_getmaps, rpcb_getaddr, rpcb_gettime, rpcb_rmtcall, rpcb_set, rpcb_unset – library routines for RPC bind service

DESCRIPTION
These routines allow client C programs to make procedure calls to the RPC binder service. rpcbind [see rpcbind(1M)] maintains a list of mappings between programs and their universal addresses.

Routines
```
#include <rpc/rpc.h>

struct rpcblist *
rpcb_getmaps(const struct netconfig *netconf, const char *host);
```
A user interface to the rpcbind service, which returns a list of the current RPC program-to-address mappings on the host named. It uses the transport specified through *netconf* to contact the remote rpcbind service on host *host*. This routine will return NULL, if the remote rpcbind could not be contacted.

```
bool_t
rpcb_getaddr(const u_long prognum, const u_long versnum,
    const struct netconfig *netconf, struct netbuf *svcaddr,
    const char *host);
```
A user interface to the rpcbind service, which finds the address of the service on *host* that is registered with program number *prognum*, version *versnum*, and speaks the transport protocol associated with *netconf*. The address found is returned in *svcaddr*. *svcaddr* should be preallocated. This routine returns 1 if it succeeds. A return value of 0 means that the mapping does not exist or that the RPC system failed to contact the remote rpcbind service. In the latter case, the global variable rpc_createerr contains the RPC status.

```
bool_t
rpcb_gettime(const char *host, time_t *timep);
```
This routine returns the time on *host* in *timep*. If *host* is NULL, rpcb_gettime returns the time on its own machine. This routine returns 1 if it succeeds, 0 if it fails. rpcb_gettime can be used to synchronize the time between the client and the remote server. This routine is particularly useful for secure RPC.

```
enum clnt_stat
rpcb_rmtcall(const struct netconfig *netconf, const char *host,
        const u_long prognum, const u_long versnum, const u_long procnum,
        const xdrproc_t inproc, const caddr_t in,
        const xdrproc_t outproc, const caddr_t out,
        const struct timeval tout, struct netbuf *svcaddr);
```

A user interface to the rpcbind service, which instructs rpcbind on *host* to make an RPC call on your behalf to a procedure on that host. The parameter **svcaddr* will be modified to the server's address if the procedure succeeds [see rpc_call and clnt_call in rpc_clnt_calls(3N) for the definitions of other parameters]. This procedure should normally be used for a ping and nothing else [see rpc_broadcast in rpc_clnt_calls(3N)]. This routine allows programs to do lookup and call, all in one step.

```
bool_t
rpcb_set(const u_long prognum, const u_long versnum,
        const struct netconfig *netconf, const struct netbuf *svcaddr);
```

A user interface to the rpcbind service, which establishes a mapping between the triple [*prognum, versnum, netconf*->nc_netid] and *svcaddr* on the machine's rpcbind service. The value of *transport* must correspond to a network token that is defined by the netconfig database. This routine returns 1 if it succeeds, 0 otherwise. [See also svc_reg in rpc_svc_calls(3N)].

```
bool_t
rpcb_unset(const u_long prognum, const u_long versnum,
        const struct netconfig *netconf);
```

A user interface to the rpcbind service, which destroys all mapping between the triple [*prognum, versnum, netconf*->nc_netid] and the address on the machine's rpcbind service. If *netconf* is NULL, rpcb_unset destroys all mapping between the triple [*prognum, versnum,* *] and the addresses on the machine's rpcbind service. This routine returns 1 if it succeeds, 0 otherwise. [See also svc_unreg in rpc_svc_calls(3N)].

SEE ALSO
rpc_clnt_calls(3N), rpc_svc_calls(3N), rpcbind(1M), rpcinfo(1M)

rusers(3N)

NAME
rusers – return information about users on remote machines

SYNOPSIS
#include <rpcsvc/rusers.h>

int rusers(char *_host_, struct utmpidlearr *_up_);

rusers fills the utmpidlearr structure with data about _host,_ and returns 0 if successful. The function will fail if the underlying transport does not support broadcast mode.

SEE ALSO
rusers(1)

rwall(3N) rwall(3N)

NAME
   rwall – write to specified remote machines

SYNOPSIS
   #include <rpcsvc/rwall.h>

   rwall(char **host*, char **msg*);

DESCRIPTION
   rwall executes wall(1M) on *host*. *host* prints the string *msg* to all its users. It returns 0 if successful.

SEE ALSO
   rwall(1M), rwalld(1M)

NAME
scandir, alphasort – scan a directory

SYNOPSIS
cc [*flag*. . .] *file* . . . -lucb

```
#include <sys/types.h>
#include <sys/dir.h>

scandir(dirname, &namelist, select, compar)
char *dirname;
struct direct **namelist;
int (*select)();
int (*compar)();

alphasort(d1, d2)
struct direct **d1, **d2;
```

DESCRIPTION
scandir reads the directory `dirname` and builds an array of pointers to directory entries using malloc(3C). The second parameter is a pointer to an array of structure pointers. The third parameter is a pointer to a routine which is called with a pointer to a directory entry and should return a non zero value if the directory entry should be included in the array. If this pointer is NULL, then all the directory entries will be included. The last argument is a pointer to a routine which is passed to qsort(3C) to sort the completed array. If this pointer is NULL, the array is not sorted. alphasort is a routine which will sort the array alphabetically.

scandir returns the number of entries in the array and a pointer to the array through the parameter *namelist*.

SEE ALSO
getdents(2), directory(3C), malloc(3C), qsort(3C) in the *Programmer's Reference Manual*

RETURN VALUE
Returns −1 if the directory cannot be opened for reading or if malloc(3C) cannot allocate enough memory to hold all the data structures.

scanf(3S)

NAME
scanf, fscanf, sscanf – convert formatted input

SYNOPSIS
#include <stdio.h>

int scanf(const char *format, ...);

int fscanf(FILE *strm, const char *format, ...);

int sscanf(const char *s, const char *format, ...);

DESCRIPTION
scanf reads from the standard input stream, stdin.

fscanf reads from the stream *strm*.

sscanf reads from the character string *s*.

Each function reads characters, interprets them according to a format, and stores the results in its arguments. Each expects, as arguments, a control string, *format*, described below and a set of pointer arguments indicating where the converted input should be stored. If there are insufficient arguments for the format, the behavior is undefined. If the format is exhausted while arguments remain, the excess arguments are simply ignored.

The control string usually contains conversion specifications, which are used to direct interpretation of input sequences. The control string may contain:

1. White-space characters (blanks, tabs, new-lines, or form-feeds) that, except in two cases described below, cause input to be read up to the next non-white-space character.

2. An ordinary character (not %) that must match the next character of the input stream.

3. Conversion specifications consisting of the character % or the character sequence %*digits*$, an optional assignment suppression character *, a decimal digit string that specifies an optional numerical maximum field width, an optional letter l (ell), L, or h indicating the size of the receiving object, and a conversion code. The conversion specifiers d, i, and n should be preceded by h if the corresponding argument is a pointer to short int rather than a pointer to int, or by l if it is a pointer to long int. Similarly, the conversion specifiers o, u, and x should be preceded by h if the corresponding argument is a pointer to unsigned short int rather than a pointer to unsigned int, or by l if it is a pointer to unsigned long int. Finally, the conversion specifiers e, f, and g should be preceded by l if the corresponding argument is a pointer to double rather than a pointer to float, or by L if it is a pointer to long double. The h, l, or L modifier is ignored with any other conversion specifier.

A conversion specification directs the conversion of the next input field; the result is placed in the variable pointed to by the corresponding argument unless assignment suppression was indicated by the character *. The suppression of assignment provides a way of describing an input field that is to be skipped. An input field is defined as a string of non-space characters; it extends to the next inappropriate character or until the maximum field width, if one is specified, is exhausted. For all descriptors except the character [and the character c, white space leading an input field is ignored.

Conversions can be applied to the *nth* argument in the argument list, rather than to the next unused argument. In this case, the conversion character % (see above) is replaced by the sequence %*digits*$ where *digits* is a decimal integer *n*, giving the position of the argument in the argument list. The first such argument, %1$, immediately follows *format*. The control string can contain either form of a conversion specification, i.e., % or %*digits*$, although the two forms cannot be mixed within a single control string.

The conversion code indicates the interpretation of the input field; the corresponding pointer argument must usually be of a restricted type. For a suppressed field, no pointer argument is given. The following conversion codes are valid:

%   A single % is expected in the input at this point; no assignment is done.

d   Matches an optionally signed decimal integer, whose format is the same as expected for the subject sequence of the strtol function with the value 10 for the *base* argument. The corresponding argument should be a pointer to integer.

u   Matches an optionally signed decimal integer, whose format is the same as expected for the subject sequence of the strtoul function with the value 10 for the *base* argument. The corresponding argument should be a pointer to unsigned integer.

o   Matches an optionally signed octal integer, whose format is the same as expected for the subject sequence of the strtoul function with the value 8 for the *base* argument. The corresponding argument should be a pointer to unsigned integer.

x   Matches an optionally signed hexadecimal integer, whose format is the same as expected for the subject sequence of the strtoul function with the value 16 for the *base* argument. The corresponding argument should be a pointer to unsigned integer.

i   Matches an optionally signed integer, whose format is the same as expected for the subject sequence of the strtol function with the value 0 for the *base* argument. The corresponding argument should be a pointer to integer.

n   No input is consumed. The corresponding argument should be a pointer to integer into which is to be written the number of characters read from the input stream so far by the call to the function. Execution of a %n directive does not increment the assignment count returned at the completion of execution of the function.

e,f,g   Matches an optionally signed floating point number, whose format is the same as expected for the subject string of the strtod function. The corresponding argument should be a pointer to floating.

scanf(3S) scanf(3S)

s   A character string is expected; the corresponding argument should be a character pointer pointing to an array of characters large enough to accept the string and a terminating \0, which will be added automatically. The input field is terminated by a white-space character.

c   Matches a sequence of characters of the number specified by the field width (1 if no field width is present in the directive). The corresponding argument should be a pointer to the initial character of an array large enough to accept the sequence. No null character is added. The normal skip over white space is suppressed.

[Matches a nonempty sequence of characters from a set of expected characters (the *scanset*). The corresponding argument should be a pointer to the initial character of an array large enough to accept the sequence and a terminating null character, which will be added automatically. The conversion specifier includes all subsequent characters in the *format* string, up to and including the matching right bracket (]). The characters between the brackets (the *scanlist*) comprise the scanset, unless the character after the left bracket is a circumflex (^), in which case the scanset contains all characters that do not appear in the scanlist between the circumflex and the right bracket. If the conversion specifier begins with [] or [^], the right bracket character is in the scanlist and the next right bracket character is the matching right bracket that ends the specification; otherwise the first right bracket character is the one that ends the specification.

A range of characters in the scanset may be represented by the construct *first* − *last*; thus [0123456789] may be expressed [0−9]. Using this convention, *first* must be lexically less than or equal to *last*, or else the dash will stand for itself. The character − will also stand for itself whenever it is the first or the last character in the scanlist. To include the right bracket as an element of the scanset, it must appear as the first character (possibly preceded by a circumflex) of the scanlist and in this case it will not be syntactically interpreted as the closing bracket. At least one character must match for this conversion to be considered successful.

p   Matches an implementation-defined set of sequences, which should be the same as the set of sequences that may be produced by the %p conversion of the printf function. The corresponding argument should be a pointer to void. The interpretation of the input item is implementation-defined. If the input item is a value converted earlier during the same program execution, the pointer that results shall compare equal to that value; otherwise, the behavior of the %p conversion is undefined.

If an invalid conversion character follows the %, the results of the operation may not be predictable.

The conversion specifiers E, G, and X are also valid and, under the −Xa and −Xc compilation modes [see cc(1)], behave the same as e, g, and x, respectively. Under the −Xt compilation mode, E, G, and X behave the same as le, lg, and lx, respectively.

Each function allows for detection of a language-dependent decimal point character in the input string. The decimal point character is defined by the program's locale (category LC_NUMERIC). In the "C" locale, or in a locale where the decimal point character is not defined, the decimal point character defaults to a period (.).

The scanf conversion terminates at end of file, at the end of the control string, or when an input character conflicts with the control string.

If end-of-file is encountered during input, conversion is terminated. If end-of-file occurs before any characters matching the current directive have been read (other than leading white space, where permitted), execution of the current directive terminates with an input failure; otherwise, unless execution of the current directive is terminated with a matching failure, execution of the following directive (if any) is terminated with an input failure.

If conversion terminates on a conflicting input character, the offending input character is left unread in the input stream. Trailing white space (including new-line characters) is left unread unless matched by a directive. The success of literal matches and suppressed assignments is not directly determinable other than via the %n directive.

EXAMPLES

The call to the function scanf:

```
int i, n; float x; char name[50];
n = scanf ("%d%f%s", &i, &x, name);
```

with the input line:

```
25 54.32E-1 thompson
```

will assign to n the value 3, to i the value 25, to x the value 5.432, and name will contain thompson\0.

The call to the function scanf:

```
int i; float x; char name[50];
(void) scanf ("%2d%f%*d %[0-9]", &i, &x, name);
```

with the input line:

```
56789 0123 56a72
```

will assign 56 to i, 789.0 to x, skip 0123, and place the characters 56\0 in name. The next character read from stdin will be a.

SEE ALSO

cc(1), printf(3S), strtod(3C), strtol(3C), strtoul(3C).

DIAGNOSTICS

These routines return the number of successfully matched and assigned input items; this number can be zero in the event of an early matching failure between an input character and the control string. If the input ends before the first matching failure or conversion, EOF is returned.

NAME

secure_rpc: authdes_seccreate, authdes_getucred, getnetname, host2netname, key_decryptsession, key_encryptsession, key_gendes, key_setsecret, netname2host, netname2user, user2netname – library routines for secure remote procedure calls

DESCRIPTION

RPC library routines allow C programs to make procedure calls on other machines across the network. First, the client calls a procedure to send a data packet to the server. Upon receipt of the packet, the server calls a dispatch routine to perform the requested service, and then sends back a reply.

RPC supports various authentication flavors. Among them are:

    AUTH_NONE   (none) no authentication.
    AUTH_SYS   Traditional UNIX®-style authentication.
    AUTH_DES   DES encryption-based authentication.

The authdes_getucred and authdes_seccreate routines implement the AUTH_DES authentication flavor. The keyserver daemon keyserv [see keyserv(1M)] must be running for the AUTH_DES authentication system to work.

Routines

See rpc(3N) for the definition of the AUTH data structure.

```
#include <rpc/rpc.h>

int
authdes_getucred(const struct authdes_cred *adc, uid_t *uidp,
        gid_t *gidp, short *gidlenp, gid_t *gidlist);
```

authdes_getucred is the first of the two routines which interface to the RPC secure authentication system known as AUTH_DES. The second is authdes_seccreate, below. authdes_getucred is used on the server side for converting an AUTH_DES credential, which is operating system independent, into an AUTH_SYS credential. This routine returns 1 if it succeeds, 0 if it fails.

uidp is set to the user's numerical ID associated with *adc*. *gidp* is set to the numerical ID of the group to which the user belongs. *gidlist* contains the numerical IDs of the other groups to which the user belongs. *gidlenp* is set to the number of valid group ID entries in *gidlist* [see netname2user, below].

secure_rpc(3N)

```
AUTH *
authdes_seccreate(const char *name, const unsigned int window,
     const char *timehost, const des_block *ckey);
```

> authdes_seccreate, the second of two AUTH_DES authentication routines, is used on the client side to return an authentication handle that will enable the use of the secure authentication system. The first parameter *name* is the network name, or *netname*, of the owner of the server process. This field usually represents a hostname derived from the utility routine host2netname, but could also represent a user name using user2netname, described below. The second field is window on the validity of the client credential, given in seconds. A small window is more secure than a large one, but choosing too small of a window will increase the frequency of resynchronizations because of clock drift. The third parameter, *timehost*, the host's name, is optional. If it is NULL, then the authentication system will assume that the local clock is always in sync with the *timehost* clock, and will not attempt resynchronizations. If a timehost is supplied, however, then the system will consult with the remote time service whenever resynchronization is required. This parameter is usually the name of the RPC server itself. The final parameter *ckey* is also optional. If it is NULL, then the authentication system will generate a random DES key to be used for the encryption of credentials. If *ckey* is supplied, then it will be used instead.

```
int
getnetname(char name[MAXNETNAMELEN+1]);
```

> getnetname installs the unique, operating-system independent netname of the caller in the fixed-length array *name*. Returns 1 if it succeeds, and 0 if it fails.

```
int
host2netname(char name[MAXNETNAMELEN+1], const char *host,
     const char *domain);
```

> Convert from a domain-specific hostname *host* to an operating-system independent netname. Return 1 if it succeeds, and 0 if it fails. Inverse of netname2host. If *domain* is NULL, host2netname uses the default domain name of the machine. If *host* is NULL, it defaults to that machine itself.

```
int
key_decryptsession(const char *remotename, des_block *deskey);
```

> key_decryptsession is an interface to the keyserver daemon, which is associated with RPC's secure authentication system (AUTH_DES authentication). User programs rarely need to call it, or its associated routines key_encryptsession, key_gendes and key_setsecret.
>
> key_decryptsession takes a server netname *remotename* and a DES key *deskey*, and decrypts the key by using the the public key of the the server and the secret key associated with the effective UID of the calling process. It is the inverse of key_encryptsession.

```
int
key_encryptsession(const char *remotename, des_block *deskey);
```

> key_encryptsession is a keyserver interface routine. It takes a server netname *remotename* and a DES key *deskey*, and encrypts it using the public key of the the server and the secret key associated with the effective UID of the calling process. It is the inverse of key_decryptsession. This routine returns 0 if it succeeds, −1 if it fails.

```
int
key_gendes(des_block *deskey);
```

> key_gendes is a keyserver interface routine. It is used to ask the keyserver for a secure conversation key. Choosing one at random is usually not good enough, because the common ways of choosing random numbers, such as using the current time, are very easy to guess.

```
int
key_setsecret(const char *key);
```

> key_setsecret is a keyserver interface routine. It is used to set the key for the effective UID of the calling process. this routine returns 0 if it succeeds, −1 if it fails.

```
int
netname2host(const char *name, char *host, const int hostlen);
```

> Convert from an operating-system independent netname *name* to a domain-specific hostname *host*. *hostlen* is the maximum size of *host*. Returns 1 if it succeeds, and 0 if it fails. Inverse of host2netname.

```
int
netname2user(const char *name, uid_t *uidp, gid_t *gidp,
    int *gidlenp, gid_t gidlist[NGROUPS]);
```

> Convert from an operating-system independent netname to a domain-specific user ID. Returns 1 if it succeeds, and 0 if it fails. Inverse of user2netname.
>
> **uidp* is set to the user's numerical ID associated with *name*. **gidp* is set to the numerical ID of the group to which the user belongs. *gidlist* contains the numerical IDs of the other groups to which the user belongs. **gidlenp* is set to the number of valid group ID entries in *gidlist*.

```
int
user2netname(char name[MAXNETNAMELEN+1], const uid_t uid,
    const char *domain);
```

> Convert from a domain-specific username to an operating-system independent netname. Returns 1 if it succeeds, and 0 if it fails. Inverse of netname2user.

SEE ALSO

chkey(1), keyserv(1M), newkey(1M), rpc(3N), rpc_clnt_auth(3N)

NAME
select – synchronous I/O multiplexing

SYNOPSIS
```
#include <sys/time.h>
#include <sys/types.h>

select(int nfds, fd_set *readfds, *writefds, *execptfds, struct
    timeval *timeout);
FD_SET(int fd, fd_set fdset);
FD_CLR(int fd, fd_set fdset);
FD_ISSET(int fd, fd_set fdset);
FD_ZERO(fd_set fdset);
```

DESCRIPTION
select examines the I/O descriptor sets whose addresses are passed in *readfds*, *writefds*, and *execptfds* to see if any of their descriptors are ready for reading, are ready for writing, or have an exceptional condition pending, respectively. *nfds* is the number of bits to be checked in each bit mask that represents a file descriptor; the descriptors from 0 to −1 in the descriptor sets are examined. On return, select replaces the given descriptor sets with subsets consisting of those descriptors that are ready for the requested operation. The return value from the call to select() is the number of ready descriptors.

The descriptor sets are stored as bit fields in arrays of integers. The following macros are provided for manipulating such descriptor sets: FD_ZERO(&*fdset*) initializes a descriptor set *fdset* to the null set. FD_SET(*fd*, &*fdset*) includes a particular descriptor *fd* in *fdset*. FD_CLR(*fd*, &*fdset*) removes *fd* from *fdset*. FD_ISSET(*fd*, &*fdset*) is nonzero if *fd* is a member of *fdset*, zero otherwise. The behavior of these macros is undefined if a descriptor value is less than zero or greater than or equal to FD_SETSIZE. FD_SETSIZE is a constant defined in sys/select.h and is normally at least equal to the maximum number of descriptors supported by the system.

If *timeout* is not a NULL pointer, it specifies a maximum interval to wait for the selection to complete. If *timeout* is a NULL pointer, the select blocks indefinitely. To affect a poll, the *timeout* argument should be a non-NULL pointer, pointing to a zero-valued timeval structure.

Any of *readfds*, *writefds*, and *execptfds* may be given as NULL pointers if no descriptors are of interest.

RETURN VALUE
select returns the number of ready descriptors contained in the descriptor sets or −1 if an error occurred. If the time limit expires, then select returns 0.

ERRORS
An error return from select indicates:

EBADF	One of the I/O descriptor sets specified an invalid I/O descriptor.
EINTR	A signal was delivered before any of the selected events occurred, or the time limit expired.

EINVAL   A component of the pointed-to time limit is outside the acceptable range: t_sec must be between 0 and 10^8, inclusive. t_usec must be greater-than or equal to 0, and less than 10^6.

SEE ALSO
poll(2), read(2), write(2)

NOTES
The default value for FD_SETSIZE (currently 1024) is larger than the default limit on the number of open files. In order to accommodate programs that may use a larger number of open files with `select`, it is possible to increase this size within a program by providing a larger definition of FD_SETSIZE before the inclusion of <sys/types.h>.

In future versions of the system, `select` may return the time remaining from the original timeout, if any, by modifying the time value in place. It is thus unwise to assume that the timeout value will be unmodified by the `select` call.

The descriptor sets are always modified on return, even if the call returns as the result of a timeout.

send(3N)

NAME
send, sendto, sendmsg – send a message from a socket

SYNOPSIS
#include <sys/types.h>

int send(int s, char *msg, int len, int flags);

int sendto(int s, char *msg, int len, int flags, caddr_t to, int tolen);

int sendmsg(int s, msghdr *msg, int flags);

DESCRIPTION
s is a socket created with socket. send, sendto, and sendmsg are used to transmit a message to another socket. send may be used only when the socket is in a *connected* state, while sendto and sendmsg may be used at any time.

The address of the target is given by *to* with *tolen* specifying its size. The length of the message is given by *len*. If the message is too long to pass atomically through the underlying protocol, then the error EMSGSIZE is returned, and the message is not transmitted.

No indication of failure to deliver is implicit in a send. Return values of −1 indicate some locally detected errors.

If no buffer space is available at the socket to hold the message to be transmitted, then send normally blocks, unless the socket has been placed in non-blocking I/O mode [see fcntl(2)]. The select call may be used to determine when it is possible to send more data.

The *flags* parameter is formed by ORing one or more of the following:

MSG_OOB   Send out-of-band data on sockets that support this notion. The underlying protocol must also support out-of-band data. Currently, only SOCK_STREAM sockets created in the AF_INET address family support out-of-band data.

MSG_DONTROUTE   The SO_DONTROUTE option is turned on for the duration of the operation. It is used only by diagnostic or routing programs.

See recv(3N) for a description of the msghdr structure.

RETURN VALUE
These calls return the number of bytes sent, or −1 if an error occurred.

ERRORS
The calls fail if:

EBADF   s is an invalid descriptor.

ENOTSOCK   s is a descriptor for a file, not a socket.

EINVAL   *tolen* is not the size of a valid address for the specified address family.

EINTR   The operation was interrupted by delivery of a signal before any data could be buffered to be sent.

EMSGSIZE	The socket requires that message be sent atomically, and the message was too long.
EWOULDBLOCK	The socket is marked non-blocking and the requested operation would block.
ENOMEM	There was insufficient user memory available for the operation to complete.
ENOSR	There were insufficient STREAMS resources available for the operation to complete.

SEE ALSO

connect(3N), getsockopt(3N), recv(3N), socket(3N).
fcntl(2), write(2) in the *Programmer's Reference Manual*.

NOTES

The type of address structure passed to accept depends on the address family. UNIX domain sockets (address family AF_UNIX) require a socketaddr_un structure as defined in sys/un.h; Internet domain sockets (address family AF_INET) require a sockaddr_in structure as defined in netinet/in.h. Other address families may require other structures. Use the structure appropriate to the address family; cast the structure address to a generic caddr_t in the call to send and pass the size of the structure in the *tolen* argument.

See "The Sockets Interface" section in the *Programmer's Guide: Networking Interfaces* for details.

NAME

setbuf, setvbuf – assign buffering to a stream

SYNOPSIS

```
#include <stdio.h>

void setbuf (FILE *stream, char *buf);

int setvbuf (FILE *stream, char *buf, int type, size_t size);
```

DESCRIPTION

setbuf may be used after a *stream* [see intro(3)] has been opened but before it is read or written. It causes the array pointed to by *buf* to be used instead of an automatically allocated buffer. If *buf* is the NULL pointer input/output will be completely unbuffered.

While there is no limitation on the size of the buffer, the constant BUFSIZ, defined in the stdio.h header file, is typically a good buffer size:

```
char buf[BUFSIZ];
```

setvbuf may be used after a stream has been opened but before it is read or written. *type* determines how *stream* will be buffered. Valid values for *type* (defined in stdio.h) are:

_IOFBF   causes input/output to be fully buffered.

_IOLBF   causes output to be line buffered; the buffer is flushed when a newline is written, the buffer is full, or input is requested.

_IONBF   causes input/output to be completely unbuffered.

If *buf* is not the NULL pointer, the array it points to is used for buffering, instead of an automatically allocated buffer. *size* specifies the size of the buffer to be used. If input/output is unbuffered, *buf* and *size* are ignored.

For a further discussion of buffering, see stdio(3S).

SEE ALSO

fopen(3S), getc(3S), malloc(3C), putc(3S), stdio(3S)

DIAGNOSTICS

If an invalid value for *type* is provided, setvbuf returns a non-zero value. Otherwise, it returns zero.

NOTES

A common source of error is allocating buffer space as an "automatic" variable in a code block, and then failing to close the stream in the same block.

Parts of buf are used for internal bookkeeping of the stream and, therefore, buf contains less than *size* bytes when full. It is recommended that the automatically allocated buffer is used when using setvbuf.

NAME

setbuf, setbuffer, setlinebuf, setvbuf – assign buffering to a stream

SYNOPSIS

cc [*flag*...] *file* ... −lucb

```
#include <stdio.h>
```

setbuf(stream, buf)
FILE *stream;
char *buf;

setbuffer(stream, buf, size)
FILE *stream;
char *buf;
int size;

setlinebuf(stream)
FILE *stream;

int setvbuf(stream, buf, type, size)
FILE *stream;
char *buf;
int type, size;

DESCRIPTION

The three types of buffering available are unbuffered, block buffered, and line buffered. When an output stream is unbuffered, information appears on the destination file or terminal as soon as written; when it is block buffered many characters are saved up and written as a block; when it is line buffered characters are saved up until a NEWLINE is encountered or input is read from stdin. fflush (see fclose(3S)) may be used to force the block out early. Normally all files are block buffered. A buffer is obtained from malloc(3C) upon the first getc or putc(3S) on the file. If the standard stream stdout refers to a terminal it is line buffered. The standard stream stderr is unbuffered by default.

setbuf can be used after a stream has been opened but before it is read or written. It causes the array pointed to by *buf* to be used instead of an automatically allocated buffer. If *buf* is the NULL pointer, input/output will be completely unbuffered. A manifest constant BUFSIZ, defined in the <stdio.h> header file, tells how big an array is needed:

    char buf[BUFSIZ];

setbuffer, an alternate form of setbuf, can be used after a stream has been opened but before it is read or written. It uses the character array *buf* whose size is determined by the *size* argument instead of an automatically allocated buffer. If *buf* is the NULL pointer, input/output will be completely unbuffered.

setvbuf can be used after a stream has been opened but before it is read or written. *type* determines how stream will be buffered. Legal values for *type* (defined in <stdio.h>) are:

_IOFBF   fully buffers the input/output.

_IOLBF   line buffers the output; the buffer will be flushed when a NEWLINE is written, the buffer is full, or input is requested.

_IONBF   completely unbuffers the input/output.

If *buf* is not the NULL pointer, the array it points to will be used for buffering, instead of an automatically allocated buffer. *size* specifies the size of the buffer to be used.

setlinebuf is used to change the buffering on a stream from block buffered or unbuffered to line buffered. Unlike setbuf, setbuffer, and setvbuf, it can be used at any time that the file descriptor is active.

A file can be changed from unbuffered or line buffered to block buffered by using freopen (see fopen(3S)). A file can be changed from block buffered or line buffered to unbuffered by using freopen followed by setbuf with a buffer argument of NULL.

NOTE

A common source of error is allocating buffer space as an "automatic" variable in a code block, and then failing to close the stream in the same block.

SEE ALSO

fclose(3S), fopen(3S), fread(3S), getc(3S), malloc(3C), printf(3S), putc(3S), puts(3S), setbuf(3S) in the *Programmer's Reference Manual*

RETURN VALUE

If an illegal value for *type* or *size* is provided, setvbuf returns a non-zero value. Otherwise, the value returned will be zero.

NAME
setbuffer, setlinebuf − assign buffering to a stream

SYNOPSIS
cc [*flag*. . .] *file* . . . -lucb

#include <stdio.h>

setbuffer(stream, buf, size)
FILE *stream;
char *buf;
int size;

setlinebuf(stream)
FILE *stream;

DESCRIPTION
The three types of buffering available are unbuffered, block buffered, and line buffered. When an output stream is unbuffered, information appears on the destination file or terminal as soon as written; when it is block buffered many characters are saved up and written as a block; when it is line buffered characters are saved up until a NEWLINE is encountered or input is read from any line buffered input stream. fflush (see fclose(3S)) may be used to force the block out early. Normally all files are block buffered. A buffer is obtained from malloc(3C) upon the first getc or putc(3S) on the file.

By default, output to a terminal is line buffered, except for output to the standard stream stderr which is unbuffered, and all other input/output is fully buffered.

setbuffer can be used after a stream has been opened but before it is read or written. It uses the character array *buf* whose size is determined by the *size* argument instead of an automatically allocated buffer. If *buf* is the NULL pointer, input/output will be completely unbuffered. A manifest constant BUFSIZ, defined in the <stdio.h> header file, tells how big an array is needed:

    char buf[BUFSIZ];

setlinebuf is used to change the buffering on a stream from block buffered or unbuffered to line buffered. Unlike setbuffer, it can be used at any time that the file descriptor is active.

A file can be changed from unbuffered or line buffered to block buffered by using freopen (see fopen(3S)). A file can be changed from block buffered or line buffered to unbuffered by using freopen followed by setbuffer with a buffer argument of NULL.

SEE ALSO
setbuf(3S)

fclose(3S), fopen(3S), fread(3S), getc(3S), malloc(3C), printf(3S), putc(3S), puts(3S), setbuf(3S) in the *Programmer's Reference Manual*

NOTE
A common source of error is allocating buffer space as an automatic variable in a code block, and then failing to close the stream in the same block.

setjmp(3C)

NAME
setjmp, longjmp – non-local goto

SYNOPSIS
```
#include <setjmp.h>

int setjmp (jmp_buf env);

void longjmp (jmp_buf env, int val);
```

DESCRIPTION
These functions are useful for dealing with errors and interrupts encountered in a low-level subroutine of a program.

setjmp saves its stack environment in env (whose type, *jmp_buf*, is defined in the <setjmp.h> header file) for later use by longjmp. It returns the value 0.

longjmp restores the environment saved by the last call of setjmp with the corresponding env argument. After longjmp is completed, program execution continues as if the corresponding call of setjmp had just returned the value val. (The caller of setjmp must not have returned in the interim.) longjmp cannot cause setjmp to return the value 0. If longjmp is invoked with a second argument of 0, setjmp will return 1. At the time of the second return from setjmp, all external and static variables have values as of the time longjmp is called (see example). The values of register and automatic variables are undefined.

Register or automatic variables whose value must be relied upon must be declared as volatile.

EXAMPLE
```
#include <stdio.h>
#include <stdlib.h>
#include <setjmp.h>

jmp_buf env;
int i = 0;
main ()
{
    void exit();

    if(setjmp(env) != 0) {
        (void) printf("value of i on 2nd return from setjmp: %d\n", i)
        exit(0);
    }
    (void) printf("value of i on 1st return from setjmp: %d\n", i);
    i = 1;
    g();
    /* NOTREACHED */
}
g()
{
    longjmp(env, 1);
    /* NOTREACHED */
}
```

If the a.out resulting from this C language code is run, the output will be:

    value of i on 1st return from setjmp: 0

    value of i on 2nd return from setjmp: 1

SEE ALSO
    signal(2), sigsetjmp(3C).

NOTES
    If longjmp is called even though env was never primed by a call to setjmp, or when the last such call was in a function that has since returned, absolute chaos is guaranteed.

setjmp(3) (BSD Compatibility Package)

NAME
setjmp, longjmp, _setjmp, _longjmp, sigsetjmp, siglongjmp – non-local goto

SYNOPSIS
cc [*flag*...] *file* ... -lucb

```
#include <setjmp.h>
```

int setjmp(env)
jmp_buf env;

longjmp(env, val)
jmp_buf env;
int val;

int _setjmp(env)
jmp_buf env;

_longjmp(env, val)
jmp_buf env;
int val;

int sigsetjmp(env, savemask)
sigjmp_buf env;
int savemask;

siglongjmp(env, val)
sigjmp_buf env;
int val;

DESCRIPTION
setjmp and longjmp are useful for dealing with errors and interrupts encountered in a low-level subroutine of a program.

setjmp saves its stack environment in *env* for later use by longjmp. A normal call to setjmp returns zero. setjmp also saves the register environment. If a longjmp call will be made, the routine which called setjmp should not return until after the longjmp has returned control (see below).

longjmp restores the environment saved by the last call of setjmp, and then returns in such a way that execution continues as if the call of setjmp had just returned the value *val* to the function that invoked setjmp; however, if *val* were zero, execution would continue as if the call of setjmp had returned one. This ensures that a "return" from setjmp caused by a call to longjmp can be distinguished from a regular return from setjmp. The calling function must not itself have returned in the interim, otherwise longjmp will be returning control to a possibly non-existent environment. All memory-bound data have values as of the time longjmp was called. The CPU and floating-point data registers are restored to the values they had at the time that setjmp was called. But, because the register storage class is only a hint to the C compiler, variables declared as register variables may not necessarily be assigned to machine registers, so their values are unpredictable after a longjmp. This is especially a problem for programmers trying to write machine-independent C routines.

setjmp and longjmp save and restore the signal mask (see sigsetmask(2)), while _setjmp and _longjmp manipulate only the C stack and registers. If the *savemask* flag to sigsetjmp is non-zero, the signal mask is saved, and a subsequent siglongjmp using the same *env* will restore the signal mask. If the *savemask* flag is zero, the signal mask is not saved, and a subsequent siglongjmp using the same *env* will not restore the signal mask. In all other ways, _setjmp and sigsetjmp function in the same way that setjmp does, and _longjmp and siglongjmp function in the same way that longjmp does.

None of these functions save or restore any floating-point status or control registers.

EXAMPLE

The following code fragment indicates the flow of control of the setjmp and longjmp combination:

function declaration
```
    ...
        jmp_buf    my_environment;
        ...
        if (setjmp(my_environment)) {
           /* register variables have unpredictable values */
```
           code after the return from longjmp
```
            ...
        } else {
           /* do not modify register vars in this leg of code */
```
           this is the return from setjmp
```
            ...
        }
```

SEE ALSO

cc(1), signal(3), sigsetmask(3), sigvec(3)

cc(1), signal(2), setjmp(3C) in the *Programmer's Reference Manual*

NOTES

setjmp does not save the current notion of whether the process is executing on the signal stack. The result is that a longjmp to some place on the signal stack leaves the signal stack state incorrect.

On some systems setjmp also saves the register environment. Therefore, all data that are bound to registers are restored to the values they had at the time that setjmp was called. All memory-bound data have values as of the time longjmp was called. However, because the register storage class is only a hint to the C compiler, variables declared as register variables may not necessarily be assigned to machine registers, so their values are unpredictable after a longjmp. When using compiler options that specify automatic register allocation (see cc(1V)), the compiler will not attempt to assign variables to registers in routines that call setjmp.

longjmp never causes setjmp to return zero, so programmers should not depend on longjmp being able to cause setjmp to return zero.

setlocale(3C)   (C Programming Language Utilities)   setlocale(3C)

NAME
setlocale – modify and query a program's locale

SYNOPSIS
```
#include <locale.h>
```
char *setlocale (int category, const char *locale);

DESCRIPTION
setlocale selects the appropriate piece of the program's locale as specified by the *category* and *locale* arguments. The *category* argument may have the following values: LC_CTYPE, LC_NUMERIC, LC_TIME, LC_COLLATE, LC_MONETARY, LC_MESSAGES and LC_ALL. These names are defined in the locale.h header file. LC_CTYPE affects the behavior of the character handling functions (isdigit, tolower, etc.) and the multibyte character functions (such as mbtowc and wctomb). LC_NUMERIC affects the decimal-point character for the formatted input/output functions and the string conversion functions as well as the non-monetary formatting information returned by localeconv. [See localeconv(3C).]. LC_TIME affects the behavior of ascftime, cftime, getdate and strftime. LC_COLLATE affects the behavior of strcoll and strxfrm. LC_MONETARY affects the monetary formatted information returned by localeconv. LC_MESSAGES affects the behavior of gettxt, catopen, catclose, and catgets. [See catopen(3C) and catgets(3C).] LC_ALL names the program's entire locale.

Each category corresponds to a set of databases which contain the relevant information for each defined locale. The location of a database is given by the following path, /usr/lib/locale/*locale*/*category*, where *locale* and *category* are the names of locale and category, respectively. For example, the database for the LC_CTYPE category for the "german" locale would be found in /usr/lib/locale/german/LC_CTYPE.

A value of "C" for *locale* specifies the default environment.

A value of "" for *locale* specifies that the locale should be taken from environment variables. The order in which the environment variables are checked for the various categories is given below:

Category	1st Env. Var.	2nd Env. Var
LC_CTYPE:	LC_CTYPE	LANG
LC_COLLATE:	LC_COLLATE	LANG
LC_TIME:	LC_TIME	LANG
LC_NUMERIC:	LC_NUMERIC	LANG
LC_MONETARY:	LC_MONETARY	LANG
LC_MESSAGES:	LC_MESSAGES	LANG

At program startup, the equivalent of
   setlocale(LC_ALL, "C")
is executed. This has the effect of initializing each category to the locale described by the environment "C".

If a pointer to a string is given for *locale*, `setlocale` attempts to set the locale for the given category to *locale*. If `setlocale` succeeds, *locale* is returned. If `setlocale` fails, a null pointer is returned and the program's locale is not changed.

For category LC_ALL, the behavior is slightly different. If a pointer to a string is given for *locale* and LC_ALL is given for *category*, `setlocale` attempts to set the locale for all the categories to *locale*. The *locale* may be a simple locale, consisting of a single locale, or a composite locale. A composite locale is a string beginning with a "/" followed by the locale of each category separated by a "/". If `setlocale` fails to set the locale for any category, a null pointer is returned and the program's locale for all categories is not changed. Otherwise, locale is returned.

A null pointer for *locale* causes `setlocale` to return the current locale associated with the *category*. The program's locale is not changed.

FILES

/usr/lib/locale/C/LC_CTYPE – LC_CTYPE database for the C locale.
/usr/lib/locale/C/LC_NUMERIC – LC_NUMERIC database for the C locale.
/usr/lib/locale/C/LC_TIME – LC_TIME database for the C locale.
/usr/lib/locale/C/LC_COLLATE – LC_COLLATE database for the C locale.
/usr/lib/locale/C/LC_MESSAGES – LC_MESSAGES database for the C locale.
/usr/lib/locale/*locale*/*category* – files containing the locale specific information for each locale and category.

SEE ALSO

ctime(3C), ctype(3C), getdate(3C), gettxt(3G), localeconv(3C), mbtowc(3C), printf(3S), strcoll(3C), strftime(3C), strtod(3C), strxfrm(3C), wctomb(3C), environ(5).

setregid(3)　　　　　　　(BSD Compatibility Package)　　　　　　　setregid(3)

NAME
setregid – set real and effective group IDs

SYNOPSIS
cc [*flag*...] *file* ... -lucb

```
int setregid(rgid, egid)
int rgid, egid;
```

DESCRIPTION
setregid is used to set the real and effective group IDs of the calling process. If *rgid* is −1, the real GID is not changed; if *egid* is −1, the effective GID is not changed. The real and effective GIDs may be set to different values in the same call.

If the effective user ID of the calling process is super-user, the real GID and the effective GID can be set to any legal value.

If the effective user ID of the calling process is not super-user, either the real GID can be set to the saved setGID from execv, or the effective GID can either be set to the saved setGID or the real GID. Note: if a setGID process sets its effective GID to its real GID, it can still set its effective GID back to the saved setGID.

In either case, if the real GID is being changed (that is, if *rgid* is not −1), or the effective GID is being changed to a value not equal to the real GID, the saved setGID is set equal to the new effective GID.

If the real GID is changed from its current value, the old value is removed from the groups access list (see getgroups(2)) if it is present in that list, and the new value is added to the groups access list if it is not already present and if this would not cause the number of groups in that list to exceed NGROUPS, as defined in /usr/include/sys/param.h.

RETURN VALUE
Upon successful completion, a value of 0 is returned. Otherwise, a value of −1 is returned and errno is set to indicate the error.

ERRORS
setregid will fail and neither of the group IDs will be changed if:

EPERM　　　　The calling process's effective UID is not the super-user and a change other than changing the real GID to the saved setGID, or changing the effective GID to the real GID or the saved GID, was specified.

SEE ALSO
setreuid(3)

exec(2), getuid(2), setuid(2) in the *Programmer's Reference Manual*

NAME

setreuid – set real and effective user IDs

SYNOPSIS

cc [*flag*...] *file* ... -lucb

```
int setreuid(ruid, euid)
int ruid, euid;
```

DESCRIPTION

setreuid is used to set the real and effective user IDs of the calling process. If *ruid* is -1, the real user ID is not changed; if *euid* is -1, the effective user ID is not changed. The real and effective user IDs may be set to different values in the same call.

If the effective user ID of the calling process is super-user, the real user ID and the effective user ID can be set to any legal value.

If the effective user ID of the calling process is not super-user, either the real user ID can be set to the effective user ID, or the effective user ID can either be set to the saved set-user ID from execv or the real user ID. Note: if a set-UID process sets its effective user ID to its real user ID, it can still set its effective user ID back to the saved set-user ID.

In either case, if the real user ID is being changed (that is, if *ruid* is not -1), or the effective user ID is being changed to a value not equal to the real user ID, the saved set-user ID is set equal to the new effective user ID.

RETURN VALUE

Upon successful completion, a value of 0 is returned. Otherwise, a value of -1 is returned and errno is set to indicate the error.

ERRORS

setreuid will fail and neither of the user IDs will be changed if:

EPERM   The calling process's effective user ID is not the super-user and a change other than changing the real user ID to the effective user ID, or changing the effective user ID to the real user ID or the saved set-user ID, was specified.

SEE ALSO

setregid(3)

exec(2), getuid(2), setuid(2) in the *Programmer's Reference Manual*

shutdown (3N)

NAME
shutdown − shut down part of a full-duplex connection

SYNOPSIS
`int shutdown(int s, int how);`

DESCRIPTION
The `shutdown` call shuts down all or part of a full-duplex connection on the socket associated with *s*. If *how* is 0, then further receives will be disallowed. If *how* is 1, then further sends will be disallowed. If *how* is 2, then further sends and receives will be disallowed.

RETURN VALUE
A 0 is returned if the call succeeds, −1 if it fails.

ERRORS
The call succeeds unless:

EBADF	*s* is not a valid descriptor.
ENOTSOCK	*s* is a file, not a socket.
ENOTCONN	The specified socket is not connected.
ENOMEM	There was insufficient user memory available for the operation to complete.
ENOSR	There were insufficient STREAMS resources available for the operation to complete.

SEE ALSO
connect(3N), socket(3N)

NOTES
The *how* values should be defined constants.

NAME
sigblock, sigmask – block signals

SYNOPSIS
cc [*flag*. . .] *file* . . . -lucb

#include <signal.h>

sigblock(mask);
int mask;

#define sigmask(signum)

DESCRIPTION
sigblock adds the signals specified in *mask* to the set of signals currently being blocked from delivery. Signals are blocked if the appropriate bit in *mask* is a 1; the macro sigmask is provided to construct the mask for a given *signum*. The previous mask is returned, and may be restored using sigsetmask(3).

It is not possible to block SIGKILL, SIGSTOP, or SIGCONT; this restriction is silently imposed by the system.

RETURN VALUE
The previous set of masked signals is returned.

SEE ALSO
sigsetmask(2), sigvec(2)

kill(2), sigaction(2), signal(2) in the *Programmer's Reference Manual*

sigfpe(3) (BSD Compatibility Package) sigfpe(3)

NAME
sigfpe – signal handling for specific SIGFPE codes

SYNOPSIS
cc [*flag*...] *file* ... -lucb

#include <signal.h>

#include <floatingpoint.h>

sigfpe_handler_type sigfpe(code, hdl)
sigfpe_code_type code;
sigfpe_handler_type hdl;

DESCRIPTION
This function allows signal handling to be specified for particular SIGFPE codes. A call to sigfpe defines a new handler *hdl* for a particular SIGFPE *code* and returns the old handler as the value of the function sigfpe. Normally handlers are specified as pointers to functions; the special cases SIGFPE_IGNORE, SIGFPE_ABORT, and SIGFPE_DEFAULT allow ignoring, specifying core dump using abort(3), or default handling respectively.

For these IEEE-related codes:

FPE_FLTINEX_TRAP	fp_inexact	floating inexact result
FPE_FLTDIV_TRAP	fp_division	floating division by zero
FPE_FLTUND_TRAP	fp_underflow	floating underflow
FPE_FLTOVF_TRAP	fp_overflow	floating overflow
FPE_FLTBSUN_TRAP	fp_invalid	branch or set on unordered
FPE_FLTOPERR_TRAP	fp_invalid	floating operand error
FPE_FLTNAN_TRAP	fp_invalid	floating Not-A-Number

default handling is defined to be to call the handler specified to ieee_handler(3M).

For all other SIGFPE codes, default handling is to core dump using abort(3).

The compilation option -ffpa causes fpa recomputation to replace the default abort action for code FPE_FPA_ERROR. Note: SIGFPE_DEFAULT will restore abort rather than FPA recomputation for this code.

Three steps are required to intercept an IEEE-related SIGFPE code with sigfpe:

1. Set up a handler with sigfpe.
2. Enable the relevant IEEE trapping capability in the hardware, perhaps by using assembly-language instructions.
3. Perform a floating-point operation that generates the intended IEEE exception.

Unlike ieee_handler(3M), sigfpe never changes floating-point hardware mode bits affecting IEEE trapping. No IEEE-related SIGFPE signals will be generated unless those hardware mode bits are enabled.

SIGFPE signals can be handled using sigvec(2), signal(3), sigfpe(3), or ieee_handler(3M). In a particular program, to avoid confusion, use only one of these interfaces to handle SIGFPE signals.

EXAMPLE

A user-specified signal handler might look like this:

```
void sample_handler( sig, code, scp, addr )
        int sig ;               /* sig == SIGFPE always */
        int code ;
        struct sigcontext *scp ;
        char *addr ;
        {
                /*
                  Sample user-written sigfpe code handler.
                  Prints a message and continues.
                  struct sigcontext is defined in <signal.h>.
                 */
                printf(" ieee exception code %x occurred at pc %X \n",
                        code, scp->sc_pc);
        }
```

and it might be set up like this:

```
        extern void sample_handler;
        main
        {
                sigfpe_handler_type hdl, old_handler1, old_handler2;
        /*
         * save current overflow and invalid handlers; set the new
         * overflow handler to sample_handler and set the new
         * invalid handler to SIGFPE_ABORT (abort on invalid)
         */
                hdl = (sigfpe_handler_type) sample_handler;
                old_handler1 = sigfpe(FPE_FLTOVF_TRAP, hdl);
                old_handler2 = sigfpe(FPE_FLTOPERR_TRAP, SIGFPE_ABORT);
                ...
        /*
         * restore old overflow and invalid handlers
         */
                sigfpe(FPE_FLTOVF_TRAP,   old_handler1);
                sigfpe(FPE_FLTOPERR_TRAP, old_handler2);
        }
```

FILES

/usr/include/floatingpoint.h
/usr/include/signal.h

sigfpe(3) (BSD Compatibility Package) **sigfpe(3)**

SEE ALSO
sigvec(2), floatingpoint(3), ieee_handler(3M), signal(3), abort(3C) in the *Programmer's Reference Manual*

RETURN VALUE
sigfpe returns BADSIG if *code* is not zero or a defined SIGFPE code.

NAME
siginterrupt – allow signals to interrupt system calls

SYNOPSIS
cc [*flag*. . .] *file* . . . -lucb

int siginterrupt(sig, flag)
int sig, flag;

DESCRIPTION
siginterrupt is used to change the system call restart behavior when a system call is interrupted by the specified signal. If the flag is false (0), then system calls will be restarted if they are interrupted by the specified signal and no data has been transferred yet. System call restart is the default behavior when the signal(3) routine is used.

If the flag is true (1), then restarting of system calls is disabled. If a system call is interrupted by the specified signal and no data has been transferred, the system call will return −1 with errno set to EINTR. Interrupted system calls that have started transferring data will return the amount of data actually transferred.

Issuing a siginterrupt call during the execution of a signal handler will cause the new action to take place on the next signal to be caught.

NOTES
This library routine uses an extension of the sigvec(2) system call that is not available in 4.2BSD, hence it should not be used if backward compatibility is needed.

RETURN VALUE
A 0 value indicates that the call succeeded. A −1 value indicates that an invalid signal number has been supplied.

SEE ALSO
sigblock(3), sigpause(3), sigsetmask(3), sigvec(3), signal(3)

signal(2) in the *Programmer's Reference Manual*

signal(3)   (BSD Compatibility Package)   signal(3)

NAME
signal – simplified software signal facilities

SYNOPSIS
cc [flag. . .] file . . . -lucb

#include <signal.h>

void (*signal(sig, func)) ()
void (*func) ();

DESCRIPTION
signal is a simplified interface to the more general sigvec(2) facility. Programs that use signal in preference to sigvec are more likely to be portable to all systems.

A signal is generated by some abnormal event, initiated by a user at a terminal (quit, interrupt, stop), by a program error (bus error, and so on), by request of another program (kill), or when a process is stopped because it wishes to access its control terminal while in the background [see termio(4)]. Signals are optionally generated when a process resumes after being stopped, when the status of child processes changes, or when input is ready at the control terminal. Most signals cause termination of the receiving process if no action is taken; some signals instead cause the process receiving them to be stopped, or are simply discarded if the process has not requested otherwise. Except for the SIGKILL and SIGSTOP signals, the signal call allows signals either to be ignored or to interrupt to a specified location. The following is a list of all signals with names as in the include file <signal.h>:

SIGHUP		hangup
SIGINT		interrupt
SIGQUIT	*	quit
SIGILL	*	illegal instruction
SIGTRAP	*	trace trap
SIGABRT	*	abort (generated by abort(3) routine)
SIGEMT	*	emulator trap
SIGFPE	*	arithmetic exception
SIGKILL		kill (cannot be caught, blocked, or ignored)
SIGBUS	*	bus error
SIGSEGV	*	segmentation violation
SIGSYS	*	bad argument to system call
SIGPIPE		write on a pipe or other socket with no one to read it
SIGALRM		alarm clock
SIGTERM		software termination signal
SIGURG	•	urgent condition present on socket
SIGSTOP	†	stop (cannot be caught, blocked, or ignored)
SIGTSTP	†	stop signal generated from keyboard
SIGCONT	•	continue after stop (cannot be blocked)
SIGCHLD	•	child status has changed
SIGTTIN	†	background read attempted from control terminal
SIGTTOU	†	background write attempted to control terminal
SIGIO	•	I/O is possible on a descriptor [see fcntl(2)]
SIGXCPU	*	cpu time limit exceeded [see getrlimit(2)

signal(3) (BSD Compatibility Package) signal(3)

SIGXFSZ	*	file size limit exceeded [see getrlimit(2)]
SIGVTALRM		virtual time alarm [see getitimer(2)]
SIGPROF		profiling timer alarm [see getitimer(2)]
SIGWINCH	•	window changed [see termio(4)]
SIGUSR1		user-defined signal 1
SIGUSR2		user-defined signal 2

The starred signals in the list above cause a core image if not caught or ignored.

If *func* is SIG_DFL, the default action for signal *sig* is reinstated; this default is termination (with a core image for starred signals) except for signals marked with • or †. Signals marked with • are discarded if the action is SIG_DFL; signals marked with † cause the process to stop. If *func* is SIG_IGN the signal is subsequently ignored and pending instances of the signal are discarded. Otherwise, when the signal occurs further occurrences of the signal are automatically blocked and *func* is called.

A return from the function unblocks the handled signal and continues the process at the point it was interrupted.

If a caught signal occurs during certain system calls, terminating the call prematurely, the call is automatically restarted. In particular this can occur during a read(2) or write(2) on a slow device (such as a terminal; but not a file) and during a wait(2).

The value of signal is the previous (or initial) value of *func* for the particular signal.

After a fork(2) or vfork(2) the child inherits all signals. An execve(2) resets all caught signals to the default action; ignored signals remain ignored.

NOTES

The handler routine can be declared:

```
void handler(sig, code, scp, addr)
int sig, code;
struct sigcontext *scp;
char *addr;
```

Here *sig* is the signal number; *code* is a parameter of certain signals that provides additional detail; *scp* is a pointer to the sigcontext structure (defined in <signal.h>), used to restore the context from before the signal; and *addr* is additional address information. See sigvec(2) for more details.

RETURN VALUE

The previous action is returned on a successful call. Otherwise, −1 is returned and errno is set to indicate the error.

ERRORS

signal will fail and no action will take place if one of the following occur:

EINVAL   *sig* is not a valid signal number, or is SIGKILL or SIGSTOP.

SEE ALSO

setjmp(3), sigblock(3), sigpause(3), sigsetmask(3), sigstack(3), sigvec(3), wait(3)

execve(2), fork(2), getitimer(2), getrlimit(2), kill(2), ptrace(2), read(2), sigaction(2) wait(2), write(2), setjmp(3C), in the *Programmer's Reference Manual*
kill(1), in the *User's Reference Manual*
termio(7) in the *System Administrator's Reference Manual*

NAME
sigpause – automically release blocked signals and wait for interrupt

SYNOPSIS
    cc [flag. . .] file . . . -lucb

    sigpause(sigmask)
    int sigmask;

DESCRIPTION
sigpause assigns *sigmask* to the set of masked signals and then waits for a signal to arrive; on return the set of masked signals is restored. *sigmask* is usually 0 to indicate that no signals are now to be blocked. sigpause always terminates by being interrupted, returning EINTR.

In normal usage, a signal is blocked using sigblock(3), to begin a critical section, variables modified on the occurrence of the signal are examined to determine that there is no work to be done, and the process pauses awaiting work by using sigpause with the mask returned by sigblock.

SEE ALSO
sigblock(3), sigvec(3), signal(3)

signal(2), sigaction(2) in the *Programmer's Reference Manual*

sigsetjmp(3C)

NAME
sigsetjmp, siglongjmp – a non-local goto with signal state

SYNOPSIS
    #include <setjmp.h>

    int sigsetjmp (sigjmp_buf *env*, int *savemask*);

    void siglongjmp (sigjmp_buf *env*, int *val*);

DESCRIPTION
These functions are useful for dealing with errors and interrupts encountered in a low-level subroutine of a program.

sigsetjmp saves the calling process's registers and stack environment [see sigaltstack(2)] in *env* (whose type, sigjmp_buf, is defined in the <setjmp.h> header file) for later use by siglongjmp. If *savemask* is non-zero, the calling process's signal mask [see sigprocmask(2)] and scheduling parameters [see priocntl(2)] are also saved. sigsetjmp returns the value 0.

siglongjmp restores the environment saved by the last call of sigsetjmp with the corresponding *env* argument. After siglongjmp is completed, program execution continues as if the corresponding call of sigsetjmp had just returned the value *val*. siglongjmp cannot cause sigsetjmp to return the value zero. If siglongjmp is invoked with a second argument of zero, sigsetjmp will return 1. At the time of the second return from sigsetjmp, all external and static variables have values as of the time siglongjmp is called. The values of register and automatic variables are undefined. Register or automatic variables whose value must be relied upon must be declared as volatile.

If a signal-catching function interrupts sleep and calls siglongjmp to restore an environment saved prior to the sleep call, the action associated with SIGALRM and time it is scheduled to be generated are unspecified. It is also unspecified whether the SIGALRM signal is blocked, unless the process's signal mask is restored as part of the environment.

The function siglongjmp restores the saved signal mask if and only if the *env* argument was initialized by a call to the sigsetjmp function with a non-zero *savemask* argument.

SEE ALSO
getcontext(2), priocntl(2), sigaction(2), sigaltstack(2), sigprocmask(2), setjmp(3C).

NOTES
If siglongjmp is called even though *env* was never primed by a call to sigsetjmp, or when the last such call was in a function that has since returned, the behavior is undefined.

NAME

sigsetmask − set current signal mask

SYNOPSIS

cc [*flag*...] *file* ... −lucb

#include <signal.h>

sigsetmask(mask);
int mask;

#define sigmask(signum)

DESCRIPTION

sigsetmask sets the current signal mask (those signals that are blocked from delivery). Signals are blocked if the corresponding bit in *mask* is a 1; the macro sigmask is provided to construct the mask for a given *signum*.

The system quietly disallows SIGKILL, SIGSTOP, or SIGCONT from being blocked.

RETURN VALUE

The previous set of masked signals is returned.

SEE ALSO

sigblock(3), sigpause(3), sigvec(3), signal(3)

kill(2), signal(2) in the *Programmer's Reference Manual*

sigsetops(3C)

NAME
sigemptyset, sigfillset, sigaddset, sigdelset, sigismember – manipulate sets of signals

SYNOPSIS
#include <signal.h>

int sigemptyset (sigset_t *set);

int sigfillset (sigset_t *set);

int sigaddset (sigset_t *set, int signo);

int sigdelset (sigset_t *set, int signo);

int sigismember (sigset_t *set, int signo);

DESCRIPTION
These functions manipulate *sigset_t* data types, representing the set of signals supported by the implementation.

sigemptyset initializes the set pointed to by *set* to exclude all signals defined by the system.

sigfillset initializes the set pointed to by *set* to include all signals defined by the system.

sigaddset adds the individual signal specified by the value of *signo* to the set pointed to by *set*.

sigdelset deletes the individual signal specified by the value of *signo* from the set pointed to by *set*.

sigismember checks whether the signal specified by the value of *signo* is a member of the set pointed to by *set*.

Any object of type *sigset_t* must be initialized by applying either sigemptyset or sigfillset before applying any other operation.

sigaddset, sigdelset and sigismember will fail if the following is true:

EINVAL   The value of the *signo* argument is not a valid signal number.

sigfillset will fail if the following is true:

EFAULT   The *set* argument specifies an invalid address.

SEE ALSO
sigaction(2), sigprocmask(2), sigpending(2), sigsuspend(2), signal(5).

DIAGNOSTICS
Upon successful completion, the sigismember function returns a value of one if the specified signal is a member of the specified set, or a value of zero if it is not. Upon successful completion, the other functions return a value of zero. Otherwise a value of -1 is returned and errno is set to indicate the error.

sigstack(3) (BSD Compatibility Package)

NAME
sigstack – set and/or get signal stack context

SYNOPSIS
cc [*flag*...] *file* ... -lucb

#include <signal.h>

int sigstack (ss, oss)
struct sigstack *ss, *oss;

DESCRIPTION
sigstack allows users to define an alternate stack, called the "signal stack," on which signals are to be processed. When a signal's action indicates its handler should execute on the signal stack (specified with a sigvec(2) call), the system checks to see if the process is currently executing on that stack. If the process is not currently executing on the signal stack, the system arranges a switch to the signal stack for the duration of the signal handler's execution.

A signal stack is specified by a sigstack structure, which includes the following members:

```
    char       *ss_sp;         /* signal stack pointer */
    int        ss_onstack;     /* current status */
```

ss_sp is the initial value to be assigned to the stack pointer when the system switches the process to the signal stack. Note that, on machines where the stack grows downwards in memory, this is *not* the address of the beginning of the signal stack area. ss_onstack field is zero or non-zero depending on whether the process is currently executing on the signal stack or not.

If *ss* is not a NULL pointer, sigstack sets the signal stack state to the value in the sigstack structure pointed to by *ss*. Note: if ss_onstack is non-zero, the system will think that the process is executing on the signal stack. If *ss* is a NULL pointer, the signal stack state will be unchanged. If *oss* is not a NULL pointer, the current signal stack state is stored in the sigstack structure pointed to by *oss*.

RETURN VALUE
Upon successful completion, a value of 0 is returned. Otherwise, a value of −1 is returned and errno is set to indicate the error.

ERRORS
sigstack will fail and the signal stack context will remain unchanged if one of the following occurs.

EFAULT   Either *ss* or *oss* points to memory that is not a valid part of the process address space.

SEE ALSO
sigvec(3), signal(3)

sigaltstack(2), in the *Programmer's Reference Manual*

NOTES
Signal stacks are not "grown" automatically, as is done for the normal stack. If the stack overflows unpredictable results may occur.

sigvec(3) (BSD Compatibility Package) sigvec(3)

NAME
sigvec – software signal facilities

SYNOPSIS
cc [*flag*. . .] *file* . . . -lucb

#include <signal.h>

int sigvec(sig, vec, ovec)
int sig;
struct sigvec *vec, *ovec;

DESCRIPTION
The system defines a set of signals that may be delivered to a process. Signal delivery resembles the occurrence of a hardware interrupt: the signal is blocked from further occurrence, the current process context is saved, and a new one is built. A process may specify a *handler* to which a signal is delivered, or specify that a signal is to be *blocked* or *ignored*. A process may also specify that a default action is to be taken by the system when a signal occurs. Normally, signal handlers execute on the current stack of the process. This may be changed, on a per-handler basis, so that signals are taken on a special *signal stack*.

All signals have the same *priority*. Signal routines execute with the signal that caused their invocation to be *blocked*, but other signals may yet occur. A global *signal mask* defines the set of signals currently blocked from delivery to a process. The signal mask for a process is initialized from that of its parent (normally 0). It may be changed with a sigblock(3) or sigsetmask(3) call, or when a signal is delivered to the process.

A process may also specify a set of *flags* for a signal that affect the delivery of that signal.

When a signal condition arises for a process, the signal is added to a set of signals pending for the process. If the signal is not currently *blocked* by the process then it is delivered to the process. When a signal is delivered, the current state of the process is saved, a new signal mask is calculated (as described below), and the signal handler is invoked. The call to the handler is arranged so that if the signal handling routine returns normally the process will resume execution in the context from before the signal's delivery. If the process wishes to resume in a different context, then it must arrange to restore the previous context itself.

When a signal is delivered to a process a new signal mask is installed for the duration of the process' signal handler (or until a sigblock or sigsetmask call is made). This mask is formed by taking the current signal mask, adding the signal to be delivered, and ORing in the signal mask associated with the handler to be invoked.

The action to be taken when the signal is delivered is specified by a sigvec structure, which includes the following members:

```
void    (*sv_handler)();   /* signal handler */
int     sv_mask;           /* signal mask to apply */
int     sv_flags;          /* see signal options */
```

```
#define  SV_ONSTACK      /* take signal on signal stack */
#define  SV_INTERRUPT    /* do not restart system on signal return */
#define  SV_RESETHAND    /* reset handler to SIG_DFL when signal taken */
```

If the SV_ONSTACK bit is set in the flags for that signal, the system will deliver the signal to the process on the signal stack specified with sigstack(2), rather than delivering the signal on the current stack.

If *vec* is not a NULL pointer, sigvec assigns the handler specified by sv_handler, the mask specified by sv_mask, and the flags specified by sv_flags to the specified signal. If *vec* is a NULL pointer, sigvec does not change the handler, mask, or flags for the specified signal.

The mask specified in *vec* is not allowed to block SIGKILL, SIGSTOP, or SIGCONT. The system enforces this restriction silently.

If *ovec* is not a NULL pointer, the handler, mask, and flags in effect for the signal before the call to sigvec are returned to the user. A call to sigvec with *vec* a NULL pointer and *ovec* not a NULL pointer can be used to determine the handling information currently in effect for a signal without changing that information.

The following is a list of all signals with names as in the include file /usr/include/signal.h:

Signal		Description
SIGHUP		hangup
SIGINT		interrupt
SIGQUIT	*	quit
SIGILL	*	illegal instruction
SIGTRAP	*	trace trap
SIGABRT	*	abort (generated by abort(3) routine)
SIGEMT	*	emulator trap
SIGFPE	*	arithmetic exception
SIGKILL		kill (cannot be caught, blocked, or ignored)
SIGBUS	*	bus error
SIGSEGV	*	segmentation violation
SIGSYS	*	bad argument to system call
SIGPIPE		write on a pipe or other socket with no one to read it
SIGALRM		alarm clock
SIGTERM		software termination signal
SIGURG	•	urgent condition present on socket
SIGSTOP	†	stop (cannot be caught, blocked, or ignored)
SIGTSTP	†	stop signal generated from keyboard
SIGCONT	•	continue after stop (cannot be blocked)
SIGCHLD	•	child status has changed
SIGTTIN	†	background read attempted from control terminal
SIGTTOU	†	background write attempted to control terminal
SIGIO	•	I/O is possible on a descriptor [see fcntl(2)]
SIGXCPU		cpu time limit exceeded [see setrlimit(2)]
SIGXFSZ		file size limit exceeded [see setrlimit(2)]
SIGVTALRM		virtual time alarm [see setitimer(2)]
SIGPROF		profiling timer alarm [see setitimer(2)]
SIGWINCH	•	window changed [see termio(4)]

| SIGUSR1 | user-defined signal 1 |
| SIGUSR2 | user-defined signal 2 |

The starred signals in the list above cause a core image if not caught or ignored.

Once a signal handler is installed, it remains installed until another sigvec call is made, or an execve(2) is performed, unless the SV_RESETHAND bit is set in the flags for that signal. In that case, the value of the handler for the caught signal will be set to SIG_DFL before entering the signal-catching function, unless the signal is SIGILL, SIGPWR, or SIGTRAP. Also, if this bit is set, the bit for that signal in the signal mask will not be set; unless the signal mask associated with that signal blocks that signal, further occurrences of that signal will not be blocked. The SV_RESETHAND flag is not available in 4.2BSD, hence it should not be used if backward compatibility is needed.

The default action for a signal may be reinstated by setting the signal's handler to SIG_DFL; this default is termination except for signals marked with • or †. Signals marked with • are discarded if the action is SIG_DFL; signals marked with † cause the process to stop. If the process is terminated, a "core image" will be made in the current working directory of the receiving process if the signal is one for which an asterisk appears in the above list [see core(4)].

If the handler for that signal is SIG_IGN, the signal is subsequently ignored, and pending instances of the signal are discarded.

If a caught signal occurs during certain system calls, the call is normally restarted. The call can be forced to terminate prematurely with an EINTR error return by setting the SV_INTERRUPT bit in the flags for that signal. The SV_INTERRUPT flag is not available in 4.2BSD, hence it should not be used if backward compatibility is needed. The affected system calls are read(2) or write(2) on a slow device (such as a terminal or pipe or other socket, but not a file) and during a wait(2).

After a fork(2) or vfork(2) the child inherits all signals, the signal mask, the signal stack, and the restart/interrupt and reset-signal-handler flags.

The execve(2) call resets all caught signals to default action and resets all signals to be caught on the user stack. Ignored signals remain ignored; the signal mask remains the same; signals that interrupt system calls continue to do so.

The accuracy of *addr* is machine dependent. For example, certain machines may supply an address that is on the same page as the address that caused the fault. If an appropriate *addr* cannot be computed it will be set to SIG_NOADDR.

RETURN VALUE

A 0 value indicates that the call succeeded. A −1 return value indicates that an error occurred and errno is set to indicate the reason.

ERRORS

sigvec will fail and no new signal handler will be installed if one of the following occurs:

| EFAULT | Either *vec* or *ovec* is not a NULL pointer and points to memory that is not a valid part of the process address space. |

EINVAL   *Sig* is not a valid signal number, or, SIGKILL, or SIGSTOP.

SEE ALSO
signal(3), sigpause(3), sigsetmask(3), wait(3)

exec(2), fcntl(2), fork(2), getrlimit(2), getitimer(2), ioctl(2), kill(2), ptrace(2), read(2), sigblock(2), signal(2), sigstack(2), umask(2), wait(2), write(2), setjmp(3) in the *Programmer's Reference Manual*

streamio(7), termio(7) in the *System Administrator's Reference Manual*

NOTES

SIGPOLL is a synonym for SIGIO. A SIGIO will be issued when a file descriptor corresponding to a STREAMS [see intro(2)] file has a "selectable" event pending. Unless that descriptor has been put into asynchronous mode [see fcntl(2)], a process must specifically request that this signal be sent using the I_SETSIG ioctl call [see streamio(4)]. Otherwise, the process will never receive SIGPOLL.

The handler routine can be declared:

```
void handler(sig, code, scp, addr)
int sig, code;
struct sigcontext *scp;
char *addr;
```

Here *sig* is the signal number; *code* is a parameter of certain signals that provides additional detail; *scp* is a pointer to the sigcontext structure (defined in signal.h), used to restore the context from before the signal; and *addr* is additional address information.

The signals SIGKILL, SIGSTOP, and SIGCONT cannot be ignored.

NAME

sinh, sinhf, cosh, coshf, tanh, tanhf, asinh, acosh, atanh − hyperbolic functions

SYNOPSIS

cc [*flag* ...] *file* ... −lm [*library* ...]

#include <math.h>

double sinh (double *x*);

float sinhf (float *x*);

double cosh (double *x*);

float coshf (float *x*);

double tanh (double *x*);

float tanhf (float *x*);

double asinh (double *x*);

double acosh (double *x*);

double atanh (double *x*);

DESCRIPTION

sinh, cosh, and tanh and the single-precision versions sinhf, coshf, and tanhf return, respectively, the hyberbolic sine, cosine, and tangent of their argument.

asinh, acosh, and atanh return, respectively, the inverse hyperbolic sine, cosine, and tangent of their argument.

SEE ALSO

matherr(3M)

DIAGNOSTICS

sinh, sinhf, cosh, and coshf return HUGE (and sinh and sinhf may return −HUGE for negative *x*) when the correct value would overflow and set errno to ERANGE.

acosh returns NaN and sets errno to EDOM when the argument *x* is less than 1. A message indicating DOMAIN error is printed on the standard error output.

atanh returns NaN and sets errno to EDOM if $|x| \geq 1$. If $|x| = 1$, a message indicating SING error is printed on the standard error output; if $|x| > 1$ the message will indicate DOMAIN error.

Except when the −Xc compilation option is used, these error-handling procedures may be changed with the function matherr. When the −Xa or −Xc compilation options are used, HUGE_VAL is returned instead of HUGE and no error messages are printed.

NAME

sleep – suspend execution for interval

SYNOPSIS

#include <unistd.h>

unsigned sleep (unsigned seconds);

DESCRIPTION

The current process is suspended from execution for the number of *seconds* specified by the argument. The actual suspension time may be less than that requested because any caught signal will terminate the sleep following execution of that signal's catching routine. Also, the suspension time may be longer than requested by an arbitrary amount because of the scheduling of other activity in the system. The value returned by sleep will be the "unslept" amount (the requested time minus the time actually slept) in case the caller had an alarm set to go off earlier than the end of the requested sleep time, or premature arousal because of another caught signal.

The routine is implemented by setting an alarm signal and pausing until it (or some other signal) occurs. The previous state of the alarm signal is saved and restored. The calling program may have set up an alarm signal before calling sleep. If the sleep time exceeds the time until such alarm signal, the process sleeps only until the alarm signal would have occurred. The caller's alarm catch routine is executed just before the sleep routine returns. But if the sleep time is less than the time till such alarm, the prior alarm time is reset to go off at the same time it would have without the intervening sleep.

SEE ALSO

alarm(2), pause(2), signal(2), wait(2).

NAME

sleep − suspend execution for interval

SYNOPSIS

cc [*flag*...] *file* ... -lucb

```
sleep(seconds)
unsigned seconds;
```

DESCRIPTION

`sleep` suspends the current process from execution for the number of seconds specified by the argument. The actual suspension time may be up to 1 second less than that requested, because scheduled wakeups occur at fixed 1-second intervals, and may be an arbitrary amount longer because of other activity in the system.

`sleep` is implemented by setting an interval timer and pausing until it expires. The previous state of this timer is saved and restored. If the sleep time exceeds the time to the expiration of the previous value of the timer, the process sleeps only until the timer would have expired, and the signal which occurs with the expiration of the timer is sent one second later.

SEE ALSO

sigpause(3), usleep(3)

getitimer(2) in the *Programmer's Reference Manual*

NAME
socket – create an endpoint for communication

SYNOPSIS
#include <sys/types.h>
#include <sys/socket.h>

int socket(int *domain*, int *type*, int *protocol*);

DESCRIPTION
socket creates an endpoint for communication and returns a descriptor.

The *domain* parameter specifies a communications domain within which communication will take place; this selects the protocol family which should be used. The protocol family generally is the same as the address family for the addresses supplied in later operations on the socket. These families are defined in the include file sys/socket.h. There must be an entry in the netconfig(4) file for at least each protocol family and type required. If *protocol* has been specified, but no exact match for the tuplet family, type, protocol is found, then the first entry containing the specified family and type with zero for protocol will be used. The currently understood formats are:

PF_UNIX   UNIX system internal protocols

PF_INET   ARPA Internet protocols

The socket has the indicated *type*, which specifies the communication semantics. Currently defined types are:

    SOCK_STREAM
    SOCK_DGRAM
    SOCK_RAW
    SOCK_SEQPACKET
    SOCK_RDM

A SOCK_STREAM type provides sequenced, reliable, two-way connection-based byte streams. An out-of-band data transmission mechanism may be supported. A SOCK_DGRAM socket supports datagrams (connectionless, unreliable messages of a fixed (typically small) maximum length). A SOCK_SEQPACKET socket may provide a sequenced, reliable, two-way connection-based data transmission path for datagrams of fixed maximum length; a consumer may be required to read an entire packet with each read system call. This facility is protocol specific, and presently not implemented for any protocol family. SOCK_RAW sockets provide access to internal network interfaces. The types SOCK_RAW, which is available only to the super-user, and SOCK_RDM, for which no implementation currently exists, are not described here.

protocol specifies a particular protocol to be used with the socket. Normally only a single protocol exists to support a particular socket type within a given protocol family. However, multiple protocols may exist, in which case a particular protocol must be specified in this manner. The protocol number to use is particular to the communication domain in which communication is to take place. If a protocol is specified by the caller, then it will be packaged into a socket level option request and sent to the underlying protocol layers.

socket(3N)

Sockets of type SOCK_STREAM are full-duplex byte streams, similar to pipes. A stream socket must be in a *connected* state before any data may be sent or received on it. A connection to another socket is created with a connect call. Once connected, data may be transferred using read and write calls or some variant of the send and recv calls. When a session has been completed, a close may be performed. Out-of-band data may also be transmitted as described on the send(3N) manual page and received as described on the recv(3N) manual page.

The communications protocols used to implement a SOCK_STREAM insure that data is not lost or duplicated. If a piece of data for which the peer protocol has buffer space cannot be successfully transmitted within a reasonable length of time, then the connection is considered broken and calls will indicate an error with −1 returns and with ETIMEDOUT as the specific code in the global variable errno. The protocols optionally keep sockets warm by forcing transmissions roughly every minute in the absence of other activity. An error is then indicated if no response can be elicited on an otherwise idle connection for a extended period (for instance 5 minutes). A SIGPIPE signal is raised if a process sends on a broken stream; this causes naive processes, which do not handle the signal, to exit.

SOCK_SEQPACKET sockets employ the same system calls as SOCK_STREAM sockets. The only difference is that read calls will return only the amount of data requested, and any remaining in the arriving packet will be discarded.

SOCK_DGRAM and SOCK_RAW sockets allow datagrams to be sent to correspondents named in sendto calls. Datagrams are generally received with recvfrom, which returns the next datagram with its return address.

An fcntl call can be used to specify a process group to receive a SIGURG signal when the out-of-band data arrives. It may also enable non-blocking I/O and asynchronous notification of I/O events with SIGIO signals.

The operation of sockets is controlled by socket level *options*. These options are defined in the file sys/socket.h. setsockopt and getsockopt are used to set and get options, respectively.

RETURN VALUE

A −1 is returned if an error occurs. Otherwise the return value is a descriptor referencing the socket.

ERRORS

The socket call fails if:

EPROTONOSUPPORT	The protocol type or the specified protocol is not supported within this domain.
EMFILE	The per-process descriptor table is full.
EACCESS	Permission to create a socket of the specified type and/or protocol is denied.
ENOMEM	Insufficient user memory is available.

socket(3N)

ENOSR   There were insufficient STREAMS resources available to complete the operation.

SEE ALSO

accept(3N), bind(3N), connect(3N), getsockname(3N), getsockopt(3N), listen(3N), recv(3N), send(3N), shutdown(3N), socketpair(3N).

close(2), fcntl(2), ioctl(2), read(2), write(2) in the *Programmer's Reference Manual*.

socketpair(3N)   socketpair(3N)

NAME
    socketpair – create a pair of connected sockets

SYNOPSIS
    #include <sys/types.h>
    #include <sys/socket.h>

    int socketpair(int d, int type, int protocol, int sv[2]);

DESCRIPTION
    The socketpair library call creates an unnamed pair of connected sockets in the specified address family *d*, of the specified *type*, and using the optionally specified *protocol*. The descriptors used in referencing the new sockets are returned in *sv*[0] and *sv*[1]. The two sockets are indistinguishable.

RETURN VALUE
    socketpair returns a −1 on failure, otherwise it returns the number of the second file descriptor it creates.

ERRORS
    The call succeeds unless:

    EMFILE   Too many descriptors are in use by this process.
    EAFNOSUPPORT   The specified address family is not supported on this machine.
    EPROTONOSUPPORT   The specified protocol is not supported on this machine.
    EOPNOSUPPORT   The specified protocol does not support creation of socket pairs.
    ENOMEM   There was insufficient user memory for the operation to complete.
    ENOSR   There were insufficient STREAMS resources for the operation to complete.

SEE ALSO
    pipe(2), read(2), write(2) in the *Programmer's Reference Manual*

NOTES
    This call is currently implemented only for the AF_UNIX address family.

spray(3N)

NAME
spray – scatter data in order to check the network

SYNOPSIS
#include <rpcsvc/spray.h>

DESCRIPTION
The spray protocol sends packets to a given machine to test the speed and reliability of communications with that machine.

The spray protocol is not a C function interface, per se, but can be accessed using the generic remote procedure calling interface clnt_call() [see rpc_clnt_calls(3N)]. The protocol sends a packet to the called host. The host acknowledges receipt of the packet. The protocol counts the number of acknowledgments and can return that count.

The spray protocol currently supports the following procedures, which should be called in the order given:

SPRAYPROC_CLEAR   This procedure clears the counter.

SPRAYPROC_SPRAY   This procedure sends the packet.

SPRAYPROC_GET   This procedure returns the count and the amount of time since the last SPRAYPROC_CLEAR.

The following XDR routines are available in librpcsvc:

xdr_sprayarr
xdr_spraycumul

EXAMPLE
The following code fragment demonstrates how the spray protocol is used:

```
#include <rpc/rpc.h>
#include <rpcsvc/spray.h>

    . . .
        spraycumul spray_result;
        sprayarr   spray_data;
        char       buf[100];       /* arbitrary data */
        int        loop = 1000;
        CLIENT     *clnt;
        struct timeval timeout0 = {0, 0};
        struct timeval timeout25 = {25, 0};

        spray_data.sprayarr_len = (u_int)100;
        spray_data.sprayarr_val = buf;

        clnt = clnt_create("somehost", SPRAYPROG, SPRAYVERS, "netpath");
        if (clnt == (CLIENT *)NULL) {
            /* handle this error */
        }
        if (clnt_call(clnt, SPRAYPROC_CLEAR,
            xdr_void, NULL, xdr_void, NULL, timeout25)) {
                /* handle this error */
```

spray(3N)

```
    }
    while (loop-- > 0) {
        if (clnt_call(clnt, SPRAYPROC_SPRAY,
            xdr_sprayarr, &spray_data, xdr_void, NULL, timeout0)) {
                /* handle this error */
        }
    }
    if (clnt_call(clnt, SPRAYPROC_GET,
        xdr_void, NULL, xdr_spraycumul, &spray_result, timeout25)) {
            /* handle this error */
    }
    printf("Acknowledged %ld of 1000 packets in %d secs %d usecs\n",
        spray_result.counter,
        spray_result.clock.sec,
        spray_result.clock.usec);
```

SEE ALSO

rpc_clnt_calls(3N), spray(1M), sprayd(1M)

NAME
sputl, sgetl – access long integer data in a machine-independent fashion

SYNOPSIS
cc [*flag* ...] *file* ... −lld [*library* ...]

```
#include <ldfcn.h>

void sputl (long value, char *buffer);

long sgetl (const char *buffer);
```

DESCRIPTION
sputl takes the four bytes of the long integer *value* and places them in memory starting at the address pointed to by *buffer*. The ordering of the bytes is the same across all machines.

sgetl retrieves the four bytes in memory starting at the address pointed to by *buffer* and returns the long integer value in the byte ordering of the host machine.

The combination of sputl and sgetl provides a machine-independent way of storing long numeric data in a file in binary form without conversion to characters.

NAME

ssignal, gsignal – software signals

SYNOPSIS

#include <signal.h>

int (*ssignal (int *sig*, int (**action*) (int))) (int);

int gsignal (int *sig*);

DESCRIPTION

ssignal and gsignal implement a software facility similar to signal(2). This facility is made available to users for their own purposes.

Software signals made available to users are associated with integers in the inclusive range 1 through 17. A call to ssignal associates a procedure, *action*, with the software signal *sig*; the software signal, *sig*, is raised by a call to gsignal. Raising a software signal causes the action established for that signal to be *taken*.

The first argument to ssignal is a number identifying the type of signal for which an action is to be established. The second argument defines the action; it is either the name of a (user-defined) *action function* or one of the manifest constants SIG_DFL (default) or SIG_IGN (ignore). ssignal returns the action previously established for that signal type; if no action has been established or the signal number is illegal, ssignal returns SIG_DFL.

gsignal raises the signal identified by its argument, *sig*:

If an action function has been established for *sig*, then that action is reset to SIG_DFL and the action function is entered with argument *sig*. gsignal returns the value returned to it by the action function.

If the action for *sig* is SIG_IGN, gsignal returns the value 1 and takes no other action.

If the action for *sig* is SIG_DFL, gsignal returns the value 0 and takes no other action.

If *sig* has an illegal value or no action was ever specified for *sig*, gsignal returns the value 0 and takes no other action.

SEE ALSO

signal(2), sigset(2), raise(3C).

stdio(3S)

NAME
stdio – standard buffered input/output package

SYNOPSIS
#include <stdio.h>

FILE *stdin, *stdout, *stderr;

DESCRIPTION
The functions described in the entries of sub-class 3S of this manual constitute an efficient, user-level I/O buffering scheme. The in-line macros getc and putc handle characters quickly. The macros getchar and putchar, and the higher-level routines fgetc, fgets, fprintf, fputc, fputs, fread, fscanf, fwrite, gets, getw, printf, puts, putw, and scanf all use or act as if they use getc and putc; they can be freely intermixed.

A file with associated buffering is called a *stream* [see intro(3)] and is declared to be a pointer to a defined type FILE. fopen creates certain descriptive data for a stream and returns a pointer to designate the stream in all further transactions. Normally, there are three open streams with constant pointers declared in the <stdio.h> header file and associated with the standard open files:

    stdin   standard input file
    stdout   standard output file
    stderr   standard error file

The following symbolic values in <unistd.h> define the file descriptors that will be associated with the C-language *stdin*, *stdout* and *stderr* when the application is started:

    STDIN_FILENO   Standard input value, stdin. It has the value of 0.
    STDOUT_FILENO   Standard output value, stdout. It has the value of 1.
    STDERR_FILENO   Standard error value, stderr. It has the value of 2.

A constant null designates a null pointer.

An integer-constant EOF (−1) is returned upon end-of-file or error by most integer functions that deal with streams (see the individual descriptions for details).

An integer constant BUFSIZ specifies the size of the buffers used by the particular implementation.

An integer constant FILENAME_MAX specifies the size needed for an array of char large enough to hold the longest file name string that the implementation guarantees can be opened.

An integer constant FOPEN_MAX specifies the minimum number of files that the implementation guarantees can be open simultaneously. Note that no more than 255 files may be opened via fopen, and only file descriptors 0 through 255 are valid.

Any program that uses this package must include the header file of pertinent macro definitions, as follows:

    #include <stdio.h>

The functions and constants mentioned in the entries of sub-class 3S of this manual are declared in that header file and need no further declaration. The constants and the following "functions" are implemented as macros (redeclaration of these names is perilous): `getc`, `getchar`, `putc`, `putchar`, `ferror`, `feof`, `clearerr`, and `fileno`. There are also function versions of `getc`, `getchar`, `putc`, `putchar`, `ferror`, `feof`, `clearerr`, and `fileno`.

Output streams, with the exception of the standard error stream `stderr`, are by default buffered if the output refers to a file and line-buffered if the output refers to a terminal. The standard error output stream `stderr` is by default unbuffered, but use of `freopen` [see fopen(3S)] will cause it to become buffered or line-buffered. When an output stream is unbuffered, information is queued for writing on the destination file or terminal as soon as written; when it is buffered, many characters are saved up and written as a block. When it is line-buffered, each line of output is queued for writing on the destination terminal as soon as the line is completed (that is, as soon as a new-line character is written or terminal input is requested). `setbuf` or `setvbuf` [both described in setbuf(3S)] may be used to change the stream's buffering strategy.

SEE ALSO

open(2), close(2), lseek(2), pipe(2), read(2), write(2), ctermid(3S), cuserid(3S), fclose(3S), ferror(3S), fopen(3S), fread(3S), fseek(3S), getc(3S), gets(3S), popen(3S), printf(3S), putc(3S), puts(3S), scanf(3S), setbuf(3S), system(3S), tmpfile(3S), tmpnam(3S), ungetc(3S)

DIAGNOSTICS

Invalid *stream* pointers usually cause grave disorder, possibly including program termination. Individual function descriptions describe the possible error conditions.

NAME
stdipc: ftok − standard interprocess communication package

SYNOPSIS
```
#include <sys/types.h>
#include <sys/ipc.h>

key_t ftok(const char *path, int id);
```

DESCRIPTION
All interprocess communication facilities require the user to supply a key to be used by the msgget(2), semget(2), and shmget(2) system calls to obtain interprocess communication identifiers. One suggested method for forming a key is to use the ftok subroutine described below. Another way to compose keys is to include the project ID in the most significant byte and to use the remaining portion as a sequence number. There are many other ways to form keys, but it is necessary for each system to define standards for forming them. If some standard is not adhered to, it will be possible for unrelated processes to unintentionally interfere with each other's operation. It is still possible to interface intentionally. Therefore, it is strongly suggested that the most significant byte of a key in some sense refer to a project so that keys do not conflict across a given system.

ftok returns a key based on *path* and *id* that is usable in subsequent msgget, semget, and shmget system calls. *path* must be the path name of an existing file that is accessible to the process. *id* is a character that uniquely identifies a project. Note that ftok will return the same key for linked files when called with the same *id* and that it will return different keys when called with the same file name but different *ids*.

SEE ALSO
intro(2), msgget(2), semget(2), shmget(2).

DIAGNOSTICS
ftok returns (key_t) −1 if *path* does not exist or if it is not accessible to the process.

NOTES
If the file whose *path* is passed to ftok is removed when keys still refer to the file, future calls to ftok with the same *path* and *id* will return an error. If the same file is recreated, then ftok is likely to return a different key than it did the original time it was called.

str(3G)

NAME
str: strfind, strrspn, strtrns – string manipulations

SYNOPSIS
cc [*flag* ...] *file* ... −lgen [*library* ...]

#include <libgen.h>

int strfind (const char *as1*, const char *as2*);

char *strrspn (const char *string*, const char *tc*);

char * strtrns (const char *str*, const char *old*, const char *new*, char *result*);

DESCRIPTION
strfind returns the offset of the second string, *as2*, if it is a substring of string *as1*.

strrspn returns a pointer to the first character in the string to be trimmed (all characters from the first character to the end of *string* are in *tc*).

strtrns transforms *str* and copies it into *result*. Any character that appears in *old* is replaced with the character in the same position in *new*. The *new* result is returned.

EXAMPLES
```
/* find pointer to substring "hello" in as1 */
i = strfind(as1, "hello");

/* trim junk from end of string */
s2 = strrspn(s1, "*?#$%");
*s2 = '\0';

/* transform lower case to upper case */
a1[] = "abcdefghijklmnopqrstuvwxyz";
a2[] = "ABCDEFGHIJKLMNOPQRSTUVWXYZ";
s2 = strtrns(s1, a1, a2, s2);
```

SEE ALSO
string(3C).

DIAGNOSTICS
If the second string is not a substring of the first string strfind returns −1.

strccpy(3G)

NAME
strccpy: streadd, strcadd, strecpy – copy strings, compressing or expanding escape codes

SYNOPSIS
cc [*flag* ...] *file* ... -lgen [*library* ...]

#include <libgen.h>

char *strccpy (char *output*, const char *input*);

char *strcadd (char *output*, const char *input*);

char *strecpy (char *output*, const char *input*, const char *exceptions*);

char *streadd (char *output*, const char *input*, const char *exceptions*);

DESCRIPTION
strccpy copies the *input* string, up to a null byte, to the *output* string, compressing the C-language escape sequences (for example, \n, \001) to the equivalent character. A null byte is appended to the output. The *output* argument must point to a space big enough to accommodate the result. If it is as big as the space pointed to by *input* it is guaranteed to be big enough. strccpy returns the *output* argument.

strcadd is identical to strccpy, except that it returns the pointer to the null byte that terminates the output.

strecpy copies the *input* string, up to a null byte, to the *output* string, expanding non-graphic characters to their equivalent C-language escape sequences (for example, \n, \001). The *output* argument must point to a space big enough to accommodate the result; four times the space pointed to by *input* is guaranteed to be big enough (each character could become \ and 3 digits). Characters in the *exceptions* string are not expanded. The *exceptions* argument may be zero, meaning all non-graphic characters are expanded. strecpy returns the *output* argument.

streadd is identical to strecpy, except that it returns the pointer to the null byte that terminates the output.

EXAMPLES
```
/* expand all but newline and tab */
strecpy( output, input, "\n\t" );

/* concatenate and compress several strings */
cp = strcadd( output, input1 );
cp = strcadd( cp, input2 );
cp = strcadd( cp, input3 );
```

SEE ALSO
string(3C), str(3G).

strcoll (3C) (C Programming Language Utilities) **strcoll (3C)**

NAME
strcoll – string collation

SYNOPSIS
    #include <string.h>

    int strcoll (const char *s1, const char *s2);

DESCRIPTION
strcoll returns an integer greater than, equal to, or less than zero in direct correlation to whether string *s1* is greater than, equal to, or less than the string *s2*. The comparison is based on strings interpreted as appropriate to the program's locale for category LC_COLLATE [see setlocale(3C)].

Both strcoll and strxfrm provide for locale-specific string sorting. strcoll is intended for applications in which the number of comparisons per string is small. When strings are to be compared a number of times, strxfrm is a more appropriate utility because the transformation process occurs only once.

FILES
/usr/lib/locale/*locale*/LC_COLLATE   LC_COLLATE database for *locale*.

SEE ALSO
setlocale(3C), string(3C), strxfrm(3C), environ(5).
colltbl(1M) in the *System Administrator's Reference Manual*.

NAME

strerror – get error message string

SYNOPSIS

#include <string.h>

char *strerror (int *errnum*);

DESCRIPTION

strerror maps the error number in *errnum* to an error message string, and returns a pointer to that string. strerror uses the same set of error messages as perror. The returned string should not be overwritten.

SEE ALSO

perror(3C).

strftime (3C)   (C Programming Language Utilities)   strftime (3C)

NAME
strftime, cftime, ascftime - convert date and time to string

SYNOPSIS
#include <time.h>

size_t *strftime (char *s, size_t maxsize, const char *format, const struct tm *timeptr);

int cftime (char *s, char *format, const time_t *clock);

int ascftime (char *s, const char *format, const struct tm *timeptr);

DESCRIPTION
strftime, ascftime, and cftime place characters into the array pointed to by s as controlled by the string pointed to by *format*. The *format* string consists of zero or more directives and ordinary characters. All ordinary characters (including the terminating null character) are copied unchanged into the array. For strftime, no more than *maxsize* characters are placed into the array.

If *format* is (char *)0, then the locale's default format is used. For strftime the default format is the same as "%c", for cftime and ascftime the default format is the same as "%C". cftime and ascftime first try to use the value of the environment variable CFTIME, and if that is undefined or empty, the default format is used.

Each directive is replaced by appropriate characters as described in the following list. The appropriate characters are determined by the LC_TIME category of the program's locale and by the values contained in the structure pointed to by *timeptr* for strftime and ascftime, and by the time represented by *clock* for cftime.

%%	same as %
%a	locale's abbreviated weekday name
%A	locale's full weekday name
%b	locale's abbreviated month name
%B	locale's full month name
%c	locale's appropriate date and time representation
%C	locale's date and time representation as produced by date(1)
%d	day of month (01 - 31)
%D	date as %m/%d/%y
%e	day of month (1-31; single digits are preceded by a blank)
%h	locale's abbreviated month name.
%H	hour (00 - 23)
%I	hour (01 - 12)
%j	day number of year (001 - 366)
%m	month number (01 - 12)
%M	minute (00 - 59)
%n	same as \n
%p	locale's equivalent of either AM or PM

%r	time as %I:%M:%S [AM|PM]
%R	time as %H:%M
%S	seconds (00 - 61), allows for leap seconds
%t	insert a tab
%T	time as %H:%M:%S
%U	week number of year (00 - 53), Sunday is the first day of week 1
%w	weekday number (0 - 6), Sunday = 0
%W	week number of year (00 - 53), Monday is the first day of week 1
%x	locale's appropriate date representation
%X	locale's appropriate time representation
%y	year within century (00 - 99)
%Y	year as ccyy (for example, 1986)
%Z	time zone name or no characters if no time zone exists

The difference between %U and %W lies in which day is counted as the first of the week. Week number 01 is the first week in January starting with a Sunday for %U or a Monday for %W. Week number 00 contains those days before the first Sunday or Monday in January for %U and %W, respectively.

If the total number of resulting characters including the terminating null character is not more than *maxsize*, strftime, cftime and ascftime return the number of characters placed into the array pointed to by *s* not including the terminating null character. Otherwise, zero is returned and the contents of the array are indeterminate. cftime and ascftime return the number of characters placed into the array pointed to by *s* not including the terminating null character.

Selecting the Output's Language
By default, the output of strftime, cftime, and ascftime appear in US English. The user can request that the output of strftime, cftime or ascftime be in a specific language by setting the *locale* for *category* LC_TIME in setlocale.

Timezone
The timezone is taken from the environment variable TZ [see ctime(3C) for a description of TZ].

EXAMPLES
The example illustrates the use of strftime. It shows what the string in str would look like if the structure pointed to by *tmptr* contains the values corresponding to Thursday, August 28, 1986 at 12:44:36 in New Jersey.

    strftime (str, strsize, "%A %b %d %j", tmptr)

This results in str containing "Thursday Aug 28 240".

FILES
/usr/lib/locale/*locale*/LC_TIME – file containing locale specific date and time information

SEE ALSO
ctime(3C), getenv(3C), setlocale(3C), strftime(4), timezone(4), environ(5).

NOTE
cftime and ascftime are obsolete. strftime should be used instead.

string (3C)

NAME
string: strcat, strdup, strncat, strcmp, strncmp, strcpy, strncpy, strlen, strchr, strrchr, strpbrk, strspn, strcspn, strtok, strstr – string operations

SYNOPSIS
#include <string.h>

char *strcat (char *s1, const char *s2);

char *strdup (const char *s1);

char *strncat (char *s1, const char *s2, size_t n);

int strcmp (const char *s1, const char *s2);

int strncmp (const char *s1, const char *s2, size_t n);

char *strcpy (char *s1, const char *s2);

char *strncpy (char *s1, const char *s2, size_t n);

size_t strlen (const char *s);

char *strchr (const char *s, int c);

char *strrchr (const char *s, int c);

char *strpbrk (const char *s1, const char *s2);

size_t strspn (const char *s1, const char *s2);

size_t strcspn (const char *s1, const char *s2);

char *strtok (char *s1, const char *s2);

char *strstr (const char *s1, const char *s2);

DESCRIPTION
The arguments *s*, *s1*, and *s2* point to strings (arrays of characters terminated by a null character). The functions strcat, strncat, strcpy, strncpy, and strtok. all alter *s1*. These functions do not check for overflow of the array pointed to by *s1*.

strcat appends a copy of string *s2*, including the terminating null character, to the end of string *s1*. strncat appends at most *n* characters. Each returns a pointer to the null-terminated result. The initial character of *s2* overrides the null character at the end of *s1*.

strcmp compares its arguments and returns an integer less than, equal to, or greater than 0, based upon whether *s1* is lexicographically less than, equal to, or greater than *s2*. strncmp makes the same comparison but looks at at most *n* characters. Characters following a null character are not compared.

strcpy copies string *s2* to *s1* including the terminating null character, stopping after the null character has been copied. strncpy copies exactly *n* characters, truncating *s2* or adding null characters to *s1* if necessary. The result will not be null-terminated if the length of *s2* is *n* or more. Each function returns *s1*.

`strdup` returns a pointer to a new string which is a duplicate of the string pointed to by *s1*. The space for the new string is obtained using malloc(3C). If the new string can not be created, a NULL pointer is returned.

`strlen` returns the number of characters in *s*, not including the terminating null character.

`strchr` (or `strrchr`) returns a pointer to the first (last) occurrence of *c* (converted to a char) in string *s*, or a NULL pointer if *c* does not occur in the string. The null character terminating a string is considered to be part of the string.

`strpbrk` returns a pointer to the first occurrence in string *s1* of any character from string *s2*, or a NULL pointer if no character from *s2* exists in *s1*.

`strspn` (or `strcspn`) returns the length of the initial segment of string *s1* which consists entirely of characters from (not from) string *s2*.

`strtok` considers the string *s1* to consist of a sequence of zero or more text tokens separated by spans of one or more characters from the separator string *s2*. The first call (with pointer *s1* specified) returns a pointer to the first character of the first token, and will have written a null character into *s1* immediately following the returned token. The function keeps track of its position in the string between separate calls, so that subsequent calls (which must be made with the first argument a NULL pointer) will work through the string *s1* immediately following that token. In this way subsequent calls will work through the string *s1* until no tokens remain. The separator string *s2* may be different from call to call. When no token remains in *s1*, a NULL pointer is returned.

`strstr` locates the first occurrence in string *s1* of the sequence of characters (excluding the terminating null character) in string *s2*. `strstr` returns a pointer to the located string, or a null pointer if the string is not found. If *s2* points to a string with zero length (that is, the string ""), the function returns *s1*.

SEE ALSO
malloc(3C), setlocale(3C), strxfrm(3C).

NOTES
All of these functions assume the default locale "C." For some locales, `strxfrm` should be applied to the strings before they are passed to the functions.

string(3)   (BSD Compatibility Package)   string(3)

NAME
string: strcasecmp, strncasecmp – string operations

SYNOPSIS
cc [*flag*...] *file* ... -lucb

int strcasecmp(s1, s2)
char *s1, *s2;

int strncasecmp(s1, s2, n)
char *s1, *s2;
int n;

DESCRIPTION
The strcasecmp and strncasecmp routines compare the strings and ignore differences in case. These routines assume the ASCII character set when equating lower and upper case characters.

These functions operate on null-terminated strings. They do not check for overflow of any receiving string.

SEE ALSO
bstring(3)

malloc(3C), string(3C) in the *Programmer's Reference Manual*

NOTES
strcasecmp and strncasecmp use native character comparison as above and assume the ASCII character set.

strtod (3C)   (C Programming Language Utilities)   strtod (3C)

NAME
strtod, strtold, atof – convert string to double-precision number

SYNOPSIS
    #include <stdlib.h>

    double strtod (const char *nptr, char **endptr);

    long double strtold (const char *nptr, char **endptr);

    double atof (const char *nptr);

DESCRIPTION
strtod returns as a double-precision floating-point number the value represented by the character string pointed to by *nptr*. The string is scanned up to the first unrecognized character.

strtod recognizes an optional string of "white-space" characters [as defined by isspace in ctype(3C)], then an optional sign, then a string of digits optionally containing a decimal-point character [as specified by the current locale; see setlocale(3C)], then an optional exponent part including an e or E followed by an optional sign, followed by an integer.

If the value of *endptr* is not (char **)NULL, a pointer to the character terminating the scan is returned in the location pointed to by *endptr*. If no number can be formed, *endptr* is set to *nptr*, and zero is returned.

strtold is equivalent to strtod except it returns a long double-precision floating-point number.

atof(nptr) is equivalent to:
    strtod(nptr, (char **)NULL).

SEE ALSO
ctype(3C), strtol(3C), scanf(3S).

DIAGNOSTICS
If the correct value would cause overflow, ±HUGE is returned (according to the sign of the value), and errno is set to ERANGE.

If the correct value would cause underflow, zero is returned and errno is set to ERANGE.

When the –Xc or –Xa compilation options are used, ±HUGE_VAL is returned instead of ±HUGE.

strtol(3C) (C Programming Language Utilities) strtol(3C)

NAME
strtol, strtoul, atol, atoi – convert string to integer

SYNOPSIS
#include <stdlib.h>

long strtol (const char *str, char **ptr, int base);

unsigned long strtoul (const char *str, char **ptr, int base);

long atol (const char *str);

int atoi (const char *str);

DESCRIPTION
strtol returns as a long integer the value represented by the character string pointed to by str. The string is scanned up to the first character inconsistent with the base. Leading "white-space" characters [as defined by isspace in ctype(3C)] are ignored.

If the value of *ptr* is not (char **)NULL, a pointer to the character terminating the scan is returned in the location pointed to by *ptr*. If no integer can be formed, that location is set to str, and zero is returned.

If *base* is positive (and not greater than 36), it is used as the base for conversion. After an optional leading sign, leading zeros are ignored, and "0x" or "0X" is ignored if *base* is 16.

If *base* is zero, the string itself determines the base as follows: After an optional leading sign a leading zero indicates octal conversion, and a leading "0x" or "0X" hexadecimal conversion. Otherwise, decimal conversion is used.

Truncation from long to int can, of course, take place upon assignment or by an explicit cast.

If the value represented by str would cause overflow, LONG_MAX or LONG_MIN is returned (according to the sign of the value), and errno is set to the value, ERANGE.

strtoul is similar to *strtol* except that *strtoul* returns as an unsigned long integer the value represented by *str*. If the value represented by *str* would cause overflow, ULONG_MAX is returned, and errno is set to the value, ERANGE.

Except for behavior on error, atol(str) is equivalent to: strtol(str, (char **)NULL, 10).

Except for behavior on error, atoi(str) is equivalent to: (int) strtol(str, (char **)NULL, 10).

DIAGNOSTICS
If strtol is given a *base* greater than 36, it returns 0 and sets errno to EINVAL.

SEE ALSO
ctype(3C), scanf(3S), strtod(3C).

NOTES
strtol no longer accepts values greater than LONG_MAX as valid input. Use strtoul instead.

NAME

strxfrm – string transformation

SYNOPSIS

```
#include <string.h>

size_t strxfrm (char *s1, const char *s2, size_t n);
```

DESCRIPTION

strxfrm transforms the string *s2* and places the resulting string into the array *s1*. The transformation is such that if strcmp is applied to two transformed strings, it returns a value greater than, equal to, or less than zero, corresponding to the result of the strcoll function applied to the same two original strings. The transformation is based on the program's locale for category LC_COLLATE [see setlocale(3C)].

No more than *n* characters will be placed into the resulting array pointed to by *s1*, including the terminating null character. If *n* is 0, then *s1* is permitted to be a null pointer. If copying takes place between objects that overlap, the behavior is undefined.

strxfrm returns the length of the transformed string (not including the terminating null character). If the value returned is *n* or more, the contents of the array *s1* are indeterminate.

EXAMPLE

The value of the following expression is the size of the array needed to hold the transformation of the string pointed to by *s*.

```
1 + strxfrm(NULL, s, 0);
```

FILES

/usr/lib/locale/*locale*/LC_COLLATE   LC_COLLATE database for *locale*.

SEE ALSO

colltbl(1M) in the *System Administrator's Reference Manual*.
setlocale(3C), strcoll(3C), string(3C), environ(5).

DIAGNOSTICS

On failure, strxfrm returns (size_t) −1.

swab(3C) (C Development Set) swab(3C)

NAME
    swab – swap bytes

SYNOPSIS
    #include <stdlib.h>

    void swab (const char *from, char *to, int nbytes);

DESCRIPTION
    swab copies *nbytes* bytes pointed to by *from* to the array pointed to by *to*, exchanging adjacent even and odd bytes. *nbytes* should be even and non-negative. If *nbytes* is odd and positive, swab uses *nbytes*–1 instead. If *nbytes* is negative, swab does nothing.

NAME

syscall – indirect system call

SYNOPSIS

cc [*flag*...] *file* ... -lucb

#include <sys/syscall.h>

int syscall(number, arg, ...)

DESCRIPTION

syscall performs the system call whose assembly language interface has the specified *number*, and arguments *arg* .... Symbolic constants for system calls can be found in the header file /usr/include/sys/syscall.h.

RETURN VALUE

When the C-bit is set, syscall returns −1 and sets the external variable errno (see intro(2)).

SEE ALSO

intro(2), pipe(2) in the *Programmer's Reference Manual*

sysconf(3C)   (C Programming Language Utilities)   sysconf(3C)

NAME
sysconf – retrieves configurable system variables

SYNOPSIS
```
#include <unistd.h>

long sysconf(int name);
```

DESCRIPTION
The `sysconf` function provides a method for the application to determine the current value of a configurable system limit or option (variable).

The *name* argument represents the system variable to be queried. The following table lists the minimal set of system variables from <limits.h> and <unistd.h> that can be returned by `sysconf`, and the symbolic constants, defined in <unistd.h> that are the corresponding values used for *name*.

NAME	RETURN VALUE
_SC_ARG_MAX	ARG_MAX
_SC_CHILD_MAX	CHILD_MAX
_SC_CLK_TCK	CLK_TCK
_SC_NGROUPS_MAX	NGROUPS_MAX
_SC_OPEN_MAX	OPEN_MAX
_SC_PASS_MAX	PASS_MAX
_SC_PAGESIZE	PAGESIZE
_SC_JOB_CONTROL	_POSIX_JOB_CONTROL
_SC_SAVED_IDS	_POSIX_SAVED_IDS
_SC_VERSION	_POSIX_VERSION
_SC_XOPEN_VERSION	_XOPEN_VERSION
_SC_LOGNAME_MAX	LOGNAME_MAX

The value of CLK_TCK may be variable and it should not be assumed that CLK_TCK is a compile-time constant. The value of CLK_TCK is the same as the value of sysconf(_SC_CLK_TCK).

SEE ALSO
fpathconf(2).

DIAGNOSTICS
If *name* is an invalid value, `sysconf` will return −1 and set `errno` to indicate the error. If `sysconf` fails due to a value of *name* that is not defined on the system, the function will return a value of −1 without changing the value of `errno`.

NOTES
A call to `setrlimit` may cause the value of OPEN_MAX to change.

NAME

sysconf – retrieves configurable system variables

SYNOPSIS

```
#include <unistd.h>

long sysconf(int name);
```

DESCRIPTION

Multiprocessing supports the following new name values:

_SC_NPROC_CONF	Number of currently configured processors.
_SC_NPROC_ONLN	Number of processors currently online.

The sysconf function provides a method for the application to determine the current value of a configurable system limit or option (variable).

The name argument represents the system variable to be queried. The following table lists the minimal set of system variables from <limits.h> and <unistd.h> that can be returned by sysconf, and the symbolic constants, defined in <unistd.h> that are the corresponding values used for *name*.

NAME	RETURN VALUE
_SC_ARG_MAX	ARG_MAX
_SC_CHILD_MAX	CHILD_MAX
_SC_CLK_TCK	CLK_TCK
_SC_NGROUPS_MAX	NGROUPS_MAX
_SC_OPEN_MAX	OPEN_MAX
_SC_PASS_MAX	PASS_MAX
_SC_PAGESIZE	PAGESIZE
_SC_JOB_CONTROL	_POSIX_JOB_CONTROL
_SC_SAVED_IDS	_POSIX_SAVED_IDS
_SC_VERSION	_POSIX_VERSION
_SC_XOPEN_VERSION	_XOPEN_VERSION
_SC_LOGNAME_MAX	LOGNAME_MAX
_SC_NPROC_CONF	# configured processors
_SC_NPROC_ONLN	# processors online

The value of CLK_TCK may be variable and it should not be assumed that CLK_TCK is a compile-time constant. The value of CLK_TCK is the same as the value of sysconf(_SC_CLK_TCK).

SEE ALSO

fpathconf(2).

DIAGNOSTICS

sysconf returns the appropriate value on success, or a negative value on failure.

Failure may result from:

EINVAL	The name argument is invalid.

sysconf(3C) (Multiprocessing) sysconf(3C)

If *name* is an invalid value, sysconf will return −1 and set errno to indicate the error. If sysconf fails due to a value of *name* that is not defined on the system, the function will return a value of −1 without changing the value of errno.

NOTES

A call to setrlimit may cause the value of OPEN_MAX to change.

syslog(3) (BSD Compatibility Package)

NAME
syslog, openlog, closelog, setlogmask – control system log

SYNOPSIS
cc [*flag*. . .] *file* . . . -lucb

#include <syslog.h>

openlog(ident, logopt, facility)
char *ident;

syslog(priority, message, parameters ...)
char *message;

closelog()

setlogmask(maskpri)

DESCRIPTION
syslog passes *message* to syslogd(1M), which logs it in an appropriate system log, writes it to the system console, forwards it to a list of users, or forwards it to the syslogd on another host over the network. The message is tagged with a priority of *priority*. The message looks like a printf(3S) string except that %m is replaced by the current error message (collected from errno). A trailing NEWLINE is added if needed.

Priorities are encoded as a *facility* and a *level*. The facility describes the part of the system generating the message. The level is selected from an ordered list:

LOG_EMERG	A panic condition. This is normally broadcast to all users.
LOG_ALERT	A condition that should be corrected immediately, such as a corrupted system database.
LOG_CRIT	Critical conditions, such as hard device errors.
LOG_ERR	Errors.
LOG_WARNING	Warning messages.
LOG_NOTICE	Conditions that are not error conditions, but that may require special handling.
LOG_INFO	Informational messages.
LOG_DEBUG	Messages that contain information normally of use only when debugging a program.

If special processing is needed, openlog can be called to initialize the log file. The parameter *ident* is a string that is prepended to every message. *logopt* is a bit field indicating logging options. Current values for *logopt* are:

LOG_PID	Log the process ID with each message. This is useful for identifying specific daemon processes (for daemons that fork).
LOG_CONS	Write messages to the system console if they cannot be sent to syslogd. This option is safe to use in daemon processes that have no controlling terminal, since syslog forks before opening the console.

LOG_NDELAY		Open the connection to `syslogd` immediately. Normally the open is delayed until the first message is logged. This is useful for programs that need to manage the order in which file descriptors are allocated.
LOG_NOWAIT		Do not wait for child processes that have been forked to log messages onto the console. This option should be used by processes that enable notification of child termination using SIGCHLD, since `syslog` may otherwise block waiting for a child whose exit status has already been collected.

The *facility* parameter encodes a default facility to be assigned to all messages that do not have an explicit facility already encoded:

LOG_KERN	Messages generated by the kernel. These cannot be generated by any user processes.
LOG_USER	Messages generated by random user processes. This is the default facility identifier if none is specified.
LOG_MAIL	The mail system.
LOG_DAEMON	System daemons, such as `ftpd`(1M), `routed`(1M), etc.
LOG_AUTH	The authorization system: `login`(1), `su`(1), `getty`(1M), etc.
LOG_LPR	The line printer spooling system: `lpr`(1), `lpc`(1M), etc.
LOG_NEWS	Reserved for the USENET network news system.
LOG_UUCP	Reserved for the UUCP system; it does not currently use `syslog`.
LOG_CRON	The cron/at facility; `crontab`(1), `at`(1), `cron`(1M), etc.
LOG_LOCAL0-7	Reserved for local use.

`closelog` can be used to close the log file.

`setlogmask` sets the log priority mask to *maskpri* and returns the previous mask. Calls to `syslog` with a priority not set in *maskpri* are rejected. The mask for an individual priority *pri* is calculated by the macro LOG_MASK (*pri*) ; the mask for all priorities up to and including *toppri* is given by the macro LOG_UPTO (*toppri*). The default allows all priorities to be logged.

EXAMPLE

This call logs a message at priority LOG_ALERT:

    syslog(LOG_ALERT, "who: internal error 23");

The FTP daemon, ftpd, would make this call to openlog to indicate that all messages it logs should have an identifying string of ftpd, should be treated by syslogd as other messages from system daemons are, and should include the process ID of the process logging the message:

```
openlog("ftpd", LOG_PID, LOG_DAEMON);
```

Then it would make the following call to setlogmask to indicate that messages at priorities from LOG_EMERG through LOG_ERR should be logged, but that no messages at any other priority should be logged:

```
setlogmask(LOG_UPTO(LOG_ERR));
```

Then, to log a message at priority LOG_INFO, it would make the following call to syslog:

```
syslog(LOG_INFO, "Connection from host %d", CallingHost);
```

A locally-written utility could use the following call to syslog to log a message at priority LOG_INFO, to be treated by syslogd as other messages to the facility LOG_LOCAL2 are treated:

```
syslog(LOG_INFO|LOG_LOCAL2, "error: %m");
```

SEE ALSO

logger(1), login(1), lpr(1), lpc(1M), syslogd(1M), printf(3S)

at(1), crontab(1), login(1) in the *User's Reference Manual*
ftpd(1M), routed(1M) in the *Network User's and Administrator's Guide*
getty(1M), cron(1M), su(1), in the *System Administrator's Reference Manual*
printf(3S) in the *Programmer's Reference Manual*

system(3S) (C Development Set) **system(3S)**

NAME
system – issue a shell command

SYNOPSIS
```
#include <stdlib.h>

int system (const char *string);
```

DESCRIPTION
system causes the *string* to be given to the shell [see sh(1)] as input, as if the string had been typed as a command at a terminal. The current process waits until the shell has completed, then returns the exit status of the shell in the format specified by waitpid(2).

If *string* is a NULL pointer, system checks if /sbin/sh exists and is executable. If /sbin/sh is available, system returns non-zero; otherwise it returns zero.

system fails if one or more of the following are true:

EAGAIN   The system-imposed limit on the total number of processes under execution by a single user would be exceeded.

EINTR   system was interrupted by a signal.

ENOMEM   The new process requires more memory than is allowed by the system-imposed maximum MAXMEM.

SEE ALSO
exec(2), waitpid(2)

sh(1) in the *User's Reference Manual*

DIAGNOSTICS
system forks to create a child process that in turn execs /sbin/sh in order to execute *string*. If the fork or exec fails, system returns −1 and sets errno.

NAME

t_accept – accept a connect request

SYNOPSIS

    #include <tiuser.h>

    int t_accept(int fd, int resfd, struct t_call *call);

DESCRIPTION

This function is issued by a transport user to accept a connect request. fd identifies the local transport endpoint where the connect indication arrived, resfd specifies the local transport endpoint where the connection is to be established, and call contains information required by the transport provider to complete the connection. call points to a t_call structure that contains the following members:

    struct netbuf addr;
    struct netbuf opt;
    struct netbuf udata;
    int sequence;

netbuf is described in intro(3N). In call, addr is the address of the caller, opt indicates any protocol-specific parameters associated with the connection, udata points to any user data to be returned to the caller, and sequence is the value returned by t_listen that uniquely associates the response with a previously received connect indication.

A transport user may accept a connection on either the same, or on a different, local transport endpoint from the one on which the connect indication arrived. If the same endpoint is specified (that is, resfd=fd), the connection can be accepted unless the following condition is true: The user has received other indications on that endpoint but has not responded to them (with t_accept or t_snddis). For this condition, t_accept will fail and set t_errno to TBADF.

If a different transport endpoint is specified (resfd!=fd), the endpoint must be bound to a protocol address and must be in the T_IDLE state [see t_getstate(3N)] before the t_accept is issued.

For both types of endpoints, t_accept will fail and set t_errno to TLOOK if there are indications (for example, a connect or disconnect) waiting to be received on that endpoint.

The values of parameters specified by opt and the syntax of those values are protocol specific. The udata argument enables the called transport user to send user data to the caller and the amount of user data must not exceed the limits supported by the transport provider as returned in the connect field of the info argument of t_open or t_getinfo. If the len [see netbuf in intro(3N)] field of udata is zero, no data will be sent to the caller.

On failure, t_errno may be set to one of the following:

TBADF   The specified file descriptor does not refer to a transport endpoint, or the user is invalidly accepting a connection on the same transport endpoint on which the connect indication arrived.

TOUTSTATE	The function was issued in the wrong sequence on the transport endpoint referenced by fd, or the transport endpoint referred to by resfd is not in the T_IDLE state.
TACCES	The user does not have permission to accept a connection on the responding transport endpoint or use the specified options.
TBADOPT	The specified options were in an incorrect format or contained invalid information.
TBADDATA	The amount of user data specified was not within the bounds supported by the transport provider as returned in the connect field of the info argument of t_open or t_getinfo.
TBADSEQ	An invalid sequence number was specified.
TLOOK	An asynchronous event has occurred on the transport endpoint referenced by fd and requires immediate attention.
TNOTSUPPORT	This function is not supported by the underlying transport provider.
TSYSERR	A system error has occurred during execution of this function.

SEE ALSO
intro(3N), t_connect(3N), t_getstate(3N), t_listen(3N), t_open(3N), t_rcvconnect(3N)

Programmer's Guide: Networking Interfaces

DIAGNOSTICS
Upon successful completion, a value of 0 is returned. Otherwise, a value of −1 is returned and t_errno is set to indicate the error.

NAME
t_alloc – allocate a library structure

SYNOPSIS
```
#include <tiuser.h>

char *t_alloc(fd, struct_type, fields)
int fd;
int struct_type;
int fields;
```

DESCRIPTION
The t_alloc function dynamically allocates memory for the various transport function argument structures as specified below. This function will allocate memory for the specified structure, and will also allocate memory for buffers referenced by the structure.

The structure to allocate is specified by struct_type, and can be one of the following:

T_BIND	struct t_bind
T_CALL	struct t_call
T_OPTMGMT	struct t_optmgmt
T_DIS	struct t_discon
T_UNITDATA	struct t_unitdata
T_UDERROR	struct t_uderr
T_INFO	struct t_info

where each of these structures may subsequently be used as an argument to one or more transport functions.

Each of the above structures, except T_INFO, contains at least one field of type struct netbuf. netbuf is described in intro(3N). For each field of this type, the user may specify that the buffer for that field should be allocated as well. The fields argument specifies this option, where the argument is the bitwise-OR of any of the following:

T_ADDR   The addr field of the t_bind, t_call, t_unitdata, or t_uderr structures.

T_OPT   The opt field of the t_optmgmt, t_call, t_unitdata, or t_uderr structures.

T_UDATA The udata field of the t_call, t_discon, or t_unitdata structures.

T_ALL   All relevant fields of the given structure.

For each field specified in fields, t_alloc will allocate memory for the buffer associated with the field, and initialize the buf pointer and maxlen [see netbuf in intro(3N) for description of buf and maxlen] field accordingly. The length of the buffer allocated will be based on the same size information that is returned to the user on t_open and t_getinfo. Thus, fd must refer to the transport endpoint through which the newly allocated structure will be passed, so that the appropriate size information can be accessed. If the size value associated with any specified field is −1 or −2 (see t_open or t_getinfo), t_alloc will be unable to determine the size of the buffer to allocate and will fail, setting t_errno to TSYSERR and errno to EINVAL. For any field not specified in fields, buf will be set to NULL and maxlen will be set to zero.

Use of t_alloc to allocate structures will help ensure the compatibility of user programs with future releases of the transport interface.

On failure, t_errno may be set to one of the following:

    TBADF   The specified file descriptor does not refer to a transport endpoint.

    TSYSERR   A system error has occurred during execution of this function.

SEE ALSO
intro(3N), t_free(3N), t_getinfo(3N), t_open(3N)

Programmer's Guide: Networking Interfaces

DIAGNOSTICS
On successful completion, t_alloc returns a pointer to the newly allocated structure. On failure, NULL is returned.

t_bind(3N) (Networking Support Utilities) t_bind(3N)

NAME
t_bind – bind an address to a transport endpoint

SYNOPSIS
```
#include <tiuser.h>

int t_bind (fd, req, ret)
int fd;
struct t_bind *req;
struct t_bind *ret;
```

DESCRIPTION
This function associates a protocol address with the transport endpoint specified by fd and activates that transport endpoint. In connection mode, the transport provider may begin accepting or requesting connections on the transport endpoint. In connectionless mode, the transport user may send or receive data units through the transport endpoint.

The req and ret arguments point to a t_bind structure containing the following members:

```
struct netbuf addr;
unsigned qlen;
```

netbuf is described in intro(3N). The addr field of the t_bind structure specifies a protocol address and the qlen field is used to indicate the maximum number of outstanding connect indications.

req is used to request that an address, represented by the netbuf structure, be bound to the given transport endpoint. len [see netbuf in intro(3N); also for buf and maxlen] specifies the number of bytes in the address and buf points to the address buffer. maxlen has no meaning for the req argument. On return, ret contains the address that the transport provider actually bound to the transport endpoint; this may be different from the address specified by the user in req. In ret, the user specifies maxlen, which is the maximum size of the address buffer, and buf, which points to the buffer where the address is to be placed. On return, len specifies the number of bytes in the bound address and buf points to the bound address. If maxlen is not large enough to hold the returned address, an error will result.

If the requested address is not available, or if no address is specified in req (the len field of addr in req is zero) the transport provider may assign an appropriate address to be bound, and will return that address in the addr field of ret. The user can compare the addresses in req and ret to determine whether the transport provider bound the transport endpoint to a different address than that requested.

req may be NULL if the user does not wish to specify an address to be bound. Here, the value of qlen is assumed to be zero, and the transport provider must assign an address to the transport endpoint. Similarly, ret may be NULL if the user does not care what address was bound by the provider and is not interested in the negotiated value of qlen. It is valid to set req and ret to NULL for the same call, in which case the provider chooses the address to bind to the transport endpoint and does not return that information to the user.

The qlen field has meaning only when initializing a connection-mode service. It specifies the number of outstanding connect indications the transport provider should support for the given transport endpoint. An outstanding connect indication is one that has been passed to the transport user by the transport provider. A value of qlen greater than zero is only meaningful when issued by a passive transport user that expects other users to call it. The value of qlen will be negotiated by the transport provider and may be changed if the transport provider cannot support the specified number of outstanding connect indications. On return, the qlen field in ret will contain the negotiated value.

This function allows more than one transport endpoint to be bound to the same protocol address (however, the transport provider must support this capability also), but it is not allowable to bind more than one protocol address to the same transport endpoint. If a user binds more than one transport endpoint to the same protocol address, only one endpoint can be used to listen for connect indications associated with that protocol address. In other words, only one t_bind for a given protocol address may specify a value of qlen greater than zero. In this way, the transport provider can identify which transport endpoint should be notified of an incoming connect indication. If a user attempts to bind a protocol address to a second transport endpoint with a value of qlen greater than zero, the transport provider will assign another address to be bound to that endpoint. If a user accepts a connection on the transport endpoint that is being used as the listening endpoint, the bound protocol address will be found to be busy for the duration of that connection. No other transport endpoints may be bound for listening while that initial listening endpoint is in the data transfer phase. This will prevent more than one transport endpoint bound to the same protocol address from accepting connect indications.

On failure, t_errno may be set to one of the following:

[TBADF]	The specified file descriptor does not refer to a transport endpoint.
[TOUTSTATE]	The function was issued in the wrong sequence.
[TBADADDR]	The specified protocol address was in an incorrect format or contained illegal information.
[TNOADDR]	The transport provider could not allocate an address.
[TACCES]	The user does not have permission to use the specified address.
[TBUFOVFLW]	The number of bytes allowed for an incoming argument is not sufficient to store the value of that argument. The provider's state will change to [T_IDLE] and the information to be returned in ret will be discarded.
TSYSERR	A system error has occurred during execution of this function.

SEE ALSO
> intro(3N), t_open(3N), t_optmgmt(3N), t_unbind(3N)
>
> *Programmer's Guide: Networking Interfaces*

DIAGNOSTICS
> t_bind returns 0 on success and −1 on failure and t_errno is set to indicate the error.

NAME

t_close – close a transport endpoint

SYNOPSIS

```
#include <tiuser.h>

int t_close(fd)
int fd;
```

DESCRIPTION

The t_close function informs the transport provider that the user is finished with the transport endpoint specified by fd, and frees any local library resources associated with the endpoint. In addition, t_close closes the file associated with the transport endpoint.

t_close should be called from the T_UNBND state [see t_getstate(3N)]. However, this function does not check state information, so it may be called from any state to close a transport endpoint. If this occurs, the local library resources associated with the endpoint will be freed automatically. In addition, close(2) will be issued for that file descriptor; the close will be abortive if no other process has that file open, and will break any transport connection that may be associated with that endpoint.

On failure, t_errno may be set to the following:

TBADF   The specified file descriptor does not refer to a transport endpoint.

SEE ALSO

t_getstate(3N), t_open(3N), t_unbind(3N).

Programmer's Guide: Networking Interfaces.

DIAGNOSTICS

t_close returns 0 on success and –1 on failure and t_errno is set to indicate the error.

NAME
t_connect – establish a connection with another transport user

SYNOPSIS
#include <tiuser.h>

int t_connect(fd, sndcall, rcvcall)
int fd;
struct t_call *sndcall;
struct t_call *rcvcall;

DESCRIPTION
This function enables a transport user to request a connection to the specified destination transport user. fd identifies the local transport endpoint where communication will be established, while sndcall and rcvcall point to a t_call structure that contains the following members:

    struct netbuf addr;
    struct netbuf opt;
    struct netbuf udata;
    int sequence;

sndcall specifies information needed by the transport provider to establish a connection and rcvcall specifies information that is associated with the newly established connection.

netbuf is described in intro(3N). In sndcall, addr specifies the protocol address of the destination transport user, opt presents any protocol-specific information that might be needed by the transport provider, udata points to optional user data that may be passed to the destination transport user during connection establishment, and sequence has no meaning for this function.

On return in rcvcall, addr returns the protocol address associated with the responding transport endpoint, opt presents any protocol-specific information associated with the connection, udata points to optional user data that may be returned by the destination transport user during connection establishment, and sequence has no meaning for this function.

The opt argument implies no structure on the options that may be passed to the transport provider. The transport provider is free to specify the structure of any options passed to it. These options are specific to the underlying protocol of the transport provider. The user may choose not to negotiate protocol options by setting the len field of opt to zero. In this case, the provider may use default options.

The udata argument enables the caller to pass user data to the destination transport user and receive user data from the destination user during connection establishment. However, the amount of user data must not exceed the limits supported by the transport provider as returned in the connect field of the info argument of t_open or t_getinfo. If the len [see netbuf in intro(3N)] field of udata is zero in sndcall, no data will be sent to the destination transport user.

t_connect(3N) (Networking Support Utilities) **t_connect(3N)**

On return, the addr, opt, and udata fields of rcvcall will be updated to reflect values associated with the connection. Thus, the maxlen [see netbuf in intro(3N)] field of each argument must be set before issuing this function to indicate the maximum size of the buffer for each. However, rcvcall may be NULL, in which case no information is given to the user on return from t_connect.

By default, t_connect executes in synchronous mode, and will wait for the destination user's response before returning control to the local user. A successful return (that is, return value of zero) indicates that the requested connection has been established. However, if O_NDELAY or O_NONBLOCK is set (via t_open or fcntl), t_connect executes in asynchronous mode. In this case, the call will not wait for the remote user's response, but will return control immediately to the local user and return -1 with t_errno set to TNODATA to indicate that the connection has not yet been established. In this way, the function simply initiates the connection establishment procedure by sending a connect request to the destination transport user.

On failure, t_errno may be set to one of the following:

TBADF
: The specified file descriptor does not refer to a transport endpoint.

TOUTSTATE
: The function was issued in the wrong sequence.

TNODATA
: O_NDELAY or O_NONBLOCK was set, so the function successfully initiated the connection establishment procedure, but did not wait for a response from the remote user.

TBADADDR
: The specified protocol address was in an incorrect format or contained invalid information.

TBADOPT
: The specified protocol options were in an incorrect format or contained invalid information.

TBADDATA
: The amount of user data specified was not within the bounds supported by the transport provider as returned in the connect field of the info argument of t_open or t_getinfo.

TACCES
: The user does not have permission to use the specified address or options.

TBUFOVFLW
: The number of bytes allocated for an incoming argument is not sufficient to store the value of that argument. If executed in synchronous mode, the provider's state, as seen by the user, changes to T_DATAXFER, and the connect indication information to be returned in rcvcall is discarded.

TLOOK
: An asynchronous event has occurred on this transport endpoint and requires immediate attention.

TNOTSUPPORT
: This function is not supported by the underlying transport provider.

TSYSERR   A system error has occurred during execution of this function.

SEE ALSO
intro(3N), t_accept(3N), t_getinfo(3N), t_listen(3N), t_open(3N), t_optmgmt(3N), t_rcvconnect(3N)

Programmer's Guide: Networking Interfaces

DIAGNOSTICS
t_connect returns 0 on success and −1 on failure and t_errno is set to indicate the error.

t_error(3N) (Networking Support Utilities) t_error(3N)

NAME
t_error – produce error message

SYNOPSIS
#include <tiuser.h>

void t_error(errmsg)
char *errmsg;
extern int t_errno;
extern char *t_errlist[];
extern int t_nerr;

DESCRIPTION
t_error produces a message on the standard error output which describes the last error encountered during a call to a transport function. The argument string errmsg is a user-supplied error message that gives context to the error.

t_error prints the user-supplied error message followed by a colon and the standard transport function error message for the current value contained in t_errno. If t_errno is TSYSERR, t_error will also print the standard error message for the current value contained in errno [see intro(2)].

t_errlist is the array of message strings, to allow user message formatting. t_errno can be used as an index into this array to retrieve the error message string (without a terminating newline). t_nerr is the maximum index value for the t_errlist array.

t_errno is set when an error occurs and is not cleared on subsequent successful calls.

EXAMPLE
If a t_connect function fails on transport endpoint fd2 because a bad address was given, the following call might follow the failure:

    t_error("t_connect failed on fd2");

The diagnostic message would print as:

    t_connect failed on fd2: Incorrect transport address format

where "t_connect failed on fd2" tells the user which function failed on which transport endpoint, and "Incorrect transport address format" identifies the specific error that occurred.

SEE ALSO
Programmer's Guide: Networking Interfaces

NAME

t_free – free a library structure

SYNOPSIS

```
#include <tiuser.h>

int t_free(ptr, struct_type)
char *ptr;
int struct_type;
```

DESCRIPTION

The t_free function frees memory previously allocated by t_alloc. This function will free memory for the specified structure, and will also free memory for buffers referenced by the structure.

ptr points to one of the six structure types described for t_alloc, and struct_type identifies the type of that structure, which can be one of the following:

T_BIND	struct t_bind
T_CALL	struct t_call
T_OPTMGMT	struct t_optmgmt
T_DIS	struct t_discon
T_UNITDATA	struct t_unitdata
T_UDERROR	struct t_uderr
T_INFO	struct t_info

where each of these structures is used as an argument to one or more transport functions.

t_free will check the addr, opt, and udata fields of the given structure (as appropriate), and free the buffers pointed to by the buf field of the netbuf [see intro(3N)] structure. If buf is NULL, t_free will not attempt to free memory. After all buffers are freed, t_free will free the memory associated with the structure pointed to by ptr.

Undefined results will occur if ptr or any of the buf pointers points to a block of memory that was not previously allocated by t_alloc.

On failure, t_errno may be set to the following:

TSYSERR   A system error has occurred during execution of this function.

SEE ALSO

intro(3N), t_alloc(3N)

Programmer's Guide: Networking Interfaces

DIAGNOSTICS

t_free returns 0 on success and −1 on failure and t_errno is set to indicate the error.

NAME

t_getinfo - get protocol-specific service information

SYNOPSIS

    #include <tiuser.h>

    int t_getinfo(fd, info)
    int fd;
    struct t_info *info;

DESCRIPTION

This function returns the current characteristics of the underlying transport protocol associated with file descriptor fd. The info structure is used to return the same information returned by t_open. This function enables a transport user to access this information during any phase of communication.

This argument points to a t_info structure, which contains the following members:

    long addr;   /* max size of the transport protocol address */
    long options;   /* max number of bytes of protocol-specific options */
    long tsdu;   /* max size of a transport service data unit (TSDU) */
    long etsdu;   /* max size of an expedited transport service data unit (ETSDU) */
    long connect;   /* max amount of data allowed on connection establishment functions */
    long discon;   /* max amount of data allowed on t_snddis and t_rcvdis functions */
    long servtype;   /* service type supported by the transport provider */

The values of the fields have the following meanings:

- addr A value greater than or equal to zero indicates the maximum size of a transport protocol address; a value of −1 specifies that there is no limit on the address size; and a value of −2 specifies that the transport provider does not provide user access to transport protocol addresses.

- options A value greater than or equal to zero indicates the maximum number of bytes of protocol-specific options supported by the provider; a value of −1 specifies that there is no limit on the option size; and a value of −2 specifies that the transport provider does not support user-settable options.

- tsdu A value greater than zero specifies the maximum size of a transport service data unit (TSDU); a value of zero specifies that the transport provider does not support the concept of TSDU, although it does support the sending of a data stream with no logical boundaries preserved across a connection; a value of −1 specifies that there is no limit on the size of a TSDU; and a value of −2 specifies that the transfer of normal data is not supported by the transport provider.

- etsdu A value greater than zero specifies the maximum size of an expedited transport service data unit (ETSDU); a value of zero specifies that the transport provider does not support the concept of ETSDU, although it does support the sending of an expedited data stream with no logical boundaries preserved across a

	connection; a value of −1 specifies that there is no limit on the size of an ETSDU; and a value of −2 specifies that the transfer of expedited data is not supported by the transport provider.
connect	A value greater than or equal to zero specifies the maximum amount of data that may be associated with connection establishment functions; a value of −1 specifies that there is no limit on the amount of data sent during connection establishment; and a value of −2 specifies that the transport provider does not allow data to be sent with connection establishment functions.
discon	A value greater than or equal to zero specifies the maximum amount of data that may be associated with the t_snddis and t_rcvdis functions; a value of −1 specifies that there is no limit on the amount of data sent with these abortive release functions; and a value of −2 specifies that the transport provider does not allow data to be sent with the abortive release functions.
servtype	This field specifies the service type supported by the transport provider, as described below.

If a transport user is concerned with protocol independence, the above sizes may be accessed to determine how large the buffers must be to hold each piece of information. Alternatively, the t_alloc function may be used to allocate these buffers. An error will result if a transport user exceeds the allowed data size on any function. The value of each field may change as a result of option negotiation, and t_getinfo enables a user to retrieve the current characteristics.

The servtype field of info may specify one of the following values on return:

T_COTS	The transport provider supports a connection-mode service but does not support the optional orderly release facility.
T_COTS_ORD	The transport provider supports a connection-mode service with the optional orderly release facility.
T_CLTS	The transport provider supports a connectionless-mode service. For this service type, t_open will return −2 for etsdu, connect, and discon.

On failure, t_errno may be set to one of the following:

TBADF	The specified file descriptor does not refer to a transport endpoint.
TSYSERR	A system error has occurred during execution of this function.

SEE ALSO
t_open(3N)

Programmer's Guide: Networking Interfaces

DIAGNOSTICS
t_getinfo returns 0 on success and −1 on failure and t_errno is set to indicate the error.

NAME

t_getstate – get the current state

SYNOPSIS

    #include <tiuser.h>

    int t_getstate(fd)
    int fd;

DESCRIPTION

The t_getstate function returns the current state of the provider associated with the transport endpoint specified by fd.

On failure, t_errno may be set to one of the following:

TBADF	The specified file descriptor does not refer to a transport endpoint.
TSTATECHNG	The transport provider is undergoing a state change.
TSYSERR	A system error has occurred during execution of this function.

SEE ALSO

t_open(3N)

Programmer's Guide: Networking Interfaces

DIAGNOSTICS

t_getstate returns the current state on successful completion and −1 on failure and t_errno is set to indicate the error. The current state may be one of the following:

T_UNBND	unbound
T_IDLE	idle
T_OUTCON	outgoing connection pending
T_INCON	incoming connection pending
T_DATAXFER	data transfer
T_OUTREL	outgoing orderly release (waiting for an orderly release indication)
T_INREL	incoming orderly release (waiting for an orderly release request)

If the provider is undergoing a state transition when t_getstate is called, the function will fail.

t_listen(3N) (Networking Support Utilities) t_listen(3N)

NAME
t_listen – listen for a connect request

SYNOPSIS
#include <tiuser.h>

int t_listen(fd, call)
int fd;
struct t_call *call;

DESCRIPTION
This function listens for a connect request from a calling transport user. fd identifies the local transport endpoint where connect indications arrive, and on return, call contains information describing the connect indication. call points to a t_call structure, which contains the following members:

    struct netbuf addr;
    struct netbuf opt;
    struct netbuf udata;
    int sequence;

netbuf is described in intro(3N). In call, addr returns the protocol address of the calling transport user, opt returns protocol-specific parameters associated with the connect request, udata returns any user data sent by the caller on the connect request, and sequence is a number that uniquely identifies the returned connect indication. The value of sequence enables the user to listen for multiple connect indications before responding to any of them.

Since this function returns values for the addr, opt, and udata fields of call, the maxlen [see netbuf in intro(3N)] field of each must be set before issuing t_listen to indicate the maximum size of the buffer for each.

By default, t_listen executes in synchronous mode and waits for a connect indication to arrive before returning to the user. However, if O_NDELAY or O_NONBLOCK is set (via t_open or fcntl), t_listen executes asynchronously, reducing to a poll for existing connect indications. If none are available, it returns −1 and sets t_errno to TNODATA.

On failure, t_errno may be set to one of the following:

TBADF   The specified file descriptor does not refer to a transport endpoint.

TBUFOVFLW   The number of bytes allocated for an incoming argument is not sufficient to store the value of that argument. The provider's state, as seen by the user, changes to T_INCON, and the connect indication information to be returned in call is discarded.

TNODATA   O_NDELAY or O_NONBLOCK was set, but no connect indications had been queued.

TLOOK   An asynchronous event has occurred on this transport endpoint and requires immediate attention.

TNOTSUPPORT	This function is not supported by the underlying transport provider.
TSYSERR	A system error has occurred during execution of this function.

NOTES

If a user issues t_listen in synchronous mode on a transport endpoint that was not bound for listening (that is, qlen was zero on t_bind), the call will wait forever because no connect indications will arrive on that endpoint.

SEE ALSO

intro(3N), t_accept(3N), t_bind(3N), t_connect(3N), t_open(3N), t_rcvconnect(3N)

Programmer's Guide: Networking Interfaces

DIAGNOSTICS

t_listen returns 0 on success and −1 on failure and t_errno is set to indicate the error.

t_look(3N) (Networking Support Utilities) t_look(3N)

NAME
t_look − look at the current event on a transport endpoint

SYNOPSIS
```
#include <tiuser.h>

int t_look(fd)
int fd;
```

DESCRIPTION
This function returns the current event on the transport endpoint specified by fd. This function enables a transport provider to notify a transport user of an asynchronous event when the user is issuing functions in synchronous mode. Certain events require immediate notification of the user and are indicated by a specific error, TLOOK, on the current or next function to be executed.

This function also enables a transport user to poll a transport endpoint periodically for asynchronous events.

On failure, t_errno may be set to one of the following:

TBADF	The specified file descriptor does not refer to a transport endpoint.
TSYSERR	A system error has occurred during execution of this function.

SEE ALSO
t_open(3N)
Programmer's Guide: Networking Interfaces

DIAGNOSTICS
Upon success, t_look returns a value that indicates which of the allowable events has occurred, or returns zero if no event exists. One of the following events is returned:

T_LISTEN	connection indication received
T_CONNECT	connect confirmation received
T_DATA	normal data received
T_EXDATA	expedited data received
T_DISCONNECT	disconnect received
T_UDERR	datagram error indication
T_ORDREL	orderly release indication

On failure, −1 is returned and t_errno is set to indicate the error.

t_open(3N) (Networking Support Utilities) t_open(3N)

NAME
t_open – establish a transport endpoint

SYNOPSIS
#include <tiuser.h>

#include <fcntl.h>

int t_open (char path, int oflag, struct t_info *info);

DESCRIPTION
t_open must be called as the first step in the initialization of a transport endpoint. This function establishes a transport endpoint by opening a UNIX file that identifies a particular transport provider (that is, transport protocol) and returning a file descriptor that identifies that endpoint. For example, opening the file /dev/iso_cots identifies an OSI connection-oriented transport layer protocol as the transport provider.

path points to the path name of the file to open, and oflag identifies any open flags [as in open(2)]. oflag may be constructed from O_NDELAY or O_NONBLOCK OR-ed with O_RDWR. These flags are defined in the header file <fcntl.h>. t_open returns a file descriptor that will be used by all subsequent functions to identify the particular local transport endpoint.

t_open also returns various default characteristics of the underlying transport protocol by setting fields in the t_info structure. The t_info argument points to a t_info structure that contains the following members:

```
long addr;        /* maximum size of the transport protocol address */
long options;     /* maximum number of bytes of protocol-specific options */
long tsdu;        /* maximum size of a transport service data unit (TSDU) */
long etsdu;       /* maximum size of an expedited transport service data unit (ETSDU) */
long connect;     /* maximum amount of data allowed on connection establishment
                     functions */
long discon;      /* maximum amount of data allowed on t_snddis and t_rcvdis
                     functions */
long servtype;    /* service type supported by the transport provider */
```

The values of the fields have the following meanings:

  addr   A value greater than or equal to zero indicates the maximum size of a transport protocol address; a value of −1 specifies that there is no limit on the address size; and a value of −2 specifies that the transport provider does not provide user access to transport protocol addresses.

  options   A value greater than or equal to zero indicates the maximum number of bytes of protocol-specific options supported by the provider; a value of −1 specifies that there is no limit on the option size; and a value of −2 specifies that the transport provider does not support user-settable options.

  tsdu   A value greater than zero specifies the maximum size of a transport service data unit (TSDU); a value of zero specifies that the transport provider does not support the concept of TSDU, although it does support the sending of a data stream with no logical

t_open (3N) (Networking Support Utilities) t_open (3N)

boundaries preserved across a connection; a value of −1 specifies that there is no limit on the size of a TSDU; and a value of −2 specifies that the transfer of normal data is not supported by the transport provider.

etsdu
A value greater than zero specifies the maximum size of an expedited transport service data unit (ETSDU); a value of zero specifies that the transport provider does not support the concept of ETSDU, although it does support the sending of an expedited data stream with no logical boundaries preserved across a connection; a value of −1 specifies that there is no limit on the size of an ETSDU; and a value of −2 specifies that the transfer of expedited data is not supported by the transport provider.

connect
A value greater than or equal to zero specifies the maximum amount of data that may be associated with connection establishment functions; a value of −1 specifies that there is no limit on the amount of data sent during connection establishment; and a value of −2 specifies that the transport provider does not allow data to be sent with connection establishment functions.

discon
A value greater than or equal to zero specifies the maximum amount of data that may be associated with the t_snddis and t_rcvdis functions; a value of −1 specifies that there is no limit on the amount of data sent with these abortive release functions; and a value of −2 specifies that the transport provider does not allow data to be sent with the abortive release functions.

servtype
This field specifies the service type supported by the transport provider, as described below.

If a transport user is concerned with protocol independence, the above sizes may be accessed to determine how large the buffers must be to hold each piece of information. Alternatively, the t_alloc function may be used to allocate these buffers. An error will result if a transport user exceeds the allowed data size on any function.

The servtype field of info may specify one of the following values on return:

T_COTS
The transport provider supports a connection-mode service but does not support the optional orderly release facility.

T_COTS_ORD
The transport provider supports a connection-mode service with the optional orderly release facility.

T_CLTS
The transport provider supports a connectionless-mode service. For this service type, t_open will return −2 for etsdu, connect, and discon.

A single transport endpoint may support only one of the above services at one time.

If info is set to NULL by the transport user, no protocol information is returned by t_open.

On failure, t_errno may be set to the following:

TSYSERR   A system error has occurred during execution of this function.

TBADFLAG   An invalid flag is specified.

DIAGNOSTICS

t_open returns a valid file descriptor on success and −1 on failure and t_errno is set to indicate the error.

NOTES

If t_open is used on a non-TLI-conforming STREAMS device, unpredictable events may occur.

SEE ALSO

open(2)

Programmer's Guide: Networking Interfaces

NAME

t_optmgmt – manage options for a transport endpoint

SYNOPSIS

```
#include <tiuser.h>
int t_optmgmt (int fd, struct t_optmgmt *req, struct t_optmgmt *ret);
```

DESCRIPTION

The t_optmgmt function enables a transport user to retrieve, verify, or negotiate protocol options with the transport provider. fd identifies a bound transport endpoint.

The req and ret arguments point to a t_optmgmt structure containing the following members:

```
struct netbuf opt;
long flags;
```

The opt field identifies protocol options and the flags field is used to specify the action to take with those options.

The options are represented by a netbuf [see intro(3N); also for len, buf, and maxlen] structure in a manner similar to the address in t_bind. req is used to request a specific action of the provider and to send options to the provider. len specifies the number of bytes in the options, buf points to the options buffer, and maxlen has no meaning for the req argument. The transport provider may return options and flag values to the user through ret. For ret, maxlen specifies the maximum size of the options buffer and buf points to the buffer where the options are to be placed. On return, len specifies the number of bytes of options returned. maxlen has no meaning for the req argument, but must be set in the ret argument to specify the maximum number of bytes the options buffer can hold. The actual structure and content of the options is imposed by the transport provider.

The flags field of req can specify one of the following actions:

T_NEGOTIATE   This action enables the user to negotiate the values of the options specified in req with the transport provider. The provider will evaluate the requested options and negotiate the values, returning the negotiated values through ret.

T_CHECK   This action enables the user to verify whether the options specified in req are supported by the transport provider. On return, the flags field of ret will have either T_SUCCESS or T_FAILURE set to indicate to the user whether the options are supported. These flags are only meaningful for the T_CHECK request.

T_DEFAULT   This action enables a user to retrieve the default options supported by the transport provider into the opt field of ret. In req, the len field of opt must be zero and the buf field may be NULL.

t_optmgmt(3N) (Networking Support Utilities) t_optmgmt(3N)

If issued as part of the connectionless-mode service, t_optmgmt may block due to flow control constraints. The function will not complete until the transport provider has processed all previously sent data units.

On failure, t_errno may be set to one of the following:

TBADF	The specified file descriptor does not refer to a transport endpoint.
TOUTSTATE	The function was issued in the wrong sequence.
TACCES	The user does not have permission to negotiate the specified options.
TBADOPT	The specified protocol options were in an incorrect format or contained illegal information.
TBADFLAG	An invalid flag was specified.
TBUFOVFLW	The number of bytes allowed for an incoming argument is not sufficient to store the value of that argument. The information to be returned in ret will be discarded.
TSYSERR	A system error has occurred during execution of this function.

SEE ALSO

intro(3N), t_getinfo(3N), t_open(3N)

Programmer's Guide: Networking Interfaces

DIAGNOSTICS

t_optmgmt returns 0 on success and −1 on failure and t_errno is set to indicate the error.

t_rcv(3N) (Networking Support Utilities) t_rcv(3N)

NAME
t_rcv – receive data or expedited data sent over a connection

SYNOPSIS
    int t_rcv (int fd, char *buf, unsigned nbytes, int *flags);

DESCRIPTION
This function receives either normal or expedited data. fd identifies the local transport endpoint through which data will arrive, buf points to a receive buffer where user data will be placed, and nbytes specifies the size of the receive buffer. flags may be set on return from t_rcv and specifies optional flags as described below.

By default, t_rcv operates in synchronous mode and will wait for data to arrive if none is currently available. However, if O_NDELAY or O_NONBLOCK is set (via t_open or fcntl), t_rcv will execute in asynchronous mode and will fail if no data is available. (See TNODATA below.)

On return from the call, if T_MORE is set in flags, this indicates that there is more data and the current transport service data unit (TSDU) or expedited transport service data unit (ETSDU) must be received in multiple t_rcv calls. Each t_rcv with the T_MORE flag set indicates that another t_rcv must follow to get more data for the current TSDU. The end of the TSDU is identified by the return of a t_rcv call with the T_MORE flag not set. If the transport provider does not support the concept of a TSDU as indicated in the info argument on return from t_open or t_getinfo, the T_MORE flag is not meaningful and should be ignored.

On return, the data returned is expedited data if T_EXPEDITED is set in flags. If the number of bytes of expedited data exceeds nbytes, t_rcv will set T_EXPEDITED and T_MORE on return from the initial call. Subsequent calls to retrieve the remaining ETSDU will have T_EXPEDITED set on return. The end of the ETSDU is identified by the return of a t_rcv call with the T_MORE flag not set.

If expedited data arrives after part of a TSDU has been retrieved, receipt of the remainder of the TSDU will be suspended until the ETSDU has been processed. Only after the full ETSDU has been retrieved (T_MORE not set) will the remainder of the TSDU be available to the user.

On failure, t_errno may be set to one of the following:

TBADF	The specified file descriptor does not refer to a transport endpoint.
TNODATA	O_NDELAY or O_NONBLOCK was set, but no data is currently available from the transport provider.
TLOOK	An asynchronous event has occurred on this transport endpoint and requires immediate attention.
TNOTSUPPORT	This function is not supported by the underlying transport provider.
TSYSERR	A system error has occurred during execution of this function.

SEE ALSO
t_open(3N), t_snd(3N)

Programmer's Guide: Networking Interfaces

DIAGNOSTICS
On successful completion, t_rcv returns the number of bytes received, and it returns −1 on failure and t_errno is set to indicate the error.

NAME

t_rcvconnect – receive the confirmation from a connect request

SYNOPSIS

#include <tiuser.h>

int t_rcvconnect (int fd, struct t_call *call);

DESCRIPTION

This function enables a calling transport user to determine the status of a previously sent connect request and is used in conjunction with t_connect to establish a connection in asynchronous mode. The connection will be established on successful completion of this function.

fd identifies the local transport endpoint where communication will be established, and call contains information associated with the newly established connection. call points to a t_call structure which contains the following members:

```
struct netbuf addr;
struct netbuf opt;
struct netbuf udata;
int sequence;
```

netbuf is described in intro(3N). In call, addr returns the protocol address associated with the responding transport endpoint, opt presents any protocol-specific information associated with the connection, udata points to optional user data that may be returned by the destination transport user during connection establishment, and sequence has no meaning for this function.

The maxlen [see netbuf in intro(3N)] field of each argument must be set before issuing this function to indicate the maximum size of the buffer for each. However, call may be NULL, in which case no information is given to the user on return from t_rcvconnect. By default, t_rcvconnect executes in synchronous mode and waits for the connection to be established before returning. On return, the addr, opt, and udata fields reflect values associated with the connection.

If O_NDELAY or O_NONBLOCK is set (via t_open or fcntl), t_rcvconnect executes in asynchronous mode, and reduces to a poll for existing connect confirmations. If none are available, t_rcvconnect fails and returns immediately without waiting for the connection to be established. (See TNODATA below.) t_rcvconnect must be re-issued at a later time to complete the connection establishment phase and retrieve the information returned in call.

On failure, t_errno may be set to one of the following:

TBADF   The specified file descriptor does not refer to a transport endpoint.

TBUFOVFLW   The number of bytes allocated for an incoming argument is not sufficient to store the value of that argument and the connect information to be returned in call will be discarded. The provider's state, as seen by the user, will be changed to DATAXFER.

	TNODATA	O_NDELAY or O_NONBLOCK was set, but a connect confirmation has not yet arrived.
	TLOOK	An asynchronous event has occurred on this transport connection and requires immediate attention.
	TNOTSUPPORT	This function is not supported by the underlying transport provider.
	TSYSERR	A system error has occurred during execution of this function.

SEE ALSO

intro(3N), t_accept(3N), t_bind(3N), t_connect(3N), t_listen(3N), t_open(3N)

Programmer's Guide: Networking Interfaces

DIAGNOSTICS

t_rcvconnect returns 0 on success and −1 on failure and t_errno is set to indicate the error.

t_rcvdis(3N) (Networking Support Utilities) t_rcvdis(3N)

NAME
t_rcvdis – retrieve information from disconnect

SYNOPSIS
#include <tiuser.h>

t_rcvdis (int fd, struct t_discon *discon);

DESCRIPTION
This function is used to identify the cause of a disconnect, and to retrieve any user data sent with the disconnect. fd identifies the local transport endpoint where the connection existed, and discon points to a t_discon structure containing the following members:

```
struct netbuf udata;
int reason;
int sequence;
```

netbuf is described in intro(3N). reason specifies the reason for the disconnect through a protocol-dependent reason code, udata identifies any user data that was sent with the disconnect, and sequence may identify an outstanding connect indication with which the disconnect is associated. sequence is only meaningful when t_rcvdis is issued by a passive transport user who has executed one or more t_listen functions and is processing the resulting connect indications. If a disconnect indication occurs, sequence can be used to identify which of the outstanding connect indications is associated with the disconnect.

If a user does not care if there is incoming data and does not need to know the value of reason or sequence, discon may be NULL and any user data associated with the disconnect will be discarded. However, if a user has retrieved more than one outstanding connect indication (via t_listen) and discon is NULL, the user will be unable to identify which connect indication the disconnect is associated with.

On failure, t_errno may be set to one of the following:

TBADF	The specified file descriptor does not refer to a transport endpoint.
TNODIS	No disconnect indication currently exists on the specified transport endpoint.
TBUFOVFLW	The number of bytes allocated for incoming data is not sufficient to store the data. The provider's state, as seen by the user, will change to T_IDLE, and the disconnect indication information to be returned in discon will be discarded.
TNOTSUPPORT	This function is not supported by the underlying transport provider.
TSYSERR	A system error has occurred during execution of this function.

SEE ALSO
intro(3N), t_connect(3N), t_listen(3N), t_open(3N), t_snddis(3N)
Programmer's Guide: Networking Interfaces

DIAGNOSTICS
t_rcvdis returns 0 on success and −1 on failure and t_errno is set to indicate the error.

NAME

t_rcvrel – acknowledge receipt of an orderly release indication

SYNOPSIS

    #include <tiuser.h>

    t_rcvrel (int fd);

DESCRIPTION

This function is used to acknowledge receipt of an orderly release indication. fd identifies the local transport endpoint where the connection exists. After receipt of this indication, the user should not attempt to receive more data because such an attempt will block forever. However, the user may continue to send data over the connection if t_sndrel has not been issued by the user.

This function is an optional service of the transport provider, and is only supported if the transport provider returned service type T_COTS_ORD on t_open or t_getinfo.

On failure, t_errno may be set to one of the following:

TBADF	The specified file descriptor does not refer to a transport endpoint.
TNOREL	No orderly release indication currently exists on the specified transport endpoint.
TLOOK	An asynchronous event has occurred on this transport endpoint and requires immediate attention.
TNOTSUPPORT	This function is not supported by the underlying transport provider.
TSYSERR	A system error has occurred during execution of this function.

SEE ALSO

t_open(3N), t_sndrel(3N)

Programmer's Guide: Networking Interfaces

DIAGNOSTICS

t_rcvrel returns 0 on success and −1 on failure t_errno is set to indicate the error.

NAME

t_rcvudata – receive a data unit

SYNOPSIS

```
#include <tiuser.h>

int t_rcvudata (int fd, struct t_unitdata *unitdata, int *flags);
```

DESCRIPTION

This function is used in connectionless mode to receive a data unit from another transport user. fd identifies the local transport endpoint through which data will be received, unitdata holds information associated with the received data unit, and flags is set on return to indicate that the complete data unit was not received. unitdata points to a t_unitdata structure containing the following members:

```
struct netbuf addr;
struct netbuf opt;
struct netbuf udata;
```

The maxlen [see netbuf in intro(3N)] field of addr, opt, and udata must be set before issuing this function to indicate the maximum size of the buffer for each.

On return from this call, addr specifies the protocol address of the sending user, opt identifies protocol-specific options that were associated with this data unit, and udata specifies the user data that was received.

By default, t_rcvudata operates in synchronous mode and will wait for a data unit to arrive if none is currently available. However, if O_NDELAY or O_NONBLOCK is set (via t_open or fcntl), t_rcvudata will execute in asynchronous mode and will fail if no data units are available.

If the buffer defined in the udata field of unitdata is not large enough to hold the current data unit, the buffer will be filled and T_MORE will be set in flags on return to indicate that another t_rcvudata should be issued to retrieve the rest of the data unit. Subsequent t_rcvudata call(s) will return zero for the length of the address and options until the full data unit has been received.

On failure, t_errno may be set to one of the following:

TBADF	The specified file descriptor does not refer to a transport endpoint.
TNODATA	O_NDELAY or O_NONBLOCK was set, but no data units are currently available from the transport provider.
TBUFOVFLW	The number of bytes allocated for the incoming protocol address or options is not sufficient to store the information. The unit data information to be returned in unitdata will be discarded.
TLOOK	An asynchronous event has occurred on this transport endpoint and requires immediate attention.
TNOTSUPPORT	This function is not supported by the underlying transport provider.

TSYSERR	A system error has occurred during execution of this function.

SEE ALSO
    intro(3N), t_rcvuderr(3N), t_sndudata(3N)
    Programmer's Guide: Networking Interfaces

DIAGNOSTICS
    t_rcvudata returns 0 on successful completion and −1 on failure and t_errno is set to indicate the error.

t_rcvuderr(3N) (Networking Support Utilities) t_rcvuderr(3N)

NAME
t_rcvuderr – receive a unit data error indication

SYNOPSIS
#include <tiuser.h>

int t_rcvuderr (int fd, struct t_uderr *uderr);

DESCRIPTION
This function is used in connectionless mode to receive information concerning an error on a previously sent data unit, and should be issued only after a unit data error indication. It informs the transport user that a data unit with a specific destination address and protocol options produced an error. fd identifies the local transport endpoint through which the error report will be received, and uderr points to a t_uderr structure containing the following members:

    struct netbuf addr;
    struct netbuf opt;
    long error;

netbuf is described in intro(3N). The maxlen [see netbuf in intro(3N)] field of addr and opt must be set before issuing this function to indicate the maximum size of the buffer for each.

On return from this call, the addr structure specifies the destination protocol address of the erroneous data unit, the opt structure identifies protocol-specific options that were associated with the data unit, and error specifies a protocol-dependent error code.

If the user does not care to identify the data unit that produced an error, uderr may be set to NULL and t_rcvuderr will simply clear the error indication without reporting any information to the user.

On failure, t_errno may be set to one of the following:

TBADF	The specified file descriptor does not refer to a transport endpoint.
TNOUDERR	No unit data error indication currently exists on the specified transport endpoint.
TBUFOVFLW	The number of bytes allocated for the incoming protocol address or options is not sufficient to store the information. The unit data error information to be returned in uderr will be discarded.
TNOTSUPPORT	This function is not supported by the underlying transport provider.
TSYSERR	A system error has occurred during execution of this function.

SEE ALSO
intro(3N), t_rcvudata(3N), t_sndudata(3N)

Programmer's Guide: Networking Interfaces

DIAGNOSTICS

t_rcvuderr returns 0 on successful completion and −1 on failure and t_errno is set to indicate the error.

NAME

t_snd - send data or expedited data over a connection

SYNOPSIS

#include <tiuser.h>

int t_snd (int fd, char *buf, unsigned nbytes, int flags);

DESCRIPTION

This function is used to send either normal or expedited data. fd identifies the local transport endpoint over which data should be sent, buf points to the user data, nbytes specifies the number of bytes of user data to be sent, and flags specifies any optional flags described below.

By default, t_snd operates in synchronous mode and may wait if flow control restrictions prevent the data from being accepted by the local transport provider at the time the call is made. However, if O_NDELAY or O_NONBLOCK is set (via t_open or fcntl), t_snd will execute in asynchronous mode, and will fail immediately if there are flow control restrictions.

Even when there are no flow control restrictions, t_snd will wait if STREAMS internal resources are not available, regardless of the state of O_NDELAY or O_NONBLOCK.

On successful completion, t_snd returns the number of bytes accepted by the transport provider. Normally this will equal the number of bytes specified in nbytes. However, if O_NDELAY or O_NONBLOCK is set, it is possible that only part of the data will be accepted by the transport provider. In this case, t_snd will set T_MORE for the data that was sent (see below) and will return a value less than nbytes. If nbytes is zero and sending of zero bytes is not supported by the underlying transport provider, t_snd() will return -1 with t_errno set to TBADDATA. A return value of zero indicates that the request to send a zero-length data message was sent to the provider.

If T_EXPEDITED is set in flags, the data will be sent as expedited data, and will be subject to the interpretations of the transport provider.

If T_MORE is set in flags, or is set as described above, an indication is sent to the transport provider that the transport service data unit (TSDU) or expedited transport service data unit (ETSDU) is being sent through multiple t_snd calls. Each t_snd with the T_MORE flag set indicates that another t_snd will follow with more data for the current TSDU. The end of the TSDU (or ETSDU) is identified by a t_snd call with the T_MORE flag not set. Use of T_MORE enables a user to break up large logical data units without losing the boundaries of those units at the other end of the connection. The flag implies nothing about how the data is packaged for transfer below the transport interface. If the transport provider does not support the concept of a TSDU as indicated in the info argument on return from t_open or t_getinfo, the T_MORE flag is not meaningful and should be ignored.

The size of each TSDU or ETSDU must not exceed the limits of the transport provider as returned by t_open or t_getinfo. If the size is exceeded, a TSYSERR with system error EPROTO will occur. However, the t_snd may not fail because EPROTO errors may not be reported immediately. In this case, a subsequent call that accesses the transport endpoint will fail with the associated TSYSERR.

t_snd(3N) (Networking Support Utilities) t_snd(3N)

If t_snd is issued from the T_IDLE state, the provider may silently discard the data. If t_snd is issued from any state other than T_DATAXFER, T_INREL or T_IDLE, the provider will generate a TSYSERR with system error EPROTO (which may be reported in the manner described above).

On failure, t_errno may be set to one of the following:

TBADF
The specified file descriptor does not refer to a transport endpoint.

TFLOW
O_NDELAY or O_NONBLOCK was set, but the flow control mechanism prevented the transport provider from accepting data at this time.

TNOTSUPPORT
This function is not supported by the underlying transport provider.

TSYSERR
A system error [see intro(2)] has been detected during execution of this function.

TBADDATA
nbytes is zero and sending zero bytes is not supported by the transport provider.

NOTES
The t_snd routine does not look for a disconnect indication (showing that the connection was broken) before passing data to the provider.

SEE ALSO
t_open(3N), t_rcv(3N)

Programmer's Guide: Networking Interfaces

DIAGNOSTICS
On successful completion, t_snd returns the number of bytes accepted by the transport provider, and it returns −1 on failure and t_errno is set to indicate the error.

t_snddis(3N) (Networking Support Utilities) t_snddis(3N)

NAME
t_snddis – send user-initiated disconnect request

SYNOPSIS
    #include <tiuser.h>

    int t_snddis (int fd, struct t_call *call):

DESCRIPTION
This function is used to initiate an abortive release on an already established connection or to reject a connect request. fd identifies the local transport endpoint of the connection, and call specifies information associated with the abortive release. call points to a t_call structure that contains the following members:

    struct netbuf addr;
    struct netbuf opt;
    struct netbuf udata;
    int sequence;

netbuf is described in intro(3N). The values in call have different semantics, depending on the context of the call to t_snddis. When rejecting a connect request, call must be non-NULL and contain a valid value of sequence to identify uniquely the rejected connect indication to the transport provider. The addr and opt fields of call are ignored. In all other cases, call need only be used when data is being sent with the disconnect request. The addr, opt, and sequence fields of the t_call structure are ignored. If the user does not want to send data to the remote user, the value of call may be NULL.

udata specifies the user data to be sent to the remote user. The amount of user data must not exceed the limits supported by the transport provider as returned in the discon field of the info argument of t_open or t_getinfo. If the len field of udata is zero, no data will be sent to the remote user.

On failure, t_errno may be set to one of the following:

TBADF	The specified file descriptor does not refer to a transport endpoint.
TOUTSTATE	The function was issued in the wrong sequence. The transport provider's outgoing queue may be flushed, so data may be lost.
TBADDATA	The amount of user data specified was not within the bounds supported by the transport provider as returned in the discon field of the info argument of t_open or t_getinfo. The transport provider's outgoing queue will be flushed, so data may be lost.
TBADSEQ	An invalid sequence number was specified, or a NULL call structure was specified when rejecting a connect request. The transport provider's outgoing queue will be flushed, so data may be lost.

TLOOK	An asynchronous event has occurred on this transport endpoint and requires immediate attention.
TNOTSUPPORT	This function is not supported by the underlying transport provider.
TSYSERR	A system error has occurred during execution of this function.

SEE ALSO

intro(3N), t_connect(3N), t_getinfo(3N), t_listen(3N), t_open(3N)

Programmer's Guide: Networking Interfaces

DIAGNOSTICS

t_snddis returns 0 on success and −1 on failure and t_errno is set to indicate the error.

t_sndrel(3N) (Networking Support Utilities) t_sndrel(3N)

NAME
t_sndrel - initiate an orderly release

SYNOPSIS
```
#include <tiuser.h>
```
int t_sndrel (int fd);

DESCRIPTION
This function is used to initiate an orderly release of a transport connection and indicates to the transport provider that the transport user has no more data to send. fd identifies the local transport endpoint where the connection exists. After issuing t_sndrel, the user may not send any more data over the connection. However, a user may continue to receive data if an orderly release indication has not been received.

This function is an optional service of the transport provider, and is only supported if the transport provider returned service type T_COTS_ORD on t_open or t_getinfo.

If t_sndrel is issued from an invalid state, the provider will generate an EPROTO protocol error; however, this error may not occur until a subsequent reference to the transport endpoint.

On failure, t_errno may be set to one of the following:

TBADF	The specified file descriptor does not refer to a transport endpoint.
TFLOW	O_NDELAY or O_NONBLOCK was set, but the flow control mechanism prevented the transport provider from accepting the function at this time.
TNOTSUPPORT	This function is not supported by the underlying transport provider.
TSYSERR	A system error has occurred during execution of this function.

SEE ALSO
t_open(3N), t_rcvrel(3N)

Programmer's Guide: Networking Interfaces

DIAGNOSTICS
t_sndrel returns 0 on success and -1 on failure and t_errno is set to indicate the error.

NAME

t_sndudata – send a data unit

SYNOPSIS

#include <tiuser.h>

int t_sndudata (int fd, struct t_unitdata *unitdata);

DESCRIPTION

This function is used in connectionless mode to send a data unit to another transport user. fd identifies the local transport endpoint through which data will be sent, and unitdata points to a t_unitdata structure containing the following members:

```
struct netbuf addr;
struct netbuf opt;
struct netbuf udata;
```

netbuf is described in intro(3N). In unitdata, addr specifies the protocol address of the destination user, opt identifies protocol-specific options that the user wants associated with this request, and udata specifies the user data to be sent. The user may choose not to specify what protocol options are associated with the transfer by setting the len field of opt to zero. In this case, the provider may use default options.

If the len field of udata is zero, and the sending of zero bytes is not supported by the underlying transport provider, t_sndudata will return –1 with t_errno set to TBADDATA.

By default, t_sndudata operates in synchronous mode and may wait if flow control restrictions prevent the data from being accepted by the local transport provider at the time the call is made. However, if O_NDELAY or O_NONBLOCK is set (via t_open or fcntl), t_sndudata will execute in asynchronous mode and will fail under such conditions.

If t_sndudata is issued from an invalid state, or if the amount of data specified in udata exceeds the TSDU size as returned in the tsdu field of the info argument of t_open or t_getinfo, the provider will generate an EPROTO protocol error. (See TSYSERR below.) If the state is invalid, this error may not occur until a subsequent reference is made to the transport endpoint.

On failure, t_errno may be set to one of the following:

TBADF   The specified file descriptor does not refer to a transport endpoint.

TFLOW   O_NDELAY or O_NONBLOCK was set, but the flow control mechanism prevented the transport provider from accepting data at this time.

TNOTSUPPORT   This function is not supported by the underlying transport provider.

TSYSERR   A system error has occurred during execution of this function.

TBADDATA	nbytes is zero and sending zero bytes is not supported by the transport provider.

SEE ALSO
intro(3N), t_rcvudata(3N), t_rcvuderr(3N)
Programmer's Guide: Networking Interfaces

DIAGNOSTICS
t_sndudata returns 0 on successful completion and −1 on failure t_errno is set to indicate the error.

t_sync(3N) (Networking Support Utilities) t_sync(3N)

NAME
t_sync – synchronize transport library

SYNOPSIS
```
#include <tiuser.h>

int t_sync (int fd);
```

DESCRIPTION

For the transport endpoint specified by fd, t_sync synchronizes the data structures managed by the transport library with information from the underlying transport provider. In doing so, it can convert a raw file descriptor [obtained via open(2), dup(2), or as a result of a fork(2) and exec(2)] to an initialized transport endpoint, assuming that file descriptor referenced a transport provider. This function also allows two cooperating processes to synchronize their interaction with a transport provider.

For example, if a process forks a new process and issues an exec, the new process must issue a t_sync to build the private library data structure associated with a transport endpoint and to synchronize the data structure with the relevant provider information.

It is important to remember that the transport provider treats all users of a transport endpoint as a single user. If multiple processes are using the same endpoint, they should coordinate their activities so as not to violate the state of the provider. t_sync returns the current state of the provider to the user, thereby enabling the user to verify the state before taking further action. This coordination is only valid among cooperating processes; it is possible that a process or an incoming event could change the provider's state *after* a t_sync is issued.

If the provider is undergoing a state transition when t_sync is called, the function will fail.

On failure, t_errno may be set to one of the following:

TBADF	The specified file descriptor does not refer to a transport endpoint.
TSTATECHNG	The transport provider is undergoing a state change.
TSYSERR	A system error has occurred during execution of this function.

SEE ALSO
dup(2), exec(2), fork(2), open(2)

Programmer's Guide: Networking Interfaces

DIAGNOSTICS
t_sync returns the state of the transport provider on successful completion and -1 on failure and t_errno is set to indicate the error. The state returned may be one of the following:

T_UNBND	unbound
T_IDLE	idle
T_OUTCON	outgoing connection pending
T_INCON	incoming connection pending
T_DATAXFER	data transfer
T_OUTREL	outgoing orderly release (waiting for an orderly release indication)
T_INREL	incoming orderly release (waiting for an orderly release request)

NAME

t_unbind – disable a transport endpoint

SYNOPSIS

```
#include <tiuser.h>
```

```
int t_unbind (int fd);
```

DESCRIPTION

The t_unbind function disables the transport endpoint specified by fd which was previously bound by t_bind(3N). On completion of this call, no further data or events destined for this transport endpoint will be accepted by the transport provider.

On failure, t_errno may be set to one of the following:

TBADF	The specified file descriptor does not refer to a transport endpoint.
TOUTSTATE	The function was issued in the wrong sequence.
TLOOK	An asynchronous event has occurred on this transport endpoint.
TSYSERR	A system error has occurred during execution of this function.

SEE ALSO

t_bind(3N)

Programmer's Guide: Networking Interfaces

DIAGNOSTICS

t_unbind returns 0 on success and −1 on failure and t_errno is set to indicate the error.

tam(3X)

NAME
tam – TAM transition libraries

SYNOPSIS
#include <tam.h>

cc -I /usr/include/tam [*flags*] *files* -ltam -lcurses [*libraries*]

DESCRIPTION
These routines are used to port UNIX PC character-based TAM programs to the 3B processor line so that they will run using any terminal supported by curses(3X), the low-level ETI library. Once a TAM program has been changed to remove machine-specific code, it can be recompiled with the standard TAM header file <tam.h> and linked with the TAM transition and curses(3X) libraries.

Note that TAM will probably not be supported in future releases.

FUNCTIONS
The following is a list of TAM routines supplied in the transition library. Those routines marked with a dagger (†) are macros and do not return a value. For a complete description of each routine, see the UNIX PC *UNIX System V User's Manual* under the entries indicated.

```
addch (c) †                              See curses(3X).
char c;

addstr (s) †
char *s;

int adf_gttok (ptr, tbl)                 See paste(3X).
char *ptr;
struct s_kwtbl *tbl;

char *adf_gtwrd (sptr, dptr)
char *sptr, *dptr;

char *adf_gtxcd (sptr, dptr)
char *sptr, *dptr;

int attroff (attrs)                      See curses(3X).
long attrs;

int attron (attrs)
long attrs;

int baudrate ()

int beep ()

int cbreak ()

int clear ()

clearok (dummy, dummy) †
int dummy;

int clrtobot ()
```

```
int clrtoeol ()
int delch ()
int deleteln ()
int echo ()
int endwin ()
erase ()†
int exhelp (hfile, htitle).          See message(3T).
char *hfile, *htitle;
int fixterm ()                       See curses(3X).
flash ()†
int flushinp ()
int form (form, op)                  See form(3X).
form_t *form;
int op;
int getch ()                         See curses(3X).
getyx (win, r, c)†
int win, r, c;
int initscr ()
int insch (ch)
char ch;
int insertln ()
int iswind ()                        See tam(3X); always returns 0.
char *kcodemap (code).               See curses(3X).
unsigned char code;
int keypad (dummy, flag)
int dummy, flag;
leaveok (dummy, dummy)†
int dummy;
int menu (menu, op)                  See menu(3X).
menu_t *menu;
int op;
int message (mtype, hfile, htitle, format [, arg ...]
                                     See message(3X).
int mtype;
char *hfile, *htitle, *format;
move (r, c)†                         See curses(3X).
int r, c;
```

tam(3X)

```
mvaddch (r, c, ch)†
int r, c;
char ch;

mvaddstr (r, c, s)†
int r, c;
char *s;

unsigned long mvinch(r, c)
int r, c;

nl()†                                       Not supported

int nocbreak()

int nodelay (dummy, bool)
int dummy, bool;

int noecho()

nonl()†                                     NOT SUPPORTED

int pb_check (stream)                       See paste(3X).
FILE *stream;

int pb_empty (stream)
FILE *stream;

int pb_gbuf (ptr, n, fn, stream)
char *ptr;
int n;
int (*fn) ();
FILE *stream;

char *pb_gets (ptr, n, stream)
char *ptr;
int n;
FILE *stream;

char *pb_name()

FILE *pb_open()

int pb_puts (ptr, stream)
char *ptr;
FILE *stream;

int pb_seek (stream)
FILE *stream;

int pb_weof (stream)
FILE *stream;

int printw (fmt[, arg1 ... argn])           See curses(3X).
char *fmt;

refresh()†
```

tam(3X)

```
int resetterm()
int resetty()
int savetty()
int track (w, trk, op, butptr, whyptr)
                                        See wgetc().
int w, op, *butptr, *whyptr;
track_t *trk;
int wcmd (wn, cp)                       See tam(3X). Outputs a null-
short wn;                               terminated string to the entry/
char *cp;                               echo line.
int wcreate (row, col, height, width, flags)
                                        Creates a window.
short row, col, height, width;
unsigned short flags;
int wdelete (wn)                        Deletes the specified window.
short wn;
void wexit (ret)                        See tam(3X).
int ret;
int wgetc (wn)
short wn;
int wgetmouse (wn, ms)                  no-op; returns 0.
short wn;
struct umdata *ms;
int wgetpos (wn, rowp, colp)            Gets the current position (row,
short wn;                               column) of the cursor in the
int *rowp, *colp;                       specified window (wn).
int wgetsel ()                          Returns the currently selected
                                        window.
int wgetstat (wn, wstatp)               Returns the information in
short wn;                               WSTAT for a window.
WSTAT *wstatp;
int wgoto (wn, row, col)                Moves the window's cursor to
short wn, row, col;                     a specified row, column.
void wicoff (wn, row, col, icp)         no-op. returns 0.
short wn, row, col;
struct icon *icp;
void wicon (wn, row, col, icp)          no-op. returns 0.
short wn, row, col;
struct icon *icp;
int wind (type, height, width, flags, pfont)
                                        See wind(3X).
```

tam(3X)

```
int type, height, width;
short flags;
char *pfont[ ];
```

`void winit ()`	Sets up the process for window access. See tam(3X).

`int wlabel (wn, cp)`
`short wn;`
`char *cp;`
	Outputs a null-terminated string to the window label area.

`int wndelay (wn, bool)` `int wn, bool;`	

`void wnl (wn, flag)`
`short wn;`
`int flag;`	

`int wpostwait ()`	Reverses the effects of *wprexec*().
`int wprexec ()`	Performs the appropriate actions for passing a window to a child process.

`int wprintf (wn, fmt [, arg1 ... argn])`
`short wn;`
`char *fmt;`	

`int wprompt (wn, cp)`
`short wn;`
`char *cp;`
	Outputs a null-terminated string to the prompt line.

`int wputc (wn, c)`
`short wn;`
`char c;`
	Outputs a character to a window (*wn*).

`int wputs (wn, cp)`
`short wn;`
`char *cp;`
	Outputs a character string to a window.

`int wrastop (w, srcbase, srcwidth, dstbase`
`        dstwidth, srcx, srcy, dstx,`
`        dsty, width, height, srcop,`
`        dstop, pattern)`
	NOT SUPPORTED.

```
int w;
unsigned short *srcbase, *dstbase, *pattern;
unsigned short srcwidth, dswidth, width, height;
unsigned short srcx, srcy, dstx, dsty;
char srcop, dstop;
```

`int wreadmouse (wn, xp, yp, bp, rp)` `short wn;`	no-op; returns 0.

tam(3X)

```
        int *xp, *yp, *bp, *rp;
        int wrefresh (wn)                       Flushes all output
        short wn;                               to the window.
        int wselect (wn)                        Selects the specified window
        short wn;                               as the current or active one.
        int wsetmouse (wn, ms)                  no-op; returns 0.
        short wn;
        struct umdata *ms;
        int wsetstat (wn, wstatp)               Sets the status for a window.
        short wn;
        WSTAT *wstatp;
        int wslk (wn, 0, slong1, slong2, sshort)
                                                Writes a null-terminated string
        short wn;                               to a set of screen-labeled keys.
        char *slong1, *slong2, *sshort;

        int wslk (wn, kn, llabel, slabel)       Writes a null-terminated string
        short wn, kn;                           to a screen-labeled key. The
        char *llabel, *slabel;                  alternate form writes all the
                                                screen-labeled keys at once
                                                more efficiently.

        int wuser (wn, cp)                      Not supported
        short wn;
        char *cp;
```
SEE ALSO
    curses(3X)

NAME

tcsetpgrp – set terminal foreground process group id

SYNOPSIS

    #include <unistd.h>

    int tcsetpgrp (int fildes, pid_t pgid)

DESCRIPTION

tcsetpgrp sets the foreground process group ID of the terminal specified by *fildes* to *pgid*. The file associated with *fildes* must be the controlling terminal of the calling process and the controlling terminal must be currently associated with the session of the calling process. The value of *pgid* must match a process group ID of a process in the same session as the calling process.

tcsetpgrp fails if one or more of the following is true:

EBADF	The *fildes* argument is not a valid file descriptor.
EINVAL	The *fildes* argument is a terminal that does not support tcsetpgrp, or *pgid* is not a valid process group ID.
ENOTTY	The calling process does not have a controlling terminal, or the file is not the controlling terminal, or the controlling terminal is no longer associated with the session of the calling process.
EPERM	*pgid* does not match the process group ID of an existing process in the same session as the calling process.

SEE ALSO

tcsetpgrp(3C), tcsetsid(3C).
termio(7) in the *System Administrator's Reference Manual*.

DIAGNOSTICS

Upon successful completion, tcsetpgrp returns a value of 0. Otherwise, a value of −1 is returned and errno is set to indicate the error.

NAME
times – get process times

SYNOPSIS
cc [*flag*. . .] *file* . . . −lucb

#include <sys/types.h>
#include <sys/times.h>

times(buffer)
struct tms *buffer;

DESCRIPTION
times returns time-accounting information for the current process and for the terminated child processes of the current process. All times are in 1/HZ seconds, where HZ is 60.

This is the structure returned by times:

```
struct tms {
        time_t tms_utime;      /* user time */
        time_t tms_stime;      /* system time */
        time_t tms_cutime;     /* user time, children */
        time_t tms_cstime;     /* system time, children */
};
```

The children's times are the sum of the children's process times and their children's times.

SEE ALSO
getrusage(3), wait(3), time(3)

time(1) in the *User's Reference Manual*
wait(2) in the *Programmer's Reference Manual*

NOTES
times has been superseded by getrusage.

NAME

timezone – get time zone name given offset from GMT

SYNOPSIS

cc [*flag*. . .] *file* . . . -lucb

char *timezone(zone, dst)

int zone
int dst

DESCRIPTION

timezone attempts to return the name of the time zone associated with its first argument, which is measured in minutes westward from Greenwich. If the second argument is 0, the standard name is used, otherwise the Daylight Savings Time version. If the required name does not appear in a table built into the routine, the difference from GMT is produced; for instance, in Afghanistan timezone(-(60*4+30), 0) is appropriate because it is 4:30 ahead of GMT and the string GMT+4:30 is produced.

SEE ALSO

ctime(3) in the *Programmer's Reference Manual*

NOTES

The offset westward from Greenwich and an indication of whether Daylight Savings Time is in effect may not be sufficient to determine the name of the time zone, as the name may differ between different locations in the same time zone. Instead of using timezone to determine the name of the time zone for a given time, that time should be converted to a struct tm using localtime [see ctime(3)] and the tm_zone field of that structure should be used. timezone is retained for compatibility with existing programs.

NAME
tmpfile – create a temporary file

SYNOPSIS
`#include <stdio.h>`

`FILE *tmpfile (void);`

DESCRIPTION
tmpfile creates a temporary file using a name generated by the tmpnam routine and returns a corresponding FILE pointer. If the file cannot be opened, a NULL pointer is returned. The file is automatically deleted when the process using it terminates or when the file is closed. The file is opened for update ("w+").

SEE ALSO
creat(2), open(2), unlink(2), fopen(3S), mktemp(3C), perror(3C), stdio(3S), tmpnam(3S)

tmpnam(3S)   (C Development Set)   tmpnam(3S)

NAME
tmpnam, tempnam – create a name for a temporary file

SYNOPSIS
```
#include <stdio.h>

char *tmpnam (char *s);

char *tempnam (const char *dir, const char *pfx);
```

DESCRIPTION
These functions generate file names that can safely be used for a temporary file.

tmpnam always generates a file name using the path-prefix defined as P_tmpdir in the <stdio.h> header file. If s is NULL, tmpnam leaves its result in an internal static area and returns a pointer to that area. The next call to tmpnam will destroy the contents of the area. If s is not NULL, it is assumed to be the address of an array of at least L_tmpnam bytes, where L_tmpnam is a constant defined in <stdio.h>; tmpnam places its result in that array and returns s.

tempnam allows the user to control the choice of a directory. The argument *dir* points to the name of the directory in which the file is to be created. If *dir* is NULL or points to a string that is not a name for an appropriate directory, the path-prefix defined as P_tmpdir in the <stdio.h> header file is used. If that directory is not accessible, /tmp will be used as a last resort. This entire sequence can be up-staged by providing an environment variable TMPDIR in the user's environment, whose value is the name of the desired temporary-file directory.

Many applications prefer their temporary files to have certain favorite initial letter sequences in their names. Use the *pfx* argument for this. This argument may be NULL or point to a string of up to five characters to be used as the first few characters of the temporary-file name.

tempnam uses malloc to get space for the constructed file name, and returns a pointer to this area. Thus, any pointer value returned from tempnam may serve as an argument to free [see malloc(3C)]. If tempnam cannot return the expected result for any reason, for example, malloc failed—or none of the above mentioned attempts to find an appropriate directory was successful, a NULL pointer will be returned.

tempnam fails if there is not enough space.

FILES
p_tmpdir   /var/tmp

SEE ALSO
creat(2), unlink(2), fopen(3S), malloc(3C), mktemp(3C), tmpfile(3S).

NOTES
These functions generate a different file name each time they are called.

Files created using these functions and either fopen or creat are temporary only in the sense that they reside in a directory intended for temporary use, and their names are unique. It is the user's responsibility to remove the file when its use is ended.

If called more than TMP_MAX (defined in stdio.h) times in a single process, these functions start recycling previously used names.

Between the time a file name is created and the file is opened, it is possible for some other process to create a file with the same name. This can never happen if that other process is using these functions or mktemp and the file names are chosen to render duplication by other means unlikely.

trig(3M) (Math Libraries) trig(3M)

NAME
trig: sin, sinf, cos, cosf, tan, tanf, asin, asinf, acos, acosf, atan, atanf, atan2, atan2f – trigonometric functions

SYNOPSIS
cc [flag ...] file ... -lm [library ...]

cc -O -Ksd [flag ...] file ... -J sfm [library ...]

#include <math.h>

double sin (double x);

float sinf (float x);

double cos (double x);

float cosf (float x);

double tan (double x);

float tanf (float x);

double asin (double x);

float asinf (float x);

double acos (double x);

float acosf (float x);

double atan (double x);

float atanf (float x);

double atan2 (double y, double x);

float atan2f (float y, float x);

DESCRIPTION
sin, cos, and tan and the single-precision versions sinf, cosf, and tanf return, respectively, the sine, cosine, and tangent of their argument, x, measured in radians.

asin and asinf return the arcsine of x, in the range $[-\pi/2,+\pi/2]$.

acos and acosf return the arccosine of x, in the range $[0,+\pi]$.

atan and atanf return the arctangent of x, in the range $(-\pi/2,+\pi/2)$.

atan2 and atan2f return the arctangent of y/x, in the range $(-\pi,+\pi]$, using the signs of both arguments to determine the quadrant of the return value.

SEE ALSO
matherr(3M).

DIAGNOSTICS
If the magnitude of the argument of asin, asinf, acos, or acosf is greater than 1, or if both arguments of atan2 or atan2f are 0, 0 is returned and errno is set to EDOM. In addition, a message indicating DOMAIN error is printed on the standard error output.

Except when the −Xc compilation option is used, these error-handling procedures may be changed with the function matherr. When the −Xa or −Xc compilation options are used, no error messages are printed.

truncate(3C) (C Development Set) truncate(3C)

NAME
truncate, ftruncate – set a file to a specified length

SYNOPSIS
#include <unistd.h>

int truncate (const char *path, off_t length);

int ftruncate (int fildes, off_t length);

DESCRIPTION
The file whose name is given by *path* or referenced by the descriptor *fildes* has its size set to *length* bytes.

If the file was previously longer than *length*, bytes past *length* will no longer be accessible. If it was shorter, bytes from the EOF before the call to the EOF after the call will be read in as zeros. The effective user ID of the process must have write permission for the file, and for ftruncate the file must be open for writing.

truncate fails if one or more of the following are true:

EACCES	Search permission is denied on a component of the path prefix.
EACCES	Write permission is denied for the file referred to by *path*.
EFAULT	*path* points outside the process's allocated address space.
EINTR	A signal was caught during execution of the truncate routine.
EINVAL	*path* is not an ordinary file.
EIO	An I/O error occurred while reading from or writing to the file system.
EISDIR	The file referred to by *path* is a directory.
ELOOP	Too many symbolic links were encountered in translating *path*.
EMFILE	The maximum number of file descriptors available to the process has been reached.
EMULTIHOP	Components of *path* require hopping to multiple remote machines and file system type does not allow it.
ENAMETOOLONG	The length of a *path* component exceeds {NAME_MAX} characters, or the length of *path* exceeds {PATH_MAX} characters.
ENFILE	Could not allocate any more space for the system file table.
ENOENT	Either a component of the path prefix or the file referred to by *path* does not exist.
ENOLINK	*path* points to a remote machine and the link to that machine is no longer active.
ENOTDIR	A component of the path prefix of *path* is not a directory.

EROFS	The file referred to by *path* resides on a read-only file system.
ETXTBSY	The file referred to by *path* is a pure procedure (shared text) file that is being executed.

ftruncate fails if one or more of the following are true:

EAGAIN	The file exists, mandatory file/record locking is set, and there are outstanding record locks on the file [see chmod(2)].
EBADF	*fildes* is not a file descriptor open for writing.
EINTR	A signal was caught during execution of the ftruncate routine.
EIO	An I/O error occurred while reading from or writing to the file system.
ENOLINK	*fildes* points to a remote machine and the link to that machine is no longer active.
EINVAL	*fildes* does not correspond to an ordinary file.

SEE ALSO
fcntl(2), open(2)

DIAGNOSTICS
Upon successful completion, a value of 0 is returned. Otherwise, a value of −1 is returned and errno is set to indicate the error.

tsearch(3C)

NAME
tsearch, tfind, tdelete, twalk – manage binary search trees

SYNOPSIS
```
#include <search.h>
```
void *tsearch (const void *key, void **rootp, int (*compar)
    (const void *, const void *));

void *tfind (const void *key, void * const *rootp, int (*compar)
    (const void *, const void *));

void *tdelete (const void *key, void **rootp, int (*compar)
    (const void *, const void *));

void twalk (void *root, void(*action) (void *, VISIT, int));

DESCRIPTION
tsearch, tfind, tdelete, and twalk are routines for manipulating binary search trees. They are generalized from Knuth (6.2.2) Algorithms T and D. All comparisons are done with a user-supplied routine. This routine is called with two arguments, the pointers to the elements being compared. It returns an integer less than, equal to, or greater than 0, according to whether the first argument is to be considered less than, equal to or greater than the second argument. The comparison function need not compare every byte, so arbitrary data may be contained in the elements in addition to the values being compared.

tsearch is used to build and access the tree. *key* is a pointer to a datum to be accessed or stored. If there is a datum in the tree equal to *key (the value pointed to by *key*), a pointer to this found datum is returned. Otherwise, *key is inserted, and a pointer to it returned. Only pointers are copied, so the calling routine must store the data. rootp points to a variable that points to the root of the tree. A NULL value for the variable pointed to by *rootp* denotes an empty tree; in this case, the variable will be set to point to the datum which will be at the root of the new tree.

Like tsearch, tfind will search for a datum in the tree, returning a pointer to it if found. However, if it is not found, tfind will return a NULL pointer. The arguments for tfind are the same as for tsearch.

tdelete deletes a node from a binary search tree. The arguments are the same as for tsearch. The variable pointed to by *rootp* will be changed if the deleted node was the root of the tree. tdelete returns a pointer to the parent of the deleted node, or a NULL pointer if the node is not found.

twalk traverses a binary search tree. *root* is the root of the tree to be traversed. (Any node in a tree may be used as the root for a walk below that node.) *action* is the name of a routine to be invoked at each node. This routine is, in turn, called with three arguments. The first argument is the address of the node being visited. The second argument is a value from an enumeration data type *typedef enum { preorder, postorder, endorder, leaf } VISIT;* (defined in the search.h header file), depending on whether this is the first, second or third time that the node has been visited (during a depth-first, left-to-right traversal of the tree), or whether the node is a leaf. The third argument is the level of the node in the tree, with the root being level zero.

The pointers to the key and the root of the tree should be of type pointer-to-element, and cast to type pointer-to-character. Similarly, although declared as type pointer-to-character, the value returned should be cast into type pointer-to-element.

EXAMPLE

The following code reads in strings and stores structures containing a pointer to each string and a count of its length. It then walks the tree, printing out the stored strings and their lengths in alphabetical order.

```
#include <string.h>
#include <stdio.h>
#include <search.h>

struct node {
      char *string;
      int length;
};
char string_space[10000];
struct node nodes[500];
void *root = NULL;

int node_compare(const void *node1, const void *node2) {
      return strcmp(((const struct node *) node1)->string,
              ((const struct node *) node2)->string);
}

void print_node(void **node, VISIT order, int level) {
      if (order == preorder || order == leaf) {
            printf("length=%d, string=%20s\n",
            (*(struct node **)node)->length,
            (*(struct node **)node)->string);
      }
}

main() {
      char *strptr = string_space;
      struct node *nodeptr = nodes;
      int i = 0;

      while (gets(strptr) != NULL && i++ < 500) {
            nodeptr->string = strptr;
            nodeptr->length = strlen(strptr);
            (void) tsearch((void *)nodeptr,
                   &root, node_compare);
            strptr += nodeptr->length + 1;
            nodeptr++;
      }
      twalk(root, print_node);
}
```

tsearch (3C)

SEE ALSO
bsearch(3C), hsearch(3C), lsearch(3C).

DIAGNOSTICS
A NULL pointer is returned by tsearch if there is not enough space available to create a new node.

A NULL pointer is returned by tfind and tdelete if *rootp* is NULL on entry.

If the datum is found, both tsearch and tfind return a pointer to it. If not, tfind returns NULL, and tsearch returns a pointer to the inserted item.

NOTES
The root argument to twalk is one level of indirection less than the *rootp* arguments to tsearch and tdelete.

There are two nomenclatures used to refer to the order in which tree nodes are visited. tsearch uses preorder, postorder and endorder to refer respectively to visiting a node before any of its children, after its left child and before its right, and after both its children. The alternate nomenclature uses preorder, inorder and postorder to refer to the same visits, which could result in some confusion over the meaning of postorder.

If the calling function alters the pointer to the root, results are unpredictable.

ttyname(3C)

NAME
ttyname, isatty – find name of a terminal

SYNOPSIS
#include <stdlib.h>

char *ttyname (int fildes);

int isatty (int fildes);

DESCRIPTION
ttyname returns a pointer to a string containing the null-terminated path name of the terminal device associated with file descriptor *fildes*.

isatty returns 1 if *fildes* is associated with a terminal device, 0 otherwise.

FILES
/dev/*

DIAGNOSTICS
ttyname returns a NULL pointer if *fildes* does not describe a terminal device in directory /dev.

NOTES
The return value points to static data whose content is overwritten by each call.

ttyslot(3C)

NAME
ttyslot – find the slot in the utmp file of the current user

SYNOPSIS
#include <stdlib.h>

int ttyslot (void);

DESCRIPTION
ttyslot returns the index of the current user's entry in the /var/adm/utmp file. The returned index is accomplished by scanning files in /dev for the name of the terminal associated with the standard input, the standard output, or the standard error output (0, 1, or 2).

FILES
/var/adm/utmp

SEE ALSO
getut(3C), ttyname(3C)

DIAGNOSTICS
A value of −1 is returned if an error was encountered while searching for the terminal name or if none of the above file descriptors are associated with a terminal device.

NAME
ualarm − schedule signal after interval in microseconds

SYNOPSIS
cc [*flag*...] *file* ... −lucb

unsigned ualarm(value, interval)
unsigned value;
unsigned interval;

DESCRIPTION
ualarm sends signal SIGALRM [see signal(3)], to the invoking process in a number of microseconds given by the *value* argument. Unless caught or ignored, the signal terminates the process.

If the *interval* argument is non-zero, the SIGALRM signal will be sent to the process every *interval* microseconds after the timer expires (for instance, after *value* microseconds have passed).

Because of scheduling delays, resumption of execution of when the signal is caught may be delayed an arbitrary amount. The longest specifiable delay time is 2147483647 microseconds.

The return value is the amount of time previously remaining in the alarm clock.

NOTES
ualarm is a simplified interface to setitimer; see getitimer(2).

SEE ALSO
sigpause(3), sigvec(3), signal(3), sleep(3), usleep(3)

alarm(2), getitimer(3) in the *Programmer's Reference Manual*

NAME

ungetc – push character back onto input stream

SYNOPSIS

#include <stdio.h>

int ungetc (int *c*, FILE *stream*);

DESCRIPTION

ungetc inserts the character specified by *c* (converted to an unsigned char) into the buffer associated with an input *stream* [see intro(3)]. That character, *c*, will be returned by the next getc(3S) call on that *stream*. ungetc returns *c*, and leaves the file corresponding to *stream* unchanged. A successful call to ungetc clears the EOF indicator for stream.

Four bytes of pushback are guaranteed.

The value of the file position indicator for *stream* after reading or discarding all pushed-back characters will be the same as it was before the characters were pushed back.

If *c* equals EOF, ungetc does nothing to the buffer and returns EOF.

fseek, rewind [both described on fseek(3S)], and fsetpos erase the memory of inserted characters for the stream on which they are applied.

SEE ALSO

fseek(3S), fsetpos(3C), getc(3S), setbuf(3S), stdio(3S).

DIAGNOSTICS

ungetc returns EOF if it cannot insert the character.

NAME
unlockpt – unlock a pseudo-terminal master/slave pair

SYNOPSIS
`int unlockpt(int fildes);`

DESCRIPTION
The function unlockpt() clears a lock flag associated with the slave pseudo-terminal device associated with its master pseudo-terminal counterpart so that the slave pseudo-terminal device can be opened. *fildes* is a file descriptor returned from a successful open of a master pseudo-terminal device.

RETURN VALUE
Upon successful completion, the function unlockpt() returns 0; otherwise it returns −1. A failure may occur if *fildes* is not an open file descriptor or is not associated with a master pseudo-terminal device.

SEE ALSO
open(2)

grantpt(3C), ptsname(3C) in the *Programmer's Guide: STREAMS*

NAME

usleep – suspend execution for interval in microseconds

SYNOPSIS

cc [*flag*. . .] *file* . . . −lucb

usleep(useconds)
unsigned useconds;

DESCRIPTION

Suspend the current process for the number of microseconds specified by the argument. The actual suspension time may be an arbitrary amount longer because of other activity in the system, or because of the time spent in processing the call.

The routine is implemented by setting an interval timer and pausing until it occurs. The previous state of this timer is saved and restored. If the sleep time exceeds the time to the expiration of the previous timer, the process sleeps only until the signal would have occurred, and the signal is sent a short time later.

This routine is implemented using setitimer [see getitimer(2)]; it requires eight system calls each time it is invoked.

SEE ALSO

sigpause(3), sleep(3), ualarm(3)

getitimer(3), alarm(2) in the *Programmer's Reference Manual*

utimes(3) (BSD Compatibility Package) **utimes(3)**

NAME
utimes – set file times

SYNOPSIS
cc [*flag*...] *file* ... -lucb

#include <sys/types.h>

int utimes(file, tvp)
char *file;
struct timeval *tvp;

DESCRIPTION
utimes sets the access and modification times of the file named by *file*.

If *tvp* is NULL, the access and modification times are set to the current time. A process must be the owner of the file or have write permission for the file to use utimes in this manner.

If *tvp* is not NULL, it is assumed to point to an array of two timeval structures. The access time is set to the value of the first member, and the modification time is set to the value of the second member. Only the owner of the file or the privileged user may use utimes in this manner.

In either case, the *inode-changed* time of the file is set to the current time.

RETURN VALUE
Upon successful completion, a value of 0 is returned. Otherwise, a value of −1 is returned and errno is set to indicate the error.

ERRORS
utimes will fail if one or more of the following are true:

ENOTDIR	A component of the path prefix of *file* is not a directory.
ENAMETOOLONG	The length of a component of *file* exceeds 255 characters, or the length of *file* exceeds 1023 characters.
ENOENT	The file referred to by *file* does not exist.
EACCES	Search permission is denied for a component of the path prefix of *file*.
ELOOP	Too many symbolic links were encountered in translating *file*.
EPERM	The effective user ID of the process is not privileged user and not the owner of the file, and *tvp* is not NULL.
EACCES	The effective user ID of the process is not privileged user and not the owner of the file, write permission is denied for the file, and *tvp* is NULL.
EIO	An I/O error occurred while reading from or writing to the file system.
EROFS	The file system containing the file is mounted read-only.

utimes(3) (BSD Compatibility Package) **utimes(3)**

       EFAULT   *file* or *tvp* points outside the process's allocated address space.

SEE ALSO
    stat(2), utime(2) in the *Programmer's Reference Manual*

NOTES
    utimes is a library routine that calls the utime system call.

NAME

vprintf, vfprintf, vsprintf – print formatted output of a variable argument list

SYNOPSIS

```
#include <stdio.h>
#include <stdarg.h>
```

int vprintf(const char *format, va_list ap);

int vfprintf(FILE *stream, const char *format, va_list ap);

int vsprintf(char *s, const char *format, va_list ap);

DESCRIPTION

vprintf, vfprintf and vsprintf are the same as printf, fprintf, and sprintf respectively, except that instead of being called with a variable number of arguments, they are called with an argument list as defined by the stdarg.h header file.

The stdarg.h header file defines the type va_list and a set of macros for advancing through a list of arguments whose number and types may vary. The argument ap to the vprint family of routines is of type va_list. This argument is used with the stdarg.h header file macros va_start, va_arg and va_end [see va_start, va_arg, and va_end in stdarg(5)]. The EXAMPLE section below shows their use with vprintf.

EXAMPLE

The following demonstrates how vfprintf could be used to write an error routine:

```
#include <stdio.h>
#include <stdarg.h>
/*
 *    error should be called like
 *         error(function_name, format, arg1, . . .);
 */
void error(char *function_name, char *format, . . .)
{
    va_list ap;

    va_start(ap, format);
    /* print out name of function causing error */
    (void) fprintf(stderr, "ERR in %s: ", function_name);
    va_arg(ap, char*);
    /* print out remainder of message */
    (void) vfprintf(stderr, format, ap);
    va_end(ap);
    (void) abort;
}
```

SEE ALSO
    printf(3S), stdarg(5)
DIAGNOSTICS
    vprintf and vfprintf return the number of characters transmitted, or return −1 if an error was encountered.

NAME
wait, wait3, WIFSTOPPED, WIFSIGNALED, WIFEXITED — wait for process to terminate or stop

SYNOPSIS
cc [*flag*. . .] *file* . . . -lucb

#include <sys/wait.h>

int wait(statusp)
union wait *statusp;

#include <sys/time.h>
#include <sys/resource.h>

int wait3(statusp, options, rusage)
union wait *statusp;
int options;
struct rusage *rusage;

WIFSTOPPED(status)
union wait status;

WIFSIGNALED(status)
union wait status;

WIFEXITED(status)
union wait status;

DESCRIPTION
wait delays its caller until a signal is received or one of its child processes terminates or stops due to tracing. If any child has died or stopped due to tracing and this has not been reported using wait, return is immediate, returning the process ID and exit status of one of those children. If that child had died, it is discarded. If there are no children, return is immediate with the value −1 returned. If there are only running or stopped but reported children, the calling process is blocked.

If *status* is not a NULL pointer, then on return from a successful wait call the status of the child process whose process ID is the return value of wait is stored in the wait union pointed to by *status*. The w_status member of that union is an int; it indicates the cause of termination and other information about the terminated process in the following manner:

- If the low-order 8 bits of w_status are equal to 0177, the child process has stopped; the 8 bits higher up from the low-order 8 bits of w_status contain the number of the signal that caused the process to stop. See ptrace(2) and sigvec(3).

- If the low-order 8 bits of w_status are non-zero and are not equal to 0177, the child process terminated due to a signal; the low-order 7 bits of w_status contain the number of the signal that terminated the process. In addition, if the low-order seventh bit of w_status (that is, bit 0200) is set, a "core image" of the process was produced; see sigvec(3).

- Otherwise, the child process terminated due to an exit call; the 8 bits higher up from the low-order 8 bits of w_status contain the low-order 8 bits of the argument that the child process passed to exit; see exit(2).

Other members of the wait union can be used to extract this information more conveniently:

- If the w_stopval member has the value WSTOPPED, the child process has stopped; the value of the w_stopsig member is the signal that stopped the process.
- If the w_termsig member is non-zero, the child process terminated due to a signal; the value of the w_termsig member is the number of the signal that terminated the process. If the w_coredump member is non-zero, a core dump was produced.
- Otherwise, the child process terminated due to an exit call; the value of the w_retcode member is the low-order 8 bits of the argument that the child process passed to exit.

The other members of the wait union merely provide an alternate way of analyzing the status. The value stored in the w_status field is compatible with the values stored by other versions of the UNIX system, and an argument of type int * may be provided instead of an argument of type union wait * for compatibility with those versions.

wait3 is an alternate interface that allows both non-blocking status collection and the collection of the status of children stopped by any means. The *status* parameter is defined as above. The *options* parameter is used to indicate the call should not block if there are no processes that have status to report (WNOHANG), and/or that children of the current process that are stopped due to a SIGTTIN, SIGTTOU, SIGTSTP, or SIGSTOP signal are eligible to have their status reported as well (WUNTRACED). A terminated child is discarded after it reports status, and a stopped process will not report its status more than once. If *rusage* is not a NULL pointer, a summary of the resources used by the terminated process and all its children is returned. Only the user time used and the system time used are currently available. They are returned in rusage.ru_utime and rusage.ru_stime, respectively.

When the WNOHANG option is specified and no processes have status to report, wait3 returns 0. The WNOHANG and WUNTRACED options may be combined by ORing the two values.

WIFSTOPPED, WIFSIGNALED, WIFEXITED, are macros that take an argument *status*, of type 'union wait', as returned by wait, or wait3. WIFSTOPPED evaluates to true (1) when the process for which the wait call was made is stopped, or to false (0) otherwise. WIFSIGNALED evaluates to true when the process was terminated with a signal. WIFEXITED evaluates to true when the process exited by using an exit(2) call.

RETURN VALUE

If wait returns due to a stopped or terminated child process, the process ID of the child is returned to the calling process. Otherwise, a value of −1 is returned and errno is set to indicate the error.

wait3 returns 0 if WNOHANG is specified and there are no stopped or exited children, and returns the process ID of the child process if it returns due to a stopped or terminated child process. Otherwise, wait3 returns a value of −1 and sets errno to indicate the error.

ERRORS

wait, or wait3 will fail and return immediately if one or more of the following are true:

ECHILD   The calling process has no existing unwaited-for child processes.

EFAULT   The *status* or *rusage* arguments point to an illegal address.

wait, and wait3 will terminate prematurely, return −1, and set errno to EINTR upon the arrival of a signal whose SV_INTERRUPT bit in its flags field is set [see sigvec(3) and siginterrupt(3)]. signal(3), in the System V compatibility library, sets this bit for any signal it catches.

SEE ALSO

sigvec(3), getrusage(3), siginterrupt(3), signal(3)

exit(2), ptrace(2), signal(2) wait(2), waitpid(2) in the *Programmer's Reference Manual*

NOTES

If a parent process terminates without waiting on its children, the initialization process (process ID = 1) inherits the children.

wait, and wait3 are automatically restarted when a process receives a signal while awaiting termination of a child process, unless the SV_INTERRUPT bit is set in the flags for that signal.

Calls to wait with an argument of 0 should be cast to type 'union wait *', as in:

    wait((union wait *)0)

Otherwise lint will complain.

xdr(3N)

NAME
xdr – library routines for external data representation

DESCRIPTION
XDR routines allow C programmers to describe arbitrary data structures in a machine-independent fashion. Data for remote procedure calls (RPC) are transmitted using these routines.

Index to Routines
The following table lists XDR routines and the manual reference pages on which they are described:

XDR Routine	Manual Reference Page
xdr_array	xdr_complex(3N)
xdr_bool	xdr_simple(3N)
xdr_bytes	xdr_complex(3N)
xdr_char	xdr_simple(3N)
xdr_destroy	xdr_create(3N)
xdr_double	xdr_simple(3N)
xdr_enum	xdr_simple(3N)
xdr_float	xdr_simple(3N)
xdr_free	xdr_simple(3N)
xdr_getpos	xdr_admin(3N)
xdr_inline	xdr_admin(3N)
xdr_int	xdr_simple(3N)
xdr_long	xdr_simple(3N)
xdr_opaque	xdr_complex(3N)
xdr_pointer	xdr_complex(3N)
xdr_reference	xdr_complex(3N)
xdr_setpos	xdr_admin(3N)
xdr_short	xdr_simple(3N)
xdr_string	xdr_complex(3N)
xdr_u_char	xdr_simple(3N)
xdr_u_long	xdr_simple(3N)
xdr_u_short	xdr_simple(3N)
xdr_union	xdr_complex(3N)
xdr_vector	xdr_complex(3N)
xdr_void	xdr_simple(3N)
xdr_wrapstring	xdr_complex(3N)
xdrmem_create	xdr_create(3N)
xdrrec_create	xdr_create(3N)
xdrrec_eof	xdr_admin(3N)
xdrstdio_create	xdr_create(3N)

SEE ALSO
xdr_admin(3N), xdr_complex(3N), xdr_create(3N), xdr_simple(3N), rpc(3N).

NAME

xdr_admin: xdr_getpos, xdr_inline, xdrrec_eof, xdr_setpos – library routines for external data representation

DESCRIPTION

XDR library routines allow C programmers to describe arbitrary data structures in a machine-independent fashion. Protocols such as remote procedure calls (RPC) use these routines to describe the format of the data.

These routines deal specifically with the management of the XDR stream.

Routines

See rpc(3N) for the definition of the XDR data structure.

```
#include <rpc/xdr.h>

u_int
xdr_getpos(const XDR *xdrs);
```

A macro that invokes the get-position routine associated with the XDR stream, *xdrs*. The routine returns an unsigned integer, which indicates the position of the XDR byte stream. A desirable feature of XDR streams is that simple arithmetic works with this number, although the XDR stream instances need not guarantee this. Therefore, applications written for portability should not depend on this feature.

```
long *
xdr_inline(XDR *xdrs; const int len);
```

A macro that invokes the in-line routine associated with the XDR stream, *xdrs*. The routine returns a pointer to a contiguous piece of the stream's buffer; *len* is the byte length of the desired buffer. Note: pointer is cast to long *.

Note: xdr_inline may return NULL (0) if it cannot allocate a contiguous piece of a buffer. Therefore the behavior may vary among stream instances; it exists for the sake of efficiency, and applications written for portability should not depend on this feature.

```
bool_t
xdrrec_eof(XDR *xdrs);
```

This routine can be invoked only on streams created by xdrrec_create. After consuming the rest of the current record in the stream, this routine returns 1 if the stream has no more input, 0 otherwise.

```
bool_t
xdr_setpos(XDR *xdrs, const u_int pos);
```

A macro that invokes the set position routine associated with the XDR stream *xdrs*. The parameter *pos* is a position value obtained from xdr_getpos. This routine returns 1 if the XDR stream was repositioned, and 0 otherwise.

Note: it is difficult to reposition some types of XDR streams, so this routine may fail with one type of stream and succeed with another. Therefore, applications written for portability should not depend on this feature.

SEE ALSO
 rpc(3N), xdr_complex(3N), xdr_create(3N), xdr_simple(3N)

NAME

xdr_complex: xdr_array, xdr_bytes, xdr_opaque, xdr_pointer, xdr_reference, xdr_string, xdr_union, xdr_vector, xdr_wrapstring – library routines for external data representation

DESCRIPTION

XDR library routines allow C programmers to describe complex data structures in a machine-independent fashion. Protocols such as remote procedure calls (RPC) use these routines to describe the format of the data. These routines are the XDR library routines for complex data structures. They require the creation of XDR stream [see xdr_create(3N)].

Routines

See rpc(3N) for the definition of the XDR data structure.

```
#include <rpc/xdr.h>

bool_t
xdr_array(XDR *xdrs, caddr_t *arrp, u_int *sizep,
      const u_int maxsize, const u_int elsize,
      const xdrproc_t elproc);
```

xdr_array translates between variable-length arrays and their corresponding external representations. The parameter *arrp* is the address of the pointer to the array, while *sizep* is the address of the element count of the array; this element count cannot exceed *maxsize*. The parameter *elsize* is the sizeof each of the array's elements, and *elproc* is an XDR routine that translates between the array elements' C form and their external representation. This routine returns 1 if it succeeds, 0 otherwise.

```
bool_t
xdr_bytes(XDR *xdrs, char **sp, u_int *sizep,
      const u_int maxsize);
```

xdr_bytes translates between counted byte strings and their external representations. The parameter *sp* is the address of the string pointer. The length of the string is located at address *sizep*; strings cannot be longer than *maxsize*. This routine returns 1 if it succeeds, 0 otherwise.

```
bool_t
xdr_opaque(XDR *xdrs, caddr_t cp, const u_int cnt);
```

xdr_opaque translates between fixed size opaque data and its external representation. The parameter *cp* is the address of the opaque object, and *cnt* is its size in bytes. This routine returns 1 if it succeeds, 0 otherwise.

```
bool_t
xdr_pointer(XDR *xdrs, char **objpp, u_int objsize,
      const xdrproc_t xdrobj);
```

Like xdr_reference except that it serializes NULL pointers, whereas xdr_reference does not. Thus, xdr_pointer can represent recursive data structures, such as binary trees or linked lists.

xdr_complex(3N)

```
bool_t
xdr_reference(XDR *xdrs, caddr_t *pp, u_int size,
     const xdrproc_t proc);
```

> xdr_reference provides pointer chasing within structures. The parameter *pp* is the address of the pointer; *size* is the sizeof the structure that **pp* points to; and *proc* is an XDR procedure that translates the structure between its C form and its external representation. This routine returns 1 if it succeeds, 0 otherwise.
>
> Note: this routine does not understand NULL pointers. Use xdr_pointer instead.

```
bool_t
xdr_string(XDR *xdrs, char **sp, const u_int maxsize);
```

> xdr_string translates between C strings and their corresponding external representations. Strings cannot be longer than *maxsize*. Note: *sp* is the address of the string's pointer. This routine returns 1 if it succeeds, 0 otherwise.

```
bool_t
xdr_union(XDR *xdrs, enum_t *dscmp, char *unp,
     const struct xdr_discrim *choices,
     const bool_t (*defaultarm)(const XDR *, const char *,
         const int));
```

> xdr_union translates between a discriminated C union and its corresponding external representation. It first translates the discriminant of the union located at *dscmp*. This discriminant is always an enum_t. Next the union located at *unp* is translated. The parameter *choices* is a pointer to an array of xdr_discrim structures. Each structure contains an ordered pair of [*value, proc*]. If the union's discriminant is equal to the associated *value*, then the *proc* is called to translate the union. The end of the xdr_discrim structure array is denoted by a routine of value NULL. If the discriminant is not found in the *choices* array, then the *defaultarm* procedure is called (if it is not NULL). Returns 1 if it succeeds, 0 otherwise.

```
bool_t
xdr_vector(XDR *xdrs, char *arrp, const u_int size,
     const u_int elsize, const xdrproc_t elproc);
```

> xdr_vector translates between fixed-length arrays and their corresponding external representations. The parameter *arrp* is the address of the pointer to the array, while *size* is is the element count of the array. The parameter *elsize* is the sizeof each of the array's elements, and *elproc* is an XDR routine that translates between the array elements' C form and their external representation. This routine returns 1 if it succeeds, 0 otherwise.

```
bool_t
xdr_wrapstring(XDR *xdrs, char **sp);
```
  A routine that calls `xdr_string`(*xdrs*, *sp*, *maxuint*); where *maxuint* is the maximum value of an unsigned integer.

  Many routines, such as `xdr_array`, `xdr_pointer` and `xdr_vector` take a function pointer of type `xdrproc_t`, which takes two arguments. `xdr_string`, one of the most frequently used routines, requires three arguments, while `xdr_wrapstring` only requires two. For these routines, `xdr_wrapstring` is desirable. This routine returns 1 if it succeeds, 0 otherwise.

SEE ALSO
  rpc(3N), xdr_admin(3N), xdr_create(3N), xdr_simple(3N)

NAME

xdr_create: xdr_destroy, xdrmem_create, xdrrec_create, xdrstdio_create – library routines for external data representation stream creation

DESCRIPTION

XDR library routines allow C programmers to describe arbitrary data structures in a machine-independent fashion. Protocols such as remote procedure calls (RPC) use these routines to describe the format of the data.

These routines deal with the creation of XDR streams. XDR streams have to be created before any data can be translated into XDR format.

Routines

See rpc(3N) for the definition of the XDR, CLIENT, and SVCXPRT data structures.

```
#include <rpc/xdr.h>

void
xdr_destroy(XDR *xdrs);
```

A macro that invokes the destroy routine associated with the XDR stream, *xdrs*. Destruction usually involves freeing private data structures associated with the stream. Using *xdrs* after invoking xdr_destroy is undefined.

```
void
xdrmem_create(XDR *xdrs, const caddr_t addr,
     const u_int size, const enum xdr_op op);
```

This routine initializes the XDR stream object pointed to by *xdrs*. The stream's data is written to, or read from, a chunk of memory at location *addr* whose length is no more than *size* bytes long. The *op* determines the direction of the XDR stream (either XDR_ENCODE, XDR_DECODE, or XDR_FREE).

```
void
xdrrec_create(XDR *xdrs, const u_int sendsz,
     const u_int recvsz, const caddr_t handle,
     const int (*readit)(const void *, char *, const int),
     const int (*writeit)(const void *, const char *, const int));
```

This routine initializes the XDR stream object pointed to by *xdrs*. The stream's data is written to a buffer of size *sendsz*; a value of 0 indicates the system should use a suitable default. The stream's data is read from a buffer of size *recvsz*; it too can be set to a suitable default by passing a 0 value. When a stream's output buffer is full, *writeit* is called. Similarly, when a stream's input buffer is empty, *readit* is called. The behavior of these two routines is similar to the system calls read and write [see read(2) and write(2), respectively], except that *handle* (CLIENT, or SVCXPRT) is passed to the former routines as the first parameter instead of a file descriptor. Note: the XDR stream's *op* field must be set by the caller.

Note: this XDR stream implements an intermediate record stream. Therefore there are additional bytes in the stream to provide record boundary information.

void
xdrstdio_create(XDR *xdrs, FILE *file, const enum xdr_op op);

This routine initializes the XDR stream object pointed to by *xdrs*. The XDR stream data is written to, or read from, the standard I/O stream *file*. The parameter *op* determines the direction of the XDR stream (either XDR_ENCODE, XDR_DECODE, or XDR_FREE).

Note: the destroy routine associated with such XDR streams calls fflush on the *file* stream, but never fclose [see fclose(3S)].

SEE ALSO

fclose(3S), read(2), rpc(3N), write(2), xdr_admin(3N), xdr_complex(3N), xdr_simple(3N)

xdr_simple(3N)

NAME
xdr_simple: xdr_bool, xdr_char, xdr_double, xdr_enum, xdr_float, xdr_free, xdr_int, xdr_long, xdr_short, xdr_u_char, xdr_u_long, xdr_u_short, xdr_void – library routines for external data representation

DESCRIPTION
XDR library routines allow C programmers to describe simple data structures in a machine-independent fashion. Protocols such as remote procedure calls (RPC) use these routines to describe the format of the data.

These routines require the creation of XDR streams [see xdr_create(3N)].

Routines
See rpc(3N) for the definition of the XDR data structure.

```
#include <rpc/xdr.h>

bool_t
xdr_bool(XDR *xdrs, bool_t *bp);
```

xdr_bool translates between booleans (C integers) and their external representations. When encoding data, this filter produces values of either 1 or 0. This routine returns 1 if it succeeds, 0 otherwise.

```
bool_t
xdr_char(XDR *xdrs, char *cp);
```

xdr_char translates between C characters and their external representations. This routine returns 1 if it succeeds, 0 otherwise. Note: encoded characters are not packed, and occupy 4 bytes each. For arrays of characters, it is worthwhile to consider xdr_bytes, xdr_opaque or xdr_string [see xdr_bytes, xdr_opaque and xdr_string in xdr_complex(3N)].

```
bool_t
xdr_double(XDR *xdrs, double *dp);
```

xdr_double translates between C double precision numbers and their external representations. This routine returns 1 if it succeeds, 0 otherwise.

```
bool_t
xdr_enum(XDR *xdrs, enum_t *ep);
```

xdr_enum translates between C enums (actually integers) and their external representations. This routine returns 1 if it succeeds, 0 otherwise.

```
bool_t
xdr_float(XDR *xdrs, float *fp);
```

xdr_float translates between C floats and their external representations. This routine returns 1 if it succeeds, 0 otherwise.

```
void
xdr_free(xdrproc_t proc, char *objp);
```

Generic freeing routine. The first argument is the XDR routine for the object being freed. The second argument is a pointer to the object itself. Note: the pointer passed to this routine is not freed, but what it points to is freed (recursively).

```
bool_t
xdr_int(XDR *xdrs, int *ip);
```
    xdr_int translates between C integers and their external representations. This routine returns 1 if it succeeds, 0 otherwise.

```
bool_t
xdr_long(XDR *xdrs, long *lp);
```
    xdr_long translates between C long integers and their external representations. This routine returns 1 if it succeeds, 0 otherwise.

```
bool_t
xdr_short(XDR *xdrs, short *sp);
```
    xdr_short translates between C short integers and their external representations. This routine returns 1 if it succeeds, 0 otherwise.

```
bool_t
xdr_u_char(XDR *xdrs, char *ucp);
```
    xdr_u_char translates between unsigned C characters and their external representations. This routine returns 1 if it succeeds, 0 otherwise.

```
bool_t
xdr_u_long(XDR *xdrs, unsigned long *ulp);
```
    xdr_u_long translates between C unsigned long integers and their external representations. This routine returns 1 if it succeeds, 0 otherwise.

```
bool_t
xdr_u_short(XDR *xdrs, unsigned short *usp);
```
    xdr_u_short translates between C unsigned short integers and their external representations. This routine returns 1 if it succeeds, 0 otherwise.

```
bool_t
xdr_void(void);
```
    This routine always returns 1. It may be passed to RPC routines that require a function parameter, where nothing is to be done.

SEE ALSO
rpc(3N), xdr_admin(3N), xdr_complex(3N), xdr_create(3N)

ypclnt(3N)

NAME
ypclnt, yp_get_default_domain, yp_bind, yp_unbind, yp_match, yp_first, yp_next, yp_all, yp_order, yp_master, yperr_string, ypprot_err – NIS client interface

SYNOPSIS
#include <rpcsvc/ypclnt.h>
#include <rpcsvc/yp_prot.h>

DESCRIPTION
This package of functions provides an interface to the NIS network lookup service. The package can be loaded from the standard library, /usr/lib/libnsl.{so,a}. Refer to ypfiles(4) and ypserv(1M) for an overview of the NIS name services, including the definitions of *map* and *domain*, and a description of the various servers, databases, and commands that comprise the NIS name service.

All input parameters names begin with *in*. Output parameters begin with *out*. Output parameters of type char ** should be addresses of uninitialized character pointers. Memory is allocated by the NIS client package using malloc(3), and may be freed if the user code has no continuing need for it. For each *outkey* and *outval*, two extra bytes of memory are allocated at the end that contain newline and NULL, respectively, but these two bytes are not reflected in *outkeylen* or *outvallen*. *indomain* and *inmap* strings must be non-NULL and NULL-terminated. String parameters which are accompanied by a count parameter may not be NULL, but may point to NULL strings, with the count parameter indicating this. Counted strings need not be NULL-terminated.

All functions in this package of type *int* return 0 if they succeed, and a failure code (ERR_*xxxx*) otherwise. Failure codes are described under DIAGNOSTICS below.

Routines
int yp_bind (char *indomain);

> To use the NIS name services, the client process must be bound to a NIS server that serves the appropriate domain using yp_bind. Binding need not be done explicitly by user code; this is done automatically whenever a NIS lookup function is called. yp_bind can be called directly for processes that make use of a backup strategy (for example, a local file) in cases when NIS services are not available.

void yp_unbind (char *indomain);

> Each binding allocates (uses up) one client process socket descriptor; each bound domain costs one socket descriptor. However, multiple requests to the same domain use that same descriptor. yp_unbind is available at the client interface for processes that explicitly manage their socket descriptors while accessing multiple domains. The call to yp_unbind make the domain *unbound*, and free all per-process and per-node resources used to bind it.

If an RPC failure results upon use of a binding, that domain will be unbound automatically. At that point, the ypclnt layer will retry forever or until the operation succeeds, provided that ypbind is running, and either the client process cannot bind a server for the proper domain or RPC requests to the server fail.

If an error is not RPC-related, or if ypbind is not running, or if a bound ypserv process returns any answer (success or failure), the ypclnt layer will return control to the user code, either with an error code, or a success code and any results.

int yp_get_default_domain (char **outdomain);

The NIS lookup calls require a map name and a domain name, at minimum. It is assumed that the client process knows the name of the map of interest. Client processes should fetch the node's default domain by calling yp_get_default_domain, and use the returned *outdomain* as the *indomain* parameter to successive NIS name service calls.

int yp_match(char *indomain, char *inmap, char *inkey,
        int inkeylen, char **outval, int *outvallen);

yp_match returns the value associated with a passed key. This key must be exact; no pattern matching is available.

int yp_first(char *indomain, char *inmap, char **outkey,
        int *outkeylen, char **outval, int *outvallen);

yp_first returns the first key-value pair from the named map in the named domain.

int yp_next(char *indomain, char *inmap, char *inkey,
        int inkeylen, char **outkey, int *outkeylen,
        char **outval, int *outvallen);

yp_next returns the next key-value pair in a named map. The *inkey* parameter should be the *outkey* returned from an initial call to yp_first (to get the second key-value pair) or the one returned from the *n*th call to yp_next (to get the *n*th + second key-value pair).

The concept of first (and, for that matter, of next) is particular to the structure of the NIS map being processing; there is no relation in retrieval order to either the lexical order within any original (non-NIS name service) data base, or to any obvious numerical sorting order on the keys, values, or key-value pairs. The only ordering guarantee made is that if the yp_first function is called on a particular map, and then the yp_next function is repeatedly called on the same map at the same server until the call fails with a reason of YPERR_NOMORE, every entry in the data base will be seen exactly once. Further, if the same sequence of operations is performed on the same map at the same server, the entries will be seen in the same order.

Under conditions of heavy server load or server failure, it is possible for the domain to become unbound, then bound once again (perhaps to a different server) while a client is running. This can cause a break in one of the enumeration rules; specific entries may be seen twice by the client, or not at all. This approach protects the client from error messages that would otherwise be returned in the midst of the enumeration. The next paragraph describes a better solution to enumerating all entries in a map.

```
int yp_all(char *indomain, char *inmap,
           struct ypall_callback *incallback);
```

yp_all provides a way to transfer an entire map from server to client in a single request using TCP (rather than UDP as with other functions in this package). The entire transaction take place as a single RPC request and response. yp_all can be used just like any other NIS name service procedure, identify the map in the normal manner, and supply the name of a function which will be called to process each key-value pair within the map. The call to yp_all returns only when the transaction is completed (successfully or unsuccessfully), or the foreach function decides that it does not want to see any more key-value pairs.

The third parameter to yp_all is

```
struct ypall_callback *incallback {
    int (*foreach)();
    char *data;
};
```

The function foreach is called

```
int foreach(int instatus, char *inkey, int inkeylen,
            char *inval, int invallen, char *indata);
```

The *instatus* parameter will hold one of the return status values defined in rpcsvc/yp_prot.h—either YP_TRUE or an error code. (See ypprot_err, below, for a function which converts a NIS name service protocol error code to a ypclnt layer error code.)

The key and value parameters are somewhat different than defined in the synopsis section above. First, the memory pointed to by the *inkey* and *inval* parameters is private to the yp_all function, and is overwritten with the arrival of each new key-value pair. It is the responsibility of the foreach function to do something useful with the contents of that memory, but it does not own the memory itself. Key and value objects presented to the foreach function look exactly as they do in the server's map—if they were not newline-terminated or NULL-terminated in the map, they will not be here either.

The *indata* parameter is the contents of the incallback->data element passed to yp_all. The data element of the callback structure may be used to share state information between the foreach function and the mainline code. Its use is optional, and no part of the NIS client package inspects its contents—cast it to something useful, or ignore it.

ypclnt(3N)

The `foreach` function is a Boolean. It should return zero to indicate that it wants to be called again for further received key-value pairs, or non-zero to stop the flow of key-value pairs. If `foreach` returns a non-zero value, it is not called again; the functional value of `yp_all` is then 0.

`int yp_order(char *indomain, char *inmap, int *outorder);`

yp_order returns the order number for a map.

`int yp_master(char *indomain, char *inmap, char **outname);`

yp_master returns the machine name of the master NIS server for a map.

`char *yperr_string(int incode);`

yperr_string returns a pointer to an error message string that is NULL-terminated but contains no period or newline.

`int ypprot_err (unsigned int incode);`

ypprot_err takes a NIS name service protocol error code as input, and returns a ypclnt layer error code, which may be used in turn as an input to yperr_string.

FILES
/usr/lib/libyp.a

SEE ALSO
ypserv(1M), malloc(3), ypupdate(3N), ypfiles(4)

DIAGNOSTICS
All integer functions return 0 if the requested operation is successful, or one of the following errors if the operation fails.

1	YPERR_BADARGS	args to function are bad
2	YPERR_RPC	RPC failure – domain has been unbound
3	YPERR_DOMAIN	can't bind to server on this domain
4	YPERR_MAP	no such map in server's domain
5	YPERR_KEY	no such key in map
6	YPERR_YPERR	internal NIS server or client error
7	YPERR_RESRC	resource allocation failure
8	YPERR_NOMORE	no more records in map database
9	YPERR_PMAP	can't communicate with RPC binder
10	YPERR_YPBIND	can't communicate with ypbind
11	YPERR_YPSERV	can't communicate with ypserv
12	YPERR_NODOM	local domain name not set
13	YPERR_BADDB	NIS database is bad
14	YPERR_VERS	NIS version mismatch
15	YPERR_ACCESS	access violation
16	YPERR_BUSY	database busy

NAME

yp_update – change NIS information

SYNOPSIS

```
#include <rpcsvc/ypclnt.h>
```

```
yp_update(char *domain, char *map, unsigned ypop, char *key,
     int keylen, char *data, int datalen);
```

DESCRIPTION

yp_update is used to make changes to the NIS database. The syntax is the same as that of yp_match except for the extra parameter *ypop*, which may take on one of four values. If it is YPOP_CHANGE then the data associated with the key will be changed to the new value. If the key is not found in the database, then yp_update will return YPERR_KEY. If *ypop* has the value YPOP_INSERT then the key-value pair will be inserted into the database. The error YPERR_KEY is returned if the key already exists in the database. To store an item into the database without concern for whether it exists already or not, pass *ypop* as YPOP_STORE and no error will be returned if the key already or does not exist. To delete an entry, the value of *ypop* should be YPOP_DELETE.

This routine depends upon secure RPC, and will not work unless the network is running secure RPC.

SEE ALSO

secure_rpc(3N)

Section 4 – File Formats

intro(4)	introduction to file formats
a.out(4)	ELF (Executable and Linking Format) files
acct(4)	per-process accounting file format
admin(4)	installation defaults file
aliases, addresses, forward(4)	addresses and aliases for sendmail
ar(4)	archive file format
archives(4)	device header file
binarsys(4)	remote system information for the ckbinarsys command
boot(4)	boot
compver(4)	compatible versions file
copyright(4)	copyright information file
core(4)	core image file
cron(4)	cron
depend(4)	software dependencies files
dfstab(4)	file containing commands for sharing resources
dir (s5)(4)	format of s5 directories
dir (ufs)(4)	format of ufs directories
dirent(4)	file system independent directory entry
dump(4)	dump
ethers(4)	Ethernet address to hostname database or domain
/dev/fd(4)	file descriptor files
filehdr(4)	file header for common object files
fs (bfs)(4)	format of the bfs file system volume
fs (s5)(4)	format of s5 file system volume
fs (ufs)(4)	format of ufs file system volume
fspec(4)	format specification in text files
fstypes(4)	file that registers distributed file system packages
group(4)	group file
hosts(4)	host name data base
hosts.equiv, .rhosts(4)	trusted hosts by system and by user
inetd.conf(4)	Internet servers database
inittab(4)	script for init
inode (bfs)(4)	format of a bfs i-node
inode (s5)(4)	format of an s5 i-node
inode (ufs)(4)	format of a ufs inode
issue(4)	issue identification file
limits(4)	header file for implementation-specific constants
login(4)	login default file
loginlog(4)	log of failed login attempts

Section 4 – File Formats

mailcnfg(4)	initialization information for mail and rmail
mailsurr(4)	surrogate commands for routing and transport of mail
mapchan(4)	Format of tty device mapping files
mdevice (4)	file format
mdevice (4)	file format
mfsys (4)	file format
mnttab(4)	mounted file system table
mtune(4)	file format
netconfig(4)	network configuration database
netmasks(4)	network mask data base
netrc(4)	file for ftp remote login data
networks(4)	network name data base
passwd(4)	password file
pathalias(4)	alias file for FACE
pkginfo(4)	package characteristics file
pkgmap(4)	package contents description file
pnch(4)	file format for card images
/proc(4)	process file system
profile(4)	setting up an environment at login time
protocols(4)	protocol name data base
prototype(4)	package information file
publickey(4)	public key database
resolv.conf(4)	configuration file for name server routines
rfmaster(4)	Remote File Sharing name server master file
routing(4)	system supporting for packet network routing
rpc(4)	rpc program number data base
rt_dptbl(4)	real-time dispatcher parameter table
sccsfile(4)	format of SCCS file
sdevice (4)	file format
services(4)	Internet services and aliases
sfsys (4)	file format
shadow(4)	shadow password file
sharetab(4)	shared file system table
space(4)	disk space requirement file
stat(4)	data returned by stat system call
strcf(4)	STREAMS Configuration File for STREAMS TCP/IP
strftime(4)	language specific strings
stune (4)	file format
su(4)	su
syslog.conf(4)	configuration file for syslogd system log daemon

Section 4 – File Formats

term(4) .... format of compiled term file
terminfo(4) .... terminal capability data base
timezone(4) .... set default system time zone
ts_dptbl(4) .... time-sharing dispatcher parameter table
ttydefs(4) .... file contains terminal line settings information for ttymon
ttysrch(4) .... directory search list for ttyname
unistd(4) .... header file for symbolic constants
updaters(4) .... configuration file for Network Information Service (NIS) updating
utmp, wtmp(4) .... utmp and wtmp entry formats
utmpx, wtmpx(4) .... utmpx and wtmpx entry formats
vfstab(4) .... table of file system defaults
ypfiles(4) .... the Network Information Service (NIS) database and directory structure

Where To Find Section 4 Manual Pages

 Section 4 manual pages describing file formats been moved to the *System Files and Devices Reference Manual*. See the "Preface" for a description of the design changes to this Reference Manual set.

Section 5 – Miscellaneous Facilities

intro(5)	introduction to miscellany
ascii(5)	map of ASCII character set
environ(5)	user environment
eqnchar(5)	special character definitions for eqn
fcntl(5)	file control options
iconv(5)	code set conversion tables
jagent(5)	host control of windowing terminal
langinfo(5)	language information constants
layers(5)	protocol used between host and windowing terminal under layers(1)
man(5)	macros to format Reference Manual pages
math(5)	math functions and constants
me(5)	macros for formatting papers
ms(5)	text formatting macros
nl_types(5)	native language data types
prof(5)	profile within a function
regexp: compile, step, advance(5)	regular expression compile and match routines
siginfo(5)	signal generation information
signal(5)	base signals
stat(5)	data returned by stat system call
stdarg(5)	handle variable argument list
term(5)	conventional names for terminals
types(5)	primitive system data types
ucontext(5)	user context
values(5)	machine-dependent values
varargs(5)	handle variable argument list
wstat(5)	wait status
xtproto(5)	multiplexed channels protocol used by xt driver

SECTION 5 - MISCELLANEOUS FACILITIES

Where To Find Section 5 Manual Pages

 Section 5 manual pages describing miscellaneous facilities have been moved to the *System Files and Devices Reference Manual*. See the "Preface" for a description of the design changes to this Reference Manual set.

Permuted Index

l3tol, ltol3 convert between integer and base-64 ASCII string	3-byte integers and long integers .... l3tol(3C)
	a64l, l64a convert between long .... a64l(3C)
abort generate an	abnormal termination signal .... abort(3)
termination signal	abort generate an abnormal .... abort(3)
value	abs, labs return integer absolute .... abs(3C)
abs, labs return integer	absolute value .... abs(3C)
floor, ceiling, remainder,	absolute value functions /remainder .... floor(3M)
t_accept	accept a connect request .... t_accept(3N)
accept	accept a connection on a socket .... accept(3N)
socket	accept accept a connection on a .... accept(3N)
utime set file	access and modification times .... utime(2)
file	access determine accessibility of a .... access(2)
elf_next sequential archive member	access .... elf_next(3E)
elf_rand random archive member	access .... elf_rand(3E)
elf object file	access library .... elf(3E)
get or set supplementary group	access list IDs /setgroups .... getgroups(2)
initialize the supplementary group	access list initgroups .... initgroups(3C)
machine-independent/ sputl, sgetl	access long integer data in a .... sputl(3X)
sdgetv synchronize shared data	access .... sdgetv(2)
waitsem, nbwaitsem await and check	access to a resource governed by a/ .... waitsem(2)
sdenter, sdleave synchronize	access to a shared data segment .... sdenter(2)
device grantpt grant	access to the slave pseudo-terminal .... grantpt(3C)
setutent, endutent, utmpname	access utmp file entry /pututline, ... getut(3C)
getutmpx, updwtmp, updwtmpx	access utmpx file entry /getutmp, ... getutx(3C)
access determine	accessibility of a file .... access(2)
acct enable or disable process	accounting .... acct(2)
accounting	acct enable or disable process .... acct(2)
release indication t_rcvrel	acknowledge receipt of an orderly .... t_rcvrel(3N)
/cos, cosf, tan, tanf, asin, asinf,	acos, acosf, atan, atanf, atan2,/ .... trig(3M)
/cosf, tan, tanf, asin, asinf, acos,	acosf, atan, atanf, atan2, atan2f/ .... trig(3M)
/cosh, coshf, tanh, tanhf, asinh,	acosh, atanh hyperbolic functions .... sinh(3M)
to a/ /mvwaddch, echochar, wechochar	add a character (with attributes) .... curs_addch(3X)
/mvaddnstr, mvwaddstr, mvwaddnstr	add a string of characters to a/ .... curs_addstr(3X)
atexit	add program termination routine .... atexit(3C)
/mvwaddchstr, mvwaddchnstr	add string of characters (and/ .... curs_addchstr(3X)
putenv change or	add value to environment .... putenv(3C)
echochar, wechochar/ curs_addch:	addch, waddch, mvaddch, mvwaddch, ... curs_addch(3X)
curs_addchstr: addchstr,	addchnstr, waddchstr, waddchnstr,/ .... curs_addchstr(3X)
waddchnstr,/ curs_addchstr:	addchstr, addchnstr, waddchstr, ... curs_addchstr(3X)
mvaddstr,/ curs_addstr: addstr,	addnstr, waddstr, waddnstr, ... curs_addstr(3X)
inet_netof, inet_ntoa Internet	address manipulation /inet_lnaof, ... inet(3N)
ethers Ethernet	address mapping operations .... ethers(3N)
object dlsym get the	address of a symbol in shared .... dlsym(3X)
mlockall, munlockall lock or unlock	address space .... mlockall(3C)
t_bind bind an	address to a transport endpoint .... t_bind(3N)
severity levels for an application/	addseverity build a list of .... addseverity(3C)
mvaddstr, mvaddnstr,/ curs_addstr:	addstr, addnstr, waddstr, waddnstr, ... curs_addstr(3X)

Permuted Index

synchronization of the system/	adjtime correct the time to allow .... adjtime(2)
uadmin	administrative control .... uadmin(2)
attributes) to a curses window and	advance cursor /a character (with .... curs_addch(3X)
characters to a curses window and	advance cursor /add a string of .... curs_addstr(3X)
and match/ regexpr: compile, step,	advance regular expression compile .... regexpr(3G)
if forms field has off-screen data	ahead or behind /data_behind tell .... form_data(3X)
alarm set a process	alarm clock .... alarm(2)
	alarm set a process alarm clock .... alarm(2)
	alloca memory allocator .... alloca(3)
t_alloc	allocate a library structure .... t_alloc(3N)
brk, sbrk change data segment space	allocation .... brk(2)
alloca memory	allocator .... alloca(3)
calloc, memalign, valloc, memory	allocator malloc, free, realloc, ... malloc(3C)
calloc, mallopt, mallinfo memory	allocator malloc, free, realloc, ... malloc(3X)
calls siginterrupt	allow signals to interrupt system .... siginterrupt(3)
clock adjtime correct the time to	allow synchronization of the system .... adjtime(2)
scandir,	alphasort scan a directory .... scandir(3)
sigaltstack set or get signal	alternate stack context .... sigaltstack(2)
window /get a string of characters	(and attributes) from a curses .... curs_inchstr(3X)
/add string of characters	(and attributes) to a curses window .... curs_addchstr(3X)
sigstack set	and/or get signal stack context .... sigstack(3)
/field_just format the general	appearance of forms .... form_field_just(3X)
panel /panel_userptr associate	application data with a panels .... panel_userptr(3X)
/field_userptr associate	application data with forms .... form_field_userptr(3X)
/form_userptr associate	application data with forms .... form_userptr(3X)
/item_userptr associate	application data with menus items .... menu_item_userptr(3X)
/menu_userptr associate	application data with menus .... menu_userptr(3X)
/a list of severity levels for an	application for use with fmtmsg .... addseverity(3C)
coordinate ELF library and	application versions elf_version .... elf_version(3E)
/set_menu_term, menu_term assign	application-specific routines for/ .... menu_hook(3X)
/set_field_term, field_term assign	application-specific routines for/ .... form_hook(3X)
elf_next sequential	archive member access .... elf_next(3E)
elf_rand random	archive member access .... elf_rand(3E)
elf_getarhdr retrieve	archive member header .... elf_getarhdr(3E)
elf_getarsym retrieve	archive symbol table .... elf_getarsym(3E)
formatted output of a variable	argument list /vsprintf print .... vprintf(3S)
getopt get option letter from	argument vector .... getopt(3C)
miscellaneous functions for IEEE	arithmetic /isnan, copysign, scalbn .... ieee_functions(3M)
mfree multiple precision integer	arithmetic /sdiv, itom, xtom, mtox, ... mp(3X)
string strftime, cftime,	ascftime convert date and time to .... strftime(3C)
between long integer and base-64	ASCII string a64l, l64a convert .... a64l(3C)
time to/ ctime, localtime, gmtime,	asctime, tzset convert date and .... ctime(3C)
/sin, sinf, cos, cosf, tan, tanf,	asin, asinf, acos, acosf, atan,/ .... trig(3M)
/sinf, cos, cosf, tan, tanf, asin,	asinf, acos, acosf, atan, atanf,/ .... trig(3M)
/sinhf, cosh, coshf, tanh, tanhf,	asinh, acosh, atanh hyperbolic/ .... sinh(3M)
	assert verify program assertion .... assert(3X)

Programmer's Reference Manual: Operating System API

assert verify program	assertion .... assert(3X)
/menu_init, set_menu_term, menu_term	assign application-specific/ .... menu_hook(3X)
/set_field_term, field_term	assign application-specific/ .... form_hook(3X)
/setbuffer, setlinebuf, setvbuf	assign buffering to a stream .... setbuf(3S)
setbuf, setvbuf	assign buffering to a stream .... setbuf(3S)
setbuffer, setlinebuf	assign buffering to a stream .... setbuffer(3S)
/set_panel_userptr, panel_userptr	associate application data with a/ .... panel_userptr(3X)
/set_field_userptr, field_userptr	associate application data with/ .... form_field_userptr(3X)
/set_form_userptr, form_userptr	associate application data with/ .... form_userptr(3X)
/set_item_userptr, item_userptr	associate application data with/ .... menu_item_userptr(3X)
/set_menu_userptr, menu_userptr	associate application data with/ .... menu_userptr(3X)
write or erase forms from	associated subwindows /unpost_form .... form_post(3X)
write or erase menus from	associated subwindows /unpost_menu .... menu_post(3X)
forms window and subwindow	association routines /scale_form .... form_win(3X)
menus window and subwindow	association routines /scale_menu .... menu_win(3X)
tanf, asin, asinf, acos, acosf,	atan, atanf, atan2, atan2f/ /tan, ... trig(3M)
asinf, acos, acosf, atan, atanf,	atan2, atan2f trigonometric/ /asin, ... trig(3M)
/acos, acosf, atan, atanf, atan2,	atan2f trigonometric functions .... trig(3M)
/asin, asinf, acos, acosf, atan,	atanf, atan2, atan2f trigonometric/ .... trig(3M)
coshf, tanh, tanhf, asinh, acosh,	atanh hyperbolic functions /cosh, ... sinh(3M)
routine	atexit add program termination .... atexit(3C)
double-precision/ strtod, strtold,	atof convert string to .... strtod(3C)
strtol, strtoul, atol,	atoi convert string to integer .... strtol(3C)
integer strtol, strtoul,	atol, atoi convert string to .... strtol(3C)
descriptor to an object in/ fattach	attach a STREAMS-based file .... fattach(3C)
segment sdget, sdfree	attach and detach a shared data .... sdget(2)
/curses character and window	attribute control routines .... curs_attr(3X)
set and get forms field	attributes /set_max_field .... form_field_buffer(3X)
/mvwinch get a character and its	attributes from a curses window .... curs_inch(3X)
/get a string of characters (and	attributes) from a curses window .... curs_inchstr(3X)
menu_pad control menus display	attributes /set_menu_pad, ... menu_attributes(3X)
format the general display	attributes of forms /field_pad .... form_field_attributes(3X)
/wechochar add a character (with	attributes) to a curses window and/ .... curs_addch(3X)
/add string of characters (and	attributes) to a curses window .... curs_addchstr(3X)
attrset, wattrset,/ curs_attr:	attroff, wattroff, attron, wattron, ... curs_attr(3X)
curs_attr: attroff, wattroff,	attron, wattron, attrset, wattrset,/ .... curs_attr(3X)
/attroff, wattroff, attron, wattron,	attrset, wattrset, standend,/ .... curs_attr(3X)
secure_rpc: authdes_seccreate,	authdes_getucred, getnetname,/ .... secure_rpc(3N)
authdes_getucred,/ secure_rpc:	authdes_seccreate, ... secure_rpc(3N)
authsys_create,/ rpc_clnt_auth:	auth_destroy, authnone_create, ... rpc_clnt_auth(3N)
client side remote procedure call	authentication /routines for .... rpc_clnt_auth(3N)
rpc_clnt_auth: auth_destroy,	authnone_create, authsys_create,/ .... rpc_clnt_auth(3N)
auth_destroy, authnone_create,	authsys_create,/ rpc_clnt_auth: .... rpc_clnt_auth(3N)
/authnone_create, authsys_create,	authsys_create_default library/ .... rpc_clnt_auth(3N)
/application-specific routines for	automatic invocation by menus .... menu_hook(3X)
and wait for interrupt sigpause	automically release blocked signals .... sigpause(3)
resource/ waitsem, nbwaitsem	await and check access to a .... waitsem(2)

Permuted Index

/mvwgetch, ungetch get (or push	back) characters from curses/ .... curs_getch(3X)
/wbkgdset, bkgd, wbkgd curses window	background manipulation routines .... curs_bkgd(3X)
elf_getbase get the	base offset for an object file .... elf_getbase(3E)
delete, firstkey, nextkey data	base subroutines /fetch, store, ... dbm(3)
dbm_open, dbm_store data	base subroutines /dbm_nextkey, ... ndbm(3)
convert between long integer and	base-64 ASCII string a64l, l64a .... a64l(3C)
forms character	based forms package .... forms(3X)
menus character	based menus package .... menus(3X)
panels character	based panels package .... panels(3X)
a path name	basename return the last element of .... basename(3G)
has_il, killchar,/ curs_termattrs:	baudrate, erasechar, has_ic, ... curs_termattrs(3X)
string operations bstring: bcopy,	bcmp, bzero, ffs bit and byte .... bstring(3)
byte string operations bstring:	bcopy, bcmp, bzero, ffs bit and .... bstring(3)
flash routines curs_beep:	beep, flash curses bell and screen .... curs_beep(3X)
field has off-screen data ahead or	behind /data_behind tell if forms .... form_data(3X)
curs_beep: beep, flash curses	bell and screen flash routines .... curs_beep(3X)
bessel: j0, j1, jn, y0, y1, yn	Bessel functions .... bessel(3M)
Bessel functions	bessel: j0, j1, jn, y0, y1, yn .... bessel(3M)
/srandom, initstate, setstate	better random number generator;/ .... random(3)
delimiter	bgets read stream up to next .... bgets(3G)
fread, fwrite	binary input/output .... fread(3S)
bsearch	binary search a sorted table .... bsearch(3C)
tfind, tdelete, twalk manage	binary search trees tsearch, ... tsearch(3C)
creatsem create an instance of a	binary semaphore .... creatsem(2)
bind	bind a name to a socket .... bind(3N)
processor_bind	bind a process to a processor .... processor_bind(2)
endpoint t_bind	bind an address to a transport .... t_bind(3N)
	bind bind a name to a socket .... bind(3N)
rpcb_unset library routines for RPC	bind service /rpcb_set, ... rpcb(3N)
bstring: bcopy, bcmp, bzero, ffs	bit and byte string operations .... bstring(3)
ffs find first set	bit .... ffs(3C)
curs_bkgd: bkgdset, wbkgdset,	bkgd, wbkgd curses window/ .... curs_bkgd(3X)
curses window/ curs_bkgd:	bkgdset, wbkgdset, bkgd, wbkgd .... curs_bkgd(3X)
sigblock, sigmask	block signals .... sigblock(3)
sync update super	block .... sync(2)
sigpending examine signals that are	blocked and pending .... sigpending(2)
sigpause automically release	blocked signals and wait for/ .... sigpause(3)
whline, vline, wvline/ curs_border:	border, wborder, box, hline, ... curs_border(3X)
/whline, vline, wvline create curses	borders, horizontal and vertical/ .... curs_border(3X)
manipulation/ panel_top: top_panel,	bottom_panel panels deck .... panel_top(3X)
curs_border: border, wborder,	box, hline, whline, vline, wvline/ .... curs_border(3X)
allocation	brk, sbrk change data segment space .... brk(2)
table	bsearch binary search a sorted .... bsearch(3C)
bit and byte string operations	bstring: bcopy, bcmp, bzero, ffs .... bstring(3)
bufsplit split	buffer into fields .... bufsplit(3G)
determine whether a character	buffer is encrypted isencrypt .... isencrypt(3G)
set and get menus pattern match	buffer /menu_pattern .... menu_pattern(3X)

Permuted Index

stdio standard	buffered input/output package	stdio(3S)
setlinebuf, setvbuf assign	buffering to a stream /setbuffer,	setbuf(3S)
setbuf, setvbuf assign	buffering to a stream	setbuf(3S)
setbuffer, setlinebuf assign	buffering to a stream	setbuffer(3S)
	bufsplit split buffer into fields	bufsplit(3G)
an application for use/ addseverity	build a list of severity levels for	addseverity(3C)
elf_fill set fill	byte	elf_fill(3E)
values between host and network	byte order /ntohl, ntohs convert	byteorder(3N)
bcopy, bcmp, bzero, ffs bit and	byte string operations bstring:	bstring(3)
ntohs convert values between host/	byteorder, htonl, htons, ntohl,	byteorder(3N)
swab swap	bytes	swab(3C)
operations bstring: bcopy, bcmp,	bzero, ffs bit and byte string	bstring(3)
mktime converts a tm structure to a	calendar time	mktime(3C)
computes the difference between two	calendar times difftime	difftime(3C)
for client side remote procedure	call authentication /routines	rpc_clnt_auth(3N)
for server side remote procedure	call errors /library routines	rpc_svc_err(3N)
syscall indirect system	call	syscall(3)
allocator malloc, free, realloc,	calloc, mallopt, mallinfo memory	malloc(3X)
allocator malloc, free, realloc,	calloc, memalign, valloc, memory	malloc(3C)
intro introduction to system	calls and error numbers	intro(2)
routines for remote procedure	calls rpc library	rpc(3N)
library routines for client side	calls /rpc_broadcast, rpc_call	rpc_clnt_calls(3N)
routines for remote procedure	calls /xdr_replymsg XDR library	rpc_xdr(3N)
for secure remote procedure	calls /library routines	secure_rpc(3N)
allow signals to interrupt system	calls siginterrupt	siginterrupt(3)
/init_pair, init_color, has_colors,	can_change_color, color_content,/	curs_color(3X)
catclose open/close a message	catalog catopen,	catopen(3C)
catclose open/close a message	catalog catopen,	catopen(3C)
	catgets read a program message	catgets(3C)
message catalog	catopen, catclose open/close a	catopen(3C)
halfdelay, intrflush,/ curs_inopts:	cbreak, nocbreak, echo, noecho,	curs_inopts(3X)
pow, powf, sqrt, sqrtf/ exp, expf,	cbrt, log, logf, log10, log10f,	exp(3M)
fabs, fabsf, rint,/ floor, floorf,	ceil, ceilf, copysign, fmod, fmodf,	floor(3M)
fabsf, rint,/ floor, floorf, ceil,	ceilf, copysign, fmod, fmodf, fabs,	floor(3M)
/fabs, fabsf, rint, remainder floor,	ceiling, remainder, absolute value/	floor(3M)
tcflush, tcflow, cfgetospeed,	cfgetispeed, cfsetispeed,/ /tcdrain,	termios(2)
/tcdrain, tcflush, tcflow,	cfgetospeed, cfgetispeed,/	termios(2)
tcflow, cfgetospeed, cfgetispeed,	cfsetispeed, cfsetospeed,/ /tcflush,	termios(2)
tcgetsid/ /cfgetispeed, cfsetispeed,	cfsetospeed, tcgetpgrp, tcsetpgrp,	termios(2)
time to string strftime,	cftime, ascftime convert date and	strftime(3C)
allocation brk, sbrk	change data segment space	brk(2)
chmod, fchmod	change mode of file	chmod(2)
yp_update	change NIS information	yp_update(3N)
putenv	change or add value to environment	putenv(3C)
sigprocmask	change or examine signal mask	sigprocmask(2)
chown, lchown, fchown	change owner and group of a file	chown(2)
nice	change priority of a process	nice(3C)

Permuted Index

process nice	change priority of a time-sharing .... nice(2)
chroot	change root directory .... chroot(2)
waitid wait for child process to	change state .... waitid(2)
waitpid wait for child process to	change state .... waitpid(2)
rename	change the name of a file .... rename(2)
chsize	change the size of a file .... chsize(2)
chdir, fchdir	change working directory .... chdir(2)
number generator; routines for	changing generators /better random .... random(3)
pipe create an interprocess	channel .... pipe(2)
/inch, winch, mvinch, mvwinch get a	character and its attributes from a/ .... curs_inch(3X)
control/ /standout, wstandout curses	character and window attribute .... curs_attr(3X)
ungetc push	character back onto input stream .... ungetc(3S)
forms	character based forms package .... forms(3X)
menus	character based menus package .... menus(3X)
panels	character based panels package .... panels(3X)
/winsch, mvinsch, mvwinsch insert a	character before the character/ .... curs_insch(3X)
isencrypt determine whether a	character buffer is encrypted .... isencrypt(3G)
ispunct, isprint, isgraph, isascii	character handling /iscntrl, ... ctype(3C)
mbtowc, mblen, wctomb multibyte	character handling mbchar: .... mbchar(3C)
cuserid get	character login name of the user .... cuserid(3S)
getc, getchar, fgetc, getw get	character or word from a stream .... getc(3S)
putc, putchar, fputc, putw put	character or word on a stream .... putc(3S)
/mvgetstr, mvwgetstr, wgetnstr get	character strings from curses/ .... curs_getstr(3X)
wdelch, mvdelch, mvwdelch delete	character under cursor in a/ /delch, ... curs_delch(3X)
/insert a character before the	character under the cursor in a/ .... curs_insch(3X)
/mvwinsnstr insert string before	character under the cursor in a/ .... curs_instr(3X)
/mvwaddch, echochar, wechochar add a	character (with attributes) to a/ .... curs_addch(3X)
dynamic_field_info get forms field	characteristics /field_info, ... form_field_info(3X)
curses/ /mvwinchnstr get a string of	characters (and attributes) from a .... curs_inchstr(3X)
curses/ /mvwaddchnstr add string of	characters (and attributes) to a .... curs_addchstr(3X)
_tolower, toascii translate	characters /tolower, _toupper, ... conv(3C)
/mvwinstr, mvwinnstr get a string of	characters from a curses window .... curs_instr(3X)
/ungetch get (or push back)	characters from curses terminal/ .... curs_getch(3X)
advance/ /mvwaddnstr add a string of	characters to a curses window and .... curs_addstr(3X)
	directory
by a/ waitsem, nbwaitsem await and	chdir, fchdir change working .... chdir(2)
spray scatter data in order to	check access to a resource governed .... waitsem(2)
read rdchk	check the network .... spray(3N)
times get process and	check to see if there is data to be .... rdchk(2)
waitid wait for	child process times .... times(2)
waitpid wait for	child process to change state .... waitid(2)
wait wait for	child process to change state .... waitpid(2)
	child process to stop or terminate .... wait(2)
and group of a file	chmod, fchmod change mode of file .... chmod(2)
	chown, lchown, fchown change owner .... chown(2)
	chroot change root directory .... chroot(2)
/elf32_xlatetof, elf32_xlatetom	chsize change the size of a file .... chsize(2)
	class-dependent data translation .... elf_xlate(3E)

/elf32_newehdr retrieve	class-dependent object file header	elf_getehdr(3E)
table /elf32_newphdr retrieve	class-dependent program header	elf_getphdr(3E)
elf_getshdr: elf32_getshdr retrieve	class-dependent section header	elf_getshdr(3E)
/wclrtobot, clrtoeol, wclrtoeol	clear all or part of a curses/	curs_clear(3X)
curs_clear: erase, werase,	clear, wclear, clrtobot, wclrtobot,/	curs_clear(3X)
inquiries ferror, feof,	clearerr, fileno stream status	ferror(3S)
leaveok, setscrreg,/ curs_outopts:	clearok, idlok, idcok immedok,	curs_outopts(3X)
with creation and manipulation of	CLIENT handles /for dealing	rpc_clnt_create(3N)
yperr_string, ypprot_err NIS	client interface /yp_master,	ypclnt(3N)
rpc_call library routines for	client side calls /rpc_broadcast,	rpc_clnt_calls(3N)
/library routines for	client side remote procedure call/	rpc_clnt_auth(3N)
listener nlsgetcall get	client's data passed via the	nlsgetcall(3N)
clnt_geterr,/ rpc_clnt_calls:	clnt_call, clnt_freeres,	rpc_clnt_calls(3N)
clnt_destroy,/ rpc_clnt_create:	clnt_control, clnt_create,	rpc_clnt_create(3N)
rpc_clnt_create: clnt_control,	clnt_create, clnt_destroy,/	rpc_clnt_create(3N)
/clnt_control, clnt_create,	clnt_destroy, clnt_dg_create,/	rpc_clnt_create(3N)
/clnt_create, clnt_destroy,	clnt_dg_create, clnt_pcreateerror,/	rpc_clnt_create(3N)
rpc_clnt_calls: clnt_call,	clnt_freeres, clnt_geterr,/	rpc_clnt_calls(3N)
/clnt_call, clnt_freeres,	clnt_geterr, clnt_perrno,/	rpc_clnt_calls(3N)
/clnt_destroy, clnt_dg_create,	clnt_pcreateerror, clnt_raw_create,/	rpc_clnt_create(3N)
/clnt_freeres, clnt_geterr,	clnt_perrno, clnt_perror,/	rpc_clnt_calls(3N)
/clnt_geterr, clnt_perrno,	clnt_perror, clnt_sperrno,/	rpc_clnt_calls(3N)
clnt_dg_create, clnt_pcreateerror,	clnt_raw_create,/ /clnt_destroy,	rpc_clnt_create(3N)
/clnt_pcreateerror, clnt_raw_create,	clnt_spcreateerror,/	rpc_clnt_create(3N)
/clnt_perrno, clnt_perror,	clnt_sperrno, clnt_sperror,/	rpc_clnt_calls(3N)
/clnt_perror, clnt_sperrno,	clnt_sperror, rpc_broadcast,/	rpc_clnt_calls(3N)
clnt_vc_create/ /clnt_spcreateerror,	clnt_tli_create, clnt_tp_create,	rpc_clnt_create(3N)
library routines/ /clnt_tli_create,	clnt_tp_create, clnt_vc_create	rpc_clnt_create(3N)
/clnt_tli_create, clnt_tp_create,	clnt_vc_create library routines for/	rpc_clnt_create(3N)
allow synchronization of the system	clock adjtime correct the time to	adjtime(2)
alarm set a process alarm	clock	alarm(2)
	clock report CPU time used	clock(3C)
close	close a file descriptor	close(2)
dlclose	close a shared object	dlclose(3X)
t_close	close a transport endpoint	t_close(3N)
	close close a file descriptor	close(2)
fclose, fflush	close or flush a stream	fclose(3S)
p2open, p2close open,	close pipes to and from a command	p2open(3G)
/telldir, seekdir, rewinddir,	closedir directory operations	directory(3C)
/telldir, seekdir, rewinddir,	closedir directory operations	directory(3C)
log syslog, openlog,	closelog, setlogmask control system	syslog(3)
/erase, werase, clear, wclear,	clrtobot, wclrtobot, clrtoeol,/	curs_clear(3X)
/clear, wclear, clrtobot, wclrtobot,	clrtoeol, wclrtoeol clear all or/	curs_clear(3X)
signal handling for specific SIGFPE	codes sigfpe	sigfpe(3)
compressing or expanding escape	codes /strccpy copy strings,	strccpy(3G)
strcoll string	collation	strcoll(3C)
/color_content, pair_content curses	color manipulation routines	curs_color(3X)

Permuted Index

/has_colors, can_change_color,	color_content, pair_content curses/	curs_color(3X)
and get maximum numbers of rows and	columns in menus /menu_format set	menu_format(3X)
open, close pipes to and from a	command p2open, p2close	p2open(3G)
subsystem form_driver	command processor for the forms	form_driver(3X)
subsystem menu_driver	command processor for the menus	menu_driver(3X)
rexec return stream to a remote	command	rexec(3N)
system issue a shell	command	system(3S)
stdipc: ftok standard interprocess	communication package	stdipc(3C)
socket create an endpoint for	communication	socket(3N)
expression regcmp, regex	compile and execute regular	regcmp(3G)
/step, advance regular expression	compile and match routines	regexpr(3G)
expression compile and/ regexpr:	compile, step, advance regular	regexpr(3G)
erf, erfc error function and	complementary error function	erf(3M)
and their names errno	complete list of the error numbers	errno(2)
entry corresponding to NETPATH	component getnetpath get netconfig	getnetpath(3N)
/strcadd, strecpy copy strings,	compressing or expanding escape/	strccpy(3G)
elf_hash	compute hash value	elf_hash(3E)
div, ldiv	compute the quotient and remainder	div(3C)
calendar times difftime	computes the difference between two	difftime(3C)
fpathconf, pathconf get	configurable pathname variables	fpathconf(2)
sysconf retrieves	configurable system variables	sysconf(3C)
sysconf retrieves	configurable system variables	sysconf(3C)
getnetconfig get network	configuration database entry	getnetconfig(3N)
doconfig execute a	configuration script	doconfig(3N)
t_rcvconnect receive the	confirmation from a connect request	t_rcvconnect(3N)
and from/ /menu_items, item_count	connect and disconnect items to	menu_items(3X)
/field_count, move_field	connect fields to forms	form_field(3X)
socket	connect initiate a connection on a	connect(3N)
t_accept accept a	connect request	t_accept(3N)
t_listen listen for a	connect request	t_listen(3N)
receive the confirmation from a	connect request t_rcvconnect	t_rcvconnect(3N)
getpeername get name of	connected peer	getpeername(3N)
socketpair create a pair of	connected sockets	socketpair(3N)
establish an outgoing terminal line	connection dial	dial(3C)
accept accept a	connection on a socket	accept(3N)
connect initiate a	connection on a socket	connect(3N)
shut down part of a full-duplex	connection shutdown	shutdown(3N)
data or expedited data sent over a	connection t_rcv receive	t_rcv(3N)
send data or expedited data over a	connection t_snd	t_snd(3N)
user t_connect establish a	connection with another transport	t_connect(3N)
listen listen for	connections on a socket	listen(3N)
a message on stderr or system	console fmtmsg display	fmtmsg(3C)
control maximum system resource	consumption getrlimit, setrlimit	getrlimit(2)
retrieve uninterpreted file	contents elf_rawfile	elf_rawfile(3E)
setcontext get and set current user	context getcontext,	getcontext(2)
set or get signal alternate stack	context sigaltstack	sigaltstack(2)
set and/or get signal stack	context sigstack	sigstack(3)

```
            swapcontext manipulate user    contexts  makecontext, .......................................... makecontext(3C)
                                elf_cntl   control a file descriptor ................................................... elf_cntl(3E)
                                   ioctl   control device ............................................................................ ioctl(2)
                              fcntl file   control ..................................................................................... fcntl(2)
     IEEE floating-point environment       control  /fpgetsticky, fpsetsticky ........................... fpgetround(3C)
       consumption  getrlimit, setrlimit   control maximum system resource ............................... getrlimit(2)
             mctl memory management        control ....................................................................................... mctl(3)
         memcntl memory management         control .................................................................................... memcntl(2)
  /menu_grey, set_menu_pad, menu_pad       control menus display attributes ................... menu_attributes(3X)
                       msgctl message      control operations ............................................................... msgctl(2)
                     semctl semaphore      control operations ............................................................... semctl(2)
                shmctl shared memory       control operations ............................................................... shmctl(2)
                priocntl process scheduler control ................................................................................. priocntl(2)
         generalized process scheduler     control  priocntlset ....................................................... priocntlset(2)
         character and window attribute    control routines  /wstandout curses ......................... curs_attr(3X)
           curses terminal input option    control routines  /typeahead ............................... curs_inopts(3X)
      nonl curses terminal output option   control routines  /scrollok, nl, ............................. curs_outopts(3X)
            is_wintouched curses refresh   control routines  /is_linetouched, .......................... curs_touch(3X)
         openlog, closelog, setlogmask     control system log  syslog, ..................................................... syslog(3)
                  uadmin administrative    control ................................................................................. uadmin(2)
           _tolower, toascii translate/    conv: toupper, tolower, _toupper, ...................................... conv(3C)
           sfconvert, sgconvert output     conversion  /gconvert, seconvert, ................................ econvert(3)
         vfprintf, vsprintf formatted output conversion  /sprintf, vprintf, ......................................... printf(3S)
                 long integers  l3tol, ltol3  convert between 3-byte integers and ................................. l3tol(3C)
              base-64 ASCII string  a64l, l64a  convert between long integer and ...................................... a64l(3C)
          /localtime, gmtime, asctime, tzset   convert date and time to string ...................................... ctime(3C)
                 strftime, cftime, ascftime  convert date and time to string ................................... strftime(3C)
         floating-point/  /decimal_to_extended  convert decimal record to .......................... decimal_to_floating(3)
              /ecvtl, fcvt, fcvtl, gcvt, gcvtl  convert floating-point number to/ ................................... ecvt(3C)
         decimal record  /extended_to_decimal  convert floating-point value to .................. floating_to_decimal(3)
         /wscanw, mvscanw, mvwscanw, vwscanw  convert formatted input from a/ .......................... curs_scanw(3X)
                      scanf, fscanf, sscanf   convert formatted input .................................................. scanf(3S)
               number  strtod, strtold, atof  convert string to double-precision .................................. strtod(3C)
                     strtol, strtoul, atol, atoi  convert string to integer ............................................. strtol(3C)
                                   getdate  convert user format date and time ................................. getdate(3C)
             network/  /htonl, htons, ntohl, ntohs  convert values between host and .......................... byteorder(3N)
                      calendar time  mktime   converts a tm structure to a .......................................... mktime(3C)
               application versions  elf_version  coordinate ELF library and ...................................... elf_version(3E)
             get curses cursor and window   coordinates  /getbegyx, getmaxyx ........................... curs_getyx(3X)
                                   copylist  copy a file into memory ................................................. copylist(3G)
            strccpy: streadd, strcadd, strecpy  copy strings, compressing or/ ...................................... strccpy(3G)
                                            copylist copy a file into memory .................................. copylist(3G)
                      rint,/  floor, floorf, ceil, ceilf,  copysign, fmod, fmodf, fabs, fabsf, ................................. floor(3M)
                ieee_functions, fp_class, isnan,   copysign, scalbn miscellaneous/ ...................... ieee_functions(3M)
             curs_overlay: overlay, overwrite,  copywin overlap and manipulate/ .................... curs_overlay(3X)
              synchronization of the/  adjtime   correct the time to allow ................................................. adjtime(2)
             menu_cursor: pos_menu_cursor   correctly position a menus cursor .......................... menu_cursor(3X)
```

Permuted Index

getnetpath get netconfig entry	corresponding to NETPATH component .... getnetpath(3N)
acos, acosf,/ trig: sin, sinf,	cos, cosf, tan, tanf, asin, asinf, ... trig(3M)
acosf, atan,/ trig: sin, sinf, cos,	cosf, tan, tanf, asin, asinf, acos, ... trig(3M)
acosh, atanh/ sinh, sinhf,	cosh, coshf, tanh, tanhf, asinh, ... sinh(3M)
atanh/ sinh, sinhf, cosh,	coshf, tanh, tanhf, asinh, acosh, ... sinh(3M)
clock report	CPU time used .... clock(3C)
an existing one	creat create a new file or rewrite .... creat(2)
tmpnam, tempnam	create a name for a temporary file .... tmpnam(3S)
mkfifo	create a new FIFO .... mkfifo(3C)
existing one creat	create a new file or rewrite an .... creat(2)
fork	create a new process .... fork(2)
socketpair	create a pair of connected sockets .... socketpair(3N)
tmpfile	create a temporary file .... tmpfile(3S)
communication socket	create an endpoint for .... socket(3N)
semaphore creatsem	create an instance of a binary .... creatsem(2)
pipe	create an interprocess channel .... pipe(2)
/dup_field, link_field, free_field,	create and destroy forms fields .... form_field_new(3X)
form_new: new_form, free_form	create and destroy forms .... form_new(3X)
menu_item_new: new_item, free_item	create and destroy menus items .... menu_item_new(3X)
menu_new: new_menu, free_menu	create and destroy menus .... menu_new(3X)
panel_new: new_panel, del_panel	create and destroy panels .... panel_new(3X)
/prefresh, pnoutrefresh, pechochar	create and display curses pads .... curs_pad(3X)
/box, hline, whline, vline, wvline	create curses borders, horizontal/ .... curs_border(3X)
syncok, wcursyncup, wsyncdown	create curses windows / wsyncup, ... curs_window(3X)
path mkdirp, rmdirp	create, remove directories in a .... mkdirp(3G)
/library routines for dealing with	creation and manipulation of CLIENT/
	.... rpc_clnt_create(3N)
umask set and get file	creation mask .... umask(2)
routines for dealing with the	creation of server handles /library .... rpc_svc_create(3N)
external data representation stream	creation /library routines for .... xdr_create(3N)
binary semaphore	creatsem create an instance of a .... creatsem(2)
optimization package curses	CRT screen handling and .... curses(3X)
functions	crypt password and file encryption .... crypt(3X)
encryption	crypt, setkey, encrypt generate .... crypt(3C)
terminal	ctermid generate file name for .... ctermid(3S)
tzset convert date and time to/	ctime, localtime, gmtime, asctime, ... ctime(3C)
isupper, isalpha, isalnum,/	ctype: isdigit, isxdigit, islower, ... ctype(3C)
endpoint t_look look at the	current event on a transport .... t_look(3N)
gethostid get unique identifier of	current host .... gethostid(3)
sethostname get/set name of	current host gethostname, ... gethostname(3)
top_row, item_index set and get	current menus items /set_top_row,
	.... menu_item_current(3X)
/field_index set forms	current page and field .... form_page(3X)
sigsetmask set	current signal mask .... sigsetmask(3)
t_getstate get the	current state .... t_getstate(3N)
uname get name of	current UNIX system .... uname(2)
getcontext, setcontext get and set	current user context .... getcontext(2)

the slot in the utmp file of the	current user ttyslot find .... ttyslot(3C)
/replace_panel get or set the	current window of a panels panel .... panel_window(3X)
getcwd get pathname of	current working directory .... getcwd(3C)
getwd get	current working directory pathname .... getwd(3)
/form_page, set_current_field,	current_field, field_index set / .... form_page(3X)
item_index set / /set_current_item,	current_item, set_top_row, top_row,
	.... menu_item_current(3X)
mvwaddch, echochar, wechochar add /	curs_addch: addch, waddch, mvaddch, ... curs_addch(3X)
waddchstr, waddchnstr, mvaddchstr, /	curs_addchstr: addchstr, addchnstr, ... curs_addchstr(3X)
waddstr, waddnstr, mvaddstr, /	curs_addstr: addstr, addnstr, ... curs_addstr(3X)
attron, wattron, attrset, /	curs_attr: attroff, wattroff, ... curs_attr(3X)
and screen flash routines	curs_beep: beep, flash curses bell .... curs_beep(3X)
wbkgd curses window background /	curs_bkgd: bkgdset, wbkgdset, bkgd, ... curs_bkgd(3X)
hline, whline, vline, wvline /	curs_border: border, wborder, box, ... curs_border(3X)
wclear, clrtobot, wclrtobot, /	curs_clear: erase, werase, clear, ... curs_clear(3X)
init_color, has_colors, /	curs_color: start_color, init_pair, ... curs_color(3X)
mvwdelch delete character under /	curs_delch: delch, wdelch, mvdelch, ... curs_delch(3X)
insdelln, winsdelln, insertln, /	curs_deleteln: deleteln, wdeleteln, ... curs_deleteln(3X)
routines curs_beep: beep, flash	curses bell and screen flash .... curs_beep(3X)
/hline, whline, vline, wvline create	curses borders, horizontal and / .... curs_border(3X)
/wstandend, standout, wstandout	curses character and window / .... curs_attr(3X)
/color_content, pair_content	curses color manipulation routines .... curs_color(3X)
optimization package	curses CRT screen handling and .... curses(3X)
getparyx, getbegyx, getmaxyx get	curses cursor and window / /getyx, ... curs_getyx(3X)
/longname, termattrs, termname	curses environment query routines .... curs_termattrs(3X)
/tgetnum, tgetstr, tgoto, tputs	curses interfaces (emulated) to the / .... curs_termcap(3X)
/tigetflag, tigetnum, tigetstr	curses interfaces to terminfo / .... curs_terminfo(3X)
pechochar create and display	curses pads /pnoutrefresh, ... curs_pad(3X)
/is_linetouched, is_wintouched	curses refresh control routines .... curs_touch(3X)
curs_set, napms low-level	curses routines /ripoffline, ... curs_kernel(3X)
/scr_init, scr_set read (write) a	curses screen from (to) a file .... curs_scr_dump(3X)
/isendwin, set_term, delscreen	curses screen initialization and / .... curs_initscr(3X)
/slk_attrset, slk_attroff	curses soft label routines .... curs_slk(3X)
/timeout, wtimeout, typeahead	curses terminal input option / .... curs_inopts(3X)
get (or push back) characters from	curses terminal keyboard /ungetch .... curs_getch(3X)
/wgetnstr get character strings from	curses terminal keyboard .... curs_getstr(3X)
/wsetscrreg, scrollok, nl, nonl	curses terminal output option / .... curs_outopts(3X)
/flushinp miscellaneous	curses utility routines .... curs_util(3X)
convert formatted input from a	curses widow /mvwscanw, vwscanw .... curs_scanw(3X)
/a character (with attributes) to a	curses window and advance cursor .... curs_addch(3X)
/add a string of characters to a	curses window and advance cursor .... curs_addstr(3X)
/bkgdset, wbkgdset, bkgd, wbkgd	curses window background / .... curs_bkgd(3X)
of characters (and attributes) to a	curses window /add string .... curs_addchstr(3X)
wclrtoeol clear all or part of a	curses window /wclrtobot, clrtoeol, ... curs_clear(3X)
delete character under cursor in a	curses window /mvdelch, mvwdelch .... curs_delch(3X)
delete and insert lines in a	curses window /winsertln .... curs_deleteln(3X)
character and its attributes from a	curses window /mvwinch get a .... curs_inch(3X)

Permuted Index

characters (and attributes) from a	curses window /get a string of	curs_inchstr(3X)
the character under the cursor in a	curses window /a character before	curs_insch(3X)
character under the cursor in a	curses window /insert string before	curs_instr(3X)
get a string of characters from a	curses window /mvwinstr, mvwinnstr	curs_instr(3X)
curs_move: move, wmove move	curses window cursor	curs_move(3X)
scroll, srcl, wscrl scroll a	curses window curs_scroll:	curs_scroll(3X)
redrawwin, wredrawln refresh	curses windows and lines /doupdate,	curs_refresh(3X)
overlap and manipulate overlapped	curses windows /overwrite, copywin	curs_overlay(3X)
print formatted output in	curses windows /mvwprintw, vwprintw	curs_printw(3X)
wcursyncup, wsyncdown create	curses windows /wsyncup, syncok,	curs_window(3X)
mvwgetch, ungetch get (or push/	curs_getch: getch, wgetch, mvgetch,	curs_getch(3X)
mvgetstr, mvwgetstr, wgetnstr get/	curs_getstr: getstr, wgetstr,	curs_getstr(3X)
getbegyx, getmaxyx get curses/	curs_getyx: getyx, getparyx,	curs_getyx(3X)
mvwinch get a character and its/	curs_inch: inch, winch, mvinch,	curs_inch(3X)
winchstr, winchnstr, mvinchstr,/	curs_inchstr: inchstr, inchnstr,	curs_inchstr(3X)
endwin, isendwin, set_term,/	curs_initscr: initscr, newterm,	curs_initscr(3X)
echo, noecho, halfdelay,/	curs_inopts: cbreak, nocbreak,	curs_inopts(3X)
mvwinsch insert a character before/	curs_insch: insch, winsch, mvinsch,	curs_insch(3X)
winsstr, winsnstr, mvinsstr,/	curs_instr: insstr, insnstr,	curs_instr(3X)
winnstr, mvinstr, mvinnstr,/	curs_instr: instr, innstr, winstr,	curs_instr(3X)
def_shell_mode, reset_prog_mode,/	curs_kernel: def_prog_mode,	curs_kernel(3X)
window cursor	curs_move: move, wmove move curses	curs_move(3X)
/getbegyx, getmaxyx get curses	cursor and window coordinates	curs_getyx(3X)
to a curses window and advance	cursor /character (with attributes)	curs_addch(3X)
to a curses window and advance	cursor /add a string of characters	curs_addstr(3X)
move, wmove move curses window	cursor curs_move:	curs_move(3X)
position forms window	cursor /pos_form_cursor	form_cursor(3X)
/mvwdelch delete character under	cursor in a curses window	curs_delch(3X)
/before the character under the	cursor in a curses window	curs_insch(3X)
string before character under the	cursor in a curses window /insert	curs_instr(3X)
correctly position a menus	cursor /pos_menu_cursor	menu_cursor(3X)
immedok, leaveok, setscrreg,/	curs_outopts: clearok, idlok, idcok	curs_outopts(3X)
copywin overlap and manipulate/	curs_overlay: overlay, overwrite,	curs_overlay(3X)
pnoutrefresh, pechochar create and/	curs_pad: newpad, subpad, prefresh,	curs_pad(3X)
mvprintw, mvwprintw, vwprintw/	curs_printw: printw, wprintw,	curs_printw(3X)
wnoutrefresh, doupdate, redrawwin,/	curs_refresh: refresh, wrefresh,	curs_refresh(3X)
mvwscanw, vwscanw convert/	curs_scanw: scanw, wscanw, mvscanw,	curs_scanw(3X)
scr_restore, scr_init, scr_set/	curs_scr_dump: scr_dump,	curs_scr_dump(3X)
scroll a curses window	curs_scroll: scroll, srcl, wscrl	curs_scroll(3X)
/getsyx, setsyx, ripoffline,	curs_set, napms low-level curses/	curs_kernel(3X)
slk_refresh, slk_noutrefresh,/	curs_slk: slk_init, slk_set,	curs_slk(3X)
erasechar, has_ic, has_il,/	curs_termattrs: baudrate,	curs_termattrs(3X)
tgetnum, tgetstr, tgoto, tputs/	curs_termcap: tgetent, tgetflag,	curs_termcap(3X)
set_curterm, del_curterm,/	curs_terminfo: setupterm, setterm,	curs_terminfo(3X)
untouchwin, wtouchln,/	curs_touch: touchwin, touchline,	curs_touch(3X)
use_env, putwin, getwin,/	curs_util: unctrl, keyname, filter,	curs_util(3X)

Permuted Index

subwin, derwin, mvderwin, dupwin,/	curs_window: newwin, delwin, mvwin, ... curs_window(3X)
the user	cuserid get character login name of .... cuserid(3S)
sdgetv synchronize shared	data access .... sdgetv(2)
tell if forms field has off-screen	data ahead or behind /data_behind .... form_data(3X)
store, delete, firstkey, nextkey	data base subroutines /fetch, ... dbm(3)
/dbm_nextkey, dbm_open, dbm_store	data base subroutines .... ndbm(3)
elf_rawdata get section	data elf_getdata, elf_newdata, ... elf_getdata(3E)
retrieve file identification	data elf_getident .... elf_getident(3E)
t_rcvuderr receive a unit	data error indication .... t_rcvuderr(3N)
sputl, sgetl access long integer	data in a machine-independent/ .... sputl(3X)
spray scatter	data in order to check the network .... spray(3N)
connection t_snd send	data or expedited data over a .... t_snd(3N)
connection t_rcv receive	data or expedited data sent over a .... t_rcv(3N)
t_snd send data or expedited	data over a connection .... t_snd(3N)
nlsgetcall get client's	data passed via the listener .... nlsgetcall(3N)
memory or unlock process, text, or	data plock lock into .... plock(2)
/library routines for external	data representation stream creation .... xdr_create(3N)
xdr library routines for external	data representation .... xdr(3N)
library routines for external	data representation /xdr_setpos .... xdr_admin(3N)
library routines for external	data representation /xdr_wrapstring .... xdr_complex(3N)
library routines for external	data representation /xdr_void .... xdr_simple(3N)
synchronize access to a shared	data segment sdenter, sdleave .... sdenter(2)
sdfree attach and detach a shared	data segment sdget, ... sdget(2)
brk, sbrk change	data segment space allocation .... brk(2)
t_rcv receive data or expedited	data sent over a connection .... t_rcv(3N)
rdchk check to see if there is	data to be read .... rdchk(2)
elf32_xlatetom class-dependent	data translation /elf32_xlatetof, ... elf_xlate(3E)
/field_type, field_arg forms field	data type validation .... form_field_validation(3X)
t_rcvudata receive a	data unit .... t_rcvudata(3N)
t_sndudata send a	data unit .... t_sndudata(3N)
/panel_userptr associate application	data with a panels panel .... panel_userptr(3X)
field_userptr associate application	data with forms /set_field_userptr, ... form_field_userptr(3X)
form_userptr associate application	data with forms /set_form_userptr, ... form_userptr(3X)
/item_userptr associate application	data with menus items .... menu_item_userptr(3X)
menu_userptr associate application	data with menus /set_menu_userptr, ... menu_userptr(3X)
forms field has/ form_data:	data_ahead, data_behind tell if .... form_data(3X)
curses interfaces to terminfo	database /tigetnum, tigetstr .... curs_terminfo(3X)
get network configuration	database entry getnetconfig .... getnetconfig(3N)
off-screen/ form_data: data_ahead,	data_behind tell if forms field has .... form_data(3X)
ftime get	date and time .... ftime(3C)
getdate convert user format	date and time .... getdate(3C)
settimeofday get or set the	date and time gettimeofday, ... gettimeofday(3)
settimeofday get or set the	date and time gettimeofday, ... gettimeofday(3C)
gmtime, asctime, tzset convert	date and time to string /localtime, ... ctime(3C)
strftime, cftime, ascftime convert	date and time to string .... strftime(3C)

Permuted Index

ftime get time and	date	ftime(2)
store, delete, firstkey, nextkey/	dbm: dbminit, dbmclose, fetch, ...	dbm(3)
dbm_delete, dbm_error,/ ndbm:	dbm_clearerr, dbm_close, ...	ndbm(3)
dbm_fetch,/ ndbm: dbm_clearerr,	dbm_close, dbm_delete, dbm_error, ...	ndbm(3)
firstkey, nextkey/ dbm: dbminit,	dbmclose, fetch, store, delete, ...	dbm(3)
ndbm: dbm_clearerr, dbm_close,	dbm_delete, dbm_error, dbm_fetch,/	ndbm(3)
/dbm_close, dbm_delete,	dbm_error, dbm_fetch, dbm_firstkey,/	ndbm(3)
/dbm_close, dbm_delete, dbm_error,	dbm_fetch, dbm_firstkey,/	ndbm(3)
/dbm_delete, dbm_error, dbm_fetch,	dbm_firstkey, dbm_nextkey,/	ndbm(3)
delete, firstkey, nextkey/ dbm:	dbminit, dbmclose, fetch, store, ...	dbm(3)
/dbm_error, dbm_fetch, dbm_firstkey,	dbm_nextkey, dbm_open, dbm_store/	ndbm(3)
/dbm_firstkey, dbm_nextkey,	dbm_open, dbm_store data base/	ndbm(3)
/dbm_nextkey, dbm_open,	dbm_store data base subroutines	ndbm(3)
/clnt_vc_create library routines for	dealing with creation and/	rpc_clnt_create(3N)
/svc_vc_create library routines for	dealing with the creation of server/	rpc_svc_create(3N)
convert floating-point value to	decimal record /extended_to_decimal	floating_to_decimal(3)
value /decimal_to_extended convert	decimal record to floating-point	decimal_to_floating(3)
/decimal_to_single,	decimal_to_double,/	decimal_to_floating(3)
record to/ /decimal_to_double,	decimal_to_extended convert decimal	decimal_to_floating(3)
decimal_to_single,/	decimal_to_floating:	decimal_to_floating(3)
decimal_to_floating:	decimal_to_single,/	decimal_to_floating(3)
/hide_panel, panel_hidden panels	deck manipulation routines	panel_show(3X)
/top_panel, bottom_panel panels	deck manipulation routines	panel_top(3X)
/panel_above, panel_below panels	deck traversal primitives	panel_above(3X)
floatingpoint IEEE floating point	definitions	floatingpoint(3)
reset_prog_mode,/ curs_kernel:	def_prog_mode, def_shell_mode, ...	curs_kernel(3X)
curs_kernel: def_prog_mode,	def_shell_mode, reset_prog_mode,/	curs_kernel(3X)
filter, use_env, putwin, getwin,	delay_output, flushinp/ /keyname, ...	curs_util(3X)
delete character under/ curs_delch:	delch, wdelch, mvdelch, mvwdelch	curs_delch(3X)
/setupterm, setterm, set_curterm,	del_curterm, restartterm, tparm,/	curs_terminfo(3X)
/winsdelln, insertln, winsertln	delete and insert lines in a curses/	curs_deleteln(3X)
/delch, wdelch, mvdelch, mvwdelch	delete character under cursor in a/	curs_delch(3X)
/dbminit, dbmclose, fetch, store,	delete, firstkey, nextkey data base/	dbm(3)
winsdelln,/ curs_deleteln:	deleteln, wdeleteln, insdelln, ...	curs_deleteln(3X)
bgets read stream up to next	delimiter	bgets(3G)
panel_new: new_panel,	del_panel create and destroy panels	panel_new(3X)
endwin, isendwin, set_term,	delscreen curses screen/ /newterm, ...	curs_initscr(3X)
mvderwin,/ curs_window: newwin,	delwin, mvwin, subwin, derwin, ...	curs_window(3X)
/newwin, delwin, mvwin, subwin,	derwin, mvderwin, dupwin, wsyncup,/	curs_window(3X)
get menus item name and	description /item_description	menu_item_name(3X)
close close a file	descriptor	close(2)
dup duplicate an open file	descriptor	dup(2)
dup2 duplicate an open file	descriptor	dup2(3C)
elf_begin make a file	descriptor	elf_begin(3E)

Permuted Index

elf_cntl control a file	descriptor	elf_cntl(3E)
elf_update update an ELF	descriptor	elf_update(3E)
a name from a STREAMS-based file	descriptor fdetach detach	fdetach(3C)
isastream test a file	descriptor	isastream(3C)
getdtablesize get	descriptor table size	getdtablesize(3)
fattach attach a STREAMS-based file	descriptor to an object in the file/	fattach(3C)
link_field, free_field, create and	destroy forms fields /dup_field,	form_field_new(3X)
new_form, free_form create and	destroy forms form_new:	form_new(3X)
new_item, free_item create and	destroy menus items menu_item_new:	menu_item_new(3X)
new_menu, free_menu create and	destroy menus menu_new:	menu_new(3X)
new_panel, del_panel create and	destroy panels panel_new:	panel_new(3X)
file descriptor fdetach	detach a name from a STREAMS-based	fdetach(3C)
sdget, sdfree attach and	detach a shared data segment	sdget(2)
sigaction	detailed signal management	sigaction(2)
access	determine accessibility of a file	access(2)
elf_kind	determine file type	elf_kind(3E)
mincore	determine residency of memory pages	mincore(2)
/fpclassl, unordered, unorderedl	determine type of floating-point/	isnan(3C)
buffer is encrypted isencrypt	determine whether a character	isencrypt(3G)
access to the slave pseudo-terminal	device grantpt grant	grantpt(3C)
ioctl control	device	ioctl(2)
makedev, major, minor manage a	device number	makedev(3C)
name of the slave pseudo-terminal	device ptsname get	ptsname(3C)
dlerror get	diagnostic information	dlerror(3X)
line connection	dial establish an outgoing terminal	dial(3C)
times difftime computes the	difference between two calendar	difftime(3C)
between two calendar times	difftime computes the difference	difftime(3C)
mkdirp, rmdirp create, remove	directories in a path	mkdirp(3G)
search for named file in named	directories pathfind	pathfind(3G)
chdir, fchdir change working	directory	chdir(2)
chroot change root	directory	chroot(2)
system independent/ getdents read	directory entries and put in a file	getdents(2)
unlink remove	directory entry	unlink(2)
get pathname of current working	directory getcwd	getcwd(3C)
mkdir make a	directory	mkdir(2)
dirname report the parent	directory name of a file path name	dirname(3G)
telldir, seekdir, rewinddir,/	directory: opendir, readdir,	directory(3C)
telldir, seekdir, rewinddir,/	directory: opendir, readdir,	directory(3C)
seekdir, rewinddir, closedir	directory operations /telldir,	directory(3C)
seekdir, rewinddir, closedir	directory operations /telldir,	directory(3C)
file mknod make a	directory, or a special or ordinary	mknod(2)
file mknod make a	directory, or a special or ordinary	mknod(2)
getwd get current working	directory pathname	getwd(3)
rmdir remove a	directory	rmdir(2)
scandir, alphasort scan a	directory	scandir(3)
name of a file path name	dirname report the parent directory	dirname(3G)

Permuted Index

t_unbind	disable a transport endpoint .... t_unbind(3N)
acct enable or	disable process accounting .... acct(2)
/menu_items, item_count connect and	disconnect items to and from/ .... menu_items(3X)
t_snddis send user-initiated	disconnect request .... t_snddis(3N)
t_rcvdis retrieve information from	disconnect .... t_rcvdis(3N)
system console fmtmsg	display a message on stderr or .... fmtmsg(3C)
menu_pad control menus	display attributes /set_menu_pad, ... menu_attributes(3X)
/field_pad format the general	display attributes of forms .... form_field_attributes(3X)
pnoutrefresh, pechochar create and	display curses pads /prefresh, ... curs_pad(3X)
hypot Euclidean	distance function .... hypot(3M)
/seed48, lcong48 generate uniformly	distributed pseudo-random numbers .... drand48(3C)
remainder	div, ldiv compute the quotient and .... div(3C)
	dlclose close a shared object .... dlclose(3X)
	dlerror get diagnostic information .... dlerror(3X)
	dlopen open a shared object .... dlopen(3X)
in shared object	dlsym get the address of a symbol .... dlsym(3X)
/res_mkquery, res_send, res_init,	dn_comp, dn_expand resolver/ .... resolver(3N)
/res_send, res_init, dn_comp,	dn_expand resolver routines .... resolver(3N)
script	doconfig execute a configuration .... doconfig(3N)
strtold, atof convert string to	double-precision number strtod, ... strtod(3C)
/single_to_decimal,	double_to_decimal,/ .... floating_to_decimal(3)
/refresh, wrefresh, wnoutrefresh,	doupdate, redrawwin, wredrawln/ .... curs_refresh(3X)
mrand48, jrand48, srand48, seed48,/	drand48, erand48, lrand48, nrand48, ... drand48(3C)
descriptor	dup duplicate an open file .... dup(2)
descriptor	dup2 duplicate an open file .... dup2(2C)
create/ form_field_new: new_field,	dup_field, link_field, free_field, ... form_field_new(3X)
dup	duplicate an open file descriptor .... dup(2)
dup2	duplicate an open file descriptor .... dup2(2C)
mvwin, subwin, derwin, mvderwin,	dupwin, wsyncup, syncok,/ /delwin, ... curs_window(3X)
form_field_info: field_info,	dynamic_field_info get forms field/ .... form_field_info(3X)
curs_inopts: cbreak, nocbreak,	echo, noecho, halfdelay, intrflush/ .... curs_inopts(3X)
/addch, waddch, mvaddch, mvwaddch,	echochar, wechochar add a character/ .... curs_addch(3X)
seconvert, sfconvert, sgconvert/	econvert, fconvert, gconvert, ... econvert(3)
gcvtl convert floating-point/	ecvt, ecvtl, fcvt, fcvtl, gcvt, ... ecvt(3C)
convert floating-point/ ecvt,	ecvtl, fcvt, fcvtl, gcvt, gcvtl .... ecvt(3C)
end, etext,	edata last locations in program .... end(3C)
effective user, real group, and	effective group IDs /get real user, ... getuid(2)
setregid set real and	effective group IDs .... setregid(3)
setreuid set real and	effective user IDs .... setreuid(3)
/getgid, getegid get real user,	effective user, real group, and/ .... getuid(2)
new process in a virtual memory	efficient way vfork spawn .... vfork(2)
insque, remque insert/remove	element from a queue .... insque(3C)
basename return the last	element of a path name .... basename(3G)
elf_update update an	ELF descriptor .... elf_update(3E)
versions elf_version coordinate	ELF library and application .... elf_version(3E)
	elf object file access library .... elf(3E)
object file type elf_fsize	elf32_fsize return the size of an .... elf_fsize(3E)

16   Programmer's Reference Manual: Operating System API

retrieve/ elf_getehdr:	elf32_getehdr, elf32_newehdr	elf_getehdr(3E)
retrieve/ elf_getphdr:	elf32_getphdr, elf32_newphdr	elf_getphdr(3E)
class-dependent/ elf_getshdr:	elf32_getshdr retrieve	elf_getshdr(3E)
elf_getehdr: elf32_getehdr,	elf32_newehdr retrieve/	elf_getehdr(3E)
elf_getphdr: elf32_getphdr,	elf32_newphdr retrieve/	elf_getphdr(3E)
class-dependent data/ elf_xlate:	elf32_xlatetof, elf32_xlatetom	elf_xlate(3E)
elf_xlate: elf32_xlatetof,	elf32_xlatetom class-dependent data/	elf_xlate(3E)
	elf_begin make a file descriptor	elf_begin(3E)
	elf_cntl control a file descriptor	elf_cntl(3E)
	elf_end finish using an object file	elf_end(3E)
handling	elf_errmsg, elf_errno error	elf_errmsg(3E)
elf_errmsg,	elf_errno error handling	elf_errmsg(3E)
	elf_fill set fill byte	elf_fill(3E)
elf_flagelf, elf_flagphdr,/	elf_flagdata, elf_flagehdr, ...	elf_flagdata(3E)
elf_flagphdr,/ elf_flagdata,	elf_flagehdr, elf_flagelf, ...	elf_flagdata(3E)
elf_flagdata, elf_flagehdr,	/elf_flagehdr, elf_flagelf, ...	elf_flagdata(3E)
/elf_flagehdr, elf_flagelf,	elf_flagelf, elf_flagphdr,/	elf_flagdata(3E)
/elf_flagelf, elf_flagphdr,	elf_flagphdr, elf_flagscn,/	elf_flagdata(3E)
/elf_flagphdr, elf_flagscn,	elf_flagscn, elf_flagshdr/	elf_flagdata(3E)
	elf_flagshdr manipulate flags	elf_flagdata(3E)
size of an object file type	elf_fsize: elf32_fsize return the	elf_fsize(3E)
member header	elf_getarhdr retrieve archive	elf_getarhdr(3E)
symbol table	elf_getarsym retrieve archive	elf_getarsym(3E)
an object file	elf_getbase get the base offset for	elf_getbase(3E)
elf_rawdata get section data	elf_getdata, elf_newdata, ...	elf_getdata(3E)
elf32_newehdr retrieve/	elf_getehdr: elf32_getehdr, ...	elf_getehdr(3E)
identification data	elf_getident retrieve file	elf_getident(3E)
elf32_newphdr retrieve/	elf_getphdr: elf32_getphdr, ...	elf_getphdr(3E)
elf_nextscn get section/	elf_getscn, elf_ndxscn, elf_newscn, ...	elf_getscn(3E)
class-dependent section header	elf_getshdr: elf32_getshdr retrieve	elf_getshdr(3E)
	elf_hash compute hash value	elf_hash(3E)
	elf_kind determine file type	elf_kind(3E)
get section/ elf_getscn,	elf_ndxscn, elf_newscn, elf_nextscn	elf_getscn(3E)
section data elf_getdata,	elf_newdata, elf_rawdata get	elf_getdata(3E)
elf_getscn, elf_ndxscn,	elf_newscn, elf_nextscn get section/	elf_getscn(3E)
access	elf_next sequential archive member	elf_next(3E)
elf_getscn, elf_ndxscn, elf_newscn,	elf_nextscn get section information	elf_getscn(3E)
access	elf_rand random archive member	elf_rand(3E)
elf_getdata, elf_newdata,	elf_rawdata get section data	elf_getdata(3E)
file contents	elf_rawfile retrieve uninterpreted	elf_rawfile(3E)
	elf_strptr make a string pointer	elf_strptr(3E)
	elf_update update an ELF descriptor	elf_update(3E)
and application versions	elf_version coordinate ELF library	elf_version(3E)
elf32_xlatetom class-dependent/	elf_xlate: elf32_xlatetof, ...	elf_xlate(3E)
/tgoto, tputs curses interfaces	(emulated) to the termcap library	curs_termcap(3X)
accounting acct	enable or disable process	acct(2)
crypt, setkey,	encrypt generate encryption	crypt(3C)
whether a character buffer is	encrypted isencrypt determine	isencrypt(3G)

Permuted Index

crypt, setkey, encrypt generate	encryption	crypt(3C)
crypt password and file	encryption functions	crypt(3X)
program	end, etext, edata last locations in	end(3C)
/getgrgid, getgrnam, setgrent,	endgrent, fgetgrent get group file/	getgrent(3C)
/gethostbyname, sethostent,	endhostent get network host entry	gethostent(3N)
/getnetbyname, setnetent,	endnetent get network entry	getnetent(3N)
socket create an	endpoint for communication	socket(3N)
bind an address to a transport	endpoint t_bind	t_bind(3N)
t_close close a transport	endpoint	t_close(3N)
at the current event on a transport	endpoint t_look look	t_look(3N)
t_open establish a transport	endpoint	t_open(3N)
manage options for a transport	endpoint t_optmgmt	t_optmgmt(3N)
t_unbind disable a transport	endpoint	t_unbind(3N)
/getprotobyname, setprotoent,	endprotoent get protocol entry	getprotoent(3N)
/getpwuid, getpwnam, setpwent,	endpwent, fgetpwent manipulate/	getpwent(3C)
/getservbyname, setservent,	endservent get service entry	getservent(3N)
getspent, getspnam, setspent,	endspent, fgetspent, lckpwdf,/	getspent(3C)
getusershell, setusershell,	endusershell get legal user shells	getusershell(3)
/getutline, pututline, setutent,	endutent, utmpname access utmp file/	getut(3C)
/getutxline, pututxline, setutxent,	endutxent, utmpxname, getutmp,/	getutx(3C)
curs_initscr: initscr, newterm,	endwin, isendwin, set_term,/	curs_initscr(3X)
getdents read directory	entries and put in a file system/	getdents(2)
nlist get	entries from name list	nlist(3E)
nlist get	entries from symbol table	nlist(3)
component getnetpath get netconfig	entry corresponding to NETPATH	getnetpath(3N)
endgrent, fgetgrent get group file	entry /getgrnam, setgrent,	getgrent(3C)
endhostent get network host	entry /gethostbyname, sethostent,	gethostent(3N)
getmntany get mnttab file	entry getmntent,	getmntent(3C)
get network configuration database	entry getnetconfig	getnetconfig(3N)
setnetent, endnetent get network	entry /getnetbyaddr, getnetbyname,	getnetent(3N)
endprotoent get protocol	entry /getprotobyname, setprotoent,	getprotoent(3N)
fgetpwent manipulate password file	entry /setpwent, endpwent,	getpwent(3C)
setservent, endservent get service	entry /getservbyname,	getservent(3N)
manipulate shadow password file	entry /fgetspent, lckpwdf, ulckpwdf	getspent(3C)
endutent, utmpname access utmp file	entry /pututline, setutent,	getut(3C)
updwtmp, updwtmpx access utmpx file	entry /getutmp, getutmpx,	getutx(3C)
getvfsany get vfstab file	entry /getvfsfile, getvfsspec,	getvfsent(3C)
putpwent write password file	entry	putpwent(3C)
putspent write shadow password file	entry	putspent(3C)
unlink remove directory	entry	unlink(2)
fpsetsticky IEEE floating-point	environment control /fpgetsticky,	fpgetround(3C)
getenv return value for	environment name	getenv(3C)
putenv change or add value to	environment	putenv(3C)
/termattrs, termname curses	environment query routines	curs_termattrs(3X)
jrand48, srand48, seed48,/ drand48,	erand48, lrand48, nrand48, mrand48,	drand48(3C)
/post_form, unpost_form write or	erase forms from associated/	form_post(3X)
/post_menu, unpost_menu write or	erase menus from associated/	menu_post(3X)

Permuted Index

clrtobot, wclrtobot,/ curs_clear:	erase, werase, clear, wclear, ... curs_clear(3X)
curs_termattrs: baudrate,	erasechar, has_ic, has_il,/ .... curs_termattrs(3X)
complementary error function	erf, erfc error function and .... erf(3M)
complementary error function erf,	erfc error function and .... erf(3M)
numbers and their names	errno complete list of the error .... errno(2)
error function erf, erfc	error function and complementary .... erf(3M)
error function and complementary	error function erf, erfc .... erf(3M)
elf_errmsg, elf_errno	error handling .... elf_errmsg(3E)
t_rcvuderr receive a unit data	error indication .... t_rcvuderr(3N)
strerror get	error message string .... strerror(3C)
t_error produce	error message .... t_error(3N)
perror print system	error messages .... perror(3C)
errno complete list of the	error numbers and their names .... errno(2)
introduction to system calls and	error numbers intro .... intro(2)
matherr	error-handling function .... matherr(3M)
server side remote procedure call	errors /library routines for .... rpc_svc_err(3N)
strings, compressing or expanding	escape codes /strcadd, strecpy copy .... strccpy(3G)
transport user t_connect	establish a connection with another .... t_connect(3N)
t_open	establish a transport endpoint .... t_open(3N)
connection dial	establish an outgoing terminal line .... dial(3C)
program end,	etext, edata last locations in .... end(3C)
ethers	Ethernet address mapping operations .... ethers(3N)
operations	ethers Ethernet address mapping .... ethers(3N)
hypot	Euclidean distance function .... hypot(3M)
t_look look at the current	event on a transport endpoint .... t_look(3N)
sigprocmask change or	examine signal mask .... sigprocmask(2)
and pending sigpending	examine signals that are blocked .... sigpending(2)
ieee_handler IEEE	exception trap handler function .... ieee_handler(3M)
execlp, execvp execute a file	exec: execl, execv, execle, execve, ... exec(2)
execlp, execvp execute a/ exec:	execl, execv, execle, execve, ... exec(2)
execute a file exec: execl, execv,	execle, execve, execlp, execvp .... exec(2)
exec: execl, execv, execle, execve,	execlp, execvp execute a file .... exec(2)
doconfig	execute a configuration script .... doconfig(3N)
execle, execve, execlp, execvp	execute a file exec: execl, execv, ... exec(2)
regcmp, regex compile and	execute regular expression .... regcmp(3G)
nap suspend	execution for a short interval .... nap(2)
microseconds usleep suspend	execution for interval in .... usleep(3)
sleep suspend	execution for interval .... sleep(3)
sleep suspend	execution for interval .... sleep(3C)
monitor prepare	execution profile .... monitor(3C)
profil	execution time profile .... profil(2)
execvp execute a file exec: execl,	execv, execle, execve, execlp, ... exec(2)
file exec: execl, execv, execle,	execve, execlp, execvp execute a .... exec(2)
execv, execle, execve, execlp,	execvp execute a file exec: execl, ... exec(2)
create a new file or rewrite an	existing one creat .... creat(2)
	exit, _exit terminate process .... exit(2)
exit,	_exit terminate process .... exit(2)

Permuted Index 19

Permuted Index

log10f, pow, powf, sqrt, sqrtf/	exp, expf, cbrt, log, logf, log10, ... exp(3M)
copy strings, compressing or	expanding escape codes /strccpy .... strccpy(3G)
t_snd send data or	expedited data over a connection .... t_snd(3N)
connection t_rcv receive data or	expedited data sent over a .... t_rcv(3N)
log10f, pow, powf, sqrt,/ exp,	expf, cbrt, log, logf, log10, ... exp(3M)
/log10f, pow, powf, sqrt, sqrtf	exponential, logarithm, power,/ .... exp(3M)
/compile, step, advance regular	expression compile and match/ .... regexpr(3G)
regex, re_comp, re_exec regular	expression handler .... regex(3)
regex compile and execute regular	expression regcmp, ... regcmp(3G)
floating-point/ /double_to_decimal,	extended_to_decimal convert .... floating_to_decimal(3)
creation /library routines for	external data representation stream .... xdr_create(3N)
xdr library routines for	external data representation .... xdr(3N)
/xdr_setpos library routines for	external data representation .... xdr_admin(3N)
/xdr_wrapstring library routines for	external data representation .... xdr_complex(3N)
/xdr_void library routines for	external data representation .... xdr_simple(3N)
/ceil, ceilf, copysign, fmod, fmodf,	fabs, fabsf, rint, remainder floor,/ .... floor(3M)
/ceilf, copysign, fmod, fmodf, fabs,	fabsf, rint, remainder floor,/ .... floor(3M)
signal simplified software signal	facilities .... signal(3)
sigvec software signal	facilities .... sigvec(3)
data in a machine-independent	fashion /sgetl access long integer .... sputl(3X)
descriptor to an object in the/	fattach attach a STREAMS-based file .... fattach(3C)
chdir,	fchdir change working directory .... chdir(2)
chmod,	fchmod change mode of file .... chmod(2)
file chown, lchown,	fchown change owner and group of a .... chown(2)
stream	fclose, fflush close or flush a .... fclose(3S)
	fcntl file control .... fcntl(2)
sfconvert, sgconvert/ econvert,	fconvert, gconvert, seconvert, ... econvert(3)
floating-point number/ ecvt, ecvtl,	fcvt, fcvtl, gcvt, gcvtl convert .... ecvt(3C)
floating-point/ ecvt, ecvtl, fcvt,	fcvtl, gcvt, gcvtl convert .... ecvt(3C)
STREAMS-based file descriptor	fdetach detach a name from a .... fdetach(3C)
fopen, freopen,	fdopen open a stream .... fopen(3S)
fopen, freopen,	fdopen open a stream .... fopen(3S)
status inquiries ferror,	feof, clearerr, fileno stream .... ferror(3S)
stream status inquiries	ferror, feof, clearerr, fileno .... ferror(3S)
nextkey/ dbm: dbminit, dbmclose,	fetch, store, delete, firstkey, ... dbm(3)
fclose,	fflush close or flush a stream .... fclose(3S)
bstring: bcopy, bcmp, bzero,	ffs bit and byte string operations .... bstring(3)
	ffs find first set bit .... ffs(3C)
from a stream getc, getchar,	fgetc, getw get character or word .... getc(3S)
/getgrnam, setgrent, endgrent,	fgetgrent get group file entry .... getgrent(3C)
in a stream fsetpos,	fgetpos reposition a file pointer .... fsetpos(3C)
/getpwnam, setpwent, endpwent,	fgetpwent manipulate password file/ .... getpwent(3C)
gets,	fgets get a string from a stream .... gets(3S)
/getspnam, setspent, endspent,	fgetspent, lckpwdf, ulckpwdf/ .... getspent(3C)
set_max_field set and get forms	field attributes /field_status, ... form_field_buffer(3X)
dynamic_field_info get forms	field characteristics /field_info, ... form_field_info(3X)
/field_type, field_arg forms	field data type validation .... form_field_validation(3X)

set forms current page and field /current_field, field_index	form_page(3X)
behind /data_behind tell if forms field has off-screen data ahead or	form_data(3X)
/field_opts_off, field_opts forms field option routines	form_field_opts(3X)
/set_field_type, field_type, field_arg forms field data type/	form_field_validation(3X)
/field_fore, set_field_back, field_back, set_field_pad,/	form_field_attributes(3X)
field_status,/ /set_field_buffer, field_buffer, set_field_status,	form_field_buffer(3X)
/set_form_fields, form_fields, field_count, move_field connect/	form_field(3X)
field_back,/ /set_field_fore, field_fore, set_field_back,	form_field_attributes(3X)
/set_current_field, current_field, field_index set forms current page/	form_page(3X)
forms field/ form_field_info: field_info, dynamic_field_info get	form_field_info(3X)
/form_term, set_field_init, field_init, set_field_term,/	form_hook(3X)
form_field_just: set_field_just, field_just format the general/	form_field_just(3X)
/field_opts_on, field_opts_off, field_opts forms field option/	form_field_opts(3X)
/set_field_opts, field_opts_on, field_opts_off, field_opts forms/	form_field_opts(3X)
form_field_opts: set_field_opts, field_opts_on, field_opts_off,/	form_field_opts(3X)
display/ /field_back, set_field_pad, field_pad format the general	form_field_attributes(3X)
bufsplit split buffer into fields	bufsplit(3G)
create and destroy forms fields /link_field, free_field,	form_field_new(3X)
field_count, move_field connect fields to forms /form_fields,	form_field(3X)
/field_buffer, set_field_status, field_status, set_max_field set and/	form_field_buffer(3X)
field_init, set_field_term, field_term assign/ /set_field_init,	form_hook(3X)
data type/ /set_field_type, field_type, field_arg forms field	form_field_validation(3X)
/link_fieldtype forms fieldtype routines	form_fieldtype(3X)
data with forms /set_field_userptr, field_userptr associate application	form_field_userptr(3X)
mkfifo create a new FIFO	mkfifo(3C)
utime set file access and modification times	utime(2)
elf object file access library	elf(3E)
access determine accessibility of a file	access(2)
chmod, fchmod change mode of file	chmod(2)
fchown change owner and group of a file chown, lchown,	chown(2)
chsize change the size of a file	chsize(2)
elf_rawfile retrieve uninterpreted file contents	elf_rawfile(3E)
fcntl file control	fcntl(2)
umask set and get file creation mask	umask(2)
(write) a curses screen from (to) a file /scr_init, scr_set read	curs_scr_dump(3X)
close close a file descriptor	close(2)
dup duplicate an open file descriptor	dup(2)
dup2 duplicate an open file descriptor	dup2(3C)
elf_begin make a file descriptor	elf_begin(3E)
elf_cntl control a file descriptor	elf_cntl(3E)
detach a name from a STREAMS-based file descriptor fdetach	fdetach(3C)
isastream test a file descriptor	isastream(3C)
fattach attach a STREAMS-based file descriptor to an object in the/	fattach(3C)
elf_end finish using an object file	elf_end(3E)

Permuted Index

get the base offset for an object	file elf_getbase	elf_getbase(3E)
crypt password and	file encryption functions	crypt(3X)
endgrent, fgetgrent get group	file entry /getgrnam, setgrent,	getgrent(3C)
getmntent, getmntany get mnttab	file entry	getmntent(3C)
fgetpwent manipulate password	file entry /setpwent, endpwent,	getpwent(3C)
ulckpwdf manipulate shadow password	file entry /fgetspent, lckpwdf,	getspent(3C)
endutent, utmpname access utmp	file entry /pututline, setutent,	getut(3C)
updwtmp, updwtmpx access utmpx	file entry /getutmp, getutmpx,	getutx(3C)
getvfsspec, getvfsany get vfstab	file entry getvfsent, getvfsfile,	getvfsent(3C)
putpwent write password	file entry	putpwent(3C)
putspent write shadow password	file entry	putspent(3C)
execve, execlp, execvp execute a	file exec: execl, execv, execle,	exec(2)
retrieve class-dependent object	file header /elf32_newehdr	elf_getehdr(3E)
elf_getident retrieve	file identification data	elf_getident(3E)
pathfind search for named	file in named directories	pathfind(3G)
copylist copy a	file into memory	copylist(3G)
link link to a	file	link(2)
directory, or a special or ordinary	file mknod make a	mknod(2)
directory, or a special or ordinary	file mknod make a	mknod(2)
ctermid generate	file name for terminal	ctermid(3S)
mkstemp make a unique	file name	mkstemp(3)
mktemp make a unique	file name	mktemp(3C)
realpath returns the real	file name	realpath(3C)
ttyslot find the slot in the utmp	file of the current user	ttyslot(3C)
creat create a new	file or rewrite an existing one	creat(2)
the parent directory name of a	file path name dirname report	dirname(3G)
fseek, rewind, ftell reposition a	file pointer in a stream	fseek(3S)
fsetpos, fgetpos reposition a	file pointer in a stream	fsetpos(3C)
lseek move read/write	file pointer	lseek(2)
read read from	file	read(2)
locking lock or unlock a	file region for reading or writing	locking(2)
remove remove	file	remove(3C)
rename change the name of a	file	rename(2)
stat, lstat, fstat get	file status	stat(2)
stat, lstat, fstat get	file status	stat(2)
symlink make a symbolic link to a	file	symlink(2)
/read directory entries and put in a	file system independent format	getdents(2)
statvfs, fstatvfs get	file system information	statvfs(2)
mount mount a	file system	mount(2)
/file descriptor to an object in the	file system name space	fattach(3C)
ustat get	file system statistics	ustat(2)
sysfs get	file system type information	sysfs(2)
umount unmount a	file system	umount(2)
utimes set	file times	utimes(3)
tmpfile create a temporary	file	tmpfile(3S)
create a name for a temporary	file tmpnam, tempnam	tmpnam(3S)
truncate, ftruncate set a	file to a specified length	truncate(3C)

22 Programmer´s Reference Manual: Operating System API

ftw, nftw walk a file tree	ftw(3C)
return the size of an object file type elf_fsize: elf32_fsize	elf_fsize(3E)
elf_kind determine file type	elf_kind(3E)
write, writev write on a file	write(2)
ferror, feof, clearerr, fileno stream status inquiries	ferror(3S)
the physical/ fsync synchronize a file's in-memory state with that on	fsync(2)
lockf record locking on files	lockf(3C)
elf_fill set fill byte	elf_fill(3E)
curs_util: unctrl, keyname, filter, use_env, putwin, getwin,/	curs_util(3X)
ffs find first set bit	ffs(3C)
ttyname, isatty find name of a terminal	ttyname(3C)
the current user ttyslot find the slot in the utmp file of	ttyslot(3C)
elf_end finish using an object file	elf_end(3E)
isnan, isnand, isnanf, isnanl, finite, finitel, fpclass, fpclassl,/	isnan(3C)
isnand, isnanf, isnanl, finite, finitel, fpclass, fpclassl,/ isnan,	isnan(3C)
/dbmclose, fetch, store, delete, firstkey, nextkey data base/	dbm(3)
elf_flagshdr manipulate flags /elf_flagphdr, elf_flagscn,	elf_flagdata(3E)
routines curs_beep: beep, flash curses bell and screen flash	curs_beep(3X)
beep, flash curses bell and screen flash routines curs_beep:	curs_beep(3X)
floatingpoint IEEE floating point definitions	floatingpoint(3)
/fpgetsticky, fpsetsticky IEEE floating-point environment control	fpgetround(3C)
definitions floatingpoint IEEE floating point	floatingpoint(3)
unorderedl determine type of floating-point number /unordered,	isnan(3C)
/fcvt, fcvtl, gcvt, gcvtl convert floating-point number to string	ecvt(3C)
scalb, scalbl manipulate parts of floating-point numbers /nextafter,	frexp(3C)
/convert decimal record to floating-point value	decimal_to_floating(3)
record /extended_to_decimal convert floating-point value to decimal	floating_to_decimal(3)
single_to_decimal,/ floating_to_decimal:	floating_to_decimal(3)
/fmodf, fabs, fabsf, rint, remainder floor, ceiling, remainder, absolute/	floor(3M)
copysign, fmod, fmodf, fabs,/ floor, floorf, ceil, ceilf,	floor(3M)
fmod, fmodf, fabs, fabsf,/ floor, floorf, ceil, ceilf, copysign,	floor(3M)
fclose, fflush close or flush a stream	fclose(3S)
/putwin, getwin, delay_output, flushinp miscellaneous curses/	curs_util(3X)
/floorf, ceil, ceilf, copysign, fmod, fmodf, fabs, fabsf, rint,/	floor(3M)
/ceil, ceilf, copysign, fmod, fmodf, fabs, fabsf, rint, remainder/	floor(3M)
for an application for use with fmtmsg /a list of severity levels	addseverity(3C)
or system console fmtmsg display a message on stderr	fmtmsg(3C)
stream fopen, freopen, fdopen open a	fopen(3S)
stream fopen, freopen, fdopen open a	fopen(3S)
tcsetpgrp set terminal foreground process group id	tcsetpgrp(3C)
fork create a new process	fork(2)
request message nlsrequest format and send listener service	nlsrequest(3N)
getdate convert user format date and time	getdate(3C)
put in a file system independent format /read directory entries and	getdents(2)
forms /set_field_just, field_just format the general appearance of	form_field_just(3X)
/set_field_pad, field_pad format the general display/	form_field_attributes(3X)
/mvscanw, mvwscanw, vwscanw convert formatted input from a curses widow	curs_scanw(3X)

Permuted Index

scanf, fscanf, sscanf convert formatted input	scanf(3S)
/vprintf, vfprintf, vsprintf formatted output conversion	printf(3S)
/mvprintw, mvwprintw, vwprintw print formatted output in curses/	curs_printw(3X)
vprintf, vfprintf, vsprintf print formatted output of a variable/	vprintf(3S)
printf, fprintf, sprintf print formatted output	printf(3S)
localeconv get numeric formatting information	localeconv(3C)
position forms window cursor form_cursor: pos_form_cursor	form_cursor(3X)
tell if forms field has off-screen/ form_data: data_ahead, data_behind	form_data(3X)
the forms subsystem form_driver command processor for	form_driver(3X)
form_fields, field_count,/ form_field: set_form_fields,	form_field(3X)
set_field_fore, field_fore,/ form_field_attributes:	form_field_attributes(3X)
set_field_buffer, field_buffer,/ form_field_buffer:	form_field_buffer(3X)
dynamic_field_info get forms field/ form_field_info: field_info,	form_field_info(3X)
field_just format the general/ form_field_just: set_field_just,	form_field_just(3X)
dup_field, link_field, free_field,/ form_field_new: new_field,	form_field_new(3X)
field_opts_on, field_opts_off,/ form_field_opts: set_field_opts,	form_field_opts(3X)
form_field: set_form_fields, form_fields, field_count,/	form_field(3X)
free_fieldtype, set_fieldtype_arg,/ form_fieldtype: new_fieldtype,	form_fieldtype(3X)
set_field_userptr, field_userptr/ form_field_userptr:	form_field_userptr(3X)
set_field_type, field_type,/ form_field_validation:	form_field_validation(3X)
form_init, set_form_term,/ form_hook: set_form_init,	form_hook(3X)
form_hook: set_form_init, form_init, set_form_term,/	form_hook(3X)
create and destroy forms form_new: new_form, free_form	form_new(3X)
new_page forms pagination form_new_page: set_new_page,	form_new_page(3X)
/form_opts_on, form_opts_off, form_opts forms option routines	form_opts(3X)
form_opts_on, form_opts_off,/ form_opts: set_form_opts,	form_opts(3X)
/set_form_opts, form_opts_on, form_opts_off, form_opts forms/	form_opts(3X)
form_opts: set_form_opts, form_opts_on, form_opts_off,/	form_opts(3X)
form_page: set_form_page,/ form_page, set_current_field,/	form_page(3X)
form_page, set_current_field,/ form_page: set_form_page,	form_page(3X)
write or erase forms from/ form_post: post_form, unpost_form	form_post(3X)
	forms character based forms package ... forms(3X)
/current_field, field_index set forms current page and field	form_page(3X)
/set_max_field set and get forms field attributes	form_field_buffer(3X)
/field_info, dynamic_field_info get forms field characteristics	form_field_info(3X)
/field_type, field_arg forms field data type validation	form_field_validation(3X)
/data_ahead, data_behind tell if forms field has off-screen data/	form_data(3X)
/field_opts_off, field_opts forms field option routines	form_field_opts(3X)
free_field, create and destroy forms fields /link_field,	form_field_new(3X)
/link_fieldtype forms fieldtype routines	form_fieldtype(3X)
move_field connect fields to forms /form_fields, field_count,	form_field(3X)
the general display attributes of forms /field_pad format	form_field_attributes(3X)
format the general appearance of forms /set_field_just, field_just	form_field_just(3X)
associate application data with forms /field_userptr	form_field_userptr(3X)
routines for invocation by forms /assign application-specific	form_hook(3X)
free_form create and destroy forms form_new: new_form,	form_new(3X)

24   Programmer's REference Manual: Operating System API

associate application data with	forms /form_userptr .... form_userptr(3X)
/unpost_form write or erase	forms from associated subwindows .... form_post(3X)
/form_opts_off, form_opts	forms option routines .... form_opts(3X)
forms character based	forms package .... forms(3X)
set_new_page, new_page	forms pagination form_new_page: .... form_new_page(3X)
command processor for the	forms subsystem form_driver .... form_driver(3X)
/set_form_sub, form_sub, scale_form	forms window and subwindow/ .... form_win(3X)
pos_form_cursor position	forms window cursor form_cursor: .... form_cursor(3X)
and/ /form_win, set_form_sub,	form_sub, scale_form forms window .... form_win(3X)
/form_init, set_form_term,	form_term, set_field_init,/ .... form_hook(3X)
form_userptr: set_form_userptr,	form_userptr associate application/ .... form_userptr(3X)
form_userptr associate application/	form_userptr: set_form_userptr, ... form_userptr(3X)
scale_form/ form_win: set_form_win,	form_win, set_form_sub, form_sub, ... form_win(3X)
set_form_sub, form_sub, scale_form/	form_win: set_form_win, form_win, ... form_win(3X)
configurable pathname variables	fpathconf, pathconf get .... fpathconf(2)
/isnanf, isnanl, finite, finitel,	fpclass, fpclassl, unordered,/ .... isnan(3C)
miscellaneous/ ieee_functions,	fp_class, isnan, copysign, scalbn .... ieee_functions(3M)
/isnanl, finite, finitel, fpclass,	fpclassl, unordered, unorderedl/ .... isnan(3C)
fpgetround, fpsetround,	fpgetmask, fpsetmask, fpgetsticky,/ .... fpgetround(3C)
fpsetmask, fpgetsticky,/	fpgetround, fpsetround, fpgetmask, ... fpgetround(3C)
/fpsetround, fpgetmask, fpsetmask,	fpgetsticky, fpsetsticky IEEE/ .... fpgetround(3C)
output printf,	fprintf, sprintf print formatted .... printf(3S)
vfprintf, vsprintf/ printf,	fprintf, sprintf, vprintf, ... printf(3S)
fpgetround, fpsetround, fpgetmask,	fpsetmask, fpgetsticky, fpsetsticky/ .... fpgetround(3C)
fpgetsticky,/ fpgetround,	fpsetround, fpgetmask, fpsetmask, ... fpgetround(3C)
/fpgetmask, fpsetmask, fpgetsticky,	fpsetsticky IEEE floating-point/ .... fpgetround(3C)
on a stream putc, putchar,	fputc, putw put character or word .... putc(3S)
puts,	fputs put a string on a stream .... puts(3S)
	fread, fwrite binary input/output .... fread(3S)
t_free	free a library structure .... t_free(3N)
mallinfo memory allocator malloc,	free, realloc, calloc, mallopt, ... malloc(3X)
valloc, memory allocator malloc,	free, realloc, calloc, memalign, ... malloc(3C)
/new_field, dup_field, link_field,	free_field, create and destroy/ .... form_field_new(3X)
form_fieldtype: new_fieldtype,	free_fieldtype, set_fieldtype_arg,/ .... form_fieldtype(3X)
form_new: new_form,	free_form create and destroy forms .... form_new(3X)
items menu_item_new: new_item,	free_item create and destroy menus .... menu_item_new(3X)
menu_new: new_menu,	free_menu create and destroy menus .... menu_new(3X)
fopen,	freopen, fdopen open a stream .... fopen(3S)
fopen,	freopen, fdopen open a stream .... fopen(3S)
modf, modff, modfl, nextafter,/	frexp, frexpl, ldexp, ldexpl, logb, ... frexp(3C)
modff, modfl, nextafter,/ frexp,	frexpl, ldexp, ldexpl, logb, modf, ... frexp(3C)
input scanf,	fscanf, sscanf convert formatted .... scanf(3S)
file pointer in a stream	fseek, rewind, ftell reposition a .... fseek(3S)
pointer in a stream	fsetpos, fgetpos reposition a file .... fsetpos(3C)
stat, lstat,	fstat get file status .... stat(2)
stat, lstat,	fstat get file status .... stat(2)
information statvfs,	fstatvfs get file system .... statvfs(2)

Permuted Index

in-memory state with that on the/	fsync synchronize a file's .... fsync(2)
a stream fseek, rewind,	ftell reposition a file pointer in .... fseek(3S)
	ftime get date and time .... ftime(3C)
	ftime get time and date .... ftime(2)
communication package stdipc:	ftok standard interprocess .... stdipc(3C)
length truncate,	ftruncate set a file to a specified .... truncate(3C)
	ftw, nftw walk a file tree .... ftw(3C)
shutdown shut down part of a	full-duplex connection .... shutdown(3N)
function erf, erfc error	function and complementary error .... erf(3M)
function and complementary error	function erf, erfc error .... erf(3M)
gamma, lgamma log gamma	function .... gamma(3M)
hypot Euclidean distance	function .... hypot(3M)
IEEE exception trap handler	function ieee_handler .... ieee_handler(3M)
libwindows windowing terminal	function library .... libwindows(3X)
matherr error-handling	function .... matherr(3M)
intro introduction to	functions and libraries .... intro(3)
j0, j1, jn, y0, y1, yn Bessel	functions bessel: .... bessel(3M)
crypt password and file encryption	functions .... crypt(3X)
logarithm, power, square root	functions /sqrt, sqrtf exponential, ... exp(3M)
ceiling, remainder, absolute value	functions /rint, remainder floor, ... floor(3M)
/copysign, scalbn miscellaneous	functions for IEEE arithmetic .... ieee_functions(3M)
mbstowcs, wcstombs multibyte string	functions mbstring: .... mbstring(3C)
asinh, acosh, atanh hyperbolic	functions /coshf, tanh, tanhf, ... sinh(3M)
sysi86 machine specific	functions .... sysi86(2)
atanf, atan2, atan2f trigonometric	functions /acos, acosf, atan, ... trig(3M)
fread,	fwrite binary input/output .... fread(3S)
gamma, lgamma log	gamma function .... gamma(3M)
	gamma, lgamma log gamma function .... gamma(3M)
/mult, mdiv, mcmp, min, mout, pow,	gcd, rpow, msqrt, sdiv, itom, xtom,/ .... mp(3X)
sgconvert/ econvert, fconvert,	gconvert, seconvert, sfconvert, ... econvert(3)
number/ ecvt, ecvtl, fcvt, fcvtl,	gcvt, gcvtl convert floating-point .... ecvt(3C)
to/ ecvt, ecvtl, fcvt, fcvtl, gcvt,	gcvtl convert floating-point number .... ecvt(3C)
/field_just format the	general appearance of forms .... form_field_just(3X)
/set_field_pad, field_pad format the	general display attributes of forms .... form_field_attributes(3X)
/tcgetpgrp, tcsetpgrp, tcgetsid	general terminal interface .... termios(2)
control priocntlset	generalized process scheduler .... priocntlset(2)
signal abort	generate an abnormal termination .... abort(3C)
crypt, setkey, encrypt	generate encryption .... crypt(3C)
ctermid	generate file name for terminal .... ctermid(3S)
/jrand48, srand48, seed48, lcong48	generate uniformly distributed/ .... drand48(3C)
rand, srand simple random number	generator .... rand(3C)
rand, srand simple random-number	generator .... rand(3C)
/setstate better random number	generator; routines for changing/ .... random(3)
generator; routines for changing	generators /better random number .... random(3)

Permuted Index

/netdir_perror, netdir_sperror	generic transport name-to-address/	netdir_getbyname(3N)
curs_getyx: getyx, getparyx,	getbegyx, getmaxyx get curses/	curs_getyx(3X)
character or word from a stream	getc, getchar, fgetc, getw get	getc(3S)
ungetch get (or push/ curs_getch:	getch, wgetch, mvgetch, mvwgetch, ...	curs_getch(3X)
or word from a stream getc,	getchar, fgetc, getw get character	getc(3S)
current user context	getcontext, setcontext get and set	getcontext(2)
working directory	getcwd get pathname of current	getcwd(3C)
and time	getdate convert user format date	getdate(3C)
put in a file system independent/	getdents read directory entries and	getdents(2)
size	getdtablesize get descriptor table	getdtablesize(3)
user,/ getuid, geteuid, getgid,	getegid get real user, effective	getuid(2)
name	getenv return value for environment	getenv(3C)
user, effective user, real/ getuid,	geteuid, getgid, getegid get real	getuid(2)
effective user,/ getuid, geteuid,	getgid, getegid get real user, ...	getuid(2)
setgrent, endgrent, fgetgrent get/	getgrent, getgrgid, getgrnam, ...	getgrent(3C)
endgrent, fgetgrent get/ getgrent,	getgrgid, getgrnam, setgrent, ...	getgrent(3C)
fgetgrent get/ getgrent, getgrgid,	getgrnam, setgrent, endgrent, ...	getgrent(3C)
supplementary group access list/	getgroups, setgroups get or set	getgroups(2)
sethostent, endhostent/ gethostent,	gethostbyaddr, gethostbyname, ...	gethostent(3N)
gethostent, gethostbyaddr,	gethostbyname, sethostent,/	gethostent(3N)
gethostbyname, sethostent,/	gethostent, gethostbyaddr, ...	gethostent(3N)
current host	gethostid get unique identifier of	gethostid(3)
name of current host	gethostname, sethostname get/set	gethostname(3)
of interval timer	getitimer, setitimer get/set value	getitimer(3C)
	getlogin get login name	getlogin(3C)
window/ /getyx, getparyx, getbegyx,	getmaxyx get curses cursor and	curs_getyx(3X)
getmntent,	getmntany get mnttab file entry	getmntent(3C)
file entry	getmntent, getmntany get mnttab	getmntent(3C)
stream	getmsg get next message off a	getmsg(2)
setnetent, endnetent/ getnetent,	getnetbyaddr, getnetbyname, ...	getnetent(3N)
get/ getnetent, getnetbyaddr,	getnetbyname, setnetent, endnetent	getnetent(3N)
configuration database entry	getnetconfig get network	getnetconfig(3N)
getnetbyname, setnetent, endnetent/	getnetent, getnetbyaddr, ...	getnetent(3N)
/authdes_getucred,	getnetname, host2netname,/	secure_rpc(3N)
corresponding to NETPATH component	getnetpath get netconfig entry	getnetpath(3N)
argument vector	getopt get option letter from	getopt(3C)
	getpagesize get system page size	getpagesize(3)
curses cursor/ curs_getyx: getyx,	getparyx, getbegyx, getmaxyx get	curs_getyx(3X)
	getpass read a password	getpass(3C)
peer	getpeername get name of connected	getpeername(3N)
and/ getpid, getpgrp, getppid,	getpgid get process, process group, ...	getpid(2)
process, process group,/ getpid,	getpgrp, getppid, getpgid get	getpid(2)
get process, process group, and/	getpid, getpgrp, getppid, getpgid	getpid(2)
process group,/ getpid, getpgrp,	getppid, getpgid get process, ...	getpid(2)
program scheduling priority	getpriority, setpriority get/set	getpriority(3)
getprotoent, getprotobynumber,	getprotobyname, setprotoent,/	getprotoent(3N)

Permuted Index

setprotoent,/ getprotoent,	getprotobynumber, getprotobyname,	getprotoent(3N)
getprotobyname, setprotoent,/	getprotoent, getprotobynumber,	getprotoent(3N)
public or secret key publickey:	getpublickey, getsecretkey retrieve	publickey(3N)
	getpw get name from UID	getpw(3C)
setpwent, endpwent, fgetpwent/	getpwent, getpwuid, getpwnam,	getpwent(3C)
fgetpwent/ getpwent, getpwuid,	getpwnam, setpwent, endpwent,	getpwent(3C)
endpwent, fgetpwent/ getpwent,	getpwuid, getpwnam, setpwent,	getpwent(3C)
maximum system resource/	getrlimit, setrlimit control	getrlimit(2)
resource utilization	getrusage get information about	getrusage(3)
stream	gets, fgets get a string from a	gets(3S)
secret/ publickey: getpublickey,	getsecretkey retrieve public or	publickey(3N)
getservent, getservbyport,	getservbyname, setservent,/	getservent(3N)
setservent, endservent/ getservent,	getservbyport, getservbyname,	getservent(3N)
getservbyname, setservent,/	getservent, getservbyport,	getservent(3N)
gethostname, sethostname	get/set name of current host	gethostname(3)
getpriority, setpriority	get/set program scheduling priority	getpriority(3)
getitimer, setitimer	get/set value of interval timer	getitimer(3C)
	getsid get session ID	getsid(2)
	getsockname get socket name	getsockname(3N)
options on sockets	getsockopt, setsockopt get and set	getsockopt(3N)
endspent, fgetspent, lckpwdf,/	getspent, getspnam, setspent,	getspent(3C)
fgetspent, lckpwdf,/ getspent,	getspnam, setspent, endspent,	getspent(3C)
mvwgetstr, wgetnstr/ curs_getstr:	getstr, wgetstr, mvgetstr,	curs_getstr(3X)
string	getsubopt parse suboptions from a	getsubopt(3C)
/reset_shell_mode, resetty, savetty,	getsyx, setsyx, ripoffline,/	curs_kernel(3X)
set the date and time	gettimeofday, settimeofday get or	gettimeofday(3)
set the date and time	gettimeofday, settimeofday get or	gettimeofday(3C)
	gettxt retrieve a text string	gettxt(3C)
get real user, effective user,/	getuid, geteuid, getgid, getegid	getuid(2)
endusershell get legal user shells	getusershell, setusershell,	getusershell(3)
getutline, pututline, setutent,/	getut: getutent, getutid,	getut(3C)
pututline, setutent,/ getut:	getutent, getutid, getutline,	getut(3C)
setutent,/ getut: getutent,	getutid, getutline, pututline,	getut(3C)
getut: getutent, getutid,	getutline, pututline, setutent,/	getut(3C)
/setutxent, endutxent, utmpxname,	getutmp, getutmpx, updwtmp,/	getutx(3C)
/endutxent, utmpxname, getutmp,	getutmpx, updwtmp, updwtmpx access/	getutx(3C)
getutxline, pututxline, setutxent,/	getutx: getutxent, getutxid,	getutx(3C)
pututxline, setutxent,/ getutx:	getutxent, getutxid, getutxline,	getutx(3C)
setutxent,/ getutx: getutxent,	getutxid, getutxline, pututxline,	getutx(3C)
getutx: getutxent, getutxid,	getutxline, pututxline, setutxent,/	getutx(3C)
getvfsent, getvfsfile, getvfsspec,	getvfsany get vfstab file entry	getvfsent(3C)
getvfsany get vfstab file entry	getvfsent, getvfsfile, getvfsspec,	getvfsent(3C)
get vfstab file entry getvfsent,	getvfsfile, getvfsspec, getvfsany	getvfsent(3C)
file entry getvfsent, getvfsfile,	getvfsspec, getvfsany get vfstab	getvfsent(3C)
stream getc, getchar, fgetc,	getw get character or word from a	getc(3S)
pathname	getwd get current working directory	getwd(3)
/keyname, filter, use_env, putwin,	getwin, delay_output, flushinp/	curs_util(3X)

Permuted Index

get curses cursor and/ curs_getyx:	getyx, getparyx, getbegyx, getmaxyx	curs_getyx(3X)
timezone get time zone name	given offset from GMT	timezone(3C)
gmatch shell	global pattern matching	gmatch(3G)
matching	gmatch shell global pattern	gmatch(3G)
time zone name given offset from	GMT timezone get	timezone(3C)
and time to/ ctime, localtime,	gmtime, asctime, tzset convert date	ctime(3C)
sigsetjmp, siglongjmp non-local	goto /longjmp, _setjmp, _longjmp,	setjmp(3)
setjmp, longjmp non-local	goto	setjmp(3C)
sigsetjmp, siglongjmp a non-local	goto with signal state	sigsetjmp(3C)
and check access to a resource	governed by a semaphore /await	waitsem(2)
pseudo-terminal device grantpt	grant access to the slave	grantpt(3C)
pseudo-terminal device	grantpt grant access to the slave	grantpt(3C)
setgroups get or set supplementary	group access list IDs getgroups,	getgroups(2)
initialize the supplementary	group access list initgroups	initgroups(3C)
/get real user, effective user, real	group, and effective group IDs	getuid(2)
/getpgid get process, process	group, and parent process IDs	getpid(2)
setgrent, endgrent, fgetgrent get	group file entry /getgrnam,	getgrent(3C)
setpgid set process	group ID	setpgid(2)
setpgrp set process	group ID	setpgrp(2)
set terminal foreground process	group id tcsetpgrp	tcsetpgrp(3C)
user, real group, and effective	group IDs /get real user, effective	getuid(2)
setregid set real and effective	group IDs	setregid(3)
setuid, setgid set user and	group IDs	setuid(2)
killpg send signal to a process	group	killpg(3)
lchown, fchown change owner and	group of a file chown,	chown(2)
send a signal to a process or a	group of processes kill	kill(2)
send a signal to a process or a	group of processes /sigsendset	sigsend(2)
ssignal,	gsignal software signals	ssignal(3C)
/cbreak, nocbreak, echo, noecho,	halfdelay, intrflush, keypad, meta,/	curs_inopts(3X)
reboot reboot system or	halt processor	reboot(3)
ieee_handler IEEE exception trap	handler function	ieee_handler(3M)
re_comp, re_exec regular expression	handler regex,	regex(3)
creation and manipulation of CLIENT	handles /routines for dealing with	rpc_clnt_create(3N)
dealing with the creation of server	handles /library routines for	rpc_svc_create(3N)
curses CRT screen	handling and optimization package	curses(3X)
isprint, isgraph, isascii character	handling /iscntrl, ispunct,	ctype(3C)
elf_errmsg, elf_errno error	handling	elf_errmsg(3E)
sigfpe signal	handling for specific SIGFPE codes	sigfpe(3)
mblen, wctomb multibyte character	handling mbchar: mbtowc,	mbchar(3C)
/start_color, init_pair, init_color,	has_colors, can_change_color,/	curs_color(3X)
hsearch, hcreate, hdestroy manage	hash search tables	hsearch(3C)
elf_hash compute	hash value	elf_hash(3E)
termattrs,/ /baudrate, erasechar,	has_ic, has_il, killchar, longname,	curs_termattrs(3X)
/baudrate, erasechar, has_ic,	has_il, killchar, longname,/	curs_termattrs(3X)
search tables hsearch,	hcreate, hdestroy manage hash	hsearch(3C)
hsearch, hcreate,	hdestroy manage hash search tables	hsearch(3C)
retrieve archive member	header elf_getarhdr	elf_getarhdr(3E)

Permuted Index

class-dependent object file	header /elf32_newehdr retrieve	elf_getehdr(3E)
retrieve class-dependent section	header elf_getshdr: elf32_getshdr	elf_getshdr(3E)
retrieve class-dependent program	header table /elf32_newphdr	elf_getphdr(3E)
deck/ panel_show: show_panel,	hide_panel, panel_hidden panels	panel_show(3X)
curs_border: border, wborder, box,	hline, whline, vline, wvline create/	curs_border(3X)
/wvline create curses borders,	horizontal and vertical lines	curs_border(3X)
ntohl, ntohs convert values between	host and network byte order /htons,	byteorder(3N)
sethostent, endhostent get network	host entry /gethostbyname,	gethostent(3N)
get unique identifier of current	host gethostid	gethostid(3)
sethostname get/set name of current	host gethostname,	gethostname(3)
/authdes_getucred, getnetname,	host2netname, key_decryptsession,/	secure_rpc(3N)
hash search tables	hsearch, hcreate, hdestroy manage	hsearch(3C)
values between host and/ byteorder,	htonl, htons, ntohl, ntohs convert	byteorder(3N)
between host and/ byteorder, htonl,	htons, ntohl, ntohs convert values	byteorder(3N)
tanh, tanhf, asinh, acosh, atanh	hyperbolic functions /cosh, coshf,	sinh(3M)
	hypot Euclidean distance function	hypot(3M)
getsid get session	ID	getsid(2)
setpgid set process group	ID	setpgid(2)
setpgrp set process group	ID	setpgrp(2)
setsid set session	ID	setsid(2)
terminal foreground process group	id tcsetpgrp set	tcsetpgrp(3C)
curs_outopts: clearok, idlok,	idcok immedok, leaveok, setscrreg,/	curs_outopts(3X)
elf_getident retrieve file	identification data	elf_getident(3E)
gethostid get unique	identifier of current host	gethostid(3)
shmget get shared memory segment	identifier	shmget(2)
setscrreg,/ curs_outopts: clearok,	idlok, idcok immedok, leaveok,	curs_outopts(3X)
set supplementary group access list	IDs getgroups, setgroups get or	getgroups(2)
process group, and parent process	IDs /getppid, getpgid get process,	getpid(2)
real group, and effective group	IDs /get real user, effective user,	getuid(2)
set real and effective group	IDs setregid	setregid(3)
set real and effective user	IDs setreuid	setreuid(3)
setuid, setgid set user and group	IDs	setuid(2)
scalbn miscellaneous functions for	IEEE arithmetic /isnan, copysign,	ieee_functions(3M)
function ieee_handler	IEEE exception trap handler	ieee_handler(3M)
floatingpoint	IEEE floating point definitions	floatingpoint(3)
/fpsetmask, fpgetsticky, fpsetsticky	IEEE floating-point environment/	fpgetround(3C)
copysign, scalbn miscellaneous/	ieee_functions, fp_class, isnan,	ieee_functions(3M)
handler function	ieee_handler IEEE exception trap	ieee_handler(3M)
curs_outopts: clearok, idlok, idcok	immedok, leaveok, setscrreg,/	curs_outopts(3X)
character and its/ curs_inch:	inch, winch, mvinch, mvwinch get a	curs_inch(3X)
mvinchstr,/ curs_inchstr: inchstr,	inchnstr, winchstr, winchnstr,	curs_inchstr(3X)
winchnstr,/ curs_inchstr:	inchstr, inchnstr, winchstr,	curs_inchstr(3X)
entries and put in a file system	independent format /read directory	getdents(2)
	index, rindex string operations	index(3)
receipt of an orderly release	indication t_rcvrel acknowledge	t_rcvrel(3N)
receive a unit data error	indication t_rcvuderr	t_rcvuderr(3N)
syscall	indirect system call	syscall(3)

30 Programmer's Reference Manual: Operating System API

Permuted Index

inet_makeaddr, inet_lnaof,/	inet: inet_addr, inet_network, ...	inet(3N)
inet_makeaddr, inet_lnaof,/ inet:	inet_addr, inet_network, ...	inet(3N)
/inet_network, inet_makeaddr,	inet_lnaof, inet_netof, inet_ntoa/	inet(3N)
inet: inet_addr, inet_network,	inet_makeaddr, inet_lnaof,/	inet(3N)
address/ /inet_makeaddr, inet_lnaof,	inet_netof, inet_ntoa Internet	inet(3N)
inet_lnaof,/ inet: inet_addr,	inet_network, inet_makeaddr, ...	inet(3N)
/inet_lnaof, inet_netof,	inet_ntoa Internet address/	inet(3N)
processor_info get	information about one processor	processor_info(2)
utilization getrusage get	information about resource	getrusage(3)
machines rusers return	information about users on remote	rusers(3N)
dlerror get diagnostic	information	dlerror(3X)
elf_newscn, elf_nextscn get section	information /elf_ndxscn, ...	elf_getscn(3E)
t_rcvdis retrieve	information from disconnect	t_rcvdis(3N)
localeconv get numeric formatting	information	localeconv(3C)
nl_langinfo language	information	nl_langinfo(3C)
statvfs, fstatvfs get file system	information	statvfs(2)
sysinfo get and set system	information strings	sysinfo(2)
sysfs get file system type	information	sysfs(2)
get protocol-specific service	information t_getinfo	t_getinfo(3N)
yp_update change NIS	information	yp_update(3N)
curs_color: start_color, init_pair,	init_color, has_colors,/	curs_color(3X)
supplementary group access list	initgroups initialize the	initgroups(3C)
/set_term, delscreen curses screen	initialization and manipulation/	curs_initscr(3X)
access list initgroups	initialize the supplementary group	initgroups(3C)
connect	initiate a connection on a socket	connect(3N)
t_sndrel	initiate an orderly release	t_sndrel(3N)
popen, pclose	initiate pipe to/from a process	popen(3S)
curs_color: start_color,	init_pair, init_color, has_colors,/	curs_color(3X)
set_term, delscreen/ curs_initscr:	initscr, newterm, endwin, isendwin, ...	curs_initscr(3X)
number generator;/ random, srandom,	initstate, setstate better random	random(3)
fsync synchronize a file's	in-memory state with that on the/	fsync(2)
mvinnstr,/ curs_instr: instr,	innstr, winstr, winnstr, mvinstr, ...	curs_instr(3X)
mvwscanw, vwscanw convert formatted	input from a curses widow /mvscanw, ...	curs_scanw(3X)
/wtimeout, typeahead curses terminal	input option control routines	curs_inopts(3X)
fscanf, sscanf convert formatted	input scanf, ...	scanf(3S)
ungetc push character back onto	input stream	ungetc(3S)
fread, fwrite binary	input/output	fread(3S)
poll	input/output multiplexing	poll(2)
stdio standard buffered	input/output package	stdio(3S)
clearerr, fileno stream status	inquiries ferror, feof, ...	ferror(3S)
insert a character/ curs_insch:	insch, winsch, mvinsch, mvwinsch	curs_insch(3X)
curs_deleteln: deleteln, wdeleteln,	insdelln, winsdelln, insertln,/	curs_deleteln(3X)
/insch, winsch, mvinsch, mvwinsch	insert a character before the/	curs_insch(3X)
/insertln, winsertln delete and	insert lines in a curses window	curs_deleteln(3X)
/mvinsnstr, mvwinsstr, mvwinsnstr	insert string before character/	curs_instr(3X)
/wdeleteln, insdelln, winsdelln,	insertln, winsertln delete and/	curs_deleteln(3X)
insque, remque	insert/remove element from a queue	insque(3C)

Permuted Index

mvinsstr,/ curs_instr: insstr,	insnstr, winsstr, winsnstr, ...	curs_instr(3X)
element from a queue	insque, remque insert/remove	insque(3C)
mvinsstr, mvinsnstr,/ curs_instr:	insstr, insnstr, winsstr, winsnstr, ...	curs_instr(3X)
process until signal sigsuspend	install a signal mask and suspend	sigsuspend(2)
creatsem create an	instance of a binary semaphore	creatsem(2)
mvinstr, mvinnstr,/ curs_instr:	instr, innstr, winstr, winnstr, ...	curs_instr(3X)
abs, labs return	integer absolute value	abs(3C)
a64l, l64a convert between long	integer and base-64 ASCII string	a64l(3C)
mtox, mfree multiple precision	integer arithmetic /itom, xtom, ...	mp(3X)
sputl, sgetl access long	integer data in a/	sputl(3X)
atol, atoi convert string to	integer strtol, strtoul, ...	strtol(3C)
l3tol, ltol3 convert between 3-byte	integers and long integers	l3tol(3C)
between 3-byte integers and long	integers l3tol, ltol3 convert	l3tol(3C)
tcgetsid general terminal	interface /tcgetpgrp, tcsetpgrp, ...	termios(2)
yperr_string, ypprot_err NIS client	interface /yp_order, yp_master, ...	ypclnt(3N)
/tgetstr, tgoto, tputs curses	interfaces (emulated) to the/	curs_termcap(3X)
/tigetnum, tigetstr curses	interfaces to terminfo database	curs_terminfo(3X)
/inet_lnaof, inet_netof, inet_ntoa	Internet address manipulation	inet(3N)
pipe create an	interprocess channel	pipe(2)
stdipc: ftok standard	interprocess communication package	stdipc(3C)
blocked signals and wait for	interrupt /automically release	sigpause(3)
siginterrupt allow signals to	interrupt system calls	siginterrupt(3)
ualarm schedule signal after	interval in microseconds	ualarm(3)
usleep suspend execution for	interval in microseconds	usleep(3)
nap suspend execution for a short	interval	nap(2)
sleep suspend execution for	interval	sleep(3)
sleep suspend execution for	interval	sleep(3C)
setitimer get/set value of	interval timer getitimer, ...	getitimer(3C)
/nocbreak, echo, noecho, halfdelay,	intrflush, keypad, meta, nodelay,/	curs_inopts(3X)
libraries	intro introduction to functions and	intro(3)
and error numbers	intro introduction to system calls	intro(2)
libraries intro	introduction to functions and	intro(3)
error numbers intro	introduction to system calls and	intro(2)
application-specific routines for	invocation by forms /assign	form_hook(3X)
/routines for automatic	invocation by menus	menu_hook(3X)
select synchronous	I/O multiplexing	select(3C)
	ioctl control device	ioctl(2)
/islower, isupper, isalpha,	isalnum, isspace, iscntrl, ispunct,/	ctype(3C)
/isxdigit, islower, isupper,	isalpha, isalnum, isspace, iscntrl,/	ctype(3C)
/iscntrl, ispunct, isprint, isgraph,	isascii character handling	ctype(3C)
	isastream test a file descriptor	isastream(3C)
ttyname,	isatty find name of a terminal	ttyname(3C)
/isupper, isalpha, isalnum, isspace,	iscntrl, ispunct, isprint, isgraph,/	ctype(3C)
isupper, isalpha, isalnum,/ ctype:	isdigit, isxdigit, islower, ...	ctype(3C)
character buffer is encrypted	isencrypt determine whether a	isencrypt(3G)
curses/ /initscr, newterm, endwin,	isendwin, set_term, delscreen	curs_initscr(3X)
/isspace, iscntrl, ispunct, isprint,	isgraph, isascii character handling	ctype(3C)

/touchline, untouchwin, wtouchln, isspace,/ ctype: isdigit, isxdigit, ieee_functions, fp_class, finite, finitel, fpclass,/ finitel, fpclass, fpclassl,/ isnan, fpclass, fpclassl,/ isnan, isnand, fpclassl,/ isnan, isnand, isnanf, /isalnum, isspace, iscntrl, ispunct, /isalpha, isalnum, isspace, iscntrl, /islower, isupper, isalpha, isalnum, system ctype: isdigit, isxdigit, islower, control/ /wtouchln, is_linetouched, isalpha, isalnum,/ ctype: isdigit, item_visible tell if menus /item_description get menus item_opts_off, item_opts menus item_value set and get menus items/ /set_menu_items, menu_items, name/ menu_item_name: item_name, /current_item, set_top_row, top_row, menu_hook: set_item_init, menus item name/ menu_item_name: /item_opts_on, item_opts_off, /set_item_opts, item_opts_on, menu_item_opts: set_item_opts, set and get current menus free_item create and destroy menus application data with menus /item_count connect and disconnect /item_init, set_item_term, data with menus/ /set_item_userptr, menu_item_value: set_item_value, visible menu_item_visible: /mout, pow, gcd, rpow, msqrt, sdiv, functions bessel: bessel: j0, bessel: j0, j1, /erand48, lrand48, nrand48, mrand48, retrieve public or secret characters from curses terminal strings from curses terminal /getnetname, host2netname, /host2netname, key_decryptsession,	is_linetouched, is_wintouched/ .... curs_touch(3X) islower, isupper, isalpha, isalnum, ... ctype(3C) isnan, copysign, scalbn/ .... ieee_functions(3M) isnan, isnand, isnanf, isnanl, ... isnan(3C) isnand, isnanf, isnanl, finite, ... isnan(3C) isnanf, isnanl, finite, finitel, ... isnan(3C) isnanl, finite, finitel, fpclass, ... isnan(3C) isprint, isgraph, isascii character/ .... ctype(3C) ispunct, isprint, isgraph, isascii/ .... ctype(3C) isspace, iscntrl, ispunct, isprint,/ .... ctype(3C) issue a shell command .... system(3S) isupper, isalpha, isalnum, isspace,/ .... ctype(3C) is_wintouched curses refresh .... curs_touch(3X) isxdigit, islower, isupper, ... ctype(3C) item is visible menu_item_visible: .... menu_item_visible(3X) item name and description .... menu_item_name(3X) item option routines /item_opts_on, ... menu_item_opts(3X) item values /set_item_value, ... menu_item_value(3X) item_count connect and disconnect .... menu_items(3X) item_description get menus item .... menu_item_name(3X) item_index set and get current/ .... menu_item_current(3X) item_init, set_item_term,/ .... menu_hook(3X) item_name, item_description get .... menu_item_name(3X) item_opts menus item option/ .... menu_item_opts(3X) item_opts_off, item_opts menus item/ .... menu_item_opts(3X) item_opts_on, item_opts_off,/ .... menu_item_opts(3X) items /top_row, item_index .... menu_item_current(3X) items menu_item_new: new_item, ... menu_item_new(3X) items /item_userptr associate .... menu_item_userptr(3X) items to and from menus .... menu_items(3X) item_term, set_menu_init,/ .... menu_hook(3X) item_userptr associate application .... menu_item_userptr(3X) item_value set and get menus item/ .... menu_item_value(3X) item_visible tell if menus item is .... menu_item_visible(3X) itom, xtom, mtox, mfree multiple/ .... mp(3X) j0, j1, jn, y0, y1, yn Bessel .... bessel(3M) j1, jn, y0, y1, yn Bessel functions .... bessel(3M) jn, y0, y1, yn Bessel functions .... bessel(3M) jrand48, srand48, seed48, lcong48/ .... drand48(3C) key /getpublickey, getsecretkey .... publickey(3N) keyboard /get (or push back) .... curs_getch(3X) keyboard /wgetnstr get character .... curs_getstr(3X) key_decryptsession,/ .... secure_rpc(3N) key_encryptsession, key_gendes,/ .... secure_rpc(3N)

Permuted Index

netname2host,/ /key_encryptsession,	key_gendes, key_setsecret,	secure_rpc(3N)
getwin,/ curs_util: unctrl,	keyname, filter, use_env, putwin,	curs_util(3X)
/echo, noecho, halfdelay, intrflush,	keypad, meta, nodelay, notimeout,/	curs_inopts(3X)
/key_encryptsession, key_gendes,	key_setsecret, netname2host,/	secure_rpc(3N)
a group of processes	kill send a signal to a process or	kill(2)
/erasechar, has_ic, has_il,	killchar, longname, termattrs,/	curs_termattrs(3X)
group	killpg send signal to a process	killpg(3)
integers and long integers	l3tol, ltol3 convert between 3-byte	l3tol(3C)
and base-64 ASCII string a64l,	l64a convert between long integer	a64l(3C)
slk_attroff curses soft	label routines /slk_attrset,	curs_slk(3X)
abs,	labs return integer absolute value	abs(3C)
nl_langinfo	language information	nl_langinfo(3C)
group of a file chown,	lchown, fchown change owner and	chown(2)
/setspent, endspent, fgetspent,	lckpwdf, ulckpwdf manipulate shadow/	getspent(3C)
/mrand48, jrand48, srand48, seed48,	lcong48 generate uniformly/	drand48(3C)
modfl, nextafter,/ frexp, frexpl,	ldexp, ldexpl, logb, modf, modff,	frexp(3C)
nextafter,/ frexp, frexpl, ldexp,	ldexpl, logb, modf, modff, modfl,	frexp(3C)
remainder div,	ldiv compute the quotient and	div(3C)
/clearok, idlok, idcok immedok,	leaveok, setscrreg, wsetscrreg,/	curs_outopts(3X)
setusershell, endusershell get	legal user shells getusershell,	getusershell(3)
ftruncate set a file to a specified	length truncate,	truncate(3C)
getopt get option	letter from argument vector	getopt(3C)
with/ /build a list of severity	levels for an application for use	addseverity(3C)
lsearch,	lfind linear search and update	lsearch(3C)
gamma,	lgamma log gamma function	gamma(3M)
intro introduction to functions and	libraries	intro(3)
tam TAM transition	libraries	tam(3X)
elf_version coordinate ELF	library and application versions	elf_version(3E)
(emulated) to the termcap	library /tputs curses interfaces	curs_termcap(3X)
elf object file access	library	elf(3E)
windowing terminal function	library libwindows	libwindows(3X)
calls /rpc_broadcast, rpc_call	library routines for client side	rpc_clnt_calls(3N)
remote/ /authsys_create_default	library routines for client side	rpc_clnt_auth(3N)
/clnt_tp_create, clnt_vc_create	library routines for dealing with/	rpc_clnt_create(3N)
the/ /svc_tp_create, svc_vc_create	library routines for dealing with	rpc_svc_create(3N)
/xdrrec_create, xdrstdio_create	library routines for external data/	xdr_create(3N)
representation xdr	library routines for external data	xdr(3N)
/xdr_inline, xdrrec_eof, xdr_setpos	library routines for external data/	xdr_admin(3N)
/xdr_vector, xdr_wrapstring	library routines for external data/	xdr_complex(3N)
/xdr_u_long, xdr_u_short, xdr_void	library routines for external data/	xdr_simple(3N)
/xprt_register, xprt_unregister	library routines for registering/	rpc_svc_calls(3N)
procedure calls rpc	library routines for remote	rpc(3N)
procedure calls /xdr_replymsg XDR	library routines for remote	rpc_xdr(3N)
/rpcb_rmtcall, rpcb_set, rpcb_unset	library routines for RPC bind/	rpcbind(3N)
/svc_run, svc_sendreply	library routines for RPC servers	rpc_svc_reg(3N)
/netname2user, user2netname	library routines for secure remote/	secure_rpc(3N)
/svcerr_systemerr, svcerr_weakauth	library routines for server side/	rpc_svc_err(3N)

t_alloc allocate a	library structure	t_alloc(3N)
t_free free a	library structure	t_free(3N)
t_sync synchronize transport	library	t_sync(3N)
function library	libwindows windowing terminal	libwindows(3X)
ulimit get and set user	limits	ulimit(2)
dial establish an outgoing terminal	line connection	dial(3C)
lsearch, lfind	linear search and update	lsearch(3C)
borders, horizontal and vertical	lines /vline, wvline create curses	curs_border(3X)
refresh curses windows and	lines /redrawwin, wredrawln	curs_refresh(3X)
winsertln delete and insert	lines in a curses window /insertln,	curs_deleteln(3X)
link link to a file	link link to a file	link(2)
read the value of a symbolic link	link readlink	readlink(2)
	link to a file	link(2)
symlink make a symbolic	link to a file	symlink(2)
destroy/ /new_field, dup_field,	link_field, free_field, create and	form_field_new(3X)
routines /set_fieldtype_choice,	link_fieldtype forms fieldtype	form_fieldtype(3X)
or set supplementary group access	list IDs getgroups, setgroups get	getgroups(2)
the supplementary group access	list initgroups initialize	initgroups(3C)
nlist get entries from name list	list	nlist(3E)
application/ addseverity build a	list of severity levels for an	addseverity(3C)
names errno complete	list of the error numbers and their	errno(2)
output of a variable argument list	/vsprintf print formatted	vprintf(3S)
t_listen	listen for a connect request	t_listen(3N)
listen	listen for connections on a socket	listen(3N)
socket	listen listen for connections on a	listen(3N)
get client's data passed via the	listener nlsgetcall	nlsgetcall(3N)
nlsrequest format and send	listener service request message	nlsrequest(3N)
modify and query a program's	locale setlocale	setlocale(3C)
information	localeconv get numeric formatting	localeconv(3C)
convert date and time to/ ctime,	localtime, gmtime, asctime, tzset	ctime(3C)
end, etext, edata last	locations in program	end(3C)
lock	lock a process in primary memory	lock(2)
text, or data plock	lock into memory or unlock process,	plock(2)
memory	lock lock a process in primary	lock(2)
reading or writing locking	lock or unlock a file region for	locking(2)
mlockall, munlockall	lock or unlock address space	mlockall(3C)
mlock, munlock	lock (or unlock) pages in memory	mlock(3C)
	lockf record locking on files	lockf(3C)
maillock manage	lockfile for user's mailbox	maillock(3X)
region for reading or writing	locking lock or unlock a file	locking(2)
lockf record	locking on files	lockf(3C)
gamma, lgamma	log gamma function	gamma(3M)
powf, sqrt, sqrtf/ exp, expf, cbrt,	log, logf, log10, log10f, pow,	exp(3M)
closelog, setlogmask control system	log syslog, openlog,	syslog(3)
sqrtf/ exp, expf, cbrt, log, logf,	log10, log10f, pow, powf, sqrt,	exp(3M)
exp, expf, cbrt, log, logf, log10,	log10f, pow, powf, sqrt, sqrtf/	exp(3M)
/pow, powf, sqrt, sqrtf exponential,	logarithm, power, square root/	exp(3M)

Permuted Index   35

Permuted Index

frexp, frexpl, ldexp, ldexpl,	logb, modf, modff, modfl,/	frexp(3C)
sqrt, sqrtf/ exp, expf, cbrt, log,	logf, log10, log10f, pow, powf,	exp(3M)
getlogin get	login name	getlogin(3C)
cuserid get character	login name of the user	cuserid(3S)
setjmp,	longjmp non-local goto	setjmp(3C)
sigsetjmp, siglongjmp/ setjmp,	longjmp, _setjmp, _longjmp,	setjmp(3)
setjmp, longjmp, _setjmp,	_longjmp, sigsetjmp, siglongjmp/	setjmp(3)
curses/ /has_ic, has_il, killchar,	longname, termattrs, termname	curs_termattrs(3X)
transport endpoint t_look	look at the current event on a	t_look(3N)
setsyx, ripoffline, curs_set, napms	low-level curses routines /getsyx,	curs_kernel(3X)
srand48, seed48,/ drand48, erand48,	lrand48, nrand48, mrand48, jrand48,	drand48(3C)
update	lsearch, lfind linear search and	lsearch(3C)
	lseek move read/write file pointer	lseek(2)
stat,	lstat, fstat get file status	stat(2)
stat,	lstat, fstat get file status	stat(2)
integers and long integers l3tol,	ltol3 convert between 3-byte	l3tol(3C)
sysi86	machine specific functions	sysi86(2)
sgetl access long integer data in a	machine-independent fashion sputl,	sputl(3X)
information about users on remote	machines rusers return	rusers(3N)
rwall write to specified remote	machines	rwall(3N)
mout, pow, gcd, rpow, msqrt,/ mp:	madd, msub, mult, mdiv, mcmp, min,	mp(3X)
maillock manage lockfile for user's	mailbox	maillock(3X)
mailbox	maillock manage lockfile for user's	maillock(3X)
makedev,	major, minor manage a device number	makedev(3C)
user contexts	makecontext, swapcontext manipulate	makecontext(3C)
device number	makedev, major, minor manage a	makedev(3C)
free, realloc, calloc, mallopt,	mallinfo memory allocator malloc,	malloc(3X)
mallopt, mallinfo memory allocator	malloc, free, realloc, calloc,	malloc(3X)
memalign, valloc, memory allocator	malloc, free, realloc, calloc,	malloc(3X)
malloc, free, realloc, calloc,	mallopt, mallinfo memory allocator	malloc(3X)
makedev, major, minor	manage a device number	makedev(3C)
tsearch, tfind, tdelete, twalk	manage binary search trees	tsearch(3C)
hsearch, hcreate, hdestroy	manage hash search tables	hsearch(3C)
maillock	manage lockfile for user's mailbox	maillock(3X)
endpoint t_optmgmt	manage options for a transport	t_optmgmt(3N)
swapctl	manage swap space	swapctl(2)
mctl memory	management control	mctl(3)
memcntl memory	management control	memcntl(2)
sigaction detailed signal	management	sigaction(2)
sigpause simplified signal	management /sigrelse, sigignore,	signal(2)
elf_flagscn, elf_flagshdr	manipulate flags /elf_flagphdr,	elf_flagdata(3E)
/overwrite, copywin overlap and	manipulate overlapped curses/	curs_overlay(3X)
/modfl, nextafter, scalb, scalbl	manipulate parts of floating-point/	frexp(3C)
/setpwent, endpwent, fgetpwent	manipulate password file entry	getpwent(3C)
/sigaddset, sigdelset, sigismember	manipulate sets of signals	sigemptyset(3C)
entry /fgetspent, lckpwdf, ulckpwdf	manipulate shadow password file	getspent(3C)
makecontext, swapcontext	manipulate user contexts	makecontext(3C)

Permuted Index

inet_ntoa Internet address manipulation /inet_netof,	inet(3N)
/for dealing with creation and manipulation of CLIENT handles	rpc_clnt_create(3N)
wbkgd curses window background manipulation routines /bkgd,	curs_bkgd(3X)
/pair_content curses color manipulation routines	curs_color(3X)
curses screen initialization and manipulation routines /delscreen	curs_initscr(3X)
panel_hidden panels deck manipulation routines /hide_panel,	panel_show(3X)
top_panel, bottom_panel panels deck manipulation routines panel_top:	panel_top(3X)
strfind, strrspn, strtrns string manipulations str:	str(3G)
mmap map pages of memory	mmap(2)
mprotect set protection of memory mapping	mprotect(2)
ethers Ethernet address mapping operations	ethers(3N)
set_menu_mark, menu_mark menus mark string routines menu_mark:	menu_mark(3X)
signal sigsuspend install a signal mask and suspend process until	sigsuspend(2)
change or examine signal mask sigprocmask	sigprocmask(2)
sigsetmask set current signal mask	sigsetmask(3)
umask set and get file creation mask	umask(2)
unlockpt unlock a pseudo-terminal master/slave pair	unlockpt(3C)
set and get menus pattern match buffer /menu_pattern	menu_pattern(3X)
regular expression compile and match routines /step, advance	regexpr(3G)
gmatch shell global pattern matching	gmatch(3G)
matherr error-handling function	matherr(3M)
in menus /menu_format set and get maximum numbers of rows and columns	menu_format(3X)
getrlimit, setrlimit control maximum system resource consumption	getrlimit(2)
multibyte character handling mbchar: mbtowc, mblen, wctomb	mbchar(3C)
handling mbchar: mbtowc, mblen, wctomb multibyte character	mbchar(3C)
functions mbstring: mbstowcs, wcstombs multibyte string	mbstring(3C)
multibyte string functions mbstring: mbstowcs, wcstombs	mbstring(3C)
character handling mbchar: mbtowc, mblen, wctomb multibyte	mbchar(3C)
msqrt,/ mp: madd, msub, mult, mdiv, mcmp, min, mout, pow, gcd, rpow,	mp(3X)
mctl memory management control	mctl(3)
rpow, msqrt,/ mp: madd, msub, mult, mdiv, mcmp, min, mout, pow, gcd,	mp(3X)
state with that on the physical medium /a file's in-memory	fsync(2)
malloc, free, realloc, calloc, memalign, valloc, memory allocator	malloc(3C)
elf_next sequential archive member access	elf_next(3E)
elf_rand random archive member access	elf_rand(3E)
elf_getarhdr retrieve archive member header	elf_getarhdr(3E)
offsetof offset of structure member	offsetof(3C)
memmove, memset memory/ memory: memccpy, memchr, memcmp, memcpy,	memory(3C)
memset memory/ memory: memccpy, memchr, memcmp, memcpy, memmove,	memory(3C)
memory/ memory: memccpy, memchr, memcmp, memcpy, memmove, memset	memory(3C)
memcntl memory management control	memcntl(2)
memory: memccpy, memchr, memcmp, memcpy, memmove, memset memory/	memory(3C)
/memccpy, memchr, memcmp, memcpy, memmove, memset memory operations	memory(3C)
alloca memory allocator	alloca(3)
realloc, calloc, memalign, valloc, memory allocator malloc, free,	malloc(3C)
realloc, calloc, mallopt, mallinfo memory allocator malloc, free,	malloc(3X)

Permuted Index

shmctl shared	memory control operations .... shmctl(2)
copylist copy a file into	memory .... copylist(3G)
spawn new process in a virtual	memory efficient way vfork .... vfork(2)
lock lock a process in primary	memory .... lock(2)
mctl	memory management control .... mctl(3)
memcntl	memory management control .... memcntl(2)
mprotect set protection of	memory mapping .... mprotect(2)
memcpy, memmove, memset memory/	memory: memccpy, memchr, memcmp, ... memory(3C)
munlock lock (or unlock) pages in	memory mlock, ... mlock(3C)
mmap map pages of	memory .... mmap(2)
munmap unmap pages of	memory .... munmap(2)
memcmp, memcpy, memmove, memset	memory operations /memccpy, memchr, ... memory(3C)
shmop: shmat, shmdt shared	memory operations .... shmop(2)
data plock lock into	memory or unlock process, text, or .... plock(2)
mincore determine residency of	memory pages .... mincore(2)
shmget get shared	memory segment identifier .... shmget(2)
msync synchronize	memory with physical storage .... msync(3C)
memchr, memcmp, memcpy, memmove,	memset memory operations /memccpy, ... memory(3C)
menu_fore, set_menu_back,/	menu_attributes: set_menu_fore, ... menu_attributes(3X)
/menu_fore, set_menu_back,	menu_back, set_menu_grey,/ .... menu_attributes(3X)
correctly position a menus cursor	menu_cursor: pos_menu_cursor .... menu_cursor(3X)
the menus subsystem	menu_driver command processor for .... menu_driver(3X)
menu_attributes: set_menu_fore,	menu_fore, set_menu_back,/ .... menu_attributes(3X)
menu_format: set_menu_format,	menu_format set and get maximum/ .... menu_format(3X)
menu_format set and get maximum/	menu_format: set_menu_format, ... menu_format(3X)
control/ /menu_back, set_menu_grey,	menu_grey, set_menu_pad, menu_pad
	.... menu_attributes(3X)
item_init, set_item_term,/	menu_hook: set_item_init, ... menu_hook(3X)
assign/ /item_term, set_menu_init,	menu_init, set_menu_term, menu_term .... menu_hook(3X)
set_current_item, current_item,/	menu_item_current: .... menu_item_current(3X)
item_description get menus item/	menu_item_name: item_name, ... menu_item_name(3X)
create and destroy menus items	menu_item_new: new_item, free_item
	.... menu_item_new(3X)
item_opts_on, item_opts_off,/	menu_item_opts: set_item_opts, ... menu_item_opts(3X)
menu_items: set_menu_items,	menu_items, item_count connect and/ .... menu_items(3X)
menu_items, item_count connect and/	menu_items: set_menu_items, ... menu_items(3X)
set_item_userptr, item_userptr/	menu_item_userptr: .... menu_item_userptr(3X)
item_value set and get menus item/	menu_item_value: set_item_value, ... menu_item_value(3X)
tell if menus item is visible	menu_item_visible: item_visible .... menu_item_visible(3X)
routines menu_mark: set_menu_mark,	menu_mark menus mark string .... menu_mark(3X)
menus mark string routines	menu_mark: set_menu_mark, menu_mark
	.... menu_mark(3X)
create and destroy menus	menu_new: new_menu, free_menu .... menu_new(3X)
/menu_opts_on, menu_opts_off,	menu_opts menus option routines .... menu_opts(3X)
menu_opts_on, menu_opts_off,/	menu_opts: set_menu_opts, ... menu_opts(3X)
/set_menu_opts, menu_opts_on,	menu_opts_off, menu_opts menus/ .... menu_opts(3X)
menu_opts: set_menu_opts,	menu_opts_on, menu_opts_off,/ .... menu_opts(3X)

Permuted Index

/menu_grey, set_menu_pad,	menu_pad control menus display/	menu_attributes(3X)
menu_pattern: set_menu_pattern,	menu_pattern set and get menus/	menu_pattern(3X)
menu_pattern set and get menus/	menu_pattern: set_menu_pattern,	menu_pattern(3X)
write or erase menus from/	menu_post: post_menu, unpost_menu	menu_post(3X)
	menus character based menus package	menus(3X)
correctly position a	menus cursor /pos_menu_cursor	menu_cursor(3X)
/set_menu_pad, menu_pad control	menus display attributes	menu_attributes(3X)
/unpost_menu write or erase	menus from associated subwindows	menu_post(3X)
/item_visible tell if	menus item is visible	menu_item_visible(3X)
/item_name, item_description get	menus item name and description	menu_item_name(3X)
/item_opts_off, item_opts	menus item option routines	menu_item_opts(3X)
item_value set and get	menus item values /set_item_value,	
		menu_item_value(3X)
item_index set and get current	menus items /set_top_row, top_row,	
		menu_item_current(3X)
free_item create and destroy	menus items /new_item,	menu_item_new(3X)
associate application data with	menus items /item_userptr	menu_item_userptr(3X)
menu_mark: set_menu_mark, menu_mark	menus mark string routines	menu_mark(3X)
numbers of rows and columns in	menus /set and get maximum	menu_format(3X)
for automatic invocation by	menus /routines	menu_hook(3X)
and disconnect items to and from	menus /item_count connect	menu_items(3X)
free_menu create and destroy	menus menu_new: new_menu,	menu_new(3X)
associate application data with	menus /menu_userptr	menu_userptr(3X)
/menu_opts_off, menu_opts	menus option routines	menu_opts(3X)
menus character based	menus package	menus(3X)
/menu_pattern set and get	menus pattern match buffer	menu_pattern(3X)
command processor for the	menus subsystem menu_driver	menu_driver(3X)
/set_menu_sub, menu_sub, scale_menu	menus window and subwindow/	menu_win(3X)
and/ /menu_win, set_menu_sub,	menu_sub, scale_menu menus window	menu_win(3X)
menu_init, set_menu_term,	menu_term assign/ /set_menu_init,	menu_hook(3X)
menu_userptr: set_menu_userptr,	menu_userptr associate application/	menu_userptr(3X)
menu_userptr associate application/	menu_userptr: set_menu_userptr,	menu_userptr(3X)
scale_menu/ menu_win: set_menu_win,	menu_win, set_menu_sub, menu_sub,	menu_win(3X)
set_menu_sub, menu_sub, scale_menu/	menu_win: set_menu_win, menu_win,	menu_win(3X)
catopen, catclose open/close a	message catalog	catopen(3C)
catgets read a program	message	catgets(3C)
msgctl	message control operations	msgctl(2)
recv, recvfrom, recvmsg receive a	message from a socket	recv(3N)
send, sendto, sendmsg send a	message from a socket	send(3N)
and send listener service request	message nlsrequest format	nlsrequest(3N)
getmsg get next	message off a stream	getmsg(2)
putmsg send a	message on a stream	putmsg(2)
fmtmsg display a	message on stderr or system console	fmtmsg(3C)
msgop: msgsnd, msgrcv	message operations	msgop(2)
msgget get	message queue	msgget(2)
strerror get error	message string	strerror(3C)
t_error produce error	message	t_error(3N)

Permuted Index

perror print system error	messages	perror(3C)
psignal, sys_siglist system signal	messages	psignal(3)
psignal, psiginfo system signal	messages	psignal(3C)
/halfdelay, intrflush, keypad,	meta, nodelay, notimeout, raw,/	curs_inopts(3X)
/msqrt, sdiv, itom, xtom, mtox,	mfree multiple precision integer/	mp(3X)
schedule signal after interval in	microseconds ualarm	ualarm(3)
suspend execution for interval in	microseconds usleep	usleep(3)
mp: madd, msub, mult, mdiv, mcmp,	min, mout, pow, gcd, rpow, msqrt,/	mp(3X)
memory pages	mincore determine residency of	mincore(2)
makedev, major,	minor manage a device number	makedev(3C)
/getwin, delay_output, flushinp	miscellaneous curses utility/	curs_util(3X)
/fp_class, isnan, copysign, scalbn	miscellaneous functions for IEEE/	ieee_functions(3M)
	mkdir make a directory	mkdir(2)
directories in a path	mkdirp, rmdirp create, remove	mkdirp(3G)
	mkfifo create a new FIFO	mkfifo(3C)
special or ordinary file	mknod make a directory, or a	mknod(2)
special or ordinary file	mknod make a directory, or a	mknod(2)
	mkstemp make a unique file name	mkstemp(3)
	mktemp make a unique file name	mktemp(3C)
calendar time	mktime converts a tm structure to a	mktime(3C)
pages in memory	mlock, munlock lock (or unlock)	mlock(3C)
address space	mlockall, munlockall lock or unlock	mlockall(3C)
	mmap map pages of memory	mmap(2)
getmntent, getmntany get	mnttab file entry	getmntent(3C)
chmod, fchmod change	mode of file	chmod(2)
frexp, frexpl, ldexp, ldexpl, logb,	modf, modff, modfl, nextafter,/	frexp(3C)
/frexpl, ldexp, ldexpl, logb, modf,	modff, modfl, nextafter, scalb,/	frexp(3C)
/ldexp, ldexpl, logb, modf, modff,	modfl, nextafter, scalb, scalbl/	frexp(3C)
utime set file access and	modification times	utime(2)
setlocale	modify and query a program's locale	setlocale(3C)
	monitor prepare execution profile	monitor(3C)
mount	mount a file system	mount(2)
	mount mount a file system	mount(2)
/madd, msub, mult, mdiv, mcmp, min,	mout, pow, gcd, rpow, msqrt, sdiv,/	mp(3X)
screen panel_move: move_panel	move a panels window on the virtual	panel_move(3X)
curs_move: move, wmove	move curses window cursor	curs_move(3X)
lseek	move read/write file pointer	lseek(2)
cursor curs_move:	move, wmove move curses window	curs_move(3X)
/form_fields, field_count,	move_field connect fields to forms	form_field(3X)
the virtual screen panel_move:	move_panel move a panels window on	panel_move(3X)
min, mout, pow, gcd, rpow, msqrt,/	mp: madd, msub, mult, mdiv, mcmp,	mp(3X)
mapping	mprotect set protection of memory	mprotect(2)
drand48, erand48, lrand48, nrand48,	mrand48, jrand48, srand48, seed48,/	drand48(3C)
	msgctl message control operations	msgctl(2)
	msgget get message queue	msgget(2)
operations	msgop: msgsnd, msgrcv message	msgop(2)
msgop: msgsnd,	msgrcv message operations	msgop(2)

Permuted Index

msgop:	msgsnd, msgrcv message operations	msgop(2)
/mcmp, min, mout, pow, gcd, rpow,	msqrt, sdiv, itom, xtom, mtox,/	mp(3X)
pow, gcd, rpow, msqrt,/ mp: madd,	msub, mult, mdiv, mcmp, min, mout, ...	mp(3X)
physical storage	msync synchronize memory with	msync(3C)
/gcd, rpow, msqrt, sdiv, itom, xtom,	mtox, mfree multiple precision/	mp(3X)
gcd, rpow, msqrt,/ mp: madd, msub,	mult, mdiv, mcmp, min, mout, pow, ...	mp(3X)
mbchar: mbtowc, mblen, wctomb	multibyte character handling	mbchar(3C)
mbstring: mbstowcs, wcstombs	multibyte string functions	mbstring(3C)
sdiv, itom, xtom, mtox, mfree	multiple precision integer/ /msqrt, ...	mp(3X)
poll input/output	multiplexing	poll(2)
select synchronous I/O	multiplexing	select(3C)
memory mlock,	munlock lock (or unlock) pages in	mlock(3C)
space mlockall,	munlockall lock or unlock address	mlockall(3C)
	munmap unmap pages of memory	munmap(2)
curs_addch: addch, waddch,	mvaddch, mvwaddch, echochar,/	curs_addch(3X)
/waddchstr, waddchnstr, mvaddchstr,	mvaddchnstr, mvwaddchstr,/	curs_addchstr(3X)
addchnstr, waddchstr, waddchnstr,	mvaddchstr, mvaddchnstr,/ /addchstr, ...	curs_addchstr(3X)
add a/ /waddstr, waddnstr, mvaddstr,	mvaddnstr, mvwaddstr, mvwaddnstr	curs_addstr(3X)
/addstr, addnstr, waddstr, waddnstr,	mvaddstr, mvaddnstr, mvwaddstr,/	curs_addstr(3X)
tputs, putp, vidputs, vidattr,	mvcur, tigetflag, tigetnum,/ /tparm, ...	curs_terminfo(3X)
under/ curs_delch: delch, wdelch,	mvdelch, mvwdelch delete character	curs_delch(3X)
/delwin, mvwin, subwin, derwin,	mvderwin, dupwin, wsyncup, syncok,/	
	....	curs_window(3X)
push/ curs_getch: getch, wgetch,	mvgetch, mvwgetch, ungetch get (or	curs_getch(3X)
curs_getstr: getstr, wgetstr,	mvgetstr, mvwgetstr, wgetnstr get/	curs_getstr(3X)
its/ curs_inch: inch, winch,	mvinch, mvwinch get a character and	curs_inch(3X)
/winchstr, winchnstr, mvinchstr,	mvinchnstr, mvwinchstr, mvwinchnstr/	curs_inchstr(3X)
/inchnstr, winchstr, winchnstr,	mvinchstr, mvinchnstr, mvwinchstr,/	curs_inchstr(3X)
/innstr, winstr, winnstr, mvinstr,	mvinnstr, mvwinstr, mvwinnstr get a/	curs_instr(3X)
curs_insch: insch, winsch,	mvinsch, mvwinsch insert a/	curs_insch(3X)
/winsstr, winsnstr, mvinsstr,	mvinsnstr, mvwinsstr, mvwinsnstr/	curs_instr(3X)
/insstr, insnstr, winsstr, winsnstr,	mvinsstr, mvinsnstr, mvwinsstr,/	curs_instr(3X)
/instr, innstr, winstr, winnstr,	mvinstr, mvinnstr, mvwinstr,/	curs_instr(3X)
curs_printw: printw, wprintw,	mvprintw, mvwprintw, vwprintw print/	
	....	curs_printw(3X)
curs_scanw: scanw, wscanw,	mvscanw, mvwscanw, vwscanw convert/	
	....	curs_scanw(3X)
curs_addch: addch, waddch, mvaddch,	mvwaddch, echochar, wechochar add a/	curs_addch(3X)
/mvaddchnstr, mvwaddchstr,	mvwaddchnstr add string of/	curs_addchstr(3X)
string of/ /mvaddchstr, mvaddchnstr,	mvwaddchstr, mvwaddchnstr add	curs_addchstr(3X)
/mvaddstr, mvaddnstr, mvwaddstr,	mvwaddnstr add a string of/	curs_addstr(3X)
of/ /waddnstr, mvaddstr, mvaddnstr,	mvwaddstr, mvwaddnstr add a string	curs_addstr(3X)
curs_delch: delch, wdelch, mvdelch,	mvwdelch delete character under/	curs_delch(3X)
curs_getch: getch, wgetch, mvgetch,	mvwgetch, ungetch get (or push/	curs_getch(3X)
strings/ /getstr, wgetstr, mvgetstr,	mvwgetstr, wgetnstr get character	curs_getstr(3X)
curs_window: newwin, delwin,	mvwin, subwin, derwin, mvderwin,/	curs_window(3X)
curs_inch: inch, winch, mvinch,	mvwinch get a character and its/	curs_inch(3X)

Permuted Index

/mvinchstr, mvinchnstr, mvwinchstr,	mvwinchnstr get a string of/	curs_inchstr(3X)
/winchnstr, mvinchstr, mvinchnstr,	mvwinchstr, mvwinchnstr get a/	curs_inchstr(3X)
mvinstr, mvinnstr, mvwinstr,	mvwinnstr get a string of/ /winnstr,	curs_instr(3X)
curs_insch: insch, winsch, mvinsch,	mvwinsch insert a character before/	curs_insch(3X)
/mvinsstr, mvinsnstr, mvwinsstr,	mvwinsnstr insert string before/	curs_instr(3X)
/winsnstr, mvinsstr, mvinsnstr,	mvwinsstr, mvwinsnstr insert string/	curs_instr(3X)
/winstr, winnstr, mvinstr, mvinnstr,	mvwinstr, mvwinnstr get a string of/	curs_instr(3X)
/printw, wprintw, mvprintw,	mvwprintw, vwprintw print/	curs_printw(3X)
curs_scanw: scanw, wscanw, mvscanw,	mvwscanw, vwscanw convert formatted/	curs_scanw(3X)
item_description get menus item	name and description /item_name,	menu_item_name(3X)
return the last element of a path	name basename	basename(3G)
directory name of a file path	name dirname report the parent	dirname(3G)
tmpnam, tempnam create a	name for a temporary file	tmpnam(3S)
ctermid generate file	name for terminal	ctermid(3S)
descriptor fdetach detach a	name from a STREAMS-based file	fdetach(3C)
getpw get	name from UID	getpw(3C)
getenv return value for environment	name	getenv(3C)
getlogin get login	name	getlogin(3C)
getsockname get socket	name	getsockname(3N)
timezone get time zone	name given offset from GMT	timezone(3C)
nlist get entries from	name list	nlist(3E)
mkstemp make a unique file	name	mkstemp(3)
mktemp make a unique file	name	mktemp(3C)
dirname report the parent directory	name of a file path name	dirname(3G)
rename change the	name of a file	rename(2)
ttyname, isatty find	name of a terminal	ttyname(3C)
getpeername get	name of connected peer	getpeername(3N)
gethostname, sethostname get/set	name of current host	gethostname(3)
uname get	name of current UNIX system	uname(2)
device ptsname get	name of the slave pseudo-terminal	ptsname(3C)
cuserid get character login	name of the user	cuserid(3S)
nlsprovider get	name of transport provider	nlsprovider(3N)
realpath returns the real file	name	realpath(3C)
to an object in the file system	name space /file descriptor	fattach(3C)
bind bind a	name to a socket	bind(3N)
pathfind search for named file in	named directories	pathfind(3G)
pathfind search for	named file in named directories	pathfind(3G)
list of the error numbers and their	names errno complete	errno(2)
/netdir_sperror generic transport	name-to-address translation	netdir_getbyname(3N)
interval	nap suspend execution for a short	nap(2)
/setsyx, ripoffline, curs_set,	napms low-level curses routines	curs_kernel(3X)
a resource governed by a/ waitsem,	nbwaitsem await and check access to	waitsem(2)
dbm_delete, dbm_error, dbm_fetch,/	ndbm: dbm_clearerr, dbm_close,	ndbm(3)
NETPATH component getnetpath get	netconfig entry corresponding to	getnetpath(3N)
netdir_getbyname, netdir_getbyaddr,	netdir_free, netdir_mergeaddr,/	netdir_getbyname(3N)
netdir_getbyname,	netdir_getbyaddr, netdir_free,/	netdir_getbyname(3N)

42   Programmer's Reference Manual: Operating System API

Permuted Index

netdir_free, netdir_mergeaddr,/	netdir_getbyname, netdir_getbyaddr, ...	netdir_getbyname(3N)
/netdir_getbyaddr, netdir_free,	netdir_mergeaddr, taddr2uaddr,/	netdir_getbyname(3N)
generic/ /taddr2uaddr, uaddr2taddr,	netdir_perror, netdir_sperror	netdir_getbyname(3N)
/uaddr2taddr, netdir_perror,	netdir_sperror generic transport/	netdir_getbyname(3N)
/key_gendes, key_setsecret,	netname2host, netname2user,/	secure_rpc(3N)
/key_setsecret, netname2host,	netname2user, user2netname library/	secure_rpc(3N)
netconfig entry corresponding to	NETPATH component getnetpath get	getnetpath(3N)
convert values between host and	network byte order /ntohl, ntohs	byteorder(3N)
entry getnetconfig get	network configuration database	getnetconfig(3N)
setnetent, endnetent get	network entry /getnetbyname, ...	getnetent(3N)
sethostent, endhostent get	network host entry /gethostbyname, ...	gethostent(3N)
scatter data in order to check the	network spray	spray(3N)
free_field, create/ form_field_new:	new_field, dup_field, link_field, ...	form_field_new(3X)
set_fieldtype_arg,/ form_fieldtype:	new_fieldtype, free_fieldtype, ...	form_fieldtype(3X)
destroy forms form_new:	new_form, free_form create and	form_new(3X)
destroy menus items menu_item_new:	new_item, free_item create and	menu_item_new(3X)
destroy menus menu_new:	new_menu, free_menu create and	menu_new(3X)
pnoutrefresh, pechochar/ curs_pad:	newpad, subpad, prefresh, ...	curs_pad(3X)
form_new_page: set_new_page,	new_page forms pagination	form_new_page(3X)
destroy panels panel_new:	new_panel, del_panel create and	panel_new(3X)
set_term,/ curs_initscr: initscr	newterm, endwin, isendwin, ...	curs_initscr(3X)
derwin, mvderwin,/ curs_window:	newwin, delwin, mvwin, subwin, ...	curs_window(3X)
bgets read stream up to	next delimiter	bgets(3G)
getmsg get	next message off a stream	getmsg(2)
/ldexpl, logb, modf, modff, modfl,	nextafter, scalb, scalbl manipulate/	frexp(3C)
/fetch, store, delete, firstkey,	nextkey data base subroutines	dbm(3)
ftw,	nftw walk a file tree	ftw(3C)
	nice change priority of a process	nice(3C)
time-sharing process	nice change priority of a	nice(2)
yp_master, yperr_string, ypprot_err	NIS client interface /yp_order, ...	ypclnt(3N)
yp_update change	NIS information	yp_update(3N)
/setscrreg, wsetscrreg, scrollok,	nl, nonl curses terminal output/	curs_outopts(3X)
	nlist get entries from name list	nlist(3E)
	nlist get entries from symbol table	nlist(3)
	nl_langinfo language information	nl_langinfo(3C)
via the listener	nlsgetcall get client's data passed	nlsgetcall(3N)
provider	nlsprovider get name of transport	nlsprovider(3N)
service request message	nlsrequest format and send listener	nlsrequest(3N)
intrflush,/ curs_inopts: cbreak,	nocbreak, echo, noecho, halfdelay, ...	curs_inopts(3X)
/halfdelay, intrflush, keypad, meta,	nodelay, notimeout, raw, noraw,/	curs_inopts(3X)
keypad,/ /cbreak, nocbreak, echo,	noecho, halfdelay, intrflush, ...	curs_inopts(3X)
control/ /wsetscrreg, scrollok, nl,	nonl curses terminal output option	curs_outopts(3X)
_longjmp, sigsetjmp, siglongjmp	non-local goto /longjmp, _setjmp, ...	setjmp(3)
setjmp, longjmp	non-local goto	setjmp(3C)
sigsetjmp, siglongjmp a	non-local goto with signal state	sigsetjmp(3C)
nodelay, notimeout, raw, noraw,/	noqiflush, qiflush, timeout,/ /meta, ...	curs_inopts(3X)

Permuted Index

/meta, nodelay, notimeout, raw,	noraw, noqiflush, qiflush, timeout,/	curs_inopts(3X)
/intrflush, keypad, meta, nodelay,	notimeout, raw, noraw, noqiflush,/	curs_inopts(3X)
seed48,/ drand48, erand48, lrand48,	nrand48, mrand48, jrand48, srand48,	drand48(3C)
host and/ byteorder, htonl, htons,	ntohl, ntohs convert values between	byteorder(3N)
byteorder, htonl, htons, ntohl,	ntohs convert values between host/	byteorder(3N)
rand, srand simple random	number generator	rand(3C)
/initstate, setstate better random	number generator; routines for/	random(3)
determine type of floating-point	number /unordered, unorderedl	isnan(3C)
major, minor manage a device	number makedev,	makedev(3C)
convert string to double-precision	number strtod, strtold, atof	strtod(3C)
gcvt, gcvtl convert floating-point	number to string /fcvt, fcvtl,	ecvt(3C)
errno complete list of the error	numbers and their names	errno(2)
uniformly distributed pseudo-random	numbers /seed48, lcong48 generate	drand48(3C)
manipulate parts of floating-point	numbers /nextafter, scalb, scalbl	frexp(3C)
to system calls and error	numbers intro introduction	intro(2)
/menu_format set and get maximum	numbers of rows and columns in/	menu_format(3X)
localeconv get	numeric formatting information	localeconv(3C)
dlclose close a shared	object	dlclose(3X)
dlopen open a shared	object	dlopen(3X)
the address of a symbol in shared	object dlsym get	dlsym(3X)
elf	object file access library	elf(3E)
elf_end finish using an	object file	elf_end(3E)
get the base offset for an	object file elf_getbase	elf_getbase(3E)
retrieve class-dependent	object file header /elf32_newehdr	elf_getehdr(3E)
elf32_fsize return the size of an	object file type elf_fsize:	elf_fsize(3E)
STREAMS-based file descriptor to an	object in the file system name/ /a	fattach(3C)
p_online turn a processor online or	offline	p_online(2)
/data_behind tell if forms field has	off-screen data ahead or behind	form_data(3X)
elf_getbase get the base	offset for an object file	elf_getbase(3E)
timezone get time zone name given	offset from GMT	timezone(3C)
offsetof	offset of structure member	offsetof(3C)
	offsetof offset of structure member	offsetof(3C)
p_online turn a processor	online or offline	p_online(2)
ungetc push character back	onto input stream	ungetc(3S)
opensem	open a semaphore	opensem(2)
dlopen	open a shared object	dlopen(3X)
fopen, freopen, fdopen	open a stream	fopen(3S)
fopen, freopen, fdopen	open a stream	fopen(3S)
command p2open, p2close	open, close pipes to and from a	p2open(3G)
dup duplicate an	open file descriptor	dup(2)
dup2 duplicate an	open file descriptor	dup2(3C)
open	open for reading or writing	open(2)
	open open for reading or writing	open(2)
catopen, catclose	open/close a message catalog	catopen(3C)
rewinddir, closedir/ directory:	opendir, readdir, telldir, seekdir,	directory(3C)
rewinddir, closedir/ directory:	opendir, readdir, telldir, seekdir,	directory(3C)
control system log syslog,	openlog, closelog, setlogmask	syslog(3)

Permuted Index

	opensem open a semaphore	opensem(2)
bzero, ffs bit and byte string	operations bstring: bcopy, bcmp,	bstring(3)
rewinddir, closedir directory	operations /telldir, seekdir,	directory(3C)
rewinddir, closedir directory	operations /telldir, seekdir,	directory(3C)
ethers Ethernet address mapping	operations	ethers(3N)
index, rindex string	operations	index(3)
memcpy, memmove, memset memory	operations /memchr, memcmp,	memory(3C)
msgctl message control	operations	msgctl(2)
msgop: msgsnd, msgrcv message	operations	msgop(2)
semctl semaphore control	operations	semctl(2)
semop semaphore	operations	semop(2)
shmctl shared memory control	operations	shmctl(2)
shmop: shmat, shmdt shared memory	operations	shmop(2)
strcasecmp, strncasecmp string	operations string:	string(3)
strcspn, strtok, strstr string	operations /strpbrk, strspn,	string(3C)
curses CRT screen handling and	optimization package	curses(3X)
typeahead curses terminal input	option control routines /wtimeout,	curs_inopts(3X)
/nl, nonl curses terminal output	option control routines	curs_outopts(3X)
getopt get	option letter from argument vector	getopt(3C)
field_opts forms field	option routines /field_opts_off,	form_field_opts(3X)
form_opts_off, form_opts forms	option routines /form_opts_on,	form_opts(3X)
item_opts_off, item_opts menus item	option routines /item_opts_on,	menu_item_opts(3X)
menu_opts_off, menu_opts menus	option routines /menu_opts_on,	menu_opts(3X)
t_optmgmt manage	options for a transport endpoint	t_optmgmt(3N)
getsockopt, setsockopt get and set	options on sockets	getsockopt(3N)
/mvgetch, mvwgetch, ungetch get	(or push back) characters from/	curs_getch(3X)
mlock, munlock lock	(or unlock) pages in memory	mlock(3C)
between host and network byte	order /ntohl, ntohs convert values	byteorder(3N)
spray scatter data in	order to check the network	spray(3N)
t_rcvrel acknowledge receipt of an	orderly release indication	t_rcvrel(3N)
t_sndrel initiate an	orderly release	t_sndrel(3N)
make a directory, or a special or	ordinary file mknod	mknod(2)
make a directory, or a special or	ordinary file mknod	mknod(2)
dial establish an	outgoing terminal line connection	dial(3C)
seconvert, sfconvert, sgconvert	output conversion /gconvert,	econvert(3)
vfprintf, vsprintf formatted	output conversion /vprintf,	printf(3S)
/vwprintw print formatted	output in curses windows	curs_printw(3X)
/vfprintf, vsprintf print formatted	output of a variable argument list	vprintf(3S)
/scrollok, nl, nonl curses terminal	output option control routines	curs_outopts(3X)
fprintf, sprintf print formatted	output printf,	printf(3S)
curses/ /overlay, overwrite, copywin	overlap and manipulate overlapped	curs_overlay(3X)
/copywin overlap and manipulate	overlapped curses windows	curs_overlay(3X)
and manipulate/ curs_overlay:	overlay, overwrite, copywin overlap	curs_overlay(3X)
manipulate/ curs_overlay: overlay,	overwrite, copywin overlap and	curs_overlay(3X)
chown, lchown, fchown change	owner and group of a file	chown(2)
from a command p2open,	p2close open, close pipes to and	p2open(3G)
to and from a command	p2open, p2close open, close pipes	p2open(3G)

Permuted Index

screen handling and optimization package	curses CRT .... curses(3X)
forms character based forms package	.... forms(3X)
menus character based menus package	.... menus(3X)
panels character based panels package	.... panels(3X)
standard buffered input/output package	stdio .... stdio(3S)
standard interprocess communication package	stdipc: ftok .... stdipc(3C)
pechochar create and display curses pads	/prefresh, pnoutrefresh, ... curs_pad(3X)
field_index set forms current page and field	/current_field, ... form_page(3X)
getpagesize get system page size	.... getpagesize(3)
mlock, munlock lock (or unlock) pages in memory	.... mlock(3C)
determine residency of memory pages mincore	.... mincore(2)
mmap map pages of memory	.... mmap(2)
munmap unmap pages of memory	.... munmap(2)
set_new_page, new_page forms pagination form_new_page:	.... form_new_page(3X)
socketpair create a pair of connected sockets	.... socketpair(3N)
a pseudo-terminal master/slave pair unlockpt unlock	.... unlockpt(3C)
/can_change_color, color_content, pair_content curses color/	.... curs_color(3X)
application data with a panels panel	/panel_userptr associate .... panel_userptr(3X)
set the current window of a panels panel	/replace_panel get or .... panel_window(3X)
panel_below panels deck traversal/ panel_above: panel_above,	.... panel_above(3X)
deck traversal/ panel_above: panel_above, panel_below panels	.... panel_above(3X)
panel_above: panel_above, panel_below panels deck traversal/	.... panel_above(3X)
panel_show: show_panel, hide_panel, panel_hidden panels deck/	.... panel_show(3X)
panels window on the virtual/ panel_move: move_panel move a	.... panel_move(3X)
create and destroy panels panel_new: new_panel, del_panel	.... panel_new(3X)
package panels character based panels	.... panels(3X)
/hide_panel, panel_hidden panels deck manipulation routines	.... panel_show(3X)
panel_top: top_panel, bottom_panel panels deck manipulation routines	.... panel_top(3X)
/panel_above, panel_below panels deck traversal primitives	.... panel_above(3X)
panels character based panels package	.... panels(3X)
associate application data with a panels panel /panel_userptr	.... panel_userptr(3X)
get or set the current window of a panels panel /replace_panel	.... panel_window(3X)
del_panel create and destroy panels panel_new: new_panel,	.... panel_new(3X)
panel_update: update_panels panels virtual screen refresh/	.... panel_update(3X)
panel_move: move_panel move a panels window on the virtual screen	.... panel_move(3X)
panel_hidden panels deck/ panel_show: show_panel, hide_panel,	.... panel_show(3X)
panels deck manipulation routines panel_top: top_panel, bottom_panel	.... panel_top(3X)
virtual screen refresh routine panel_update: update_panels panels	.... panel_update(3X)
panel_userptr: set_panel_userptr, panel_userptr associate application/	.... panel_userptr(3X)
panel_userptr associate/ panel_userptr: set_panel_userptr,	.... panel_userptr(3X)
replace_panel get or set the/ panel_window: panel_window,	.... panel_window(3X)
set the current/ panel_window: panel_window, replace_panel get or	.... panel_window(3X)
path name dirname report the parent directory name of a file	.... dirname(3G)
get process, process group, and parent process IDs /getpgid	.... getpid(2)
getsubopt parse suboptions from a string	.... getsubopt(3C)
clrtoeol, wclrtoeol clear all or part of a curses window /wclrtobot,	.... curs_clear(3X)
shutdown shut down part of a full-duplex connection	.... shutdown(3N)

Permuted Index

/nextafter, scalb, scalbl manipulate	parts of floating-point numbers	frexp(3C)
nlsgetcall get client's data	passed via the listener	nlsgetcall(3N)
functions crypt	password and file encryption	crypt(3X)
endpwent, fgetpwent manipulate	password file entry /setpwent,	getpwent(3C)
lckpwdf, ulckpwdf manipulate shadow	password file entry /fgetspent,	getspent(3C)
putpwent write	password file entry	putpwent(3C)
putpsent write shadow	password file entry	putspent(3C)
getpass read a	password	getpass(3C)
create, remove directories in a	path mkdirp, rmdirp	mkdirp(3G)
return the last element of a	path name basename	basename(3G)
the parent directory name of a file	path name dirname report	dirname(3G)
variables fpathconf,	pathconf get configurable pathname	fpathconf(2)
named directories	pathfind search for named file in	pathfind(3G)
getwd get current working directory	pathname	getwd(3)
directory getcwd get	pathname of current working	getcwd(3C)
pathconf get configurable	pathname variables fpathconf,	fpathconf(2)
/menu_pattern set and get menus	pattern match buffer	menu_pattern(3X)
gmatch shell global	pattern matching	gmatch(3G)
	pause suspend process until signal	pause(2)
process popen,	pclose initiate pipe to/from a	popen(3S)
/subpad, prefresh, pnoutrefresh,	pechochar create and display curses/	curs_pad(3X)
getpeername get name of connected	peer	getpeername(3N)
signals that are blocked and	pending sigpending examine	sigpending(2)
	perror print system error messages	perror(3C)
in-memory state with that on the	physical medium /a file's	fsync(2)
msync synchronize memory with	physical storage	msync(3C)
	pipe create an interprocess channel	pipe(2)
popen, pclose initiate	pipe to/from a process	popen(3S)
p2open, p2close open, close	pipes to and from a command	p2open(3G)
process, text, or data	plock lock into memory or unlock	plock(2)
curs_pad: newpad, subpad, prefresh,	pnoutrefresh, pechochar create and/	curs_pad(3X)
floatingpoint IEEE floating	point definitions	floatingpoint(3)
elf_strptr make a string	pointer	elf_strptr(3E)
rewind, ftell reposition a file	pointer in a stream fseek,	fseek(3S)
fsetpos, fgetpos reposition a file	pointer in a stream	fsetpos(3C)
lseek move read/write file	pointer	lseek(2)
	poll input/output multiplexing	poll(2)
offline	p_online turn a processor online or	p_online(2)
a process	popen, pclose initiate pipe to/from	popen(3S)
window cursor form_cursor:	pos_form_cursor position forms	form_cursor(3X)
/pos_menu_cursor correctly	position a menus cursor	menu_cursor(3X)
form_cursor: pos_form_cursor	position forms window cursor	form_cursor(3X)
a menus cursor menu_cursor:	pos_menu_cursor correctly position	menu_cursor(3X)
erase forms from/ form_post:	post_form, unpost_form write or	form_post(3X)
erase menus from/ menu_post:	post_menu, unpost_menu write or	menu_post(3X)
/msub, mult, mdiv, mcmp, min, mout,	pow, gcd, rpow, msqrt, sdiv, itom,/	mp(3X)
/cbrt, log, logf, log10, log10f,	pow, powf, sqrt, sqrtf exponential,/	exp(3M)

Permuted Index

sqrt, sqrtf exponential, logarithm,	power, square root functions /powf,	exp(3M)
/log, logf, log10, log10f, pow,	powf, sqrt, sqrtf exponential,/	exp(3M)
itom, xtom, mtox, mfree multiple	precision integer arithmetic /sdiv,	mp(3X)
create/ curs_pad: newpad, subpad,	prefresh, pnoutrefresh, pechochar	curs_pad(3X)
monitor	prepare execution profile	monitor(3C)
lock lock a process in	primary memory	lock(2)
panel_below panels deck traversal	primitives /panel_above,	panel_above(3X)
/mvprintw, mvwprintw, vwprintw	print formatted output in curses/	curs_printw(3X)
vprintf, vfprintf, vsprintf	print formatted output of a/	vprintf(3S)
printf, fprintf, sprintf	print formatted output	printf(3S)
perror	print system error messages	perror(3C)
formatted output	printf, fprintf, sprintf print	printf(3S)
vfprintf, vsprintf formatted/	printf, fprintf, sprintf, vprintf,	printf(3S)
mvwprintw, vwprintw/ curs_printw:	printw, wprintw, mvprintw,	curs_printw(3X)
	priocntl process scheduler control	priocntl(2)
scheduler control	priocntlset generalized process	priocntlset(2)
get/set program scheduling	priority getpriority, setpriority	getpriority(3)
nice change	priority of a process	nice(3C)
nice change	priority of a time-sharing process	nice(2)
/routines for client side remote	procedure call authentication	rpc_clnt_auth(3N)
routines for server side remote	procedure call errors /library	rpc_svc_err(3N)
rpc library routines for remote	procedure calls	rpc(3N)
XDR library routines for remote	procedure calls /xdr_replymsg	rpc_xdr(3N)
library routines for secure remote	procedure calls /user2netname	secure_rpc(3N)
acct enable or disable	process accounting	acct(2)
alarm set a	process alarm clock	alarm(2)
times get	process and child process times	times(2)
exit, _exit terminate	process	exit(2)
fork create a new	process	fork(2)
IDs /getppid, getpgid get process,	process group, and parent process	getpid(2)
setpgid set	process group ID	setpgid(2)
setpgrp set	process group ID	setpgrp(2)
tcsetpgrp set terminal foreground	process group id	tcsetpgrp(3C)
killpg send signal to a	process group	killpg(3)
process, process group, and parent	process IDs /getppid, getpgid get	getpid(2)
efficient way vfork spawn new	process in a virtual memory	vfork(2)
lock lock a	process in primary memory	lock(2)
change priority of a time-sharing	process nice	nice(2)
nice change priority of a	process	nice(3C)
kill send a signal to a	process or a group of processes	kill(2)
/sigsendset send a signal to a	process or a group of processes	sigsend(2)
pclose initiate pipe to/from a	process popen,	popen(3S)
/getpgrp, getppid, getpgid get	process, process group, and parent/	getpid(2)
priocntl	process scheduler control	priocntl(2)
priocntlset generalized	process scheduler control	priocntlset(2)
plock lock into memory or unlock	process, text, or data	plock(2)
times get process and child	process times	times(2)

48 Programmer's Reference Manual: Operating System API

Permuted Index

times get	process times	times(3C)
processor_bind bind a	process to a processor	processor_bind(2)
waitid wait for child	process to change state	waitid(2)
waitpid wait for child	process to change state	waitpid(2)
wait wait for child	process to stop or terminate	wait(2)
/WIFSIGNALED, WIFEXITED wait for	process to terminate or stop	wait(3)
ptrace	process trace	ptrace(2)
pause suspend	process until signal	pause(2)
install a signal mask and suspend	process until signal sigsuspend	sigsuspend(2)
sigsem signal a	process waiting on a semaphore	sigsem(2)
a signal to a process or a group of	processes kill send	kill(2)
a signal to a process or a group of	processes sigsend, sigsendset send	sigsend(2)
form_driver command	processor for the forms subsystem	form_driver(3X)
menu_driver command	processor for the menus subsystem	menu_driver(3X)
p_online turn a	processor online or offline	p_online(2)
processor_bind bind a process to a	processor	processor_bind(2)
get information about one	processor processor_info	processor_info(2)
reboot reboot system or halt	processor	reboot(3)
	processor_bind bind a process to a	processor_bind(2)
about one processor	processor_info get information	processor_info(2)
t_error	produce error message	t_error(3N)
	profil execution time profile	profil(2)
monitor prepare execution	profile	monitor(3C)
profil execution time	profile	profil(2)
assert verify	program assertion	assert(3X)
end, etext, edata last locations in	program	end(3C)
retrieve class-dependent	program header table /elf32_newphdr	elf_getphdr(3E)
catgets read a	program message	catgets(3C)
raise send signal to	program	raise(3C)
getpriority, setpriority get/set	program scheduling priority	getpriority(3)
atexit add	program termination routine	atexit(3C)
setlocale modify and query a	program's locale	setlocale(3C)
mprotect set	protection of memory mapping	mprotect(2)
setprotoent, endprotoent get	protocol entry /getprotobyname,	getprotoent(3N)
information t_getinfo get	protocol-specific service	t_getinfo(3N)
nlsprovider get name of transport	provider	nlsprovider(3N)
generate uniformly distributed	pseudo-random numbers /lcong48	drand48(3C)
grantpt grant access to the slave	pseudo-terminal device	grantpt(3C)
ptsname get name of the slave	pseudo-terminal device	ptsname(3C)
unlockpt unlock a	pseudo-terminal master/slave pair	unlockpt(3C)
psignal, messages	psiginfo system signal messages	psignal(3C)
messages	psignal, psiginfo system signal	psignal(3C)
	psignal, sys_siglist system signal	psignal(3)
	ptrace process trace	ptrace(2)
pseudo-terminal device	ptsname get name of the slave	ptsname(3C)
getpublickey, getsecretkey retrieve	public or secret key publickey:	publickey(3N)
getsecretkey retrieve public or/	publickey: getpublickey,	publickey(3N)

Permuted Index

/mvgetch, mvwgetch, ungetch get (or	push back) characters from curses/	curs_getch(3X)
stream ungetc	push character back onto input	ungetc(3S)
puts, fputs	put a string on a stream	puts(3S)
putc, putchar, fputc, putw	put character or word on a stream	putc(3S)
getdents read directory entries and	put in a file system independent/	getdents(2)
character or word on a stream	putc, putchar, fputc, putw put	putc(3S)
or word on a stream putc,	putchar, fputc, putw put character	putc(3S)
environment	putenv change or add value to	putenv(3C)
	putmsg send a message on a stream	putmsg(2)
/restartterm, tparm, tputs,	putp, vidputs, vidattr, mvcur,/	curs_terminfo(3X)
	putpwent write password file entry	putpwent(3C)
stream	puts, fputs put a string on a	puts(3S)
entry	putspent write shadow password file	putspent(3C)
/getutent, getutid, getutline,	pututline, setutent, endutent,/	getut(3C)
/getutxent, getutxid, getutxline,	pututxline, setutxent, endutxent,/	getutx(3C)
stream putc, putchar, fputc,	putw put character or word on a	putc(3S)
/unctrl, keyname, filter, use_env,	putwin, getwin, delay_output,/	curs_util(3X)
/notimeout, raw, noraw, noqiflush,	qiflush, timeout, wtimeout,/	curs_inopts(3X)
	qsort quicker sort	qsort(3C)
setlocale modify and	query a program's locale	setlocale(3C)
termname curses environment	query routines /termattrs,	curs_termattrs(3X)
remque insert/remove element from a	queue insque,	insque(3C)
msgget get message	queue	msgget(2)
qsort	quicker sort	qsort(3C)
div, ldiv compute the	quotient and remainder	div(3C)
	raise send signal to program	raise(3C)
generator	rand, srand simple random number	rand(3C)
generator	rand, srand simple random-number	rand(3C)
elf_rand	random archive member access	elf_rand(3E)
rand, srand simple	random number generator	rand(3C)
/srandom, initstate, setstate better	random number generator; routines/	random(3)
setstate better random number/	random, srandom, initstate,	random(3)
rand, srand simple	random-number generator	rand(3C)
/keypad, meta, nodelay, notimeout,	raw, noraw, noqiflush, qiflush,/	curs_inopts(3X)
to be read	rdchk check to see if there is data	rdchk(2)
getpass	read a password	getpass(3C)
catgets	read a program message	catgets(3C)
file system independent/ getdents	read directory entries and put in a	getdents(2)
read	read from file	read(2)
check to see if there is data to be	read rdchk	rdchk(2)
	read read from file	read(2)
bgets	read stream up to next delimiter	bgets(3G)
readlink	read the value of a symbolic link	readlink(2)
/scr_restore, scr_init, scr_set	read (write) a curses screen from/	curs_scr_dump(3X)
rewinddir,/ directory: opendir,	readdir, telldir, seekdir,	directory(3C)
rewinddir,/ directory: opendir,	readdir, telldir, seekdir,	directory(3C)
lock or unlock a file region for	reading or writing locking	locking(2)

50   Programmer's Reference Manual: Operating System API

Permuted Index

open open for	reading or writing	open(2)
symbolic link	readlink read the value of a	readlink(2)
lseek move	read/write file pointer	lseek(2)
setregid set	real and effective group IDs	setregid(3)
setreuid set	real and effective user IDs	setreuid(3)
realpath returns the	real file name	realpath(3C)
/get real user, effective user,	real group, and effective group IDs	getuid(2)
/geteuid, getgid, getegid get	real user, effective user, real/	getuid(2)
memory allocator malloc, free,	realloc, calloc, mallopt, mallinfo	malloc(3X)
memory allocator malloc, free,	realloc, calloc, memalign, valloc,	malloc(3C)
	realpath returns the real file name	realpath(3C)
processor	reboot reboot system or halt	reboot(3)
reboot	reboot system or halt processor	reboot(3)
indication t_rcvrel acknowledge	receipt of an orderly release	t_rcvrel(3N)
t_rcvudata	receive a data unit	t_rcvudata(3N)
recv, recvfrom, recvmsg	receive a message from a socket	recv(3N)
indication t_rcvuderr	receive a unit data error	t_rcvuderr(3N)
over a connection t_rcv	receive data or expedited data sent	t_rcv(3N)
connect request t_rcvconnect	receive the confirmation from a	t_rcvconnect(3N)
handler regex,	re_comp, re_exec regular expression	regex(3)
floating-point value to decimal	record /extended_to_decimal convert	floating_to_decimal(3)
lockf	record locking on files	lockf(3C)
/decimal_to_extended convert decimal	record to floating-point value	decimal_to_floating(3)
message from a socket	recv, recvfrom, recvmsg receive a	recv(3N)
from a socket recv,	recvfrom, recvmsg receive a message	recv(3N)
socket recv, recvfrom,	recvmsg receive a message from a	recv(3N)
/wrefresh, wnoutrefresh, doupdate,	redrawwin, wredrawln refresh curses/	curs_refresh(3X)
regex, re_comp,	re_exec regular expression handler	regex(3)
/is_wintouched curses	refresh control routines	curs_touch(3X)
/doupdate, redrawwin, wredrawln	refresh curses windows and lines	curs_refresh(3X)
update_panels panels virtual screen	refresh routine panel_update:	panel_update(3X)
doupdate, redrawwin,/ curs_refresh:	refresh, wrefresh, wnoutrefresh,	curs_refresh(3X)
regular expression	regcmp, regex compile and execute	regcmp(3G)
expression regcmp,	regex compile and execute regular	regcmp(3G)
expression handler	regex, re_comp, re_exec regular	regex(3)
regular expression compile and/	regexpr: compile, step, advance	regexpr(3G)
locking lock or unlock a file	region for reading or writing	locking(2)
/library routines for	registering servers	rpc_svc_calls(3N)
regexpr: compile, step, advance	regular expression compile and/	regexpr(3G)
regex, re_comp, re_exec	regular expression handler	regex(3)
regcmp, regex compile and execute	regular expression	regcmp(3G)
for interrupt sigpause automicaly	release blocked signals and wait	sigpause(3)
acknowledge receipt of an orderly	release indication t_rcvrel	t_rcvrel(3N)
t_sndrel initiate an orderly	release	t_sndrel(3N)
/rint, remainder floor, ceiling,	remainder, absolute value functions	floor(3M)
div, ldiv compute the quotient and	remainder	div(3C)

Permuted Index

/fmod, fmodf, fabs, fabsf, rint,	remainder floor, ceiling,/	floor(3M)
rexec return stream to a	remote command	rexec(3N)
return information about users on	remote machines rusers	rusers(3N)
rwall write to specified	remote machines	rwall(3N)
/library routines for client side	remote procedure call/	rpc_clnt_auth(3N)
/library routines for server side	remote procedure call errors	rpc_svc_err(3N)
rpc library routines for	remote procedure calls	rpc(3N)
/XDR library routines for	remote procedure calls	rpc_xdr(3N)
/library routines for secure	remote procedure calls	secure_rpc(3N)
rmdir	remove a directory	rmdir(2)
mkdirp, rmdirp create,	remove directories in a path	mkdirp(3G)
unlink	remove directory entry	unlink(2)
remove	remove file	remove(3C)
	remove remove file	remove(3C)
queue insque,	remque insert/remove element from a	insque(3C)
	rename change the name of a file	rename(2)
panel_window: panel_window,	replace_panel get or set the/	panel_window(3X)
clock	report CPU time used	clock(3C)
a file path name dirname	report the parent directory name of	dirname(3G)
stream fseek, rewind, ftell	reposition a file pointer in a	fseek(3S)
stream fsetpos, fgetpos	reposition a file pointer in a	fsetpos(3C)
/library routines for external data	representation stream creation	xdr_create(3N)
library routines for external data	representation xdr	xdr(3N)
library routines for external data	representation /xdr_setpos	xdr_admin(3N)
library routines for external data	representation /xdr_wrapstring	xdr_complex(3N)
library routines for external data	representation /xdr_void	xdr_simple(3N)
format and send listener service	request message nlsrequest	nlsrequest(3N)
t_accept accept a connect	request	t_accept(3N)
t_listen listen for a connect	request	t_listen(3N)
the confirmation from a connect	request t_rcvconnect receive	t_rcvconnect(3N)
send user-initiated disconnect	request t_snddis	t_snddis(3N)
/def_prog_mode, def_shell_mode,	reset_prog_mode, reset_shell_mode,/	curs_kernel(3X)
/def_shell_mode, reset_prog_mode,	reset_shell_mode, resetty, savetty,/	curs_kernel(3X)
/reset_prog_mode, reset_shell_mode,	resetty, savetty, getsyx, setsyx,/	curs_kernel(3X)
mincore determine	residency of memory pages	mincore(2)
resolver, res_mkquery, res_send,	res_init, dn_comp, dn_expand/	resolver(3N)
dn_comp, dn_expand/ resolver,	res_mkquery, res_send, res_init,	resolver(3N)
res_init, dn_comp, dn_expand/	resolver, res_mkquery, res_send,	resolver(3N)
res_init, dn_comp, dn_expand	resolver routines /res_send,	resolver(3N)
setrlimit control maximum system	resource consumption getrlimit,	getrlimit(2)
/await and check access to a	resource governed by a semaphore	waitsem(2)
getrusage get information about	resource utilization	getrusage(3)
dn_expand/ resolver, res_mkquery,	res_send, res_init, dn_comp,	resolver(3N)
/setterm, set_curterm, del_curterm,	restartterm, tparm, tputs, putp,/	curs_terminfo(3X)
gettxt	retrieve a text string	gettxt(3C)
elf_getarhdr	retrieve archive member header	elf_getarhdr(3E)
elf_getarsym	retrieve archive symbol table	elf_getarsym(3E)

52 Programmer's Reference Manual: Operating System API

Permuted Index

file/ /elf32_getehdr, elf32_newehdr	retrieve class-dependent object	elf_getehdr(3E)
/elf32_getphdr, elf32_newphdr	retrieve class-dependent program/	elf_getphdr(3E)
header elf_getshdr: elf32_getshdr	retrieve class-dependent section	elf_getshdr(3E)
elf_getident	retrieve file identification data	elf_getident(3E)
disconnect t_rcvdis	retrieve information from	t_rcvdis(3N)
/getpublickey, getsecretkey	retrieve public or secret key	publickey(3N)
contents elf_rawfile	retrieve uninterpreted file	elf_rawfile(3E)
variables sysconf	retrieves configurable system	sysconf(3C)
variables sysconf	retrieves configurable system	sysconf(3C)
remote machines rusers	return information about users on	rusers(3N)
abs, labs	return integer absolute value	abs(3C)
rexec	return stream to a remote command	rexec(3N)
name basename	return the last element of a path	basename(3G)
type elf_fsize: elf32_fsize	return the size of an object file	elf_fsize(3E)
getenv	return value for environment name	getenv(3C)
realpath	returns the real file name	realpath(3C)
pointer in a stream fseek,	rewind, ftell reposition a file	fseek(3S)
/opendir, readdir, telldir, seekdir,	rewinddir, closedir directory/	directory(3C)
/opendir, readdir, telldir, seekdir,	rewinddir, closedir directory/	directory(3C)
creat create a new file or	rewrite an existing one	creat(2)
command	rexec return stream to a remote	rexec(3N)
index,	rindex string operations	index(3)
/copysign, fmod, fmodf, fabs, fabsf,	rint, remainder floor, ceiling,/	floor(3M)
/resetty, savetty, getsyx, setsyx,	ripoffline, curs_set, napms/	curs_kernel(3X)
rmdir remove a directory		rmdir(2)
in a path mkdirp,	rmdirp create, remove directories	mkdirp(3G)
chroot change	root directory	chroot(2)
logarithm, power, square	root functions /sqrtf exponential,	exp(3M)
atexit add program termination	routine	atexit(3C)
panels virtual screen refresh	routine /update_panels	panel_update(3X)
and window attribute control	routines /curses character	curs_attr(3X)
flash curses bell and screen flash	routines curs_beep: beep,	curs_beep(3X)
window background manipulation	routines /bkgd, wbkgd curses	curs_bkgd(3X)
curses color manipulation	routines /pair_content	curs_color(3X)
initialization and manipulation	routines /delscreen curses screen	curs_initscr(3X)
terminal input option control	routines /typeahead curses	curs_inopts(3X)
curs_set, napms low-level curses	routines /setsyx, ripoffline,	curs_kernel(3X)
terminal output option control	routines /nl, nonl curses	curs_outopts(3X)
slk_attroff curses soft label	routines /slk_attron, slk_attrset,	curs_slk(3X)
termname curses environment query	routines /longname, termattrs,	curs_termattrs(3X)
curses refresh control	routines /is_wintouched	curs_touch(3X)
miscellaneous curses utility	routines /delay_output, flushinp	curs_util(3X)
by/ /assign application-specific	routines for automatic invocation	menu_hook(3X)
/better random number generator;	routines for changing generators	random(3)
/rpc_broadcast, rpc_call library	routines for client side calls	rpc_clnt_calls(3N)
/authsys_create_default library	routines for client side remote/	rpc_clnt_auth(3N)
and/ /clnt_vc_create library	routines for dealing with creation	rpc_clnt_create(3N)

Permuted Index

creation of/ /svc_vc_create library	routines for dealing with the	rpc_svc_create(3N)
/xdrstdio_create library	routines for external data/	xdr_create(3N)
representation xdr library	routines for external data	xdr(3N)
/xdrrec_eof, xdr_setpos library	routines for external data/	xdr_admin(3N)
/xdr_vector, xdr_wrapstring library	routines for external data/	xdr_complex(3N)
/xdr_u_short, xdr_void library	routines for external data/	xdr_simple(3N)
/assign application-specific	routines for invocation by forms	form_hook(3X)
/xprt_unregister library	routines for registering servers	rpc_svc_calls(3N)
rpc library	routines for remote procedure calls	rpc(3N)
/xdr_replymsg XDR library	routines for remote procedure calls	rpc_xdr(3N)
/rpcb_set, rpcb_unset library	routines for RPC bind service	rpcbind(3N)
/svc_run, svc_sendreply library	routines for RPC servers	rpc_svc_reg(3N)
/netname2user, user2netname library	routines for secure remote/	secure_rpc(3N)
procedure/ /svcerr_weakauth library	routines for server side remote	rpc_svc_err(3N)
field_opts forms field option	routines /field_opts_off,	form_field_opts(3X)
link_fieldtype forms fieldtype	routines /set_fieldtype_choice,	form_fieldtype(3X)
form_opts forms option	routines /form_opts_off,	form_opts(3X)
window and subwindow association	routines /scale_form forms	form_win(3X)
item_opts menus item option	routines /item_opts_off,	menu_item_opts(3X)
menu_mark menus mark string	routines menu_mark: set_menu_mark,	menu_mark(3X)
menu_opts menus option	routines /menu_opts_off,	menu_opts(3X)
window and subwindow association	routines /scale_menu menus	menu_win(3X)
panels deck manipulation	routines /hide_panel, panel_hidden	panel_show(3X)
panels deck manipulation	routines /top_panel, bottom_panel	panel_top(3X)
expression compile and match	routines /step, advance regular	regexpr(3G)
dn_comp, dn_expand resolver	routines /res_send, res_init,	resolver(3N)
/set and get maximum numbers of	rows and columns in menus	menu_format(3X)
rpcb_unset library routines for	RPC bind service /rpcb_set,	rpcbind(3N)
procedure calls	rpc library routines for remote	rpc(3N)
svc_sendreply library routines for	RPC servers /svc_run,	rpc_svc_reg(3N)
rpcbind: rpcb_getmaps,	rpcb_getaddr, rpcb_gettime,/	rpcbind(3N)
rpcb_gettime,/ rpcbind:	/rpcb_getmaps, rpcb_getaddr,	rpcbind(3N)
/rpcb_getmaps, rpcb_getaddr,	rpcb_getaddr, rpcb_gettime,/	rpcbind(3N)
rpcb_getaddr, rpcb_gettime,/	rpcb_gettime, rpcb_rmtcall,/	rpcbind(3N)
/rpcb_getaddr, rpcb_gettime,	rpcbind: rpcb_getmaps,	rpcbind(3N)
/clnt_sperrno, clnt_sperror,	rpcb_rmtcall, rpcb_set, rpcb_unset/	rpcbind(3N)
/rpcb_gettime, rpcb_rmtcall,	rpc_broadcast, rpc_call library/	rpc_clnt_calls(3N)
bind/ /rpcb_rmtcall, rpcb_set,	rpcb_set, rpcb_unset library/	rpcbind(3N)
/clnt_sperror, rpc_broadcast,	rpcb_unset library routines for RPC	rpcbind(3N)
authnone_create, authsys_create,/	rpc_call library routines for/	rpc_clnt_calls(3N)
clnt_freeres, clnt_geterr,/	rpc_clnt_auth: auth_destroy,	rpc_clnt_auth(3N)
clnt_create, clnt_destroy,/	rpc_clnt_calls: clnt_call,	rpc_clnt_calls(3N)
xprt_register,/ rpc_svc_calls:	rpc_clnt_create: clnt_control,	rpc_clnt_create(3N)
svc_unreg, xprt_register,/	rpc_reg, svc_reg, svc_unreg,	rpc_svc_calls(3N)
svc_destroy, svc_dg_create,/	rpc_svc_calls: rpc_reg, svc_reg,	rpc_svc_calls(3N)
svcerr_decode, svcerr_noproc,/	rpc_svc_create: svc_create,	rpc_svc_create(3N)
svc_getargs, svc_getreqset,/	rpc_svc_err: svcerr_auth,	rpc_svc_err(3N)
	rpc_svc_reg: svc_freeargs,	rpc_svc_reg(3N)

xdr_authsys_parms, xdr_callhdr,/	rpc_xdr: xdr_accepted_reply, ... rpc_xdr(3N)
/mdiv, mcmp, min, mout, pow, gcd,	rpow, msqrt, sdiv, itom, xtom,/ .... mp(3X)
users on remote machines	rusers return information about .... rusers(3N)
machines	rwall write to specified remote .... rwall(3N)
/reset_shell_mode, resetty,	savetty, getsyx, setsyx,/ .... curs_kernel(3X)
allocation brk,	sbrk change data segment space .... brk(2)
/modf, modff, modfl, nextafter,	scalb, scalbl manipulate parts of/ .... frexp(3C)
modff, modfl, nextafter, scalb,	scalbl manipulate parts of/ /modf, ... frexp(3C)
IEEE/ /fp_class, isnan, copysign,	scalbn miscellaneous functions for .... ieee_functions(3M)
/form_win, set_form_sub, form_sub,	scale_form forms window and/ .... form_win(3X)
/menu_win, set_menu_sub, menu_sub,	scale_menu menus window and/ .... menu_win(3X)
scandir, alphasort	scan a directory .... scandir(3)
	scandir, alphasort scan a directory .... scandir(3)
formatted input	scanf, fscanf, sscanf convert .... scanf(3S)
vwscanw convert/ curs_scanw:	scanw, wscanw, mvscanw, mvwscanw, ... curs_scanw(3X)
network spray	scatter data in order to check the .... spray(3N)
microseconds ualarm	schedule signal after interval in .... ualarm(3)
priocntl process	scheduler control .... priocntl(2)
priocntlset generalized process	scheduler control .... priocntlset(2)
setpriority get/set program	scheduling priority getpriority, ... getpriority(3)
scr_set read/ curs_scr_dump:	scr_dump, scr_restore, scr_init, ... curs_scr_dump(3X)
beep, flash curses bell and	screen flash routines curs_beep: .... curs_beep(3X)
scr_set read (write) a curses	screen from (to) a file /scr_init, ... curs_scr_dump(3X)
package curses CRT	screen handling and optimization .... curses(3X)
/set_term, delscreen curses	screen initialization and/ .... curs_initscr(3X)
move a panels window on the virtual	screen panel_move: move_panel .... panel_move(3X)
/update_panels panels virtual	screen refresh routine .... panel_update(3X)
curses/ /scr_dump, scr_restore,	scr_init, scr_set read (write) a .... curs_scr_dump(3X)
doconfig execute a configuration	script .... doconfig(3N)
curs_scroll: scroll, srcl, wscrl	scroll a curses window .... curs_scroll(3X)
window curs_scroll:	scroll, srcl, wscrl scroll a curses .... curs_scroll(3X)
/leaveok, setscrreg, wsetscrreg,	scrollok, nl, nonl curses terminal/ .... curs_outopts(3X)
(write) a/ curs_scr_dump: scr_dump,	scr_restore, scr_init, scr_set read .... curs_scr_dump(3X)
/scr_dump, scr_restore, scr_init,	scr_set read (write) a curses/ .... curs_scr_dump(3X)
to a shared data segment	sdenter, sdleave synchronize access .... sdenter(2)
data segment sdget,	sdfree attach and detach a shared .... sdget(2)
shared data segment	sdget, sdfree attach and detach a .... sdget(2)
access	sdgetv synchronize shared data .... sdgetv(2)
/min, mout, pow, gcd, rpow, msqrt,	sdiv, itom, xtom, mtox, mfree/ .... mp(3X)
shared data segment sdenter,	sdleave synchronize access to a .... sdenter(2)
bsearch binary	search a sorted table .... bsearch(3C)
lsearch, lfind linear	search and update .... lsearch(3C)
directories pathfind	search for named file in named .... pathfind(3G)
hcreate, hdestroy manage hash	search tables hsearch, ... hsearch(3C)
tfind, tdelete, twalk manage binary	search trees tsearch, ... tsearch(3C)
econvert, fconvert, gconvert,	seconvert, sfconvert, sgconvert/ .... econvert(3)
getsecretkey retrieve public or	secret key /getpublickey, ... publickey(3N)

Permuted Index   55

Permuted Index

elf_newdata, elf_rawdata get	section data elf_getdata,	elf_getdata(3E)
retrieve class-dependent	section header /elf32_getshdr	elf_getshdr(3E)
elf_newscn, elf_nextscn get	section information /elf_ndxscn,	elf_getscn(3E)
/user2netname library routines for	secure remote procedure calls	secure_rpc(3N)
authdes_getucred, getnetname,/	secure_rpc: authdes_seccreate,	secure_rpc(3N)
/nrand48, mrand48, jrand48, srand48,	seed48, lcong48 generate uniformly/	drand48(3C)
/opendir, readdir, telldir,	seekdir, rewinddir, closedir/	directory(3C)
/opendir, readdir, telldir,	seekdir, rewinddir, closedir/	directory(3C)
shmget get shared memory	segment identifier	shmget(2)
synchronize access to a shared data	segment sdenter, sdleave	sdenter(2)
attach and detach a shared data	segment sdget, sdfree	sdget(2)
brk, sbrk change data	segment space allocation	brk(2)
	select synchronous I/O multiplexing	select(3C)
semctl	semaphore control operations	semctl(2)
create an instance of a binary	semaphore creatsem	creatsem(2)
opensem open a	semaphore	opensem(2)
semop	semaphore operations	semop(2)
signal a process waiting on a	semaphore sigsem	sigsem(2)
access to a resource governed by a	semaphore /await and check	waitsem(2)
semget get set of	semaphores	semget(2)
	semctl semaphore control operations	semctl(2)
	semget get set of semaphores	semget(2)
	semop semaphore operations	semop(2)
t_sndudata	send a data unit	t_sndudata(3N)
send, sendto, sendmsg	send a message from a socket	send(3N)
putmsg	send a message on a stream	putmsg(2)
group of processes kill	send a signal to a process or a	kill(2)
group of/ sigsend, sigsendset	send a signal to a process or a	sigsend(2)
connection t_snd	send data or expedited data over a	t_snd(3N)
message nlsrequest format and	send listener service request	nlsrequest(3N)
message from a socket	send, sendto, sendmsg send a	send(3N)
killpg	send signal to a process group	killpg(3)
raise	send signal to program	raise(3C)
request t_snddis	send user-initiated disconnect	t_snddis(3N)
socket send, sendto,	sendmsg send a message from a	send(3N)
a socket send,	sendto, sendmsg send a message from	send(3N)
receive data or expedited data	sent over a connection t_rcv	t_rcv(3N)
elf_next	sequential archive member access	elf_next(3E)
for dealing with the creation of	server handles /library routines	rpc_svc_create(3N)
errors /library routines for	server side remote procedure call	rpc_svc_err(3N)
library routines for registering	servers /xprt_unregister	rpc_svc_calls(3N)
library routines for RPC	servers /svc_run, svc_sendreply	rpc_svc_reg(3N)
setservent, endservent get	service entry /getservbyname,	getservent(3N)
t_getinfo get protocol-specific	service information	t_getinfo(3N)
nlsrequest format and send listener	service request message	nlsrequest(3N)
library routines for RPC bind	service /rpcb_set, rpcb_unset	rpcbind(3N)
getsid get	session ID	getsid(2)

setsid set	session ID .... setsid(2)
truncate, ftruncate	set a file to a specified length .... truncate(3C)
alarm	set a process alarm clock .... alarm(2)
/set_top_row, top_row, item_index	set and get current menus items .... menu_item_current(3X)
umask	set and get file creation mask .... umask(2)
/field_status, set_max_field	set and get forms field attributes .... form_field_buffer(3X)
and/ /set_menu_format, menu_format	set and get maximum numbers of rows .... menu_format(3X)
/set_item_value, item_value	set and get menus item values .... menu_item_value(3X)
/set_menu_pattern, menu_pattern	set and get menus pattern match/ .... menu_pattern(3X)
sigstack	set and/or get signal stack context .... sigstack(3)
ffs find first	set bit .... ffs(3C)
sigsetmask	set current signal mask .... sigsetmask(3)
getcontext, setcontext get and	set current user context .... getcontext(2)
times utime	set file access and modification .... utime(2)
utimes	set file times .... utimes(3)
elf_fill	set fill byte .... elf_fill(3E)
/current_field, field_index	set forms current page and field .... form_page(3X)
semget get	set of semaphores .... semget(2)
getsockopt, setsockopt get and	set options on sockets .... getsockopt(3N)
context sigaltstack	set or get signal alternate stack .... sigaltstack(2)
setpgid	set process group ID .... setpgid(2)
setpgrp	set process group ID .... setpgrp(2)
mprotect	set protection of memory mapping .... mprotect(2)
setregid	set real and effective group IDs .... setregid(3)
setreuid	set real and effective user IDs .... setreuid(3)
setsid	set session ID .... setsid(2)
IDs getgroups, setgroups get or	set supplementary group access list .... getgroups(2)
sysinfo get and	set system information strings .... sysinfo(2)
group id tcsetpgrp	set terminal foreground process .... tcsetpgrp(3C)
/panel_window, replace_panel get or	set the current window of a panels/ .... panel_window(3X)
gettimeofday, settimeofday get or	set the date and time .... gettimeofday(3)
gettimeofday, settimeofday get or	set the date and time .... gettimeofday(3C)
stime	set time .... stime(2)
setuid, setgid	set user and group IDs .... setuid(2)
ulimit get and	set user limits .... ulimit(2)
setvbuf assign buffering to a/	setbuf, setbuffer, setlinebuf, ... setbuf(3S)
a stream	setbuf, setvbuf assign buffering to .... setbuf(3S)
buffering to a stream	setbuffer, setlinebuf assign .... setbuffer(3S)
assign buffering to a/ setbuf,	setbuffer, setlinebuf, setvbuf .... setbuf(3S)
context getcontext,	setcontext get and set current user .... getcontext(2)
/set_form_page, form_page,	set_current_field, current_field,/ .... form_page(3X)
set_top_row,/ menu_item_current:	set_current_item, current_item, ... menu_item_current(3X)
curs_terminfo: setupterm, setterm,	set_curterm, del_curterm,/ .... curs_terminfo(3X)
/set_field_fore, field_fore,	set_field_back, field_back,/ .... form_field_attributes(3X)
form_field_buffer:	set_field_buffer, field_buffer,/ .... form_field_buffer(3X)
form_field_attributes:	set_field_fore, field_fore,/ .... form_field_attributes(3X)

Permuted Index

/set_form_term, form_term,	set_field_init, field_init,/ .... form_hook(3X)
the general/ form_field_just:	set_field_just, field_just format .... form_field_just(3X)
field_opts_off,/ form_field_opts:	set_field_opts, field_opts_on, ... form_field_opts(3X)
/set_field_back, field_back,	set_field_pad, field_pad format the/
	.... form_field_attributes(3X)
/set_field_buffer, field_buffer,	set_field_status, field_status,/ .... form_field_buffer(3X)
/set_field_init, field_init,	set_field_term, field_term assign/ .... form_hook(3X)
field_arg/ form_field_validation:	set_field_type, field_type, ... form_field_validation(3X)
new_fieldtype, free_fieldtype,	set_fieldtype_arg,/ form_fieldtype: .... form_fieldtype(3X)
/free_fieldtype, set_fieldtype_arg,	set_fieldtype_choice,/ .... form_fieldtype(3X)
associate/ form_field_userptr:	set_field_userptr, field_userptr .... form_field_userptr(3X)
field_count,/ form_field:	set_form_fields, form_fields, ... form_field(3X)
set_form_term,/ form_hook:	set_form_init, form_init, ... form_hook(3X)
form_opts_off,/ form_opts:	set_form_opts, form_opts_on, ... form_opts(3X)
set_current_field,/ form_page:	set_form_page, form_page, ... form_page(3X)
form_win: set_form_win, form_win,	set_form_sub, form_sub, scale_form/ .... form_win(3X)
/set_form_init, form_init,	set_form_term, form_term,/ .... form_hook(3X)
associate/ form_userptr:	set_form_userptr, form_userptr .... form_userptr(3X)
set_form_sub, form_sub,/ form_win:	set_form_win, form_win, ... form_win(3X)
setuid,	setgid set user and group IDs .... setuid(2)
getgrent, getgrgid, getgrnam,	setgrent, endgrent, fgetgrent get/ .... getgrent(3C)
group access list IDs getgroups,	setgroups get or set supplementary .... getgroups(2)
host/ /gethostbyaddr, gethostbyname,	sethostent, endhostent get network .... gethostent(3N)
host gethostname,	sethostname get/set name of current .... gethostname(3)
set_item_term,/ menu_hook:	set_item_init, item_init, ... menu_hook(3X)
item_opts_off,/ menu_item_opts:	set_item_opts, item_opts_on, ... menu_item_opts(3X)
/set_item_init, item_init,	set_item_term, item_term,/ .... menu_hook(3X)
associate/ menu_item_userptr:	set_item_userptr, item_userptr .... menu_item_userptr(3X)
get menus item/ menu_item_value:	set_item_value, item_value set and .... menu_item_value(3X)
timer getitimer,	setitimer get/set value of interval .... getitimer(3C)
	setjmp, longjmp non-local goto .... setjmp(3C)
sigsetjmp, siglongjmp non-local/	setjmp, longjmp, _setjmp, _longjmp, ... setjmp(3)
siglongjmp/ setjmp, longjmp,	_setjmp, _longjmp, sigsetjmp, ... setjmp(3)
crypt,	setkey, encrypt generate encryption .... crypt(3C)
stream setbuffer,	setlinebuf assign buffering to a .... setbuffer(3S)
buffering to a/ setbuf, setbuffer,	setlinebuf, setvbuf assign .... setbuf(3S)
program's locale	setlocale modify and query a .... setlocale(3C)
syslog, openlog, closelog,	setlogmask control system log .... syslog(3)
/set_field_status, field_status,	set_max_field set and get forms/ .... form_field_buffer(3X)
/set_menu_fore, menu_fore,	set_menu_back, menu_back,/ .... menu_attributes(3X)
set_menu_back,/ menu_attributes:	set_menu_fore, menu_fore, ... menu_attributes(3X)
and get maximum/ menu_format:	set_menu_format, menu_format set .... menu_format(3X)
/set_menu_back, menu_back,	set_menu_grey, menu_grey,/ .... menu_attributes(3X)
/set_item_term, item_term,	set_menu_init, menu_init,/ .... menu_hook(3X)
item_count connect and/ menu_items:	set_menu_items, menu_items, ... menu_items(3X)

string routines menu_mark:	set_menu_mark, menu_mark menus mark .... menu_mark(3X)
menu_opts_off,/ menu_opts:	set_menu_opts, menu_opts_on, ... menu_opts(3X)
menus/ /set_menu_grey, menu_grey,	set_menu_pad, menu_pad control .... menu_attributes(3X)
and get menus/ menu_pattern:	set_menu_pattern, menu_pattern set .... menu_pattern(3X)
menu_win: set_menu_win, menu_win,	set_menu_sub, menu_sub, scale_menu/ .... menu_win(3X)
/set_menu_init, menu_init,	set_menu_term, menu_term assign/ .... menu_hook(3X)
associate/ menu_userptr:	set_menu_userptr, menu_userptr .... menu_userptr(3X)
set_menu_sub, menu_sub,/ menu_win:	set_menu_win, menu_win, ... menu_win(3X)
entry /getnetbyaddr, getnetbyname,	setnetent, endnetent get network .... getnetent(3N)
pagination form_new_page:	set_new_page, new_page forms .... form_new_page(3X)
associate/ panel_userptr:	set_panel_userptr, panel_userptr .... panel_userptr(3X)
	setpgid set process group ID .... setpgid(2)
	setpgrp set process group ID .... setpgrp(2)
scheduling priority getpriority,	setpriority get/set program .... getpriority(3)
/getprotobynumber, getprotobyname,	setprotoent, endprotoent get/ .... getprotoent(3N)
getpwent, getpwuid, getpwnam,	setpwent, endpwent, fgetpwent/ .... getpwent(3C)
group IDs	setregid set real and effective .... setregid(3)
user IDs	setreuid set real and effective .... setreuid(3)
resource consumption getrlimit,	setrlimit control maximum system .... getrlimit(2)
sigdelset, sigismember manipulate	sets of signals /sigaddset, ... sigemptyset(3C)
nl,/ /idlok, idcok immedok, leaveok,	setscrreg, wsetscrreg, scrollok, ... curs_outopts(3X)
/getservbyport, getservbyname,	setservent, endservent get service/ .... getservent(3N)
	setsid set session ID .... setsid(2)
sockets getsockopt,	setsockopt get and set options on .... getsockopt(3N)
lckpwdf,/ getspent, getspnam,	setspent, endspent, fgetspent, ... getspent(3C)
random, srandom, initstate,	setstate better random number/ .... random(3)
/resetty, savetty, getsyx,	setsyx, ripoffline, curs_set, napms/ .... curs_kernel(3X)
/initscr, newterm, endwin, isendwin,	set_term, delscreen curses screen/ .... curs_initscr(3X)
curs_terminfo: setupterm,	setterm, set_curterm, del_curterm,/ .... curs_terminfo(3X)
and time gettimeofday,	settimeofday get or set the date .... gettimeofday(3)
and time gettimeofday,	settimeofday get or set the date .... gettimeofday(3C)
/set_current_item, current_item,	set_top_row, top_row, item_index/
	.... menu_item_current(3X)
	setuid, setgid set user and group .... setuid(2)
IDs	setupterm, setterm, set_curterm, ... curs_terminfo(3X)
del_curterm,/ curs_terminfo:	setusershell, endusershell get .... getusershell(3)
legal user shells getusershell,	setutent, endutent, utmpname access/ .... getut(3C)
/getutid, getutline, pututline,	setutxent, endutxent, utmpxname,/ .... getutx(3C)
/getutxid, getutxline, pututxline,	setvbuf assign buffering to a .... setbuf(3S)
stream setbuf,	setvbuf assign buffering to a/ .... setbuf(3S)
setbuf, setbuffer, setlinebuf,	severity levels for an application .... addseverity(3C)
for/ addseverity build a list of	sfconvert, sgconvert output/ .... econvert(3)
/fconvert, gconvert, seconvert,	sgconvert output conversion .... econvert(3)
/gconvert, seconvert, sfconvert,	sgetl access long integer data in a .... sputl(3X)
machine-independent fashion sputl,	shadow password file entry .... getspent(3C)
/lckpwdf, ulckpwdf manipulate	shadow password file entry .... putspent(3C)
putspent write	

Permuted Index

sdgetv synchronize	shared data access .... sdgetv(2)
sdleave synchronize access to a	shared data segment sdenter, ... sdenter(2)
sdget, sdfree attach and detach a	shared data segment .... sdget(2)
shmctl	shared memory control operations .... shmctl(2)
shmop: shmat, shmdt	shared memory operations .... shmop(2)
shmget get	shared memory segment identifier .... shmget(2)
dlclose close a	shared object .... dlclose(3X)
dlopen open a	shared object .... dlopen(3X)
get the address of a symbol in	shared object dlsym .... dlsym(3X)
system issue a	shell command .... system(3S)
gmatch	shell global pattern matching .... gmatch(3G)
endusershell get legal user	shells getusershell, setusershell, ... getusershell(3)
operations shmop:	shmat, shmdt shared memory .... shmop(2)
operations	shmctl shared memory control .... shmctl(2)
shmop: shmat,	shmdt shared memory operations .... shmop(2)
identifier	shmget get shared memory segment .... shmget(2)
operations	shmop: shmat, shmdt shared memory .... shmop(2)
nap suspend execution for a	short interval .... nap(2)
panel_hidden panels/ panel_show:	show_panel, hide_panel, ... panel_show(3X)
connection shutdown	shut down part of a full-duplex .... shutdown(3N)
full-duplex connection	shutdown shut down part of a .... shutdown(3N)
library routines for client	side calls /rpc_broadcast, rpc_call .... rpc_clnt_calls(3N)
/library routines for client	side remote procedure call/ .... rpc_clnt_auth(3N)
/library routines for server	side remote procedure call errors .... rpc_svc_err(3N)
management	sigaction detailed signal .... sigaction(2)
sigemptyset, sigfillset,	sigaddset, sigdelset, sigismember/ .... sigemptyset(3C)
alternate stack context	sigaltstack set or get signal .... sigaltstack(2)
	sigblock, sigmask block signals .... sigblock(3)
sigemptyset, sigfillset, sigaddset,	sigdelset, sigismember manipulate/ .... sigemptyset(3C)
sigdelset, sigismember manipulate/	sigemptyset, sigfillset, sigaddset, ... sigemptyset(3C)
sigismember/ sigemptyset,	sigfillset, sigaddset, sigdelset, ... sigemptyset(3C)
sigfpe signal handling for specific	SIGFPE codes .... sigfpe(3)
SIGFPE codes	sigfpe signal handling for specific .... sigfpe(3)
sigpause/ signal, sigset,	sighold, sigrelse, sigignore, ... signal(2)
signal, sigset, sighold, sigrelse,	sigignore, sigpause simplified/ .... signal(2)
interrupt system calls	siginterrupt allow signals to .... siginterrupt(3)
/sigfillset, sigaddset, sigdelset,	sigismember manipulate sets of/ .... sigemptyset(3C)
signal state sigsetjmp,	siglongjmp a non-local goto with .... sigsetjmp(3C)
_setjmp, _longjmp, sigsetjmp,	siglongjmp non-local goto /longjmp, ... setjmp(3)
sigblock,	sigmask block signals .... sigblock(3)
semaphore sigsem	signal a process waiting on a .... sigsem(2)
generate an abnormal termination	signal abort .... abort(3C)
microseconds ualarm schedule	signal after interval in .... ualarm(3)
sigaltstack set or get	signal alternate stack context .... sigaltstack(2)
signal simplified software	signal facilities .... signal(3)
sigvec software	signal facilities .... sigvec(3)
codes sigfpe	signal handling for specific SIGFPE .... sigfpe(3)

60   Programmer's Reference Manual: Operating System API

Permuted Index

sigaction detailed	signal management .... sigaction(2)
sigignore, sigpause simplified	signal management /sigrelse, ... signal(2)
until signal sigsuspend install a	signal mask and suspend process .... sigsuspend(2)
sigprocmask change or examine	signal mask .... sigprocmask(2)
sigsetmask set current	signal mask .... sigsetmask(3)
psignal, sys_siglist system	signal messages .... psignal(3)
psignal, psiginfo system	signal messages .... psignal(3C)
pause suspend process until	signal .... pause(2)
sigignore, sigpause simplified/	signal, sigset, sighold, sigrelse, ... signal(2)
mask and suspend process until	signal sigsuspend install a signal .... sigsuspend(2)
facilities	signal simplified software signal .... signal(3)
sigstack set and/or get	signal stack context .... sigstack(3)
siglongjmp a non-local goto with	signal state sigsetjmp, ... sigsetjmp(3C)
killpg send	signal to a process group .... killpg(3)
processes kill send a	signal to a process or a group of .... kill(2)
sigsend, sigsendset send a	signal to a process or a group of/ .... sigsend(2)
raise send	signal to program .... raise(3C)
/automically release blocked	signals and wait for interrupt .... sigpause(3)
sigblock, sigmask block	signals .... sigblock(3)
sigismember manipulate sets of	signals /sigaddset, sigdelset, ... sigemptyset(3C)
ssignal, gsignal software	signals .... ssignal(3C)
pending sigpending examine	signals that are blocked and .... sigpending(2)
siginterrupt allow	signals to interrupt system calls .... siginterrupt(3)
blocked signals and wait for/	sigpause automically release .... sigpause(3)
sighold, sigrelse, sigignore,	sigpause simplified signal/ /sigset, ... signal(2)
blocked and pending	sigpending examine signals that are .... sigpending(2)
signal mask	sigprocmask change or examine .... sigprocmask(2)
signal, sigset, sighold,	sigrelse, sigignore, sigpause/ .... signal(2)
a semaphore	sigsem signal a process waiting on .... sigsem(2)
to a process or a group of/	sigsend, sigsendset send a signal .... sigsend(2)
process or a group of/ sigsend,	sigsendset send a signal to a .... sigsend(2)
sigignore, sigpause/ signal,	sigset, sighold, sigrelse, ... signal(2)
goto with signal state	sigsetjmp, siglongjmp a non-local .... sigsetjmp(3C)
setjmp, longjmp, _setjmp, _longjmp,	sigsetjmp, siglongjmp non-local/ .... setjmp(3)
	sigsetmask set current signal mask .... sigsetmask(3)
stack context	sigstack set and/or get signal .... sigstack(3)
and suspend process until signal	sigsuspend install a signal mask .... sigsuspend(2)
	sigvec software signal facilities .... sigvec(3)
rand, srand	simple random number generator .... rand(3C)
rand, srand	simple random-number generator .... rand(3C)
/sigrelse, sigignore, sigpause	simplified signal management .... signal(2)
facilities signal	simplified software signal .... signal(3)
asin, asinf, acos, acosf,/ trig:	sin, sinf, cos, cosf, tan, tanf, ... trig(3M)
asinf, acos, acosf,/ trig: sin,	sinf, cos, cosf, tan, tanf, asin, ... trig(3M)
floating_to_decimal:	single_to_decimal,/ .... floating_to_decimal(3)
tanhf, asinh, acosh, atanh/	sinh, sinhf, cosh, coshf, tanh, ... sinh(3M)
asinh, acosh, atanh/ sinh,	sinhf, cosh, coshf, tanh, tanhf, ... sinh(3M)

Permuted Index

getdtablesize get descriptor table	size	getdtablesize(3)
getpagesize get system page	size	getpagesize(3)
chsize change the	size of a file	chsize(2)
elf_fsize: elf32_fsize return the	size of an object file type	elf_fsize(3E)
grantpt grant access to the	slave pseudo-terminal device	grantpt(3C)
ptsname get name of the	slave pseudo-terminal device	ptsname(3C)
interval	sleep suspend execution for	sleep(3)
interval	sleep suspend execution for	sleep(3C)
/slk_touch, slk_attron, slk_attrset,	slk_attroff curses soft label/	curs_slk(3X)
/slk_clear, slk_restore, slk_touch,	slk_attron, slk_attrset,/	curs_slk(3X)
/slk_restore, slk_touch, slk_attron,	slk_attrset, slk_attroff curses/	curs_slk(3X)
/slk_noutrefresh, slk_label,	slk_clear, slk_restore, slk_touch,/	curs_slk(3X)
slk_noutrefresh,/ curs_slk:	slk_init, slk_set, slk_refresh,	curs_slk(3X)
/slk_refresh, slk_noutrefresh,	slk_label, slk_clear, slk_restore,/	curs_slk(3X)
/slk_init, slk_set, slk_refresh,	slk_noutrefresh, slk_label,/	curs_slk(3X)
curs_slk: slk_init, slk_set,	slk_refresh, slk_noutrefresh,/	curs_slk(3X)
slk_attrset,/ /slk_label, slk_clear,	slk_restore, slk_touch, slk_attron,	curs_slk(3X)
curs_slk: slk_init,	slk_set, slk_refresh,/	curs_slk(3X)
/slk_label, slk_clear, slk_restore,	slk_touch, slk_attron, slk_attrset,/	curs_slk(3X)
current user ttyslot find the	slot in the utmp file of the	ttyslot(3C)
accept accept a connection on a	socket	accept(3N)
bind bind a name to a	socket	bind(3N)
connect initiate a connection on a	socket	connect(3N)
communication	socket create an endpoint for	socket(3N)
listen listen for connections on a	socket	listen(3N)
getsockname get	socket name	getsockname(3N)
recvmsg receive a message from a	socket recv, recvfrom,	recv(3N)
sendmsg send a message from a	socket send, sendto,	send(3N)
connected sockets	socketpair create a pair of	socketpair(3N)
setsockopt get and set options on	sockets getsockopt,	getsockopt(3N)
create a pair of connected	sockets socketpair	socketpair(3N)
slk_attrset, slk_attroff curses	soft label routines /slk_attron,	curs_slk(3X)
signal simplified	software signal facilities	signal(3)
sigvec	software signal facilities	sigvec(3)
ssignal, gsignal	software signals	ssignal(3C)
qsort quicker	sort	qsort(3C)
bsearch binary search a	sorted table	bsearch(3C)
brk, sbrk change data segment	space allocation	brk(2)
an object in the file system name	space /file descriptor to	fattach(3C)
munlockall lock or unlock address	space mlockall,	mlockall(3C)
swapctl manage swap	space	swapctl(2)
memory efficient way vfork	spawn new process in a virtual	vfork(2)
mknod make a directory, or a	special or ordinary file	mknod(2)
mknod make a directory, or a	special or ordinary file	mknod(2)
sysi86 machine	specific functions	sysi86(2)
sigfpe signal handling for	specific SIGFPE codes	sigfpe(3)
truncate, ftruncate set a file to a	specified length	truncate(3C)

Permuted Index

rwall write to	specified remote machines	rwall(3N)
bufsplit	split buffer into fields	bufsplit(3G)
check the network	spray scatter data in order to	spray(3N)
printf, fprintf,	sprintf print formatted output	printf(3S)
vsprintf/ printf, fprintf,	sprintf, vprintf, vfprintf,	printf(3S)
data in a machine-independent/	sputl, sgetl access long integer	sputl(3X)
/logf, log10, log10f, pow, powf,	sqrt, sqrtf exponential, logarithm,/	exp(3M)
/log10, log10f, pow, powf, sqrt,	sqrtf exponential, logarithm,/	exp(3M)
exponential, logarithm, power,	square root functions /sqrt, sqrtf	exp(3M)
generator rand,	srand simple random number	rand(3C)
generator rand,	srand simple random-number	rand(3C)
/lrand48, nrand48, mrand48, jrand48,	srand48, seed48, lcong48 generate/	drand48(3C)
random number generator;/ random,	srandom, initstate, setstate better	random(3)
curs_scroll: scroll,	srcl, wscrl scroll a curses window	curs_scroll(3X)
scanf, fscanf,	sscanf convert formatted input	scanf(3S)
	ssignal, gsignal software signals	ssignal(3C)
set or get signal alternate	stack context sigaltstack	sigaltstack(2)
sigstack set and/or get signal	stack context	sigstack(3)
package stdio	standard buffered input/output	stdio(3S)
package stdipc: ftok	standard interprocess communication	stdipc(3C)
/attron, wattron, attrset, wattrset,	standend, wstandend, standout,/	curs_attr(3X)
/wattrset, standend, wstandend,	standout, wstandout curses/	curs_attr(3X)
has_colors,/ curs_color:	start_color, init_pair, init_color,	curs_color(3X)
	stat, lstat, fstat get file status	stat(2)
	stat, lstat, fstat get file status	stat(2)
ustat get file system	statistics	ustat(2)
feof, clearerr, fileno stream	status inquiries ferror,	ferror(3S)
stat, lstat, fstat get file	status	stat(2)
stat, lstat, fstat get file	status	stat(2)
information	statvfs, fstatvfs get file system	statvfs(2)
fmtmsg display a message on	stderr or system console	fmtmsg(3C)
input/output package	stdio standard buffered	stdio(3S)
communication package	stdipc: ftok standard interprocess	stdipc(3C)
compile and/ regexpr: compile,	step, advance regular expression	regexpr(3G)
	stime set time	stime(2)
wait wait for child process to	stop or terminate	wait(2)
wait for process to terminate or	stop /WIFSIGNALED, WIFEXITED	wait(3)
synchronize memory with physical	storage msync	msync(3C)
dbm: dbminit, dbmclose, fetch,	store, delete, firstkey, nextkey/	dbm(3)
string manipulations	str: strfind, strrspn, strtrns	str(3G)
compressing or/ strccpy: streadd,	strcadd, strccpy copy strings,	strccpy(3G)
operations string:	strcasecmp, strncasecmp string	string(3)
strncmp, strcpy, strncpy,/ string:	strcat, strdup, strncat, strcmp,	string(3C)
copy strings, compressing or/	strccpy: streadd, strcadd, strccpy	strccpy(3G)
/strncmp, strcpy, strncpy, strlen,	strchr, strrchr, strpbrk, strspn,/	string(3C)
string: strcat, strdup, strncat,	strcmp, strncmp, strcpy, strncpy,/	string(3C)
	strcoll string collation	strcoll(3C)

Permuted Index 63

Permuted Index

/strdup, strncat, strcmp, strncmp,	strcpy, strncpy, strlen, strchr,/	string(3C)
/strchr, strrchr, strpbrk, strspn,	strcspn, strtok, strstr string/	string(3C)
strcpy, strncpy,/ string: strcat,	strdup, strncat, strcmp, strncmp,	string(3C)
strings, compressing or/ strccpy:	streadd, strcadd, strccpy copy	strccpy(3G)
for external data representation	stream creation /library routines	xdr_create(3N)
fclose, fflush close or flush a	stream	fclose(3S)
fopen, freopen, fdopen open a	stream	fopen(3S)
fopen, freopen, fdopen open a	stream	fopen(3S)
reposition a file pointer in a	stream fseek, rewind, ftell	fseek(3S)
reposition a file pointer in a	stream fsetpos, fgetpos	fsetpos(3C)
getw get character or word from a	stream getc, getchar, fgetc,	getc(3S)
getmsg get next message off a	stream	getmsg(2)
gets, fgets get a string from a	stream	gets(3S)
putw put character or word on a	stream putc, putchar, fputc,	putc(3S)
putmsg send a message on a	stream	putmsg(2)
puts, fputs put a string on a	stream	puts(3S)
setvbuf assign buffering to a	stream /setbuffer, setlinebuf,	setbuf(3S)
setvbuf assign buffering to a	stream setbuf,	setbuf(3S)
setlinebuf assign buffering to a	stream setbuffer,	setbuffer(3S)
ferror, feof, clearerr, fileno	stream status inquiries	ferror(3S)
rexec return	stream to a remote command	rexec(3N)
push character back onto input	stream ungetc	ungetc(3S)
bgets read	stream up to next delimiter	bgets(3G)
fdetach detach a name from a	STREAMS-based file descriptor	fdetach(3C)
object in the/ fattach attach a	STREAMS-based file descriptor to an	fattach(3C)
or/ strccpy: streadd, strcadd,	strccpy copy strings, compressing	strccpy(3G)
	strerror get error message string	strerror(3C)
manipulations str:	strfind, strrspn, strtrns string	str(3G)
date and time to string	strftime, cftime, ascftime convert	strftime(3C)
long integer and base-64 ASCII	string a64l, l64a convert between	a64l(3C)
/mvwinsstr, mvwinsnstr insert	string before character under the/	curs_instr(3X)
strcoll	string collation	strcoll(3C)
tzset convert date and time to	string /localtime, gmtime, asctime,	ctime(3C)
convert floating-point number to	string /fcvt, fcvtl, gcvt, gcvtl	ecvt(3C)
gets, fgets get a	string from a stream	gets(3S)
mbstowcs, wcstombs multibyte	string functions mbstring:	mbstring(3C)
getsubopt parse suboptions from a	string	getsubopt(3C)
gettxt retrieve a text	string	gettxt(3C)
str: strfind, strrspn, strtrns	string manipulations	str(3G)
/mvwinchstr, mvwinchnstr get a	string of characters (and/	curs_inchstr(3X)
/mvwaddchstr, mvwaddchnstr add	string of characters (and/	curs_addchstr(3X)
/mvinnstr, mvwinstr, mvwinnstr get a	string of characters from a curses/	curs_instr(3X)
window/ /mvwaddstr, mvwaddnstr add a	string of characters to a curses	curs_addstr(3X)
puts, fputs put a	string on a stream	puts(3S)
bcmp, bzero, ffs bit and byte	string operations bstring: bcopy,	bstring(3)
index, rindex	string operations	index(3)
string: strcasecmp, strncasecmp	string operations	string(3)

strspn, strcspn, strtok, strstr	string operations /strpbrk, ... string(3C)
elf_strptr make a	string pointer .... elf_strptr(3E)
set_menu_mark, menu_mark menus mark	string routines menu_mark: .... menu_mark(3X)
string operations	string: strcasecmp, strncasecmp .... string(3)
strcmp, strncmp, strcpy, strncpy,/	string: strcat, strdup, strncat, ... string(3C)
strerror get error message	string .... strerror(3C)
ascftime convert date and time to	string strftime, cftime, ... strftime(3C)
strtod, strtold, atof convert	string to double-precision number .... strtod(3C)
strtol, strtoul, atol, atoi convert	string to integer .... strtol(3C)
strxfrm	string transformation .... strxfrm(3C)
/streadd, strcadd, strecpy copy	strings, compressing or expanding/ .... strccpy(3G)
/mvwgetstr, wgetnstr get character	strings from curses terminal/ .... curs_getstr(3X)
get and set system information	strings sysinfo .... sysinfo(2)
/strcmp, strncmp, strcpy, strncpy,	strlen, strchr, strrchr, strpbrk,/ .... string(3C)
string: strcasecmp,	strncasecmp string operations .... string(3)
strncpy,/ string: strcat, strdup,	strncat, strcmp, strncmp, strcpy, ... string(3C)
/strcat, strdup, strncat, strcmp,	strncmp, strcpy, strncpy, strlen,/ .... string(3C)
/strncat, strcmp, strncmp, strcpy,	strncpy, strlen, strchr, strrchr,/ .... string(3C)
/strncpy, strlen, strchr, strrchr,	strpbrk, strspn, strcspn, strtok,/ .... string(3C)
/strcpy, strncpy, strlen, strchr,	strrchr, strpbrk, strspn, strcspn,/ .... string(3C)
manipulations str: strfind,	strrspn, strtrns string .... str(3G)
/strlen, strchr, strrchr, strpbrk,	strspn, strcspn, strtok, strstr/ .... string(3C)
strpbrk, strspn, strcspn, strtok,	strstr string operations /strrchr, ... string(3C)
string to double-precision number	strtod, strtold, atof convert .... strtod(3C)
/strrchr, strpbrk, strspn, strcspn,	strtok, strstr string operations .... string(3C)
string to integer	strtol, strtoul, atol, atoi convert .... strtol(3C)
double-precision number strtod,	strtold, atof convert string to .... strtod(3C)
to integer strtol,	strtoul, atol, atoi convert string .... strtol(3C)
str: strfind, strrspn,	strtrns string manipulations .... str(3G)
offsetof offset of	structure member .... offsetof(3C)
t_alloc allocate a library	structure .... t_alloc(3N)
t_free free a library	structure .... t_free(3N)
mktime converts a tm	structure to a calendar time .... mktime(3C)
	strxfrm string transformation .... strxfrm(3C)
getsubopt parse	suboptions from a string .... getsubopt(3C)
pechochar create/ curs_pad: newpad,	subpad, prefresh, pnoutrefresh, ... curs_pad(3X)
delete, firstkey, nextkey data base	subroutines /fetch, store, ... dbm(3)
dbm_open, dbm_store data base	subroutines /dbm_nextkey, ... ndbm(3)
command processor for the forms	subsystem form_driver .... form_driver(3X)
command processor for the menus	subsystem menu_driver .... menu_driver(3X)
curs_window: newwin, delwin, mvwin,	subwin, derwin, mvderwin, dupwin,/ .... curs_window(3X)
/scale_form forms window and	subwindow association routines .... form_win(3X)
/scale_menu menus window and	subwindow association routines .... menu_win(3X)
or erase forms from associated	subwindows /unpost_form write .... form_post(3X)
or erase menus from associated	subwindows /unpost_menu write .... menu_post(3X)
sync update	super block .... sync(2)
getgroups, setgroups get or set	supplementary group access list IDs .... getgroups(2)

Permuted Index 65

Permuted Index

initgroups initialize the supplementary group access list	initgroups(3C)
interval nap suspend execution for a short	nap(2)
microseconds usleep suspend execution for interval in	usleep(3)
sleep suspend execution for interval	sleep(3)
sleep suspend execution for interval	sleep(3C)
pause suspend process until signal	pause(2)
/install a signal mask and suspend process until signal	sigsuspend(2)
svc_dg_create,/ rpc_svc_create: svc_create, svc_destroy,	rpc_svc_create(3N)
rpc_svc_create: svc_create, svc_destroy, svc_dg_create,/	rpc_svc_create(3N)
/svc_create, svc_destroy, svc_dg_create, svc_fd_create,/	rpc_svc_create(3N)
svcerr_noproc,/ rpc_svc_err: svcerr_auth, svcerr_decode,	rpc_svc_err(3N)
rpc_svc_err: svcerr_auth, svcerr_decode, svcerr_noproc,/	rpc_svc_err(3N)
/svcerr_auth, svcerr_decode, svcerr_noproc, svcerr_noprog,/	rpc_svc_err(3N)
/svcerr_decode, svcerr_noproc, svcerr_noprog, svcerr_progvers,/	rpc_svc_err(3N)
/svcerr_noproc, svcerr_noprog, svcerr_progvers, svcerr_systemerr,/	rpc_svc_err(3N)
/svcerr_noprog, svcerr_progvers, svcerr_systemerr, svcerr_weakauth/	rpc_svc_err(3N)
/svcerr_progvers, svcerr_systemerr, svcerr_weakauth library routines/	rpc_svc_err(3N)
/svc_destroy, svc_dg_create, svc_fd_create, svc_raw_create,/	rpc_svc_create(3N)
svc_getreqset,/ rpc_svc_reg: svc_freeargs, svc_getargs,	rpc_svc_reg(3N)
rpc_svc_reg: svc_freeargs, svc_getargs, svc_getreqset,/	rpc_svc_reg(3N)
/svc_freeargs, svc_getargs, svc_getreqset, svc_getrpccaller,/	rpc_svc_reg(3N)
/svc_getargs, svc_getreqset, svc_getrpccaller, svc_run,/	rpc_svc_reg(3N)
/svc_dg_create, svc_fd_create, svc_raw_create, svc_tli_create,/	rpc_svc_create(3N)
rpc_svc_calls: rpc_reg, svc_reg, svc_unreg, xprt_register,/	rpc_svc_calls(3N)
/svc_getreqset, svc_getrpccaller, svc_run, svc_sendreply library/	rpc_svc_reg(3N)
RPC/ /svc_getrpccaller, svc_run, svc_sendreply library routines for	rpc_svc_reg(3N)
/svc_fd_create, svc_raw_create, svc_tli_create, svc_tp_create,/	rpc_svc_create(3N)
/svc_raw_create, svc_tli_create, svc_tp_create, svc_vc_create/	rpc_svc_create(3N)
rpc_svc_calls: rpc_reg, svc_reg, svc_unreg, xprt_register,/	rpc_svc_calls(3N)
/svc_tli_create, svc_tp_create, svc_vc_create library routines for/	rpc_svc_create(3N)
swab swap bytes	swab(3C)
swab swap bytes	swab(3C)
swapctl manage swap space	swapctl(2)
contexts makecontext, swapcontext manipulate user	makecontext(3C)
swapctl manage swap space	swapctl(2)
dlsym get the address of a symbol in shared object	dlsym(3X)
elf_getarsym retrieve archive symbol table	elf_getarsym(3E)
nlist get entries from symbol table	nlist(3)
readlink read the value of a symbolic link	readlink(2)
symlink make a symbolic link to a file	symlink(2)
file symlink make a symbolic link to a	symlink(2)
sync update super block	sync(2)
adjtime correct the time to allow synchronization of the system clock	adjtime(2)
state with that on the/ fsync synchronize a file's in-memory	fsync(2)
segment sdenter, sdleave synchronize access to a shared data	sdenter(2)
storage msync synchronize memory with physical	msync(3C)
sdgetv synchronize shared data access	sdgetv(2)

Programmer's Reference Manual: Operating System API

Permuted Index

t_sync	synchronize transport library	t_sync(3N)
select	synchronous I/O multiplexing	select(3C)
/derwin, mvderwin, dupwin, wsyncup,	syncok, wcursyncup, wsyncdown/	curs_window(3X)
	syscall indirect system call	syscall(3)
system variables	sysconf retrieves configurable	sysconf(3C)
system variables	sysconf retrieves configurable	sysconf(3C)
information	sysfs get file system type	sysfs(2)
	sysi86 machine specific functions	sysi86(2)
information strings	sysinfo get and set system	sysinfo(2)
setlogmask control system log	syslog, openlog, closelog,	syslog(3)
psignal,	sys_siglist system signal messages	psignal(3)
syscall indirect	system call	syscall(3)
intro introduction to	system calls and error numbers	intro(2)
allow signals to interrupt	system calls siginterrupt	siginterrupt(3)
to allow synchronization of the	system clock /correct the time	adjtime(2)
display a message on stderr or	system console fmtmsg	fmtmsg(3C)
perror print	system error messages	perror(3C)
directory entries and put in a file	system independent format /read	getdents(2)
statvfs, fstatvfs get file	system information	statvfs(2)
sysinfo get and set	system information strings	sysinfo(2)
	system issue a shell command	system(3S)
closelog, setlogmask control	system log syslog, openlog,	syslog(3)
mount mount a file	system	mount(2)
descriptor to an object in the file	system name space /file	fattach(3C)
reboot reboot	system or halt processor	reboot(3)
getpagesize get	system page size	getpagesize(3)
/setrlimit control maximum	system resource consumption	getrlimit(2)
psignal, sys_siglist	system signal messages	psignal(3)
psignal, psiginfo	system signal messages	psignal(3C)
ustat get file	system statistics	ustat(2)
sysfs get file	system type information	sysfs(2)
umount unmount a file	system	umount(2)
uname get name of current UNIX	system	uname(2)
sysconf retrieves configurable	system variables	sysconf(3C)
sysconf retrieves configurable	system variables	sysconf(3C)
bsearch binary search a sorted	table	bsearch(3C)
retrieve archive symbol	table elf_getarsym	elf_getarsym(3E)
class-dependent program header	table /elf32_newphdr retrieve	elf_getphdr(3E)
nlist get entries from symbol	table	nlist(3)
getdtablesize get descriptor	table size	getdtablesize(3)
hdestroy manage hash search	tables hsearch, hcreate,	hsearch(3C)
	t_accept accept a connect request	t_accept(3N)
/netdir_free, netdir_mergeaddr,	taddr2uaddr, uaddr2taddr,/	netdir_getbyname(3N)
structure	t_alloc allocate a library	t_alloc(3N)
	tam TAM transition libraries	tam(3X)
tam	TAM transition libraries	tam(3X)
acosf,/ trig: sin, sinf, cos, cosf,	tan, tanf, asin, asinf, acos,	trig(3M)

Permuted Index

trig: sin, sinf, cos, cosf, tan,	tanf, asin, asinf, acos, acosf,/	trig(3M)
sinh, sinhf, cosh, coshf,	tanh, tanhf, asinh, acosh, atanh/	sinh(3M)
sinh, sinhf, cosh, coshf, tanh,	tanhf, asinh, acosh, atanh/	sinh(3M)
transport endpoint	t_bind bind an address to a	t_bind(3N)
tcgetattr, tcsetattr, tcsendbreak,	tcdrain, tcflush, tcflow,/ termios:	termios(2)
/tcsendbreak, tcdrain, tcflush,	tcflow, cfgetospeed, cfgetispeed,/	termios(2)
/tcsetattr, tcsendbreak, tcdrain,	tcflush, tcflow, cfgetospeed,/	termios(2)
tcdrain, tcflush, tcflow,/ termios:	tcgetattr, tcsetattr, tcsendbreak,	termios(2)
general/ /cfsetispeed, cfsetospeed,	tcgetpgrp, tcsetpgrp, tcgetsid	termios(2)
/cfsetospeed, tcgetpgrp, tcsetpgrp,	tcgetsid general terminal interface	termios(2)
	t_close close a transport endpoint	t_close(3N)
with another transport user	t_connect establish a connection	t_connect(3N)
termios: tcgetattr, tcsetattr,	tcsendbreak, tcdrain, tcflush,/	termios(2)
tcflush,/ termios: tcgetattr,	tcsetattr, tcsendbreak, tcdrain,	termios(2)
process group id	tcsetpgrp set terminal foreground	tcsetpgrp(3C)
terminal/ /cfsetospeed, tcgetpgrp,	tcsetpgrp, tcgetsid general	termios(2)
trees tsearch, tfind,	tdelete, twalk manage binary search	tsearch(3C)
form_data: data_ahead, data_behind	tell if forms field has off-screen/	form_data(3X)
menu_item_visible: item_visible	tell if menus item is visible	menu_item_visible(3X)
directory: opendir, readdir,	telldir, seekdir, rewinddir,/	directory(3C)
directory: opendir, readdir,	telldir, seekdir, rewinddir,/	directory(3C)
temporary file tmpnam,	tempnam create a name for a	tmpnam(3S)
tmpfile create a	temporary file	tmpfile(3S)
tmpnam, tempnam create a name for a	temporary file	tmpnam(3S)
/has_ic, has_il, killchar, longname,	termattrs, termname curses/	curs_termattrs(3X)
curses interfaces (emulated) to the	termcap library /tgoto, tputs	curs_termcap(3X)
ctermid generate file name for	terminal	ctermid(3S)
id tcsetpgrp set	terminal foreground process group	tcsetpgrp(3C)
libwindows windowing	terminal function library	libwindows(3X)
/timeout, wtimeout, typeahead curses	terminal input option control/	curs_inopts(3X)
tcsetpgrp, tcgetsid general	terminal interface /tcgetpgrp,	termios(2)
push back) characters from curses	terminal keyboard /ungetch get (or	curs_getch(3X)
get character strings from curses	terminal keyboard /wgetnstr	curs_getstr(3X)
dial establish an outgoing	terminal line connection	dial(3C)
/scrollok, nl, nonl curses	terminal output option control/	curs_outopts(3X)
ttyname, isatty find name of a	terminal	ttyname(3C)
WIFEXITED wait for process to	terminate or stop /WIFSIGNALED,	wait(3)
exit, _exit	terminate process	exit(2)
wait for child process to stop or	terminate wait	wait(2)
atexit add program	termination routine	atexit(3C)
abort generate an abnormal	termination signal	abort(3C)
tigetstr curses interfaces to	terminfo database /tigetnum,	curs_terminfo(3X)
tcsendbreak, tcdrain, tcflush,/	termios: tcgetattr, tcsetattr,	termios(2)
/killchar, longname, termattrs,	termname curses environment query/	curs_termattrs(3X)
	t_error produce error message	t_error(3N)
isastream	test a file descriptor	isastream(3C)
lock into memory or unlock process,	text, or data plock	plock(2)

Permuted Index

gettxt retrieve a	text string	gettxt(3C)
search trees tsearch,	tfind, tdelete, twalk manage binary	tsearch(3C)
	t_free free a library structure	t_free(3N)
tgetstr, tgoto,/ curs_termcap:	tgetent, tgetflag, tgetnum,	curs_termcap(3X)
tputs/ curs_termcap: tgetent,	tgetflag, tgetnum, tgetstr, tgoto,	curs_termcap(3X)
service information	t_getinfo get protocol-specific	t_getinfo(3N)
curs_termcap: tgetent, tgetflag,	tgetnum, tgetstr, tgoto, tputs/	curs_termcap(3X)
	t_getstate get the current state	t_getstate(3N)
/tgetent, tgetflag, tgetnum,	tgetstr, tgoto, tputs curses/	curs_termcap(3X)
/tgetflag, tgetnum, tgetstr,	tgoto, tputs curses interfaces/	curs_termcap(3X)
/putp, vidputs, vidattr, mvcur,	tigetflag, tigetnum, tigetstr/	curs_terminfo(3X)
vidputs, vidattr, mvcur, tigetflag,	tigetnum, tigetstr curses/ /putp,	curs_terminfo(3X)
/mvcur, tigetflag, tigetnum,	tigetstr curses interfaces to/	curs_terminfo(3X)
/raw, noraw, noqiflush, qiflush,	timeout, wtimeout, typeahead curses/	curs_inopts(3X)
setitimer get/set value of interval	timer getitimer,	getitimer(3C)
the difference between two calendar	times difftime computes	difftime(3C)
times	times get process and child process	times(2)
	times get process times	times(3C)
times get process and child process	times	times(2)
times get process	times	times(3C)
set file access and modification	times utime	utime(2)
utimes set file	times	utimes(3)
nice change priority of a	time-sharing process	nice(2)
offset from GMT	timezone get time zone name given	timezone(3C)
request	t_listen listen for a connect	t_listen(3N)
a transport endpoint	t_look look at the current event on	t_look(3N)
mktime converts a	tm structure to a calendar time	mktime(3C)
	tmpfile create a temporary file	tmpfile(3S)
temporary file	tmpnam, tempnam create a name for a	tmpnam(3S)
read (write) a curses screen from	(to) a file /scr_init, scr_set	curs_scr_dump(3X)
/tolower, _toupper, _tolower,	toascii translate characters	conv(3C)
popen, pclose initiate pipe	to/from a process	popen(3S)
conv: toupper, tolower, _toupper,	_tolower, toascii translate/	conv(3C)
toascii translate/ conv: toupper,	tolower, _toupper, _tolower,	conv(3C)
endpoint	t_open establish a transport	t_open(3N)
manipulation routines panel_top:	top_panel, bottom_panel panels deck	panel_top(3X)
current/ /current_item, set_top_row,	top_row, item_index set and get	menu_item_current(3X)
transport endpoint	t_optmgmt manage options for a	t_optmgmt(3N)
curs_touch: touchwin,	touchline, untouchwin, wtouchln,/	curs_touch(3X)
wtouchln,/ curs_touch:	touchwin, touchline, untouchwin,	curs_touch(3X)
translate/ conv: toupper, tolower,	_toupper, _tolower, toascii	conv(3C)
_tolower, toascii translate/ conv:	toupper, tolower, _toupper,	conv(3C)
vidattr,/ /del_curterm, restartterm,	tparm, tputs, putp, vidputs,	curs_terminfo(3X)
/tgetflag, tgetnum, tgetstr, tgoto,	tputs curses interfaces (emulated)/	curs_termcap(3X)
/del_curterm, restartterm, tparm,	tputs, putp, vidputs, vidattr,/	curs_terminfo(3X)
ptrace process	trace	ptrace(2)
strxfrm string	transformation	strxfrm(3C)

Permuted Index

```
                          tam TAM  transition libraries ............................................................... tam(3X)
      _toupper, _tolower, toascii  translate characters   /tolower, ......................................... conv(3C)
elf32_xlatetom class-dependent data  translation   /elf32_xlatetof, ....................................... elf_xlate(3E)
    generic transport name-to-address  translation   /netdir_sperror ...................... netdir_getbyname(3N)
          t_bind bind an address to a  transport endpoint ............................................................. t_bind(3N)
                    t_close close a  transport endpoint ............................................................. t_close(3N)
     look at the current event on a  transport endpoint t_look .......................................... t_look(3N)
             t_open establish a  transport endpoint ............................................................. t_open(3N)
     t_optmgmt manage options for a  transport endpoint ...................................................... t_optmgmt(3N)
             t_unbind disable a  transport endpoint ...................................................... t_unbind(3N)
                t_sync synchronize  transport library ............................................................. t_sync(3N)
  translation  /netdir_sperror generic  transport name-to-address ....................... netdir_getbyname(3N)
        nlsprovider get name of  transport provider ...................................................... nlsprovider(3N)
  establish a connection with another  transport user  t_connect ........................................ t_connect(3N)
   ieee_handler IEEE exception  trap handler function ......................................... ieee_handler(3M)
         panel_below panels deck  traversal primitives   /panel_above, ................... panel_above(3X)
      data sent over a connection  t_rcv receive data or expedited ............................... t_rcv(3N)
   confirmation from a connect/  t_rcvconnect receive the .............................. t_rcvconnect(3N)
                    disconnect  t_rcvdis retrieve information from ........................... t_rcvdis(3N)
         orderly release indication  t_rcvrel acknowledge receipt of an .......................... t_rcvrel(3N)
                              t_rcvudata receive a data unit ................... t_rcvudata(3N)
              error indication  t_rcvuderr receive a unit data ................. t_rcvuderr(3N)
            ftw, nftw walk a file  tree ........................................................................... ftw(3C)
tdelete, twalk manage binary search  trees  tsearch, tfind, ............................................ tsearch(3C)
     tanf, asin, asinf, acos, acosf,/  trig: sin, sinf, cos, cosf, tan, ...................................... trig(3M)
     acosf, atan, atanf, atan2, atan2f  trigonometric functions   /acos, ...................................... trig(3M)
                specified length  truncate, ftruncate set a file to a ................................. truncate(3C)
     manage binary search trees  tsearch, tfind, tdelete, twalk ....................................... tsearch(3C)
              over a connection  t_snd send data or expedited data .................................. t_snd(3N)
              disconnect request  t_snddis send user-initiated ......................................... t_snddis(3N)
                       release  t_sndrel initiate an orderly ............................................ t_sndrel(3N)
                              t_sndudata send a data unit ................. t_sndudata(3N)
                        library  t_sync synchronize transport ........................................ t_sync(3N)
                       terminal  ttyname, isatty find name of a ..................................... ttyname(3C)
      file of the current user  ttyslot find the slot in the utmp ................................ ttyslot(3C)
                       endpoint  t_unbind disable a transport ....................................... t_unbind(3N)
                       p_online  turn a processor online or offline .............................. p_online(2)
           tsearch, tfind, tdelete,  twalk manage binary search trees ............................... tsearch(3C)
    return the size of an object file  type  elf_fsize: elf32_fsize ......................................... elf_fsize(3E)
        elf_kind determine file  type ........................................................................... elf_kind(3E)
          sysfs get file system  type information ........................................................ sysfs(2)
/unordered, unorderedl determine  type of floating-point number .......................................... isnan(3C)
          field_arg forms field data  type validation   /field_type, ................. form_field_validation(3X)
   option/   /qiflush, timeout, wtimeout,  typeahead curses terminal input ............................ curs_inopts(3X)
       ctime, localtime, gmtime, asctime,  tzset convert date and time to/ ......................................... ctime(3C)
   /netdir_mergeaddr, taddr2uaddr,  uaddr2taddr, netdir_perror,/ ................... netdir_getbyname(3N)
                              uadmin administrative control ......................................... uadmin(2)
```

70   Programmer's Reference Manual: Operating System API

interval in microseconds ualarm schedule signal after	ualarm(3)
getpw get name from UID	getpw(3C)
file/ /endspent, fgetspent, lckpwdf, ulckpwdf manipulate shadow password	getspent(3C)
ulimit get and set user limits	ulimit(2)
mask umask set and get file creation	umask(2)
umount unmount a file system	umount(2)
system uname get name of current UNIX	uname(2)
putwin, getwin,/ curs_util: unctrl, keyname, filter, use_env,	curs_util(3X)
input stream ungetc push character back onto	ungetc(3S)
/getch, wgetch, mvgetch, mvwgetch, ungetch get (or push back)/	curs_getch(3X)
/srand48, seed48, lcong48 generate uniformly distributed pseudo-random/	drand48(3C)
elf_rawfile retrieve uninterpreted file contents	elf_rawfile(3E)
mkstemp make a unique file name	mkstemp(3)
mktemp make a unique file name	mktemp(3C)
gethostid get unique identifier of current host	gethostid(3)
t_rcvuderr receive a unit data error indication	t_rcvuderr(3N)
t_rcvudata receive a data unit	t_rcvudata(3N)
t_sndudata send a data unit	t_sndudata(3N)
uname get name of current UNIX system	uname(2)
unlink remove directory entry	unlink(2)
writing locking lock or unlock a file region for reading or	locking(2)
master/slave pair unlockpt unlock a pseudo-terminal	unlockpt(3C)
mlockall, munlockall lock or unlock address space	mlockall(3C)
mlock, munlock lock (or unlock) pages in memory	mlock(3C)
plock lock into memory or unlock process, text, or data	plock(2)
master/slave pair unlockpt unlock a pseudo-terminal	unlockpt(3C)
munmap unmap pages of memory	munmap(2)
umount unmount a file system	umount(2)
/finite, finitel, fpclass, fpclassl, unordered, unorderedl determine/	isnan(3C)
/fpclass, fpclassl, unordered, unorderedl determine type of/	isnan(3C)
from/ form_post: post_form, unpost_form write or erase forms	form_post(3X)
from/ menu_post: post_menu, unpost_menu write or erase menus	menu_post(3X)
pause suspend process until signal	pause(2)
a signal mask and suspend process until signal sigsuspend install	sigsuspend(2)
curs_touch: touchwin, touchline, untouchwin, wtouchln,/	curs_touch(3X)
elf_update update an ELF descriptor	elf_update(3E)
lsearch, lfind linear search and update	lsearch(3C)
sync update super block	sync(2)
refresh routine panel_update: update_panels panels virtual screen	panel_update(3X)
/utmpxname, getutmp, getutmpx, updwtmp, updwtmpx access utmpx file/	getutx(3C)
/getutmp, getutmpx, updwtmp, updwtmpx access utmpx file entry	getutx(3C)
levels for an application for use with fmtmsg /a list of severity	addseverity(3C)
curs_util: unctrl, keyname, filter, use_env, putwin, getwin,/	curs_util(3X)
setuid, setgid set user and group IDs	setuid(2)
setcontext get and set current user context getcontext,	getcontext(2)
makecontext, swapcontext manipulate user contexts	makecontext(3C)
get character login name of the user cuserid	cuserid(3S)

Permuted Index

/geteuid, getgid, getegid get real	user, effective user, real group,/	getuid(2)
getdate convert	user format date and time	getdate(3C)
setreuid set real and effective	user IDs	setreuid(3)
ulimit get and set	user limits	ulimit(2)
/getegid get real user, effective	user, real group, and effective/	getuid(2)
endusershell get legal	user shells /setusershell,	getusershell(3)
a connection with another transport	user t_connect establish	t_connect(3N)
in the utmp file of the current	user ttyslot find the slot	ttyslot(3C)
secure/ /netname2host, netname2user,	user2netname library routines for	secure_rpc(3N)
t_snddis send	user-initiated disconnect request	t_snddis(3N)
maillock manage lockfile for	user's mailbox	maillock(3X)
rusers return information about	users on remote machines	rusers(3N)
elf_end finish	using an object file	elf_end(3E)
interval in microseconds	usleep suspend execution for	usleep(3)
	ustat get file system statistics	ustat(2)
flushinp miscellaneous curses	utility routines /delay_output,	curs_util(3X)
get information about resource	utilization getrusage	getrusage(3)
modification times	utime set file access and	utime(2)
	utimes set file times	utimes(3)
setutent, endutent, utmpname access	utmp file entry /pututline,	getut(3C)
ttyslot find the slot in the	utmp file of the current user	ttyslot(3C)
/pututline, setutent, endutent,	utmpname access utmp file entry	getut(3C)
getutmpx, updwtmp, updwtmpx access	utmpx file entry /getutmp,	getutx(3C)
/pututxline, setutxent, endutxent,	utmpxname, getutmp, getutmpx,/	getutx(3C)
field_arg forms field data type	validation /field_type,	form_field_validation(3X)
free, realloc, calloc, memalign,	valloc, memory allocator malloc,	malloc(3C)
abs, labs return integer absolute	value	abs(3C)
decimal record to floating-point	value /decimal_to_extended convert	decimal_to_floating(3)
elf_hash compute hash	value	elf_hash(3E)
getenv return	value for environment name	getenv(3C)
floor, ceiling, remainder, absolute	value functions /rint, remainder	floor(3M)
readlink read the	value of a symbolic link	readlink(2)
getitimer, setitimer get/set	value of interval timer	getitimer(3C)
/convert floating-point	value to decimal record	floating_to_decimal(3)
putenv change or add	value to environment	putenv(3C)
/htonl, htons, ntohl, ntohs convert	values between host and network/	byteorder(3N)
item_value set and get menus item	values /set_item_value,	menu_item_value(3X)
print formatted output of a	variable argument list /vsprintf	vprintf(3S)
pathconf get configurable pathname	variables fpathconf,	fpathconf(2)
retrieves configurable system	variables sysconf	sysconf(3C)
retrieves configurable system	variables sysconf	sysconf(3C)
get option letter from argument	vector getopt	getopt(3C)
assert	verify program assertion	assert(3X)
ELF library and application	versions elf_version coordinate	elf_version(3E)
curses borders, horizontal and	vertical lines /wvline create	curs_border(3X)
virtual memory efficient way	vfork spawn new process in a	vfork(2)

Programmer's Reference Manual: Operating System API

printf, fprintf, sprintf, vprintf, vfprintf, vsprintf formatted output/	printf(3S)
output of a variable/ vprintf, vfprintf, vsprintf print formatted	vprintf(3S)
getvfsspec, getvfsany get vfstab file entry /getvfsfile,	getvfsent(3C)
nlsgetcall get client's data passed via the listener	nlsgetcall(3N)
/tparm, tputs, putp, vidputs, vidattr, mvcur, tigetflag,/	curs_terminfo(3X)
/restartterm, tparm, tputs, putp, vidputs, vidattr, mvcur, tigetflag,/	curs_terminfo(3X)
vfork spawn new process in a virtual memory efficient way	vfork(2)
move a panels window on the virtual screen /move_panel	panel_move(3X)
panel_update: update_panels panels virtual screen refresh routine	panel_update(3X)
item_visible tell if menus item is visible menu_item_visible:	menu_item_visible(3X)
/wborder, box, hline, whline, vline, wvline create curses/	curs_border(3X)
printf, fprintf, sprintf, vprintf, vfprintf, vsprintf/	printf(3S)
formatted output of a variable/ vprintf, vfprintf, vsprintf print	vprintf(3S)
sprintf, vprintf, vfprintf, vsprintf formatted output/ /fprintf,	printf(3S)
a variable/ vprintf, vfprintf, vsprintf print formatted output of	vprintf(3S)
in/ /wprintw, mvprintw, mvwprintw, vwprintw print formatted output	curs_printw(3X)
/scanw, wscanw, mvscanw, mvwscanw, vwscanw convert formatted input/	curs_scanw(3X)
echochar,/ curs_addch: addch, waddch, mvaddch, mvwaddch,	curs_addch(3X)
/addchstr, addchnstr, waddchstr, waddchnstr, mvaddchstr,/	curs_addchstr(3X)
curs_addchstr: addchstr, addchnstr, waddchstr, waddchnstr, mvaddchstr,/	curs_addchstr(3X)
/addstr, addnstr, waddstr, waddnstr, mvaddstr, mvaddnstr,/	curs_addstr(3X)
curs_addstr: addstr, addnstr, waddstr, waddnstr, mvaddstr,/	curs_addstr(3X)
state waitid wait for child process to change	waitid(2)
state waitpid wait for child process to change	waitpid(2)
terminate wait wait for child process to stop or	wait(2)
release blocked signals and wait for interrupt /automically	sigpause(3)
/WIFSTOPPED, WIFSIGNALED, WIFEXITED wait for process to terminate or/	wait(2)
or terminate wait wait for child process to stop	wait(2)
WIFSIGNALED, WIFEXITED wait for/ wait, wait3, WIFSTOPPED,	wait(3)
WIFEXITED wait for process/ wait, wait3, WIFSTOPPED, WIFSIGNALED,	wait(3)
change state waitid wait for child process to	waitid(2)
sigsem signal a process waiting on a semaphore	sigsem(2)
change state waitpid wait for child process to	waitpid(2)
access to a resource governed by a/ waitsem, nbwaitsem await and check	waitsem(2)
ftw, nftw walk a file tree	ftw(3C)
wattrset,/ curs_attr: attroff, wattroff, attron, wattron, attrset,	curs_attr(3X)
/attroff, wattroff, attron, wattron, attrset, wattrset,/	curs_attr(3X)
/wattroff, attron, wattron, attrset, wattrset, standend, wstandend,/	curs_attr(3X)
curs_bkgd: bkgdset, wbkgdset, bkgd, wbkgd curses window background/	curs_bkgd(3X)
background/ curs_bkgd: bkgdset, wbkgdset, bkgd, wbkgd curses window	curs_bkgd(3X)
wvline create/ curs_border: border, wborder, box, hline, whline, vline,	curs_border(3X)
curs_clear: erase, werase, clear, wclear, clrtobot, wclrtobot,/	curs_clear(3X)
/werase, clear, wclear, clrtobot, wclrtobot, clrtoeol, wclrtoeol/	curs_clear(3X)
/clrtobot, wclrtobot, clrtoeol, wclrtoeol clear all or part of a/	curs_clear(3X)
mbstring: mbstowcs, wcstombs multibyte string functions	mbstring(3C)
mbchar: mbtowc, mblen, wctomb multibyte character handling	mbchar(3C)

Permuted Index   73

Permuted Index

/mvderwin, dupwin, wsyncup, syncok,	wcursyncup, wsyncdown create curses/ .... curs_window(3X)
character under/ curs_delch: delch,	wdelch, mvdelch, mvwdelch delete .... curs_delch(3X)
insertln,/ curs_deleteln: deleteln,	wdeleteln, insdelln, winsdelln, ... curs_deleteln(3X)
/mvaddch, mvwaddch, echochar,	wechochar add a character (with/ .... curs_addch(3X)
wclrtobot,/ curs_clear: erase,	werase, clear, wclear, clrtobot, ... curs_clear(3X)
get (or push/ curs_getch: getch,	wgetch, mvgetch, mvwgetch, ungetch .... curs_getch(3X)
/wgetstr, mvgetstr, mvwgetstr,	wgetnstr get character strings from/ .... curs_getstr(3X)
wgetnstr get/ curs_getstr: getstr,	wgetstr, mvgetstr, mvwgetstr, ... curs_getstr(3X)
encrypted isencrypt determine	whether a character buffer is .... isencrypt(3G)
/border, wborder, box, hline,	whline, vline, wvline create curses/ .... curs_border(3X)
formatted input from a curses	widow /mvwscanw, vwscanw convert .... curs_scanw(3X)
/wait3, WIFSTOPPED, WIFSIGNALED,	WIFEXITED wait for process to/ .... wait(3)
process/ wait, wait3, WIFSTOPPED,	WIFSIGNALED, WIFEXITED wait for .... wait(3)
wait for process to/ wait, wait3,	WIFSTOPPED, WIFSIGNALED, WIFEXITED .... wait(3)
character and its/ curs_inch: inch,	winch, mvinch, mvwinch get a .... curs_inch(3X)
/inchstr, inchnstr, winchstr,	winchnstr, mvinchstr, mvinchnstr,/ .... curs_inchstr(3X)
curs_inchstr: inchstr, inchnstr,	winchstr, winchnstr, mvinchstr,/ .... curs_inchstr(3X)
/(with attributes) to a curses	window and advance cursor .... curs_addch(3X)
a string of characters to a curses	window and advance cursor /add .... curs_addstr(3X)
/form_sub, scale_form forms	window and subwindow association/ .... form_win(3X)
/menu_sub, scale_menu menus	window and subwindow association/ .... menu_win(3X)
/wstandout curses character and	window attribute control routines .... curs_attr(3X)
/wbkgdset, bkgd, wbkgd curses	window background manipulation/ .... curs_bkgd(3X)
getmaxyx get curses cursor and	window coordinates /getbegyx, ... curs_getyx(3X)
(and attributes) to a curses	window /add string of characters .... curs_addchstr(3X)
clear all or part of a curses	window /clrtoeol, wclrtoeol .... curs_clear(3X)
under cursor in a curses	window /mvwdelch delete character .... curs_delch(3X)
delete and insert lines in a curses	window /insertln, winsertln .... curs_deleteln(3X)
and its attributes from a curses	window /mvwinch get a character .... curs_inch(3X)
(and attributes) from a curses	window /get a string of characters .... curs_inchstr(3X)
under the cursor in a curses	window /before the character .... curs_insch(3X)
under the cursor in a curses	window /string before character .... curs_instr(3X)
string of characters from a curses	window /mvwinstr, mvwinnstr get a .... curs_instr(3X)
curs_move: move, wmove move curses	window cursor .... curs_move(3X)
pos_form_cursor position forms	window cursor form_cursor: .... form_cursor(3X)
scroll, srcl, wscrl scroll a curses	window curs_scroll: .... curs_scroll(3X)
/get or set the current	window of a panels panel .... panel_window(3X)
/move_panel move a panels	window on the virtual screen .... panel_move(3X)
libwindows	windowing terminal function library .... libwindows(3X)
redrawwin, wredrawln refresh curses	windows and lines /doupdate, ... curs_refresh(3X)
and manipulate overlapped curses	windows /overwrite, copywin overlap .... curs_overlay(3X)
print formatted output in curses	windows /mvwprintw, vwprintw .... curs_printw(3X)
wcursyncup, wsyncdown create curses	windows /dupwin, wsyncup, syncok, ... curs_window(3X)
curs_instr: instr, innstr, winstr,	winnstr, mvinstr, mvinnstr,/ .... curs_instr(3X)
character/ curs_insch: insch,	winsch, mvinsch, mvwinsch insert a .... curs_insch(3X)
/deleteln, wdeleteln, insdelln,	winsdelln, insertln, winsertln/ .... curs_deleteln(3X)

Programmer's REFERENCE Manual: Operating System API

/insdelln, winsdelln, insertln,	winsertln delete and insert lines/	curs_deleteln(3X)
/insstr, insnstr, winsstr,	winsnstr, mvinsstr, mvinsnstr,/	curs_instr(3X)
curs_instr: insstr, insnstr,	winsstr, winsnstr, mvinsstr,/	curs_instr(3X)
curs_instr: instr, innstr,	winstr, winnstr, mvinstr, mvinnstr,/	curs_instr(3X)
/echochar, wechochar add a character	(with attributes) to a curses/	curs_addch(3X)
curs_move: move,	wmove move curses window cursor	curs_move(3X)
curs_refresh: refresh, wrefresh,	wnoutrefresh, doupdate, redrawwin,/	curs_refresh(3X)
fgetc, getw get character or	word from a stream getc, getchar,	getc(3S)
fputc, putw put character or	word on a stream putc, putchar,	putc(3S)
chdir, fchdir change	working directory	chdir(2)
getcwd get pathname of current	working directory	getcwd(3C)
getwd get current	working directory pathname	getwd(3)
vwprintw/ curs_printw: printw,	wprintw, mvprintw, mvwprintw,	curs_printw(3X)
/wnoutrefresh, doupdate, redrawwin,	wredrawln refresh curses windows/	curs_refresh(3X)
redrawwin,/ curs_refresh: refresh,	wrefresh, wnoutrefresh, doupdate,	curs_refresh(3X)
/scr_restore, scr_init, scr_set read	(write) a curses screen from (to) a/	curs_scr_dump(3X)
write, writev	write on a file	write(2)
form_post: post_form, unpost_form	write or erase forms from/	form_post(3X)
menu_post: post_menu, unpost_menu	write or erase menus from/	menu_post(3X)
putpwent	write password file entry	putpwent(3C)
putspent	write shadow password file entry	putspent(3C)
rwall	write to specified remote machines	rwall(3N)
	write, writev write on a file	write(2)
write,	writev write on a file	write(2)
unlock a file region for reading or	writing locking lock or	locking(2)
open open for reading or	writing	open(2)
convert/ curs_scanw: scanw,	wscanw, mvscanw, mvwscanw, vwscanw	curs_scanw(3X)
curs_scroll: scroll, srcl,	wscrl scroll a curses window	curs_scroll(3X)
/idcok immedok, leaveok, setscrreg,	wsetscrreg, scrollok, nl, nonl/	curs_outopts(3X)
/attrset, wattrset, standend,	wstandend, standout, wstandout/	curs_attr(3X)
/standend, wstandend, standout,	wstandout curses character and/	curs_attr(3X)
/wsyncup, syncok, wcursyncup,	wsyncdown create curses windows	curs_window(3X)
/subwin, derwin, mvderwin, dupwin,	wsyncup, syncok, wcursyncup,/	curs_window(3X)
/noraw, noqiflush, qiflush, timeout,	wtimeout, typeahead curses terminal/	curs_inopts(3X)
/touchwin, touchline, untouchwin,	wtouchln, is_linetouched,/	curs_touch(3X)
/wborder, box, hline, whline, vline,	wvline create curses borders,/	curs_border(3X)
data representation	xdr library routines for external	xdr(3N)
/xdr_rejected_reply, xdr_replymsg	XDR library routines for remote/	rpc_xdr(3N)
xdr_authsys_parms,/ rpc_xdr:	xdr_accepted_reply,	rpc_xdr(3N)
xdrrec_eof, xdr_setpos library/	xdr_admin: xdr_getpos, xdr_inline,	xdr_admin(3N)
xdr_pointer,/ xdr_complex:	xdr_array, xdr_bytes, xdr_opaque,	xdr_complex(3N)
rpc_xdr: xdr_accepted_reply,	xdr_authsys_parms, xdr_callhdr,/	rpc_xdr(3N)
xdr_enum, xdr_float,/ xdr_simple:	xdr_bool, xdr_char, xdr_double,	xdr_simple(3N)
xdr_complex: xdr_array,	xdr_bytes, xdr_opaque, xdr_pointer,/	xdr_complex(3N)
/xdr_authsys_parms,	xdr_callhdr, xdr_callmsg,/	rpc_xdr(3N)
/xdr_authsys_parms, xdr_callhdr,	xdr_callmsg, xdr_opaque_auth,/	rpc_xdr(3N)

Permuted Index

xdr_float,/ xdr_simple: xdr_bool,	xdr_char, xdr_double, xdr_enum,	xdr_simple(3N)
xdr_opaque, xdr_pointer,/	xdr_complex: xdr_array, xdr_bytes,	xdr_complex(3N)
xdrmem_create, xdrrec_create,/	xdr_create: xdr_destroy,	xdr_create(3N)
xdrrec_create,/ xdr_create:	xdr_destroy, xdrmem_create,	xdr_create(3N)
xdr_simple: xdr_bool, xdr_char,	xdr_double, xdr_enum, xdr_float,/	xdr_simple(3N)
/xdr_bool, xdr_char, xdr_double,	xdr_enum, xdr_float, xdr_free,/	xdr_simple(3N)
/xdr_char, xdr_double, xdr_enum,	xdr_float, xdr_free, xdr_int,/	xdr_simple(3N)
/xdr_double, xdr_enum, xdr_float,	xdr_free, xdr_int, xdr_long,/	xdr_simple(3N)
xdr_setpos library/ xdr_admin:	xdr_getpos, xdr_inline, xdrrec_eof,	xdr_admin(3N)
library/ xdr_admin: xdr_getpos,	xdr_inline, xdrrec_eof, xdr_setpos	xdr_admin(3N)
/xdr_enum, xdr_float, xdr_free,	xdr_int, xdr_long, xdr_short,/	xdr_simple(3N)
/xdr_float, xdr_free, xdr_int,	xdr_long, xdr_short, xdr_u_char,/	xdr_simple(3N)
xdr_create: xdr_destroy,	xdrmem_create, xdrrec_create,/	xdr_create(3N)
xdr_complex: xdr_array, xdr_bytes,	xdr_opaque, xdr_pointer,/	xdr_complex(3N)
/xdr_callhdr, xdr_callmsg,	xdr_opaque_auth,/	rpc_xdr(3N)
/xdr_array, xdr_bytes, xdr_opaque,	xdr_pointer, xdr_reference,/	xdr_complex(3N)
/xdr_destroy, xdrmem_create,	xdrrec_create, xdrstdio_create/	xdr_create(3N)
xdr_admin: xdr_getpos, xdr_inline,	xdrrec_eof, xdr_setpos library/	xdr_admin(3N)
/xdr_bytes, xdr_opaque, xdr_pointer,	xdr_reference, xdr_string,/	xdr_complex(3N)
XDR/ /xdr_callmsg, xdr_opaque_auth,	xdr_rejected_reply, xdr_replymsg	rpc_xdr(3N)
for remote/ /xdr_rejected_reply,	xdr_replymsg XDR library routines	rpc_xdr(3N)
/xdr_getpos, xdr_inline, xdrrec_eof,	xdr_setpos library routines for/	xdr_admin(3N)
/xdr_free, xdr_int, xdr_long,	xdr_short, xdr_u_char, xdr_u_long,/	xdr_simple(3N)
xdr_double, xdr_enum, xdr_float,/	xdr_simple: xdr_bool, xdr_char,	xdr_simple(3N)
for/ /xdrmem_create, xdrrec_create,	xdrstdio_create library routines	xdr_create(3N)
/xdr_pointer, xdr_reference,	xdr_string, xdr_union, xdr_vector,/	xdr_complex(3N)
xdr_int, xdr_long, xdr_short,	xdr_u_char, xdr_u_long,/ /xdr_free,	xdr_simple(3N)
/xdr_long, xdr_short, xdr_u_char,	xdr_u_long, xdr_u_short, xdr_void/	xdr_simple(3N)
/xdr_reference, xdr_string,	xdr_union, xdr_vector,/	xdr_complex(3N)
/xdr_short, xdr_u_char, xdr_u_long,	xdr_u_short, xdr_void library/	xdr_simple(3N)
routines/ /xdr_string, xdr_union,	xdr_vector, xdr_wrapstring library	xdr_complex(3N)
external/ /xdr_u_long, xdr_u_short,	xdr_void library routines for	xdr_simple(3N)
/xdr_string, xdr_union, xdr_vector,	xdr_wrapstring library routines for/	xdr_complex(3N)
/rpc_reg, svc_reg, svc_unreg,	xprt_register, xprt_unregister/	rpc_svc_calls(3N)
/svc_reg, svc_unreg, xprt_register,	xprt_unregister library routines/	rpc_svc_calls(3N)
pow, gcd, rpow, msqrt, sdiv, itom,	xtom, mtox, mfree multiple/ /mout,	mp(3X)
bessel: j0, j1, jn,	y0, y1, yn Bessel functions	bessel(3M)
bessel: j0, j1, jn, y0,	y1, yn Bessel functions	bessel(3M)
bessel: j0, j1, jn, y0, y1,	yn Bessel functions	bessel(3M)
/yp_match, yp_first, yp_next,	yp_all, yp_order, yp_master,/	ypclnt(3N)
ypclnt, yp_get_default_domain,	yp_bind, yp_unbind, yp_match,/	ypclnt(3N)
yp_bind, yp_unbind, yp_match,/	ypclnt, yp_get_default_domain,	ypclnt(3N)
/yp_all, yp_order, yp_master,	yperr_string, ypprot_err NIS client/	ypclnt(3N)
/yp_bind, yp_unbind, yp_match,	yp_first, yp_next, yp_all,/	ypclnt(3N)
yp_unbind, yp_match,/ ypclnt,	yp_get_default_domain, yp_bind,	ypclnt(3N)
NIS/ /yp_next, yp_all, yp_order,	yp_master, yperr_string, ypprot_err	ypclnt(3N)
yp_all,/ /yp_bind, yp_unbind,	yp_match, yp_first, yp_next,	ypclnt(3N)

/yp_unbind, yp_match, yp_first,	yp_next, yp_all, yp_order,/	ypclnt(3N)
/yp_first, yp_next, yp_all,	yp_order, yp_master, yperr_string,/	ypclnt(3N)
/yp_order, yp_master, yperr_string,	ypprot_err NIS client interface	ypclnt(3N)
/yp_get_default_domain, yp_bind,	yp_unbind, yp_match, yp_first,/	ypclnt(3N)
	yp_update change NIS information	yp_update(3N)
timezone get time	zone name given offset from GMT	timezone(3C)